Angela Thomas

A Subversive G

Angela Thomas

A Subversive Gleam
Max Bill and His Time
1908–1939

Translated by Fiona Elliott

Hauser & Wirth Publishers

Preface to the English Edition

Michaela Unterdörfer

Max Bill (1908–1994)—designer, artist, sculptor, architect—took a stand on social and political topics with the same commitment that he engaged with artistic and cultural issues. This first volume of his biography provides an insight into his early career and the circles the Swiss artist moved in.

It was toward the end of 1931 in Zurich that the idea of founding an anti-Fascist publication was first discussed. In the end, eighteen issues of *information*—the only critical, left-leaning periodical in Switzerland—were published between June 1932 and February 1934. The individuals who initiated this undertaking may well have met somewhere in Zurich's city center—possibly in the splendid "Zum Baumwollhof" in Stadelhoferstrasse, the home of Aline Valangin, who had come up with the idea of a political periodical in the first place, and her husband, the Jewish lawyer Wladimir Rosenbaum, who helped to fund *information.* Or they may have met in one of the nearby cafés—the Odéon, Café Select—or over lunch at the Kronenhalle. However, it is more likely—even if this is pure speculation—that meetings with sponsors, the publisher, editors, and supporters took place in the premises of the future Europa-Verlag, at Rämistrasse 5, where the husband-and-wife team Emil and Emmie Oprecht had run a bookshop since 1925 and had already founded their first publishing house.

Max Bill was a member of the circle of intellectuals and others who were involved with *information* and worked on its design. In the 1930s he designed numerous publications, book covers, and an edition of the Oprechts' sales catalogue. Bill would make repeated visits to the publishing house in connection with these commissions. On those occasions he would certainly not only have met with the publisher but would also have come into contact with writers who had fled Nazi Germany and Fascist Italy and who had found a new publishing home at the Europa-Verlag. The publishing house and the Oprechts' apartment had become a centre of resistance against National Socialism, and Oprecht is especially remembered as a publisher of books by authors in exile. Everyone involved with *information* was by definition openly anti-Fascist and, as such, exposed to potential danger at a time in Zurich when right-wing Frontists were marching raucously through the city and actively intimidating local residents. Many of the authors published by the Europa-Verlag adopted pseudonyms.

Nine decades later, in the same rooms on the first floor of Rämistrasse 5 —now home to Hauser & Wirth Publishers—the first discussions were held regarding the English edition of *mit subversivem glanz. max bill und seine zeit,* the first volume of Angela Thomas's comprehensive monograph on Max Bill. In conversations with the author we learned about our neighborhood as it was in the 1920s and 1930s and about the lives of political émigrés in Switzerland. She told us about Aline Valangin —poet, grande dame, wife to Wladimir Rosenbaum—and Valangin's salon, where writers and poets, musicians, visual artists and intellectuals came and went, figures such as Jean Arp, Sophie Taeuber-Arp, Max Ernst, Kurt Tucholsky, C. G. Jung, Elias Canetti, and Ignazio Silone. And we learned that in 1933 Silone's anti-Fascist novel *Fontamara* was published by Oprecht in his newly founded Europa-Verlag, with a dust jacket design by Max Bill.

In her wide-ranging monograph on Max Bill, Thomas adeptly highlights historic, social, and personal connections in Bill's life, all of which is underpinned by her years of meticulous research and the numerous cross-references she uncovers. She has a fascinating ability to breathe life into history and stories. By creating this temporal and geographical web of connections with Bill at its center she avoids simple linearity and gives her narrative—this chronology of a life—an unusual immediacy. Although volume one of this monograph guides the reader along the loosely spun thread of the biography of Max Bill—from his childhood and youth, through his time at the Bauhaus and his return to Zurich, and on into the late 1930s—Thomas nevertheless also invites the reader to leaf forward and backward through the book. Her style gives the narrative a special, lively presence. Its fluid, open structure grants the reader a welcome freedom in the sense that Thomas never goes into how things might have been, nor does she succumb to the temptation to embellish facts or to psychologize Bill's life. Instead she leaves readers free to pursue connections and to draw their own conclusions.

In order to orchestrate this abundance of information, facts, references, and sources, Thomas devised an inspired narrative technique and created a second voice that introduces additional narrative strands. It is as if she takes us, the readers, momentarily to one side and adds a pertinent comment without interrupting the flow of the narrative. None of these comments is gratuitous or superfluous. As a result, the reader can easily follow the traces of Bill's life and work, in the same way that the visitor to Haus Bill in Zumikon follows Angela Thomas through the rooms housing her library, all the way to a particular shelf where she unerringly selects a particular book and, just as unerringly, opens it at a particular passage . . .

Editorial Note for the English Edition

The German first edition of this volume, which was published by Verlag Scheidegger & Spiess in 2008, adheres to the consistent use of lower case that was adopted at the Bauhaus in Dessau and by Max Bill around 1930. In view of the difficulties this convention can present to English-speaking readers, the English edition uses both lower and upper case.

In comparison to the German edition, the "second voice" is given greater prominence and is integrated more closely into the main body of the text.

Special thanks are due to the translator, Fiona Elliott, whose joyous commitment to the task, linguistic flair, and perseverance have led to this excellent English version of Angela Thomas's text. Her experience informed fundamental editorial decisions and this preface alike.

By Lake Lauenen

Max Bill and I set out contentedly for a walk round Lake Lauenen in the Bernese Uplands. Unusually light-hearted, he followed the tracks that his mother's stories had left in his memory. As a young unmarried woman, Marie Geiger had walked by this same lake two years before Max was born, and it was as if Max were now able to share her delight in the landscape. As a rule Max Bill rarely took time to go out for walks, at least not during the twenty years when we were close—from 1974 up until his death in December 1994.

It was in late October 1906 that Marie Geiger traveled to Lauenen in the canton of Bern to meet up with her favorite brother, Ernst, who was staying there in a wooden mountain cabin on the invitation of Gertrud Züricher and her siblings, Ulrich Wilhelm and Bertha. Gertrud had bought and renovated the seventeenth-century cabin—the Hubelhüsi or "Hübi"—in 1904, and it was now well stocked with books for the many guests who came and went.

With her brother and sister spending most of their time abroad and her parents no longer alive, Gertrud Züricher bought the cabin in the mountains as a place where she and her siblings could meet up and invite friends and acquaintances to stay.

When Marie arrived, Ernst had already been there for some months: "Not having a job at the time—a free-spirited painter (a ne'er-do-well in my family's eyes)—I went to the mountains and whittled wood ... and spent time with the many visitors who found their way to the Hübi.... My sister Marie also came to stay for a while."[1] At the Hübi Geiger drew decorative borders on page after page in the new family log book—the Hubelhüsi chronicle—and made a gilded ex libris label for Gertrud Züricher, whom he was clearly fond of.

No sooner than she had arrived, Marie Geiger made herself useful at the Hübi, setting a fire (with some difficulty at first) to warm up the cabin.

The Hubelhüsi chronicle mentions a small fire caused by "Marie Giiger from Brugg" (this spelling of her surname derives from the Swiss-German pronunciation). Evidently she had forgotten that there were still two fabric "coffee cozies" on the stove—used on coffee pots, just like tea cozies, in those days—which then caught fire.

At this point she was twenty-three years of age and although she had led a relatively sheltered existence so far, she certainly did not share her parents' opinion that Ernst was a "ne'er-do-well." She was happy to be at his side, went hiking with him, and admired his paintings of the area around Lauenen. Marie basked in that carefree time before she married

Erwin Bill on 23 March 1908 in her native town of Brugg. Did Marie perhaps first meet her future husband up there in the mountains? Whatever the case, she felt at ease there, far away from the usual social niceties and constraints, and was happy and relaxed in the company of her maverick brother.

Marie stayed at the Hübi for nearly six weeks, from 30 October to 13 December 1906. A photograph of a young woman in a long winter coat standing in the snow with a man, probably her brother Ernst, is pasted in below Marie's farewell in the Hubelhüsi chronicle—"Addio, auf Wiedersehen!"

Ernst Geiger had first met the Züricher siblings when he and Ulrich Wilhelm were students together. Known to his friends as U.W.Z., Ulrich Wilhelm Züricher's given names recalled both the Reformation leader Ulrich Zwingli, and the Swiss national hero Wilhelm Tell. During that summer of 1906 Ernst and U.W.Z. started painting patterns on the wooden beams in the cabin.

Years later, in articles in the *Brugger Neujahrsblätter* (1937) and in the *Aargauer Tagblatt* (1956), Ulrich Wilhelm Züricher (1877–1961) looked back at the time he spent in Zurich with Ernst Geiger.

Bertha Züricher was also a painter and spent most of her time in Paris. In 1903 she, U.W.Z., and Ernst had all participated in an exhibition at the Helmhaus in Zurich.[2] Gertrud Züricher was a qualified drawing teacher, which meant that she was in a position to earn her own living. Four years before Ernst and Marie Geiger were at the Hübi together, Gertrud had published a collection of Bernese children's songs.[3] In her free time Gertrud painted botanical studies and, since Ernst Geiger also had a keen interest in plants, they greatly enjoyed each other's company.

Gertrud Züricher donated the ten-volume herbarium she had devised and painted to the Burgerbibliothek in Bern.

Ernst Geiger had already resolved to abstain from alcohol when he was at school in Aarau and he remained true to his convictions.

1 Geiger 1969, p. 27

2 For the titles of their works, see *Gemäldeausstellung im Helmhaus,* 15 November–2 December, Zurich, 1903: Ernst Geiger (cat. nos. 1–65), Bertha Züricher (cat. nos. 66–88) and Wilhelm Züricher (cat. nos. 89–128)

3 Gertrud Züricher, *Kinderlied und Kinderspiel im Kanton Bern,* Schweizerische Gesellschaft für Volkskunde (Zurich, 1902)

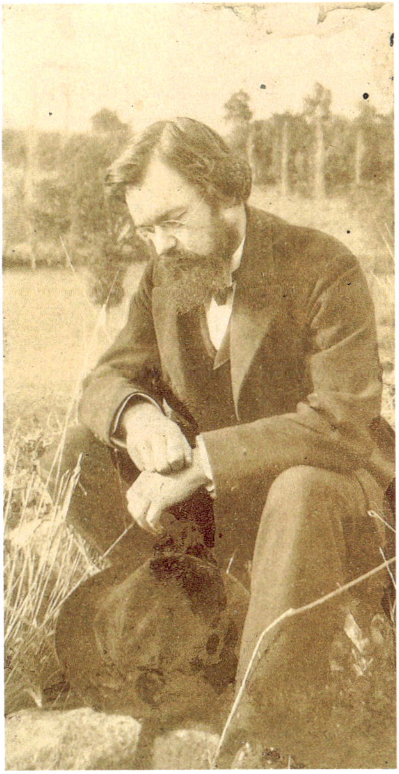

Ernst Geiger at Lake Lauenen, 1906

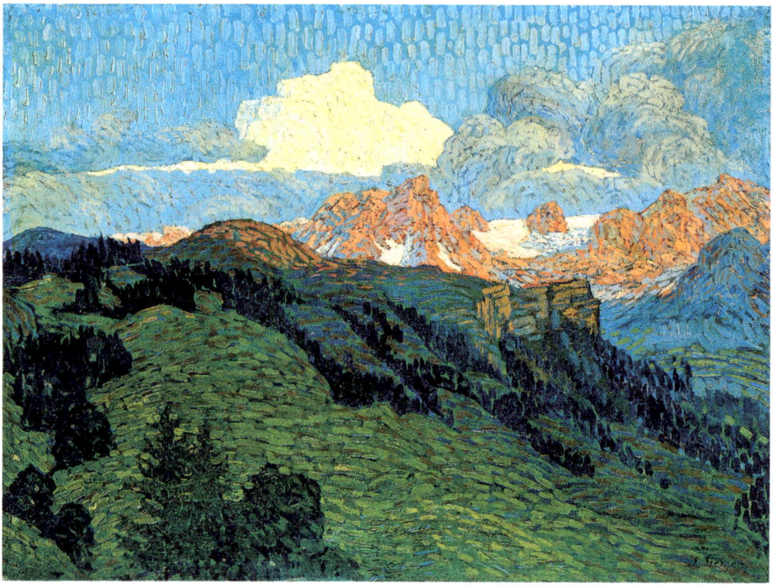

Ernst Geiger, *Geltenfall bei Lauenen* (also known as *Paysage près de Lauenen*), 1906, oil on canvas, 44×61 cm

Marie Geiger and her brother Ernst, 1906, india ink, gouache, and photograph on paper

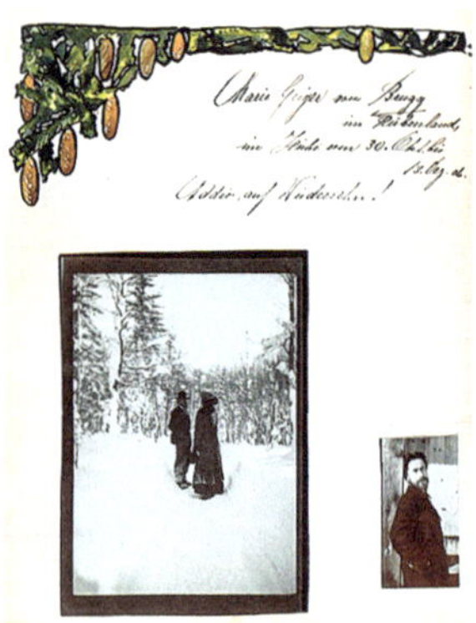

As it happens, Ernst Geiger attended the same school in Aarau as Albert Einstein, who was in the class above him; Max Bill once told me that his uncle Ernst knew Albert Einstein "from when they were boys." Later on Max Bill bought various books about Einstein (e.g. *Helle Zeit—Dunkle Zeit, in Memoriam Albert Einstein,* ed. Carl Seelig [Zurich: Europa, 1956]). Einstein, like so many others, had needed to flee Nazi Germany and Bill later made sculptures in memory of two prominent émigrés: a red, Ukrainian-granite monument to Albert Einstein (1979–82) in his native city of Ulm and a homage to the philosopher Ernst Bloch—a granite sculpture, *endlose treppe, monument für ernst bloch* (1988–90)—which stands in Bloch's native city of Ludwigshafen am Rhein. Max Bill also designed monuments (unrealized) to two more great thinkers, Karl Marx and Georg Büchner, both of whom dared to resist the politics of their own time.

As students in Zurich both he and U.W.Z. joined Libertas, a student-run teetotallers' association; Ernst's good nature made him a popular member, whereas U.W.Z.—who had lost his parents at a young age—was generally regarded as more melancholy. Many of the Libertas students, including Ernst and U.W.Z., actively campaigned for their beliefs; they were determined to fight the evil of alcohol abuse, above all because it self-evidently brought yet more misery to the poor and the disadvantaged.

U.W.Z. later looked back at the time when he and Geiger had been students together: "In those days, in Zurich, we happily looked to the future.... You were busy with your forestry, and I with my architecture. We had so many social pursuits ... how often we went hiking together! Nature and art beckoned to us—do you still remember lugging your beloved alphorn over those eight passes in the Ticino and the Valais—giving concerts on mountainsides and in lonely villages? ... Paris [was] our destination—not long before that we had been in Soglio and the two of us had stood on the very spot where Segantini composed his monumental *Werden* (1896–99). And then Paris captivated us with its endless excitement."[4]

The alphorn mentioned here was the kind known as a "büchel." "In Hergiswil I bought myself a büchel from a famous alphorn player—the type of alphorn made in Unterwalden, which is curled up, or rather, bent twice with a straight flare that makes the perfect holder for my sun and rain roof [which he always took with him when he went hiking]. A sturdy cord attached to it allows me to sling it on my back like a rifle."[5]

4 Ulrich Wilhelm Züricher, "Zum 80. Geburtstag des Malers Ernst Geiger 1. Februar 1956," in *Aargauer Tagblatt,* 24 January 1956

5 Ernst Geiger, Archiv Christoph Geiger

In Zurich U.W.Z. and Ernst Geiger were also members of a literary and debating circle where they encountered the politics of the charismatic Dr. Fritz Brupbacher, a leftist physician who had a practice in a working-class district of the city.[6] It may well be that Ernst Geiger and his sister Marie discussed some of those political issues, although there is no knowing for certain if she shared or was even aware of his political opinions.

". . . les gens hors série"

However, there is no doubt that Ernst Geiger later passed some of Brupbacher's political views on to Marie's son Max—born in 1908—and that those views would have a formative influence on him. As it were following in his uncle's footsteps, Max later on made contact with members of the progressive temperance movement in Zurich and was clearly keen to put his design skills to good use for *Die junge Schweiz,* a temperance magazine that first came out in 1926.

"Dear Uncle Ernst!

I was sorry not to see you at the Libertas Foundation Day, so many of your old comrades asked after you and I told them all they should visit you . . . I've designed a cover for Die Junge Schweiz . . . Very best wishes!"[7]

It seems the cover design mentioned in Bill's letter was not used. There is no sign of it in Max Bill's typography estate.

It was in the early 1930s that Max Bill first met Fritz Brupbacher, whose autobiography, *60 Jahre Ketzer: "Ich log so wenig als möglich,"* was published in Zurich by B. Ruppli in 1935. Over the years Brupbacher evolved from anarchist to anarcho-syndicalist to socialist; he and Bill also met in connection with the anti-Fascist periodical *information,* which was published from 1932 to 1934; Bill designed the typography for *information* and Brupbacher's wife, the physician Dr. Paula Brupbacher, was a

6 See Geiger 1969, pp. 23–24

7 Max Bill, Winterthur, to Ernst Geiger (26 December 1925), Archiv Christoph Geiger

8 Dr. Paula Brupbacher, "Der vorbereitende Kongress der Weltliga für Sexualreform," in *information* 1:3 (August/September 1932), p. 45; and "Die Bevölkerungspolitik im Dritten Reich," *information* 2:2 (September 1933), p. 19

9 See Gautschi-Züricher [1988]

10 Ernst Geiger, handwritten text, n.d., Archiv Christoph Geiger

contributor.[8] Fritz Brupbacher was always drawn to outsiders or "les gens hors série," to quote the French writer Jean-Paul Samson (as Max Bill told me), who was a close friend of Brupbacher's and later on also of Bill's. And it may be that, for Brupbacher, both Ernst Geiger and (some years later) Geiger's rebellious nephew, Max Bill, fell into that category of interesting outsiders.

In 1900 Ernst Geiger and Ulrich Wilhelm Züricher—by now an architecture graduate but more interested in painting than architecture—traveled to Paris to see the Exposition Universelle. They then decided to stay on in Paris for a while to concentrate on painting. Initially they worked in Montparnasse in the studio used by Ulrich's sister, Bertha, who was painting and making colored woodcuts. Other regular visitors to Bertha's studio included the German artists Clara Westhoff and Paula Modersohn-Becker.[9]

U.W.Z. and Ernst Geiger then rented a small studio of their own in Paris. However, Ernst quickly lost patience with U.W.Z.'s fondness for reading out loud from French books so, on the spur of the moment, he moved again, to the studio of a Swiss architect, Albert "Bärti" Frölich, who also happened to be a distant relative on his mother's side. Frölich and Geiger often spent time in the company of Russian émigrés, which soon attracted the attention of the French police, who now regarded them as persons of interest.

In view of the imminent visit to Paris by the Russian czar, the French authorities were fearful of attacks being mounted against him and determined to thwart any hostile acts.

Bärti Frölich, a craftsman's son, was always ready for a challenge, unlike Ernst Geiger, who was quieter and calmer. Ernst and Bärti had grown up in the small town of Brugg, which was just starting to become a manufacturing center in those days. As young men they used to go on "painting hikes" together, seeking out interesting local motifs such as the thatched houses that still survived in those days in the canton of Aargau.

"The little town contrasted sharply with the surrounding area, with its scattered grand estates and isolated, humble little dwellings. Although Frölich lived in the main street and Geiger was from the baronial estate that stretched from the present-day town hall to the Süssbach, they grew up together under the huge trees in the estate's parklands and in the crooked lanes of the town."[10]

The same Albert Frölich, now working as an architect, would later fulfill various private and public commissions in Brugg, including the Vindonissa Museum (1911), which very much has the look of that time. As it happens, there is another connection between the Geiger family and that museum. Ulrich Geiger-Schwarz, father to Ernst and Marie and grandfather to Max Bill, was a member of the first board of the Gesellschaft Pro Vindonissa (the Pro Vindonissa society) and would later donate the Geiger Collection—containing Roman coins and ceramics found in the canton of Aargau—to the Gesellschaft Pro Vindonissa.

The cover of the magazine *SVZ Revue Onst* 8 (1934) devoted to the Swiss Grand Prix in Bern—from which the description of Vindonissa is taken—was designed by Max Bill ("Bill-Zürich," see fig. p. 534).

Vindonissa was once the largest Roman encampment in the territory now covered by Switzerland. "Outside the military camp, which was occupied throughout the first century AD, is the imposing amphitheater with seating for an audience of 10,000. . . . Not far from the amphitheater there was a sprawling marketplace, frequented by traders from north and south, east and west: the most important military and trade routes intersected at Vindonissa . . . so there was an abundance of bronze and silver coins to be retrieved from the ground, sometimes even wonderful gold artifacts."[11]

A Visit from Maria Bockhoff

Although Ernst Geiger had lost patience with U.W.Z. in Paris, they met up again in Switzerland in 1906 when Ernst accepted the Züricher siblings' invitation to stay at the Hübi in Lauenen, where U.W.Z. generally spent the summer months. Ernst was also keen to travel to the mountains because he felt especially drawn to Gertrud. According to a note in the Hübi chronicle, she stayed at the cabin from 23 December 1906 to 6 January 1907.

But the story of their friendship, which once had romantic overtones, then took a very different turn—not even anticipated by Ernst Geiger: "Winter came, bringing deep snow with it. . . . and on Christmas Eve in 1906 Fräulein Züricher brought a friend with her. I collected the two young

11 Dr. Simonett, "Vindonissa," *SVZ Revue Onst* 8, official travel magazine of the Schweizerische Verkehrszentrale, Bern, 26 August 1934, pp. 30–31
12 Geiger 1969, p. 27
13 In the Hubelhüsi chronicle
14 "Bertha Züricher—Ausstellung von Bildern und Studien, 23. April–12. Mai" (no year given). The exhibition took place in 1907 (information kindly supplied by Judith Durrer, Registrar, Kunstmuseum Bern, 2008)
15 See Gautschi-Züricher [1988]

ladies from Gstaad with the toboggan.... I had given no particular thought to the student who was coming to stay. As it turned out she was a fresh German girl who gazed at me—a rather unkempt lad—very trustingly.... From that first moment Maria Bockhoff and I were friends. We soon became much closer friends and realized we belonged together."[12] On the day of her departure Maria Bockhoff wrote in the chronicle, expressing her thanks "for the unforgettably lovely days I spent at the welcoming Hübi, 5 January 1907. Maria Bockhoff." And Ernst Geiger, who left the following day, wrote directly below her words: "I have spent a rich six months at the Hübi. This dear little house has become a new Heimat for me. Thank you and good bye. 4 July 1906–6 January 1907. Ernst Geiger."[13] There are three photographs pasted in below these two entries, one with Maria Bockhoff and Ernst Geiger.

Although the Züricher siblings subsequently interpreted that sudden turn of events as evidence that Maria Bockhoff had "spoiled" the relationship between Gertrud Züricher and Ernst Geiger, Gertrud and Maria clearly remained friends. In the spring holiday in 1907 Gertrud and Maria were both back at the Hübi. Gertrud's sister, Bertha, now had an upcoming solo exhibition at Kunstmuseum Bern (23 April–12 May 1907), and Ernst Geiger designed the invitation cards for her.[14]

Bertha Züricher made no distinction between her artistic work and her active interest in the problems of her own time. She became "one of the first members of the Women's International League for Peace and Freedom. In 1927 Bertha attended the pacifist congress along with figures such as Romain Rolland, Mahatma Gandhi, and Albert Schweitzer, all of whom sat for portraits by her."[15]

In Marie Geiger's memories of the month and a half that she spent at the Hübi in 1906, the outcome of that first encounter between her brother and Maria Bockhoff had a lot to do with the landscape around Lake Lauenen. Ernst and Maria married within a few months and just a year later, in March 1908, Marie married Erwin Bill—and on 22 December 1908 Max Bill was born in Winterthur.

Hodler, Segantini, and Geiger: Artists and Nature

In August 1907 Bertha Züricher, her brother U.W.Z., Johannes Widmer (an art critic), and Ernst Geiger set out from the Hübi for a five-day hike over the Rawil Pass to the Wildstrubelhütte on the Weisshorn. Writing about the Lauenen area, Ulrich Wilhelm Züricher later declared that few other locations in Switzerland combined "the quiet charm of a valley with such a splendid mountainscape," and Ernst Geiger made up a little ditty about the place, which approximately translates as "From Lauenen to the mountain ridge / the many paths may make you blink / but even if you step in the mud / you won't immediately sink" ("Von Lauenen zum Bergeskamm / sieht man viel Pfade winken. / Und triffst du auch ein bisschen Schlamm, / du wirst nicht gleich versinken ...").[16] The paintings done in these high mountains by Ernst Geiger, Ferdinand Hodler, and Giovanni Segantini vividly communicate the strong feelings these artists had for the landscapes where they walked and climbed—exhaustingly, never giving up—and still seem to exude the fresh mountain air that they breathed. These paintings could not be further removed from touristic voyeurism.

Das Bergell: Forstbotanische Monographie

In 1901, in keeping with his father's wishes, Ernst Geiger concluded his botanical studies with a doctoral dissertation on the forest botany of the Bregaglia.[17]

"After one semester as a medical student at the University of Basel, [Ernst Geiger] transferred to Zurich Polytechnic, where he studied the subjects he felt would prepare him for a career in forestry. It seems that, as a young man, he was as interested in geology, ancient history, and philosophy as in trees.... Geiger ultimately graduated with a PhD in botany. He was only the second forester in Switzerland to gain a doctorate. Geiger's lively intelligence, wide-ranging interests, and love of travel took him to many countries...."[18]

16 In the Hubelhüsi chronicle

17 *Das Bergell. Forstbotanische Monographie.* A dissertation submitted in partial fulfillment of the requirements for the degree of doctor of philosophy in the Mathematical and Natural Section of the Faculty of Philosophy at the University of Zurich by Ernst Geiger, Dipl. Forestry, Brugg (canton of Aargau), examined by Prof. Dr. Hans Schinz, Prof. Dr. C. Schröter, Chur, printed by Jos. Casanova, 1901

18 See Fischer [1966]

19 Geiger 1949

20 Geiger 1949

In the foreword to his dissertation, Geiger thanks—among others—Prof. Dr. C. Schröter, director of the botanical museum at the Eidgenössisches Polytechnikum (the future ETH Zürich i.e., the Swiss Federal Institute of Technology), and a certain Prof. Heim—that is, the geologist Albert Heim.

In the summer of 1899, during the course of his research into the forest botany of the Bregaglia, Ernst Geiger and U.W.Z. had gone hiking there only to find, on one occasion, that they were stopped by the local Swiss border guards on suspicion of smuggling illicit goods. In fact, the students' bulging rucksacks were filled with nothing more incriminating than rock samples and provisions for their trip, so they were allowed to go on their way—until Italian border guards spotted them and the two had their rucksacks checked yet again.

"In those days there were barely any hiking clubs yet, with the first just being founded; it was up to the individual. The isolated Val Bregaglia on the southern border of the country beckoned, and we wanted to reach it by less-trodden paths . . . via Göschenen, the Lukmanier Pass . . . the Valle di Blenio . . . Roveredo . . . until suddenly we were stopped by a gendarme, out on the lookout for thieves; he had taken our bulging rucksacks to mean that he had captured two villains. . . . The fact was that I knew there were all kinds of rare minerals in the scree on the steep slopes of the Grenzkamm, so we often left the bridle paths and clambered about among the rocks, avidly seeking out specimens—not noticing, on that occasion, that we had aroused the curiosity of an Italian border guard."[19]

It seems highly likely that Geiger would have told his nephew Max Bill about hiking along those paths as yet untrodden by tourists, maybe still smiling at being stopped by border guards. "By the time we arrived at Gravedona it was already late. My companion's breeches were very much the worse for wear after clambering about so much. . . . The next day we traveled by boat and post coach and on foot, via Chiavenna, to Soglio, high up in the Bregaglia, which we at last reached in the evening."[20]

Ernst Geiger Waiting for Giovanni Segantini

In Soglio, Ernst Geiger and U.W.Z. spent some months in what was once the palazzo of the Counts de Salis-Soglio and was now the Hotel Willy. Although Ernst was mainly working on his dissertation, he and U.W.Z.

also painted the mountains and scenes in the village. The owner of the hotel was expecting the artist Giovanni Segantini to arrive in the autumn. U.W.Z. had to leave before then but Ernst stayed on, now the only guest in the hotel; nothing would have persuaded him to miss this chance to spend time under the same roof as Segantini. Not far from the village, along the footpath to Vicosoprano, there was a podium that Segantini had had constructed so that he could work there with the Sciora Massif in the distance.

"As the evenings drew in, the owner of the hotel opened up a room containing an easel belonging to Segantini; he was expected to return to Soglio in the late autumn, to finish work on 'Werden,' for his triptych. . . . The podium by the path and the easel in the hotel room seemed to hold out promise for the future. . . . but then the great Alpine painter's life was cut short on the Schafberg, high up above Pontresina, while he was still working on the central painting of his triptych."[21] At the age of just forty-one Segantini was suddenly taken acutely ill and died.

"In September Segantini set himself up on the Schafberg (2,700 m) to work on the central section of his Alpine triptych. Segantini died of peritonitis on 28 September 1899 in his mountain cabin on the Schafberg; present at his death were his friend, the physician Oscar Bernhard, his son Mario, and his partner Bice."[22]

Although Ernst Geiger was fully aware of his father's expectations for him (his father was in fact funding his research project), high up in the Bregaglia, far away from Brugg, his urge to focus on art—on Segantini—suddenly overwhelmed him. He gave in to his artistic sensibilities and desires. How great must his disappointment have been when the hoped-for encounter never came about. "Death overtook Segantini high up in the mountains." Segantini could not be moved and it was impossible to operate on him because of the cold on the Schafberg. "And so it was that at that young age, not yet even at the height of his powers, in the midst of the mountains he loved so deeply, he lost his life—high up in those deserted regions. Here in Soglio we are all devastated and overcome with grief."[23]

Ernst Geiger and Giovanni Giacometti met at Segantini's funeral in Maloja, and the two later showed works in the same exhibitions.

21 Geiger 1949
22 "Biografie—Giovanni Segantini, 1858–1899," 2004, p. 153
23 Geiger 1949
24 Geiger 1949
25 Giovanni Segantini to Max Liebermann, in Maciejewski 2008, p. 134
26 Geiger 1949
27 Geiger 1949

"I saw the deceased's family and his home, and—a great bonus on that unforgettable day—I also met the painter Giovanni Giacometti."[24] Geiger's nephew Max Bill met Giovanni Giacometti's son Alberto in the 1930s.

As it happens, just over a year before Segantini died, Sigmund Freud also paid a visit to Maloja. In 1898 he signed the visitors' book at Hotel Schweizerhaus, as "Dr. Sigm. Freud and Frau," only his companion was his wife's sister, not his legally wedded wife.

Sabine Richebächer, a psychoanalyst in Zurich, reports that some members of the "psychoanalytical establishment" have still not forgiven Sigmund Freud for that.

Segantini's lodgings were directly opposite the hotel where Freud and Minna stayed in room 11, and at that time he was expecting a visit from the artist Max Liebermann—just one of a steady stream of visitors to the now-famous artist Segantini.

"Maloja, 13 August 1898. I have received your esteemed letter and will be happy to shake your hand. I will be at home on the 14th and 15th inst."[25]

When Ernst Geiger was preparing to leave Soglio, the owner of the hotel gave him two small works by Segantini, as he recalled: "... two sketches by Segantini for the panorama that he had originally planned to show at the Exposition Universelle in Paris in 1900 but had then abandoned. The panorama was replaced by the triptych that is now known to so many."[26]

The sketches by Segantini, which Ernst Geiger received as gifts in Soglio, have passed down to his son Christoph Geiger.

Ernst set out alone from Soglio and for a time followed in Segantini's footsteps, like a pilgrim. As he went he wondered which country would claim Segantini as its own, given that Segantini had been born in Austria, had spent his youth in Italy and had so dearly loved the Swiss canton of Grisons.

Giovanni Segantini was born as an Austrian citizen on 15 January 1858 in the small town of Arco, Austria (now Italy) , at the northern end of Lake Garda.

Geiger walked on "over the Duana Pass and the Septimer Pass ... reaching Stalla in the evening and going on from there to Savognin, the village where Segantini first settled in Switzerland so that he could paint the mountains."[27]

Roman Shards

Marie Geiger and her siblings, including her eldest brother Ernst, grew up in a grand house, which is now the town hall in Brugg. The house had "an excellent cellar," which was a great help to their father, a wine merchant, who was soon in a position to extend his property.

This Rococo house, built in 1748 by Johann Jakob Frölich, was sometimes referred to (along with its grounds) as the "Frölich estate." As the private secretary to John Montagu, 4th Earl of Sandwich, Frölich had amassed a considerable fortune. After his death the house was successively owned by his sister (until 1782), the cotton manufacturer Kaspar Meier von Rüfenach and his descendants (until 1873), G. Angst (until 1879) and Ulrich Geiger-Schwarz (until 1908). Following a break-in and after the death of his wife, Geiger-Schwarz sold this handsome property to the town of Brugg for 100,000 Swiss francs "on 23 December 1908"—as a plaque still in place on the house today states. Family legend has it that this occurred under pressure from the "local dignitaries" in Brugg, who had put the fear of repeated break-ins into Ulrich Geiger-Schwarz. Ever since then the house has served as the town hall. Max Bill once specifically took me to Brugg to show me the grand Rococo house that his mother had grown up in.

Far away from home, at the Hübi in 1906, Marie and Ernst looked back at those days in Brugg, remembering the people in their neighborhood and their ways. Their neighbors had laughed and had mocked their father when he had deep trenches dug out for his new apple trees. Only in the end it was Ulrich Geiger-Schwarz, the wily wine merchant, who had the last laugh. "Since there were excavations under way at the time in connection with the renovations at the Königsfelden Monastery (which had been a grain store for a while and then a salt store for the canton Aargau), my father had cartloads of centuries-old rubble delivered to his orchard; we children delighted in the arrival of every new cartload, which also brought us Roman shards and golden buttons once worn by knights who had fought in the Battle of Sempach. And the scoffers were proved wrong, when—year after year—our father harvested heavenly fruit from his large orchard."[28]

In later years Marie, now Marie Bill-Geiger, would always dig for Roman shards with Max when they visited her native canton of Aargau: "My mother and I roamed through the countryside around Brugg, and I helped her look for Roman shards. Afterward we would glue any matching pieces back together."[29]

28 Geiger 1957, p. 34
29 Max Bill in conversation with Angela Thomas, 1979

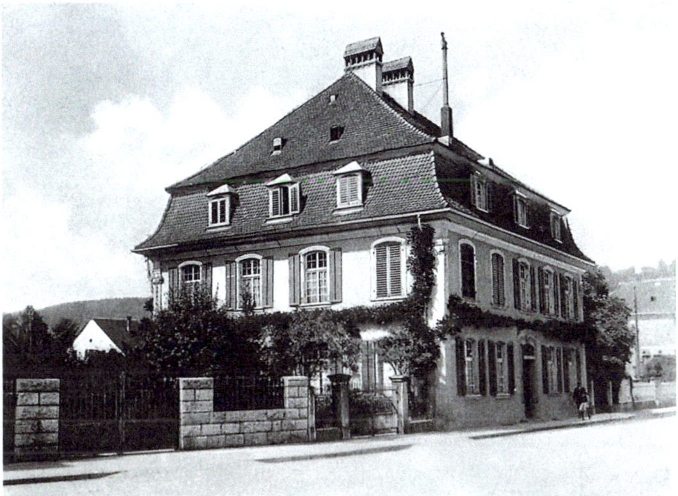

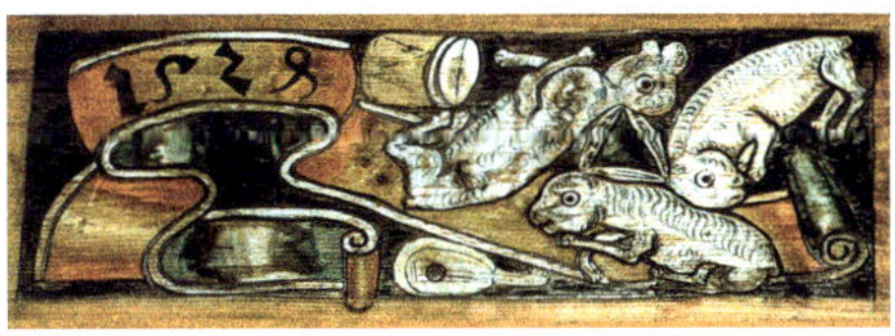

The Rococo house in Brugg, canton of Aargau, built in 1748; photographed in the first quarter of the 20th century

Three hares whose ears form a triangle in the Late Gothic church in Lauenen

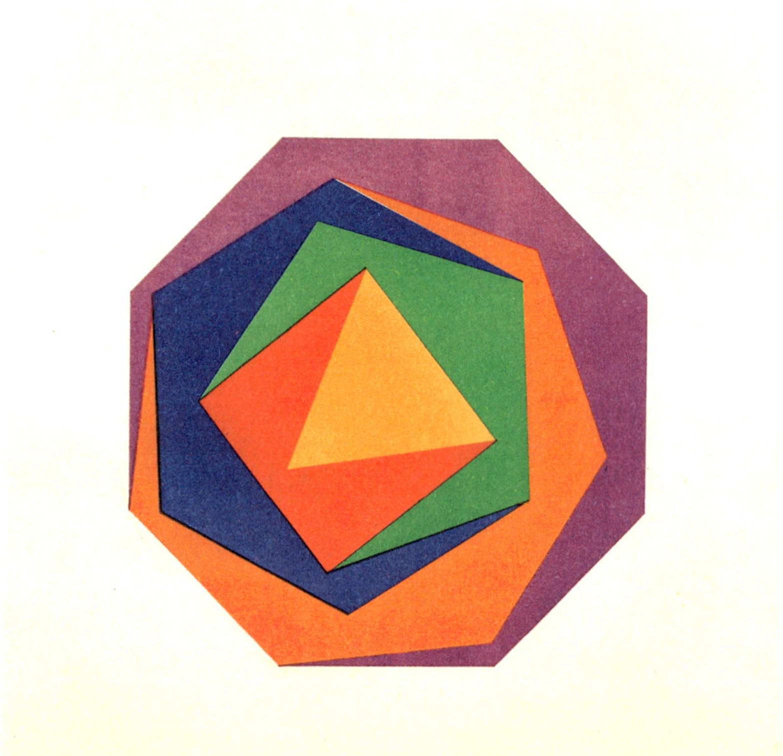

Max Bill, Sheet from the series *fünfzehn variationen über ein thema,* 1935–38, lithograph on paper, 32 × 30 cm

Hare's Ears

Marie Bill-Geiger learned a certain amount about botany from her brother and passed this on to her sons Max (born in 1908) and Hugo (born in 1911); Max also remembered her talking fondly of Lake Lauenen when he was a boy. She once told Max a strange story about three hares: in the chancel arch in the late Gothic church in Lauenen there was a painting of three white hares. Even if Max's mother had not visited that church herself (although it is likely she had, because she was always interested in local places of interest), she would certainly have heard of this story, which was recounted in the Hubelhüsi chronicle for 1904 by a certain Professor Dr. R. Steck. He describes the three white hares whose "ears form a triangle: each hare has one ear of its own and shares its other ear with its neighbor."

A geometric reworking of those "shared" hare's ears appears much later on in Max Bill's epoch-making series of prints *fünfzehn variationen über ein thema* (1935–38, see pp. 24, 238, 672). The memorable theme of this set of variations is a spiral that starts as an equilateral triangle, then becomes a square, a pentagon, a hexagon, a heptagon and finally an octagon before the process reverses back to its starting point. Notably—as in the case of the hares' ears—one side of each figure always also belongs to the next figure.

It may be that Max told his father about the white hares and their ears. Whatever the case, his father certainly dinned into him that (in German) a hare's ears are called "spoons," not ears. Much later on, when we were staying at the Hotel am Zoo in Berlin and Max started to describe that traumatic moment, his late father emerged so overpoweringly from the shadows that Max could not continue with his story. He was literally lost for words and suffered a cerebral bleed, after which—in the coming days and weeks—he had to painstakingly reacquire the ability to speak, word by word.

Years after her time at the Hübi, Marie Bill-Geiger still had *Anke* (butter) sent from Lauenen to Winterthur. (Max Bill almost always spoke High German with me; however, when he did switch into Swiss German, he used words like *Anke* and *Nidel* for butter and cream—pronouncing the "i" in *Nidel* in a particularly seductive manner.) Those blocks of butter were imprinted with special patterns that Max always loved, even as a small child. As an adult, in 1938, Max Bill recalled those geometric folk-art patterns—seen not only in the carved wooden blocks used to decorate butter pats but also in traditional Swiss furniture—and he illustrated some in his essay "Les paysans Suisses et la forme absolue" for *XXe siècle* 4 (1938).

"In the 16th century, gothic peasant furniture, worked using primitive carpentry techniques, started to appear in the canton of grisons. artist-craftsmen sculpted wonderful, extremely diverse rosettes on large boards."[30]

"Io son pittore"

During his protracted stay in Lauenen Ernst Geiger did more than just sun himself and recoup his strength; he also painted watercolors and made oil paintings of motifs in the high mountains. His friends (including the Züricher siblings) already knew that, having gained his doctorate as his father had wanted him to do, Ernst had now finally decided to be a painter. While this "most heartfelt" decision had already given him and his paintings an aura of optimism, he still had to tell his father that he was determined to become a painter and pursue a career as an artist. When it came to it, he conveyed the news to his father not in his native Swiss German, which the family used at home, but in Italian—"Io son pittore"—"I am a painter." In all likelihood Ernst used Italian as a way of maintaining a certain distance to his father because this news, as he very well knew, would be far from welcome.

"Dear Papa,

... and if it's not possible, then that's that, then one just does one's duty, in the green forests, working for the state so that one has bread to eat; but he who has the freedom pities the imprisoned man, until he himself sits imprisoned on a round office chair! That is how I feel, you see, I haven't lost my sense of humor. But at the same time I also sing; I'm a painter, but not just a painter: an artist. An artist with my whole heart. Love of nature is the call of life for me!

... best regards to everyone Ernst."[31]

Years later Ernst Geiger's nephew, Max Bill, would find himself embroiled in a similar dispute between father and son, when he—having completed an apprenticeship as a silversmith—had to stand up to his father and insist that he was indeed going to go to the Bauhaus. At least Max Bill was able to rely on moral support from his uncle Ernst, who was only too familiar with this type of conflict.

30 Bill 1938 [c], p. 29

31 Ernst Geiger, letter to his father, Ulrich, Brugg, n.d., Archiv Christoph Geiger

32 As told by Marie's brother Ernst Geiger, Archiv Christoph Geiger

33 See Geiger 1957

Winterthur, Canton of Zürich

At 4:30 in the afternoon of 22 December 1908 Max Bill was born in Winterthur, a manufacturing town in East Switzerland, where his father was a deputy station inspector. A midwife tended to his mother, Marie, at the Bills' home at Rudolfstrasse 2, not far from the main station. The young Max spent the first years of his life in Rudolfstrasse with his parents and his brother Hugo, who was born in 1911.

The clattering of trains approaching and leaving the station formed a constant backdrop to Max's life in those years, waking and sleeping. Would Max's mother have regarded the move from the grand Rococo family home in Brugg to a relatively modest house near the station in Winterthur as a step down the social ladder? Everything in Brugg seemed to be on a larger scale compared to Winterthur, where Marie always felt hemmed in, particularly since the house in Rudolfstrasse (owned by the railway company) also had another apartment that was occupied by another family. By contrast, when she had gazed out of the windows in the Rococo house in Brugg, she had been able to "see for miles: to the Siggental in the east, to Habsburg, Gislifluh, and the Linner Linde in the west.... With its outhouses, yard, vegetable garden, orchards, and parklands the house in Brugg still had the air of a noble country seat."[32]

"The elevated terrace on the west side, with lovely evening views of the Jura landscape, raised the house up above the courtyard and the gardens. The broad passage with its Rotberg tiles and two huge glass doors exuded gracious comfort and led into the living areas, with precious stoves, stucco ceilings, beautiful panelling and deep window niches.... The passage on the upper floor also had glass doors. Dark nutwood doors, with elegant brass door knobs opened into the rooms.

The passages were divided up like rooms, and it was a wonderful feeling in winter when the doors (in the passage) to the 'fire niches' that served the stoves in the rooms were opened and the kindling was lit.... The lively décor in individual rooms, with golden profiles in green panelling, added not inconsiderably to the joyful spirit of the house.... After supper people gathered around the white tiled stove...."[33]

"The garden, to the west of the courtyard and laid out in the strict French style, was divided into elaborate beds and roundels with box hedges lining gravel and bark paths. It was generously planted with fine pear trees. A raised promenade, with an avenue of plane trees and bordered by high thuja hedges, separated the garden from the orchards.

In summer we used to do our homework at a stone table shaded by the plane trees. In the southeast corner of the garden there was a well-stocked greenhouse with heating; the plants in pots and tubs survived the winter in there . . .

But the most beautiful part of our paradise was the park. It was laid out in the English style with paths meandering between groups of trees and shrubs. At the center of our park there was a fountain in a semi-circular pool . . . where we kept all kinds of fish . . . the garden house was built against the south wall of the park, a small open room . . . with large ammonites (fossils) from Bolzano lying in the corners . . ."[34] The family's love of ammonites would later re-emerge in Marie Bill-Geiger's son Max.

For more on the town hall in Brugg, see Michael Stettler and Emil Maurer, *Die Bezirke Lenzburg und Brugg* (*Die Kunstdenkmäler des Kantons Aargau,* vol. 2) (Basel, 1953).

Marie's Paradise Lost

Marie's mother died from pneumonia in 1908 and just one month later —one day after Max was born—her father sold the Rococo house. Marie, who was still grieving for her mother and had sorely lacked maternal support during the final weeks of her pregnancy, now found that all of a sudden there was no way back to the place where she had spent her idyllic childhood and youth. All she could do was sink into memories of that time. Besides her favorite brother Ernst, Marie also had another brother—Hans Karl.

A family photograph taken in 1927 shows a relaxed-looking Max Bill before he left for the Bauhaus. To his left are his Uncle Ernst, casually reading a paper, and Marie Bill-Geiger (also reading) wearing a pinafore, as housewives did in those days. A note on the back of the photograph reads, "This is how Max looks when the uncle who helps him is there." (see p. 139).

Marie thought of Hans Karl as "absent" because he lived in Vienna, but he had not forgotten home and always did his best to interest friends and acquaintances in Austria in paintings done by Ernst.

In 1905 another Swiss painter—Ferdinand Hodler—whom Marie greatly admired, had had an extremely successful exhibition at the Vienna Secession. By now Hodler's paintings were gaining recognition

34 Geiger 1957

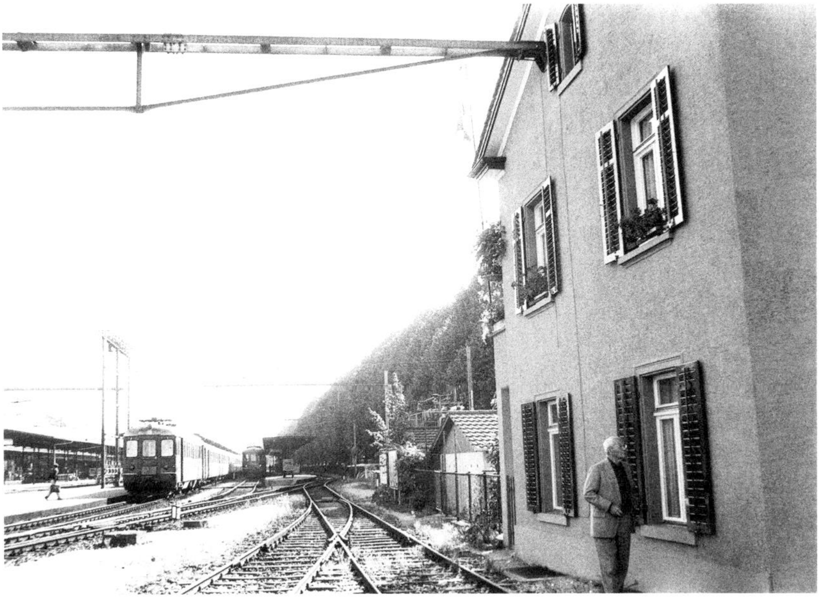

Max Bill in September 1978, Winterthur, outside the house where he was born and lived in as a young child

Ulrich Geiger on the bench of a tiled stove in his Rococo house in Brugg; a painting by his son Ernst Geiger is displayed on the wall

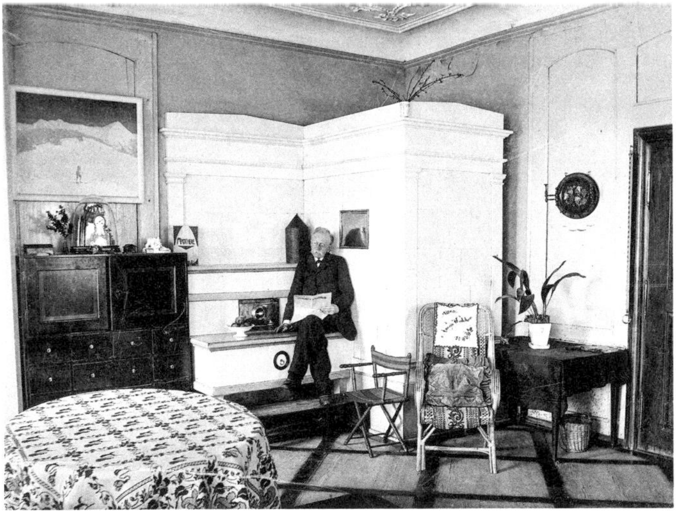

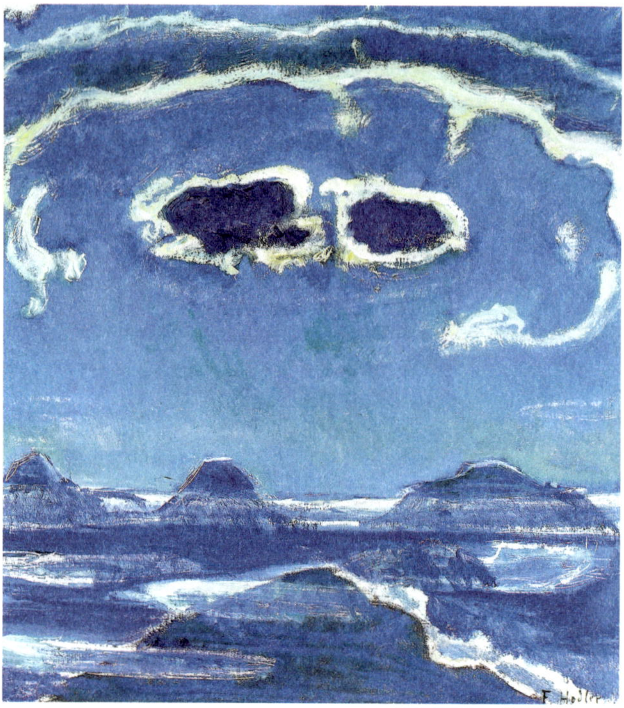

Ferdinand Hodler, *Mondnacht (Eiger, Mönch und Jungfrau),* ca. 1909, oil on canvas, 32×41.2 cm

Paul Klee, *Bern ursprüngl. Stadteingang II, 1911, 8,* 1911, pen on paper on cardboard, 9.8×17 cm

Niklaus Bill's watchmaker's pincers

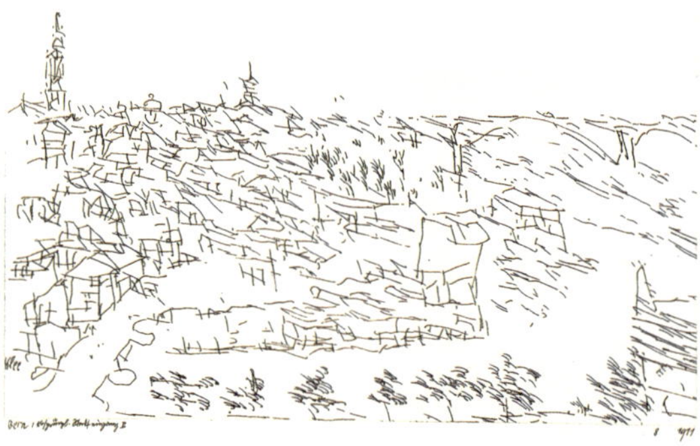

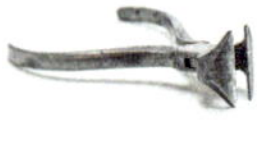

abroad, not only in Austria but also in Germany. However, in August 1914 the First World War broke out and in September 1914 the cathedral in Reims was hit by a volley of German artillery shells. The war not only caused untold human suffering, it also affected the reception of works of art. Indeed, when Hodler spoke out against the destruction of the cathedral in Reims, his art was immediately viewed less favorably in Germany. Meanwhile in France, leading collectors criticized his work for a "lack of sensibility." However, as the Belgian art critic and architect Henry van de Velde rightly points out in his obituary for Hodler, the landscapes he had painted since 1900 "put paid to any accusations of a lack of sensibility."[35] Guillaume Apollinaire resisted Hodler's art, claiming that it was more "Prussian" than Swiss: "we want no truck with the brutal parallelism of Hodler, which seems intrinsically to be more Prussian than Swiss."[36]

Politically biased critiques lingered on. In France, during the Second World War, Max Beckmann (1884–1950)—who fled the Nazis in 1937 and lived in exile in the Netherlands before finally settling in the United States in 1948—was, somewhat grotesquely, accused of producing "Germanic" art, an accusation that significantly delayed wider recognition of his oeuvre.

Hans Karl Geiger wrote from Vienna to his brother Ernst about the sale of their parental home in Brugg: "as to the sale of the house, to judge by the details that Papa has communicated to me, I also believe that the business is no longer working to his advantage. In principle I am in favor of the sale and have advised Papa accordingly, albeit on condition that [illegible].... By the way, you do him an injustice when you claim he didn't know how to develop the house properly. I don't think his intentions were to blame. I think the reason was a lack of accessible funds because it goes more or less without saying that Papa had almost all his capital tied up in the land and in his wine cellar. Taking into account the cost of supporting a large family, I doubt whether much will have been left over that could have been used for any development plans.... Although it's true that we never had to complain of abundant superfluity at home, I still wouldn't describe Papa as stingy, the opposite if anything. So any penny-pinching was merely a painful necessity ..."[37]

35 Henry van de Velde, "Ferdinand Hodler," *Die weissen Blätter* 5:3 (September 1918): 125–37, here p. 135

36 Guillaume Apollinaire in *L'intransigeant,* 14 November 1913

37 Hans Geiger, Vienna, to his brother Ernst Geiger [1908], Archiv Christoph Geiger

As foreigners in Vienna at the outbreak of war, Hans Karl Geiger and his wife Olga were interned (it has not been possible to retrieve any further details regarding Olga). On his return to Switzerland after the war, Max Bill's uncle Hans became director of the gasworks in Schlieren, not far from Zurich. Later on he ran Polyglott, a translation office in Zurich. Hans Karl Geiger died in 1934, not yet sixty, and was outlived by his sister Marie by three decades.

Unlike his brother, Ernst Geiger took the view that there was "something dubious" about the sale of his parents' property to the town of Brugg: "Our father's study was in the southwest corner of the upper ground floor, on the same level as the terrace. That was also where he kept his collection of antiquities. It was the easiest room to access from outside, and that was where the journeymen used to come asking for work and to receive their pay. I don't know if the thief who broke in and stole a sack of worthless, foreign copper coins and some bonds was one of those journeymen. In any case, thanks to the swift progress from theft to police action, the perpetrator was arrested that same morning in Neuenburg and sent to the Black Tower for a year. Following that, neighbors of the anxious, quite elderly homeowner managed to instil in him a constant fear of similar events recurring and above all a fear of a revenge attack by the condemned man. In short, he was persuaded to promise not to say anything about the impending sale until the terms had been agreed.... And by that means the bank got its construction site and the town got its town hall."[38]

The collection of antiquities that Ulrich Geiger-Schwarz had built up was not only of interest to the thief; Ernst Geiger noted that it had also "been seen by various scholars." The Geiger siblings were thus used to meeting intellectuals and academics. So Marie's move from Brugg to Winterthur required a very considerable adjustment; as well as setting up a new household, she also had to learn to deal with a very different situation.

Anyone who has lived in Switzerland will be well aware that when people move from one canton to another, they are often treated like alien interlopers in their new place of residence, even if they are Swiss nationals. Max Bill himself explained to me that in Switzerland a person's sense of belonging is mainly rooted in his or her canton.

And in 1974, when Max wanted to make love to me for the first time, he specifically took me to his mother's native canton. He had reserved

38 See Geiger 1957

39 "Jungfraubahn Schweiz," Gebr. Fretz A.G., Zurich, n.d., p.13

40 Information kindly supplied by Daniel Mani, Stiftung Historisches Erbe der SBB/SBB Heritage Foundation

a hotel room for us in Lenzburg, canton of Aargau. From the outset, as he later told me, his aim was to establish a secure emotional relationship with me.

Marie, who had been brought up as a Protestant, was intrigued when she came into contact with the largely unionized railwaymen that her husband worked with; Erwin Bill, unlike his new wife, had no links to any organized religion, which was rather unusual in those days. Nevertheless, although he was from another canton, he already enjoyed a certain degree of social recognition in Winterthur since he was a member of the leading workforce.

Max Bill's Father

Alfred Erwin Bill, known as Erwin, was born to Niklaus Bill, an independent watchmaker in Emmental, and Anna Maria Bill, née Witschi. In 1894 Erwin started work as an apprentice with SBB (Swiss Federal Railways). After the inauguration in September 1898 of the lower section of the Jungfraubahn, the highest-altitude railway in Europe, Erwin Bill—now a fully-qualified railwayman and a public servant—was assigned to the Jungfraubahn. He relished the pure mountain air and the sight of the impressive landscape all around him.

The Jungfraubahn follows "an open line along the height of the pass, with the Lauterbrunnen valley to its right and the Grindelwald valley to its left. . . . Suddenly the train dives into a little tunnel, just 87 meters long; a mere thirty seconds later a flood of dazzling sunshine bursts in and we see before us, almost in touching distance, the vast glaciers of the ice giants, the Eiger, the Mönch and the Jungfrau! We have arrived at the Eigergletscher station (2,000 meters to the Kleine Scheidegg, 2,323 meters above sea level, inaugurated on 19 September 1898)."[39]

The final breakthrough to the Jungfraujoch came in 1912, some ten years after Erwin Bill had been transferred to the main station in Winterthur (September 1902). Although he now found himself working in an entirely different, urban situation, he was as punctilious as ever.

Erwin Bill's career as a railwayman in Switzerland is recorded in full in the SBB archives: "The SBB's index of employees notes that on 1 September 1902 he took up the post of station assistant, 1st class, in Winterthur. On 15 February 1904 he became a deputy, 3rd class, and on 1 April 1908 he became a sous-chef, 1st class. The last list of employees in which he is named was compiled in 1930."[40]

On 23 March 1908 Marie Geiger and Erwin Bill "of Moosseedorf/Münchenbuchsee, resident in Winterthur" married in Brugg. In the register of marriages, which has been preserved in the municipal archive, Erwin is described as "assistant station master." A week after the wedding he took up a new post as "deputy station inspector, 1st class." Did the wine merchant Ulrich Geiger-Schwarz pull some strings to advance his new son-in-law's career? Marie's brother, Ernst, once mentioned that her father was friends with "a railways director"; "social capital was just as important in those days, even if it wasn't called that yet."[41] Whatever the case, as Erwin Bill embarked on married life he was also entrusted with more responsibility at work and now exuded the greater authority that was expected of him by the other railway employees in Winterthur. Erwin Bill, due to his occupation and to his upbringing by a watchmaker, but also by nature, was meticulous, punctual, and reliable.

The People of the Moosseetal

As a boy Max generally spoke in the local dialect of his native Winterthur, peppered with expressions inherited from his father, which he pronounced with a Bernese accent. As is still the norm in Switzerland today, Max was registered in his father's *Bürgerort,* in his case a parish in the canton of Bern with the poetic name of Moosseedorf/Münchenbuchsee. "Moosseedorf, an off-shoot of Münchenbuchsee, had its own church and ran its own affairs."[42]

All Swiss citizens have a "Bürgerort," a municipality where one is registered for life (not necessarily the same as one's place of birth). It used to be of considerable importance: if any citizens fell into poverty, it was their "Bürgerort" (not their place of birth or residence) that had to provide for them in the local workhouse.

One very famous son of Münchenbuchsee was the artist Paul Klee; his father taught music at the nearby teachers' training college in Hofwil. This would matter to Max Bill later on when he enrolled at the Bauhaus in Dessau, where Paul Klee was a master. Far away from home Max Bill

41 Ernst Geiger, Archiv Christoph Geiger
42 König 1920, p. 96
43 *Tagebücher von Paul Klee 1898–1918,* 1957, p. 11
44 Paul Klee to Lily Stumpf (1901), cited in *Ferdinand Hodler,* exh. cat. Kunsthaus Zürich (Bern: Benteli, 1998), p. 129
45 Ernst Geiger to Ida Geiger, Brugg, 1952, Archiv Christoph Geiger

and Klee discovered that they had the same geographical roots and could thus communicate in Swiss German—incomprehensible to most High German speakers—and enjoy their own little language oasis with its echoes of home.

Paul Klee: "I shall preface my childhood memories with the remark that I am said to have been born in the schoolhouse at Münchenbuchsee, near Bern, on 18 December 1879. I was a few months old when my father ... in his capacity as a teacher of music at Hofwyl's teachers' college, was granted permission to live permanently in Bern."[43] From a young age Paul Klee also admired the work of the Swiss artist Ferdinand Hodler—providing yet more for Max Bill and Paul Klee to discuss at the Bauhaus.

In July 1901 the city council in Bern decided to buy four paintings by Hodler: *Die Nacht, Die enttäuschten Seelen, Eurythmie* and *Der Tag.* Paul Klee, who saw these canvases by Hodler at Kunstmuseum Bern, described them in a letter to his future wife Lily Stumpf as the "most important compositions of the present day."[44]

The Watchmaker in Emmental

Niklaus Bill, Max's paternal grandfather, had his own clock- and watch-making business in Emmental and was naturally used to working with the utmost precision. Max Bill always claimed he had inherited his grandfather's "Emmental stubbornness" (as it is called in Switzerland). He also inherited one of his grandfather's tools: a beautifully made pair of watchmaker's pincers. And it may well be that it was those pincers that introduced Max Bill to the idea of "good form" that he would strive for and defend as long as he lived.

Childhood in Winterthur and on Holiday in Sternenberg

As a child, Max had a teddy bear called Bez, whose nose, ears, and paws he lovingly chewed off. Naturally enough his earliest drawings were of the trains passing by his window. His uncle Ernst described him as a chatterbox.

"Max Bill is no longer the chatterbox that he was as a little boy. He doesn't say much unprompted ..."[45]

The Bill family generally spent their holidays in Sternenberg, the highest village in the canton of Zürich, in a welcoming holiday house, where they felt much more at ease than in the house by the railway tracks. In their home in Winterthur there were portrait photographs of Max's maternal grandparents. Each of those daguerreotypes—astonishingly detailed and lifelike—was a unique treasure in its own right, a rarity that not every family could afford.

Once, when the family was on holiday in Sternenberg, Marie Bill-Geiger painted a picture of her sons playing while her husband read a newspaper.

This portrait, done in Sternenberg, is the only painting of Max Bill's mother known to me. It used to hang on a wall in his painting studio in Zumikon; after his death it went to his son Jakob.

Max Bill, in what was for him an unusually tender tone of voice, "how should I describe my mother?" After a long pause: "she could do anything. that's to say, she ran the house, but she also had a lot of imagination—she told us children all sorts of interesting things."[46]

On the walls of the room in this little picture she painted the daguerreotype portraits that she had temporarily hung in the holiday house.

"i mainly inherited my interest in art from my mother. she often painted for pleasure, but i was even more influenced by her brother, dr. ernst geiger, and her brother-in-law, prof. adolf weibel (aarau) who was also my godfather and had a formative impact on my life."[47]

Max's maternal grandmother, Sophie Geiger-Schwarz, was born into a respected farming family in Villigen (canton of Aargau) and was said to have been a straightforward, intelligent woman. Meanwhile, Max's grandfather, Ulrich Geiger-Schwarz, was renowned in the family for having been the "biggest wine merchant in Switzerland"—only, as a child, Max could not really picture what that meant.

Max Bill's Mother and Her Family

Max's mother, Marie Geiger (1882–1963), grew up in the small town of Brugg in the canton of Aargau with her siblings: Ernst Samuel (b. 1876), Hans Karl (b. 1877), Sophie (b. 1879), Ida (b. 1883), and Rosa (b. 1887). She

46 Bill, 1942 [b]
47 Max Bill in conversation with Angela Thomas, 22 April 1975
48 Max Bill in conversation with Angela Thomas
49 Geiger 1969, pp. 23–24

and her brother Ernst had a particularly strong bond. Later on, Marie's son, Max Bill, would find that he could always count on Ernst Geiger, his favorite uncle, for moral support and a sympathetic ear.

The Geiger family had numerous relatives in the villages around Brugg and, even after her marriage to Erwin Bill, Marie Geiger always kept in touch with them. Or, as Max Bill once said to me, his mother actively cultivated any contacts with her own relatives—be they close or distant—but never took any interest in her husband's relatives.

As to the education of the Geiger-Schwarz siblings in Brugg, the sons—as was generally the case in those days—received preferential treatment. To their father's delight Marie's brother Hans Karl "had a feel for business." He left for Austria shortly before Marie's wedding and spent several years in Vienna, with the result that Max initially barely knew him. However, in his mother's extended family there was another uncle (by marriage) whom Max did get to know as a young boy, the painter Adolf Weibel in Aarau, who was married to Marie's older sister, Sophie.

Close Up

"Right from the start, Ernst Geiger had a considerable influence on me. He was part of the Cuno Amiet–Giovanni Giacometti circle. Back then my uncle Ernst knew a lot of Russian émigrés."[48] Both in Zurich and when he was in Paris (having stayed on there after visiting the Paris Exposition in 1900), Ernst Geiger used to sing in Russian student choirs—which the French police openly regarded as deeply suspect.

"During my time in Zurich I widened my horizons by getting to know some Russian students. For a while various Swiss friends and I ate in the Russian kitchen; I also made a serious attempt to learn Russian. Later on I applied for a forester's job in the Caucasus.... But in Paris the fact that we loyal Swiss subjects were associating with Russian students aroused suspicion in the minds of the French police, who in no time at all were making inquiries at the magistrate's office in Brugg, which gave my father an entirely unnecessary fright."[49]

I once asked Max Bill to tell me more about the way his uncle Ernst painted; he extended his left hand and then drew it back in toward himself, with the words "close up!" In fact, Ernst Geiger's snowscapes, which he painted three years before Max was born, secured his reputation as a member of the European avant-garde; take his *Wintersonne,* for instance, painted in 1905—although the motif is a snowdrift and a thatched house near the small town of Gränichen in the canton of Aargau, the real subject of the painting is the light.

Giovanni Segantini, a neo-Impressionist, also demonstrated a very particular interest in light effects in his paintings. Like Georges Seurat, whose paintings Max Bill would later admire, Segantini used pure, unmixed colors, however "he would draw them across the picture plane like fine, long threads. Between those threads there were narrow strips of bare canvas, which he would then fill in with complementary colors or fine lines of gold, intensifying the impression of light."[50] In 1911 Cuno Amiet (a friend of Ernst Geiger's), Ferdinand Hodler, and the French painter Robert Delaunay all showed work at the Gereons Club in Cologne.
The Gereons Club was founded in January 1911 by the painter Olga Oppenheimer, her friend Emmy Worringer, and Franz M. Jansen: "Oppenheimer the painter, one of those highly cultured, sensitive Jewish women with strong support in wealthy intellectual circles, her enthusiastic friend Emmy and I started the Gereons Club.... We were the first to exhibit paintings by Delaunay and Derain, we showed works by Klimt, Hodler and Amiet, and the first Picasso."[51]

Hodler's influence extended well beyond Switzerland, and it was on his recommendation that Ernst Geiger was accepted into the Deutscher Künstlerbund (Association of German artists).
In 1908 Hodler was elected president of the Society of Swiss Painters, Sculptors, and Architects (GSMBA). He appointed the author Carl Albert Loosli as the society's general secretary and as editor of the GSMBA magazine, *Schweizer Kunst.* At the time "the battle against the reactionary, inner Swiss 'secession,' which was supported and instrumentalised by conservative politicians" was the main focus of the GSMBA's art policy.[52]

It should be noted at this point that, as it developed in the post-Hodler era, the GSMBA appears to have changed its ideological direction of travel. By the 1930s and 1940s it was no longer the GSMBA that took a stand against conservatism, but rather the new artists' group Allianz, which had been founded in opposition to the GSMBA.

50 Frehner 2004, p. 99
51 Jansen 1989, p. 172
52 Lerch and Marti 2008, p. 12
53 Mühlestein and Schmidt 1942, p. 16
54 Mühlestein and Schmidt 1942, p. 16
55 "Max Bill Winterthur, 20.–23.IV.26" and "Dr. Joh. Widmer, Genf," in Ernst Geiger's visitors' books, Museum Neuhaus, Biel
56 Exh. cat. for the April exhibition at Kunsthalle Basel, 5–25 April 1915, cat. nos. 59–67

Allianz, which Max Bill later joined, would go on to protest against all forms of conservativism in art and architecture by GSMBA members.

The list of members in the Deutscher Künstlerbund (Association of German Artists) in 1914 includes Swiss artists such as Ferdinand Hodler, Ernst Geiger, to name just two. The German artist Käthe Kollwitz is also on the list.

Besides debating artistic issues, Hodler and Geiger also discussed another topic that was very important to both of them: nature and the natural world. Max Bill's uncle Ernst—always addressed as "Dr. Geiger" by Hodler—had something of an advantage in this area thanks to his training as a scientist. Hodler, who had grown up in a large family living on the breadline, was more of an amateur enthusiast and regretted not having been able to study and qualify as a serious scientist.

"I actually wanted to become a natural scientist; my whole thinking and doing was secretly designed to achieve that goal." (Ferdinand Hodler)[53]

As an apprentice painter in Thun the young Ferdinand Hodler "keenly collected beetles and butterflies, pieces of beautiful rock crystal and other minerals; he also built up a herbarium.... That was the only kind of 'scientific research' that he had access to, and he pursued it with the most inadequate of means, with no money and no instructions. But with real passion!"[54] Hodler—like two of his Swiss compatriots, Le Corbusier and of course Max Bill—never completed his apprenticeship, bidding farewell to his master before his time was up.

Ernst Geiger's acceptance into the Deutscher Künstlerbund, thanks to Hodler's recommendation, meant that besides exhibiting his work in Switzerland, he could now also regularly participate in exhibitions in Germany. However, his increasing renown and these additional opportunities to earn an income were suddenly halted by the outbreak of the First World War. Fortunately, he was still able to exhibit in Switzerland despite the ongoing hostilities across the border.

Johannes Widmer, philologist and art critic, was also a friend of Ernst Geiger and Ulrich Wilhelm Züricher—all three were members of Libertas. Widmer, who lived in Geneva, wrote on Hodler and his contemporaries for *Der Bund,* a daily paper in Bern, and—as an art manager of sorts—also helped to promote the work of Ernst Geiger. Max Bill first met Widmer in April 1926, when the latter was on a three-day visit to his uncle in Ligerz. Widmer and Bill signed the visitors' book one after the other.[55]

In April 1915 paintings by Ernst Geiger and other artists in his circle of friends were presented at Kunsthalle Basel. Geiger showed nine items; the most expensive—*Unterengadin im Winter* (1914)—was priced at 1,000 Swiss francs.[56] Cuno Amiet showed seventeen works; his prices went up to a handsome 3,500 Swiss francs. Meanwhile, Giovanni Giacometti was represented with twenty-one works; at 8,000 Swiss francs, his *Weiblicher Akt* (1914) was the most expensive item on display and twice the price of the two new paintings by Hodler in the same exhibition. To his fellow artists' disappointment, Giacometti did not put in an appearance at the opening.

Letter from Cuno Amiet to Giovanni Giacometti in Stampa:

"Oschwand, 28 May 1915, Dear Giovanni, We thought you were coming to the exhibition in Basel & and expected to see you there ... in old friendship, your C. Amiet."[57]

The two works from Ferdinand Hodler's studio that were on sale in that exhibition were listed in the catalogue as *Eiger and Jungfrau (Temps d'orage)* and priced at 4,000 Swiss francs each. Hodler—by now widely renowned—was in fact the dominant presence in the exhibition, which also included a very large group of "works by Ferd. Hodler from private collections" (nos. 129–166 in the catalogue). At this point Hodler was still in deep mourning for his beloved Valentine Godé-Darel, who had given birth to their daughter in October 1913 and had died on 25 January 1915, just a few months before the Basel exhibition opened.

Hodler entrusted his daughter Pauline (known as Paulette) to his wife. What must that have been like for the child and for her stepmother? Ferdinand Hodler's portraits of the ailing, dying, and deceased Valentine Godé-Darel were exhibited in Bern in 2008; the exhibition catalogue contains an essay on these paintings by the editor, Katharina Schmidt.[58]

Ernst Geiger may have known at least some of Hodler's portraits of his lover after her cancer diagnosis. It seems that Geiger's wife, Maria Geiger-Bockhoff, copied some of these portrait drawings and paintings by Hodler; she also copied works by Édouard Manet.[59] These are now in the collection of Museum Neuhaus in Biel.

Did Max's mother maybe take her elder son to that exhibition in Basel to see paintings not only by her brother, Ernst, but also by Hodler,

57 Radlach 2000, letter no. 378
58 See *Ferdinand Hodler*, exh. cat. Kunstmuseum Bern, Szépmüvészeti Museum Budapest, (Ostfildern-Ruit: Hatje Cantz, 2008), pp. 275–96
59 Information kindly supplied by Christoph Geiger
60 Mühlestein and Schmidt 1942, p. 511
61 Van de Velde, "Ferdinand Hodler" (see note 35), p. 125
62 Van de Velde, "Ferdinand Hodler," p. 125
63 Noted in Max Burgmeier's first book of minutes for the GSMBA Aargau, Archiv Christoph Geiger

who so generously supported Ernst's artistic development? Whatever the case, she must have been proud of her brother's achievement—and, as the wife of a Swiss Federal Railways employee, she would not have had to pay to travel to Basel by train. Ferdinand Hodler had long been successful in Austria, but it was not until two years after the Basel exhibition—when his own death was only a matter of months away—that he could celebrate his "greatest triumph" in Switzerland "in the peerless display of his life's work that the Kunsthaus in Zurich presented throughout the summer of 1917."[60] Hodler died in Geneva on Whit Sunday in 1918.

"Switzerland has lost its greatest painter, the first great painter it has ever had": Henry van de Velde in his obituary for Ferdinand Hodler.[61]

In the autumn of that year, shortly before his tenth birthday, Max Bill and his father visited the Kunstmuseum in Winterthur to see the exhibition *Selbstbildnisse Schweizer Künstler der Gegenwart* (Self-portraits by contemporary Swiss artists), which included Hodler's confidently stubborn self-portrait, done in 1916.

Van de Velde especially admired Hodler's paintings, regarding them as an equivalent to the contemporary "urge for transformation" in architecture: "Hodler's enduring, highest aims run in parallel to that which has been transforming architecture for the last quarter of a century.... Were one to seek to fathom the parameters of Hodler's formula in terms of the latest architecture, one might best imagine his compositions transferred onto the wall of some grand station concourse, onto the walls of one of the recent great edifices by the Dresden architect Hans Poelzig or the walls of my theater at the exhibition in Cologne in 1914. The dominant factor in all of these works is their capacity to uplift ..."[62]

Adolf Weibel—
The Other Uncle Who Paints

Four years before Max Bill was born, his two painter uncles had already appeared on a public platform together: in 1904 Adolf Weibel and Ernst Geiger became two of the eight founding members of the Aargau section of the GSMBA (*Gesellschaft Schweizer Maler, Bildhauer und Architekten,* Society of Swiss painters, sculptors and architects). Geiger was regarded by his fellow artists as something of an intellectual who liked debating; however, he soon found the canton of Aargau too restrictive. Adolf Weibel was the first president of the GSMBA Aargau.[63]

In October 1906 Adolf Weibel and Ernst Geiger spent a few days together in the Hübi, Gertrud Züricher's wooden cabin in the mountains.

"I had a lovely time at the Hübi with Ernst Geiger from 23 to 27 October ... with heartfelt thanks to the welcoming mistress of the beautiful little Hübi house. Adolf Weibel, 27 October 1906."[64]

One their most successful excursions was a hike to the Windspillen in the Valais. When he left, just three days before Marie Geiger arrived, Weibel drew a mountain panorama in the Hubelhüsi chronicle.

"uncle adolf painted nicely—but like a philistine. only, as a person, my 'götti' [godfather] adolf weibel was anything but a philistine."[65] Later on Max Bill no longer remembered which of his uncles had given him his first paint box.

As well as acting as "treasurer for the Aargauischer Kunstverein, Weibel became the keeper of the Aargauische Kunstsammlung (Aargau art collection) in 1927 and continued in that capacity until 1942. At that time the collection was housed in the top-lit rooms of the Aargauisches Gewerbemuseum. The Aargauer Kunsthaus in Aarau, as we now know it, opened in 1959."[66] Adolf Weibel's wife, Sophie Geiger, died young from tuberculosis, as Max told me.

Max Bill's Grandfather: A Wine Trader in Brugg

Ulrich Geiger-Schwarz (see p. 44)—somewhat countrified, with spectacles and a narrow face tilted to one side in the portrait by his son Ernst—gazes curiously out at us with a canny, witty air. His ears are large and his chin is not especially well defined. Although, according to Ernst, he was not necessarily physically robust, it seems that Max's grandfather had a countryman's native intelligence combined with a dash of small-town sophistication. When Ernst Geiger and his siblings were growing up, their home—now the town hall in Brugg—was in a relatively sparsely populated area. "Toward the town, where the post office now stands, there used to be ... an old tannery. We knew it well, with its tanning devices and beautiful greenery along its south wall. When it was demolished it showered rich blessings on our father: urn after urn from a Roman burial site

64 In the Hubelhüsi chronicle
65 Max Bill in conversation with Angela Thomas
66 Information kindly supplied by Stephan Kunz, Aargauer Kunsthaus, 2007

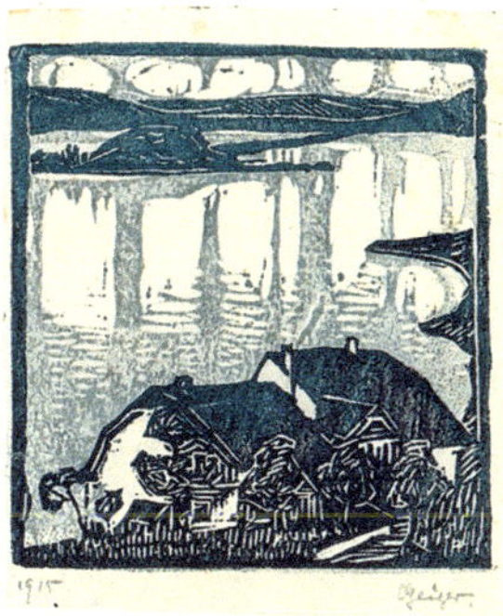

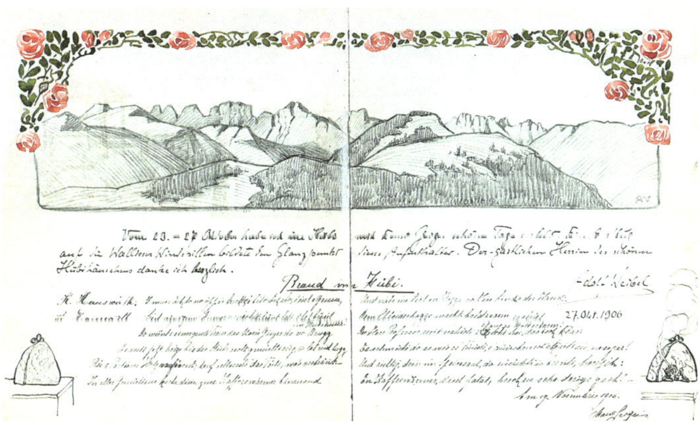

Ernst Geiger, Untitled (View of Lake Biel from the Kapf), 1915, color woodcut, 12×8.6cm

Adolf Weibel, Mountain panorama in the Bernese Uplands, drawing with monogram; decorative border by Ernst Geiger, 1906, graphite, india ink, and watercolor on paper

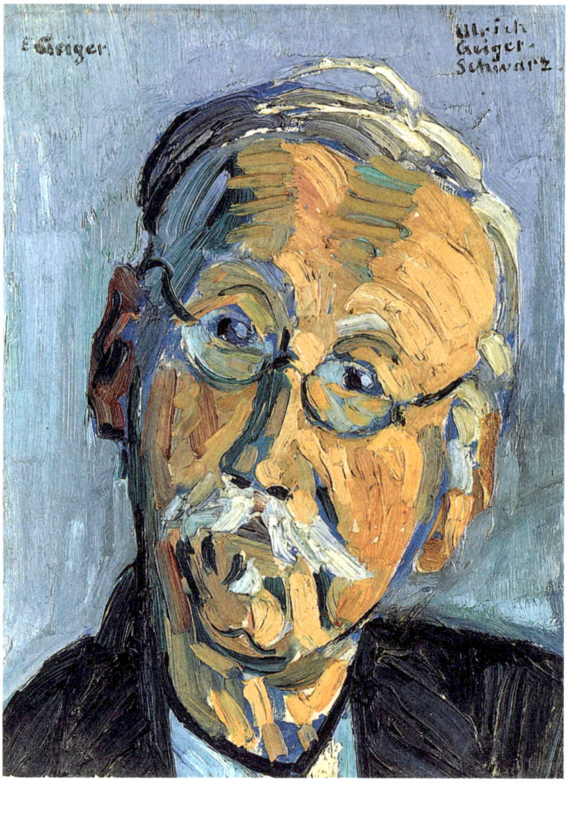

Ernst Geiger, *Ulrich Geiger-Schwarz,*
oil on canvas, 25 × 18 cm

appeared before our very eyes. Besides diverse artifacts, one of the urns contained a beautiful silvered mirror. All those items found their way into my father's study—into a tiny collection that later sowed the seed for the collection in the grandiose Vindonissa Museum. At least that ensured that all those finds stayed in Brugg."[67]

Ernst Geiger

"I was born on 1 February 1876, the first child of Ulrich and Sophie Geiger-Schwarz in Turgi, in the house opposite the Krone. It seems I was a delicate little boy with pale blond curls, so that people were often heard to say it was a 'shame little Ernst wasn't a girl.'"[68] In fact, as a boy Ernst was rather shy of girls, "and when the dance floor was set up under the plane trees by the Schützenhaus [the marksmen's club house], my dear Mama had the greatest trouble persuading me, her favorite child, to get up and dance."[69] Meanwhile Hans Karl, his younger brother by one year, never missed a chance to take to the floor. "We went to see the *Turnus* exhibition [a touring exhibition] when it came to Aarau—that was my first contact with modern art. There had never been an art exhibition in Aarau before."[70]

Heinrich Ganter taught mathematics at the cantonal school in Aarau from 1886 to 1915. As to the exhibition, it is worth noting that after 1929 Erwin Bill in Winterthur, father to Max Bill, was active as secretary for the *Turnusausstellung.*

"It was when I was at the cantonal school that I was converted to temperance, and I have remained true to my oath ever since. My Papa, the wine merchant, was not entirely averse to the idea—even if it was not in his own interest as a businessman—he was well aware of the dangers of a tipple for students."[71]

"My father, Ulrich Geiger-Schwarz, who owned the Meier estate for 25 years (the present Brugg town hall and its garden occupy just a small part of it), was born into a long line of farmers in the Rhine valley. He had come to Turgi as a bookkeeper. As an officer in the 15th battalion and as the husband of a Schwarz from Villigen, he became a proper Aargauer. The people of Brugg and the local marksmen's society welcomed him into their ranks....

67 Geiger 1957, pp. 34–35
68 Geiger 1969
69 Geiger 1969
70 Geiger 1969
71 Geiger 1969

As a member of the electricity committee he was an asset to the community. He collected antiquities and helped to found the Antiquarian Society (now the Gesellschaft Pro Vindonissa); he also helped to pave the way for the society to buy the amphitheater."[72]

However, this did not stop Ernst from now "dancing the night away."

In the summer of 1906 Ernst Geiger set up his easel in the open air near Lauenen and painted a number of strikingly atmospheric landscapes. Looking at those paintings one has a sense that he was very much at ease there. And of course within six months, he would meet his future wife, Maria Bockhoff, there and fall for her impish smile. Oddly, he only ever painted her from behind or with her head bowed.

Ernst Geiger and Maria Bockhoff soon married and moved to Bern, where they made contact with kindred spirits who also saw themselves as progressive teetotallers. These included some young Russians who had come to study in Switzerland; it was through them that Ernst Geiger met the Swiss artist Otto Morach, who painted in his own distinctly willful, expressive style. As it turned out, Otto Morach and Ernst Geiger had a certain amount in common: both "first studied science, then joined the teaching profession but ultimately turned to painting."[73] They remained in close contact. Morach visited five of the eight exhibitions that Geiger put on in his studio in 1908; by contrast Geiger's brother-in-law, Adolf Weibel, only visited two of his studio exhibitions, and Gertrud and Bertha Züricher and the artist Hanni Bay each only went to one.[74]

Other visitors to Geiger's studio exhibitions included "Mr. Frey, Mrs. Kümmerly & son" from the firm of Kümmerly & Frey; all three were teetotallers. On 1 November 1908 a certain Maja Einstein signed the visitors' book; this may or may not have been Albert Einstein's sister of that name. On 7 March 1909 fellow artist Otto Morach again features among the visitors to a studio exhibition.[75]

In 1911 Ernst Geiger was awarded a Swiss federal study grant for art, and that same year he and his wife left Bern. They spent 1913–14 in the Engadine and from 1915 onward Ernst regularly spent the winter months in the Ticino. In 1918 Ernst Geiger bought the "Hof zu Schafis" on Lake Biel, a property on the west edge of the village of Ligerz, where he subsequently presented an art exhibition each autumn.[76]

72 Geiger 1957, p. 34
73 Bill 1976, p. 15
74 Noted in Ernst Geiger's visitors' books, Museum Neuhaus, Biel
75 Ernst Geiger's visitors' books, Museum Neuhaus, Biel
76 See Fischer [1966]

The "farm" was a country residence with a half-hipped roof, corner towers, and external stone steps leading up to a knight's hall with Gothic windows and beyond that to the family's private quarters. It stood in grounds that had run wild, where Geiger—who had a diploma in forestry—had planted a cypress and fig tree coppice. Vines grew on the slopes leading down to Lake Biel. This estate had once been the seat of a prominent family in Ligerz, which had adopted the name and coat of arms of a noble family that had died out in the fifteenth century.

The young Max Bill, who turned 10 in December 1918, loved going to the "farm" in Ligerz with his mother to visit his Uncle Ernst and his "intelligent Aunt Marie" from Germany.

He may have been in a position to buy the "Hof" because he had received his share of the legacy left by his father Ulrich Geiger-Schwarz, who had died in 1916. By now Geiger was also enjoying increasing success as an artist and was able to make a living from sales of his oil paintings.

At the time Ernst Geiger set the prices of his oil paintings very high, between 400 and 1200 Swiss francs. In 1919 Ernst Geiger made a note in his accounts book: "93 'Lake Biel' oil paintings sold so far." By way of a comparison: in the 1930s paintings by Piet Mondrian sold in Switzerland for around 300 Swiss francs.

However, it may be that it was that same financial success that prevented Ernst Geiger from venturing into more daring territory in his paintings. He never made the move into pure abstraction; his work never became truly modern—it remained moderate. Nevertheless, as a boy Max Bill was clearly inspired by his favorite uncle's paintings.

From 1918 to 1920 Geiger and his family spent the winter months in Comano, in the canton of Ticino, where they always stayed in the "house with the pillared hallway." In 1920 Geiger painted the view looking up toward the chapel of the hermit San Bernardo; this painting, the *Oratorio des San Bernardo,* later went to his nephew Max.

Aunts Ida and Rosa in Brugg

Ida and Rosa Geiger were godmothers to Max and his brother Hugo. If Hugo was given a woolly hat with a red pom-pom, Max would be given a woolly hat with a blue pom-pom. Marie Geiger's two sisters were spinsters, as people used to say. Ida worked as a secretary and Rosa was a nurse. After their mother died they moved together from the Rococo house to the "Zimmermannhaus" on the outskirts of Brugg.

The "Zimmermann house" had been built in the so-called Bernese country house style, which combined rural and baronial features. Now home to the municipal art gallery, the house has a many-windowed façade looking out to the street and a mansard roof, a terraced garden and a two-story, open arcade.

When the Bill brothers and their mother went to visit her younger sisters—who always looked to the past rather than the future—they would find themselves surrounded by furniture from a bygone era and had to be on their best behavior. Ida and Rosa Geiger saw themselves as the guardians of those "beautiful old household effects."

"In Miss Geiger's salon" there was "furniture in styles ranging from Louis XVI to Biedermeier, and especially rare items in the Empire style."[77]

A Self-Portrait and Life in Brugg

Ernst Geiger, Ida and Rosa's brother, had in fact painted a self-portrait before he painted a portrait of his father Ulrich Geiger-Schwarz (see p. 44). In that self-portrait Ernst is wearing spectacles, his chin is hidden under a beard, and he does not have the same canny air as his father. He looks more vulnerable and more sensitive. As it happens, Ernst Geiger's myopia led to his being exempted from military service in the Swiss army. His nephew, Max, also already wore spectacles as a boy, with the result that he, too, was initially not deemed fit for the army. It was only later, during the Second World War, that he was called up for military service. Ernst Geiger could never have been described as intrepid. Although he did travel around to a certain extent, he was never really adventurous—he preferred to be in close contact with nature. At the time when he painted this self-portrait, he had already been happily married to Maria Bockhoff for some years and was father to Max's cousin Hans.

As a wine trader Max's grandfather, Ulrich Geiger-Schwarz, had numerous contacts with suppliers abroad. And when little Max was in Brugg, visiting his relatives, he was always entranced by the special aroma of the wooden crates filled with bottles of wine. They excited his childish imagination, as did the images on the exotic-looking foreign stamps stuck to the crates. Max Bill never met his maternal grandmother, Sophie

77 See "Führungen durch Alt-Brugg, Vorstadt," *Brugger Tagblatt,* 5 October 1946

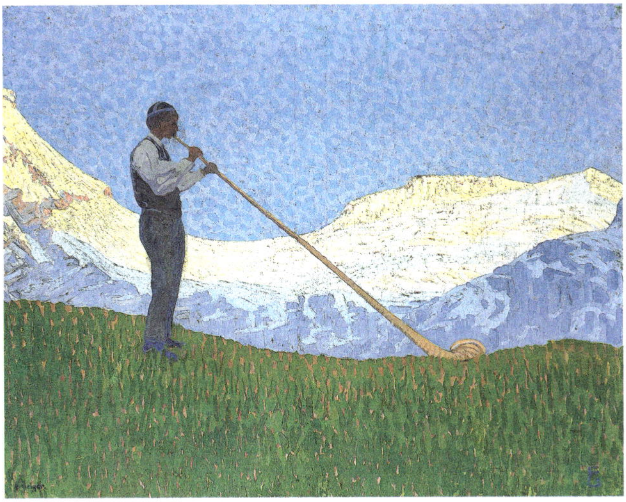

Ernst Geiger, *Alphornbläser,* ca. 1906, oil on canvas, 70×90cm

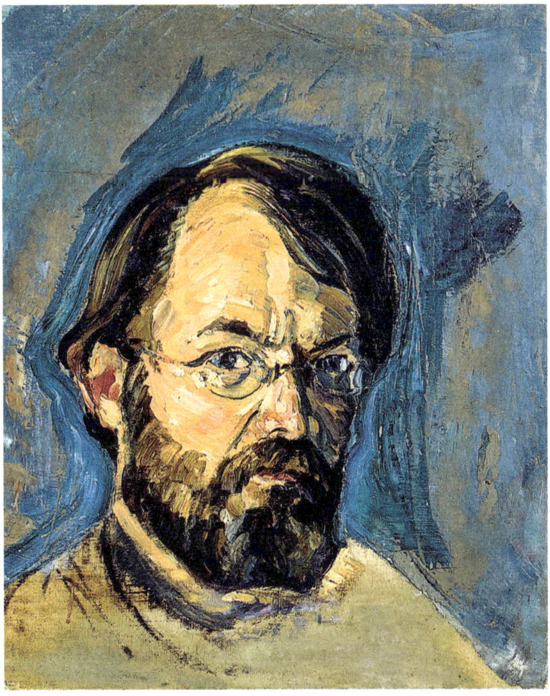

Ernst Geiger, Self-portrait, ca. 1912, oil on canvas, 46×38cm

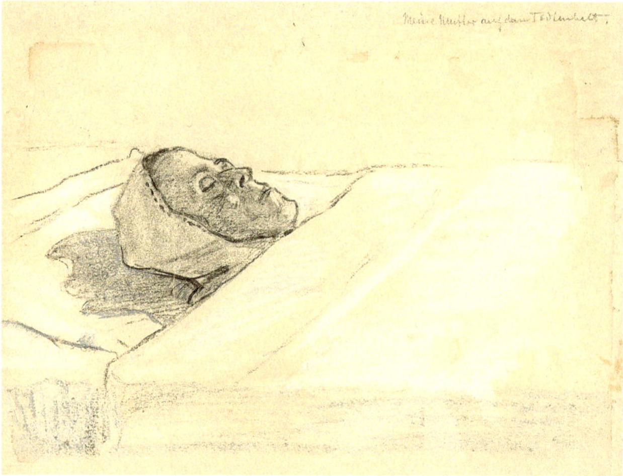

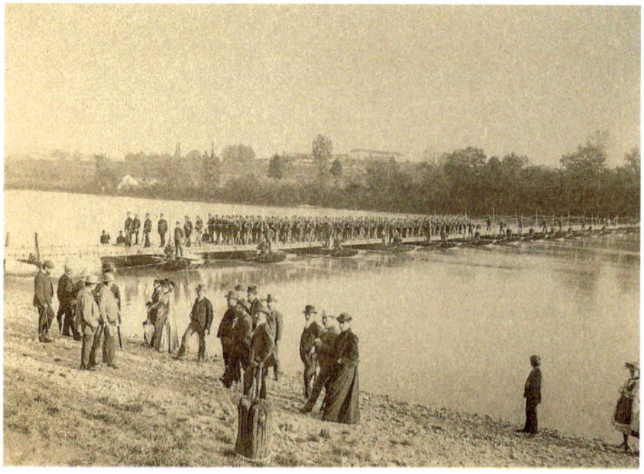

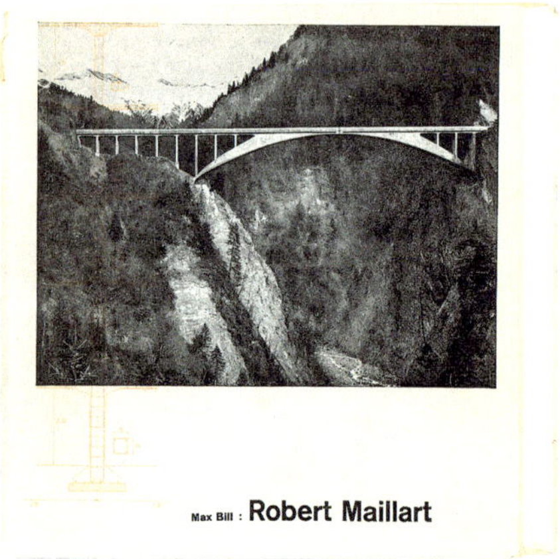

Ernst Geiger, *Sophie Geiger-Schwarz on her deathbed* (d. 10 November 1908), 1908, graphite on paper, 23.8×31 cm

Pontoon bridge at Brugg, 1890

Max Bill, Book cover featuring the world-renowned Salginatobel Bridge near Schiers, 1949

Geiger-Schwarz. Ernst Geiger had drawn her on her death bed; the style of that drawing is reminiscent of Hodler's series of portraits of Valentine Godé-Darel in her last days.

Although Ulrich Geiger-Schwarz had sold the Rococo house to the town of Brugg, just one month after his wife died, he still owned "Badenerstrasse 7, a large property with a stone dwelling house with a tiled roof. The rest of the property consisted of orchards and arable land and meadows."[78] Once he was installed in his Badenerstrasse, Max's grandfather, whose military mementos included an officer's cap and a weighty officer's sabre from about 1870, took in a lodger—a Swiss army colonel whose son had died.

A Love of Bridges Is Kindled

The lodger was very kind to little Max. He let him play with his collection of tin soldiers, showed him how to arrange them in battle formation, and took him to the Swiss National Day celebrations on 1 August. The colonel gave a speech at the celebrations and Max, just five years old, was proud to stand next to him on the speakers' platform.

Nevertheless, when the colonel took Max to the barracks afterward, the little boy was much more impressed by the models of military bridge building—there was a pontoniers' training school in Brugg.

"The pontoons were in three sections, made from larch wood and oak, with strong iron hooks so that they could be uncoupled. The center section was a rectangular box, the two outer sections were tapered." (Christoph Geiger)

As an adult, Max Bill frequently returned to the topic of bridge construction. During the Second World War, entirely on his own account, he embarked on a wide-ranging study and—despite having to enter military exclusion zones—photographed Swiss bridges built by Robert Maillart for a monograph that came out in 1949.[79] Two decades after that, in 1966–67, he even designed a bridge of his own, the Lavina-Tobel Bridge near Tamins in the canton of Grisons. The aesthetics of this bridge are perfectly captured in Erich Schmid's film *Bill—Das absolute Augenmass* (2008).

Bill's interest in bridges never waned. In September 1975 he brought me a copy of the magazine *China im Bild 7* (1975) to show me the color photographs of painted Chinese bridges.

78 Information kindly supplied by Titus J. Meier, Stadtarchiv Brugg

79 See Bill 1949 [c]

However, despite being initiated into military matters as a child, and despite his mother's preferences (in her apartment she had a framed letter written by the Swiss General Henri Guisan), Max Bill never expressed the slightest enthusiasm for military life and the Swiss army. In those days that did him no favors in certain social circles in Switzerland.

Winterthur, Brühlbergstrasse 8

In the outskirts of Winterthur, on the Brühlberg, Marie Bill-Geiger found a villa—the Hegnergüetli—with an almost enchanted air, and the Bill family moved in on 14 October 1915.[80] Two months later, on 22 December 1915, in their new home at Brühlbergstrasse 8, the Bills celebrated Max's seventh birthday. That same day his parents took out a mortgage for 17,000 Swiss francs. As to the Hegnergüetli's architecture, ambience, and setting, Marie Bill-Geiger would no doubt have regarded her new home as a considerable improvement on the house in Rudolfstrasse that the family had left. And even if the Hegnergüetli (literally, "little Hegner estate") did not compare with the property and grounds where Marie Bill-Geiger had grown up, it nevertheless reminded her of youth.

In the grounds of her parental home in Brugg there had been a wide variety of trees—spruce, a mighty birch, "a red horse chestnut ... probably all dating to the mid-eighteenth century. Two catalpas reached up out of the shrubbery, delighting us with their blossoms and long seed pods.... And then there were all sorts of smaller exotic trees and plants in our park—almonds, Japanese apple, woody mallows ... and a whitebeam, which bore such large berries that we ate them out of pure curiosity—even although they tasted of nothing. Near the shrubbery there was a strange little tree with large black-and-red blossoms with a delicious scent ... and a little farther away there was a slender tulip tree that we always noticed for its striking leaves."[81]

There are also exotic trees in the garden of Max Bill's studio-and-home, built in Zumikon in 1967–68: a *Davidia,* a number of giant redwoods, and a tulip tree that has now grown taller than the house.

The Hegnergüetli had a large, overgrown garden and an abandoned vineyard. Wine was stored in a cellar cut deep into the hillside. The previous occupants of the house had supplied fruit to the Rieter family,

80 Noted in the citizens' register in the Winterthur city archive, information kindly supplied by Lilian Banholzer

81 See Geiger 1957

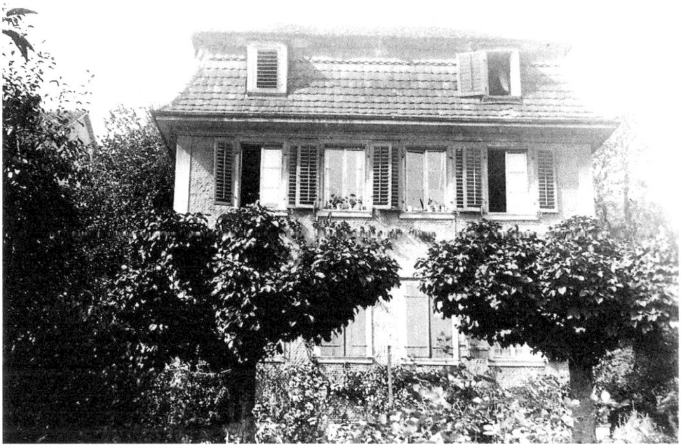

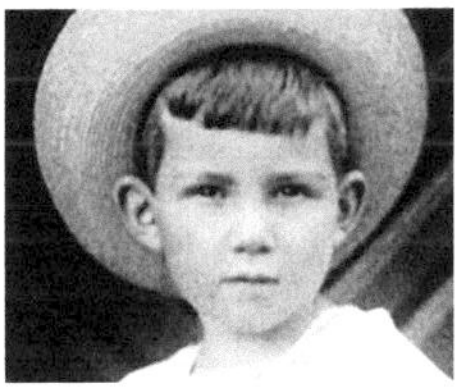

The Hegnergüetli, Brühlberg-
strasse 8, in the outskirts of
Winterthur in 1942

Max Bill, around six years old

Max Bill (left) and his brother
Hugo, Winterthur

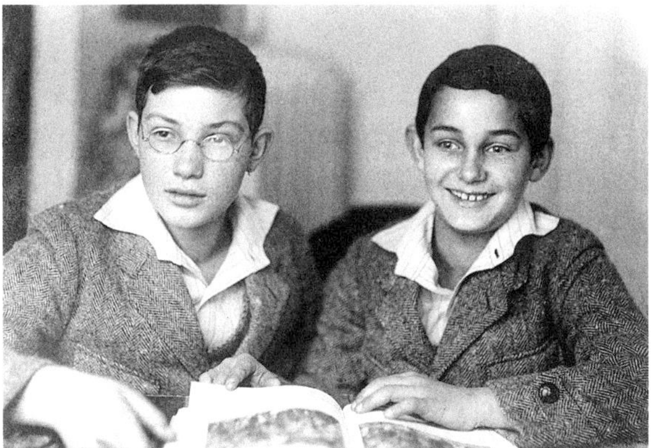

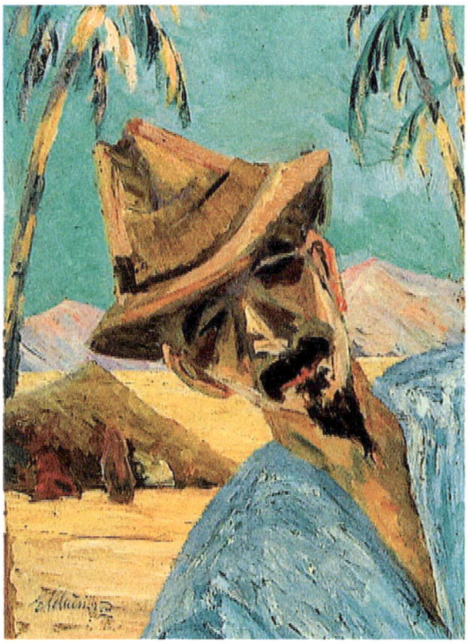

Ernst Schiess, *Self-portrait,* 1918, oil on canvas, 58 × 41 cm

Marie Bill-Geiger, Ex Libris Alfred Erwin Bill

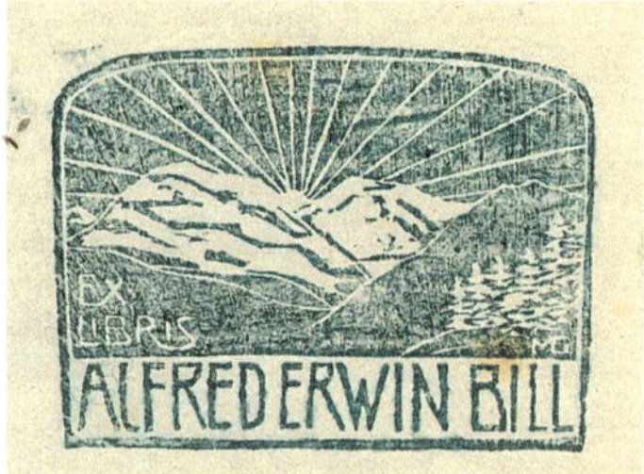

owners of a major manufacturing plant in Winterthur. After the Bill family moved in, Marie was able to harvest "pears and wonderful mirabelle plums." These were mainly for the family's own use but she also sold some of the yield in the neighborhood and regularly sent boxes of fruit to her sisters Ida and Rosa in Brugg. And she baked cakes for her favorite brother, Ernst, which she sent to him by parcel post, first to his home near Twann on Lake Biel and later on, after 1918, to Ligerz.

Although the Bills now lived far away from the sound of the trains that had provided the backdrop to Max's early years, the main station in Winterthur still played an important part in their daily lives. When Max's mother, the deputy station inspector's wife, went to the station to distribute jars of syrup to soldiers wounded in the First World War—handing it in through the open windows of the trains they were in—Max was with her and heard the soldiers' muffled cries. The Hegnergüetli was the Bills' family home until April 1927, when Max and Hugo's parents separated.

Marie Bill-Geiger had a wide knowledge of plant names; she also knew a great deal about medicinal herbs and how to use them to make healing teas. She demonstrated considerable "didactic skill" in her sons' upbringing, although Max later bemoaned the fact that she had favored his younger brother: she had "positively doted on" Hugo. He also said that Hugo had been "prettier," which was why girls had always preferred him—at least that was how Max saw it.

Félix Vallotton in Winterthur

When the newly built Kunstmuseum opened in Winterthur in 1916, the collection it would now house included a number of paintings by the Swiss artist Félix Vallotton. As a young boy Max Bill thus already saw and absorbed some of Vallotton's paintings. Hedy Hahnloser-Bühler, a leading collector in Winterthur, regularly invited Félix Vallotton to stay; he made the first of many visits in 1909 and painted numerous works at the Hahnloser-Bühlers' house over the years.

Hedy Hahnloser-Bühler's daughter-in-law wrote an empathetic text on the relationship that developed between Vallotton and his collector, in which she mentions that Vallotton and Hedy Hahnloser-Bühler sometimes discussed the bouts of depression that both occasionally experienced.[82]

82 See Hahnloser-Ingold 2007

When Max Bill encountered people or works that excited him and made a positive impact on him, he remained faithful to them for many years, often for the rest of his life. As an adult he thus successfully campaigned to persuade Kunsthaus Zürich to purchase Vallotton's action-packed *Bad am Sommerabend* (1932). Bill also greatly admired Vallotton's novel *Corbehaut*[83] and lent me his own copy to read.

Excerpt from the French flyleaf text:

"The plot is seemingly simple: a young Parisian retreats to a small port in Morbihan in the hope of finishing a serial novel he is working on, but the decaying village conceals within it a tangle of dark, mysterious destinies that make any invented intrigues pale into insignificance."

Self-Portraits by Contemporary Swiss Painters

However, Marie Bill-Geiger clearly preferred another Swiss painter to Félix Vallotton. For her the greatest Swiss painter was Ferdinand Hodler, whose work combines realism, symbolism, and idealism. On Sundays, from an early age, Max would be taken by either his mother or his father to see the art collection and the exhibitions at the Kunstmuseum. Designed by Robert Rittmeyer, the Kunstmuseum also contained a museum of natural history, where Max was always irresistibly drawn to a large ammonite.

The salient feature of the structure of an ammonite is its spiral formation. The spiral would re-emerge later on as a theme in the life of Max Bill the artist. He would return to it again and again, as in his contrary motion *spirale* (1944–48) and in his granite sculpture *einheit aus kugel und endloser spirale* (1978–83, see p. 257).

Shortly before his tenth birthday, Max Bill and his father visited the Kunstmuseum to see the exhibition *Selbstbildnisse Schweizer Künstler der Gegenwart* (Self-portraits by contemporary Swiss artists).[84] In Max Bill's library

83 Félix Vallotton, *Corbehaut* [ca. 1920] (Lausanne: Le Livre du Mois, 1970), foreword by Gustave Roud, Bibliothek Max Bill, collection of Angela Thomas

84 *Selbstbildnisse Schweizer Künstler der Gegenwart,* with an introduction and biographical sketches relating to the exhibition of Swiss artists' portraits at Kunstverein Winterthur, ed. Georg Reinhart and Dr. Paul Fink (Zurich: Kommissionsverlag Art. Institut Orell Füssli, 1918)

there is a copy of the catalogue for that exhibition of 1918, with an *ex libris* inside it in the name of his father, Alfred Erwin Bill.

Some of the paintings in that exhibition made a deep impression on the young boy—notably the *Selbstporträt* (1916) by the recently deceased Ferdinand Hodler. Besides Hodler's very confident self-portrait, other images that made an enduring impression on Max were the self-portraits by Alice Bailly, a young Otto Morach, Ignaz Epper, and Augusto Giacometti. In Alice Bailly's elegantly elongated self-portrait (1917) there are echoes of her time in Paris (1906–14). Her hair is cut in a short bob, and she draws attention to her breasts. Her hands are pointed, too pointed—maybe alluding to the pointedness of the art she creates using her hands. Bailly presents herself as a modern, enlightened, intelligent city dweller.

Having initially studied science in Bern, Otto Morach spent time in Paris, Munich, Prague, Cologne, and Berlin. When he was in Paris, Vallotton kindly advised him to position his style as far away from Hodler as possible—and Morach took that advice. Having been prevented from traveling back to Paris by the outbreak of the First World War, Morach's only option was to return to his parent's house in Solothurn. Despite declaring his beliefs as a pacifist, Morach was called up for military service. In the melancholy self-portrait (1918) that was shown in Winterthur, Morach's arms and shoulders visibly droop. Evidently he has tried in vain to give flowers to the woman who is turning her back on him and disappearing from sight at the lower edge of the picture. She is already a long way off; all we know about her is that she has a long plait reaching to her waist.

In this painting Morach lays bare a dramatic moment in his own private life. His self-portrait has a modern feel. The area around the nose is particularly complex; the lines on his forehead seem to merge into the natural formations and layers of the barely recognizable location seen behind him, suggesting that for him this moment is as traumatic as some unforeseen event in the natural world. (Some years later Max Bill and Otto Morach would meet in person at the Kunstgewerbeschule in Zurich.)

In Ignaz Epper's self-portrait (1918) an unhappy, slight figure appears to be confined in a cramped space, yet there is also something defiant about him as he gazes steadily at the viewer with his large eyes. His father earned a living designing embroidery patterns and Epper followed him into the same work until 1915, when he struck out on his own as a self-taught artist.

The last of the images that lingered on in Bill's memory was the self-portrait by Augusto Giacometti (1913); the artist's face, headwear, shirt collar, and the edge of his jacket look more like pieces in a puzzle, only approximately connected in a mosaic-like configuration. There are gaps between them, as if encrustations have split open. Many years later, during the Second World War, Max Bill's thoughts again turned to Augusto Giacometti and he bought a copy of Erwin Poeschel's monograph *Augusto Giacometti,* which includes a color illustration of that same self-portrait. Augusto Giacometti can certainly be described as a kindred spirit among Max Bill's predecessors. As early as 1900 Giacometti was already working on his first small pastel compositions—color studies with no hint of figurative motifs. "His interest was not in optical fantasies, nor in turning external reality into a picture but in turning the inner image, his vision, into reality. That is very clear in these small abstract studies from 1900, which so determinedly spurn reality and avoid any traces of figuration."[85]

There was another reason why Max had such indelible memories of that visit to the exhibition at Kunstmuseum Winterthur in the autumn of 1918. When he and his father paused at a painting in muted beige, blue, and pink tones, the *Selbstbildnis* (1918) by Ernst Schiess, Max was heard to say, in Swiss German, "der ist in der Wüste" (he's in the desert). However, his father misheard his comment as "der ist ein wüster" (he looks a mess). Erwin Bill, painfully embarrassed, was not going to tolerate that kind of comment—most certainly not in a public place. He immediately told his son that he must never say that sort of thing about a work of art and cuffed his ear to make sure the boy learned his lesson. But in fact, although Max had never been abroad, when he looked at Schiess's painting—and he looked very closely—he saw that this must be some exotic, faraway place. He saw tall palm trees and something like a pyramid in the background. Reaching diagonally upward into this landscape—a "desert" in Max's mind—is the figure of the artist, with a bushy moustache, a very distinctive goatee, and an air of passive resignation as he is tossed to and fro by fate. In this painting Schiess is not looking for adventure. His eyes are almost closed; he is not revealing his innermost thoughts. His hat, recalling a type associated with Swiss traditional costumes, seems out of place in this setting. This is clearly a foreigner, all on his own—as if he were lost in a desert.

In 1908, the year Max Bill was born, Ernst Schiess moved to Paris. From there he set out on numerous trips abroad and he spent the three years before the Winterthur exhibition in Algiers—so Max's response to the foreign look of the setting was not at all far from the mark. It is interesting to note that this early conflict between the boy and his father was in fact triggered by a painting, with the father not listening properly, not

85 Poeschel 1922, p. 15
86 See Jahn 1917

listening carefully enough, although the boy was observing very keenly and expressing himself as precisely as he could at the time. That unpleasant memory of his father angrily cuffing his ear never left Max Bill.
Years later, the adult Max Bill would make every effort to paint as precisely as possible in his own work—and also to formulate his theory of art as precisely as possible.

At exactly this time, not far from Winterthur, the Dadaists were unsettling the bourgeoisie in the city of Zurich. But as a child, Max knew nothing of that, and his parents were never at any of the events put on by Cabaret Voltaire, the artists' haunt at Spiegelgasse 1. As it happens, in 1916–17 Vladimir Ilyich Ulyanov Lenin had lived in that same narrow street in Zurich's old town, reading and studying avidly in Zurich's libraries, preparing the ground for his imminent participation in the Russian Revolution. And decades before that, in the autumn and winter of 1836–37, the German dramatist and natural scientist Georg Büchner had lived at Spiegelgasse 12 before dying of typhoid fever in February 1937, at the age of twenty-three. Outside Zurich, on the Zürichberg, a memorial stone to Georg Büchner is still accessible to the public today.

During the Second World War Max Bill purchased an edition of the collected works of Georg Buchner: *Georg Büchner gesammelte Werke, mit einem Lebensbild,* ed. Carl Seelig (Zurich: Artemis, 1944). And in the 1950s, he engaged intensely—from the point of view of a visual artist—with Büchner's ideas and thinking. Bill also designed a memorial to this German who had died in Switzerland, far from home. In this memorial, which only exists as a model, the "rational"—surrounded by the "irrational"—strives to define its own contours and to communicate a sense of clarity.

A Battle over Roman Shards

When Max was not yet eight years old, his maternal grandfather, Ulrich Geiger-Schwarz, died. Ernst Geiger created a bronze relief for his father's tombstone and an obituary was published to mark the passing of this respected citizen.[86]
The grave stone with the bronze relief is now on display in the museum of winemaking Ligerz, and there is another bronze relief in the collection of Christoph Geiger in Freienbach.
However, Ernst Geiger was very disappointed that his father did not leave his collection of Roman finds to his "descendants, who had a keen interest in archaeology" and who had unearthed many of those items themselves.

As a student at the ETH Ernst Geiger had attended lectures in geology and prehistory by professors Albert Heim, Wilhelm Öchsli, and Jakob Heierli. Among his fellow students at those lectures was Otto Hauser, who would later become famous for his archaeological finds in France. It was Professor Öchsli who introduced Geiger and Hauser to each other.

When Otto Hauser "arrived in Windisch [in the district of Brugg] to work on a dig," Ernst Geiger "lent his assistance." However, when Hauser "dared to start digging at the amphitheater, he came into conflict with the antiquarian society in Brugg." Ernst Geiger found himself in an awkward situation. He felt that rather than taking sides with the archaeologist, Hauser, with whom he had studied, he had to bow to the will of the "gentlemen in Brugg," all the more so since his own father was on the committee of the antiquarian society. He described that moment later on; "... when the animosity had reached the point where Hauser spoke out angrily against the gentlemen in Brugg, I had no choice other than to break off contact with him, despite my own mixed feelings toward the antiquarian society.... In the end it was the antiquarian society that excavated and preserved the amphitheater after it was bought by the Confederation."[87]

"Without a care for his descendants who had a keen interest in archaeology, my father disposed of his collection, i.e., first he deposited it in the museum and then he gifted it to the museum.

I was sorry to see that singular little collection go, which I had sorted and catalogued in the past; I had even pieced some of those items back together with the greatest of difficulty. From time to time experts had come to our house to view the collection."[88]

Although Ernst Geiger had not taken Hauser's side in Brugg, he later joined Hauser to France and made watercolor paintings of the Dolmen de Saint-Fort-sur-le-Né (Charente) in June 1906.

87 Geiger 1969, pp. 22–23
88 Geiger 1969, pp. 22–23
89 Geiger 1969, p. 30
90 Maria Geiger-Bockhoff, *Die Visio Philiberti des Heinrich von Neustadt* (Tübingen: J. C. B. Mohr, 1912)
91 Geiger-Bockhoff, *Die Visio Philiberti*

"... remorseless death wrenched her from us"

Some years after the death of Ulrich Geiger-Schwarz, Marie Bill-Geiger received the devastating news of the death of her sister-in-law, Maria Geiger-Bockhoff, following the birth of her second son, Wolfgang, on 17 July 1921. It was a cruel end to the love story that had begun for Marie's brother at Lake Lauenen. Having made every effort to tell Max as gently as possible of the tragic loss suffered by his favorite uncle, Marie immediately set off for Ligerz to be with Ernst.

In December 1906, when Ernst Geiger first met Maria Bockhoff in Lauenen, she was a student in her third semester at the university in Bern. Soon after that, Ernst visited the Bockhoff family in Gelsenkirchen, where he introduced himself as their future son-in-law. And on 11 March 1907, just three months after he and Maria first got to know each other, they married in Bern "in a very simple ceremony"—after which Maria returned to her studies. "In April 1908 she gave me the gift of a son (Hans-Ulrich), but then she fell ill and, due to the wrong treatment from a foolish doctor, was bedridden for weeks. A change of air in Duisburg, where I joined her, did her good and she was able to continue with her studies and her dissertation."[89] In those days it was still unusual for women to study for a university degree. Their ambitions were misconstrued and scorned by certain "colleagues," whose behavior toward them was far from collegial. But Maria Geiger-Bockhoff was not to be deterred and gained her doctorate just two years after giving birth.[90]

"When she graduated summa cum laude (1910) and I was awarded a federal study grant shortly afterward, we decided to move out of Bern and found a vacant house for rent in the Kapf, up above Twann ... where we lived until autumn 1918." The Kapf was, however, very isolated, so the Geigers handed in their notice and searched "everywhere in Twann and Ligerz. By chance we found the "Hof" in Ligerz ... and managed to buy first the front section and then, the following summer, the rear section as well, thereby reinstating the old seat of the von Ligerz family.... Now all that was needed to complete our cup of happiness was a brother or sister for Hans, the second child that Maria had so longed for. However, destiny would not grant her such happiness. She was allowed the joy of anticipation but only one glance at her newborn child. And then remorseless death wrenched her from us. That was on Sunday, 17 July 1921, in the hospital in Biel.... Her sisters immediately came to help us because we were all on our own, Hans and I. On the day of the cremation I collected the baby from the hospital."[91]

After the funeral Ernst and his sisters discussed what would be best for his newborn son, Wolfgang—known as Wölfi. When he was just a few months old, in October 1921, his unmarried aunts, Ida and Rosa, took him into their home in Brugg. Hans, who had been taught at home by his mother up until then, stayed in Ligerz and continued his education with his father.

Aunt Ida would outlive her sister Rosa Geiger and inherit the latter's estate. Ida Geiger bequeathed her antique furniture and her money to Hans Geiger, her brother Ernst's oldest son. Her nephews Max and Hugo and their mother, Marie Bill, were left empty-handed.

Ernst Geiger's friend, the artist Cuno Amiet, was deeply shocked when the news of Maria's death reached him. He and his wife Anna wrote a letter of condolence to Ernst Geiger: "Dear Friend, what terrible news we have received from you. Your dear, good wife has died. We have such fond memories of her. How often we have talked of you, whenever the occasion arose—a card, a picture, your name in the papers—and of your happy family life.... We might try to comfort you by reminding you how lucky you are to have the children. But that is no comfort. Nothing can ever make up for the wife you have lost. Although there is one comfort. It resides within you, in your artistic gift.

May your art, time, and peace come to your aid.

Yours, the Amiets"[92]

At the Hodler Exhibition in Bern

Max Bill later told me that some years after he and his father visited the exhibition of self-portraits by contemporary Swiss artists in Winterthur, he and his mother traveled to Bern together to see the major exhibition in memory of Ferdinand Hodler, the *Hodler Gedächtnis-Ausstellung,* which ran from August to October 1921 in two venues at once, the Kunstmuseum and the Kunsthalle.

Hodler Gedächtnis-Ausstellung: A memorial exhibition for Hodler: 20 August–23 October 1921, illustrated catalogue, Kunstmuseum Bern, 1921; oddly, the cover picture is not a work by Hodler, who was being honored in this exhibition, but a portrait of a woman by Cuno Amiet, the president of the exhibition committee, who thus stole the limelight for himself.

92 Letter of condolence from Cuno Amiet and his wife Anna Oschwand, to Dr. Ernst Geiger, Ligerz (19 July 1921), Archiv Christoph Geiger

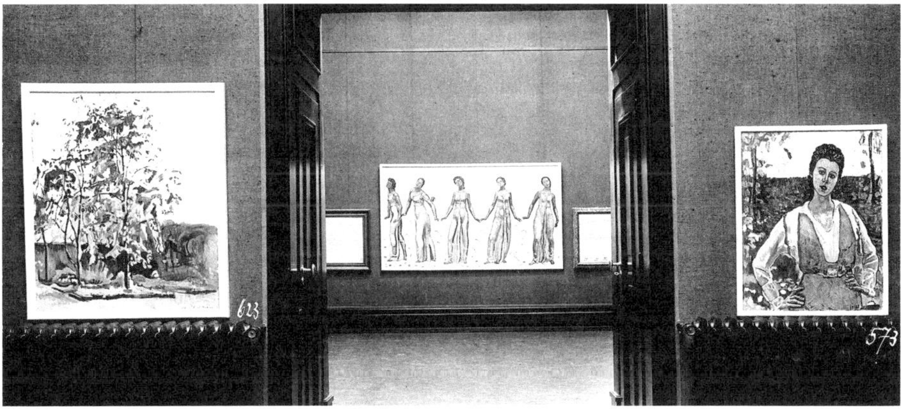

View of the *Hodler Gedächtnis-Ausstellung* in Bern, 1921

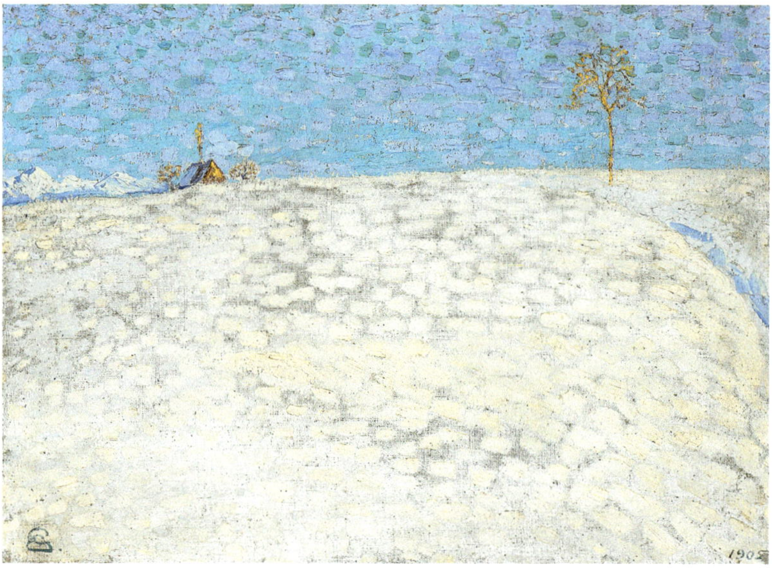

Ernst Geiger, *Wintersonne,* 1905,
oil on canvas, 35×50cm

It was impressive—with over 800 works on display. Numerous black-and-white photographs have survived, showing the exhibits as Max Bill saw them then. These photographs now fill three albums in the archives of Kunstmuseum Bern, and in one of them the large-format painting *Blick in die Unendlichkeit* (1913–16) is visible in the background. Two years later—at school in Oetwil am See—Max Bill would take that painting as his topic for his first-ever lecture on art. Might the grieving Ernst Geiger have accompanied his sister Marie and her son Max when they went to the Hodler exhibition—or did they perhaps take the time to visit him in Ligerz?

That same year, in 1921, the Aargau Section of the GSMBA—Ernst Geiger and Adolf Weibel (Max's uncle by marriage) were both founder members—was invited to present an exhibition at Kunsthalle Bern; that exhibition also included works by the now renowned Alice Bailly and Paul Klee.

Max, nearly ten, had already seen a self-portrait by Alice Bailly in the Kunstmuseum in Winterthur in 1918, and later on, Paul Klee would be one of Max Bill's Bauhaus masters in Dessau. Klee and Ernst Geiger were also members of the Die Walze, an association of Swiss artist-printmakers (co-founded in 1903 by Carl Theodor Meyer, Albert Welti, and others). A list of "members of the Walze, 1912" compiled by Max's uncle includes "Geiger, Giacometti, Klee, . . . Albert Welti, Bertha Züricher."[93]

Early Role Models

In a curriculum vitae written in the early 1940s, Max Bill named various individuals who influenced him as he was growing up: "From my father I inherited craft skills and an interest in technology and in history, after all, he was on the committee of the Winterthur Historical Antiquarian Society for years. . . ."[94]

"The Historisch-Antiquarischer Verein (Historical-Antiquarian Association) brought together expert librarians, archivists, and technicians, and was very exclusive for a long time. Their main activities included promoting historical research (through regular lectures on history and art history), excursions, caring for historic monuments, and overseeing the museum in Mörsburg Castle (owned by the city of Winterthur)."[95]

93 Note by Ernst Geiger, Museum Neuhaus archive, Biel

94 Max Bill, 1942 [b]

95 Information kindly supplied by Peter Niederhäuser, Winterthur, 2008

In fact his father audited the association's books from 1917–18 onward. In 1920 the association had around fifty or sixty members. Although there is no mention in the association's minutes of Erwin Bill delivering a lecture himself, he would most probably have attended talks now and then, possibly taking note of interesting reading matter and passing that on to Max. Besides reading newspapers at home, Erwin Bill certainly also read works by Gotthold Ephraim Lessing and by the pacifist Bertha von Suttner. This meant that Max, too, had the opportunity to read a book such as Suttner's *Die Waffen nieder!,* which significantly contributed to the emergence of a peace movement in Switzerland.[96] Many railwaymen in Switzerland were active on the political left; however, there are no records of Erwin Bill ever having been a member of the Swiss railwaymen's union. As to the influence of his mother and his two uncles who painted, Max made the following statement: "I mainly inherited my interest in art from my mother. But a greater influence was exerted on me by her brother, Dr. Ernst Geiger, and by her brother-in-law, Prof. Adolf Weibel (Aarau), who was also my godfather."[97]

"If you don't behave, you'll be in the paper!"

One day, when Max was in his second year at high school, he kept lookout for another boy who was trying to steal crime-fiction magazines from a newsstand—in vain, as they were caught in the act. Whenever Max was refusing to behave, if he was playing up, his mother always threatened him with the words, "If you don't behave, you'll be in the paper!" Only now, instead of a report appearing in the local paper, Max's parents took him out of his school in Winterthur and, in late April 1923, sent him—"for improvement"—to a reform school, the so-called Waldheim (Forest Home) in Oetwil am See (canton of Zürich).

96 Bertha von Suttner, *Die Waffen Nieder!* (Dresden: Pierson, 1902); this edition is still in the Bibliothek Max Bill (now in the collection of Angela Thomas)

97 Max Bill, 1942 [b]

98 Divorce certificate, district court, Winterthur, 1 April 1927, state archives of the canton of Zürich

99 (Zurich: Bürgi & Wagner, 1914)

A woman working the land lower down the hill from the Waldheim told me that the "toffee noses from the city used to send children that weren't doing well" there.

Evidently Marie Bill-Geiger had resigned herself to the idea that her son Max—never an easy child, in fact an exhausting child who was more than she could handle—would never make the most of school. She later complained that her husband had never fully supported her with regard to their son's education.

Marie Bill-Geiger, as it says in her petition for divorce, complained not only about her "somewhat wayward son Max," but also about the fact that, when it came to the boy's upbringing, Max's father "had not stepped in energetically enough." However, the complainant also admits that she herself "had no influence over her elder son."[98]

The Waldheim, which took both day pupils and boarders, was run by a married couple, Frau Dr. Phil. Clara Keller-Hürlimann and Herr Dr. Phil. Wilhelm Keller-Hürlimann. The boarders were encouraged to keep a record of events in the school "chronicle." The Keller-Hürlimanns are never referred to by name in the chronicle, only by their titles, Herr Doktor and Frau Doktor. Although the idea was that, besides attending lessons, Max would also be disciplined there, the reports he wrote are mostly very cheerful. He felt at ease in the school's rural setting.

One of the other boys at the school—ahead of Max in the sense that he had been sent away there a year earlier—was a certain Wolfgang Vogel. His grandparents, originally from Germany, had opened a bookshop (Buchhandlung Vogel) in Winterthur, which was where Max's father bought his books, including Lessing's *Nathan the Wise.* Wolfgang had an aunt in Oetwil am See. It may be that she had recommended the Waldheim to Wolfgang's parents—and Max's parents may in turn have heard about the school in Vogel's bookshop.

The boy that Max Bill had kept watch for at the kiosk in Winterthur later became a "notorious criminal." But then, as Bill himself went on to say in the same conversation with me, he felt that he, too, could easily have pursued a career as a gangster—if he hadn't become an artist and an architect.

Of course Erwin Bill may also have read about the school, for instance in *Bürgis Illustrierter Reiseführer: Sommer in der Schweiz:*[99] "Oetwil am See (near Zurich, Forchbahn). The boarding school run by Dr. Phil. Wilh. and Dr. Phil. Klara Keller-Hürlimann, certified secondary teachers with many years experience teaching middle school, comprises a lower school and an upper school, with a curriculum that largely conforms to that followed by schools in Zurich; the school prepares boys and girls between 12 and 16 years of age, thoroughly and according to the precepts of modern pedagogy, to enter either public middle schools or the world of work. The small number of pupils (with a maximum of 12 boarders), which is kept low as a matter of principle, allows each one to receive close, individual attention ... combining intellectual work with physical activity in the garden and the workshop.... The simple lifestyle, the pursuit of games and sports in the eminently suitable surroundings, the wholly rural, elevated situation on the edge of extensive woodlands are all immensely beneficial to physical well being."

In the school brochure the directors specifically highlight the aims of their educational institution: "The boarding school ... is intended to serve pupils in the countryside whose parents prefer not to send them to the city too soon; it is also intended for pupils from the city who, for whatever reason, would benefit from being transplanted into a boarding school and into a rural environment.... The fees for teaching, education, and boarding are 2,400 francs per academic year."[100] Evidently Max's parents were prepared to pay out a considerable sum to shield him from the small town of Winterthur and its "dangers" and to keep him in boarding school in the countryside. The annual fees for the Waldheim were in fact roughly equivalent to a year's wages for a laborer. Could it be that Marie Bill-Geiger was able to cover the cost thanks to the legacy left to her by her father?

The brochure promised that pupils would sleep "in light, airy rooms with 2 to 3 beds" and be given "a simple, hearty, varied diet in 5 meals daily with copious milk, fruit, and vegetables." And as to "visits to the parental home" ... "there was no objection to not overly frequent visits to the parental home on Sundays; as a rule pupils who live not too far away make such visits once a quarter."[101]

Erwin Bill's ambivalent, carrot-and-stick attitude to Max's education would not change in the coming years.

100 "Schülerheim Oetwil am See, Kanton Zürich, Bezirk Meilen," archive of Ortsmuseum Oetwil am See

101 "Schülerheim Oetwil am See, Kanton Zürich, Bezirk Meilen"

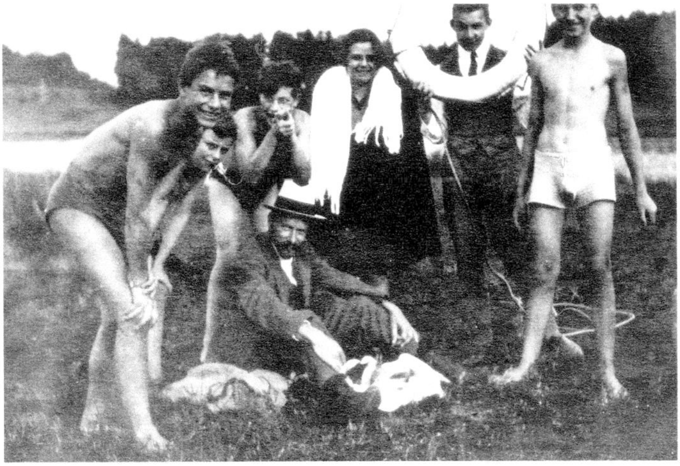

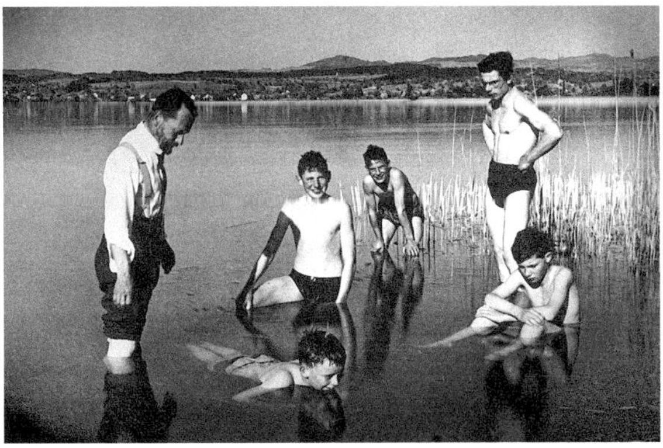

Max Bill (third from left, wearing glasses) with other pupils and one of the school's directors, Dr. Keller (seated), by Lake Greifen, May 1923

Boys and a teacher from the Waldheim, with Max Bill, second from right

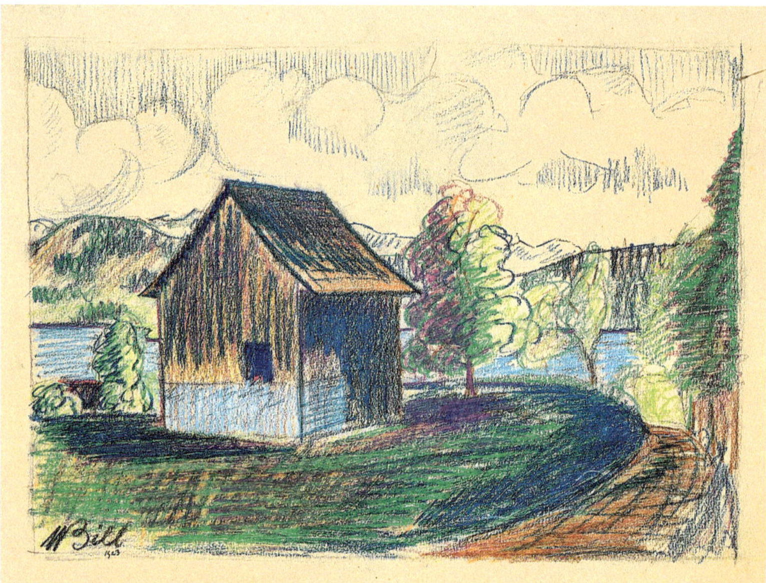

Max Bill, *Oberhalb dem Waisenhaus Stäfa,* Late May/early June 1923, colored pencil on paper, 25×34cm

Wolfgang Vogel

Wolfgang was an obstreperous boy and in the Vogel family legend still has it that he once even made a tram jump the tracks.[102] As a seasoned Waldheim chronicler, Wolfgang Vogel recorded the arrival of two new boys from Winterthur—one must have been Max Bill, although he is not named in that entry. There were four boarders from Winterthur at the Waldheim: Wolfgang Vogel, Max Bill, Arnold Mötteli, and Robert Freitag.

"On 29 April things livened up at the Waldheim, the two boys who have already been here for some time were joined by two new boys, both from Winterthur."[103]

Wolfgang also reports on the weather, on the boys' activities, and on the arrival of a certain Herr Wegmann, a new teacher from Zurich: "We had splendid weather for the first two weeks.... This year we could already go swimming in Lake Seeweid in May, with the temperature around 18°. In the evenings we went for walks or did gymnastics on the high bar and the parallel bars."[104]

According to the school rules, pupils were not allowed to go anywhere on their own; they always had to be accompanied by at least one other pupil. Wolfgang describes more outings: "On Wednesday afternoon we went down to Stäfa to go rowing on the lake. We went out to the Stäfener rock where we off-loaded Herr Wegmann. He just sat there, gazing dreamily out at the water.... 5–12 May: On Sunday we had splendid weather ... and after lunch Herr Dr. said we could go swimming in Lake Greifen.... We splashed happily around in the water and Herr Wegmann took some photographs."[105]

"28 May–4 June: The weather on the next Sunday was not very promising, but we still decided to risk an outing. Herr Dr. and we 4 boarders went over to Männedorf where we took the steamer, the Stadt Rapperswil, to the Au peninsula. We walked down to the station, passing the Au inn on our way. Then we went up toward the Zimmerberg. We explored a ravine and went on a little climbing expedition; by the time we arrived at the other side our Sunday best was pretty filthy. We quenched our thirst at the next well and cleaned ourselves off again. On we went, up hill and down dale, until we spotted the little church at Schönenberg, but we didn't

102 Information kindly supplied by Wolfgang Vogel's daughter, Christine Geiser, 2006

103 Wolfgang Vogel, 29 April–27 May 1923, Waldheim chronicle

104 Vogel, 29 April–27 May 1923, Waldheim chronicle

105 Vogel, 29 April–27 May 1923, Waldheim chronicle

want to go any farther. My corns were aching and the others' knees were buckling. Herr Dr. said we would go to Wädenswil ... so we went down at top speed. In the café, teetotal, we had coffee and cake. There was a tightrope walker at the jetty and we watched for a quarter of an hour ... then we took the Stadt Rapperswil back to Männedorf. We were allowed to take the boats out for another hour or so ... so we rowed around in the lake for an hour and arrived back in the evening very pleased with our day out.... On Monday it was pouring with rain again.... On Wednesday we took our football down to the Weidenbad and had a kick-about as the rain got heavier and heavier ... we had to head back home. We broke into a barn on the Türli and dried ourselves off a bit."[106] "On Friday we drew an idyllic spot up above the orphanage."[107] Max, who had been sent away from home as a punishment, was also on that drawing trip in the hills above Lake Zurich.

Wolfgang and Max soon became firm friends, which some of the other boys were somewhat jealously suspicious of and sometimes even "denounced." Whenever boys misbehaved, the teachers imposed punishments and expected them to "work off" their misdeeds. "On Saturday, working off, we had to weed the games pitch; afterward we built a dam in the ravine. Barefooted, we hauled huge rocks and filled the gaps ... mud splattered all over our bare skin and our clothes and by the evening we looked more like pigs than people. At 9 we went satisfied to bed."[108]

On another excursion a new boy from the canton of Grisons had a mishap: "Luzi lost his footing in the water and tried to cling on to Herr Wegmann's rucksack, but of course pulled it into the water with him, including the camera and the plates. Luzi was transfixed, but Herr Wegmann, who was barefoot, leaped into the water and rescued his camera, which was immediately laid out in the warm sun and soon dried off again."[109] Wolfgang also notes that the boys objected to choir practice "because our voices [are] breaking."

Two years before he was sent to the Waldheim, Max Bill and his mother had been to see the Hodler exhibition in Bern. Now, as a fourteen-year-old, preparing to deliver his first-ever lecture on art, he chose a painting by Hodler as his topic and made a small poster for the lecture based

106 Wolfgang Vogel, 28 May–4 June 1923, in the Waldheim chronicle

107 Vogel, 28 May–4 June 1923, Waldheim chronicle

108 Wolfgang Vogel, 5–12 June 1923, Waldheim chronicle

109 Vogel, 5–12 June 1923, Waldheim chronicle

110 Van de Velde, "Ferdinand Hodler" (see note 35), pp. 129–30

111 Max Bill in conversation with Angela Thomas, 25 September 1975

on Hodler's painting *Blick in die Unendlichkeit.* Maybe he hoped this choice might somewhat placate his mother when he told her what he was doing —as he surely must have done.

"... his longing for that which is eternal"

In 1918 Henry van de Velde—who also painted—wrote a heartfelt obituary for Ferdinand Hodler: "We see Hodler reaching out for eternal symbols.... The master's motifs are all assimilated into his synthetic formula and his longing for that which is eternal: the day, the chosen one, the hours, the truth ... gazing into infinity.... His method is distinguished by its negation of perspective.... Hodler's lines have a strength that elevates his compositions into a strangely musical sphere."[110]

Hodler's *Blick in die Unendlichkeit* had come to Winterthur, Max's place of birth, as a "gift of the gallery association, the Friends of Kunstmuseum Winterthur." Just a few months before his death, Hodler painted a large mural of the same name for Kunsthaus Zürich. Max would certainly have known the painting in Winterthur, and may also have known the mural in Zurich. And as to Max Bill's opinion of Ferdinand Hodler, he shared his mother's view. Looking back at that time, he once told me that "When it came to Hodler, who lived very freely, people were extremely divided back then.... and yet, just look at what he achieved!"[111] Bill's reference to Hodler living "very freely" no doubt related to the fact that, despite being married, Hodler also had a lover whom he was deeply attached to. But Hodler never came to any clear conclusion regarding his situation vis-à-vis the two women in his life; unlike Max Bill (I would say), Hodler was not at all able to act "freely," unable to resolve his emotions. Whatever the case, during his own lifetime Hodler's reputation in social circles was very different to his reputation as an artist.

At the Bauhaus in 1928—as we know from notes by Hanns Fischli (who later on spelled his first name with just one *n*), Max Bill initially chose Hodler as his role model, before entering his "Klee phase" (see Fischli 1968). Later on in the life of Max Bill (as a married man), he entered into similar love relationships to the relationship once lived out by Hodler. Like his onetime role model, Bill repeatedly found himself juggling time, venues and emotions with (at least) two women—the married partner and the lover. Thus Bill never "freely" entirely devoted his feelings to any one of the women in question.

Although Hodler could never contemplate abandoning his lover, the mother of his daughter, in 1913 he and his wife moved into a new, luxurious apartment at Quai du Mont-Blanc 29 in Geneva. And it was at exactly that time, when—according to his biographer Hans Mühlestein—Hodler was working on "his many hundreds of studies" for *Blick in die Unendlichkeit,* that his beloved Valentine Godé-Darel's health was starting to fail. Hodler devoted an extensive series of paintings and sketches to the insidious effects of the cancer that would end her life. In real life he could never fully commit to her, but he ensured that posterity would not forget her.

In the early 1930s Bill got to know the leading Hodler expert Hans Mühlestein, who—working in close contact with Hodler—had written a biography of the artist between 1910 and 1914, which was published in late 1914.[112] It may be that Bill's mother, a self-confessed Hodler devotee, had acquired a copy of that biography, which would have meant that Bill already had access to it as a boy. In autumn 1917, a few years after the publication of the biography and not long before Hodler's death, Mühlestein (a Swiss citizen living abroad) had returned to Switzerland and volunteered for military service. Before he left the country again, he stayed with Hodler in Geneva. Toward the end of October 1917 Hodler painted Mühlestein's portrait as a token of his gratitude and as a souvenir to take with him on his travels.

In March 1939, a quarter of a century after the publication of Mühlestein's first book on Hodler and some years after he and Max Bill first became acquainted, a publisher offered Mühlestein the opportunity to rework the biographical section of his book. In the intervening years Mühlestein had evolved from a "philosophical idealist" to a "decided realist"; this led to "such a major reversal in his evaluation of Hodler's art that even the narration of Hodler's biography demanded a fundamentally new structure for the book," as the reader is told in the foreword to the new biography, which was published in 1942, having been rewritten by Hans Mühlestein in collaboration with Dr. Georg Schmidt, an art historian born and bred in Basel.[113]

It is as if Mühlestein and Hodler traveled in opposite ideological directions during the upheavals of the Second World War. Hodler, who started life as a realist, became much more of an idealist by the time of his death in 1918. And these two very different positions in his art are in fact exemplified in two of Hodler's "core works" (as Mühlestein

112 See Mühlestein 1914
113 Mühlestein and Schmidt 1942, p. VIII
114 Mühlestein and Schmidt 1942, p. VIII
115 Mühlestein and Schmidt 1942, pp. 426–27

calls them): the realistic *Das mutige Weib* (1886) and the idealistic *Aufgehen im All* (1892), both now in Kunstmuseum Basel.

Ferdinand Hodler

Hodler himself regarded *Blick in die Unendlichkeit* (1913–16) as the "pinnacle of his life's work." However, in their reworking of Mühlestein's earlier Hodler biography, Mühlestein and Schmidt are more objectively critical of this painting: "Even if we cannot share that view, there is no denying that this work is in a sense the cupola on the temple of his hymnic idealism.... In February and March 1914—in midst of the tragic turn of events that befell Madame Darel—I found Hodler in a positive frenzy of work."[114] Mühlestein and Schmidt talk of "hymnic female figures," of "gigantic women" filling the space in an almost "Michelangelesque" manner, of the "opposition of delicate upper realms and sturdy lower reaches.... In contrast to their ladylike demeanor in their hands and heads, from the hips downward these figures emanate a quite tremendous sculptural strength.... And the masterfully shaped folds in their floor-length gowns are no less sculptural than the calves and thighs they reveal. Hodler positively wallows in these mountainous legs, as if to disclaim responsibility for the pseudo-spiritual posturing in the upper stories of this huge edifice."[115] It is hardly surprising that this highly contradictory, monumental painting by Hodler, which even disconcerts experienced art historians, should have seemed confusing to the adolescent Max Bill.

As a man Ferdinand Hodler generally adopted a "macho" air, but it seems that his love for Valentine Godé-Darel awakened a gentler side in him. Unlike his overpowering, monumental *Blick in die Unendlichkeit,* his paintings and drawings devoted to Valentine Godé-Darel, with their wide range of subtle emotions, will—in my view—ultimately hold their own much longer in the future reception of his work. On the other hand, it is also true to say that the unsettling "architecture" of *Blick in die Unendlichkeit* invites viewers to actively engage with it.

As a small boy, gazing at the parallel lines of the railway tracks running past the house he was born in, Max Bill was already struck by the notion of infinity and he would return to it later on in his own work as an artist. It is perhaps not even too far-fetched to suggest that in so doing, he was also responding to a certain aspect of Hodler's work. But Bill does not follow

Hodler into some extreme metaphysical realm; instead he takes a purely rational approach to the subject—as in his sculpture *unendliche schleife* (*ruban sans fin*), (1935, see p. 559), or, as the art historian Will Grohmann puts it: "... few people see Bill's sculptures in the same way that he sees and shapes them—for instance, as a space that starts on one side and ends differently on the other side, which is also the same side ... or is it infinity that returns into itself as the present?"[116]

James N. Wood also sees echoes of Hodler's work in Bill's symmetrical reflections: "Bill's use of the reflection recalls the work of another Swiss, Ferdinand Hodler, who was equally determined to capture the spiritual intensity of nature's contradictions. His *Silvaplanersee* exploits the only straight line in the Swiss landscape—the surface of a body of water—to contrast the identical curves of massive peaks and their immaterial reflection."[117]

In the catalogue Wood illustrated his theory with reproductions of Hodler's painting *Silvaplanersee* (1907) and Bill's sculpture *konstruktion aus einem kreisring* (1942–44). Wood was associate director at the Albright-Knox Art Gallery in Buffalo, New York, at the time when the gallery mounted a major Bill retrospective. Another pertinent example of Hodler's use of reflections is seen in his painting *Thunersee mit Symmetrischer Spiegelung* (1909).

However, when Bill worked with elements and reflections, he did not replicate configurations, as Hodler had done in *Silvaplanersee* —copying the natural world; instead Bill rotated one of the two main elements of the sculpture by 180 degrees. But one thing that Bill did share with Hodler was his *élan vital,* his utter determination to work as hard as humanly possible. "Hodler would tackle a problem with no role models to look to and nothing more to rely on than his own will. His innate tenacity, which rightly or wrongly has been ascribed to his Bernese roots, saw him triumph over every obstacle."[118] Hodler had the patience to work through countless preparatory stages for his paintings, and, in 1944, when Max Bill was designing the poster for the exhibition *Konkrete Kunst* at Kunsthalle Basel, he made over two hundred preparatory sketches. Whether "rightly or wrongly," Max Bill—who also had Bernese forefathers—did not hesitate to allude to his own "Emmental stubbornness," which he had inherited from his watchmaker grandfather.

116 Grohmann 1968, p. 19
117 Wood 1974, p. 36
118 Van de Velde, "Ferdinand Hodler" (see note 35), p. 132
119 Max Bill, late June/early July 1923, Waldheim chronicle

Continuing the Waldheim Chronicle

After his friend Wolfgang's contributions to the Waldheim chronicle, it was Max's turn to write up the reports.

The staff at the Waldheim instructed Max to take over the report-writing for the chronicle. He devoted himself to this task with enthusiasm and filled a good six pages describing events at the school between 26 August and 1 September 1923.

He looked very closely at what was going on—with a draftsman's eye—and wrote witty, mischievous entries. His character was starting to show.

"We passed a run-down inn ... and climbed up to the top, from where we could see the whole valley. Then we walked along the Hüttkopf before going down to the Tössscheide, where we bathed our feet in the Töss and ate damsons, bananas, and chocolate, building up our strength for the climb to the Tössstock. It is a well-known fact that the Tössstock is a reserve for the chamois that have been released there. We didn't see any chamois, but we did see hoof prints. We wanted to prove to the others back at home that there were chamois there. But we couldn't very well extricate a hoof print, so we took the next best thing that we could lay our hands on, not literally of course, something that a chamois had left there and that you can see in any goat shed, except not left by a chamois. Nobody wanted to touch it, so we picked it up with little sticks and put it in an envelope and Herr Doktor put it in his pocket.... Then we went merrily up the Tössstock and, from there, down to an alp where the herdsman made soup for us. It was midday and we lay and roasted in the midday sun. Then we ate soup, bread, sausages, oranges and more that our good Frau Doktor had tucked into our rucksacks. When the intensest heat was over we did up our rucksacks and climbed up the Welschenberg and from there went on to the Schwarzenberg, where we admired the view. Then we set off down again, at a smart pace because a storm was approaching and it would still take some time to reach the wood. But it already started raining, so we put on our rain capes and went happily on our way. Soon the rain eased off and we reached the sanatorium.... But then it started raining again and we huddled under a big lime tree and had something more to eat. When the rain stopped, we walked down to Wald where we conquered [a literal translation of a slip of the tongue by Max Bill when he meant to say 'caught'] the train and traveled home via Rüti and Uster. Max Bill."[119]

In his report Max wrote the word "fröhlich" ("merrily") without an "h," although there are barely any other orthographic errors. However, five years later, after his parents' divorce in 1927, he occasionally lost his grasp on spelling and old mistakes reappeared. Even after Max's time at the Bauhaus, slips of that kind led his father to bitterly reproach him, saying that it was high time Max made an effort to spell correctly in his letters: "If you are clearly not even trying to maintain the most rudimentary of decencies, no one can put their trust in you."[120]

Away from home, Max was evidently relaxed and enjoyed being with the other boarders. A small spelling mistake by the fourteen-and-a-half-year-old toward the end of his report looks a lot like a superb Freudian slip: he writes "besiegen" instead of "bestiegen," suggesting that they "conquered" the train rather than merely "catching" it. Was Max subconsciously thinking of getting the better of his own father, the railwayman?

As he roamed through the countryside around Oetwil am See, Max often used to see an odd, bizarrely dressed woman. He soon found out that her name was Helen Dahm and that she was a painter. She and her companion, Else Strantz, had set up home in Oetwil in 1919. After a life of deprivation, in 1954 Helen Dahm became the first female artist to be awarded the Art Prize of the City of Zurich. Ten years later Max Bill's thoughts returned to her and her paintings, so he went to see her in Oetwil am See, having decided to exhibit one of her paintings at *Expo '64* in Lausanne, as part of the "Human Being" display that he designed in the section "Bilden und Gestalten."

At the same *Expo* more works on the theme of "the ordering idea" were exhibited, including Concrete art paintings by Verena Loewensberg and Richard Paul Lohse and a sculpture by Max Bill.

The Fest

"On Tuesday we spent every free minute working on preparations for the Fest; in the evening there was a rehearsal, so no reading out loud. On Wednesday we were busy preparing again, so we didn't go on an outing. As soon as we had eaten we got ready to dig and build. Two of us went to Esslingen to collect the cement. Meanwhile, the rest of us went to the ravine in the woods and cut out steps while others sawed wood to secure

120 Erwin Bill to Max Bill, May 1929, Archiv Max Bill

121 Max Bill, 26 August–1 September 1923, Archiv Max Bill

the steps, we also put up little posts. By now the Esslingen team was back and got the cement ready and carried it to the ravine, where I flung it in between the rocks that they had put in front of the little bench. Then we finished repairing the bridge. The others were still working hard on the steps, but couldn't get them finished before supper; there were just a few where the planks weren't fixed in place yet....

That evening there was no wood devils' meeting [the pupils' parliament] because we were rehearsing for 1st September again. Afterward some people went up to the attic to work on a 'Schnitzelbank' [a comedic call-and-answer song].... On Friday evening there was still a lot to do, and another rehearsal, the last one before the dress rehearsal....

Then it was Saturday, with all its mysteries. We got up at the usual time, but at breakfast Frau Doktor told Herr Doktor that we were all going on strike.... Then two of the little ones came and gave everyone a snap dragon and a little maxim, written by Frau Doktor.... After breakfast everyone set to. The reading room was turned into a kitchen and hostelry. Then we searched through the charades box for suitable items of clothing for the various players. After that, we had the dress rehearsal for the boarding house comedy, penned by Frau Doktor. The dress rehearsal ended with a chocolate treat....

At 11:30 the trio played to mark the start of the Fest and the others went into the reading room. Then all the players went onto the stage, apart from the boarder who had to deliver a note. After a while the latter arrived and gave the landlord a lunch order.... After that we all went into the dining room for a meal together, during which the Fest herald delivered a speech in rhyming verses, written by Frau Doktor. The Schnitzelbank director led the singing, keeping the verses and the pictures in the right order. After supper there were old-fashioned charades: a Bible studies class, Sunday checks, and a 'gypsy' charade.... Then we went out for the lantern procession, first to the ravine and then into the village, with the Schnitzelbank singers leading the way, then Herr Alder with his mandolin and all the rest from the boarding house, in pairs, bringing up the rear. So, singing and dinning we made our way to the Waldheim linden tree and back to the boarding house again, where we all paraded round the garden and then went up to the parapet, where we hung up our lanterns one by one. Then we all had meringue and finally went to bed at about half past ten. Max Bill."[121]

Later on Arnold "Noldi" Mötteli, another boarder from Winterthur, like Wolfgang and Max, also took his turn to write the chronicle. It seems that Max Bill was punished after an excursion to the Pfannenstiel, only there is no mention of exactly what happened: "Thursday. It rained again.

Max was suspended. In the afternoon Wolfgang and Max had to build a barrier to keep the cats out up above the stairs to the top attic."[122] In 1923 the autumn half term was in early October and the boarders were allowed to go home. When they came back to school it was Max's turn to write the chronicle again. But he made no mention of what he did during the break.

"... with their fiery eyes"

It was a school outing to Männedorf, to attend a slide lecture on Tunisia, that first kindled Max Bill's interest in architecture. "We saw the most wonderful pictures of ancient Roman buildings in Carthage and the surroundings area, pictures of the way they built there, and the explanations all had a good dose of wit, the room was filled with roars of laughter, we even got a bottle of Meilen fruit juice and bread rolls.... After the lecture we went cheerily back to Oetwil and gazed at the lake and at the villages on the other side, which looked back at us with their fiery eyes."[123]

The bond between Max Bill and Wolfgang Vogel had grown stronger. They often went off on their own. Other boys complained about their "secret talks." A younger boy recorded one such occasion: "It was a beautiful starry evening. Max and Wolfgang went up toward the woods to look at the sky. Like before, some of the others said they were talking secretly.... In the evening we had reading out loud and Rudolf accused Max of having secret conversations."[124]

Kurt Bindschedler, who wrote that report, was a local boy from Männedorf and not exactly the best behaved. (The Rudolf he mentioned in his report was a certain Rudolf Stiefel from Turbenthal.) Once when Kurt had to "work off" bad behavior, he was ordered to carry "10 watering cans of manure"; elsewhere he writes that "as a punishment for using insulting language we had to help to hang the shutters ... after lunch there was a

122 Arnold "Noldi" Mötteli, 16–22 September 1923, Waldheim chronicle
123 Max Bill, late October–11 November 1923, Waldheim chronicle
124 Kurt Bindschedler, 12–17 November 1923, Waldheim chronicle
125 Kurt Bindschedler, 12–17 November 1923, Waldheim chronicle
126 Information kindly supplied by Peter Niederhäuser, Winterthur, 2008
127 Wolfgang Vogel, 7–12 January 1924, Waldheim chronicle
128 Max Bill, 13–19 January 1924, Waldheim chronicle

clothes, shoes, and overalls check. After the four o'clock snack we had exercise books check. I had such a long exercise books check that I still wasn't finished by the evening."[125]

From 16 to 23 December 1923 it was Noldi's turn again. There is no mention of Max in the report for that week. Maybe he had been allowed to leave early for the Christmas break so that he could celebrate his fifteenth birthday on 22 December with his parents in Winterthur.

The Historical Antiquarian Society

In 1924 Max's father Erwin Bill, who audited the books of the Historical Antiquarian Society in Winterthur, featured in the society's minutes. The society was planning to celebrate the fiftieth anniversary of its founding with an excursion to Mörsburg castle, which was and still is owned by the town of Winterthur. So the railwayman, Erwin Bill, arranged that the 14:14 train from Winterthur to Frauenfeld would, by way of an exception, stop at the village of Wiesendangen so the celebration party could alight there. As a rule Erwin Bill's role in the society was mainly concerned with book keeping. Two years after he specially organized that "stop," he was elected as the society's "quaestor" (cashier).[126]

"... two wonderful little birch trees with huge veils"

The first report in the chronicle at the beginning of Max Bill's second year at the Waldheim was again written by his friend Wolfgang Vogel: "On Tuesday, 7 January, the boarding house came to life again. We were all back together again for the four o'clock snack ... magnificent skiing weather so in no time at all we were out on our skis, playing around on the slopes.... Wednesday. School had properly started again ... in the afternoon we could go skating or skiing. Max and I chose skiing.... We went to see the skaters on the top pond and sallied out onto the ice with our skis, which was rather slippery.... Max flew right up in the air over a ditch and tore the binding on one ski."[127]

The events of the following week were recorded in Max's right-slanting handwriting: "Herr Doktor said we would take our skis up to the Pfannenstiel and maybe go on to the Forch from there."[128]

For Max Bill this landscape was associated with enduringly heart-warming memories. Forch is a municipality in the canton of Zürich. In those days—as now—it was connected to the city by a local train service, the Forchbahn. The Waldheim school was not far from Esslingen, the terminus. Traveling back again in the opposite direction toward Zurich, the first station after Forch is Zumikon, where Max Bill later built his second studio and home in 1967–68.

We got ready and set off. We climbed higher and higher toward the Pfannenstiel, with the mist becoming brighter and brighter. The higher we went, the more beautiful the landscape, especially the woods. In the end we arrived at the huntsman's lookout at Egg, where there were two wonderful little birch trees with huge veils. And then we just went on and on, until we had reached the lower section of the ski slopes. Now we were so high that we could look down on a wonderful sea of mist. Our heads were above it, our feet were in it.

But we couldn't stay there long, gazing at the billowing drama, and we climbed up to the edge of the forest, where Herr Doktor gave us chocolate.... some people said they wanted to stay there. Others said they wanted to go to the Forch. It was put to the vote twice but still everyone wasn't agreed. So Herr Doktor suggested a compromise that pleased everyone. One group set off for the Forch, the other group stayed at the Pfannenstiel. We flew like arrows through the magnificent landscape down into a wide valley, on the other side a long run took us to the Forch.... then we caught the little train to Esslingen, from where we tramped back home.... Saturday afternoon was filled with the usual working off, cleaning out the rabbit hutches and the chicken coop. Max Bill."[129]

Max could see a long way out into the landscape from the Waldheim in Oetwil am See; on a clear day he could see as far as the Bachtel, a peak in the Appenzeller Alps. His favorite uncle and role model, Ernst Geiger, passed on to him a love of rocks and rock formations, and Max decided he wanted to study science. However, he was not able to realize his dream of becoming a geologist because he left school without any formal qualifications. Instead, during the course of his adult life he developed his own very tactile connection with rocks and stones, marble and granite.

129 Max Bill, 13–19 January 1924, Waldheim chronicle

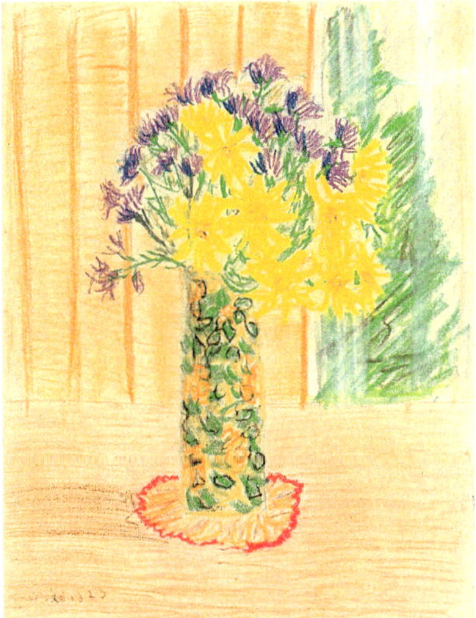

Max Bill, Untitled [Vase with flowers],
1923, Drawing on paper, 30×22.8 cm

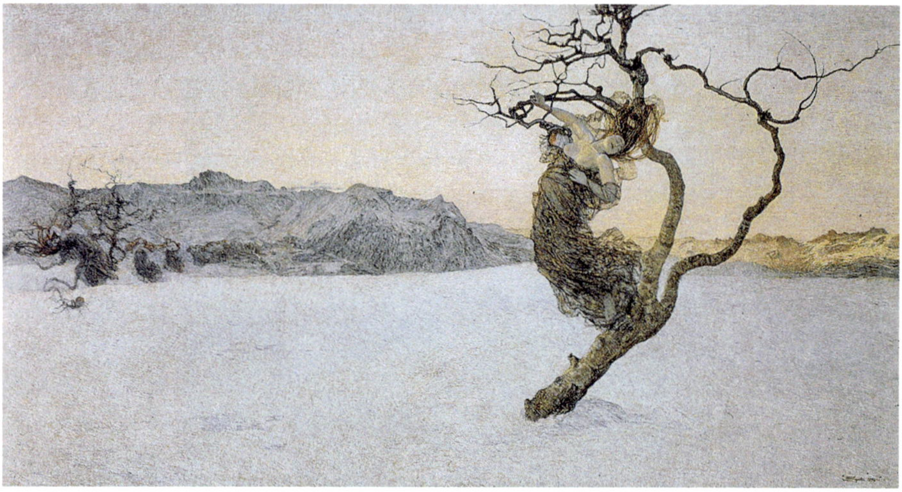

Giovanni Segantini, *Die bösen Mütter,*
1894, oil on canvas, 105×200cm

Bad Mothers

In the last of the Waldheim chronicles preserved in the local history museum in Oetwil am See, there is an entry by a certain Steffi: "... in the afternoon we couldn't find our sleds. Luckily Ernst [Ernst Sieber] and Luzi went to the ravine, where they found the missing sleds. One, Noldi's, was lying by the stream, Luzi's was hanging on a branch, and the boarding house sled was lying on the ice near the ravine. We were all sure it had been Max who had wanted to play a trick on us."[130] And it seems it was indeed young Max who decided to play a funny prank—"taking care" of the sleds and hanging one in a tree.

Could it be that Max had Giovanni Segantini's *Die bösen Mütter* (1894) in the back of his mind—a painting that his uncle Ernst might well have introduced him to? The "bad mothers" in the painting are suspended in trees, banned to the icy wastes in a bleak mountain landscape. Segantini painted *Die bösen Mütter* on the Tussagn alp up above Savognin.

I should like to add here that with this motif Segantini went out on much more of a limb than Hodler.

Art historian Matthias Frehner regards this painting as a key work in the transition from nineteenth- to twentieth-century attitudes: "The many images of a mother and child in Segantini's work, one of his main motifs, connect with basic, existential issues in his own life. As an adult he had a distinctly unreal relationship to his own mother, who died when he was just seven. On one hand he felt he was to blame for her death because she never fully recovered after giving birth to him; on the other hand she never gave him the comfort that a child of that age would normally expect from its mother."

In a Freudian interpretation of Segantini's autobiography, the psychoanalyst Karl Abraham has concluded that "the haunting story of Segantini's childhood is like an individual myth." All his variations on that theme, from genre-like cradle scenes ... to the "bad mothers" abandoned in ice fields, are permeated with the individual myths of Segantini's relationship to his mother."[131]

As long as he lived Max Bill was jealous of his younger brother Hugo, who he felt had stolen his mother's love from him. When a mother withdraws from her first-born child and instead allows the next child, the younger one, to suckle at her breast, the older child feels that his mother's

130 "Steffi," 4–9 February 1924, Waldheim chronicle

131 Frehner 2004, p. 97

love for him has gone cold. And so it was for Max, the first-born child; when Hugo was born he suddenly felt he had been abandoned to that terrible cold. First-born sons like Max Bill—and of course Sigmund Freud—are the ones who are sent out into the cold by their mothers. Segantini reverses the process: he banishes the "bad mothers" to the icy cold, along with their newborn infants.

Another source that might have given the unruly Max Bill the idea of hanging a sled in a tree was a story about the young Hodler that featured in his obituary in the *Neue Zürcher Zeitung.* It is entirely possible that Max's father (a keen reader) or his mother (a great admirer of Hodler's art) recounted that story to the boy.

Hodler, eighteen years old at the time, was staying in Langenthal, where a friend of his, Luise Rölli, witnessed certain events first hand: "A strange old woodcutter, you know, the type you see in Spitzweg drawings, lived not far from us. Rumor had it in the village that each morning he would take his Black Forest wall clock into the woods with him and hang it up in a nearby fir tree. In the evening he would take it back home again. That was exactly Hodler's sort of thing. He couldn't wait to see for himself if it was true. So one morning we set out for the woods and followed the sound of an axe. Quietly we crept closer, one behind the other with Hodler leading the way. In the middle of the wood there was a clearing, where the woodcutter was chopping wood. We watched him ... every once in a while he would stop chopping and gaze thoughtfully into the fir tree facing him. And it was true, hanging in the fir tree there was a wall clock, ticking away.... Hodler climbed up the tree, removed the clock and hung it on a much higher branch. So when the woodcutter looked back again to check the time, all he saw was a brown fir cone, dangling on a chain."[132]

132 P. Schmuziger, "Aus Hodlers Jugendzeit," *Neue Zürcher Zeitung,* 7 June 1918
133 Max Bill's Waldheim report is in the archive of the Ortsmuseum Oetwil am See
134 Max Bill in conversation with Angela Thomas
135 Bill 1942 [b]

A Waldheim School Report

A school report for Max Bill[133] records that the only subject where he achieved a 6 (the best grade in the Swiss marking system) was singing. He was given a 5 (good) in writing/stenography, bookkeeping, freehand drawing, geometry, geometric drawing, history, and chemistry/physics. His algebra/arithmetic wavered between satisfactory and good. He managed a 4 (satisfactory) in geography and also in Greek/English. The subject that evidently interested him least in Oetwil am See was French, where his results were only "adequate to satisfactory."

Maybe Bill's singing was more pleasing because, unlike his younger classmates, his voice had already broken. Whether Bill had lessons in both Greek and English or whether he had to choose one or the other is unclear. I myself never heard him utter anything in Greek; as to English, in the late 1930s he made a serious effort to improve his English. Max Bill was not taught Latin or natural history and had no religious studies lessons. Around ten years after leaving school he set about improving his French.

The Apprentice Gold- and Silversmith

Erwin Bill felt that the best thing for his son would be to learn a trade.[134] So Max decided he wanted to become a gold- and silversmith. "That was also traditional. As far back as the Middle Ages gold- and silversmiths also became sculptors, or practiced other artistic skills—such as engraving copper. In spring 1924 I enrolled at the Kunstgewerbeschule in Zurich as a student in the department for silversmiths and engravers. However, since the rule was that every new student had to spend at least one or two semesters in the general class before being allowed to join a workshop, they counted my first semester as a general class, which meant that I spent more time in the modeling classes and in the metal department than the other students."[135]

Ernst Ludwig Kirchner in Winterthur

Although Bill was now a student at the Kunstgewerbeschule in Zurich, he was still living with his parents in Winterthur and commuting to Zurich. Naturally he continued to participate in cultural activities in Winterthur, as he had done since he was a child. In June 1924, for instance, he attended the first solo exhibition of works by Ernst Ludwig Kirchner at Kunstmuseum Winterthur (organized by the Kunstverein Winterthur).

Up until then the main focus in exhibitions at the Kunstmuseum had been on French art from the nineteenth century. In those days Kirchner's art, including his painting *Bauernmittag* (1920), was widely met with stubborn non-comprehension and the solo exhibition of his work in 1924 caused a major scandal despite Georg Schmidt (the art critic for the *National-Zeitung* and librarian of the Basler Kunstverein) leading a group of visitors through the exhibition and doing his utmost to explain and mediate the work. He was met with a chorus of whistles from outraged museum-goers. As they did their best to drown him out, Max Bill found himself on the other side of the argument. Young and open-minded, Max took the same view as Schmidt—a progressive thinker who was more than willing to defend Kirchner.

It seems that Paul Fink, the keeper of the collection at Kunstmuseum Winterthur, had initially assured Schmidt that he could introduce Kirchner's art at the opening of the exhibition (which Kirchner had installed in person), only to then change his mind: "Since we in fact deprecate this art, we are concerned that an official introduction to the exhibition could be taken to suggest that we value these paintings and wished to recommend them by dint of the introduction."[136]

Schmidt was only able to deliver his highly informative talk on the second Sunday of the exhibition, on 29 June 1924. The museum's management team had already distanced itself in advance of the event: "On the request of the artist . . . the art writer Georg Schmidt from Basel will talk on the work of E. L. Kirchner by the paintings on the ground floor of the museum. However, art connoisseurs in our area repudiate these works (without in the slightest feeling like backwoodsmen)."[137]

136 Cited in Stutzer 2007, pp. 281–82
137 Cited in Stutzer 2007, p. 282
138 Beat Stutzer, "'Der Bauernmittag.' Zu einem Bild von Ernst Ludwig Kirchner," *Neue Zürcher Zeitung,* 5–6 December 1992
139 Ernst Ludwig Kirchner to Nele van de Velde, 29 July 1924, cited in Stutzer 2007, p. 284

Georg Schmidt subsequently published a text with a lengthy title that translates as "What I would like to have said on 29 June in Winterthur, but which I was somewhat prevented from saying by the friendly mood of my audience. Also with some responses to some reviews of the exhibition" ("Was ich am 29 June in Winterthur gerne gesagt hätte, was zu sagen mich aber die freundliche Gesinnung meiner Zuhörer einigermassen behindert hat. Zugleich einige Antworten auf einige Besprechungen der Ausstellung," in *Expressionismus aus den Bergen,* ed. Beat Stutzer, Samuel Vitali, Han Steenbruggen and Matthias Frehner [Zurich: Scheidegger & Spiess, 2007], pp. 287–303). Less than a decade later Georg Schmidt and Max Bill found themselves working closely together on the small-format, anti-Fascist periodical *information* in Zurich, which was printed at the Genossenschaftsdruckerei Aarau (printers' cooperative in Aarau); Schmidt wrote articles and Bill provided the typographic design for each issue.

Following the uproar in Winterthur, Kirchner wrote to Nele van de Velde, one of Henry van de Velde's daughters: "I enclose herewith the photographs of my exhibition. . . . They may give you an impression of the exhibition that met with such hostility yet was one of the biggest and best I have ever done. . . . In fact my works were utterly at odds with the contents of the collection at the museum, which may explain the public's bafflement and insults. Well-meaning individuals suggested that my art was 'too German' to be understood by the people of Winterthur, only nothing is 'more German' than the little town of Winterthur. . . . However, one very nice, pleasing thing was the response of the young artists, the way they took my side."[138] One of the young audience members at Georg Schmidt's talk, alluded to by Kirchner, was Max Bill; although he had always drawn since he was a small child and throughout his schooldays, at that point he would not yet have described himself as a "young artist."

Max Bill particularly admired Ludwig Kirchner's *Drei Akte im Walde* (see p. 661)—painted some years after the Winterthur exhibition—because of the very unusual way that Kirchner uses light as a creative tool. In 1937 Kirchner's *Bauernmittag,* which had been shown in the Winterthur exhibition and in the meantime bought by the Hamburger Kunsthalle for 3,000 Swiss francs, was suddenly ridiculed as a "shoddy piece of work" and, following Hitler's removal of every trace of "degenerate art" in German museum collections, was shown from 19 July to 30 November in Munich in its native land, alongside other spoils of this art theft, and derided with derogatory comments ("German farming folk—a Yiddish gaze").[139]

Georg Reinhart, one of the leading collectors in Winterthur and managing director of the trading company Gebrüder Volkart, met Ernst Ludwig Kirchner in person in December 1917. At the time Kirchner was in the care of the psychiatrist Ludwig Binswanger at the Bellevue Sanatorium in Kreuzlingen, where Henry van de Velde was also undergoing treatment. And it was in fact Van de Velde who introduced Kirchner to Georg Reinhart at the sanatorium.[140] Following that meeting, Reinhart started to acquire "hand done" prints by Kirchner—42 in total by 1922—despite apparently having trouble understanding them: "I wrote to Kirchner openly telling him that this newest mode of expression is still incomprehensible to me; despite his ailing hands, he took the trouble to write me a long letter of explanation. It is starting to dawn on me ... but I would be grateful for more help."[141]

Whereas Reinhart honestly sought to understand Kirchner's art, other influential collectors in Winterthur, who were generally fixated on French art, flatly refused to make that kind of an effort for a German artist who was being treated in Switzerland for substance abuse. In July 1924, in connection with the Kirchner exhibition at Kunstmuseum Winterthur, Reinhart contacted the board of the Kunstverein and proposed gifting a large-format landscape by Kirchner, *Davos im Schnee* (1923), to their collection, "however, the board, dominated by proponents of French art, declined Reinhart's offer of a gift, so the latter ultimately acquired the painting for his own collection."[142]

It was not only Kirchner who confounded the people of Winterthur; a similar controversy had erupted in the past—in the year when Max Bill was born—over the purchase of a work by Ferdinand Hodler. "In those days people still had to fight for Hodler. In 1908, when the new Kunstverein Winterthur board had purchased his *Abendruhe,* there was a burst of outrage, upon which the Hahnlosers sought a detailed evaluation from Vallotton, whose response was unequivocal: 'I think that within a few years Winterthur will be proud to have been one of the first Swiss cities with limited means to have granted itself the luxury of a Hodler painting, and that time will come sooner rather than later because the power that a work of art carries within it is an irresistible force.... If, however, your fellow citizens should be too pained by the sight of it and their walls should seem to them dishonored by it, I know of others who would gladly offer it shelter.'"[143]

140 See Schoop 1992, p. 50
141 Georg Reinhart to Hans Mardersteig, 19 May 1919, cited in Schwarz 1998, p. 353
142 Schwarz 1998, pp. 353–54
143 Félix Vallotton, cited in Hahnloser 1973, p. 23

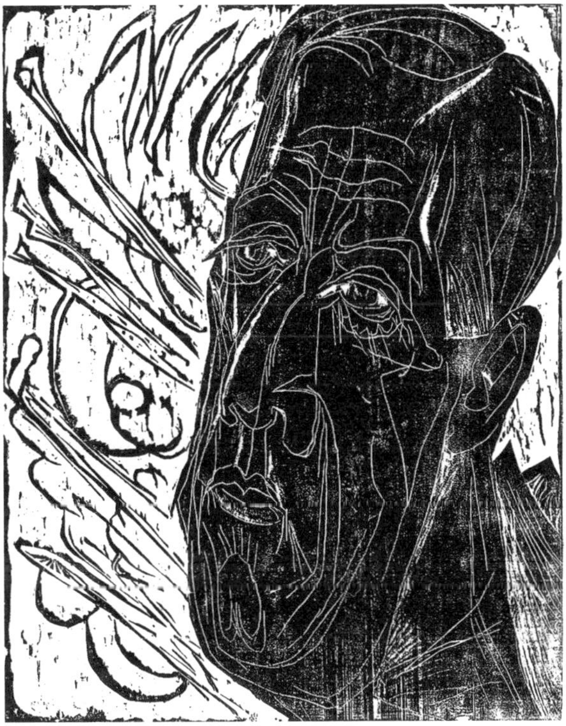

Ernst Ludwig Kirchner,
Kopf Van de Velde, dunkel, 1917,
woodcut, 49.9 × 39.5 cm

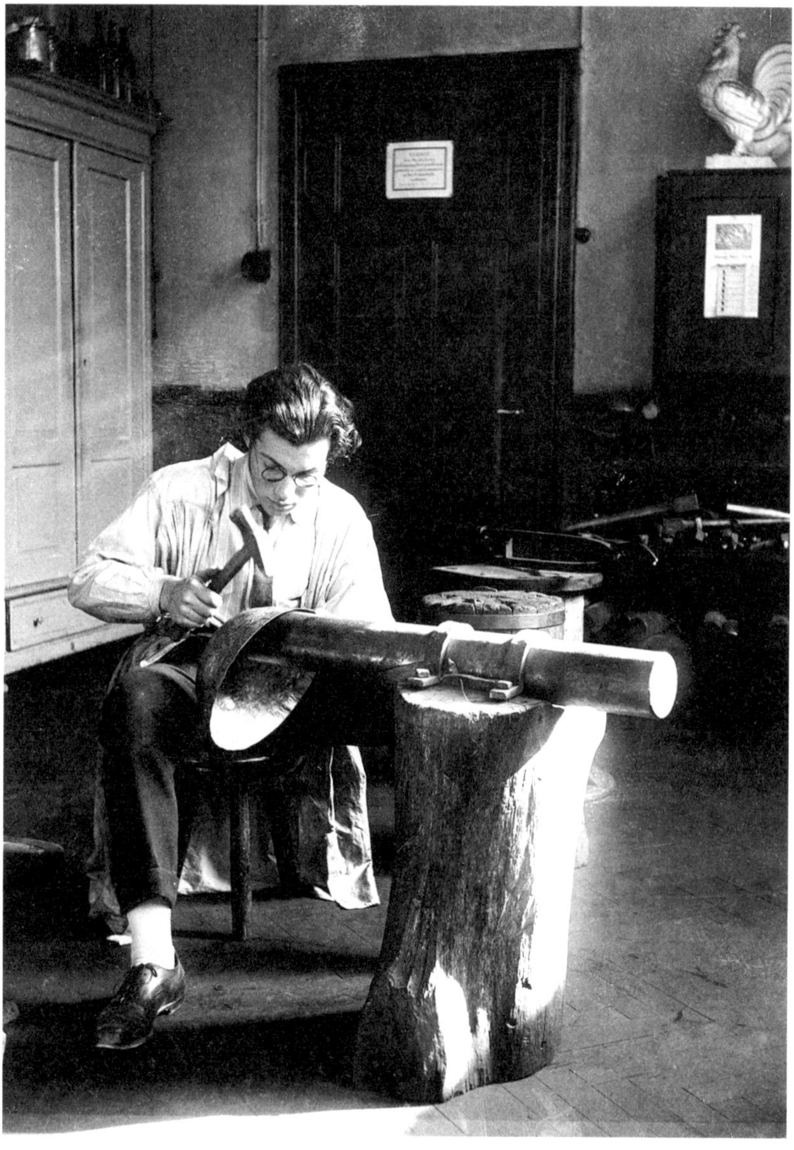

Max Bill (with a full head of wavy hair) training as a silversmith at the Kunstgewerbeschule, Zurich, 1925–26

Those other collectors in Winterthur who declined Georg Reinhart's offer of a painting by Kirchner were in fact Hedy and Arthur Hahnloser-Bühler and Hedy's cousin Richard Bühler, the long-time president of the Kunstverein Winterthur.

Having again proposed donating his Kirchner landscape with its innocuous subject matter to the museum in Winterthur in 1939, only to have his offer rejected for a second time, in 1944 Georg Reinhart "donated it to Kunstmuseum Basel, where Georg Schmidt enthusiastically took delivery of it."[144] As it turned out, Kirchner proved to be Reinhart's "most adventurous foray into modern art, given that Reinhart was just as reluctant to engage with Cubism and non-representational art as other collectors in Winterthur."[145]

At that time, collectors who (sometimes) allowed members of the public access to privately purchased works of art by lending or gifting them to museums often held considerable sway over matters of taste. And while various collectors in Winterthur owned high-quality works by artists such as Vallotton, Bonnard and Vuillard—with "painterly qualities" that Max Bill always valued—it is also true to say that many of those French artists, such as Bonnard, and Vuillard, never really ventured outside the boudoirs and the grand salons of the bourgeoisie. Vallotton did at least dare to go out into the landscape, where he painted works that have a particular appeal of their own. By contrast, Hodler's large-format compositions opened up new possibilities and could, given the right situation, hold their own in public buildings, even in a station concourse.

In the young Max Bill's native town attitudes to art were thus largely shaped by wealthy collectors.

When the young Max found himself in serious financial difficulties in 1929, he wrote to Georg Reinhart. In January 1929, and again in early April 1929, he sent a number of works to Reinhart, only to have them returned "without comment." Reinhart withheld his support.[146]

Bearing that in mind, one can readily understand the sense of relief that swept over the eighteen-year-old Max in 1927 when he enrolled at the Bauhaus in Dessau. A completely new, contemporary cultural climate awaited him there. Having first found his feet and successfully reset his course, he soon managed to make his own contribution to the mercurial, optimistic mood of the school.

144 Schwarz 1998, p. 354, for a detailed account see Stutzer 1979

145 Schwarz 1998, p. 354

146 Mebold 2008, p. 206

The Kunstgewerbeschule in Zurich

During Max Bill's first three semesters at the Kunstgewerbeschule in Zurich, Eduard Bick was the tutor for clay and plaster modeling. Although Bick had plenty to say about what he had seen and done abroad, Max Bill had no time for Bick's sculptures. Bick was from the town of Wil in the canton of St. Gallen. Having completed his apprenticeship as a goldsmith in Innsbruck, he moved on to Hanau (Germany) and then to Munich, where he studied at the art academy in 1906. His next stop was Rome, where he made his first sculptures. He then spent 1910–14 in Berlin before returning to Italy. In 1916 Bick met the art collector Baron August von der Heydt and moved back to Berlin. After the First World War, Bick returned to his native Switzerland and finally settled in Zurich in 1921.

"I remember that we were a very small class, and that everyone just modeled what they wanted. I don't remember Bick ever correcting me or giving me advice. Eduard Bick was always well turned out; at the start of the day he would sit in a corner reading the paper. Then he would disappear into Café Esplanade on the little square where Bahnhofstrasse and Rennweg meet Oetenbachgasse, which is where the modeling studio was. He had two favorite students, my friend Alfred 'Fredi' Bühler from the metalwork class and a woman, Alis Guggenheim, who lived in Oetenbachgasse in those days. She was half a generation older than me, with Fredi exactly between the two of us. As a political being, Fredi saw himself as a 'comrade' of Alis Guggenheim's. Those were the students that Bick bothered with. They started off by making busts of each other."[147]

Bill, ignored by the tutor, Bick, sometimes took his cello with him and practiced in the modeling studio when Alis was working there. Decades later Bill still remembered her "gazing intensely" at her model. Like Max's mother, Alis had grown up in the canton of Aargau. As Fredi became increasingly attracted to her, Max sometimes found himself missing his friend's company. He was disconcerted to find himself left on his own. In a self-portrait dated 1925 (see p. 115), a thin-faced Max Bill

147 Bill 1993
148 Max Bill in conversation with Angela Thomas
149 Max Bill in conversation with Angela Thomas
150 Thomas 1991 [b], p. 91
151 Alis Guggenheim, draft letter to Georg Schmidt, n.d., in Thomas 1991 [b], p. 94 and note 30
152 Max Bill in conversation with Angela Thomas

gazes out sombrely. His long, wavy hair covers his ears. Although he appears somewhat forlorn, his wide-open eyes create the impression that he is trying to draw the world in toward him through the lenses of his spectacles. At the time when Max Bill created that self-portrait, he also made a jug (see p. 107) and an electric samovar (see p. 101). "I did well in student competitions for new metal items, new vases, big cast-iron plant pots. Most of my designs won first prize."[148]

Sometimes Fredi did, after all, take Max with him when he went to visit Alis Guggenheim, who was full of stories about her time working as a seamstress for a Soviet company, witnessing the Revolution in Moscow first hand. While it was not that Max had no interest in those revolutionary events in Moscow, he found Alis "too severe" and he was "almost a little afraid of her."[149]

Alis Guggenheim had lived in Moscow in 1919–20, after which she returned to Switzerland with her daughter and enrolled at the Kunstgewerbeschule. In any free time in Moscow she had visited art galleries "enriched by works of art that had been confiscated from private owners" and filled with "masses of visitors." In Zurich, in late 1924, she met the Swiss figurative sculptor Karl Geiser, with whom she then had a series of excruciating sexual encounters—those encounters no doubt partly failed due to the fact Geiser actually preferred men. Alis ultimately came to the conclusion that her life would only "have meaning" if she lived as a practicing artist.[150] Meanwhile in Zurich she felt hemmed in by prejudice on all sides, as she wrote in a letter to the leftist art historian Georg Schmidt: "To the Swiss I am just a Jew, to the Jews just a Communist, to the Communists just an artist, to the male artists just a woman, and to women just a Miss with a child."[151]

Having absorbed his parents' interest in art, Max was already "very well aware" of the Swiss art world: "In Zurich the dominant Bernese artists, following in Ferdinand Hodler's wake, were Hermann Haller, Hermann Hubacher, and, somewhat younger, Karl Geiser."[152] Bill, at the age of nine, had already seen works by Hermann Hubacher when his parents took him to the exhibition *Selbstbildnisse Schweizer Künstler der Gegenwart* (1917) at Kunstmuseum Winterthur.

At that exhibition the Winterthur collector and art patron Georg Reinhart met the sculptor Hermann Hubacher and soon afterward decided to support him. Reinhart and Hubacher visited Egypt together in 1929–30 and remained friends. Reinhart also supported the sculptor Karl Geiser for many years, financing "trips to Paris and the production of casts." Georg Reinhart was in fact following in the footsteps of his father, Dr. Theodor Reinhart, a successful entrepreneur who in

1908 had crucially helped to ensure that the commission to design new Swiss bank notes went to the "still controversial" artist Ferdinand Hodler.[153]

Years later, in group exhibitions, Max Bill's own work could be measured against that of Hermann Haller, Hermann Hubacher, and Karl Geiser, all of whom lived and worked in Zurich. One such event was the exhibition *Schweizer Bildhauer und Maler 1941* (December 1941–February 1942), by which time Max Bill had already forged ahead into the much more modern realms of Concrete art, leaving behind him his compatriots' figurative sculptures. In 1953 figurative works by Karl Geiser and Concrete works by Max Bill were seen in company with each other at the group show *Schweizer Kunst der Gegenwart* at Kunsthalle Baden-Baden (29 March–28 June 1953). The two older artists, Haller and Hubacher, were not represented in that exhibition in Baden-Baden, which was explicitly devoted to contemporary art. It thus seems a little surprising that the exhibits by Geiser, two bronzes, in fact dated to 1928 and 1929; meanwhile Max Bill's much more recent exhibits, sculptures made between 1944 and 1952, attracted considerable attention (see *Schweizer Kunst der Gegenwart: Gemälde, Plastik, Graphik, Kunstgewerbe* [Baden-Baden 1953] for illustrations of Geiser's bronzes [cat. nos. 126 and 127] and Bill's sculptures [cat. nos. 116–20]).

In-Fighting at Libertas

In the early twentieth century two different factions emerged in the Zurich branch of Libertas. The group on the left, influenced by Fritz Brupbacher, included Ernst Geiger and Ulrich Wilhelm Züricher (U.W.Z.) "There was an appetite for conflict, both internal and external. In the Zurich branch of Libertas the two factions were well matched ... one side was happiest dancing and singing, the other side was obsessed with critical thought, hoping to

153 Schwarz 1998, pp. 353 and 345

154 Ernst Geiger, "fin de siècle," *Korrespondenzblatt Für Studierende Abstinenten 9* (July/August 1925), Archiv Christoph Geiger

155 Information kindly supplied by Christoph Geiger

156 Chronology by Ulrich Wilhelm Züricher, in Gautschi-Züricher 1988, pp. 8–9

157 U. W. Züricher, "Man wünscht Libertaserinnerungen von mir," *Korrespondenzblatt Für Studierende Abstinenten* 9 (July/August 1925), Archiv Christoph Geiger

use Turgenev and Brupbacher's pamphlet on female emancipation to revolutionise the Helvetians. There were tough clashes sometimes."[154]

When Ernst Geiger was a student at the Polytechnic in Zurich he was elected president of the student society Libertas. And it seems he was not only active in the Zurich branch of Libertas: an undated lithograph made for Libertas in Bern, depicting a mountain landscape near Lauenen, bears his initials.[155]

U.W.Z. was a revolutionary with a strong religious streak. On his return to Zurich in 1906 he made contact again with Brupbacher and the workers' movement. "Found Russian society in Zurich changed; imminent revolution palpable ... first contact with Leonhard Ragaz, university chaplain in Zurich. Religious-social outlook, close to the workers' movement, struggle against militarism ... visit to Kropotkin in Cannobbio."[156]

In connection with the celebrations for the thirtieth anniversary of Libertas, U.W.Z. recounted how he had first become involved with Libertas and the "Brupbacher faction." He had gone to hear an evening lecture with the title "Should We Drown Misery and Boredom in Alcohol?" The speaker "had a rare intelligence and his talk was both sentimental and blasé, a mixture of scepticism and belief, long-suffering acerbity and suppressed fire, which immensely impressed me as a young man striving for knowledge. During my student days in Zurich that same physician (it was Fritz Brupbacher) would have a hand in my fate. How many times did we stay up all night talking, our ideas converging and diverging again ... I still regard him as one of the most psychologically gifted people of our time.... Life as a member of Libertas was filled with walks, meetings, and endless debates.... Goethe and Keller were trumps, as were Nietzsche and Dostoevsky ... Böcklin and Segantini, Ibsen and Tolstoy, Marx, Bakunin ... of course more so for some, less so for others (the 'merely-teetotallers' as this writer calls them). There were often harsh words and sometimes we were close to splitting into two societies."[157]

In the mid-1920s Max Bill designed a cover for *Die junge Schweiz,* the progressive temperance magazine:

"Dear Uncle Ernst!

I was sorry not to see you at the Libertas Foundation Day, so many of your old comrades asked after you and I told them all they should visit you, that it's beautiful where you are, and so on.—I saw there was nothing of yours at the G.S.M.B.A. exhibition, and there was also no sign of the painting of yours that the museum is supposed to have, despite the extension.—The brushes and paints from Paris never came, just a letter saying that it was too complicated to send those sorts of things, etc.—So I didn't do anything more about it. I've designed a cover for *Die Junge*

Schweiz, but I haven't yet done the membership card for Dr. Oettli, he also wants something to put on a wall! Very best wishes! Max."[158]
Die Junge Schweiz first came out one year later, in 1926. This suggests Max Bill may have had insider information. Neither the cover design mentioned in Bill's letter nor the membership card for Dr. Oettli—a progressive anti-alcohol campaigner—have survived in Max Bill's typography estate. A note in the *Korrespondenzblatt* of June 1925 states that "a member of Humanitas Winterthur"—that may well have been Max Bill—had won the competition to design a "letter head" and had received a copy of *Das Leben Tolstois* by Romain Rolland in recognition of his efforts. An article by Geiger's friend U.W.Z. provides an insight into Dr. Max Oettli: "Max Oettli, our bustling secretary in Lausanne, burst forth in scientific profusion. He was convinced that every serious natural scientist is infinitely more important to humankind than all the verbalists and art figures like Goethe and all the rest."[159]

First Successes in the Applied Arts

One day, at Kunsthaus Zürich, Max Bill came across "a half-size girl, cast in bronze." It was by Eduard Bick: "a figure without gestures, without 'artistic interpretation,' carefully worked and almost imperceptibly stylized, otherwise utterly faithful to nature, a figure that represents nothing more nor less than naked stillness.... I realized that his favorite students were the ones who wanted to achieve a similar degree of precision. It is interesting that those two [Alis Guggenheim and Alfred Bühler] were the only young sculptors who continued to cultivate Bick's singular naturalism."[160]
The estate of the sculptor Eduard Bick would later go to the Aargau art collection—which would also be gifted works by Max's godfather Adolf Weibel.[161]

158 Max Bill, Winterthur, to Ernst Geiger (26 December 1925), Archiv Christoph Geiger
159 U. W. Züricher, "Man wünscht Libertas-erinnerungen von mir" (see note 157)
160 Bill 1993
161 See Widmer 1974, p. 131
162 Max Bill in one of his drafts of a curriculum vitae
163 Sophie Taeuber-Arp to Hans Arp, n.d., in the dossier "Lettres de Sophie," no. 14, Stiftung Hans Arp und Sophie Taeuber-Arp, Rolandseck

Bill already knew that he would not be following that path of "singular naturalism" and he very distinctly started to strike out on his own. Some years later, in one of his drafts for a curriculum vitae, he looked back at that time: "My main tutor at the school in Zurich, Herr Vermeulen, allowed me to realize my own ideas and I was always encouraged to do that, also by the director, Herr Altherr. At that time there were a number of student competitions at the Kunstgewerbeschule (for new pewterware, new ceramic vases, modern objects made from lead ... and so on), I did well in all those competitions, I was often awarded first prize."[162]

Alfred Altherr, director of the Kunstgewerbeschule in Zurich, was always at the forefront of things. He was also director of the Kunstgewerbemuseum Zürich, which had connections to the Kunstgewerbeschule, and founder-president of the Schweizerischer Werkbund (SWB).

Max Bill's teachers were evidently aware of his artistic talent, but they also repeatedly complained about what they regarded as his recalcitrance. The apprentice silversmith did not find the obligatory curriculum particularly appealing and he took much greater interest in what was going on around him, notably the thematic exhibitions put on by Alfred Altherr in the Kunstgewerbemuseum, which were filled with all kinds of compelling information and made a deep impression on the young Bill, who was always keen to widen his horizons.

There were some outstanding artists among the teachers at the Kunstgewerbeschule, including Sophie Taeuber-Arp in the textiles department and Otto Morach (already a longstanding friend of Ernst Geiger's), who taught ornamental drawing. In a letter to her husband Jean (originally Hans) Arp, whom she married in 1922, Sophie Taeuber-Arp commented on the social situation in Zurich at the time: "Zurich is forever beautiful and boring. In the minds of the people of Zurich it's only at a salary of 15,000 [francs] that you start to count as a human being."[163]

Otto Morach was born in a village in the canton of Solothurn and as a boy lived in the town of Solothurn; he was unhappy there and felt constrained by the town's provincialism. Although his parents were not wealthy, they made sure he could take his Abitur (the certificate qualifying him for university). In 1906 Morach moved to Bern and in 1908 gained his certificate as a high school teacher of mathematics and science. He then spent two semesters at university and at the Kunstgewerbeschule, training as a drawing teacher.

During his time in Bern, Morach (a follower of the abstinence movement) became friends with the painters Carl Fischer (a future colleague at the Kunstgewerbeschule in Zurich) and Johannes Itten (a future master at the Bauhaus in Weimar and later director of

Kunstgewerbeschule in Zurich), who was studying mathematics and science in Bern (1910–12); all three friends loved hiking in Switzerland.

In 1918, Morach participated in the exhibition *Das neue Leben* in Basel, alongside Sophie Taeuber, Jean Arp, and others. "The Basel exhibition was then presented, with some changes, at Kunsthaus Zürich in early 1919, and in early 1920 the *2. Ausstellung Das neue Leben* opened at Kunsthalle Bern."[164]

Morach, along with others such as Arp, Giacometti, Marcel Janco and Hans Richter, was a signatory to a radical artistic manifesto that was published in the *Neue Zürcher Zeitung* in May 1919.

As a nine-year-old Bill had of course seen Otto Morach's self-portrait in the exhibition at Kunstmuseum Winterthur and he had remembered the tortured loneliness of that face; and now it was Otto Morach who accompanied a group of Kunstgewerbe students, including Max Bill, on a trip to Paris in 1925. Morach knew the city well from having stayed there on numerous occasions before the First World War; for a time he had rented an atelier in La Ruche in the Montparnasse district, not far from Marc Chagall's studio. When Morach was teaching at the Kunstgewerbeschule in Zurich, he fell in love with a student, Hermana Sjövall, who made tapestries, among other things. She was born in Paris, her mother was from Geneva, and her father was from Sweden, but she and her mother left France when the First World War broke out. In the early 1920s Otto Morach and Hermana Sjövall became a couple, causing something of a scandal in Zurich. Initially Hermana's mother refused to let her daughter go on any trips with Morach, although she did then allow her to marry him in August 1923, before Bill arrived at the Kunstgewerbeschule. However, even after Hermana was married, it seems she was never really able to break away from her family.

The teaching staff at the Kunstgewerbeschule also included artists such as Ernst Keller,[165] Wilhelm Kienzle, and Carl Fischer.

Fischer attended the Kunstgewerbeschule in Bern in 1908–9, which is where he met his future colleague and lifelong friend Otto Morach. Morach's wife Hermana was also a follower of the Mazdaznan movement

164 Schaller 1983, p. 63

165 *Ernst Keller, Graphiker, 1891–1968. Gesamtwerk,* ed. Hansjürg Budliger, exh. cat. Kunstgewerbemuseum Zürich, 2 May–13 June 1976, Bibliothek Max Bill; this catalogue also includes an illustration of Keller's gravestone for Kienzle: "Grabstein Wilhelm Kienzle," Fluntern cemetery, 1958, p. 120

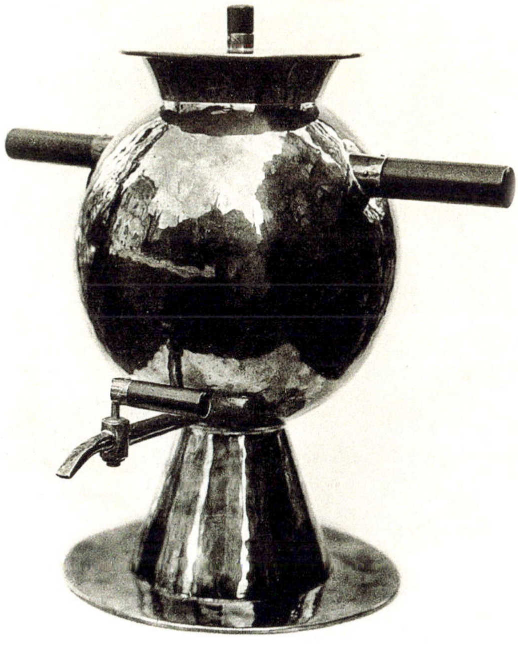

Max Bill, Electric samovar, 1925,
tombac, height ca. 40 cm

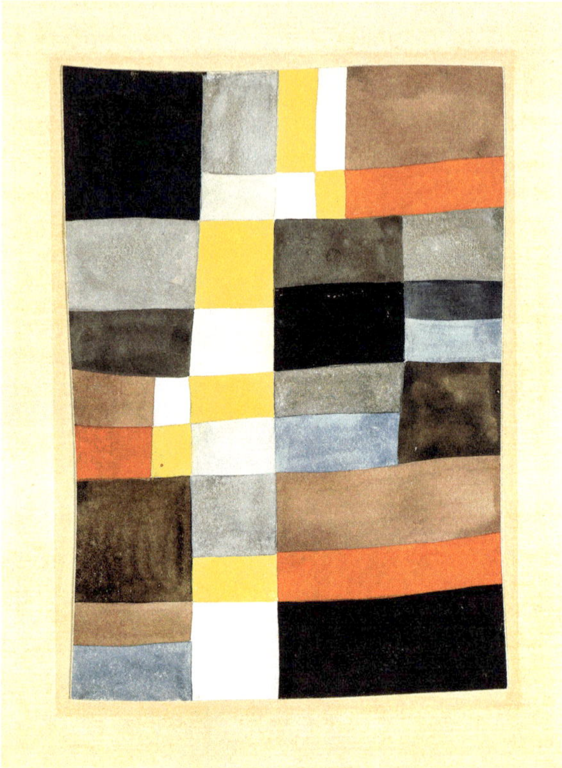

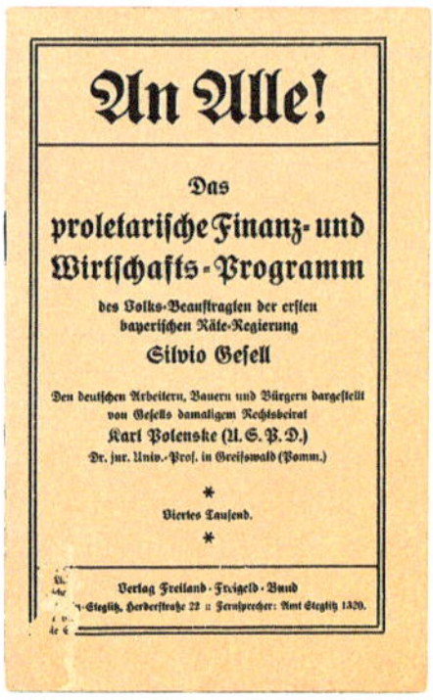

An Alle!

Das
proletarische Finanz- und
Wirtschafts-Programm
des Volks-Beauftragten der ersten
bayerischen Räte-Regierung
Silvio Gesell

Den deutschen Arbeitern, Bauern und Bürgern dargestellt
von Gesells damaligem Rechtsbeirat
Karl Polenske (U.S.P.D.)
Dr. jur. Univ.-Prof. in Greifswald (Pomm.)

*
Viertes Tausend.
*

Verlag Freiland-Freigeld-Bund
-Steglitz, Herderstraße 22 :: Fernsprecher: Amt Steglitz 1320.

Sophie Taeuber, *Rythmes verticaux-horizontaux libres,* 1919, gouache and graphite on paper pasted on board, 30.8 × 23.2 cm

Silvio Gesell, *An alle! Das proletarische Finanz—und Wirtschafts-Programm,* 1919, booklet, Bibliothek Max Bill

and often visited Carl Fischer and his wife Bertie in Herrliberg am Zürisee (sometimes accompanied by Morach) to stock up with health foods.[166]

A fellow student of Max Bill's recalled Keller's appeal: "The door would crash open and Ernst Keller—back from the library, waving a sheet of paper —would storm in: 'Just look!' In an instant the students would be crowding round him. Rapt, intent awe. Every gaze followed his pointing finger. He would usually bring prints from Nuremberg, Gothic woodcuts, prints with blocks of color. But he never explained anything, he just showed us things."[167]

It was Ernst Keller who designed the face of the clock (over eight meters in diameter) on the Church of St. Peter in Zurich that every tourist has seen; he also designed the logo for the trams in Zurich. He is regarded as an important graphic designer—even if Bill, looking back, described him as "traditional." In so saying, Bill may have been referring to the fact that Keller's main sources of inspiration were master craftsmen from long ago—book printers and type cutters working in the sixteenth century; Bill felt that Keller looked backward rather than forward. Keller had no interest in contemporary industrial design. Yet "without doubt he created an important body of work. But sometimes it almost seems ... that the most important thing he did was to be there, in the twenties and thirties, in the midst of a small group of eager, young students. That was how Zurich graphic design came about ... and that was what paved the way for me to develop what the world now calls Swiss graphic design."[168]

Wilhelm Kienzle produced various objects; today he would be described as a "designer." Carl Fischer, a modest man, was appointed to teach modeling and wood carving in 1914. And it was Fischer who realized the marionettes designed by Sophie Taeuber for the theater that the school's director, Alfred Altherr, was reviving and that would have a seminal influence on the stagecraft of that time. Altherr had commissioned Taeuber to design an ensemble of marionettes for Carlo Gozzi's *König Hirsch,* to be performed at the exhibition of the Swiss Werkbund (Association of artists, architects, designers, and industrialists) in 1918. Max Bill later remarked that the only comparisons to Taeuber's marionettes were Oskar Schlemmer's costume designs for his *Triadic Ballet* and Pablo Picasso's Cubist sets and costumes for Diaghilev.[169]

Carl Fischer's aim as a teacher (with Bill among his students) was "to nurture every student's personal aptitudes, to guide them—depending on

166 Schaller 1983, p. 75
167 Steiner 1976, pp. 21–22
168 Steiner 1976, pp. 21–22
169 Bill 1943, p. 170

their individual way of seeing, feeling, and thinking—toward impressive, expressive, or constructive creativity. . . . His 'theory of temperaments,' which he used to assess his students, was derived from Mazdaznan beliefs—an Oriental philosophy that is all about mastering life and staying young in body and mind by dint of fresh air and a vegetarian diet. In the twenties a number of Mazdaznan devotees, including Carl Fischer, settled in Herrliberg"[170] in the canton of Zürich.

Evidently influenced by his teacher Carl Fischer, one day Max Bill emphatically, defiantly made an announcement at the family dining table in Winterthur: "I will no longer eat the flesh of dead animals!" Erwin Bill was exasperated by his son's "vegetarian phase," which lasted some time, until 1930 or 1931. Max now no longer felt entirely at ease with his parents and did not always return home at night. When he fell in love with a girl in Zurich, his father took away his rail pass and forbade him to visit her. So Max mutinously set out on foot—it took him four and a half hours to walk from Winterthur to Zurich, but he and the girl were "still children," as he put it, and nothing happened. Since Erwin Bill's confiscation of his son's rail pass was not just a temporary measure, and he now also ceased to gave his son any free travel tickets (and hitchhiking was not yet a solution), Max also walked to Brugg to visit relatives and all the way to the Rheintal to see friends.

He felt an emotional-geographic connection to the Rhine valley, since his maternal grandfather came from a long line of farmers in that region.

170 "70 Jahre Bildhauer, Ausstellung von Carl Fischer," in *Zürichseezeitung,* 19 March 1975

171 In Max Bill's library there are several publications on the free economy and barter trading, such as – Heinrich Nidecker, *Gesundung des Sozialen Organismus nach den Vorschlägen von Rudolf Steiner und Silvio Gesell oder Dreigliederung und Freiwirtschaft* (Bern: Pestalozzi-Fellenberghaus [P.F.H.], 1926); this includes a chapter on "maternal annuities." In conversation with me, Max Bill often spoke in favor of the idea of the state providing financial support for mothers. Nidecker suggested that all those benefiting from the land should pay rent to the state; this rent would be administered by a land rent office, which would provide "all mothers with monthly payments depending on the number of children up to a certain age (16 years old)" (p. 26)

Encouraged by his uncle Ernst, by now a highly respected painter who was also one of the founders of the progressive temperance movement in Switzerland, in 1924–26 Max sometimes associated with members of a group of teetotal students and school pupils in Winterthur. It was there that he got to know Hans Hinterreiter—six years older than him and another native of Winterthur with its long history in engineering and manufacturing.

Hinterreiter's father, who worked as a tailor, was Austrian by birth; Max's new friend's mother was Swiss.

Hinterreiter had a particular interest in political economy and regarded himself as a "free economist." Having initially enrolled at Zurich University in 1920 to study mathematics, he then transferred to the ETH and graduated with a degree in architecture in 1925. Although Max sometimes spent time with Hans at the Hinterreiters' house in Winterthur, they generally met at the home of the Hess family. The elder of the Hess sons, Willy Hess, another free economist, played piano duets with Hinterreiter and was close to his sister Lilli (known as Züsy). Max knew the younger of the Hess sons from their time together as boy scouts in Winterthur. Hans, Züsy, and Willy took Max, the silversmith apprentice, to events put on by the free economy (*Freiwirtschaft*) movement. Enthused by the free economists' idea of abolishing profits gained through interest and by their arguments for a barter system instead of normal commerce, Max radically revised his own political outlook.[171]

Max Bill: "... i first heard about the idea of a 'free economy' in 1925, and have been a member of the f.k.b. [Fisokratischer Kampfbund: Physiocratic Activists' League] for nearly as long."[172]

– Philip Pye, *Gesell's Monetary and Social Reform: Free-Economy* (Berlin-Frohnau: Neo-Verlag, reprinted 1930)
– Theophile Christen, *Das Geldwesen, ein dynamisches System* (Bern: Verlag des Schweizer Freiland-Freigeld-Bundes, 1920); inside this publication Max wrote his name, "bill," with a lower-case "b," suggesting that he bought it a good ten years after it came out, since he used conventional upper- and lower-case until 1930
– Theophile Christen, *Ordnung und Gesundung des Schweizer Geldwesens, Drei Denkschriften an das eidgenössische Finanzdepartement,* (Bern: Pestalozzi-Fellenberg, 1919); again signed "bill" inside, suggesting this was purchased around 1930/31

172 Max Bill to Fritz Schwarz, 18 September 1932, private archives of Fritz and Elly Schwarz

First Trip to France

In 1925 Max Bill made his first ever trip to France: he and other students from the Kunstgewerbeschule went with Otto Morach to the *Exposition Internationale des Arts Décoratifs* in Paris. Morach and the students were all attending the *Exposition Internationale* as exhibitors, and Max could not have dreamed of a better place than the Grand Palais to show his work. He had every right to be happy, satisfied, and proud. The Grand Palais—a steel-and-glass construction with excellent light and spacious exhibition areas—was a fabulous venue. This was where the foundation stone of Max Bill's career was laid. It all started there. Ever after that he felt a special connection to Paris—*on y reviendra.*

Joseph Gantner, editor-in-chief of *Das Werk* (the official organ of the Association of Swiss Architects), attended the opening of the *Exposition Internationale des Arts Décoratifs* on 27 April 1925 and reported on his first impressions. Since it was not yet possible to visit the Swiss section, which would not open until mid-May, Gantner focuses on the venue itself: "The exhibition site is one of the most beautiful in Paris. Its main axis lies along the wide thoroughfare that, as Avenue Alexandre III, runs from the Champs-Élysées across Pont Alexandre III and, as Avenue du Général Gallieni, across the middle of the Esplanade des Invalides to the main entrance of the Hôtel des Invalides, always guided by the dome of the church of Les Invalides.... At the Esplanade des Invalides, in the most important part of the exhibition, France is wholly dominant. With the exception of a series of exhibition halls (to one side) for foreign nations—Switzerland takes its place there—everything is reserved for the French arts industry in the widest sense.... The most interesting part of the exhibition takes the form of a double row of pavilions laid out on the right bank of the Seine, from the Place de la Concorde ... to Place de l'Alma.... And it is in the Grand Palais, finally, that one last, important part [of the exhibition] is housed ... with the foreign schools of applied arts on the top floor. In the very first of these rooms to be set up, there are the displays of work from the schools of applied arts in Zurich and Basel, which immediately attracted considerable attention."[173]

Bill kept a copy of Gantner's article. The same issue of *Das Werk* contains a detailed article by Werner Moser entitled "Frank Lloyd Wright und amerikanische Architektur," with numerous black-and-white illustrations. In all likelihood this was Bill's first encounter with buildings by

173 Joseph Gantner, "Die internationale Kunstgewerbeausstellung in Paris, erste Eindrücke," *Das Werk* 12:5 (1925), pp. 154–58, here pp. 154–55

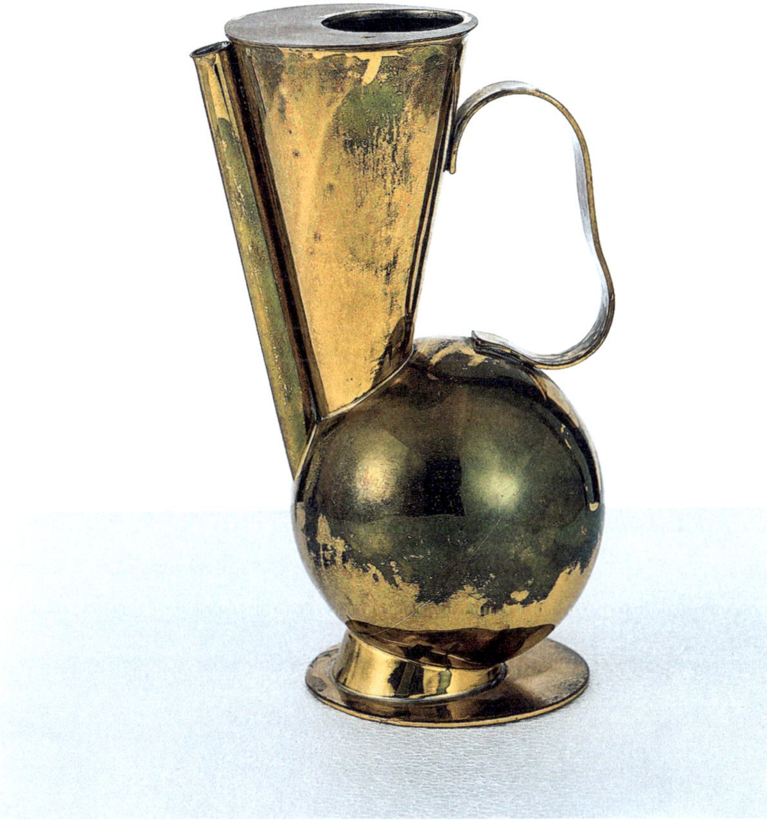

Max Bill, Jug, 1925,
brass, 26.5 × 17.5 × 12 cm

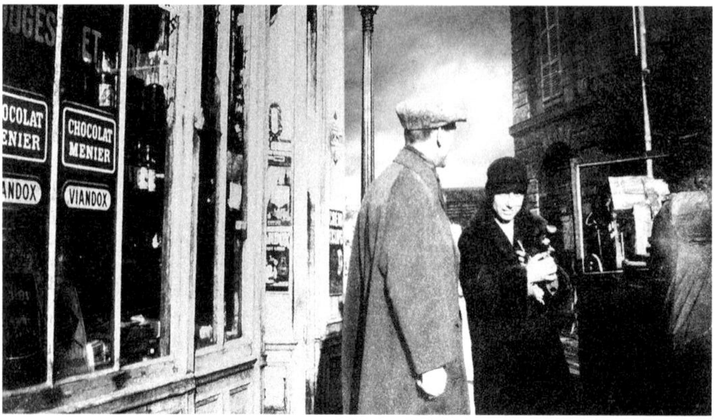

From left: Otto Morach in a peaked cap and Sophie Taeuber-Arp, wearing a hat, Paris, ca. May 1925

Max Bill on his first visit to Paris, for the *Exposition Internationale des Arts Décoratifs,* ca. May 1925

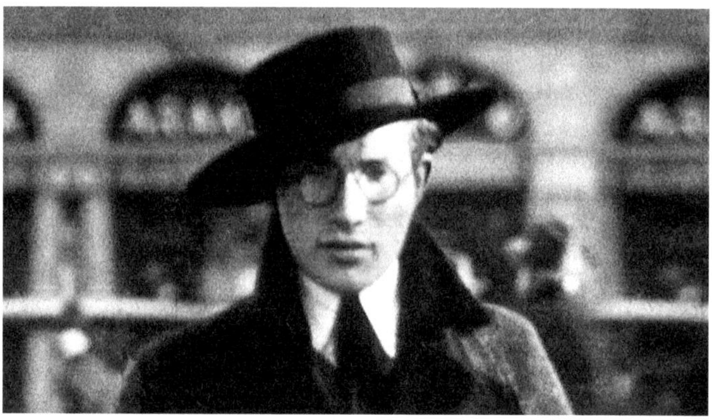

Wright, whose mentor, the architect Louis Sullivan, had died just one year previously, in May 1924. Later in life Bill would become friends with Edgar Kaufmann Jr., whose parents famously commissioned Frank Lloyd Wright to build their home, Fallingwater.

Sophie Taeuber-Arp, who had been given the task of choosing objects for the Swiss applied-arts display at the *Exposition Internationale des Arts Décoratifs,* included in her selection a metal jug—a beautiful, bulbous, no-nonsense shape—made at the Kunstgewerbeschule in Zurich by the young apprentice silversmith, Max Bill. A year later Bill would make another welded jug (see p. 107).

Bill's vessel is illustrated in *Travaux d'art appliqué exécutés dans les ateliers de l'École des Arts et Métiers de Zurich* (Zurich: Eugen Rentsch Verlag, 1926), with a foreword by the director Alfred Altherr. However, the publication only lists the name of the relevant members of staff, not the students who made the works. The copy in Max Bill's library has a pencil note: "of 17 metal items ... 2 by Bill, Bill: illustrations p. 20 below + p. 30."

Otto Morach's exhibits at *Exposition Internationale des Arts Décoratifs* included a stained-glass window, a tourism mural, and a number of posters, some of which received awards.

An earlier generation had visited the vast exhibition on the same site and had gazed in awe at the Eiffel Tower built to mark that world's fair in 1889. Max's uncle, Ernst Geiger, as we know, had made sure not to miss the Paris Exposition in 1900 and must surely have told his nephew all about that visit.

Morach of course also found time to take the students out into the city to see Paris. Sophie Taeuber-Arp joined Morach and the students from Zurich on their excursions to various attractions, such as the Eiffel Tower, which Bill had already studied in detail at home; it featured in the two-volume catalogue for the Exposition Universelle in Paris in 1889, which he had inherited from his paternal grandfather.

Length—Width—Height

Max Bill, who was all too familiar with the immense length of the railway tracks by his childhood home—leading into the distance and disappearing into unimaginable infinity—now found in the metropolis of Paris the hugest expanses he had ever witnessed, with the Eiffel Tower vastly taller than anything he had ever seen.

"People have to *want* to see. With our sense of hearing alone we would never have worked our way to such complete, universal knowledge, and without the perceptive potential of our sense of sight we would have come to a halt at some repetitive motion, at a ticking clock, so to speak." This statement comes in an early text by Robert Delaunay, "La Lumière" (translated into German as "Über das Licht" by Paul Klee, published in Herwarth Walden's journal *Der Sturm* in February 1913), and exactly chimed with Max Bill's own artistic instincts: he *wanted* to see.
By that time the French painter Robert Delaunay was already known for his oil paintings of the Eiffel Tower (ca. 1910–11), in which he transformed and reconfigured his motif. Following those experiments in theory and practice he took another decisive step. "For as long as art cannot escape the object," he concluded, "it remains description, literature, it demeans itself in its use of defective means of expression, it condemns itself to the slavery of imitation. And this is also holds true when it accentuates the light effects of an object or the light conditions of several objects, without light being elevated to representational independence."[174]

It would be a good few years before Max Bill not only took on board this theory of Robert Delaunay's (introduced to the German-speaking world by Paul Klee) but also backed it and used it as an argument.

Thus, looking at other people's paintings with Bill, I often heard him say that a figurative motif—an object as a compositional motif—was not appropriate (any longer) in the new art of the twentieth century, with the only possible exception being literature.

During the Italian Renaissance, painting had gained legitimacy through its proximity to literature. Aristocratic patrons of the arts expected "their" court painters to create compositions that breathed new life into scenes described by classical authors.[175]

In Paris, the sightseeing party led by Morach also visited the Louvre, the Madeleine, and the Bourse, where Max—who was just starting to widen his cultural horizons—commented on the "canon of Greek forms." It reminded him of the town hall in Winterthur, a classicizing building by

174 Delaunay 1989. pp. 403–4
175 On this, see, Andreas Tönnesmann, *Die Kunst der Renaissance* (Munich: C. H. Beck, 2007)
176 Bill 1966, p. 3
177 Otto Morach to Bertie Fischer-Rettenmund, n.d., in Schaller 1983, p. 27
178 Otto Morach, Positano, to Hermana Sjövall, Zurich, 23 July 1923, in Schaller 1983, p. 91
179 Max Bill in conversation with Angela Thomas

Gottfried Semper, which the young Bill admired as an example of "Greek" architecture, where "the interior and the exterior are in perfect harmony: the columns, the balustrades on the stairs, the stone treatments." Although it impressed him at the time, in reality, as Bill later remarked, it is a far remove from Greek architecture.[176]

As the group roamed through Paris, Bill fell into conversation with Morach, who was generally regarded as somewhat taciturn. Max opened with a reference to Morach's friendship with Ernst Geiger and that set the ball rolling. Morach and Bill also had another potential topic of conversation, having both grown up in provincial Switzerland.

When Morach still lived in Solothurn, he had often bemoaned his fate in letters: "It's dreadful living like this in a small town where one is so unfree, especially if one is a freedom fanatic. And it's also not pleasant to find oneself regarded as a misfit—until that's what one becomes."[177]

Before Morach married Hermana Sjövall, he traveled alone to Italy in the summer of 1923. Did he perhaps tell Bill about that trip? Did he perhaps describe the ancient town perched on a mountainside, "which was once, a 1,000 years ago, as big as Lausanne today, but which now has almost no one living there, just palaces and about 30 churches. . . . Positano in moonlight (see p. 257), it is impossible to describe, so remarkable."[178] During their conversation in Paris, Morach divulged the secret of his origins to Bill. In the past the family name had been Morachi—they had been Saracens who ultimately settled in the canton of Valais and who still had a Moor in their coat of arms. That last fact particularly impressed Max Bill. In Zurich, that same year, Bill had his first opportunity to see a major exhibition of paintings by Otto Morach: "It was at the Kunstgewerbemuseum in Zurich—a wonderful, memorable sight to behold. Alfred Altherr had had the walls in the museum painted in pale colors and the paintings, well distributed, were set directly into the partition walls."[179]

Melnikov and Le Corbusier

The sight of Konstantin Melnikov's wooden pavilion for the USSR and, even more so, Le Corbusier's *Pavillon de l'Esprit Nouveau* in Paris in 1925 had an immense, lasting impact on the young Max Bill.[180] These examples of the most modern architecture of the day crucially opened his eyes. El Lissitzky noted that the "little structure" by the "radical" architect Melnikov had been designed for a "utilitarian purpose"; that is to say, the architect had devised an architectural shell for a specific function.[181] It seems that Melnikov's decision to use wood was an economic necessity, given that the USSR had only allocated a budget of 15,000 rubles at most for the pavilion—equivalent to around 7,500 US dollars at the time. Melnikov was thus obliged to design a "light" structure; cheap, roughly cut wood was transported by train from Moscow to Paris, where the Soviet pavilion was then built at great speed and painted red, gray, and white.[182]

Melnikov's approach and construction methods made a deep impression on Bill and left its mark on his work. To name but one example, Bill's sculpture *rhythmus im raum,* now on the shore of the Aussenalster in Hamburg, is constructed in such a way that it looks the same from both sides. This phenomenon cannot properly be conveyed in photographs or drawings (see p. 666); it can only be fully understood face to face with the original or by viewing a film sequence—as in Erich Schmid's film *Bill—Das absolute Augenmass* (2008).

180 By way of an aside—in 1925 Alexander Rodchenko, already famous worldwide, was in Paris. Max Bill later acquired two of Rodchenko's works on paper for his own collection (estate of Max Bill left to Angela Thomas). A photograph taken by Rodchenko of Melnikov's pavilion with the hammer and sickle on the roof is illustrated in Victor Margolin, *The Struggle for Utopia: Rodchenko, Lissitzky, Moholy-Nagy 1917–1946* (Chicago: University of Chicago Press, 1997), p. 131. The exhibition attracted large numbers of visitors, including Piet Mondrian and Georges Vantongerloo, as a photograph shows (probably taken by Lucia Moholy), which is illustrated, for instance, in *Georges Vantongerloo,* exh. cat., (Zurich: Kunsthaus Zürich, 1981), p. 14

181 "In this case the idea was to leaven the body by freeing up the steps. The floor plan has a diagonal symmetry, which is rotated by 180 degrees. Thus the whole is taken out of its normal symmetrical equilibrium and set in motion. The tower is turned into an open mast system. The building is constructed honestly, in wood; it is a modern wooden construction, not block-built in the nationalist manner. It is transparent, [it has] unbroken colors, so no fake monumentality. A new mindset." El Lissitzky 1965, pp. 14, 16

182 Chatwin 1989, p. 96

And El Lissitzky's description of Melnikov's architecture—with "a new spirit," avoiding "false monumentality"—would also later apply to the work of Max Bill, who would himself develop a new, contemporary spirit in his art. He, too, wanted nothing to do with misconceived monumentality. He took human beings as his yardstick—as in his *Monument for the Unknown Political Prisoner* (1951), which he submitted as a competition entry to the Institute of Contemporary Art in London in 1952.

In 1988 Max Bill and I traveled to Moscow. We were assigned an interpreter who mentioned that she had previously worked at the Soviet embassy in Bern; we found her somewhat disconcerting. After an event with the GDR author Heiner Müller, someone asked us if we would like to see the house that Melnikov designed for himself in Moscow. We immediately agreed and decided to slip away without saying anything to our interpreter-minder. And as it turned out, we were able to see the whole house, only we were not able to converse with Melnikov's son, who still lived there, because he only spoke Russian. We noticed various religious icons, placed here and there by the architect's son, which we felt clashed with the design as a whole.

Although we made that trip to the USSR during the Gorbachev era and Bill delivered a public lecture in Moscow on his sculpture *kontinuität* (now outside the Deutsche Bank headquarters in Frankfurt am Main), the state security department in Switzerland felt it merited yet another entry in its record of Max Bill's political activities. The note on the relevant file (the last on Max Bill) reads: "10.10.1988. . . . Prof. B. . . . invited to a conference in the USSR, together with Frau Dr. Thomas . . ."[183]

Le Corbusier's *Pavillon de l'Esprit Nouveau,* which was officially opened on 10 July 1925, looked to Bill like a "white cube with big dark openings."[184] As one approached, it was possible to see into the pavilion, which had a tree growing up through it—right in the center, cutting through the terraces and the roof. The pavilion was in fact a model duplex apartment, with a double-height living space. This residential unit, with a strikingly innovative internal layout, also had a double-height terrace garden. Bill particularly remembered that Le Corbusier had included very beautiful, modern paintings by Fernand Léger in the large living space on the ground floor, which also had furniture by Thonet. The bedroom and other facilities were on the upper floor. The simplicity of the external design, the whiteness of the overall impression, the ambience that was utterly new to Bill—all of that excited him, it took his breath away. Above all

183 Max Bill's fiche state security files, (315:0)815, in Bundesarchiv, Bern

184 Max Bill in conversation with Angela Thomas

he remembered "the brightness," "the whiteness." Yet there was also color inside the pavilion, in the dining room in particular: blue, brown and white, yellow.

However, the unveiling of this avant-garde design did not go smoothly for Le Corbusier, who was met with obstruction and insults. In fact, the building committee at the exhibition displayed "the most marked hostility" to his design: "It was only owing to the presence of M. de Monzie, then Minister of Fine Arts, who came to inaugurate the exhibition, that the committee agreed to remove the 18-ft. palisade it had had erected in front of the pavilion to screen it from the public gaze."[185]

The prominent architectural historian Arthur Rüegg has described Le Corbusier's pavilion as one of the most important endeavors in the twentieth century to "bridge the gap between 'arts majeurs' and 'arts mineurs.'" He sees the living space in the *Pavillon de l'Esprit Nouveau* as a "rebuff" to the then prevailing "art of the ensemble," namely, "space, furniture, and art blended to form an indissoluble, uniform whole." Accordingly, in his view the real innovation in Le Corbusier's pavilion was the "juxtaposition of a new, austere architecture with a minimum of mass-produced objects ... signaling a departure from bespoke items made by artist-craftsmen." Rüegg regards "the pavilion's interior as a provocation, as an anti-applied-arts manifesto ... which was reinforced by the tin model airplane in the library niche, placed like a Crucifix above an altar; that airplane—which makes such a striking visual impact—represents the triumph of technology, the dawn of a new age."

The other main feature of the pavilion, in Rüegg's view, is its interior color scheme, which was achieved using "just a few, commercially available powder paints," chosen *subjectively* by Le Corbusier: "Blue expands a space, but it also has associations with the outside world, with the sky; brown tones are reminiscent of brick or woody atmospheres, yellow ocher recalls sand." Rüegg concludes that "the interiors Le Corbusier and Pierre Jeanneret were creating around 1925 can be described as *spatial still lifes,* which constantly change depending on the user's movements within them and on the way the objects they contain are handled. Despite selecting anonymous, commercially manufactured items of furniture for these interiors, Le Corbusier was in fact aiming to create an innovative entity that addressed the problems that were intrinsic not only to contemporary art but also to industrialization and modern product design."[186]

185 See *Le Corbusier und Pierre Jeanneret* 1930, pp. 100–101

186 Arthur Rüegg, "Le Corbusiers Innenräume um 1925," *Zeitschrift für Schweizerische Archäologie und Kunstgeschichte* 45:1 (1988), p. 32

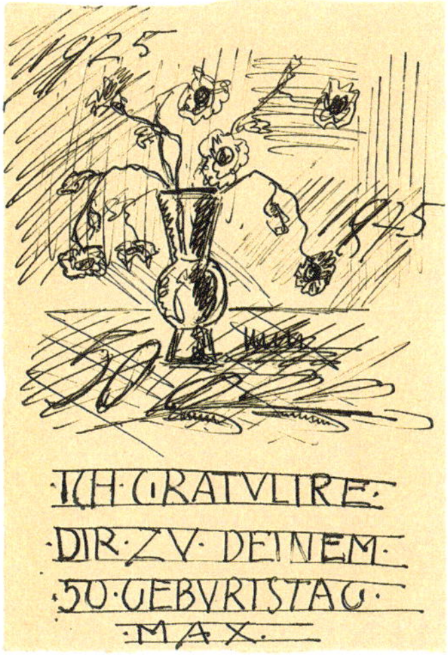

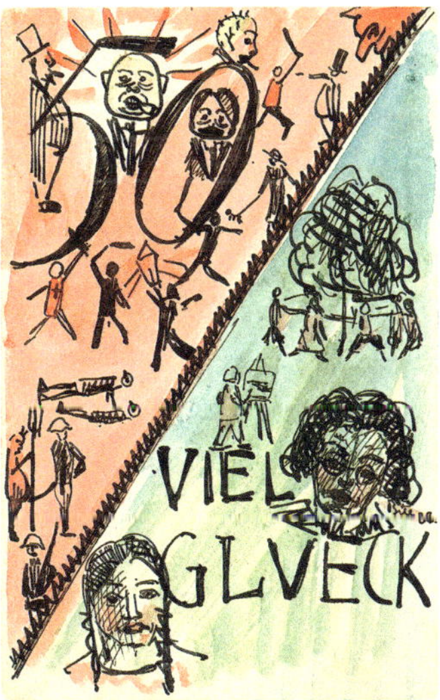

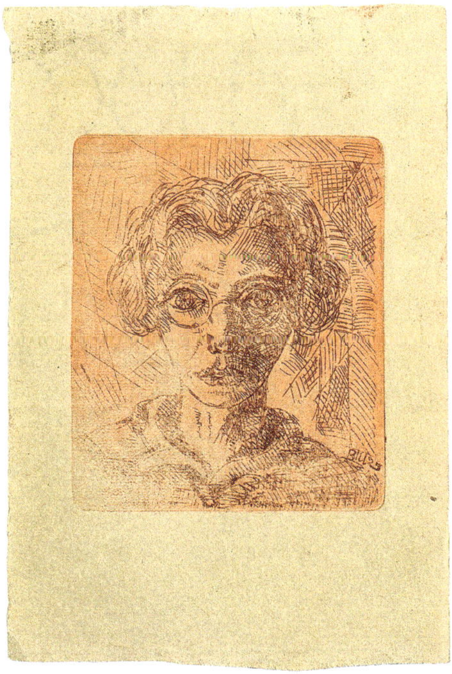

Max Bill, Birthday card for his father, 1925, ink on paper, 16.3 × 11.1 cm

Max Bill, Gift to his uncle Ernst Geiger on his 50th birthday, 1926, drawing on paper, 11.7 × 7.5 cm

Max Bill, *Self-portrait,* 1925, etching with red ink and wash on paper, 9.1 × 7.7 cm

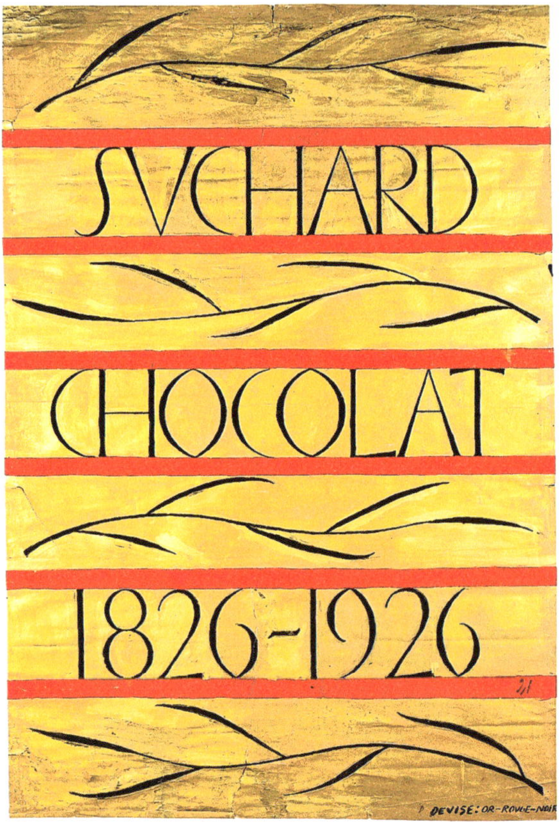

Max Bill, *Suchard Chocolat 1826–1926,* Poster design, 1925, gouache on paper, 128 × 90.5 cm

The international jury wanted to give the top award to Le Corbusier's design, but the vice president exercised his veto, declaring that "there was no architecture" in Le Corbusier's pavilion (*Le Corbusier: Œuvre complète, vol 1, 1910–1929,* 1995, p. 104).

The year 1925 marked Max Bill's first participation in a public exhibition of applied-arts objects outside of Switzerland—the *Exposition Internationale des Arts Décoratifs* in Paris. It was also the year when Erwin Bill turned fifty (9 September) and Max turned seventeen (22 December). The birthday card that Max made for his father creates a mixed impression. While he did not take very great trouble over the drawing, he clearly paid attention to the text, using stylized uppercase letters, replacing the letter "U"with a "V" and separating each word with a dot (see p. 115).

Professor Albert Heim, Geologist

As a student Ernst Geiger went on excursions led by Professor Albert Heim to the caves in Schaffhausen, the Black Forest, the Jura mountains and, particularly often, the canton of Glarus.[187] "Those hikes could be severe—carrying a rucksack with rock samples that couldn't be too small; it was heavier than a botanical box, and the more exhausted we were, the more incredibly the little man with a slight limp would forge ahead—on purpose. The Beer State Lions [carnival characters], great big fellows, couldn't even keep up sometimes. It was an object lesson. We teetotallers now also have some astounding drawings done by Heim in our geological sketchbooks. It was like this: whenever we had climbed up to a spot with a good view, Heim would ask, 'Who has sharp colored pencils?' And depending on who got to him first, Heim would take that person's sketchbook and, with masterly skill, draw a picture of the geological conditions

187 In the 1930s, on the ground floor of the "farm" in Ligerz Ernst Geiger created "a little private museum," which contained, among other things, "rocks that he had collected on excursions with Albert Heim, professor of geology." This little museum no longer exists, having been "removed by restoration" (Christoph Geiger). Ernst Geiger's sketch books with drawings by Albert Heim are still in the family's safekeeping

he wanted to discuss—instead of using a wall chart. I don't think the Beer State boys came by many of those works of art. By the time they arrived, we were already setting off again ... although I would like to add that we *all* revered that man."[188] Since Heim publicly approved of temperance, he was an important support for the students' Libertas group.

Albert Heim's brother Ernst was a musician with a very keen ear, and the two of them regularly went on excursions to listen to the sounds of Alpine waterfalls.[189] Ever curious, Albert Heim also used to take trips with the balloonist Eduard Spelterini and in October 1898, his fourth "air voyage" with Spelterini took him across the Alps in what was in fact the first ever crossing of the Alps by a manned balloon.

Heim described his experiences during the first-ever balloon flight across the Alps in a detailed essay.[190] His text, "Albert Heim erzählt von der ersten Ballonfahrt über die Alpen (1898)," was published under the rubric "Pioneering Deeds in Science" in the Swiss monthly *du* 11:6 (June 1952), pp. 50ff.

In those distant times Eduard Spelterini, the pioneering balloonist and captain on that flight, was feted in Switzerland like a national hero. In mid-flight Spelterini took magnificent, astoundingly sharp photographs that were republished (for the first time since 1928) in *Eduard Spelterini—Fotografien des Ballonpioniers,* ed. Thomas Kramer and Hilar Stadler (Zurich: Scheidegger & Spiess, 2007).

Years later the young Max Bill was similarly fascinated by Professor Heim and his geological finds; indeed for a while Bill pictured himself becoming a geologist—no doubt encouraged by his uncle Ernst's tales: "At that time I was intending to study natural sciences, I had a particular interest in chemistry and geology. But my idea was to pursue my studies as an amateur, so that later on I could devote myself to art, as

188 [Probably Ernst Geiger], "Geologie-Professor Albert Heim," *Die junge Schweiz / La jeune Suisse* 12 (September 1937), Archiv Christoph Geiger

189 Professor Albert Heim wrote a short essay on this subject ("Töne der Wasserfälle") which he delivered as a talk in 1873 to a meeting of the *Schweizerische Naturforschende Gesellschaft Schaffhausen.* His essay is reprinted in the Swiss monthly *du* 2:7 (July 1942), p. 17, and a portrait photograph of the geologist, taken by R. Zinggler, is reproduced in a text by Werner Lüdi, "Zürich als Stätte der botanischen Forschung und Lehre," *du* 14:2 (February 1954), fig. p. 10

190 Albert Heim, Julius Maurer and Eduard Spelterini, *Die Fahrt der "Wega" über Alpen und Jura am 3. Oktober 1898* (Basel: Schwabe, 1898)

191 Bill 1942 [b]

192 Guggenheim 1999, p. 193

in the rose-tinted image I had of my uncle. But this plan did not come to fruition. The general view was that if I wanted to paint later on, a university degree would be an extravagance—a trade apprenticeship would be a better starting point."[191]

It seems Max Bill already knew for certain at a young age that he also wanted "to paint on the side" like his favorite uncle Ernst Geiger. Like his uncle, Bill was also keenly interested in geology. Later on Bill also added a two-page picture report on Minya Gongkar (the highest mountain in Sichuan province, China) to his library; this report by Arnold Heim, the son of Professor Albert Heim, had been published in *Kentiku Sekai, Japanese Journal of Building and Living Culture* 9 (1936). And the Swiss writer Kurt Guggenheim once commented that if ever "a cruel fate should drive him abroad," he would take the following three books with him: *Flora der Schweiz* by Schinz and Keller, *Die Geologie der Schweiz* by Albert Heim, and the official timetable guide published by Swiss railways. "I would be able to visit my entire homeland in these three books. These are books to dream with."[192]

At home in Winterthur, with a new air of self-confidence, he now insisted that his father and everyone else should just call him "Bill"—"Max" was a good name for a dog, not for a human being. However, later in life he never objected when I addressed him as "Max"—or even, affectionately, "Maximilian Billinsky."

Or–Rouge–Noir

One evening in late September 1925, at one of the temperance parties Ernst Geiger occasionally organized at the Hof in Ligerz, Max and others could be seen dancing around a tree by the light of the full moon. Having recently been to the *Exposition Internationale des Arts Décoratifs* in the company of Ernst Geiger's friend, Otto Morach, Bill took the chance to brag a little—which he sometimes rather enjoyed doing as a young man. Later, when he drew a card for his uncle's fiftieth birthday on 1 February 1926, he included a reminder of that carefree evening. On this card, besides a self-portrait of Max there is also a portrait of a young girl—the fact that her image is the same size as his suggests a certain emotional importance. It could be that she had accompanied him to the party at Ligerz, or maybe Bill met her there, or maybe it was the girl he had fallen for in Zurich—once even walking four-and-a-half hours from Winterthur to Zurich to see her in defiance of his authoritarian father.

In 1925 the Swiss chocolate maker Suchard announced a poster competition—with a very generous prize—to celebrate its centenary; entries were to be submitted anonymously. Max Bill sent in a gouache with the code name "or–rouge–noir" and, to his astonishment, won first prize. He had done the sketches for his Suchard poster in the inspiring surroundings of the ancient Hof, in the fond care of his uncle Ernst—very possibly on his visit for the full moon celebrations, given that he drew those sketches on a page from a Kümmerly + Frey calendar for 1925, of the kind that was to be had in Ligerz. There is not much in the way of sketches on the front side of the calendar page (for the week Sunday 8–Saturday 14 November), but in his gouache design on the back of the page Bill makes use of the horizontal lines showing through from the front (separating the days of the week).

The calendar page that Bill availed himself of in Ligerz, seemingly in the absence of any other kind of paper, as it were anticipated events—in the sense that the decision regarding the winning design must have been made before that week, given that the winner's check was already sent from Neuenburg to Bill in Winterthur on 9 November 1925.

He left his preliminary sketches at the "farm." The calendar page later passed from Ernst Geiger's estate to his son Christoph from his second marriage; Bill retrospectively signed it for the latter on 15 January 1994.

The atmosphere at the Hof kindled Max's creativity. He could work well there, far away from the tensions in his parents' house. Although Ernst Geiger had already passed the peak of his own powers as an artist some years earlier—after the death of his young wife, Maria Geiger-Bockhoff, he had "completely lost . . . any urge to pursue power and recognition"—he still tended to his garden and he "brought life into the rooms at the Hof with his historical and geological collections."[193] In addition, each autumn he organized an exhibition at the Hof with works of his own, sometimes also with works by other artists, too, such as Clara Woerner, for instance, who initially took care of his sons after the death of their mother.

Clara Woerner was a student in the class of Johannes Itten and sometimes wove wall hangings. Max Bill liked her and painted a portrait of her during a summer holiday visit to Ligerz (see p. 170).

On Bill's card for his father's fiftieth birthday in early September 1925 he had deliberately replaced the letter "U" with a "V"; and when this is seen again in the poster design for "SVCHARD" it almost looks like a typographic marker for the young artist.

193 Information kindly supplied by Christoph Geiger

It is tempting to suggest that Max's replacement of a "U" with a "V" was a form of creative self-defense. There is a certain irony in the fact that he took a weakness that his father so often angrily reproached him with—his poor spelling—and turned it into an advantage, which became something of a trademark. On the other hand, for the sake of historical accuracy, it is worth pointing out that the special typography of Otto Morach's "pvnkt 5 vhr" (illustrated in Marie-Louise Schaller, *Otto Morach (1887–1973)* [Solothurn: Vogt-Schild and Munich: Prestel, 1983], p. 82, fig. 194) was already in existence by then, and Bill may well have been aware of it.

When the Suchard competition result came out, Bill assumed the jury must have imagined that his design had been done by someone older than himself—was he thinking of Morach? At any rate, he felt it was pure chance that he, a complete newcomer, had won.

Congratulations and a Check

Max Bill's Suchard poster design is a gouache with black lettering between pairs of horizontal red lines. Above and below the lettering there are stylized stems with leaves that seem faintly reminiscent of Jugendstil; all these elements are on a gold ground. The minimal variations in the stems and leaves (alternately facing in different directions) introduce subtle movement into the two-dimensional image—as if a breath of air were passing across it. The lettering is fine, albeit not exaggeratedly delicate, and the subtle manipulation of the company's name catches the viewer's eye unawares. Yet Suchard accepted that potentially disconcerting difference—which seems to me a remarkably open-minded response for that time. On 9 November 1925 the Suchard board in Neuenburg sent a letter of congratulations to the young artist—"Monsieur Max Bill, Winterthur, Bruhlbergstrasse 8"—which also included a handsome check for 2,500 Swiss francs.

"Sir, we are pleased to inform you that the jury of the Suchard poster competition has awarded your project, with the motto 'Gold, Red and Black,' the first prize, i.e. 2,500 francs (two thousand five hundred), which we are enclosing in a check ... With warm congratulations ... Suchard."

By 14–15 November 1925, soon after the check arrived, Max Bill was back in Ligerz and gave his uncle Ernst the good news.

According to entries in the visitors' book—"Max Bill 14.–15.XI.1925 Winterthur" "Rosa Geiger Brugg"[194]—Max visited Ligerz in 1925 with his unmarried aunt, Rosa Geiger, who still lived in Brugg.

Max later told me that he then "somehow or other came up with the idea of indulging in a consultation with an astrologist." Having studied Max's horoscope, the astrologist told him that, due to the powerful opposition between "the influences of Neptune and Uranus," Max must have a strong "interest in both technology and the arts." The astrologist then—extraordinarily—went on to predict that Max Bill would "start a whole new direction in art."[195] Max also mentioned that "around 1926, at any rate before [he] was a student at the Bauhaus," he painted a portrait of the astrologist "with geometric motifs in the background." However, he had no information as to the whereabouts of that painting.

A biography of Max Bill published in 2008 claimed that he "had been expelled from the Kunstgewerbeschule because he had illicitly entered the poster competition and had then even gone on to win it."[196] That was not in fact the case. While Bill was indeed expelled from the Kunstgewerbeschule, that was not until early 1927, in other words, well over a year after the Suchard poster competition result came out in November 1925. That alone militates against a direct connection, added to which, the suggestion that Bill had "illicitly" participated in the competition is simply nonsensical.

Far from being expelled for entering a competition—the real reason for his expulsion was that one morning, having been at a Carnival party the night before, he failed to remove his make-up before going to class. And that was the last straw; the staff at the Kunstgewerbeschule had simply run out of patience with Bill, who seemed to be utterly determined to resist any form of discipline.

194 Ernst Geiger's visitors' books, Museum Neuhaus, Biel

195 Max Bill in conversation with Angela Thomas, 15 April 1976

196 Koella 2008, p. 28

197 Ernst Geiger, "Erinnerungen an Frau von St. Leger," in *Schweizer Frauenblatt,* 21 and 28 May 1948

198 Ernst Geiger, "Erinnerungen an Frau von St. Leger"

First Trip to Italy, 1926

In the coming years, when Max visited his uncle Ernst at his home on Lake Bieler, he was met by a melancholy, increasingly withdrawn figure. After 1927, Max would also occasionally seek out his uncle in Porto Ronco.

At the age of seventeen Max at last had his first chance to spend some time away from home, where he no longer felt at ease. He caught a train and left the straitlaced, stuffy town of Winterthur with its many factories, traveling along the very tracks that he had gazed at throughout his childhood, hoping they would one day take him far away. Now, with the prospect of escaping for three weeks Max Bill's destination was Italy, with an initial stop at Lake Maggiore in the Ticino to visit his uncle Ernst at Casa al Porto, a traditional, stone-built *rustico* that he owned. Ernst Geiger, who was there with his younger son Wölfi, greeted Max with a bowl of sour milk. There was a fly floating in Wölfi's milk, which he now did not want to touch, but Ernst Geiger told his son just to drink the fly down.

During his stay in the *rustico,* Max helped his uncle to build a simple fireplace, with a seat on either side. The house was right by the little harbor in Porto Ronco, which had clearly suffered considerable damage due to the strong northerly Föhn winds from the Alps. Max was interested to find out how his uncle had happened to buy this house and Ernst was happy to tell the story. He started by pointing out the Brissago islands in Lake Maggiore, which are just a few minutes away from Ronco by boat. In the nineteenth century, explosives to be used in the construction of the Gotthardbahn were made on both islands. He then went on to explain that he had become acquainted with a mysterious baroness of Russian descent living there in the Ticino; the locals viewed her with open suspicion but she and Ernst Geiger soon grew to trust each other. The baroness was in fact Antoinette Bayer, baroness of Saint Leger, whom Max's uncle described as a very wealthy industrialist; she had even studied with Franz Liszt for a time. In 1885 the baroness purchased the Brissago islands. At the time when the contract was signed, there was nothing there other than "old stone walls and a deserted church on each island. The baroness built herself a tastefully restrained yet spacious country residence on one of them."[197] It was when Antoinette found herself in financial difficulties that Ernst was able to buy his *rustico,* taking over from the old lady as its legal owner. He later recalled his astonishment when he read the bill of sale with its references to "any number of half attics, half rooms, and a whole list of locations," with the result that for a moment it seemed he had acquired "half a village."[198]

Geiger had partly gained the baroness's trust with his knowledge of Russian, dating back to his student days, but mainly due to his background as a trained botanist. The baroness had had garden soil ferried to the island at great expense from a property on the mainland. She had in fact bought that property specifically so that she could use soil from its grounds to create her own private gardens on her islands. Naturally Max's uncle, whose thesis had been on forest botany, was extremely interested in her gardens and once, when the baroness was going on a trip to Italy, she asked him to look after the islands—above all he was to keep unwanted visitors away.

The family still owns a handwritten account by Ernst Geiger of his time looking after the island, entitled "Robinsonade im Langensee," which his son Christoph Geiger in Freienbach kindly alerted me to.

"The baroness wanted to leave her hermitage for a few days to go to Milan. She had urgent business with her lawyer and of course could not leave her islands unattended."[199] However, in the spring of 1926, when Geiger went across to the island where she had built her residence, the baroness found she so enjoyed talking to him that she immediately put off her departure and started regaling him with all sorts of wild tales from her past. And since the old lady had so much to say in the evenings "in the glow of the oil lamp by the crackling fire," Geiger in fact stayed there for several weeks, which also allowed him to study the many plants in her gardens. When he finally contemplated returning to the mainland, the baroness "at last decided to set off. But when she arrived back, she had yet more stories: Just think what I saw in Milan and what I did there ... so I really had no option other than to extend the time I had already been on the island by a few more days."[200] The gardens laid out by the baroness seemed like a horticultural paradise to Geiger, with their fig trees, bamboos, ranks of palm trees, eucalyptus copses, exotic conifers, and water lilies.

199 Ernst Geiger, "Robinsonade im Langensee," Archiv Christoph Geiger

200 Ernst Geiger, "Robinsonade im Langensee," Archiv Christoph Geiger

201 Information kindly supplied by Christoph Geiger

202 Ernst Geiger, "Eine Unternehmungslustige Neunzigerin," in *Brugger Tagblatt,* 22 June 1940

203 Ernst Geiger, "Zur Ehrenrettung einer Frau," in *Schweizer Frauenblatt,* 6 April 1952

204 The watercolor painting *Südliches Dorf (Porto Ronco),* 1927, is illustrated in black and white in *Max Bill,* Jakob Bill, p. 32

Max Bill once saw the slight figure of the baroness, when she pulled into the harbor in her boat. He particularly remembered that she was wearing several skirts, one on top of the other; he had heard that she had a pistol hidden somewhere in their folds because she never felt entirely welcome there. And there was a certain amount of ill-feeling toward her. Some maintained she had a *mal occhio* (an evil eye), which she used to curse her enemies. The fisherman called her *la vipera* (the viper) or *la strega* (the witch). As it happens, there is no reference in Ernst Geiger's recollections to the baroness carrying a pistol—Max Bill was the source of that intriguing detail.

A photograph from 1926–27 shows Max Bill outside open shutters on the balcony of the Casa al Porto in Porto Ronco. In another photograph taking during his visit to the Ticino he is seen posing under palm trees. Although both photographs are the property of the Geiger family, their locations are currently unknown. In addition to the *rustico,* Ernst Geiger also owned a plot of land higher up in Ronco, where Max Bill was also photographed.[201]

In articles he wrote in later life, Ernst Geiger often remembered the indomitable baroness, who had received a multi-lingual education in Smolna at an institute for the offspring of Russian aristocrats. He remained loyal to her in his own way. At one point, however, the friendship between the baroness on the Brissago islands and the forest botanist, painter, and teetotaller Dr. Ernst Geiger did take something of a comic turn when she came up with the somewhat bizarre idea of distilling alcohol from peat.

Having been driven away from her islands in Lake Maggiore by her creditors, the baroness was ultimately admitted to a charitable hospice in Intragna. When she marked her ninetieth birthday in impoverished circumstances on 20 June 1940 she still wore "the precious meteorite necklace given to her so long ago by the Tsarina on board a Russian war ship."[202] And on 2 April 1952, when the larger of the Brissago islands was at last opened to the public, Ernst Geiger did not miss the opportunity to remind his readers of the grand lady, once a pupil of Franz Liszt, who died in such reduced circumstances. He wanted the world to recognize the achievements of "Frau Antonietta von St. Leger, who acquired this barren island in 1886 and turned it into a horticultural paradise."[203]

On one of his visits to Porto Ronco, Ernst Geiger made a painting of the harbor entrance with its storm-damaged walls, and in 1927, a year after his first trip to Italy, Max Bill painted a portrait of the village when he returned to spend a few days there in his favorite uncle's stone house.[204] At around that time Ernst Geiger painted the view from

Fontana Martina looking toward Italy (*Blick von Fontana Martina Richtung Italien*); in it he seems to have been exploring the same colors as Max, namely yellow, red, and blue. Max felt unusually relaxed in Porto Ronco, in the southern reaches of his native country—as do so many visitors from northern Switzerland. They visibly flourish. The vegetation and the colors of the houses by Lake Maggiore are very different to what they know in German-speaking Switzerland. A change is a good as a rest and there is so much for them to feast their eyes on there—not to mention the beautiful sunshine.

"Not that unusual, typical"

Max's short visit to his uncle in Porto Ronco in 1926 gave him just a foretaste of the much greater vistas—looking out to the Mediterranean—that he would soon encounter in Genoa. At almost eighteen years of age, Max saw the sea for the first time. In his hotel in Genoa, he met "two very nice Swiss boys"; they were both working as waiters and one evening they took him with them to a brothel by the harbor, where there was a "new girl.... They went in, one after the other, and then I went in, too. The girl was very meek and just lay straight down on the bed. I didn't really know what I was supposed to do, so I lay on top of her and before I knew it I'd come. Not that unusual, typical."

So I asked Max "typical in what way?"

"Typically inept."

He went back again the next day, in the afternoon, because he wanted to paint a portrait of the girl, but the madam at the brothel sent him packing: "She's sleeping, she doesn't work at this time of day. Come back this evening."

Bill left Genoa and traveled on to Naples via Rome. In Naples he met a German who took him to a *dormitorio* (night refuge) filled with a very strange array of people, everything from cranks to Carabinieri. Max then took a boat to Capri before returning to Rome via Naples. In Rome he visited the Porta Pia and the colonnades at St. Peter's Square and saw all sorts of things "in palaces and entrances to small houses that had been introduced there after the Greek example."[205]

Having all but run out of money, Max went to the Swiss consulate to ask for a loan. In August 1926 he finally arrived in Florence, climbed up the hill to Fiesole, and knocked on the door of a monastery

205 Bill 1966, pp. 3–6

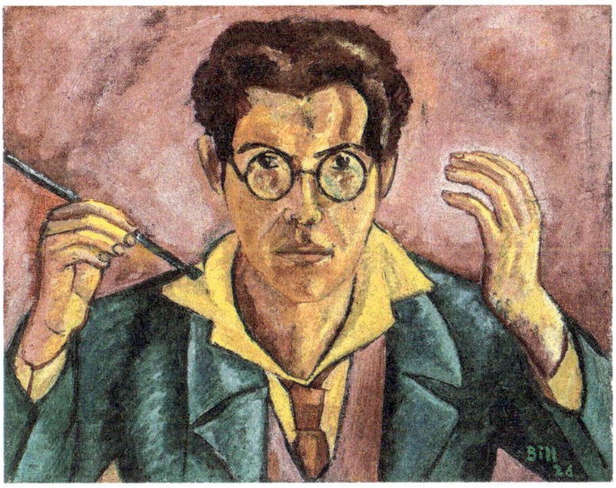

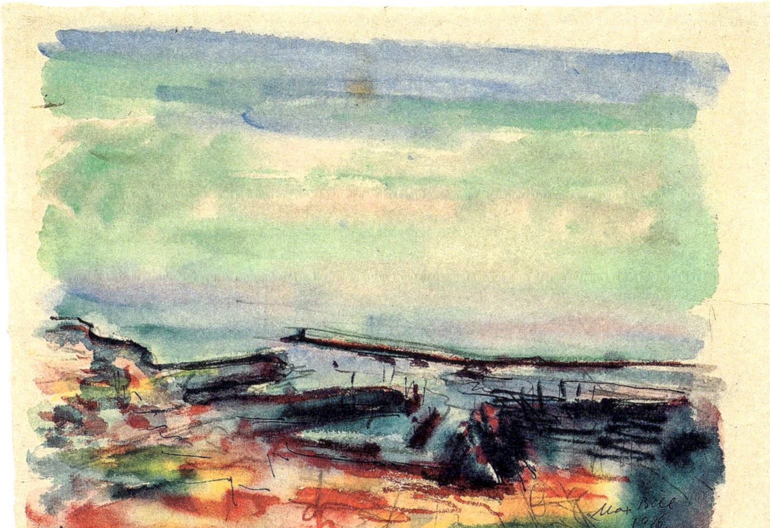

Max Bill, *Self-portrait,* 1926,
oil on canvas, 50×65cm

Max Bill, *Genova,* 1926,
watercolor and india ink on
Japan paper, 22.4×29.5cm

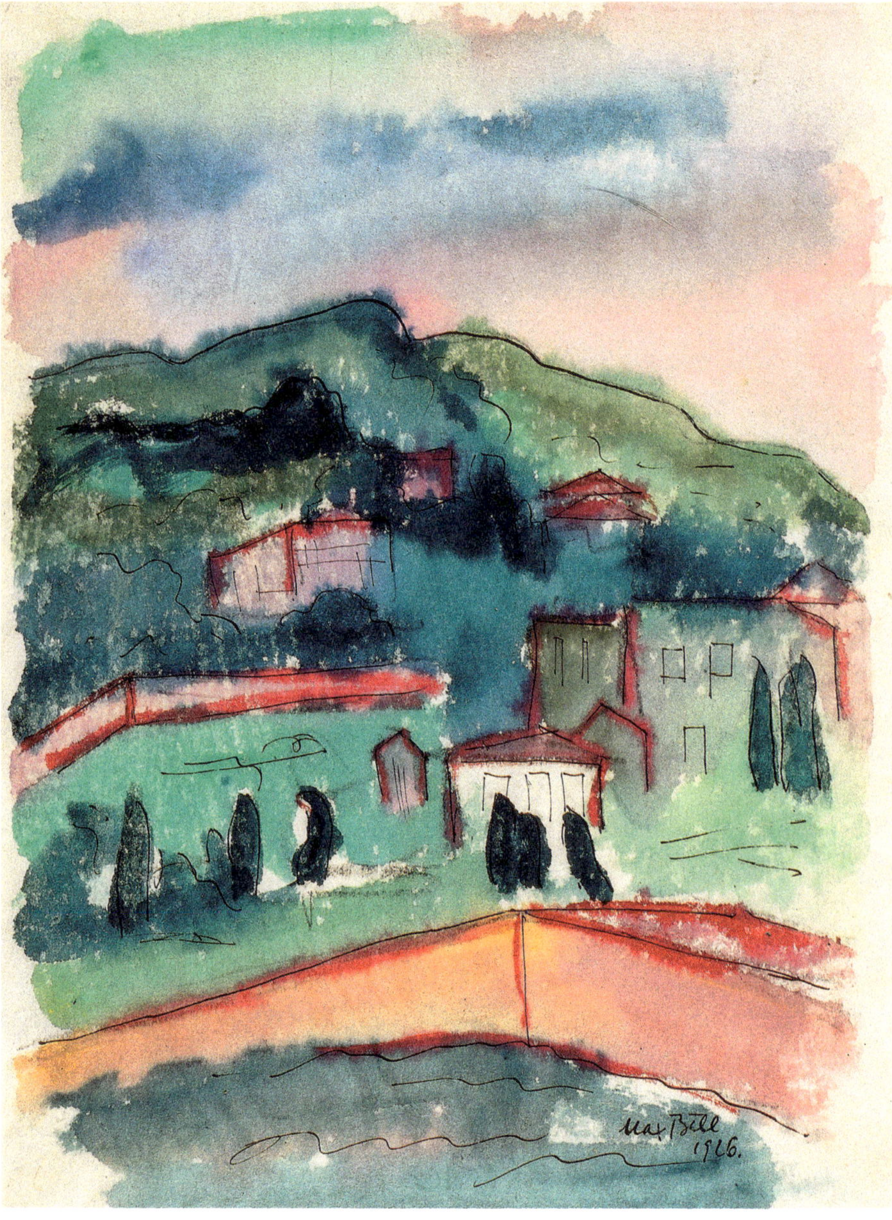

Max Bill, *Bei Florenz (Fiesole)*, 1926,
india ink over watercolor on Japan paper,
30.3×22cm

where Franciscan monks took him in for a few days. Up in Fiesole Max found time to paint some more watercolors, as he had previously done in Genoa and Naples. He described the feeling he had on that trip through Italy as "vagabonding"—the French word *bon*, which is contained in his made-up verb, seems appropriate. In Florence he caught a train to Venice, where he just wandered about as the mood took him—not visiting the usual tourist attractions. He was especially amazed by the alleys that led into canals. After a while he sent a telegram to his father, asking for funds, and was indeed able to collect a modest sum in Milan, which was to be the vagabond's point of departure for his return to Switzerland.

Another watercolor painted by Bill on that trip to Italy—titled *Napoli*—is illustrated (fig. 3) along with *Genova and Bei Florenz (Fiesole)* in *Max Bill*, Catalogo di Arturo Carlo Quintavalle, Università di Parma (Parma 1977).

In conversation with Otto Morach in Paris a year earlier, Bill had been fascinated to hear that Morach had Saracens in his ancestry. And he was reminded of that connection on Capri where he was excited to find "Saracen architecture." Maybe Morach had even told him to go there. Whatever the case, aside from St. Peter's Basilica in Rome, it was the "Saracen architecture" that made the deepest impression on him.

That same year, in 1926, maybe more self-confident after his trip to Italy and still relishing his success in Paris, he painted another self-portrait (see p. 127).

Winterthur: Factories and a Shunting Yard

Back in Winterthur after his trip to Italy, Max painted a watercolor, which he dedicated to his father for his fifty-first birthday on 10 September 1926 (see p. 131). It reflects life in Winterthur: factories and a shunting yard (*Rangierbahnhof* in German, but misspelled by Bill as *Rangschierbahnhof*). The trees in the foreground look as though they are being seen from a fast-moving train. They are blurred and have an exotic air, almost like palms—a faint echo of Bill's trip to Italy. Erwin Bill immediately pounced on his son's orthographic slip, all the more irritating for a meticulous railwayman father. At the same time, Bill's dedication is also strangely distant: "To his Father on his birthday, 10 September 1926. Max."

However, it was not only Max who was distancing himself from Erwin Bill at that point. On 14 December 1926 his wife, Marie Bill-Geiger, went to the Winterthur justice of the peace and filed a petition for an "immediate divorce." A "reconciliation session" just four days later proved fruitless, with the result that—as the official records show—"the complaint lodged on 24 February was declared pending in this place on 11 March 1927."[206] As it turned out, it took a few more weeks before Erwin and Marie Bill's divorce came through.

Architecture and Society's Needs

After Max's liberating (if not sexually fulfilling) trip to Italy, the next memorable event for him was a lecture given in Zurich in late November 1926 by Le Corbusier, one of the first of a number of lectures he gave in Zurich on the invitation of both the Ingenieur- und Architektenverein (Society of engineers and architects) and the Swiss Werkbund. Given his interests, the young Bill was in the right place at the right time. Le Corbusier delivered his exceptionally lucid lectures without notes. Public speaking came easily to him, and on that occasion he soon persuaded Max that architecture is the only art form that can meet society's needs. Having already been extremely impressed by Le Corbusier's *Pavillon de l'Esprit Nouveau,* Max was now just as taken by Le Corbusier's lecture in Zurich, and when he was allowed to select a book-prize for an internal competition he had won at the Kunstgewerbeschule, he chose Hans Hildebrandt's newly published German translation (*Kommende Baukunst,* 1926) of Le Corbusier's *Vers une architecture* (1923). He was presented with his chosen prize two days before his eighteenth birthday.[207]

206 Divorce certificate, district court, Winterthur, 1 April 1927, state archives of the canton of Zürich

207 Le Corbusier, *Kommende Baukunst,* trans. and ed. Hans Hildebrandt (Stuttgart: Deutsche Verlagsanstalt, 1926), 256 pages, 230 black-and-white illustrations, in the Bibliothek Max Bill. A typed letter is pasted into the beginning of the book: "On the occasion of a pewterware competition, the work of Mr. Max Bill was commended. Zurich, 20 December 1926"; the statement is hand-signed by the director of the Gewerbeschule der Stadt Zürich and stamped "Altherr." Since Max Bill's French was still rather rudimentary at that point, he needed a translation. French had been Bill's weakest subject at the boys' school in Oetwil am See

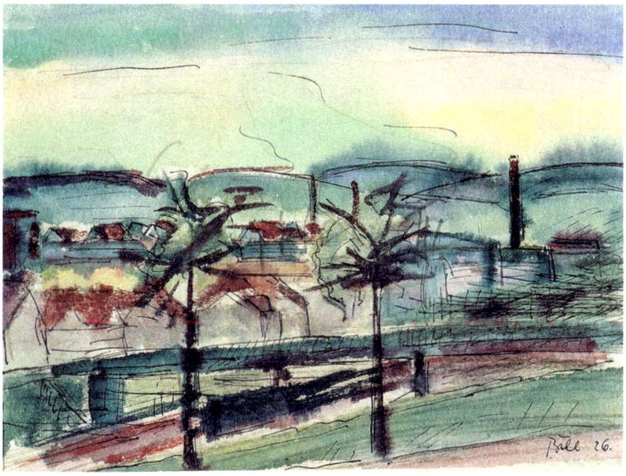

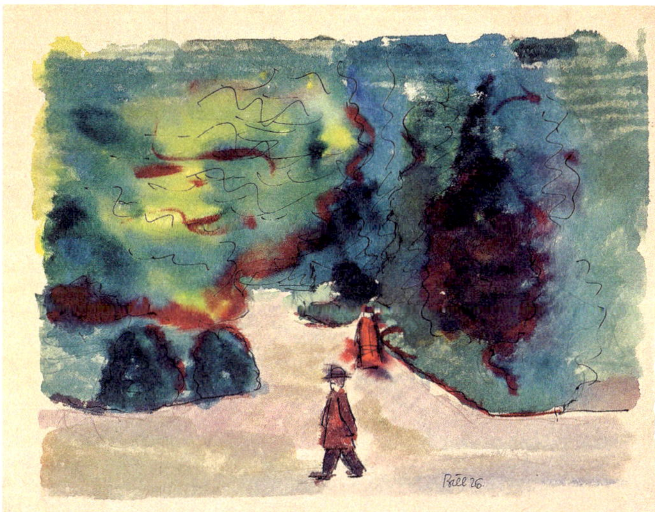

Max Bill, *Winterthur, Rangschierbahnhof und Fabriken,* 1926, gouache and ink over watercolor on laid paper, 21.5×30.5cm

Max Bill, Untitled (In the park), 1926, watercolor and india ink on Japan paper, 22.3×30cm

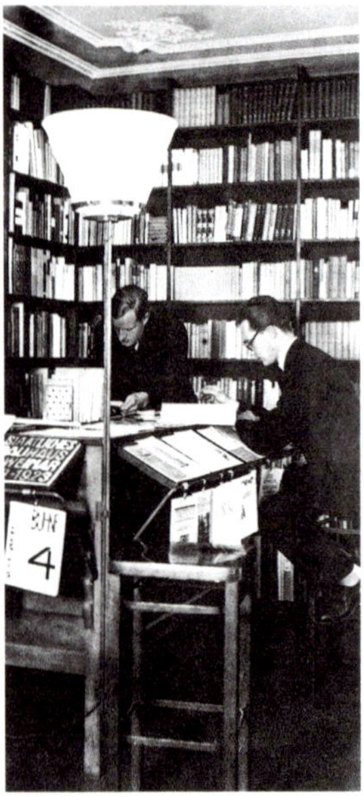

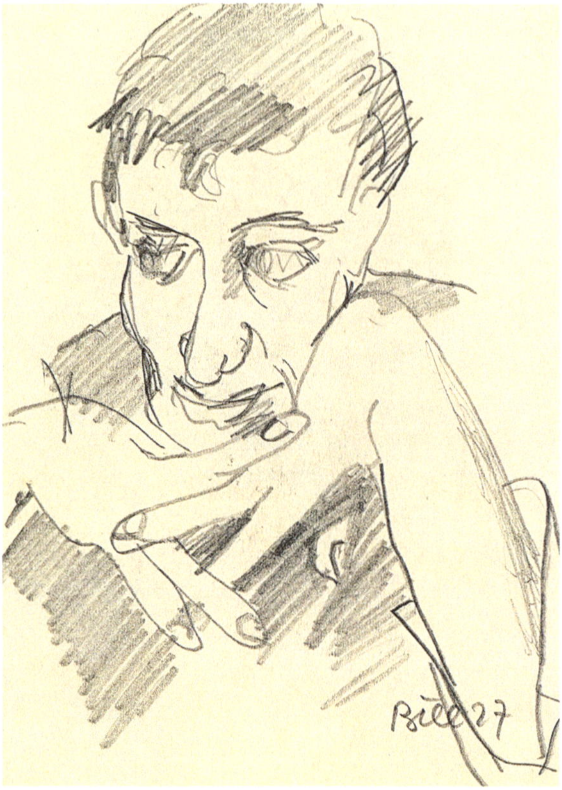

The book bar in Girsberger's bookshop, Kirchgasse 17, Zurich. The Bauhaus catalogue *Staatliches Bauhaus Weimar 1919–1923* is laid out in the foreground

Max Bill, *Auf den Händen getragener Kopf,* 1927, graphite on wove paper, 16.8×12.3 cm

Max Bill, *Fabrik,* 1926, graphite on Japan paper, 21×22.2 cm

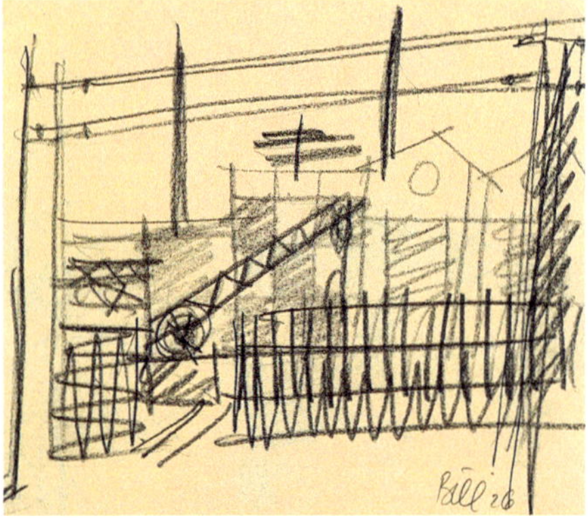

The images at the beginning of Le Corbusier's book are astonishingly raw, dry shots of grain silos and elevators. These are then followed by a far-sighted prediction: "The great problems of modern construction will be solved through geometry." (*Toward an Architecture,* trans. John Goodman [Los Angeles: Getty Research Institute, 2007], p. 86) That almost seems like a light showing the way for Max Bill, who—after a few unavoidable detours—would come to share that same ideological goal and lay claim to it as a method. In *Kommende Baukunst,* which Max would no doubt instantly have devoured, "it was already clear that Le Corbusier's language—the terms he coined in order to describe certain ideas with greater precision—is an important part of his creative achievement."[208]

Creative Aims Plus Politics

The young apprentice silversmith was impressed both by Le Corbusier's *Kommende Baukunst* and by *Staatliches Bauhaus in Weimar 1919–1923* (Munich: Bauhausverlag Weimar, 1923), another book that he found in the well-stocked library of the Kunstgewerbeschule. Both books opened up new avenues that he could explore in the pursuit of his own goals. Moreover, he could readily identify with the young Le Corbusier who grew up in the Swiss Jura Mountains and left school at thirteen and a half to become an apprentice engraver. As it happened, it was not until 1938 that Le Corbusier and Bill first met in person. Bill recognized in Le Corbusier's creative goals a political element that mattered to him, too. He was struck by the fact that Le Corbusier wanted nothing to do with the commercialization of architecture; above all his aim was to humanize architecture.

Girsberger's Bookshop

Max Bill always kept abreast of the latest publications at Hans Girsberger's bookshop at Kirchgasse 17 in Zurich—with its progressive book-buying policy and an entrance door designed by Ernst Keller, a graphic artist and teacher at the Kunstgewerbeschule in Zurich.

Hans Girsberger had commissioned a young architect, Max Ernst Haefeli, to refurbish the interior of his bookshop, which now acted as a

208 Bill 1968

draw for a lot of Haefeli's colleagues. Regular visitors included architects such as Werner Moser, Alfred Roth, Ernst F. Burckhardt and his wife Elsa Burckhardt-Blum; Max Bill became good friends with the last three.[209]

Inside the shop there was a "book bar" with metal-and-wood bar stools and adjustable reading stands. Visitors could dip into Carl von Ossietzky's *Weltbühne,* as Bill regularly did; by 1927–28 at the latest he had taken out a subscription himself. It was here that he happened to come across Will Grohmann's *Wassily Kandinsky* (Leipzig: Klinkhardt & Biermann, 1921).[210] In this slim volume Grohmann attempts to mediate between different reactions to Kandinsky, the "ill-willed" on one side and the "all too keen" on the other: "The trouble with Kandinsky is his withdrawal from reality. This is in fact one of the most controversial moves anyone has had made in twentieth century art.... Some see it as a form of artistic and moral anarchy, the others see it as the dawn of new age or even as the true beginning of art." In the biographical outline that Grohmann compiled using information from Kandinsky himself, he noted that Kandinsky painted his first abstract work in 1911. Grohmann's book also refers to the fact that Herwarth Walden opened court proceedings on Kandinsky's behalf in response to defamatory articles that were appearing in the press.

It was also in Girsberger's bookshop that the young Max Bill bought the first issue of *bauhaus,* in which he learned that a new Bauhaus had been built in Dessau, a town with a flourishing economy in the heart of the Central German coal-mining region.

The first issue of *bauhaus* was published in Dessau on 4 December 1926, with Walter Gropius and László Moholy-Nagy as its editors-in-chief; the photographs reproduced in it are by Lucia Moholy and others.

209 Divorce certificate, district court, Winterthur, 1 April 1927, state srchives of the canton of Zürich

210 Will Grohmann, *Wassily Kandinsky* (Leipzig: Klinkhardt & Biermann, 1924), with a résumé of the artist's life and work, thirty-two plates, and a colored cover picture. Inside the front cover there is a pencilled date, "12.II.25" (possibly the date the book came into the bookshop), and a pasted-in label that reads "Max Bill Ex Libris" with a year date (1926) pencilled in below it (Bibliothek Max Bill). This suggests that Max Bill read the book in 1926, certainly before he arrived at the Bauhaus in Dessau as a student in April 1927, where he would later study under Kandinsky and others

211 Divorce certificate, district court, Winterthur, 1 April 1927, state archives of the canton of Zürich

212 Max Bill, *Hugo,* 1927, pencil on paper, 20×13cm; illustrated in Arturo Carlo Quintavalle, *Max Bill,* (Parma: Università di Parma, 1977), fig. 6

Parental Conflict

As Max's mother became ever more determined to seek a divorce and increasingly suffered from psychosomatic headaches, her sons' lives also started to be affected. Max now no longer had any desire to spend time in the family home, where he could not help but witness his mother's frustrations and the taunts between his parents as they bickered and argued. By that point, Marie Bill-Geiger and Erwin Bill had "not engaged in sexual intercourse for years."[211] As a rule matters of that sort would not be aired at family mealtimes, but children generally know only too well if their mother is not happy (any more). The consequences of a mother (lacking affection from her husband) redirecting suppressed, smothered desires toward her own sons is a vast topic, best handled by psychotherapists—although none were consulted by the Bill family.

In 1927 Max drew a portrait of his brother, Hugo. It shows him wearing a tie and a waistcoat, in other words, dressed properly, not at all casually. Hugo has dark rings round his eyes, his mouth is sensual—clearly this is Max's brother—and he is resting his head on clenched fists.[212]

At this point I remember Max Bill saying to me that his mother had "positively doted on" his younger brother Hugo. Max had never fulfilled his mother's longing for a Prince Charming.

By contrast, another little work by Max from the same year looks almost like a child's drawing—maybe it was prompted by a memory from childhood.[213] It has no title as such, but it has the names "Mama," "Naira," and "Max" interwoven into it. All three names are in uppercase letters and, as such, all have the same emotional importance. In addition there are also a number of motifs drawn in a childlike manner: in the upper right there may even be an abstract portrait of Erwin Bill with a straight line for a mouth. He is seen next to a very small house and the sun, which is shining down on what appears to be a hare lying on its back—unless this is in fact Bez, Max's childhood teddy bear.

Max later told me that Naïra, the girl whose name he included in that drawing, was "a distant cousin." She and Max met up again in Paris after it was liberated. She had worked in London under Charles de Gaulle during the war and now used the name "Naïra France"; for a time she and Max were lovers.

213 Max Bill, Untitled, 1927, colored pencil and watercolor on paper [measurements not known]; illustrated in Quintavalle, *Max Bill*, fig. 7

In her divorce petition Marie Bill-Geiger complained that her husband was "an extraordinarily surly man, always finding fault, whom it is impossible to please." Moreover, he had often been rude to her and had berated her. He had never grown out of his bachelor's ways ... there had been disagreements over the children's upbringing. Above all, the accused had not tried energetically enough to discipline their somewhat wayward son Max, indeed he had even taken no action when Max, in his presence, had insulted the petitioner. It was now time for the marriage to be dissolved, otherwise their other son, Hugo, would also be damaged.

Marie Bill-Geiger lamented the fact that for years she had suffered both sexual and cultural deprivation. When her husband had a free Sunday, he would often go out very early, leaving her at home on her own. Indeed he had never done anything to give her pleasure, he had never taken her to the theater or a concert. And he never told her where he was going when he left the house on his own.

It is very possible that the young Marie, born to the wine merchant and officer Ulrich Geiger and known in the family to have a notoriously soft spot for Swiss militia, fell for Erwin Bill because of his railwayman's uniform with its oak-leaf motif on a jaunty cap, which maybe made Erwin Bill seem stylish and smart—and desirable.

Erwin Bill responded by bemoaning the fact that he was constantly reproached by his wife—in his sons' presence—as if their foolish escapades were his fault, and he added that he was weary of living in that kind of a marriage. The judge summed up: "Every little thing led to arguments, which—particularly with regard to the children's upbringing—so fundamentally upset the relationship between the two parties that they no longer shrink from abusing each other in front of their children."[214] The divorce finally came through on 1 April 1927.

If it is true of Erwin Bill that in his leisure time, when he went in for "bachelor pursuits," he frequented inns in Winterthur, played the card game Jass, and drank alcohol—as the locals used to say in Ligerz on Lake Bieler where he lived later on—then this may be another reason why Max took the same path as his intellectual Uncle Ernst and joined the progressive abstinence movement in 1925.

Any children that came into contact with Erwin Bill in Ligerz tended to be afraid of him. The daughter of a shop owner in Ligerz

214 Divorce certificate, district court, Winterthur, 1 April 1927, state archives of the canton of Zürich

215 Max Bill in conversation with Angela Thomas, 22 April 1975

remembers Erwin Bill "snatching" letters addressed to the shop out of her hand because he so badly wanted the stamps for his collection.

Unsettled by the public impact of his parents' failed marriage and subsequent divorce, Max now started taking all the more "willful liberties" at the Kunstgewerbeschule. As he himself said, that was "absolutely not welcome." Both at home—now a battlefield rather than a warm, protective environment—and at the Kunstgewerbeschule he had the feeling that he was somehow in the way. Clearly the staff and the other students saw him as a troublemaker, but no one ever thought to ask why he was so intractable.

Max Bill soon started to skip classes. He would escape out into the fresh air, going to the zoo, for instance, to the elephant enclosure to see the pachyderms—maybe hoping he, too, might acquire a thicker skin to protect him from hurt. He now only attended the Kunstgewerbeschule so that he could "somehow" complete the course and "only worked at his drawing board." He completely lost interest in doing anything in the workshop. Although two of his objects had been shown in Paris in 1925, his mother still referred to him in her petition for divorce as "somewhat wayward." Nevertheless, she also used the birth of her first son as an explanation for the fact that she had not filed for divorce a long time ago. And her lawyer added a note: "If the complainant had not given birth very soon, presumably the marriage would have ended in divorce much earlier on."

Max Bill: "my father was very patient, but my mother got more and more headaches. when i was at the bauhaus they divorced. my brother stayed with her in winterthur. . . . our mother had the house in winterthur, didn't need to pay rent and survived on the vegetables that she grew in the garden there."

Angela Thomas: "did your mother suffer from headaches all her life?"

Max Bill: "no, she went on a diet, lost weight, and didn't get any more headaches."[215]

Expelled from the Kunstgewerbeschule

In early 1927, when Max appeared in class still wearing make-up from a Carnival party the night before, the school's director, Alfred Altherr, demitted responsibility for his punishment to the city of Zurich education committee. Max Bill was thus expelled from the Kunstgewerbeschule despite his early successes and self-evident talent. His father took every opportunity to reproach him with the fact that he had spoiled his chance to qualify as a silversmith. But for Max, this new situation had the advantage that he could now try to work toward something that he had previously only dreamed of, having had no idea how to make it happen. So he presented his father with an idea that he had held ever since he attended Le Corbusier's lecture: he wanted to become an architect—a modern, rationalist architect. And he wanted to do this in the architecture department at the newly opened Bauhaus in Dessau. Bearing in mind his winnings of 2,500 Swiss francs from the Suchard poster competition, Max proposed that he would pay half the cost of studying in Dessau himself, and eventually his father agreed to pay the other half. Having submitted a folio of work to the Bauhaus, Max Bill was accepted, and on 20 April 1927 he enrolled in Dessau. Fortunately, the exchange rate for Swiss francs to German Reichsmarks was very much in his favor at the time.

The Issue of Light

Having so often tried to escape his parents' marital disputes by simply avoiding the dark atmosphere at home in Winterthur, Max—rather astutely and understandably—started to turn his attention to the "question of light," partly in the hope of restoring his own inner equilibrium.

Even when he contemplated his Uncle Ernst's early paintings, Max Bill must already have been struck by the way Geiger handled light. "Geiger was always fascinated with the idea of portraying sunlight. Sun rays filtering through profuse foliage on trees, the ensuing interplay of extreme contrasts of color and brightness were among the recurrent challenges Geiger set himself."[216]

"Toward the end of my time as an apprentice silversmith I started to consider issues to do with light. In the spring of 1927, when I arrived at the Bauhaus, I was very struck by the wide array of luminaires throughout the building, so many different kinds depending on the requirements of each situation."[217] At a time when his parents were already at odds with each other, Max had had to work through a conflict of his own with his father; he was determined to go to the Bauhaus and to pursue the life that he had chosen for himself. He had immediately been offered moral support by his uncle Ernst, who traveled from Ligerz to Winterthur for that specific purpose—Ernst Geiger was all too familiar with that kind of conflict from his own past.

216 See Fischer [1966]
217 Bill 1979 [b], p. 71

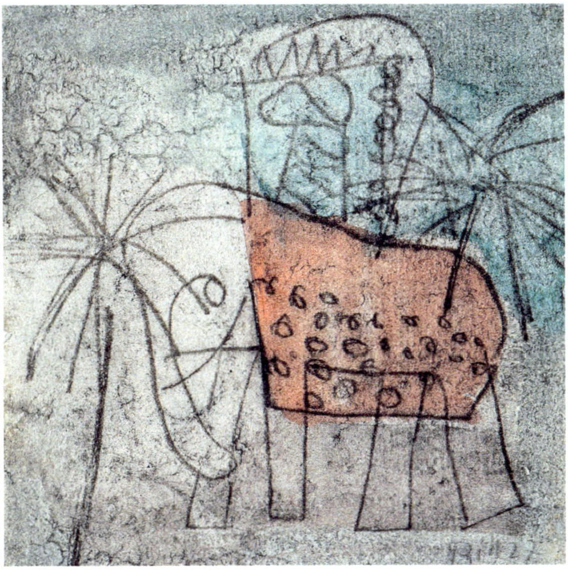

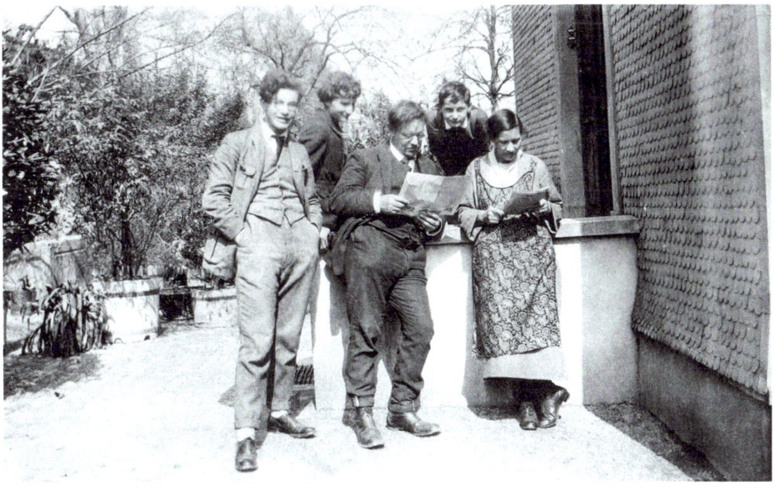

Max Bill, *Portrait eines Elefanten,* 1927, gouache and graphite over watercolor on laid paper, 12×10.8cm

Max Bill, Ernst Geiger, Marie Bill-Geiger, and two boys outside the Hegnergüetli, probably in spring 1927. Photograph inscribed verso: "This is what Max looks like when the uncle who helps *him* is there."

Ernst Geiger, Ex Libris Marie Bill Geiger, with a stamp mark concealing the name "Bill"

As letters between family members show, Ernst Geiger was firmly convinced that Max had inherited his artistic aptitude from his mother, Marie Geiger—and he always stood up for the Geiger side of the family against the Bill side.

At this critical moment in his life, Max developed a new energy. It helped him to shake off the constraints and frustrations of living in Winterthur and to choose his own unconventional path—and to become one of the *gens hors série* that Fritz Brupbacher had always found so interesting. Max now felt an urge to move forward, to become better informed, and to gain "clarity," and it may even be that Max's father also felt a certain sense of relief to know that there would be some distance between himself and his older son for the next few months. As it happened, he too was starting a new life. He and his new partner Lina Wolf—Aunt Lina to Max later on—moved into Stadthausstrasse 131 in Winterthur and married on 1 October 1928.

Now at his new address, in 1929 Erwin Bill became the secretary of the *Turnusausstellung* of the Schweizerischer Kunstverein in Winterthur. He stopped working for Swiss railways in 1930.[218] In December 1931 Erwin Bill and Lina Wolf moved to Ligerz on Lake Bieler.

> According to the divorce settlement, the defendant "transferred" the property at Brühlbergstrasse 8 to Marie Geiger:
> "to the complainant, regarding property to the value of 45,000 francs, which is calculated as follows:
> aa) the sum of 17,000 francs; the complainant is advised of the existing mortgage, in the terms of the mortgage note issued by the Zürcher Kantonalbank on 22 December 1915, to the value of 17,000 francs.
> bb) 28,000 francs are calculated as the complainant's share of the matrimonial property;
> sum total: 45,000 francs."[219]

In those days divorce was still the exception to the rule and a divorced woman—perhaps more so than a divorced man—might well find herself excluded from certain social circles where she had previously been welcome. Was that what happened to Marie Geiger, who was forty-four years old by now and who reverted to her maiden name? Did she have to endure disapproving looks from her neighbors? It seems from a letter written by

218 Information kindly supplied by Daniel Mani, Stiftung Historisches Erbe der SBB /SBB Heritage Foundation

219 Divorce certificate, district court, Winterthur, 1 April 1927, state archives of the canton of Zürich

Ernst Geiger to his son Christoph-Beat in 1962 that Marie Geiger did have to live with the consequences of her actions for many decades.

"Dear Chr.-Beat ... a card has just come from your aunt Marie, who is very much looking forward to your visit (Brühlberg 8). Take the opportunity to go to see her on your first free Sunday. She is very fond of us here in Brugg, even if the other Bruggers are not so fond of her and just race past Brühlberg in their cars.... We should be all the kinder to her and take the chance to bring a smile to her face in her old age.... She has had to pay a heavy price for marrying that scoundrel Erwin Bill."[220]

After the divorce Marie Bill-Geiger added a stamped mark to her *ex libris* labels (designed by her brother Ernst Geiger) concealing the name "Bill" and leaving just "Marie Geiger" visible. She continued to live at the Hegnergüetli with her younger son, Hugo, who was now in her sole custody—to the envy of Max. According to the divorce settlement Max was now in the sole custody of his father, who had what the documents called "*Erziehungsgewalt*"—literally, the "power of upbringing"—over his son.

On one occasion, years later, Hugo Bill in fact picked up a rifle (all Swiss men who have completed their military service can retain a rifle) and aimed it at his mother. Marie Geiger believed he fully intended to shoot her. In fact, Hugo Bill had a serious problem with alcohol and was admitted to a psychiatric clinic, where he remained for several years. He was convinced that he would one day make a major discovery that he would then patent. Hugo Bill died in 1989 and was given a pauper's funeral in Winterthur.

Although Hugo was still alive when I entered into a relationship with Max Bill, I never met him personally. Once, when Max Bill visited his brother in the cantonal care home in Winterthur-Wülflingen (a neo-classical former spinning mill built in 1818), I had to wait outside. Afterward we went to the gourmet restaurant in Wülflingen Castle. He said little about his fraternal rival, other than that it never failed to astonish him how his brother's charm made women "cluster around him," and that they even still came to visit him in his pitiable situation in the care home.

220 Ernst Geiger to Christoph-Beat Geiger, [1962], Archiv Christoph Geiger

221 Rudolf Steiger in *information* 1:6 (December 1932), p. 25

222 Sigfried Giedion, "Mode oder Zeiteinstellung," *information* 1:1 (June 1932), p. 9

223 Rudolf Steiger in *information* 1:6 (December 1932), p. 25

Two New Arrivals from Switzerland

Up until 1925 the Bauhaus occupied a Jugendstil building in Weimar designed by Henry van de Velde. However, as the political majority in the Weimar town council shifted to the right, the Bauhaus ceased to receive state funding and had to close, making the masters temporarily redundant until the town of Dessau, where a coalition of social democrats and conservatives were in power, agreed to meet the cost of a new art school designed by Walter Gropius. Dessau's willingness to take on responsibility, not only for the construction of the new premises but also for its upkeep, ultimately led to the inauguration of the new buildings for the Staatliches Bauhaus in Dessau in 1926. In April 1927 Hannes Meyer, a Swiss architect, took up his appointment as a master at the Bauhaus in Dessau, where he was to be head of the architecture department. In that same month the young Max Bill enrolled in Dessau.

Hannes Meyer is the same Meyer who, together with Hans Wittwer, created the daring competition entry for the League of Nations building in Geneva in 1926–27, which was then awarded third prize. Their competition entry was reproduced in *bauhaus* (1:4, p. 6), put together by Hannes Meyer himself and published in Dessau in October 1927.

The competition remit stipulated a building cost of 13 million francs, "which only the Le Corbusier-Jeanneret project had respected"; despite this, in 1927 the League of Nations' building committee gave the contract to a group of architects who would work together—Carlo Broggi, Camille Lefèvre, Henri-Paul Nénot, and Joseph Vago,—although the "average cost of their projects was 37 million francs"[221] Sigfried Giedion was critical of that decision: "If the League of Nations builds a palace, that palace should be both timeless and modern. In 1927, when we protested in Geneva against that decision on behalf of a Swiss association, the secretary of the Swiss delegation met us with the words, 'Columns have been beautiful for two thousand years, why shouldn't they be beautiful for another thousand years?'"[222] In 1928 the planned site was relocated from the lake to Ariana Park. The "architects reworked their design and in effect adopted Corbusier's ground plan."[223] In 1930 Le Corbusier filed a lawsuit against the League of Nations for a gross violation of the competition brief and for plagiarism.

The Meyer family now moved into one of the masters' villas designed by Walter Gropius and situated close to the Bauhaus. The villa, a two-family home, already had one other occupant, the Bauhaus master Oskar Schlemmer, who wrote to his wife about the new arrivals: "The Hannes Meyers arrived yesterday evening at ten. Two nice, chubby children—older than ours—a small wife, bright, all of them tanned."[224] Schlemmer's wife, Tut (née Tutein), had left Dessau for the Ticino with their children not long before the Meyers arrived. The plan was that she and the children would remain in the Ticino for the coming year. She had not enjoyed life in Dessau, partly because her husband's salary was so low.

Paul Klee's son described their move from Weimar to the Bauhaus in Dessau: "In the midst of gloomy industrial sites (sugar, gas, Agfa, Junkers) the little capital city drowsed like Sleeping Beauty. A courageous city father managed to transport the entire Weimar Bauhaus there, produced a magnificent school for these revolutionaries of art, and lent each master an atelier and eight rooms. In July 1926 we moved into 'our' house ... which was delightfully situated in a grove of pine trees.... My father felt that he was very fortunate between his four big walls, living right next door to his friend Kandinsky."[225]

So Oskar Schlemmer now occupied the studio, an upstairs room in the villa and the roof terrace, "which I will beautify for myself." Schlemmer (whose stagecraft class Max Bill would join the following year) kept his wife informed of his social contacts: "On Sundays I regularly dine at the Klees. On Fridays at the Feiningers. Midday coffee at the Schepers."[226]

Schlemmer also wrote, at greater length, to the artist Otto Meyer-Amden, about the new arrival: "... so Hannes Meyer has arrived. He was at the inauguration, which is where I first met him. He was very critical of all sorts of things about the Bauhaus. Boldly objective, often very pertinent, he talked about things like 'over applied arts,' 'Dornach,' 'decorative aesthetics.' He stayed for a day and a bit, longer than the other guests, and got to know various aspects of the Bauhaus. He clearly made a good impression and people sensed something new, something

224 Oskar Schlemmer, Dessau, to Tut Schlemmer, 1 April 1927, in Schlemmer 1958, p. 205

225 Klee 1968, pp. 416–17

226 Oskar Schlemmer, Dessau, to Tut Schlemmer, 11 April 1927, in Schlemmer 1958, p. 206

227 Oskar Schlemmer, Dessau, to Otto Meyer, 17 April 1927, in Schlemmer 1958, pp. 207–8

228 Schlemmer to Meyer. 17 April 1927, pp. 207–8

229 Oskar Schlemmer, Dessau, to Tut Schlemmer, 25 April 1927, in Schlemmer 1958, p. 208

that's missing at the Bauhaus. Gropius has been looking for someone to lead the long-awaited architecture department. He first asked the architect Mart Stam—he and Hannes Meyer had been here together. Stam turned him down, citing a lack of pedagogical skill and desire. So Hannes Meyer was invited to come back to Dessau and to meet the architecture students. He put on a little exhibition of works, including his very interesting League of Nations project in Geneva. One of his architectural maxims is 'organizing needs'—albeit needs in the widest sense, and certainly not forgetting inner, spiritual needs."[227]

Schlemmer then turned his attention to works by Bauhaus masters that Meyer saw on his visit—and what he liked best. He reported that Meyer said "that the strongest impact was made by some of the paintings (mine and Moholy's). As to mine in particular, he liked the abstracts. Klee's work didn't interest him; it seemed to him that Klee must always be in some kind of a trance. He didn't like Feininger's. Nor Kandinsky's, because of its theoretical side. By nature Meyer is perhaps closest to Moholy, although he is also very critical of him—his manner (his interpersonal dealings), his misguided teaching (the students also regard it as such and reject it).... Gropius can count himself lucky to be able to have this honest fellow as a new feather in his cap."[228] It soon became clear that the likes and dislikes that Schlemmer observed in Meyer applied not only to certain works but also to the people who had made those works and who would all, in due course, play a part in the hotly contested ideological disputes that later flared up at the Bauhaus.

Within a month of Hannes Meyer and his family moving into the villa, Schlemmer noticed a less-pleasing side of Meyer's character and wrote to Tut about it: "Meyer is often very boisterous. And it seems his wife has some woes. There is no denying that he is stubborn, a man of principles, but perhaps also—for all that he loves his family—inconsiderate. It just goes to show that all that glisters is not gold."[229] A year later, on 1 April 1928 Hannes Meyer took over from Walter Gropius as the director of the Bauhaus.

For his part, Max Bill now had to find his feet in among an entirely new set of fellow students and teaching staff and to work out what the masters expected of him. Given the protracted feuding between his parents, from whom he had now distanced himself—at least geographically—he did not initially find it at all easy to work out the social intricacies at the Bauhaus, the overall situation, and who was on whose side.

With the contraceptive pill still a thing of the distant future, it seems that Meyer had children with at least three women. Very little is known of Meyer's first wife other than her name, Nathalie Meyer-Herkert, and Schlemmer's sparse description of her as "small" and "bright."

There are various spellings of her given name, Nathalie and Natalie. Her full name was Louise Bianca Nathalie Herkert. Hannes and Nathalie had known each other since they were in Basel as young people and had married in 1917.[230]

After Nathalie Meyer-Herkert had left Dessau, she and her daughters, Claudia and Livia, first lived in Munich before finally moving to Zurich.[231] Livia Meyer later married Felix Klee, Paul Klee's son, and took the name Livia Klee-Meyer. She died, after a long life well lived, in 2011.

In Dessau Meyer, still living with his wife, had a love affair with his student Lotte Beese. By the time he was summarily dismissed for political reasons from his post as director of the Bauhaus (1 August 1930) he was, as he himself put it, living "separately" from his family.

"... Swiss, 40 years old, married, living apart from my family; 174 cm tall, salt-and-pepper hair, gray-blue eyes, according to my Confederation passport my nose, mouth and forehead are "medium," distinguishing features: none externally."[232]

However, Meyer does not specify whether that separation was because of his love affair with Lotte Beese or possibly because of another relationship, that is to say, with his secretary Margret Mengel. When Meyer was dismissed from the Bauhaus, Margret Mengel also left, "under protest." Meyer was the father of her son, Johannes Mengel.

Within a few months of his dismissal Meyer traveled to the USSR, where he taught at the school of architecture in Moscow and drew up a development plan for greater Moscow. At the same time, he continued to connect with various women. It seems that his relationships

230 See Kieren 1990, p. 28
231 Information kindly supplied by Erich Wagner, Deutsches Architekturmuseum, Frankfurt am Main
232 Meyer 1993, p. 117
233 Droste and Fiedler 1988, p. 421
234 Barbara Kreis, "Zwischen Funktionalismus und Sozialistischem Realismus—Hannes Meyer in der Sowjetunion" *archithese* 4 (1990), p. 31
235 Muscheler 2016, pp. 118–19
236 Droste and Fiedler 1988, p. 421

tended to overlap. Lotte Beese, previously a student at the Bauhaus alongside Max Bill, also went to Moscow; she gave birth to Hannes Meyer's son Peter on 31 July 1931. However, it was not Lotte Beese who became Meyer's second wife, but another former Bauhaus student, Helene "Lena" Bergner. She and Meyer married in 1937.

For a while Max Bill and Lena Bergner had been at the Bauhaus at the same time. In 1926 she completed the preliminary course, taught by Josef Albers, and in 1927–28 she attended Paul Klee's free (i.e. optional) painting class. Max Bill joined Klee's class in 1928. Lena also "took classes with Kandinsky, Moholy-Nagy, Schlemmer, and Joost Schmidt. Studied in the weaving workshop, worked in the advertising workshop. After attending a dyeing school, she became head of dyeing at the Bauhaus."[233] In 1930 Bergner followed Hannes Meyer to the Soviet Union, where she developed designs for the textile industry.

"Lena Meyer-Bergner reported how she, as a volunteer helping to build the Moscow metro, witnessed the enthusiasm and pride of the workers: they even made detours so that they could take the metro to work. They reverentially stroked the smooth marble with their hands and showed others the sections that they had worked on."[234]

In 1935 she also worked with members of the Bauhaus Brigade on the construction of the first station for the Moscow metro. She and Meyer married in 1937.

In 1931 Meyer's onetime secretary at the Bauhaus, Margret Mengel, accompanied by one Heinrich Vogeler, arrived in Moscow with her son Johannes (fathered by Hannes Meyer). Before moving to Moscow, Margret and her child had lived in Bremen with Heinrich Vogeler's family. As a member of the German Communist Party, Vogeler was in fact seeking refuge in Moscow.

Earlier on Heinrich Vogeler had lived from time to time in the Ticino, in the agricultural commune, Fontana Martina, that he and Fritz Jordi had set up in 1928 and that Max Bill and his uncle Ernst Geiger once visited.

After Hannes Meyer and Lena Bergner left the USSR for Switzerland in 1936, his former lover Margret Mengel remained in Moscow where she was later arrested; like many foreigners she was condemned to death by firing squad, without even going to trial. Her son, Johannes Mengel, "survived in a state-run children's home; it was only during the Khrushchev era that he learned of his mother's violent death. She was posthumously pardoned as a result of de-Stalinization reforms."[235] Having initially relocated to Geneva, "in 1939 Lena Bergner and Meyer settled in Mexico."[236]

Even this very brief foray into Meyer's complicated relationships with women indicates that it is hardly surprising that Meyer's first wife—she is never named in Schlemmer's reports—already appeared to have "some woes" soon after their arrival in Dessau.

Admiration—Toleration—Rejection

In those days it took a good two hours for the train from Berlin to reach Dessau, a provincial town with mainly single- and two-story buildings, just south of a loop in the River Elbe. The flat landscape around the town was scattered with mines and red-brick chimney stacks. Although Dessau had few famous sons and daughters, it was the birthplace of the philosopher Moses Mendelssohn and the composer Kurt Weill, who wrote the music for Brecht's *Dreigroschenoper* (*Threepenny Opera*) and who would soon have no option other than to leave Germany. He emigrated to the United States in 1935.

As Stefana Sabin puts it in her review of Dominique Bourel's book *Moses Mendelssohn: Begründer des modernen Judentums. Eine Biografie* (Zurich: Amman, 2007), Mendelssohn "was just as famous for his learning and elegant use of the German language as for the rigor of his arguments. He was a devout Jew who favored the division of state and church and who extrapolated an element of reason from Judaism that towed it into modernity." She makes particular reference to the way that Bourel conveys an impression of "Mendelssohn's precarious position on the fringes of the German republic of letters, where he was met with everything from admiration to toleration to rejection. The fact that he was awarded a prize by the Royal Prussian Academy of Sciences but was never admitted as a member is also seen by Bourel as symptomatic of an intellectual openness that was not backed up by any equivalent social permeability."[237]

The admiration, toleration, and rejection that Moses Mendelssohn encountered in Berlin in the eighteenth century would be felt again, in a sense, at the Bauhaus in Dessau in the twentieth century: the products created at the Bauhaus were admired by some, tolerated by others, but rejected and prohibited by the Nazi regime.

237 Stefana Sabin, "Am Rande der Gelehrtenrepublik. Dominique Bourel über Moses Mendelssohn," *Neue Zürcher Zeitung*, 17 October 2007

238 Max Bill, in *Deutschlandsender Kultur*, Berlin, first transmitted on 28 July 1991

Kasimir Malevich in Dessau

At Easter 1927 Kasimir Malevich, born and bred in Ukraine, visited the Bauhaus with the Polish poet Tadeusz Peiper, having previously been to see the architect Mies van der Rohe in Berlin. Peiper had in fact invited Malevich to Poland and then proposed that they take a spontaneous trip to Germany together. That same year Tadeusz Peiper published an account of their trip in the June issue of the avant-garde journal *Zwrotnica* that he had edited on and off in Kraków since 1922 (which is also the source of the following quotes).

Zwrotnica was a forum for a group of writers and artists inspired by Constructivism; their credo was in part shaped by the situation in Poland: in order to survive today our country has to reach the same level as Europe, we have to think in the categories of the present day.

Walter Gropius was in Dessau at the time and invited them to stay with him that night. He drove his official director's car to the café where Malevich and Peiper were waiting. Peiper recalled his "noble face, veiled in fatigue, hardened by truth." A number of Bauhaus masters were not in Dessau because the school was on its Easter break, but Gropius telephoned some who were still there. The first to arrive was László Moholy-Nagy, "painter and photoformer.... As he spoke, his face seemed to be shrunk together by his overexposed teeth." Soon after him Hannes Meyer arrived, and Peiper especially remembered him as having "the healthy face of a master."

Everyone was fascinated to meet Malevich, who spoke neither German nor French, so Tadeusz Peiper—a talented linguist with a good grounding in theory—acted as interpreter. Peiper had studied not only in Kraków and Berlin but also in Paris, where he became acquainted with the artist Robert Delaunay. Peiper noted that while he, for one, was interested in cultural developments in Europe, the masters at the Bauhaus expressed no interest at all in what was happening in Poland.

However, in an interview recorded decades later, Bill recalled that as a student he had seen Malevich in Dessau. He remembered "sitting in the bauhaus cafeteria ... from where [he] saw malevich."[238]

The next to arrive was Kandinsky. "One might have expected a curious, if not effusive, greeting between the Russian working in Germany and the Pole working in Russia. But no. Kandinsky made a violent bow, touching the floor quickly with his hand, and its trace disappeared immediately. Even the hope that Kandinsky might at least relieve me of the dull task of translating for a while came to nothing. Of his conversation in Russian with

Malevich, Kandinsky translated only the parts that pertained to his own recent failure in Russia."[239]

On the following day the guests from abroad were taken on a tour of the Bauhaus. "The buildings are divided into the trade school, the workshops, and the student apartments. The workshops are an important element of the Bauhaus, and there metalwork, carpentry, architecture, and wall painting are practiced. The overview is impressive. Unusual formal and material effects. Each perspective offers another set of solutions. If more proof is needed of the epochal value of the achievements of the new art, here it is. Iron, reinforced concrete, and glass.[240] The Bauhaus is a school of design. Through instruction in forms, training in crafts, and technical instruction it enables the student to build houses, to design interiors and prototypes for industry, and to work in the crafts. The relationship between the instruction in easel painting and the other scientific goals of the Bauhaus is not entirely clear."[241]

Masters' Houses in Dessau—Workers' Housing in Törten

Peiper also reported on the masters' houses: "They, too, were built by the city and are its property. They lie in a secluded boulevard, far from the school buildings, separated from them by a large section of the city. Their walls are a white glow, surrounded by the green glow of the lawns and trees."[242] "After lunch with Herr and Frau Gropius, a trip to Törten, where Gropius is building workers housing. Two long rows of small houses, each with four small rooms, comprising a dwelling. Modern methods of serial production reduce the costs to such an extent that a worker who pays a thousand Reichsmarks at the beginning and then the normal rent will be the owner of the little house he occupies after a period of fifteen years."[243]

239 Tadeusz Peiper, "At the Bauhaus" (1927), trans. Steven Lindberg, in *Between Two Worlds: A Sourcebook of Central European Avant-Gardes, 1910–1930* (Cambridge, MA: MIT Press, 2002)

240 On the colors used on the Bauhaus façade, see the drawings by Hinnerk Scheper, illustrated in Renate Scheper, *Farbenfroh! Colorful! Die Werkstatt für Wandmalerei am Bauhaus: The Wall Painting Workshop at the Bauhaus* (Berlin: Bauhaus Archiv, 2005), p. 28

241 Peiper, "At the Bauhaus" (see note 239)

242 Peiper, "At the Bauhaus" (see note 239)

243 Peiper, "At the Bauhaus" (see note 239)

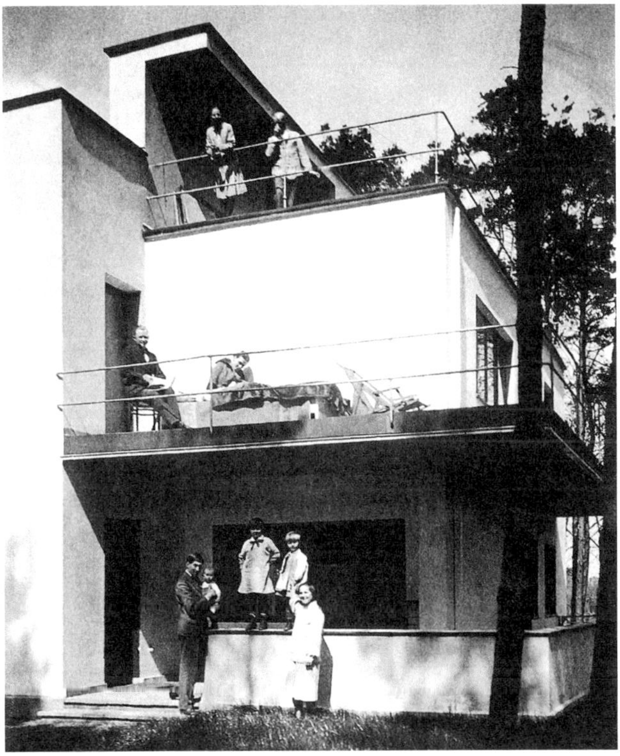

One of the masters' villas in Dessau with masters and family members, ca. 1927–28. Top floor, from left: Lou Scheper, Oskar Schlemmer. Middle floor: Georg Muche, Lucia Moholy. Ground floor: Hinnerk Scheper with his daughter Britta; Nathalie Meyer-Herkert with her daughters Claudia and Livia

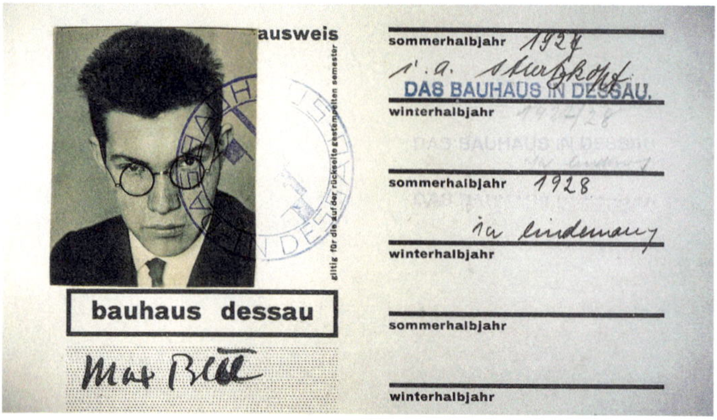

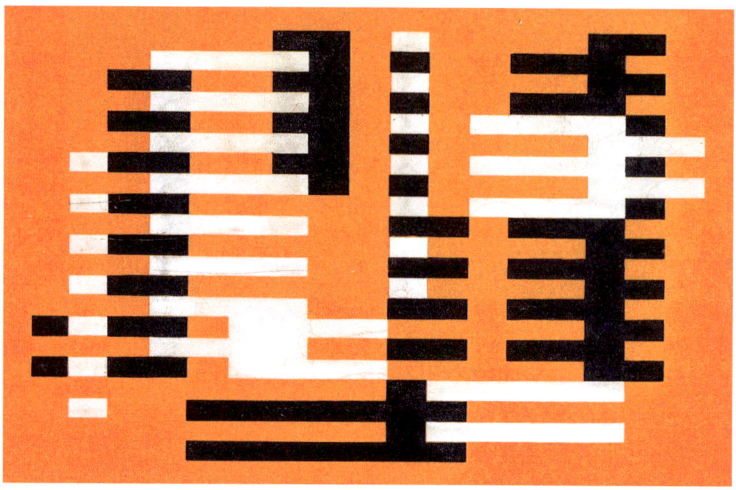

Max Bill's Bauhaus student card

Josef Albers, *Tectonische Gruppe,* 1925, sand blasted orange opaque glass, white etching, black paint, 29.6 × 45.6 cm

Bill's Arrival in Dessau, April 1927

Max Bill always remembered that morning when, coming from the station in Dessau, he was suddenly confronted by the Bauhaus—he had never seen anything like it: white walls and large, dark glass façades and a student residence with balconies and "minium-red doors." Max's folio submission had been accepted and he was able to enroll for the summer semester, which began on 20 April 1927, a few days after Malevich's visit. His matriculation number was 151.[244]

Looking back at his early days at the Bauhaus, Bill wrote (in a curriculum vitae from around 1930): "Bauhaus in Dessau. Initially keen study of mathematics, structures, etc. Theoretical exercises with Kandinski, Klee, Moholy-Nagy, Albers."[245] Much later on, looking back in 1978, he wrote: "Teaching at the Bauhaus, particularly in the preliminary course led by Josef Albers, largely consisted of questioning everything known and replacing it with new problematics. Above all in Albers's classes, and later on in Moholy-Nagy's classes, each person tried to produce something that was unlike anything that had ever been done before, which he then had to justify and discuss in a group situation. . . . In addition to these experiments we had elementary design theory with Wassily Kandinsky and then with Paul Klee. . . . So at the Bauhaus theory, experimentation, and practice always interconnected dialectically, and what's more, this all took place in a community of students, masters, and guests, the like of which has scarcely been seen since."[246]

"Insight through Experience"—Josef Albers

Although Max Bill had almost completed an apprenticeship at the Kunstgewerbeschule in Zurich, he first had to take a foundation class at the Bauhaus, since that was obligatory for everyone in their first semester. So he had to start from the basics again. The preliminary course director was Josef Albers, who was just twenty years older than Bill. Having studied painting in the class of Franz von Stuck in Munich—like Kandinsky and

244 For a list of students matriculated at the Bauhaus Dessau, see Wingler 1962, p. 534

245 Bill [ca. 1930]

246 Bill 1979 [b], p. 66

Klee in the mid-1890s—Albers had enrolled as a student at the Bauhaus in Weimar in 1920, where he took the preliminary course led by Johannes Itten. Albers immediately set off to the "town's rubbish dumps with a hammer and a rucksack, looking for pieces of colored glass and bottles. All the other students in his class constructed objects from combinations of materials, but Albers wanted just *one* single material—colored glass—in different thicknesses, with different shapes, colors, patterns, and translucencies; he mounted these bits of glass on sheets of metal and evolved a whole new way of creating compositions from non-transparent, colored glass."[247] The Bauhaus masters' council, having taken note of his experiments with shards of glass, wrote to him and invited him to set up a glass workshop at the Bauhaus.

A contemporary publication describes the way the foundation year teaching was shared by Albers and Moholy-Nagy: "Albers and Moholy were jointly entrusted with giving a new direction to the *Vorkurs* (or preliminary course), which was obligatory for all newly enrolled Bauhaus students.... Albers was originally appointed as 'young master' (even though he was Moholy's senior by seven years), Moholy as 'master of form,' with considerable difference in hierarchical and financial status. Moholy, for instance, was accommodated in one of the master houses designed by Gropius.... Albers moved into Moholy's house when the latter resigned from the Bauhaus in 1928."[248]

Albers became a full master after the Bauhaus moved to Dessau, although initially he was a young master, which meant that he of course earned less than a master.

"Since glass painting had [hitherto] been restricted to certain motifs used in sacred settings, there were no craftsmen able to develop the designs needed for the new approach to architecture.

The glass windows were to serve the new architectural concept of more open interiors and planar walls. Thus Albers not only became the first head of the workshop, but also the first practicing head: skills master and master of design in one. The official master of design, Paul Klee, paid little attention to this realm, even if Albers's designs may have been influenced by Klee's checkerboard sequences.

247 Herzogenrath 1979–80, p. 253
248 Borchardt-Hume 2006, p. 70 and note 16
249 Herzogenrath 1979–80, p. 255
250 Dietzsch 1990, vol. 1, p. 102, and vol. 2., pp. 39, 302, "Anlage" 20
251 Dietzsch 1990, vol. 1, p. 41

The commissions Albers mentioned initially came from the Bauhaus itself: a large window for Haus Sommerfeld in Berlin, designed by Gropius in Frank Lloyd Wright's prairie style and with furniture and fixtures designed by all the various Bauhaus workshops ..."[249]

In Dessau he and his wife, Anni, moved into the Prellerhaus, designed by Walter Gropius and unofficially named after the painter Friedrich Preller: "on the four upper floors there were 28 studio flats with a kitchenette on each level. These studios were allocated to students according to merit. The remaining students found private lodgings."

Around eight per cent of the students in Dessau were married. "As to marriages between staff and students before or after graduation: ten ... masters and seven young masters married Bauhaus students."[250] On the same floor as Albers in the Prellerhaus were Marcel "Lajko" Breuer, Herbert Bayer, and the student Alexander "Xanti" Schawinsky.

The young masters married to Bauhaus students were Josef Albers (to Anneliese "Anni," née Fleischmann), Alfred Arndt, Herbert Bayer, Marcel Breuer, Joost Schmidt, Hinnerk Scheper (to Louise "Lou," née Berenkamp). And the only female "young master," Gunta Stölzl, married a Bauhaus student, Arieh Sharon. In addition, "there are 57 documented cases of marriages between Bauhaus students. Regarding the age distribution in these marriages, in 24 out of these 64 marriages the husbands were younger than their wives." The same study reports that on average 150 students signed up for the courses in Dessau each semester.[251]

"... ideal communication stations"

The Prellerhaus had a very international feel; the languages spoken there ranged from Hungarian, Polish, Italian, German, Swiss German, Russian, and Yiddish to Japanese and Hindi. "The studios on the east side had balconies ... just big enough for a table for three.... Those balconies were ideal communication stations; you could make contact with your neighbors just by calling out.... Whenever Albers had a new joke he wanted to tell, he just needed to shout out the names of the others on his floor—Lajko, Herbert, Xanti—and they could 'meet' on their little balconies. People could also look into each other's studios from their balconies, through the big glass walls, unless, of course, the curtains were drawn. That 'transparency' was part of daily life, a very positive aspect of it....

At the Bauhaus complex the Prellerhaus stood out like a symbolic fulfillment of modern life and needs. It had a lower ground floor with baths and showers; above that was a canteen with a large kitchen. There were also terraces on every floor, a roof terrace, a kitchen on each of the four studio floors, and several toilets.... Internally, each studio had built-in cupboards, a sofa niche, a sink, tubular steel chairs, stools, small tables, and a big work table designed by Breuer."[252]

When Max Bill arrived in Dessau in April 1927 and all the studios in the Prellerhaus were already allocated, he found lodgings elsewhere: an attic room about two kilometers away from the Bauhaus, at Fichtenbreite 32, in an area where most of the residents worked at the nearby Junkers factory. Although he had been very impressed by the look of Le Corbusier's model of modern living two years earlier in Paris, his full-length "loft" was not at all furnished in a rational, modern style. It was more of a second-hand hodgepodge, with a hanging bookcase, two divan beds, easels and tables, and a huge blue velvet curtain concealing the kitchen area. He took everything over from the previous occupant—including the velvet curtain—and just left it as it was. When Hanns Fischli arrived from Switzerland a year later to enroll at the Bauhaus in April 1928, and went home one day with Bill to his loft, Max had clearly still not made any changes to the furnishings—neither adding a personal touch nor seeking to create a Bauhaus-worthy ambience.

Was that purely for financial reasons? Could it be that in those days he just had no interest whatsoever in the look of his surroundings? His seeming indifference is perhaps all the more perplexing given that, as Fischli recalled, Bill himself was always turned out "like a new edition of Ferdinand Hodler."[253]

To judge by Fischli's eyewitness account, at this point in the spring of 1928 Max had not yet developed his own personal style—neither in his dress nor in his décor. Was this a form of regression? Did he miss a mother's touch? Apart from the time when he had been sent away from home to the Waldheim in Oetwil am See, as a form of punishment, Marie Geiger had been a constant presence in his life, that is, until she filed a petition for divorce and decided during the divorce proceedings that, from April 1927 onward, she would only have custody of Max's younger brother Hugo, leaving Erwin Bill to take custody of Max.

252 Schawinsky 1927
253 Fischli 1968, p. 20
254 Schawinsky 1927
255 Herzogenrath 1979–80, p. 257
256 Herzogenrath 1979–80, p. 245

Max Bill would certainly have seen the very different, modern Breuer furniture in the Prellerhaus when he went to visit friends there, such as Xanti Schawinsky and Clemens Röseler. However, living in lodgings some distance away from the Bauhaus did have at least one advantage, namely that Max could avoid some of the social constraints that prevailed at the Prellerhaus, despite its otherwise progressive ethos. Away from other Bauhauslers, as they called themselves, he could explore and enjoy that taste for "vagabonding" that he had acquired on his trip to Italy.

One aspect of the Prellerhaus that certainly appealed to his architectural instincts—besides the striking shadows cast by the balconies (captured in numerous photographs)—was the light that flooded the stairwells and corridors. "In architectural terms the whole thing—inside and out—was all of a piece: logical, functional, uplifting." It was not only the light streaming in during the day that played a big part in the Prellerhaus, in the evenings it was the music that filled the building. "Anyone who had a new record to share would put his gramophone out on the balcony in the evening. That was the signal for others to join in—and that could turn into a whole musical evening."[254]

The Preliminary Course

Josef Albers, who was appointed a young master when the Bauhaus opened in Dessau, ran the first-semester preliminary course. He treated his students "caringly, but also with all the authority of a strong personality." For their part the students appreciated the "calm yet determined way" that he set tasks for them and "discussed different solutions."[255]

The newcomers—including Max Bill—starting out on the preliminary course were initially presented with just paper and scissors. "They were to fold and cut. Albers would give a precise description of the task: an 'exercise in stability and construction from one sheet without waste, using positive and negative motion' . . . or he would come into the classroom with a stack of newspapers, distribute them, and define a method: 'use no additional materials, be economical with the given material, exploit the possibilities of this material'—and then leave the students alone for several hours."[256] Albers regarded his own pedagogical principle as a learning method, not a teaching method, which the art historian Wulf Herzogenrath described as "insight through experience" and which later (after Albers emigrated to the United States) became known as "learning by doing." "The point of departure is simple and the means are constrained because even in those circumstances creative individuals will still come up with endless, multifarious solutions.... Albers never provided any examples, everyone had to come up with his or her own solution, which were then up for discussion. Albers felt very strongly that one must never interfere in the students' work processes, and that fundamentally there was no 'best solution,' just 'different works with different advantages.'"[257] In Albers's preliminary course Max Bill learned how to take a clear-sighted approach to a task, how to solve a problem, and how to defend a creative solution to his fellow students and to Albers.

Herzogenrath's research has shown that "in Hannes Meyer's time a few Communist-minded students' reproached Albers "for having no teaching method, no basic knowledge to pass on, no established guidelines to introduce." And Herzogenrath finds it unsurprising that the majority of students with Marxist views opposed anyone who cast doubt on the old values and questioned the viability of a single, logical solution: "The innovative nature of Albers's preliminary course is seen in the consideration given to a number of different responses to one and the same task: relativity of the art object, anonymity, reproducibility, material-led, economical composition."[258]

"As political forces in Germany became increasingly polarised, the number of card-carrying members of various parties among the students in Dessau went up each semester. In 1927, the formation of a Communist cell at the bauhaus led to an increase in Communist Party members. Party factions started to form. Between 1926 and 1932 over 50 students in Dessau were members of the Communist Party of Germany (KPD). At least eight were members of the Social Democratic Party of Germany (SPD)."[259]

257 Herzogenrath 1979–80, p. 258
258 Herzogenrath 1979–80, pp. 264 and 266
259 Dietzsch 1990, p. 40
260 Suzanne Markos-Ney in Kandinsky 1976, p. 132
261 Max Bill in Nina Kandinsky 1976, p. 175
262 Nina Kandinsky 1976, pp. 133–34

Learning at the Bauhaus

Suzanne Markos-Ney—a student at the Bauhaus some time after Bill—later commented that Wassily Kandinsky had the ability "to endlessly contemplate and interpret everything from different sides ... drawing on his universal knowledge.... At the Bauhaus we learned first to forget everything else. The real outcome of Kandinsky's teaching was that we learned to see the world with a painter's eyes."[260] Max Bill, however, also pointed out that when Kandinsky wanted to talk about contemporary art to his students, he would cite only himself as an example, making no mention of any other artists working at the time. "He only discussed art history in terms of the present day. He explained contemporary art and provided the students with a useful access to it. For instance, he would take Monet's *Haystacks* and deduce from that the developments that led to contemporary art. However, for Kandinsky contemporary art only went as far as Kandinsky."[261] He generally spoke in metaphors—and could not bear to be contradicted. And if "the conversation took a political turn, things would become difficult."[262]

Later on in life, both as a collector and as someone with an active interest in the future of art, Max Bill returned to what he had learned from Kandinsky and put it into practice when he purchased Roy Lichtenstein's response to Monet's *Haystacks* (Roy Lichtenstein, Untitled [*Haystacks* 7], 1969, lithograph, 52×77.5cm, estate of Max Bill left to Angela Thomas).

After the Bauhaus in Dessau closed in 1932, Kandinsky, Josef Albers, and Anni Albers all taught at the newly established Bauhaus in Berlin until it closed in 1933. Josef and Anni Albers were then invited to teach at Black Mountain College in North Carolina and remained there until 1949. For many years Josef Albers and Max Bill corresponded on the subject of art. Of all the people the young Bill encountered at the Bauhaus, Albers was his most enduring contact. In Dessau Albers taught Bill various things about the wider relationship of a creative individual to his or her environment. And it was Albers who kindled Bill's determination always to investigate the legitimacy of anything he did, to take responsibility for it, and never to allow anything he had made—be it a painting, a sculpture, or an object he had designed—to be seen by others or to go out into society without good reason.

After the Second World War Bill and Albers met up again in Peru, and Bill managed to persuade Albers not only to return to postwar Germany in the early 1950s but also to play a part in developing a preliminary course for the Hochschule für Gestaltung in Ulm. The new school of design in Ulm was not only masterminded and designed by Max Bill, he was also its first rector.

"... and disappeared off to the banks of the Elbe"

In Dessau Max Bill found himself surrounded by bright, intelligent, seemingly self-confident, fashionably urbane Bauhaus students. In Germany, barely a decade after the end of the First World War, there was still a distinct feeling among members of the younger generation of starting anew; they were curious about the world and had a relish for life that was entirely unfamiliar to the young Swiss student whose own native country had scarcely been touched by the war.

In the preliminary course, taught first by Albers and then by Moholy-Nagy, Bill—like his fellow students—strove to produce something "that was unlike anything that had ever been done before" and then discussed his work with others afterward, only he soon found himself suffering from the "Bauhaus hangover": "that business of discussing things, which had no visible purpose tested everyone's powers of reasoning. However, even although everyone enthusiastically participated and hot battles were fought, after a few weeks most people found themselves plagued by doubts; they fell victim to the Bauhaus hangover and disappeared off to the banks of the Elbe. In the end, especially if it started raining, they would come back, feeling bad, until they realized that this affliction was not dangerous, indeed it was a well-known aspect of a necessary process."[263]

And as to the students' pastimes in the winter semester, Bill suggested "not without reason, that beds replaced the banks of the Elbe." The concept of free love found widespread favor and, young and full of enthusiasm, the students eagerly set about integrating it into life at the Bauhaus. T. Lux Feininger (actually Theodore), one of the youngest students at the Bauhaus, who had moved from Weimar to Dessau with his parents, felt that Dessau was "much more urbane" than the little town where Goethe had lived. He also felt that the political climate in Dessau was "more attuned to new ideas."[264]

263 Max Bill in conversation with Angela Thomas
264 Feininger 2006, p. 72

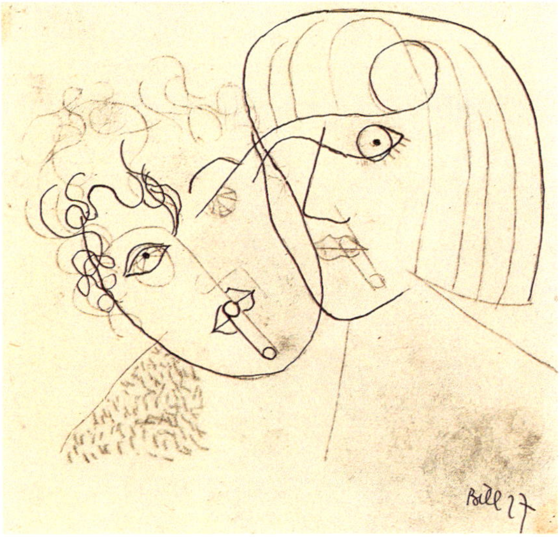

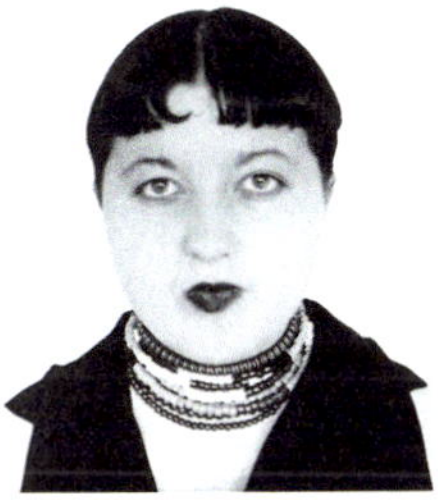

Max Bill, *Zwei Freundinnen* (Hilde Rantzsch and Katt Both), 1927, frottage on paper, 18×21cm

Grit Kallin-Fischer, *Portrait of Hilde Rantzsch,* Berlin, ca. 1927, photograph, vintage print, 21.5×15.4cm, Galerie Berinson, Berlin

Hilde Rantzsch, *Krankes Mädchen,* 1927, India ink on paper, 20.7×23.2cm

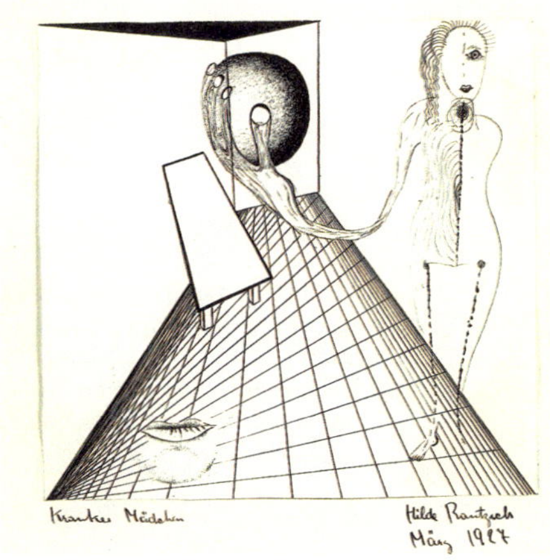

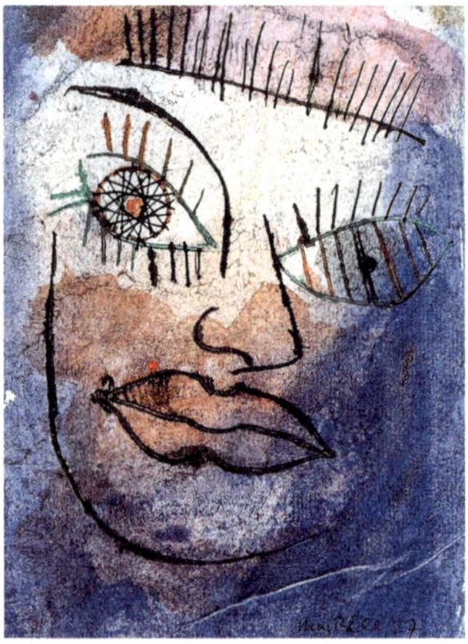

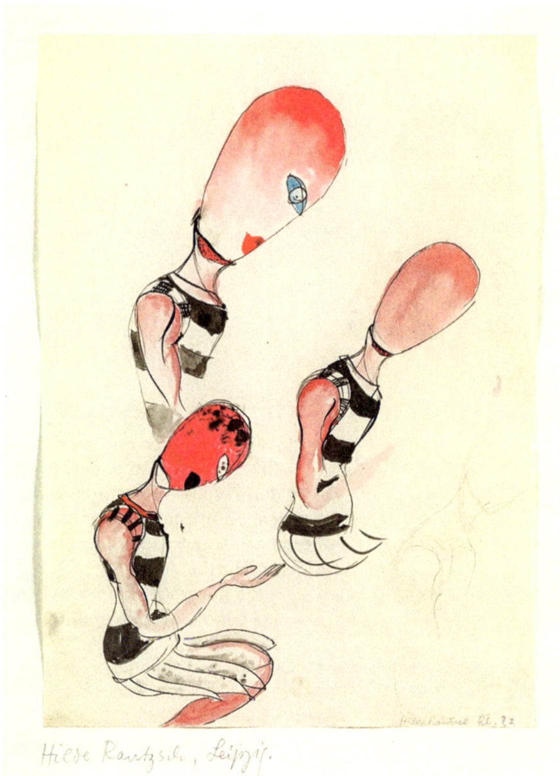

Max Bill, *Ich, ein Katzenmensch,* 1927, india ink over watercolor on paper, 17.2×13 cm

Hilde Rantzsch, Untitled, 1927, watercolor and india ink on paper, 28.5×20.5 cm

An emissary from the site management team at the Bauhaus in Dessau went to see the Feininger family, "... to meet my parents in order to discuss the colors they wanted for the interior of their half of Master House no. 1, which was allocated to the Feiningers and the Moholy-Nagys. This was the first of three duplexes ... that were externally identical but had individual interiors. I was very surprised, but it was even more of a boost to my self-esteem...."[265]

Kattja Both and Hilde Rantzsch

Some of the young women studying at the Bauhaus smoked and had their hair cut in a bob to signal their emancipation; at Bauhaus parties they danced the Charleston, with some of them even wearing dresses that exposed their knees. Max Bill soon started to relish the company of these refreshingly astute women. And as he made friends with Kattja Both and Hilde Rantzsch he discovered his own erotic appeal. But it was not just the women who enjoyed his company, he was also popular among the other young men. One later described him as an "incredibly lively," gifted person.[266]

Katt Both's given name was in fact Anna Elisabeth Mathilde. She answered to Kattina, Katt, and Kattja, and was number 4 on the Bauhaus matriculation list; Hilde Rantzsch was number 64,[267] which meant that they were both already at the Bauhaus when Max arrived. As old hands, experienced Bauhauslers, they took the young Swiss student under their wing and showed him the ropes. Katt, an attractive young woman, who was three years older than Max, was a journeyman in Marcel Breuer's carpentry workshop. "In her subsequent training—with Mart Stam, Walter Gropius, and Hannes Meyer—Katt Both concentrated on architecture and furniture design."[268] Looking back, Gropius remembered not only her artistic talent but also her "great intelligence, energy, and ability." He felt that she was "more than capable of handling even very demanding structural tasks on her own."[269] During the course of her studies Katt worked for three months in Berlin at the architectural practice Luckhardt & Anker.

265 Feininger 2006, p. 71
266 Max Gebhardt to Konrad Püschel, March 1976, Archiv Stiftung Bauhaus
267 See Wingler 1962, p. 558
268 Maasberg and Prinz 2004, p. 73
269 Walter Gropius in Maasberg and Prinz 2004, p. 74

Berlin, the metropolis, naturally exerted a pull on the students in Dessau and from May to September 1927 it was host to the *Grosse Berliner Kunst-Ausstellung.* It seems Bill may well have visited that exhibition himself, maybe with other students, because there is a copy of the exhibition catalogue in the Bibliothek Max Bill. Hugo Häring and Ludwig Hilberseimer, representing the architects' collective Der Ring, were on the exhibition committee. In 1928 Katt Both left the Bauhaus and returned to Berlin to work at Luckhardt & Anker.

Later on Bill often went to southern Germany to visit Hugo Häring about original works by Malevich, which were in Häring's care.

Katt Both's friend, Hilde Rantzsch (from Leipzig), features in an autobiographical recollection by Hanns Fischli: "Hilde's face was wide, like a wonder-cat. Everything about her physique was rounded; she had delicate limbs with fingers like a lizard's feet. Her lips were luxuriant and, had I but known it at the time, I would have to say, full of joy.... However, there were also days when she didn't know where the next meal was coming from; no one would let her put anything more on a tab; so then she just worked obsessively in the weaving workshop, slaving away until she had earned an advance."[270]

Hilde Rantzsch was an offbeat student with very little money. A small-format work of hers, from August 1927, called *Meiner grünen Laternen-Schwester* (To my green lantern sister), subsequently found its way into the Misawa Bauhaus Collection, Tokyo, and is illustrated in color in Fiedler 1999, p. 163. Another two works by Hilde Rantzsch, *Krankes Mädchen* (March 1927) and an untitled work done in June 1927 were both in Max Bill's estate (see pp. 161, 162).

Ever since Max's first visit to Paris, where the beauty of the city and the special light had raised his spirits and seems to have cast him in a special glow—"qu'il était beau!"—"how handsome he was!"—he had increasingly gained in self-confidence, which is clearly reflected in his self-portrait as a "cat person" (*Ich, ein Katzenmensch,* see p. 162). Max Bill later told me that he fell in love "four times' in total at the Bauhaus.

He was also relatively comfortable in financial terms because the exchange rate for Swiss francs to German Reichsmarks was in his favor. However, life was much harder for some of his fellow students, as it was for Hilde Rantzsch: "Rich fathers' sons were a tiny minority" among the student cohort at the Bauhaus.[271]

270 Fischli 1968, p. 54
271 Fischli 1968, p. 52
272 Dietzsch 1990, pp. 35–36
273 Fischli 1968, p. 56
274 Brandt 2001, p. 47

Folke F. Dietzsch has investigated the social backgrounds of Bauhaus students: "... the majority came from the middle or lower-middle classes. The number who could be described as working class—just ten—is relatively small. Walter Gropius described the students' circumstances as follows: 'the student body at the state-run Bauhaus largely consists of impecunious young people, who have to get by without any external financial support.' Although this may appear to contradict the above findings, it is in fact the truth; at that time middle class families, too, often found themselves facing financial and existential difficulties."[272]

One of the few wealthy students was "Flake, the poet's son": "He kept a good two meters away from everyone else, he didn't just seem more elegant, he was more elegant; he wore stylish flannels, his long hair was parted, and he spoke like a North German. He joined Gropius's department of building in 1927."[273] Marianne Brandt, who worked with Moholy-Nagy, remembered that the students "who had no money at all" used to sleep in the gymnasium on the lower ground floor of the Bauhaus building in Dessau, although that was in fact strictly forbidden: "there was a big, soft carpet there ... showers, baths." At the same time there were a few potential sources of income for a small number of students. Taking members of the public on tours of the Bauhaus on Sundays, for instance, could earn them a portion of the takings, although sometimes they were met with anger rather than gratitude: "I will never forget one tour with 200 book printers. When I told them about us only using lowercase letters and how that saved time, they went berserk. They were even waving their sticks at me."

Although the exclusive use of lower case was the norm at the Bauhaus, it was only after Bill had left the Bauhaus and returned to Switzerland that he adopted the same practice.

Another fairly meager source of income for some students came from the production licenses that were awarded to certain manufacturers. "As far as I remember the Bauhaus retained half of the fee that was paid for licenses for our models"; the other half was divided "among the master, the designer, and the workshop."[274]

Visitors from Zurich

In 1927 the artists Carl Fischer and Otto Morach, who were still on the staff at the Kunstgewerbeschule in Zurich, traveled to Dessau to learn more about the progressive teaching methods at the Bauhaus and of course also to see Max Bill. He was very pleased to make them welcome—it was Fischer who had inspired him to become a vegetarian (much to his father's annoyance) and it was Morach who taken Bill and the other students to Paris in 1925. Now the roles were reversed and Bill was proud to be able show Morach and Fischer the Bauhaus and Dessau.

Wilhelm Ostwald at the Bauhaus

Walter Gropius and Wilhelm Ostwald—winner of the Nobel Prize for Chemistry and a philosopher—first became acquainted as members of the German Werkbund. In late November 1926 Gropius wrote to Ostwald on Bauhaus paper, in lowercase of course—"we always write in lowercase because that saves us time": "dear herr ostwald ... please find enclosed a small pamphlet setting out how form and color theory are integrated into our institute ... yours, with great respect, gropius."[275] A few weeks later master Moholy-Nagy also wrote to Ostwald: "dear privy councillor, on my return i passed on to herr gropius your wish to give some lectures here at the bauhaus. he, as we all are, is very happy with this idea ... yours, with the greatest respect from all of us, moholy-nagy."[276]

275 Walter Gropius, Dessau, to Wilhelm Ostwald, 20 November 1926, Grossbothen, Saxony, Wilhelm Ostwald Archiv

276 László Moholy-Nagy, Dessau, to Wilhelm Ostwald, 22 January 1927, Grossbothen, Saxony, Wilhelm Ostwald Archiv

277 Walter Gropius, Dessau, to Wilhelm Ostwald, 2 February 1927, Wilhelm Ostwald Archiv

278 Max Bill's library contains the following publications by Ostwald (whose ideas were much disputed by Bauhaus students), although these titles only came out after this series of lectures:
– *Wege der Technik. Die Pyramide der Wissenschaften* (Stuttgart and Berlin: J. G. Cotta'sche, 1929)
– *Mathetische Farbenlehre. Die Farbenlehre,* vol. 1, 3rd enlarged and improved edition. With 42 illustrations (Leipzig: Unesma, 1930, 1st ed. 1921).
The latter is marked inside with "bill," a lower-case signature, indicating that Max Bill valued it enough to include it in his private library

Wilhelm Ostwald confirmed that he would visit the Bauhaus and Gropius wrote back by return: "dear professor ostwald, i gratefully acknowledge receipt of your kind letter. we are extremely happy that you would like to talk to us here. my wife and i will be delighted to welcome you as our guest . . . with heartfelt thanks to you for so kindly consenting to acquaint us with your immense learning. i look forward to very exciting days. if at all possible, please do also bring slides with you. with heartfelt thanks on behalf of the entire bauhaus i send warm regards, yours, with great respect, gropius."[277]

Due to various scheduling problems, it was not until 10–15 June 1927 that Ostwald delivered his lectures.[278] Thus Max Bill, as a new arrival, was able to benefit from the Nobel laureate's talks. Looking back, he remembered that there were not large audiences for the guest speaker during that week: "Wilhelm Ostwald led a seminar on color, which sparked off a 'religious war' between those who supported his theory, grounded in exact physics, and those who opposed that theory on the basis that it was physiologically erroneous."[279]

With the students now engaging in heated debates on the merits of Ostwald's color theory compared to Goethe's, Gropius wrote to Ostwald: "i would like to convey to you very special thanks to you from all of us for enriching our bauhaus. your week of lectures was very productive and will certainly leave its mark on our people. may i also formally ask you to do us the honor of joining the board of our friends of the bauhaus? . . . yours, with great respect, Gropius."[280] And indeed, shortly after that series of lectures Herbert Bayer, head of typography and advertising at the Bauhaus, expressed a keen interest "in acquiring (uncoated) papers tinted according to the color circle."

Bayer's sent his request on writing paper with a letterhead—"hochschule für gestaltung"—designed by himself and the postal

Max Bill's library also contains
– *Goethes Farbenlehre,* ed. and intro. by Hans Wohlbold (Jena: Eugen Diederichs, [1928]), with 1 portrait, 27 optical charts, 22 color plates, and 8 black-and-white plates after originals by Goethe, new special edition, in a blackletter font, purchased on "3.8.37"
– *Taschenbücher zum Studium von Goethes Farbenlehre.* Colors seen through a prism, with experimental prisms, presented in black-and-white and six-color plates by H. O. Proskauer, vol. 1 (Basel: Zbinden, 1951), which Bill acquired much later than the books by Ostwald.
There are no markings in any of the above books

279 Bill 1979 [b], p. 66

280 Walter Gropius, Dessau, to Wilhelm Ostwald, 25 June 1927, Wilhelm Ostwald Archiv

address "bauhaus in dessau." His letter is dated 21 June 1927 and addressed to the "farbenlaboratorium prof. ostwald, grossboten bei leipzig" (Wilhelm Ostwald Archiv).

Light, Space, and Matter

Ostwald maintained that "matter is solely determined by the energy it releases." According to his theory "the universe is filled with a network of diverse energies ... including radiation energy, a type of energy that is least connected to matter" and it is this radiation energy that determines color. "The energy that impacts on our eyes and thus induces a sensation of color is called light."[281]

Art historian Janos Brendel has mooted the possibility that, judging by Moholy-Nagy's experiments with light and transparency in the mid- to late 1920s, he may well have been influenced by Ostwald's theory. And, as Brendel rightly presumes, it was not only Ostwald who influenced Moholy-Nagy but also the writer Paul Scheerbart, specifically his utopian "glass architecture," which was much debated in Berlin around 1920 when Moholy moved there. Brendel also persuasively suggests that the idea of "double-paned" architecture (derived from Scheerbart's thinking) also informed Moholy-Nagy's paintings, which in turn clearly distinguished his position from that of the Russian Constructivists.

In keeping with Scheerbart's thinking, the new architecture was to be "glass architecture, built on metal constructions with double panes of colored glass. The elimination of brick-built walls will achieve a special effect: the rooms will be flooded with the natural light of the sun, the starts and the moon, and the use of double panes of colored glass will enhance this effect.... Evidence of the widespread interest in Scheerbart ... is seen in the publication of Adolf Behne's *Wiederkehr der Kunst,* large sections of which were also published in the journal *Ma* under the rubric 'Kunst und Revolution.'"[282]

As he contemplated László Moholy-Nagy's *q IV* (1923)—a very characteristic example of his work—it struck Bill that Moholy-Nagy's work was in a sense midway between Russian Constructivism and Dutch Neoplasticism.[283]

281 Cited in Brendel 1986, pp. 177, 178
282 Brendel 1986, p. 173
283 See Max Bill 1976 [b], p. 39

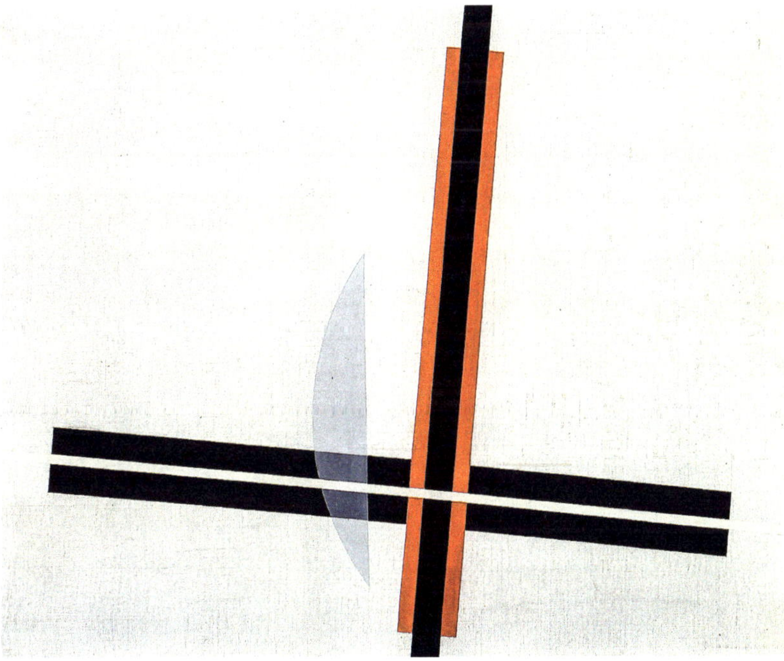

László Moholy-Nagy, *Q IV,* 1923,
oil on white-grounded canvas, 76×96 cm

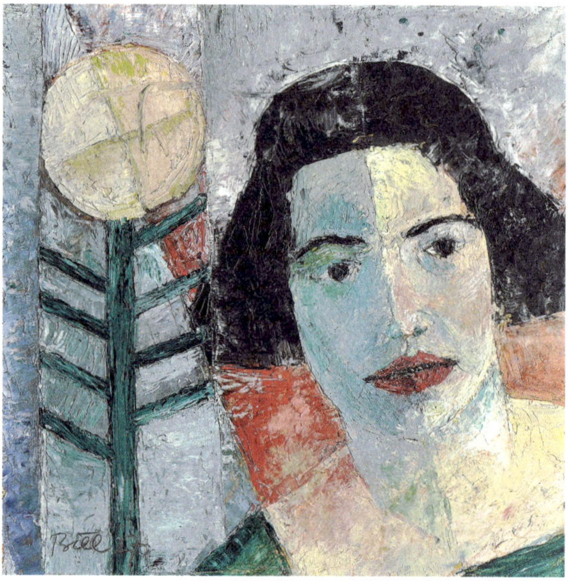

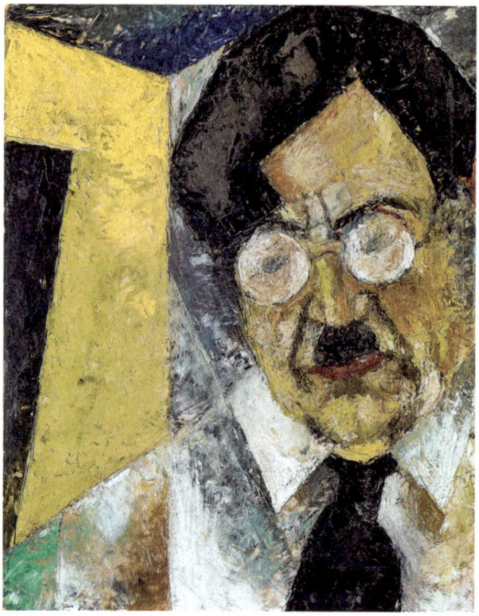

Max Bill, *Clara Woerner,* Ligerz, 1927, oil on card, 35×35cm

Max Bill, *Portrait von Dr. Ernst Geiger,* Ligerz, 1927, oil on card, 32×25cm

Luminaires

The young Max Bill was very taken with the various luminaires and lighting fixtures at the Bauhaus. Given his own strong "preference for elementary solutions," he was especially fascinated by the spherical pendant light that was used in the seminar rooms.

Looking back at the spherical pendant lamp, Bill described that dazzle-free light fixture, which "radiates light directly upward," as an example of "problems being posed with exemplary clarity and, as a result, the typical form for a particular purpose being identified."[284]

In 1944 he designed his own *indirektleuchte mit spiegelreflektor* for B.A.G. Turgi; in March 1947 he sent an image of this lamp—published in *Werk* 33:5 (May 1946)—which would have to be "reproduced" for publication purposes, to Xanti Schawinsky in the United States (Max Bill to Xanti Schawinsky, Zurich, 11 March 1947, Schawinsky-Archiv), along with a reprint of his own text "Erfahrungen bei der Formgestaltung von Industrieprodukten" from the same May 1946 issue of *Werk,* which includes reproductions of his own sketches and models.

On 3 August 1927, when he arrived at his uncle Ernst's house in Ligerz during the summer vacation—not yet sure how long he would stay—he boldly signed the visitors' book as "Max Bill, architect Winterthur, Bauhaus in Dessau."

An entry made during a visit in 1940 is even shorter: "bill, zürich swb" (Schweizerischer Werkbund), and on later visits to Ligerz in 1962 and 1963 it was reduced to just "bill" (in Ernst Geiger's visitors' books).

Overflowing with ideas from the Bauhaus, the young student immediately proposed that his uncle should allow him to add some color to the rear bedroom. Ernst Geiger agreed to Bill's idea of modernizing the room by redecorating it in primary colors and trustingly gave him a free hand. Bill launched into the task. On its completion—and happy with the result—Bill expressed his gratitude for the opportunity by painting a portrait of his uncle against the backdrop of the newly decorated room—henceforth known as the Max Bill room. Bill's portrait of Ernst Geiger includes a corner of the newly painted blue ceiling and part of a yellow border on one wall. The portrait has an air of mature seriousness; at the same time, as if Bill were promoting his own talent for design, it also documents his latest creative achievement. Bill was now well on the way to adulthood.

In 1963, two years before he died, Ernst Geiger sold that portrait to the town of Brugg "because he was in financial straits" and would be

284 Bill 1979 [a], p. 71

paid more for a picture by his nephew than for one of his own. It is now in the Brugg town hall, as Bill told me.

During that holiday by Lake Biel he also painted a portrait of Clara Woerner (just six years older than himself), who had cared for his cousins Hans and Wölfi.

"... with active help from Ernst Geiger, Hans Geiger (Ernst's eldest son from his first marriage) and his wife designed the interior for a well-known handweaving business in Ligerz" (Guido Fischer, "Nachruf auf Ernst Geiger 1 February 1876–16 December 1965," in *Brugger Neujahrsblätter,* 1966, Archiv Christoph Geiger); and Christoph Geiger, Ernst's son from his second marriage, notes that "as a textile artist and rival in the same village, Clara Geiger-Woerner was a thorn in the side of Elsi Giauque. So the latter was always plotting against Ernst Geiger and his daughter-in-law. Her husband, my step-brother Hans, turned wooden bowls on a lathe, and almost lost an eye in a lathe accident" (Christoph Geiger to Angela Thomas, Freienbach, 27 November 2007). Later on Bill would be on friendly terms with Giauque, who had studied under Sophie Taeuber-Arp and lived in the "Festi" up above Ligerz.

Red, yellow, and green dominate the portrait of Clara Woerner; one half of her face is cast in a dark, greenish shadow while the other half is much brighter with a yellow highlight on her forehead. The eye in the shaded side appears introverted, whereas the eye in the brighter side has a clear, unerring gaze, and although her lips are red and her hair is cut in a fashionable bob, it seems that the aspect she presented to Bill as she sat for him was serious rather than sensual. As to the style of this portrait, in some respects Bill's use of color calls to mind earlier paintings by artists such as Gino Severini or Sonia and Robert Delaunay.

The portrait of Clara hangs by the entrance to the Zurich home of Hans Ulrich Geiger, the son of Clara Woerner and Hans Geiger. On my visit, he approvingly remarked that "Bill captured my mother very well."

One oddity in this portrait is the schematic plant to one side of Clara. Does this unsettling plant—bereft of emotion—perhaps relate to either the artist or the sitter's state of mind? Be it a product of Ernst Geiger's otherwise exuberant garden or of Max Bill's imagination, it seems more likely to reflect the artist's mood, given that the main aspect of the sitter's persona appears to be a certain clarity gained from facing reality, looking both within herself and out into the world. Clara Woerner, a woman who knew what she wanted, would later join the Swiss Werkbund;

285 Reprinted in Frey 2003, p. 240
286 Bill 1990 [a]

in 1935 she married her onetime ward, Hans Geiger, and they then set up and ran a hand-weaving business together, with active support from Ernst Geiger.

An Architectural Proposal for Osaka

The official starting date for Bill's second semester at the Bauhaus was 5 September 1927. But some masters, including Paul Klee, were still away on vacation. It seems that Klee's yearning for freedom prevented him from returning to Dessau just yet, and he decided to extend his holiday. Still absent from the Bauhaus, on 24 September 1927 he received a letter from the masters' council: "dear herr klee! work at the bauhaus resumed three weeks ago. we miss your presence here and ask you to return immediately. it is to our disadvantage, to the town's, but above all to the students' disadvantage that some masters have taken longer holidays and have been so slow to inform the school of this that it has not even been possible to reorganize their teaching in time ... yours, kandinsky, moholy-nagy, albers, breuer, h. meyer, g. stölzl, schlemmer, schmidt, bayer, gropius."[285]

Max Bill quickly found his feet at the Bauhaus again. Having already absorbed a certain amount of architectural theory from lectures on building construction and structures, he was determined to put his new knowledge into practice as soon as possible. He decided—entirely on his own account, as he once told me—to enter a Japanese architectural competition for a high-rise building in Osaka. There are two short written references to this by Bill himself: "I won third prize, as the only European entrant, in an international architectural competition for a mixed-use building in Osaka" (Bill [ca. 1930]). Many years later he briefly mentioned it again: "As a young man I greatly admired Japanese cultural artifacts, the objects they use in daily life, the famous woodcuts, and their wonderful built structures. My first contact with Japan was an architectural competition run by a Japanese architectural magazine. I won third prize. At the time (1928) I was a student at the Bauhaus."[286]

In all the many catalogues relating to the work of Max Bill, I have never seen any reproductions of his proposal for that early competition. It may be that time ran short as he finalized his drawings in Dessau, with the result that it was no longer possible to have them photographed before they had to be sent to Japan.

All the entries were retained by the newspaper that had instigated the competition. Bill's original plans may therefore still be somewhere in a Japanese archive.

In 2007 I asked the English architect, Jason Bill, and his Japanese wife, Atsuko Bill, to try to track down his submission, which they did with great success. As a result, these long-unseen materials have been retrieved from oblivion.

The competition was run by the magazine *Shinkenchiku.* 30 October 1927 was the final date for submissions and the results were announced on 1 December 1927.

In total 114 entries were submitted in Osaka, from Manchuria, Korea, and Japan, and "it was particularly pleasing to receive an entry from the Bauhaus in Dessau"; Max Bill was the only foreign participant from the West.[287]

"Max Bill, Dessau, Bauhaus" was awarded third prize, which came with prize money of 20 yen. A few months later, the magazine published Bill's proposal along with a glowing review of his work.

"Max Bill, who came at the third place of the third prize, was an unusual overseas entrant. This must be the first incident in which a Westerner submitted to a design competition organized in Japan. It is understood that Mr. Mizutani, who is currently studying at Bauhaus, contributed the Japanese on his drawing."[288]

The report on Max Bill's entry, written in a very traditional style, was published in the magazine *Shinkenchiku* in 1928, was translated into German by Riyoko Probala and translated into English by Atsuko Bill.

When he first heard of the competition Max Bill had immediately been keen to enter and produced a strikingly meticulous proposal on a scale of 1:200 for what the magazine described as a "business establishing building" in the Chuo-Ku district of Osaka.

At that time the city of Osaka, which as yet had no high-rise buildings, was flourishing. Concrete was still regarded by the locals as an extremely unusual building material; most of the city was built from wood. As Shiina Taneo writes in the review (published in English), Max Bill did not resort to any tricks and the pleasing rationalism of his design called to mind the Bauhaus ethos. The ground floor "is dedicated to a bookshop and associated offices spaces"; on the next floor there was an apartment for the owner of the bookshop; the apartments in the floors above would

287 Shiina Taneo: [Results of the competition for business building organized by *Shinkenchiku* magazine] *Shinkenchiku* (The Japan Architect), 4:2 (1928), p. 56

288 Taneo, [Results of the competition], p. 56

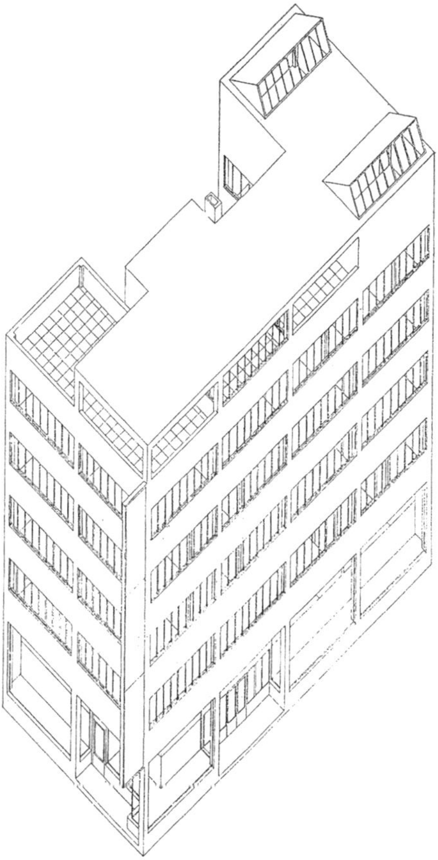

參等當選圖案　透視圖

マツクス・ビル君作品

—【46】—

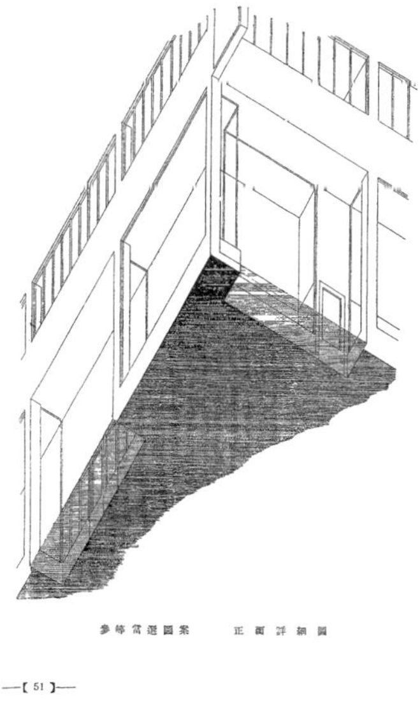

參等當選圖案　正面詳細圖

—【51】—

Max Bill, Facsimile of drawings for a five-story building with roof terrace in Osaka, 1927

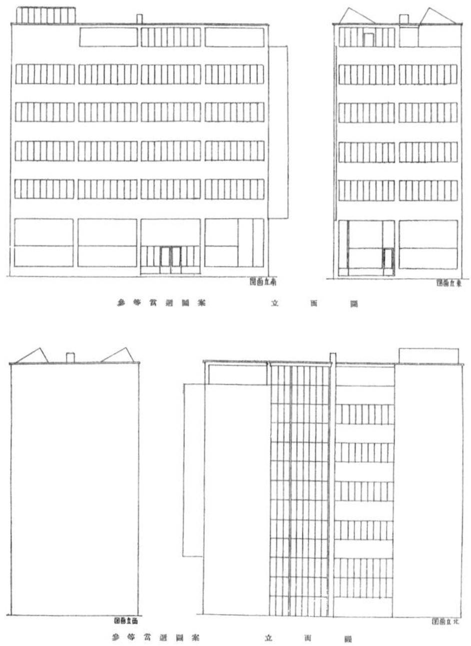

Max Bill, Facsimile of drawings for a five-story building with roof terrace in Osaka, 1927

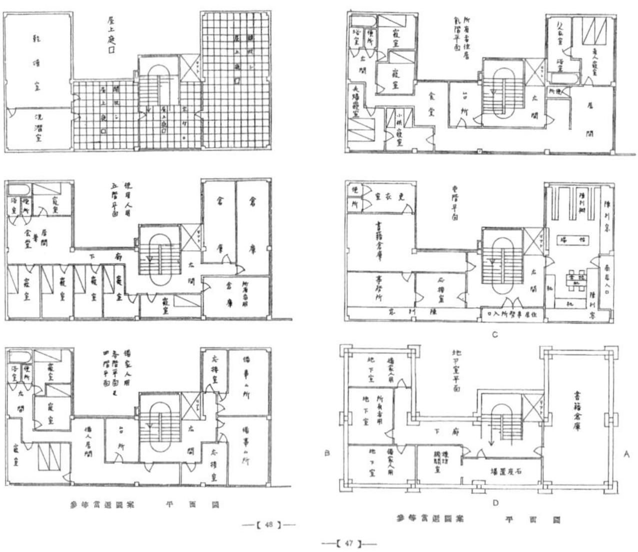

be available for rent. These were designed to accommodate a married couple with three children and a domestic servant—presumably rather too generous for the Japanese client. "The staircase and landing is well laid out. The drawing presents some distinctive ideas: installing display windows on the entire area of the two sections of the building facing a street; placing a reception room behind a display window benefiting from natural lighting coming through it; and installing retail signage in the most effective position."[289] Nothing comparable was seen in any of the other competition entries.

Bill's submission (in English) also specifies other aspects of the building: "retail signage. the projected wall for retail signage will be fitted on the exterior, made with milk-white glass, lit from inside. space above the doorway will be used for signage." The new building, located on a sloping site, was to be constructed from aerated concrete blocks with an outer coating of cork. Naturally it was designed to withstand fire and earthquakes. Bill, with help from Takehiko Mizutani (a fellow student at the Bauhaus), added various remarks to his list of building materials, such as the need for a coating on the steel sections to prevent them rusting:

> building structure
> steel-frame
> external walls: steel panel "zellbeton" + (air filled cavity) +
> cork panel + (air filled cavity) + steel frame
> basic frame: reinforced concrete . . .
> all the rooms are thoughtfully laid out for practical use,
> and particular attention is paid to allow daylight in each room.
> construction specifications
> lift: goes through all floors
> window frames: z-shape steel and crystal glass
> doors: steel
> staircases and corridors: ribbed rubber lining
> office and residential space: linoleum lining

Mizutani painstakingly inserted the Japanese specifications into Bill's very detailed drawings using a brush and ink. In a spirit of collegial solidarity he not only translated the competition remit for Bill, he also translated Bill's specifications into Japanese.

289 Taneo, [Results of the competition], p. 56

It was probably also Takehito Mizutani, who attended Josef Albers's foundation course with Max Bill, who alerted Bill to the architecture competition in the magazine *Shinkenchiku.* Mizutani, whose matriculation number was 150 (Max Bill's was 151), enrolled at the Bauhaus in Dessau in April 1927.[290]

A particularly striking feature of Bill's competition entry is that it has a partial roof terrace; the rest of the top level is roofed over and has two raised windows. His proposal provides for a laundry on this level, where washing can be dried out in the open air, even under a starry sky, far away from the street.

As my Japanese friend Riyoko Probala assured me, in those days Bill's inclusion of a roof garden in his proposal would have been "very unusual." At that time Japanese women everywhere would still have washed their laundry in the open air at a public well.

Much later on Bill returned to this (unrealized) idea of a partially covered roof terrace in his design for an apartment block with an integrated cinema, Cinevox, in Neuhausen am Rheinfall (Switzerland)—in effect recycling his own earlier idea.

Like Bill, Takehiko Mizutani attended the preliminary course run by Josef Albers at the Bauhaus, which later became world famous for the tasks he set, such as his "exercises in stability and construction from one sheet without wastage, using positive and negative motion. Paper-based tasks of this kind can be fully explained by the aims Albers was pursuing in his preliminary course teaching, but there is no easy explanation for the work Mizutani produced. Even his choice of material was more testing; rather than working with a simple, readily available, cheap material such as paper, he took brass discs, cut them and rolled them in on themselves. Mathematically exact arcs give rise to free curves with great aesthetic appeal. The articulation around a single axis and the distribution of spatial volumes into an upper and a lower section produces an attractive opposition of two equal yet unequal parts of a whole."[291] Josef Albers was so impressed by the way that Mizutani had "changed the properties of a material by bending it" that he showed this piece at the Bauhaus exhibition in New York in 1938 "as one of the few three-dimensional examples of his preliminary coursework" and in 1967 he left it to the Bauhaus-Archiv in Berlin as an exhibit.[292]

290 Wingler 1962, p. 534
291 Schaarschmidt 2003, p. 21
292 See Wollsdorff 1988, p. 28
293 Fiedler and Feierabend 1999, p. 377
294 Hin Bredendieck, "Vorkurs und Entwurf," *form + zweck,* 11:3 (1979), p. 63

This object by Mizutani has a formal assurance and sweeping elegance that is not so very different to the sculptures—with their subversive sheen—that Bill would later make. Bill's sculptures were also made from metal, which was then gilded in a specially made tank. Takehiko Mizutani and Max Bill were kindred spirits—they were both "different" to the other students.

Mizutani's work only survives in a small number of illustrations in European publications. The metal objects illustrated here are also lost. "Calibrated toward a precisely determined center of gravity, this piece by Mizutani is both elegant and dynamic. The concentration on the intrinsic nature of the material is characteristic of many of the items produced during Albers's preliminary course: a working method that in effect allows the material to speak for itself."[293]

Against Excessive Individualism

On 14 October 1927 Béla Bartók gave a piano recital at the Bauhaus, and on 29 November 1927 Adolf Busch (violin) and Rudolf Serkin (piano) presented a program of works by Mozart, Beethoven, and Busoni. It is highly likely that Max Bill, with his active interest in music, would not have missed either of those concerts.

Following his return to Switzerland from the Bauhaus, Max Bill made contact with two former students of Ferruccio Busoni: Robert Blum, who would become a fellow-performer at the "semi-political" cabaret theater, the Krater, and Wladimir Vogel—to whom we will return in due course. Hin Bredendieck, the source of this quote, studied at the Bauhaus in Dessau from 1927 to 1930.

At the end of the obligatory preliminary course with Albers, "each student displayed his or her work, which was then assessed by the entire teaching staff to determine whether the student demonstrated sufficient ability to continue studying at the Bauhaus. There were no grades given."[294] A photograph has survived of a work made by Max Bill when he was a preliminary course student, although it looks more like a response to a task set by Moholy-Nagy than one set by Albers. As teachers Moholy and Albers shared one important ideological principle: they had no time for any hint of excessive individualism.

"Albers and Moholy were united in their rejection of excessive individualism. Rather than expressing the sentiments of its maker, their art was first and foremost intended to provide an "enlightening" experience for the viewer."[295]

And Bill, having gladly taken on board their teaching, would later on always reject any form of excessive individualism, any overdone introspection—of the kind seen, for example, in the floods of images produced by the so-called Neue Wilde artists.

Bill was not able to study in the architecture department at the Bauhaus, as he had so dearly wished, because he had no relevant training, for instance as an architectural draftsman. In October 1927 he received a letter from the director, Walter Gropius, setting out his future direction: "At today's admissions meeting you were approved for entry to the second semester. It was agreed that it is particularly important for your ongoing training that you engage in practical work and tasks. Please inform us forthwith which workshop you intend to join."[296]

In the Metal Workshop at the Bauhaus

Under László Moholy-Nagy's guidance the metal workshop at the Bauhaus was the first workshop to produce affordable designs.

"Moholy was put in charge of the Metal Workshop. . . . Under his tutelage this became the first workshop to achieve the goal of affordable and economically viable Bauhaus design."[297]

Max later told me that Moholy-Nagy had instructed him to make pieces designed by Marianne Brandt (née Liebe). Brandt, who had married the Norwegian artist Erik Brandt in 1919, enrolled in the preliminary course at the Bauhaus in Weimar in 1923 and, on the express advice of Moholy-Nagy, subsequently joined the metal workshop. During her training at the Bauhaus in Weimar Brandt had already designed some exceptionally beautiful items, including the legendary tea and coffee service, which now fetches huge prices at auction. However, as a woman working with metal she was still very much the exception to the rule, and her male colleagues in Dessau initially liked to remind her of this: "At first I wasn't exactly welcomed with open arms; people felt that the metal workshop was

295 Borchardt-Hume 2006, p. 74
296 Walter Gropius, Bauhaus, Dessau, to Max Bill, 13 October 1927, Bibliothek Max Bill
297 Borchardt-Hume 2006, p. 69

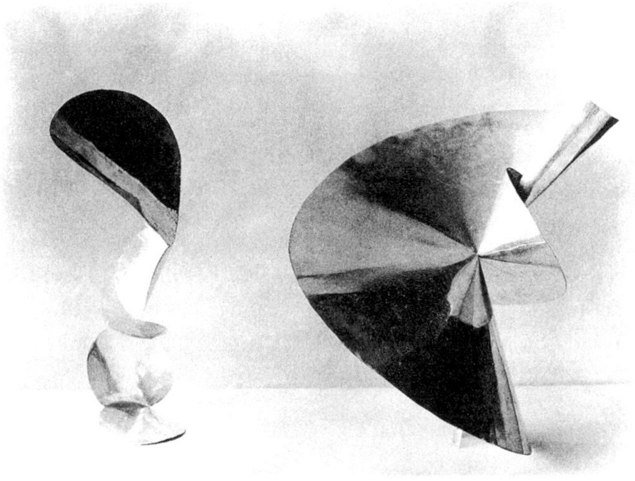

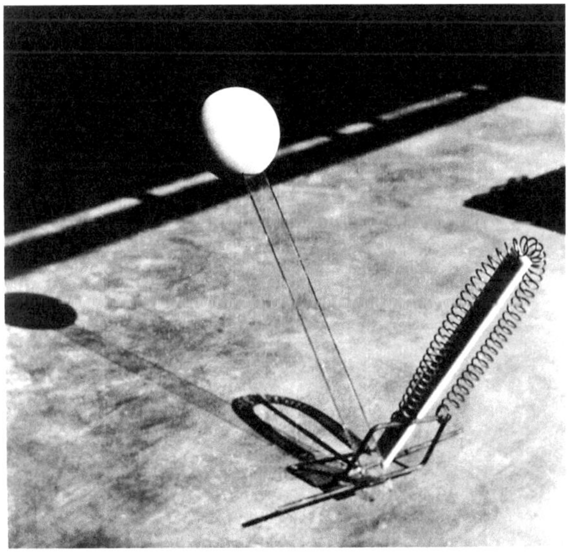

Takehito Mizutani, Plastic-dynamic assignment for Albers's preliminary course, 1926–27, metal discs, cut and rolled, freestanding

Max Bill, Balance exercise for Albers's preliminary course (Challenge: Combine any number of materials), 1927–28

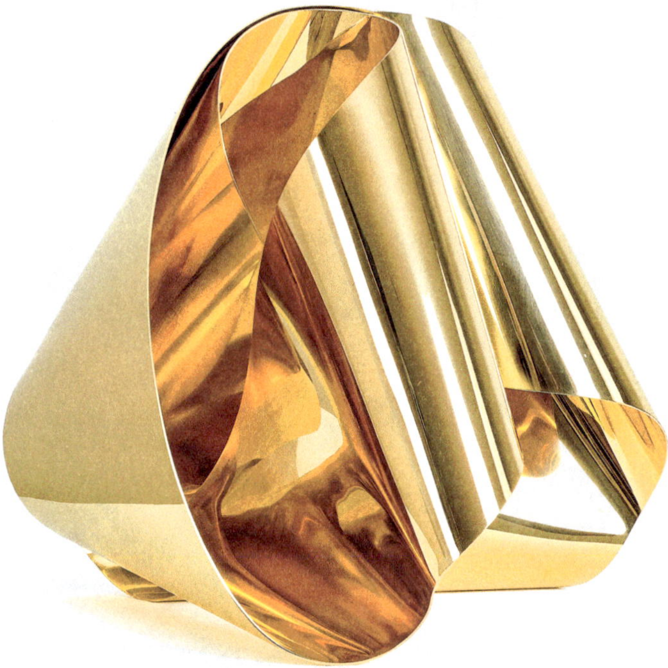

Max Bill, *Kontinuität,* 1946/1982, gold-plated polished copper, 41×36×48cm

not the place for a woman. And they showed me how they felt by mainly giving me boringly tedious tasks."[298]

At the new Bauhaus in Dessau four ex-Weimar Bauhaus students, all outstanding artist-craftsmen, were appointed as masters: Josef Albers as head of the preliminary course, Herbert Bayer as head of the newly constituted typography and advertising department, Marcel Breuer as head of the wall painting workshop, and Joost Schmidt as head of the advertising workshop; Schmidt subsequently became head of the sculpture workshop and succeeded Herbert Bayer in 1928.

Bayer was born in Austria in 1900. He studied painting at the Bauhaus under Kandinsky and became a master at the Bauhaus in Dessau, where he taught typography and layout from 1925 to 1928. Bill, in his later years at least, did not speak very well of Bayer. In 1980 we ran into him in the Bonaventure Hotel in Los Angeles, where we were attending a prize ceremony to which Ray Eames, who was receiving an award, had invited Max Bill and myself.

The workshops "were in the most modern part of the building, the wing with a large glass façade: the stage, printing, dyeing, and sculpture workshops were all on the lower ground floor; the carpentry workshop was on the ground floor, with weaving and the preliminary course on the first floor and wall painting and the metal workshop on the second floor. The latter had modern machines and apparatuses," which made it possible to produce bespoke items and to "equip the masters" houses with metal furniture, lights, and such like."[299]

Marianne Brandt arrived in Dessau in April 1927—the same month that Bill enrolled on Josef Albers's preliminary course. Marianne Brandt joined the metal workshop as an assistant and in April 1928 she became its "deputy head."

In the *Dessauer Kalender 1977* there are illustrations of the spherical pendant lamp (1926) by Marianne Brandt (p. 86) and of the rise-and-fall pendant reflector lamp (1926) by Marianne Brandt and H. Przyrembel (p. 87). Ulla Machlitt and Hans Harksen identified a number of contracts fulfilled in Dessau and the surroundings by bauhaus staff and students; however, as they point out, "unfortunately in most cases no photographs have survived." The real financial breakthrough came in 1928, when "for the first time the workshops took in the planned profit of 10,000 marks. That was no doubt due to the steel furniture and the luminaires."[300]

298 Brandt 2001, p. 46
299 Machlitt and Harksen 1977, pp. 76–87
300 Machlitt and Harksen 1977, p. 78

By that time, however, Bill no longer had anything to do with the metal workshop and Brandt because he did not at all like the metalwork tasks he was set. "I had trained as a silversmith so I was channelled into the metal department. But I left that metalwork class again within a relatively short space of time; I just didn't go any more. At the time the head of the metalwork class was Moholy-Nagy, a Hungarian Constructivist artist, still very young; when I stopped going ... he asked me what was up. So I said I wasn't interested in attending metalwork classes any more. He invited me to come and see him—and I have to say he immediately understood why I didn't want to do that any more, so I joined the stagecraft class."[301] Could it be that, having almost completed his apprenticeship as a silversmith, Max Bill felt it was beneath his dignity to make objects designed by Marianne Brandt? Was it male pride? The main reason for Bill's behavior may in fact have been his disappointment at not being admitted to the newly opened architecture department with Hannes Meyer at the helm. However, although he was not officially an architecture student, Bill did—of his own accord, already in his first semester—attend lectures in Meyer's department, "mainly on building construction, structures, and town planning."[302]

Although Bill certainly balked at the tasks he was set in the metal workshop, the time he spent in proximity to the politically radical Bauhaus master Moholy-Nagy did leave its mark on the young rebel wrestling with feelings of frustration. It is a well-known fact that any mental processing takes time and does not necessarily synchronize with external events—indeed it usually follows at some later stage. Looking back at that time, Bill wrote in a curriculum vitae: "I tried working in the metal workshop again, but that kind of work no longer appealed to me, I knew new ways of doing things, I didn't want the old ways any more; that was when I started drawing and painting again."[303]

301 Max Bill in Scheidegger 1998
302 Bill 1942 [b]
303 Bill [ca. 1930]
304 See *Kassák Lajos 1887–1967* 1987, pp. 20–22

An Extremely Keen Eye

Walter Gropius appointed László Moholy-Nagy as a Bauhaus master in Weimar in 1923. Lucia Moholy, his wife, who had a gift for languages, an unusually sharp intellect, and intense light blue eyes, had studied art history and philosophy in Prague. However, in Dessau, where she was neither a Bauhaus student nor a member of staff, she found herself cast solely in the role of Moholy-Nagy's wife.

Even before the Moholy-Nagys arrived in Dessau, Lucia had been photographing her husband's work, which she continued to do. With an extremely keen eye and her own interest in the subject matter she also documented changes at the Bauhaus over the course of five years, first in Weimar and then in Dessau. In 1926 Lucia Moholy set up her own photographic laboratory and started to develop her own striking images of the new Bauhaus buildings; she also photographed new items produced in the workshops. Without her immensely skilled photographs of Bauhaus objects—images that in effect serve as a quality mark, tested and approved—there would have been no visual reception history of the Bauhaus as we know it.

Lucia and László Moholy-Nagy first met in Berlin in April 1920. László had arrived in Berlin with a letter of recommendation to Herwarth Walden.

Walden's real name was Georg Levin; his father was a physician and his mother a Rosenthal by birth. In the late 1920s, when Hannes Meyer was director of the Bauhaus in Dessau, Ernst Kállai became editor-in-chief of *bauhaus;* he later corresponded with Max Bill.

In 1913 Walden had presented an exhibition in Budapest, during which he established personal contact with a number of Hungarian artists, notably Lajos Kassák.

Kassák arrived in Berlin in November 1922. He came with his wife, the actress Jolán Simon, "who was a very persuasive advocate for avant-garde poetry."[304]

As editor of the avant-garde, leftist Hungarian magazine *MA,* Kassák was a committed anti-militarist. Due to various political developments, in 1920 the magazine had to relocate to Vienna. Moholy-Nagy, who signed Nell and Herwarth Walden's guestbook on 27 April 1920, was to be the representative for *MA* in Germany. Ernst Kállai, who was also in Berlin at the time, wrote reviews for *MA.* At that time Herwarth Walden's gallery in Berlin was directly opposite a bookshop, Buchhandlung Twardy, which also displayed art. A young Russian woman who worked in the bookshop remembered often seeing Moholy-Nagy there; another regular visitor was Wassily Kandinsky.

"Moholy-Nagy, who seemed rather conceited to me, complimented me in his drawling Hungarian accent; Kandinsky spoke Russian with me."[305]

Lucia and László Moholy-Nagy married in Berlin in January 1921; a year later, in 1922, Moholy-Nagy had his first solo exhibition at the Sturm gallery, which was also the same year that the first ever exhibition of Russian art (*Erste Russische Kunstausstellung*) was presented in Berlin. Lajos Kassák was keen to see that exhibition, so Moholy-Nagy and Ernst Kállai prepared a program for his visit.

Kassák and his wife, Jolán Simon, met Herwarth Walden and artists in his circle within a few days of their arrival. "These important encounters partly came about so quickly because Moholy-Nagy's studio and the Sturm gallery (where the Kassáks must have regularly looked in) were well-established meeting places for Berlin's avant-garde writers and artists."[306] In the Moholy-Nagy household in Berlin Lucia was the breadwinner, thanks to her employment at Ernst Rowohlt's publishing house. This changed when László became a master at the Bauhaus in Weimar in 1923; shortly before his appointment he had already started planning the enamel paintings that later became so famous.

In his gallery and shop, Der Sturm, in Potsdamer Strasse, Herwarth Walden had a reading room with newspapers and magazines. Every Wednesday there was a cabaret show, followed by a dance with a live jazz band.[307] Visitors to the gallery might also come across the Russian artist El Lissitzky, who was working on his *Proun* compositions at the time. The word *Proun* derives from the Russian "pro-UNOVIS," meaning "project for the advancement of the new." Lissitzky himself declared that "*Proun* is where painting changes trains for architecture."

Lissitzky's experimental *Proun* compositions—with planes and bodies that appear to be floating in space, often seen at an angle from above—were all part of his search for new creative tools. And, to cite the Dutch architect Mart Stam, who met Lissitzky in Berlin, these compositions made an extraordinarily powerful, spatial impact. They created the impression of things hovering in space, rather than standing or being fixed somewhere. There was no longer "any above or any below."[308]

Mart Stam arrived at the Bauhaus in Dessau as a visiting professor of town planning and elementary building theory in mid-1928 and stayed until 1929; Max Bill attended lectures by Stam.

305 Liessner-Blomberg 1990, pp. 336–37
306 See *Kassák Lajos 1887–1967* 1987
307 See Brühl 1983
308 Stam 1976, p. 394

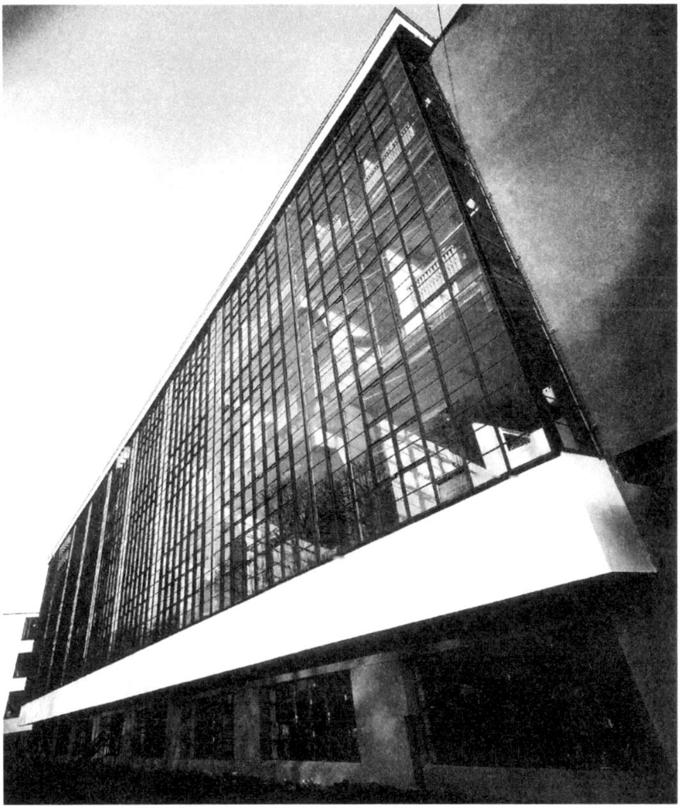

Lucia Moholy, *Bauhaus Dessau,* ca. 1925

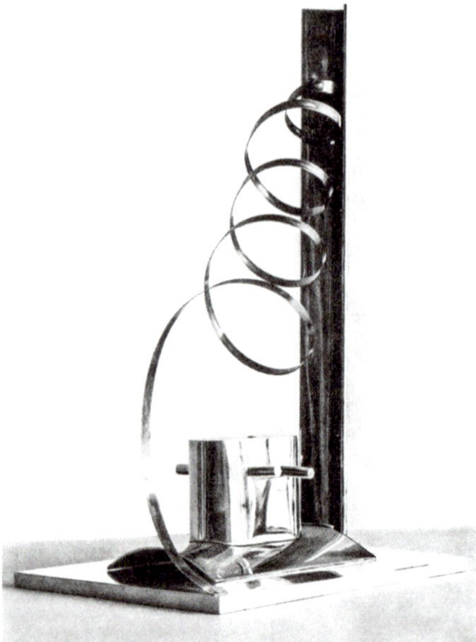

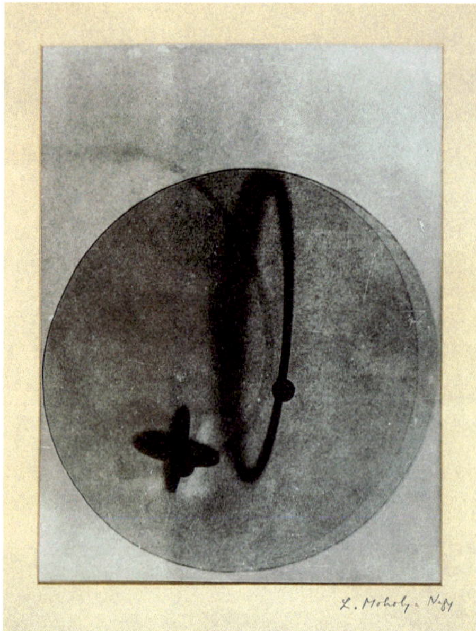

László Moholy-Nagy, *Nickel-Plastik,* 1921, metal, welded, 35.9 × 17.5 × 23.8 cm

László Moholy-Nagy, *Fotogramm (positiv),* 1924, photogram on paper, 39.7 × 29.7 cm

Lissitzky, who had a studio in a Berlin attic, participated in the *Grosse Berliner Kunst-Ausstellung* in 1923, which was also the year when hyperinflation led to banknotes being issued with a face value of 100 billion Reichsmarks.

When his day's work was done Lissitzky either went to the Romanisches Café or to see Moholy-Nagy, "whose clever wife Lucia took a great interest in her husband's theoretical writings and was a great help to him. Raoul Hausmann, Hannah Höch, Hans Richter, and Werner Graeff would meet up there in his studio—talking, planning, eagerly devouring all the latest ideas and taking them further, each according to his or her talents."[309]

"Moholy-Nagy has been in Berlin since 1921 [in fact since 1920], where his studio has become a meeting place for the international avant-garde; El Lissitzky is often there. He is young, full of ideas and enthusiasm, undogmatic and open-minded; above all he is keen to absorb and pass on anything new. El Lissitzky is thus another creative catalyst at the Bauhaus. Moholy-Nagy, who has replaced Johannes Itten [in March 1923 at the Bauhaus in Weimar] is taking over Itten's foundation course; he will also be head of the metal workshop and oversee printed materials for the Bauhaus exhibition. Moholy-Nagy's clear, objective attitude has ousted Itten's emotional approach."[310]

Another visitor to Moholy-Nagy's Berlin studio, the artist Werner Graeff remembered the impression Lissitzky made in Berlin at the time: "small, slight, mobile, nippy, often impatient.... Lissitzky had very lively, restless dark eyes and a quick, sharp mind. He worked very deftly and cleanly. He already had trouble with his lungs by then; he often coughed and generally talked in a quiet voice. Like Gabo, he could also speak German."[311]

During his time in Berlin, Moholy-Nagy became friends not only with Lissitzky but also with Jean Arp and Kurt Schwitters. But he was particularly close to Lissitzky: "Moholy instinctively embraced the leftist-orientated notion of art as a contributing force to social reform. His position at this point was close to that of other avant-garde artists such as Theo van Doesburg and El Lissitzky who defined 'art, just as much as science and technology, as a method for organizing life in general.' However, Moholy soon became frustrated with the rhetorical rivalries among his peers, especially their paranoid protestations of 'originality,' and criticized their self-centered debate as bourgeois and elitist. This criticism

309 Lissitzky-Küppers 1976, p. 22

310 Nonne-Schmidt 1984 [c], p. 19

311 Werner Graeff, in Richter 1958, unpaginated

coincided with his taking up a position at the Bauhaus, whose principal ambition was to further social progress by making good design affordable to a wider public."[312]

When Lissitzky and his partner Sophie Küppers visited the Bauhaus in Dessau and went to see Paul Klee and Wassily Kandinsky in their masters' houses they were—as Ingeborg Prior puts it—"fascinated by the simplicity and functionality of the houses designed by Gropius." By contrast, the writer Ilja Ehrenburg, who accompanied them on that occasion, found everything boring.[313]

Ehrenburg made a note: "... in Dessau ... the Bauhaus—the school for modern art. A glass building. The style of our epoch has been found: the cult of dry reason. The architect Gropius's home is filled with knobs and levers; laundry shoots through pneumatic tubes, plates sidle out of the kitchen into the dining room. Everything is perfectly thought through, even the buckets. Everything is immaculate and unimaginably boring ... in the home of Kandinsky, the painter, there are a few concessions to art: Novgorod School icons, landscapes by Rousseau Le Douanier."[314]

To judge by a photograph of Lissitzky at the Bauhaus in Weimar in 1923—assuming the date on the photograph is correct—it would seem that he was already interested in the Bauhaus in its earliest phase.

In 1928 Lissitzky was commissioned to design the Soviet pavilion at the international press exhibition, *Pressa,* in Cologne, which was why he was traveling in Europe that year. First he went to Cologne "to install designs by numerous Soviet artists," following which he made his way to the Bauhaus in Dessau—there is no knowing if Max Bill caught sight of him there in 1928—and then on to Paris, "where he used Ehrenburg's camera to take photographs of the city."[315]

During that visit to Dessau—by which time Hannes Meyer had been appointed director of the Bauhaus—Lissitzky participated in an event that was subsequently described as an "informal conversation on modern architecture and student assignments with particular reference to the Bauhaus and VKhUTEMAS, the Russian state institute in Moscow." And a month later, during the week of 2–9 November, there was a series of four lectures by another avant-garde pioneer, the Soviet artist Naum

312 Borchardt-Hume 2006, p. 74
313 Prior 2002, p. 116
314 From Ilja Ehrenburg's memoirs, cited in Prior 2002, p. 116
315 Tupitsyn 1999, p. 227
316 *bauhaus,* zeitschrift für gestaltung 3:1 (January 1929), p. 25
317 Borchart-Hume 2006, p. 28

Gabo. At Gabo's first talk, "Bauhaus members became acquainted with his Constructivist sculptures, their principles, and aims." These visits from Lissitzky and Gabo, both of whom also spoke German, were listed in the January 1929 issue of *bauhaus* in the section "Events at the Bauhaus," which summarized the most important events during the previous quarter.[316] Given that Max Bill only "officially" left the Bauhaus in October or November 1928, it is entirely possible that he attended those lectures on topics that were of the greatest interest to him.

The photograph of Lissitzky at the Bauhaus in Weimar is illustrated in Margarita Tupitsyn, *El Lissitzky jenseits der Abstraktion* (Munich: Schirmer and Mosel, 1999), p. 226; the same publication also contains a portrait photograph taken by Josef Albers, with the caption "El Lissitzky, bauhaus 1928." The latter may have been taken during Lissitzky's visit to Dessau, mentioned by Ingeborg Prior, when he was accompanied by Sophie Küppers and Ilja Ehrenburg. It seems that on that visit Lissitzky met not only Klee and Kandinsky, but also Josef Albers with his camera at the ready.

A recent publication[317] includes a whole series of photographs of "El Lissitzky at the Bauhaus" taken by Albers. However, the dates given are a rather vague 1928–30. Albers appears to have been on very direct, uncomplicatedly trusting terms with El Lissitzky. Whatever the case, his portrait photographs of the visiting professor depict a relaxed, sensitive, humorous colleague.

Walter Gropius and His Bauhaus Colleagues

Most of the masters that Walter Gropius appointed at the Bauhaus in Weimar, which opened in 1919, had already exhibited at Herwarth Walden's gallery (Der Sturm) in Berlin. Besides Moholy-Nagy, there were Johannes Itten, Wassily Kandinsky, Georg Muche, Oskar Schlemmer, Lothar Schreyer, Lyonel Feininger, and Paul Klee. The writer Walter Mehring later remembered an encounter with Paul Klee in Walden's gallery: "When I saw him for the first time at Walden's gallery, he and I were both wearing remnants from His Majesty's service, berets and faded, baggy foot-soldiers' jackets; one as gauche as the other. . . . I looked at him standing there, unspeaking, next to the rather dandyish, myopic Herwarth Walden, who was talking animatedly to him. . . . I would not have recognized Klee, were it not for his eyes—that dual gaze, far and wide, the same as in his paintings. In Weimar Lyonel Feininger twice took me to see him. They were close friends—close through their love of Bach's music, ghost ships, gable ends in old towns ... both shy, both taciturn—they haltingly discussed a few well-worn Bauhaus topics."[318] Meanwhile, Walter Mehring described Lyonel Feininger, an American citizen, as "lanky, long-legged, elastic, and willowy, with a sharp greyhound's nose, a pointed chin, and finely drawn lips, firmly closed yet gentle."[319] Lothar Schreyer, who observed Feininger at the home of Nell and Herwarth Walden, described him as a silent cigar smoker with a "noble" face.

"Lyonel Feininger sat in an armchair, saying nothing. But he was positioned in such a way that the rest of us sat around him and he was the real center of things, the hub of a wheel with the spokes turning around it."[320]

Lyonel Feininger died in his eighties, on 13 January 1956, just two blocks away from where he had been born, near the honky-tonks of Manhattan. As the obituary in the *New York Times* stated, he was survived by his second wife, Julia (they married in 1908), their three sons, Andreas—a photographer for *Life* magazine—Theodore, and Laurence, and two daughters from his first marriage, Lore Feininger and Marianne Noack.

Like a number of other Bauhaus masters, Feininger moved from Weimar to Dessau, where he and his family shared a master's house with the Moholy-Nagys. Feininger only made that move after some hesitation; he was uneasy about the ill feeling between Johannes Itten and Walter Gropius in Weimar. Lyonel Feininger, born in New York in 1871 to German parents who were both professional musicians, already had a career as a caricaturist and cartoonist behind him. His cartoons—often quite unrestrained—could be absurdly anarchic and witty. He was employed as a comic-strip artist by the *Chicago Tribune,* partly because Chicago had a large community with German roots. His comic strip, the *Kin-der-Kids,* which first appeared in late April 1906, featured "the adventures of Daniel Webster the bookworm, Pie-Mouth the boy with the huge appetite, and the incredibly strong Strenuous Teddy, all of whom—hunted by, among others, Aunt Jim-Jam, with her family-sized bottle of

318 Mehring 1965, pp. 88–89
319 Mehring 1965, p. 61
320 Schreyer 1956, p. 132
321 Christian Gasser, "In der Badewanne um die Welt. Der Künstler Lyonel Feininger als Comic-Zeichner," in *Neue Zürcher Zeitung,* 26 February 2004
322 Schreyer 1956, p. 238
323 See "C. J. Jucker, Lampen 1923–24," special issue of *tropi,* 132, 1978

castor oil—sail around the world in an old bathtub from the Arctic Ocean via England to Siberia, where they are taken for spies and end up in goal."[321] In Dessau Feininger was often seen on his bicycle, as were the aristocratic-looking Kandinskys, who were both avid cyclists—to some people's surprise. Director Gropius, on the other hand, preferred to swish through the town in his limousine.

In this obituary Lyonel Feininger, the son of German immigrants, was described as the "most famous of the American expressionists" (*New York Times,* 14 January 1956). Mention is made of this in the exhibition catalogue *Lyonel Feininger. Menschenbilder. Eine unbekannte Welt,* Hamburger Kunsthalle (Ostfildern-Ruit: Hatje Cantz, 2003), p. 138.

Alma Mahler-Werfel, Walter Gropius's first wife (1915–20), had written imploringly to the Feiningers: "It gives me such comfort that you are there in Weimar—at the Bauhaus, with Gropius. You mustn't leave him. Hold out. Take a long vacation, but remain true to the project that you co-founded. Your friend, Alma Maria" (Alma Mahler-Werfel to Lyonel and Julia Feininger, 3 July 1922).

There are many intriguing accounts of the people at the Bauhaus and their very diverse characters. Lothar Schreyer, for example, a master at the Bauhaus in Weimar who did not make the move to Dessau, had a poor impression of Moholy-Nagy: "Moholy-Nagy brought a new world into the Bauhaus—entirely alien—which seemed to pose a threat to us. The leading apprentices and journeymen in Weimar wanted nothing to do with him, not as an artist but as a person."[322] Schreyer specifically made the point that it was Moholy-Nagy's persona, not his art, that was at issue. Moholy-Nagy, a very young Bauhaus master, was uncompromisingly avant-garde in his art production. However, Carl J. Jucker—a Swiss student at the Bauhaus—responded very differently to a photograph of Moholy-Nagy with students in the metal workshop in 1924: "The students said he didn't so much teach them as give them the feeling of living and working with him."[323]

Born in Zurich in the early twentieth century, Carl J. Jucker had completed an apprenticeship as a silversmith in the metal course at the Kunstgewerbeschule in Zurich—as Max Bill would do a few years later. Since he found no work at all because of the financial crisis that was already very much making itself felt in Switzerland in the early 1920s, he spent 1923–25 as a student at the Bauhaus, where he studied under Paul Klee, Oskar Schlemmer and László Moholy-Nagy.

Eleonore "Lore" Hertzberger, née Katz, whose father launched the journal *International Textiles,* the most important trade magazine for the textile business, wrote of her father's respect for Moholy-Nagy, whom he greatly admired. When Moholy-Nagy arrived in Amsterdam, having fled the Nazi regime, he was offered a position by her Austrian-born father, Ludwig Katz. Eleonore, who would become a notable resistance fighter, was photographed by Moholy-Nagy at the time; that black-and-white photograph is reproduced in her memoir.[324]

Ludwig Katz had a particular interest in typography and printing, and was an enthusiastic supporter of the functional aesthetics developed at the Bauhaus. "My father was particularly proud that he managed to appoint Professor Moholy-Nagy—a bauhaus pioneer—as the journal's art director.

Although he was only thirty years old, Moholy-Nagy already had gray hair and wore spectacles as thick as magnifying glasses because he was so very short-sighted. I have very clear memories of the way he always used to push his spectacles up into his hair so that he could hold whatever he was looking at right up to his eyes."[325]

Following a short stay in Brussels when he was working at the 1935 world's fair, Moholy-Nagy traveled on to England and ultimately emigrated to the United States—all countries where he, a Hungarian by birth, would have difficulties with the language.

According to Lothar Schreyer a "farcical incident" occurred soon after Moholy-Nagy was appointed, which "set in motion the course of events that was so painful to us all: unfortunately Moholy-Nagy had some difficulty speaking German. That in itself was not a reason for our discomfort, but it did exacerbate the situation. At any rate, late one afternoon as it was starting to get dark Moholy-Nagy arrived at the Bauhaus completely distraught and out of breath, and blurted out a sentence that we somehow managed to disentangle: 'Hi wanted to have mi back with a rivolvir!' It turned out that on the short walk through the park to the Bauhaus, Moholy-Nagy had become seriously convinced that a man was following him with a gun aimed at his back. We all had a good laugh. Unfortunately, news of this episode spread through the Bauhaus like wildfire."[326]

Looking back years later Lucia Moholy, Moholy-Nagy's closest confidante during his time at the Bauhaus, wrote a brief, precisely, formulated account of that period in an effort to demystify the Moholy-Nagy myth. She set out her own personal memories of Moholy-Nagy:

324 Hertzberger 1993, illustration section
325 Hertzberger 1993, pp. 20–21
326 Schreyer 1956, pp. 238–39
327 Moholy 1972, pp. 10–11

"By nature he had strong instincts, he was unwaveringly intuitive, and had an unusual capacity to absorb ideas and to take rapid action. He abandoned a law degree (he did not complete it, contrary to what people have been saying) and instead—alert, open-minded and ready to be enthused—just let things happen. Whenever, wherever, and in whatever circumstances a spark leapt across to him it could instigate a process that would captivate him, set him on fire, and sweep him along with it. He had scant interest in the methodical study of scholarly, let alone scientific literature; he mainly left that to those who were better suited to it. And 'the treasure trove of technological utopias buried in the footnotes in the Bauhaus book *Malerei, Photographie, Film*' that [Otto] Stelzer referred to in his afterword to the re-issue of that book (in 1967), was the outcome of a collective effort. At that time Moholy-Nagy's overriding concern was that any statements he made should be incisive, he had no interest in convoluted thought processes. German did not come easily to him. However, that was not an issue in his personal interaction with others. He used words and sentence structures of his own making, which—despite often not being correct—were nevertheless immensely expressive and allowed him to exchange views, to discuss things, to learn, to convince and to win others over to his ideas—always with an eye to today and tomorrow, never looking back at yesterday.... Moholy and I soon established a kind of symbiotic working relationship that helped to provide fertile ground for his abundant, burgeoning ideas."[327]

Lucia Moholy Remembers

In February 1985 Lucia Moholy, ninety-one years old, told me that she had deliberately kept her distance from Wassily Kandinsky's wife, Nina. Although, as she said, Nina—seemingly somewhat capricious—spoke warmly of the music scene in Dessau, Lucia did not feel at all comfortable living there, so far away from Berlin, the metropolis. On 5 May 1927, soon after the young Max Bill had arrived in Dessau, Lucia made a note in her diary: "Dessau is like a place you might find yourself in if you were traveling and had missed a connection and now had to wait for the next train. Just waiting for the next train. One would never have alighted from the train there otherwise." Remarkably, for all her disappointment Lucia was very active; she did not succumb to depression, and—with a better grasp of German than her Hungarian husband—she started to edit his theoretical texts. Moreover, inspired by activities at the Bauhaus, she developed her skills as a photographer to a professional level and she and László experimented with photograms.[328]

When Lucia, a Schulz by birth, was still living at home in the Prague suburb of Karlín, she spoke German to other members of the family and Czech to domestic servants. She went to a German-speaking girls' high school in Prague, where she also learned English and French, and gained her school leaving certificate in 1910. Her father was a lawyer, who championed the rights of Czechs in Prague, which was still under the rule of the Austro-Hungarian empire at that point. Her mother came from a German-speaking family. Having attended lectures in art history and philosophy and having done some work in her father's law office, in 1915 Lucia left home for Germany.

Despite Lucia Moholy's many talents and the outstanding photographs she took, the Bauhaus masters' council never offered her a position teaching photography. As she herself remarked with some regret, at the Bauhaus she was only ever seen as László's wife, whereas he was recognized by everyone as the great master. And yet, his photographic works, his photographs and photograms would never have come about without her input. But of course it was always a two-way process: "László ... was a very important person in [her] life."

On another occasion she pointed out that anyone coming into contact with László Moholy-Nagy during his time at the Bauhaus "very soon realized that he was one of those people who make barely any distinction between today and tomorrow, between being and becoming, wanting and doing. Those years at the Bauhaus presented the artist Moholy-Nagy with a wealth of new—very new—possibilities. At the same time, however, they were challenging years, years of dedication to teaching, which of course makes demands on the whole person."[329]

Lucia Moholy had been particularly close to the Austrian architect Franz Singer, who had been born into a Jewish family in Vienna in 1896. In 1917 Singer enrolled at a private art school in Vienna (set up by Johannes Itten), where he met Friedl Dicker, who was born in 1898. In 1919, when Itten went to the Bauhaus in Weimar, they both followed him there. Once they had completed the preliminary course Dicker went into the printing workshop and the textiles workshop and Singer worked toward a career as an architect. In 1925 Singer and Dicker opened a studio for architecture and interior design in Vienna. Lucia Moholy, who first met Franz Singer at the Bauhaus in Weimar, was—as she told me—"very close"

328 See Valdivieso 2000
329 Moholy 1972, p. 40

View from the Prellerhaus balcony. Foreground, from left: Anni Albers, Gunta Stölzl. Standing below, center: Max Bill. Seated below, from left: Bruno Streiff, Shlomoh Ben-David (Georg Gross), Gerda Marx, 1927

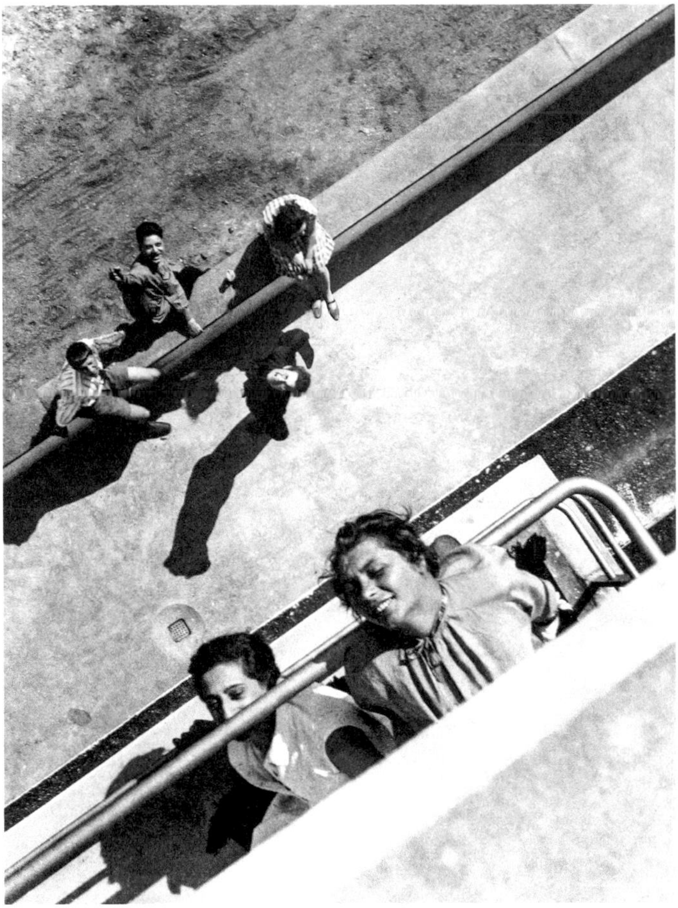

View from the Prellerhaus balcony at the Bauhaus in Dessau. Foreground, from left: Ursula Schneider, Anni Albers, Gunta Stölzl. Standing below: Max Bill, unidentified man. Seated below, from left: Bruno Streiff, Shlomoh Ben-David (Georg Gross), Gerda Marx, unidentified man, 1927

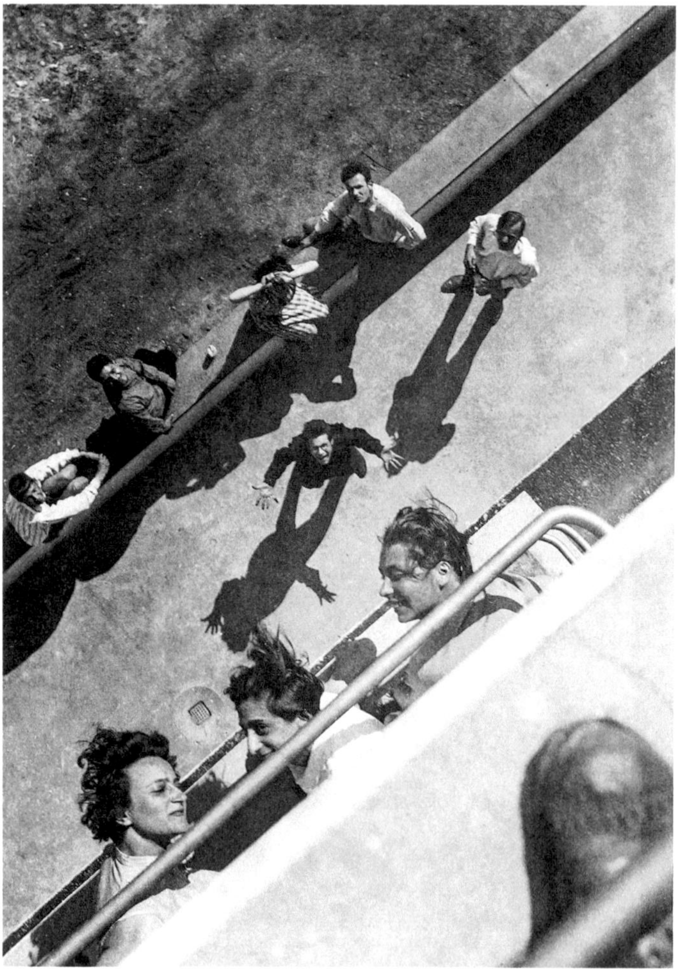

to him. Later on she photographed many of the buildings he designed in Vienna. "Franz Singer was one of the most talented Bauhaus people—but he was never showy."

"The spatial concepts devised by the collective practice run by Friedl Dicker and Franz Singer are among the most extraordinary artistic achievements of the Weimar Republic.... Their inspired stackable, foldable furniture adds a transformative dimension to any space."[330]

In 1921 Friedl Dicker took over the graphic design for the magazine *Utopia,* edited by Bruno Maria Adler, who published Johannes Itten's analyses of works by old masters that formed the basis of his preliminary course teaching at the Bauhaus. "In 1923 Itten's preliminary course and the influence of *Utopia* led to conflicts with Gropius, the Bauhaus director. Four years before the annexation of Austria, Singer emigrated to London. Lucia Moholy also fled to London, via Prague, as did László Moholy-Nagy somewhat later (independently of her, since the two were no longer living together). When László arrived Lucia helped him to find his feet there. Singer survived the war in England and died on his way to Berlin on 5 October 1954. 'The brilliant Jewish Singer–Adler group became too exuberant and unfortunately also seriously influenced Itten. They wanted to use that lever to take control of the whole Bauhaus.... It was clear to me that people like Singer and Adler should not be at the Bauhaus and at some point must leave if peace were to be restored.'"[331]

While Lucia Moholy, an intellectual by nature, certainly avoided Nina Kandinsky, it seems that this was a case of mutual mistrust; indeed in her memoirs Nina Kandinsky makes no mention at all of Lucia Moholy and there is only one brief reference to László Moholy-Nagy. There is little hint of human warmth in those few lines, when she reports that Kandinsky and Moholy-Nagy more or less remained "strangers to each other... with the result that we barely ever met privately."[332]

The Kandinskys lived in one half of a masters' house, at Burgkühnerallee 6–7, not far from the Bauhaus complex, and the Klees lived in the other half. The Feiningers and the Moholy-Nagys lived in the second masters' house and the third was home to the Muches and Oskar

330 Stephan Templ, "Wenn Vergangenheit Zukunft Bedeutet—eine Werkschau der Bauhausschülerin Friedl Dicker in Wien," in *Neue Zürcher Zeitung,* 9 November 1999, p. 68

331 Lucia Moholy, cited in Maasberg and Prinz 2004, p. 79 and note 63

332 Kandinsky 1976, p. 130

Schlemmer. All three, designed by Walter Gropius and located in a small, open wood with tall pine trees, were completed in late autumn 1926. Although the Muches were committed to the Mazdaznan movement, Georg Muche's very beautiful wife, Elsa, was always elegantly turned out. Walter Gropius also built a detached director's house for himself on the same avenue, which was subsequently destroyed during the Second World War, as was the Moholy-Nagy house. In 2014 these two houses were reinterpreted, rather than reconstructed, by the Berlin-based architects Bruno Fioretti Marquez, and are now open to the public.

Nina Kandinsky—unlike Lucia Moholy—never complained of the lack of cultural events in Dessau. She and her husband frequently went to the theater and to concerts: "Each season we took out a subscription for a box with the Klees in the Friedrich-Theater in Dessau, where there were also orchestral concerts.... Paul Klee regularly used to invite three members of the theater orchestra to play string quartets. There were also very high-quality concerts at the Bauhaus." The Kandinskys used to put on special parties in their home for New Year's Eve and Carnival. "Kandinsky only ever allowed himself to be persuaded to dance a waltz once a year, on New Year's Eve."[333]

"The landscape around Dessau was quite varied and inviting. We thoroughly investigated that landscape, exploring it on foot and on bicycles. We went on long walks through the Elbe plain, which Kandinsky loved for its blithe atmosphere, for its singular natural beauty and, above all, for the light. He felt at ease there ... each year we waited eagerly for the lilac trees to blossom in Dessau. Then we and the Klees would rent a two-horse landau and ask the coachman to drive us to the castles on the outskirts of the town. We were very taken by the architecture of Wörlitz Castle and of Oranienbaum Castle. Klee and Kandinsky always proved to be excellent guides on these excursions and fine architectural connoisseurs. In the idyllic parklands around Wörlitz Castle there was a beautiful large lake. So we often rented a boat, had the boatman row us across the lake and drank our obligatory afternoon tea as we went."[334]

333 Kandinsky 1976, p. 121
334 Kandinsky 1976, pp. 113–14
335 Loew 1984 [a], p. 78 and fig. p. 79
336 Loew 1984 [a], p. 79, note 279
337 Xanti Schawinsky in Lauterbach 1958
338 Oskar Schlemmer to Tut Schlemmer, 5 December 1927, in Schlemmer 1990, p. 185

"... the poets' guillotine"

In 1927 the Bauhaus stagecraft class participated in a theater exhibition in Magdeburg, and it is entirely possible that Max Bill, either alone or with other Bauhaus students, went to see it. After all Magdeburg was closer to Dessau than Berlin, so it would not have been a long train journey. In the "Bauhaus booth" in Magdeburg, which the writer Thomas Mann described as "the poets' guillotine" in his opening address at the exhibition, there was a "mechanical stage model" by Heinz Loew, a Bauhaus student.[335] "The Bauhaus stage exhibition excited people. The Danish magazine *Kritisk Revu* (1, March 1928) asked why the Bauhaus didn't also cut the actor into two parts, revealing his innards."[336] Whatever the case, Bill's interest in the stage emerged around this time, and Oskar Schlemmer, head of the stage workshop at the Bauhaus in Dessau, allowed Bill to become an active member of the stagecraft class in mid-January 1928.

Max Bill's fellow-student Xanti Schawinsky credited Schlemmer, the head of stage design, with "... courage. In jest and in serious situations his courage was positively audacious, making us laugh and then think again, until the two became one."[337]

Bauhaus Master Gunta Stölzl

"So: yesterday we had the Schlagwörterfest [catchword party].... Unfortunately they forgot to invite the masters in time, not until the afternoon. As a result, Moholy and I [Oskar Schlemmer] were the only 'old ones' there. I was in a tuxedo and a red paper collar with a white band that read 'the band that hold us all together'; on the front of my shirt I had a red cardboard dot (circular) with the words 'the dark, the raw, the salient point.' Red rags with 'the loose tongue' protruded from my shoes. Gunta was a servant in a white pinafore with 'the social issue' on it, on her back she had 'workers insurance' and 'liberté, egalité, fratellinité' (the Fratellini clowns are in Berlin at the moment). Katt Both came as a 'naked fact.' The party ended at three o'clock."[338]

The Gunta that Schlemmer mentions in his letter to his wife was Adelgunde "Gunta" Stölzl, born in Munich, who first became an assistant master (*Werkmeister*) and then head of the Bauhaus weaving workshop from 1925 to 1931. Gunta's first impression of Dessau was that it was a terrible town. In November 1927 she wrote to her brother about her situation as a "civil servant and teacher, barely creating anything myself."

In that letter she uses masculine nouns in her description of herself, in the same way that she never referred to herself as a *Meisterin* (a female master), but always as a *Meister.* "At the moment we are snowed under with commissions, fitting out a large café." In the winter semester of 1927–28 there were "3 masters' council meetings per week going on until midnight. . . . the masters are exhausted from discussing the program."[339] From 1 April 1927 onward Stölzl, the only female master at the Bauhaus, received a monthly salary of 345 marks, plus a studio that she could use rent-free. Fabric for a divan cover by Stölzl is illustrated in the quarterly journal *bauhaus* 1:4 (1927), with editors-in-chief Gropius and Moholy-Nagy (fig. 2), above an illustration of a tea glass designed by Josef Albers in 1926 (fig. 3).

A portrait photograph of Katt Both (ca. 1929), the other woman mentioned in Schlemmer's letter—and the same woman that features, with Hilde Rantzsch, in a drawing by Max Bill (see p. 161)—is illustrated in *Bauhaus: Ex Libris 11* (sale catalogue from 1985 of the now closed Ex Libris bookstore in New York), fig. 81.

"Silent Night"

"christmas at the bauhaus is on the seventeenth of december.
not a word is to be uttered.
but word cards will be distributed.
for one word (one pfennig), ten words, one hundred words.
communication solely by means of gesture.
monitored by the wopo (word police)"[340]

Max Bill, who was already famed at the Kunstgewerbeschule for his love of masked balls, now also became infected by the Bauhaus craze for witty wordplay, as in Gunta Stölzl's "fraternité/fratellinité" or Xanti Schawinsky's claim that the German for holidays—*Ferien*—was derived from the French for "to do nothing"—*faire rien*—which sounds a lot like the German pronunciation of *Ferien.*

339 Stölzl 1987, p. 30
340 See Stölzl 1987

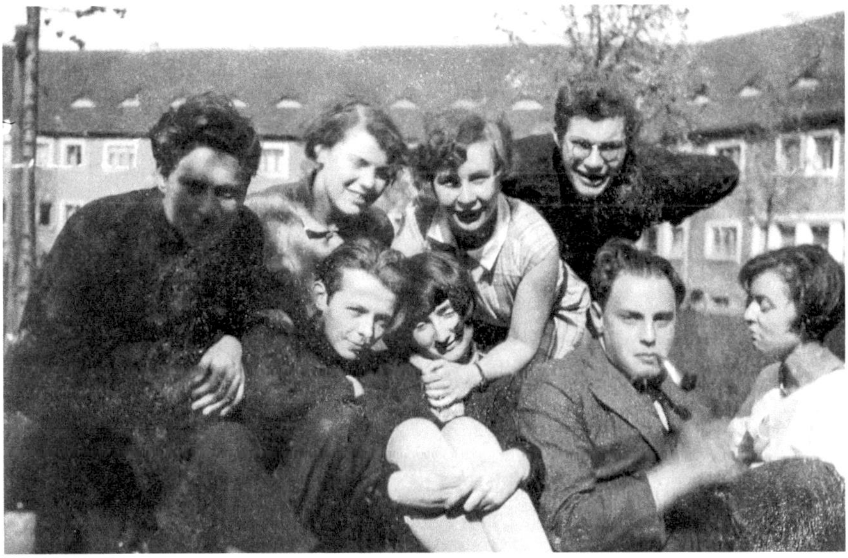

Life in Dessau, group photograph of Bauhaus students. Bottom row, left to right: Friedel Knopp, unidentified woman, Erich Comeriner (smoking a pipe), unidentified woman. Top row: Arnold-Fernand Mehl (face obscured by shadow), two unidentified women, Max Bill (wearing glasses), ca. 1927

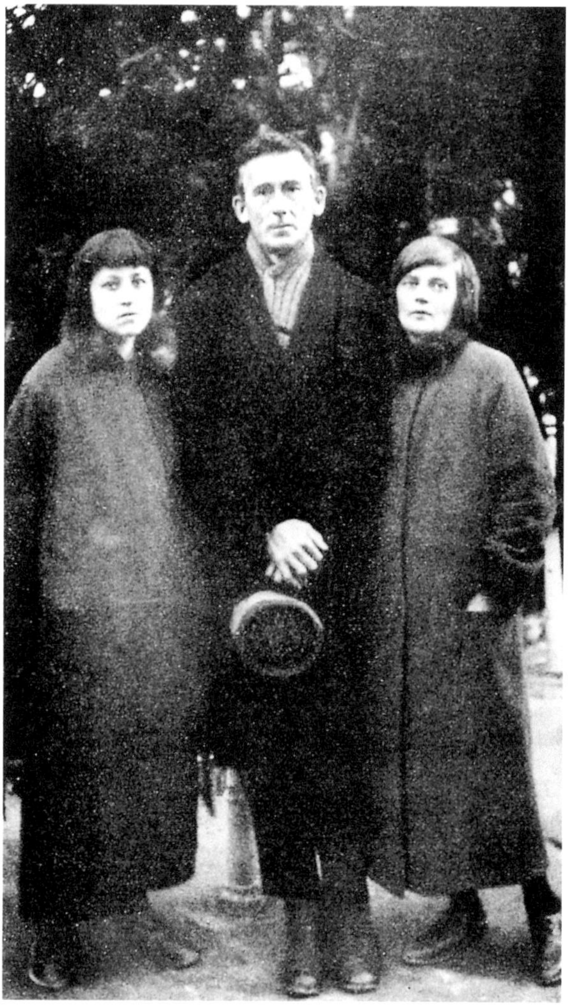

From left: Annemarie Hennings,
Hugo Ball, and Emmy Ball-Hennings,
1926, one year before Ball's death

Emmy Ball-Hennings and Annemarie Hennings

In late December 1927 Annemarie Hennings and her mother, Emmy Ball-Hennings—a writer and onetime Dada *diseuse* in Zurich—traveled to Dessau. With a difficult period in their lives behind them, they were now looking for an educational institution that would suit Annemarie. Hugo Ball, who had moved with Emmy Hennings from Munich to Zurich in 1915, was not Annemarie's biological father. She had been born in Germany in 1906 when her mother was on the road with a traveling circus.[341]

Following the sad death of Hugo Ball in September 1927 at the age of forty-one, Anna Baumann-Kienast, a wealthy Swiss artist, invited Annemarie to stay with her at her home in Lugano-Castagnola. Working in Anna Baumann-Kienast's studio, Annemarie designed and painted a series of frescos with 700 figures telling the story of King David; the full series, with a frieze in Hebrew, covered thirty-five square meters. Annemarie was paid a fee for her work by her hostess and she now wanted to use those funds to finance her studies.[342]

Emmy Ball-Hennings and Annemarie traveled to Dessau only after first making a stop in Berlin, where they turned to the writer and physician Richard Huelsenbeck and the artist Max "Mopp" Oppenheimer for advice on art schools. Annemarie was attracted by a painting school in Kantstrasse in Berlin but Mopp suggested she would be better off at the Bauhaus. "Mopp immediately said Dessau," and Emmy Ball-Hennings felt that the Bauhaus would offer Annemarie a "greater degree of concentration" than she would find in Berlin. In her diary she also added that their "finances were rapidly dwindling" and that she had "asked Moholy-Nagy what the costs would be at the Bauhaus."[343] Emmy Ball-Hennings and Annemarie did then decide on the Bauhaus and after her arrival in Dessau Annemarie was invited for a meal by the Moholy-Nagys—as it happened, on the same day as they also invited the young student Max Bill. Max immediately fell for Annemarie; she was exactly his type—albeit two years older than him, which was still significant at his age.

341 See Ball-Hennings 1987

342 A photograph of Annemarie Hennings's *König David* series (1927–28) is reproduced in Angela Thomas, *mit unverstelltem blick—bericht zu drei künstlerinnen: anna baumann-kienast, alis guggenheim, sophie taeuber-arp,* with typography by Max Bill (Bern: Benteli, 1991), p. 79. Hennings's series was destroyed by Walter Boven

343 Ball-Hennings 1999, pp. 208–9

At that time Moholy-Nagy's art—compared with that of Mondrian, Klee, and Kandinsky—was Constructivist, daring, groundbreaking, cutting edge. Might Max have been so distracted by Annemarie that he took no proper notice of the compositions in the lounge and the dining room by his former master in the metal workshop? It was on that evening that Moholy-Nagy inquired again why Max had stopped going to the metal workshop. Bill replied that he had caught the *maladie de la peinture*—the painting sickness. Moholy of course had strong views on painting and it was in one of his slide lectures that Bill first encountered the work of Piet Mondrian. Moholy talked to the students about "purity" in art, which he felt was only to be found in the work of the (Russian) Constructivists and in the paintings of the Dutch artist Piet Mondrian. In fact, Moholy described Mondrian as the "purest" contemporary painter and Bill never forgot that stamp of approval. Little did Max Bill realize then that in just six years time, in Paris in December 1933, he would come face to face with the artist that Moholy so greatly respected.

Evidently still well able to concentrate on what was going on around him, despite the spell cast over him by Annemarie, Bill took in all that Moholy said on that evening and treasured it as a yardstick for the future. Looking back, Bill commented that in conversation and in his teaching Moholy always had "very interesting things" to say. "We conducted very interesting experiments with him, for instance about 'the surfaces of things.'"

The evolution of Moholy-Nagy's own style has been very lucidly outlined by the curator of the major Albers and Moholy-Nagy retrospective presented in London at Tate Modern in 2006: "Moholy's move into abstraction was motivated by the fervent desire to be part of an artistic and social avant-garde. Dada's irreverence, which aimed to offend middle-class notions of good taste, taught Moholy to refuse the limitations of traditional definitions of art, and to appreciate the artistic potential of mundane subject matter such as railway bridges, machines and mathematical numbers, and the value of humor and irony as

344 Borchardt-Hume 2006, p. 68

345 Max Bill in Scheidegger 1998

346 Max Bill, *tanzendes mädchen* (1927–28), oil on canvas, 146.5×110.5cm, estate of Max Bill left to Jakob Bill, is reproduced in Max Bill. Maler, Bildhauer, Architekt, Designer (Ostfildern: Hatje Cantz, 2005), p. 22). Max Raphael's book was published in 1913: *Von Monet zu Picasso: Grundzüge einer Ästhetik und Entwicklung der modernen Malerei von Max Raphael,* with 32 illustrations (Munich and Leipzig: Delphin, 1913)

creative strategies. From Constructivism, on the other hand, Moholy borrowed the principle that art should be pure, creating its compositional constituents that were void of any representational references. 'to be an artist is to surrender to the elements that give form,' he proclaimed. Moholy's idiosyncratic type of constructivism was characterized by its emphasis on transparency and light. Built from opaque areas of color, the geometric shapes in Moholy's paintings seemingly float on top of each other . . . though there is pictorial depth in paintings . . . there is no spatial 'illusion'. . . . Overlapping translucent planes explored in a wide range of different media remained a recurrent theme in Moholy's art throughout his career."[344]

Representing an Idea

"I showed Moholy some of my works and got a critical response. He then gave me an idea as to how I might approach things. He took Picasso as his example; Picasso was basically completely unknown to us students at the Bauhaus at the time."[345] In late December 1927 or possibly early January 1928, Moholy pointed out to Max Bill that it was not viable to simply enlarge a drawing and use that as the basis for a painting, as Bill had done in his *tanzendes mädchen* (1927–28), because paintings and drawings are governed by different laws. And Moholy lent weight to his argument by showing Max reproductions of paintings by Picasso that obeyed the innate laws of painting; he explained how Picasso composed a painting, how he structured it and shaped it. The reproductions he showed Bill were in *Von Monet zu Picasso* by Max Raphael (1913).[346]

In the early 1930s Bill met the Marxist cultural philosopher Max Raphael in Zurich, at a time when Bill had taken over as typographic designer for the small-format, anti-Fascist periodical *information,* which counted Max Raphael among its writers. More on this will follow in due course.

Raphael, who had studied art history in Munich under Heinrich Wölfflin, conducted some of his research in Paris where he made personal contact with Picasso, Rodin, and Matisse. However, when he submitted his doctoral dissertation based on these conversations in Paris, Wölfflin deemed it substandard, thereby preventing his own student from ever pursuing a career as an academic. Or, to put it rather differently, that research allowed Raphael to escape the clutches of academia and to strike out into an entirely new world. He posed questions that needed to be asked.

"Annemarie cast an angel"

Before Emmy Ball-Hennings left Dessau again, she and her daughter Annemarie spent the last day of 1927 together. They tried to "artificially get into the New Year's Eve mood by already casting lead in the stove with a spoon at five in the afternoon. Annemarie cast an angel."[347] A few months later Annemarie Hennings enrolled at the Bauhaus in Dessau for the summer semester of 1928 (matriculation no. 256), not long after the Swiss student Hanns Fischli (no. 217). Once Fischli had completed the preliminary course led by Albers, he joined the class of Oskar Schlemmer and, like Max Bill, also attended the free (optional) painting classes offered by Klee and by Kandinsky.

Bill and Fischli: Housemates

Max Bill regarded Fischli—the new arrival, whom he described as "alternately pensive or full of fire"—as a decent sort, and the two agreed that Fischli would move in with Bill at Fichtenbreite 32. Annemarie Hennings visited the new housemates from time to time and sometimes went to the free painting classes with them. Both masters, Kandinsky and Klee, were "careful" about the way they talked to Annemarie. Fischli, the new boy at the Bauhaus, regarded Klee as a "wise man" but felt that Kandinsky's teaching was often "too theoretical." He noticed that Annemarie only had one black dress; her black hair was "long, lank, unkempt, and her almond-shaped eyes glowed feverishly in her pale face.... She used opaque tempera paints, with a lot of black and golden yellow, to paint elongated figures of girls with olive eyes and big round pupils gazing at you, asking questions with closed lips."[348] Annemarie wanted to be a painter. Bill described her style as "somehow Byzantine."

At that point Annemarie, painfully fragile, was also to be found in the weaving workshop at the Bauhaus. She seemed to be surviving on breadcrumbs alone and Hanns Fischli later recalled that she was constantly in a state of "not quite starving." In Gunta Stölzl's class she used "one of the low chairs because she wasn't actually weaving, certainly not upholstery fabrics; she didn't guide her yarn with a weaver's shuttle but with a needle. Stitch by stitch, line by line she made yarn replicas of her own tempera paintings, with black wool for the dresses and gleaming silk for the eyes."

347 Ball-Hennings 1999, p. 210
348 Fischli 1968, p. 54

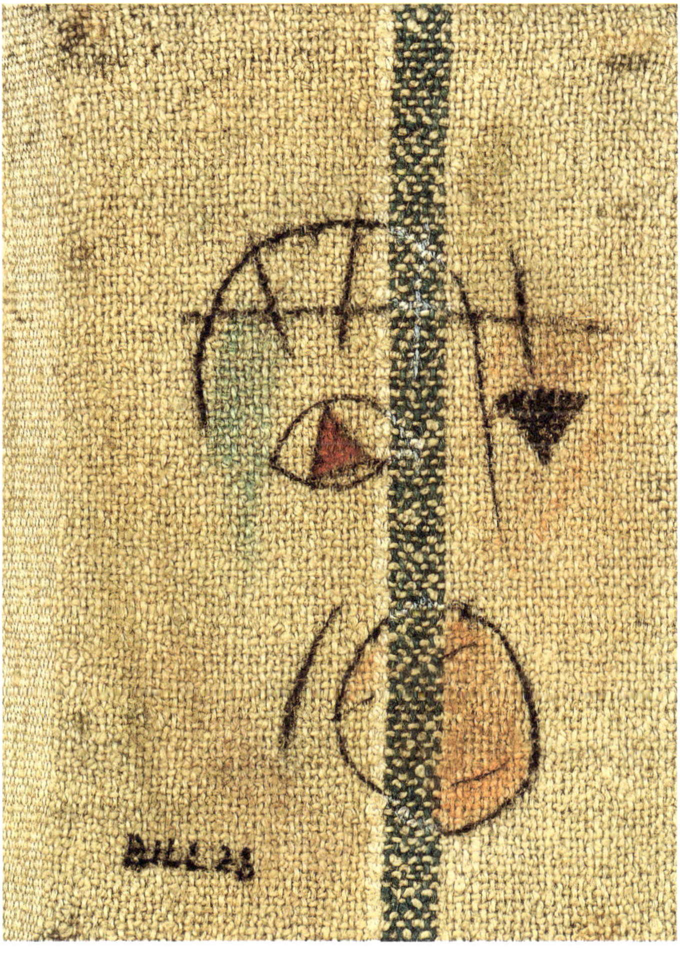

Max Bill, *Was man nur auf dem Bilde sieht,* 1928, india ink and paint on textile, 19×13 cm

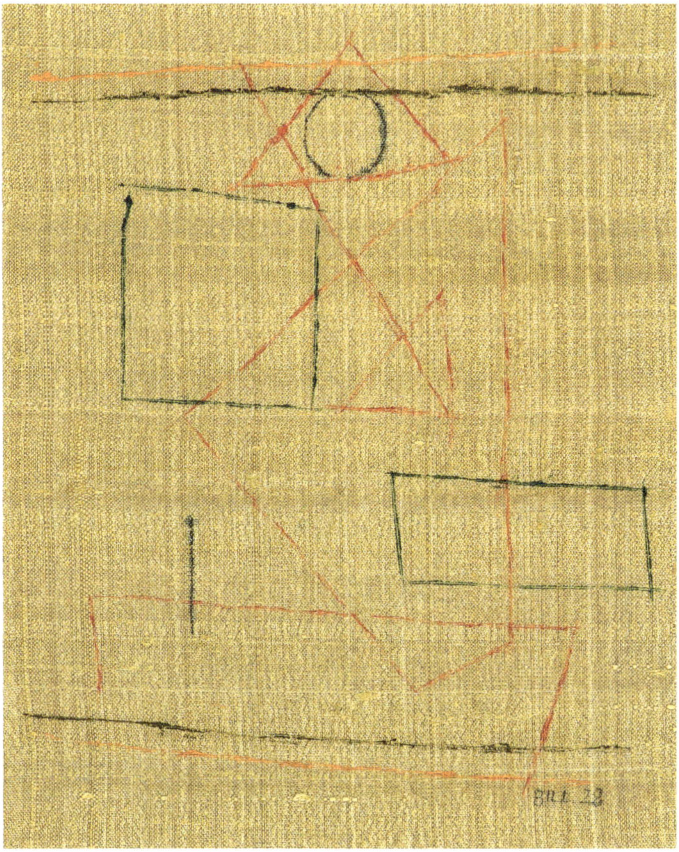

Max Bill, Untitled, 1928,
ink and color on yellow textile,
17 × 13.8 cm

Max was not the only one who was drawn to Annemarie: "The teachers' wives used to involuntarily gently stroke her forehead, as you would do with a kitten."[349] Possibly as a way of seeing her and striking up a conversation, Bill went to the weaving workshop one day to source fabric for a small-format work with the mysterious title *was man nur auf dem bilde sieht* (What you only see in the picture). The motif is an abstract face—Bill's own face?—with inquisitive triangular eyes, one looking up and the other down. Bill was still searching for answers. As yet he had no art-historical overview, and it would be a long time before he would be at the forefront of things like Moholy-Nagy, who made connections between all kinds of human creativity. Nevertheless—perhaps after a private conversation with Moholy—all of a sudden Max drew a completely geometric composition on a small piece of fabric.

Bill bought Moholy-Nagy's book *Von Material zu Architektur,* no. 14, *Bauhausbücher* (Munich: Albert Langen, 1929) in 1930.

Moholy-Nagy's Departure

Moholy's political views were very clear: "Those engaged in the struggle must always remember that ultimately the class struggle is not about capital, not about the means of production, but in truth it is about the right to a satisfying occupation and internally fulfilling work, it is about leading a healthy life.... There are very few aspects of today's economy that are conducive to self-fulfillment. Given the present pace of life there is rarely a chance nowadays to get to the heart of things or of oneself.... Production today is the harshest extortion of profit.... And it is not only the worker, the proletarian who is in this situation; everyone working within the current production system is just as hard done by. At best there are only differences of degree. The mad pursuit of money and power influences all of life today, right down to the individual's basic state of mind: when he should be taking care of his internal security, he thinks only of his external safety."[350]

In January 1928, shortly after Walter Gropius had decided to step down as director at the end March of that year and hand over to Hannes Meyer, Moholy-Nagy announced that he would resign from his position at the Bauhaus "because of increasing political pressure."[351] And in that same month, January 1928, Max Bill—who in any case was no longer

349 Fischli 1968, p. 54
350 See Moholy-Nagy 1929
351 Weitemeier 1974, p. 67

attending Moholy's metal workshop—joined the stage workshop at the Bauhaus. Oskar Schlemmer, politely addressing him as "herr bill," had informed him that there was "nothing to prevent him being accepted into the stage workshop."[352]

Entries in Oskar Schlemmer's diary record that Moholy was still in Dessau in early March 1928 when a group of Bauhauslers met to celebrate the Kandinskys' new status as German citizens. "Our Kandinsky evening was very merry. Breuer, Scheper, Wittwer, and I went as Prussian militia, Moholy as an old Dessauer (in costume) . . . Hannes Meyer as a representative of the people, Klee as a Turk, Kandinsky as a hybrid being, comical. The women were mixed. Reason: the Kandinskys have now become Anhaltiner (residents of Sachsen-Anhalt), Germans."[353]

Not long after that, László and Lucia Moholy-Nagy finally left Dessau, where Lucia had never really felt at ease. "On 31 March 1928 the Moholys are leaving Dessau. Whatever reasons may be given for this exodus. . . . it is primarily connected with the departure of Walter Gropius. That Moholy-Nagy, of all people, could not have worked under Hannes Meyer as director is perfectly demonstrated by a letter from Meyer, in which he claims that the Bauhaus preliminary course (judging by its results) has *anthroposophical* tendencies"—the reference here is to the bio-mechanical principles that Moholy-Nagy used to discuss in his preliminary course teaching—"whereas the theoretical basis of Meyer's Bauhaus pedagogy could not have been more different. It was grounded in rigorous historical materialism, which relegates all biologisms to the realms of the irrational."[354]

Rolf Sachsse regards Meyer's observation in this letter as "correct, if exaggerated."[355]

Lucia Moholy, whose *Marginalien* shed new light on some aspects of her life with László Moholy-Nagy, cited 1928 as the year of their departure but did not specify a month. She would have preferred to return to Berlin

352 Oskar Schlemmer, Dessau, to Max Bill, 20 January 1928, Bibliothek Max Bill
353 Oskar Schlemmer, Dessau, to Tut Schlemmer, 13 March 1928, in Schlemmer 1958, pp. 232–33
354 Sachsse 1985, p. 42
355 Sachsse 1985, p. 42
356 Lucia Moholy to László Moholy-Nagy, 24 May 1927, in Berger 2000, p. 77
357 Oskar Schlemmer, Dessau to Tut Schlemmer, 1 June 1927 and 17 October 1927, in Schlemmer 1990, pp. 173, 181
358 Schlemmer, Dessau, to Otto Meyer-Amden, 23 January 1928, Schlemmer 1990, p. 189

sooner than that. "Dear Laci," she wrote to her husband, "Why can you not bring yourself to believe that it is the capital city that I am attracted by?—I was reluctant to go with you to Weimar back then and reluctant to come to Dessau—now, four years later, I simply can't stand it any more, despite taking a few trips—time mounts up and it's not like someone occasionally needing some meat because he doesn't want to eat spinach every day. Believe me—I need bustling surroundings—and since I can rarely afford the trip to the city, I have to find a way of combining it with a work project.—My aim is not to leave you—but to find you again."[356]

Bauhaus Funding Issues

On 1 June 1927 Oskar Schlemmer, the master of the stage workshop, wrote to his wife, Tut, in the Ticino: "The ensemble often rehearses into the night, starting at eight o'clock. Individual rehearsals are in the mornings, often in the afternoon, too, from three to seven o'clock." In another letter to Tut a few months later, on 17 October 1927, Schlemmer wrote: "Tomorrow the stage rehearsals start again, each evening at nine. Another student has joined the stage, so now we're five or six. The atmosphere is good ... we're preparing a new program: lighting sketch, noises sketch, salon sketch, comic, ancient, political, horror drama, all in the form of excerpts, as it were excerpts from possible works, short and to the point ... and then a performance for the Bauhaus ... maybe more after that, to get some money into the coffers."[357]

Fundraising was an ongoing problem at the Bauhaus; funds were constantly needed not only for the (often impoverished) Bauhaus students but also to keep all the Bauhaus workshops going. Schlemmer had noticed a striking discrepancy in the distribution of funds: whereas his stage workshop and the sculpture workshop each received just twenty-five Reichsmarks, Moholy-Nagy's specially privileged metal workshop received a thousand Reichsmarks. And, as he also pointed out in a letter to Otto Meyer-Amden, the parties at the Bauhaus were a thorn in the side of certain local politicians: "The town ... prohibits parties at the Bauhaus. The second one we had already planned was also ultimately banned ..."[358]

In daily life at the Bauhaus Walter Gropius seemed to Bill to be "tough, proper, and sharp." Anyone wanting to access the Bauhaus library—which Bill only found out about later on—had to cross through the director's office. But after work Gropius enjoyed the Bauhaus parties and celebrations as much as anyone else. "everyone who was there has enduring memories of the Bauhaus parties, where there was such a strong feeling of oneness, as it said in a banner from that time: 'in dieser saubucht herrscht die bausucht' (a play on words, including a German place name—Saubucht, literally 'sow's cove'—meaning that in this 'sow's cove' everyone is obsessed with building.) The parties made up for all our hard, serious work, and all those who were privileged enough to be part of that pioneering era are grateful to Walter Gropius for making it possible."[359]

The Bauhaus Family

Whenever Bauhauslers met up in later years, as I saw for myself, more often than not they were heartily glad to see each other and easily fell back into conversation—that was very much the case in May 1985 for Bill and Lotte Beese when they met again (after many long years) at the Bauhaus-Archiv in Berlin (see p. 292).

During the memorial to Max Bill at Schauspielhaus Zürich on 12 February 1995, Dirk Scheper, Hinnerk and Lou Scheper's son, made particular mention of the "Bauhaus family": "The descendants of members of the Bauhaus family are also assured of being part of that myth, the all-embracing bauhaus family." Max Bill already touched on what this means in 1985—of course in lower case and with a twinkle in his eye—in his thanks to Philip Rosenthal, his predecessor as chair of the board of the Bauhaus-Archiv in Berlin: 'as an old bauhausler and in the name of all those individuals who are still inspired by those glorious times, i would like to thank you for your crucial part in turning the bauhaus archive into a resource that will continue to sustain the bauhaus idea.' Bill, who always preferred to look forward, regarded the archive more as a place for active use than as a museum.

He always had a warm welcome for members of the Bauhaus family, but he maintained a more critical distance when the Bauhaus idea was only seen as something to feed off. The Bauhaus family comprises

359 Bill 1969 [b], p. 1145
360 Walter Gropius to Wilhelm Ostwald, 21 March 1928 and 5 July 1928, in Wilhelm Ostwald Archiv
361 Walter Gropius to Wilhelm Ostwald, 13 August 1928, Wilhelm Ostwald Archiv
362 Joost Schmidt to Wilhelm Ostwald, 3 October 1928, Wilhelm Ostwald Archiv
363 Josef Albers to Wilhelm Ostwald, 22 April 1929, Wilhelm Ostwald Archiv

Bauhauslers, Bauhaus children, Bauhaus descendants, Bauhaus grandchildren, and so on, until it will fade away into infinity, when—and I am very sure of this—Marcel Breuer's slatted chair will still be the epitome of modern seating. Besides still respecting their masters, the true old Bauhauslers can be recognized by the special way they respond to the descendants of members of the family: warmly, openly, free of prejudice, and filled with curiosity, always ready to provide help or advice—neither self-important nor ingratiating—in command of their own views and attitudes and never reluctant to pass these on: for young people an ideal form of partnership that ignores any generation gaps, for older people an orientation aid in a time that is uncertain and bereft of past yardsticks. That, I now realize, is what Max Bill was to me."

In March 1928 Walter Gropius wrote to Wilhelm Ostwald to tell him of his imminent departure from the Bauhaus on 1 April and to ask Ostwald to help his colleague and successor "hannes meyer, from basel, to continue to expand the circle of friends of the bauhaus."[360] Gropius, for his part, was planning to concentrate more on his own work as an architect.

Ostwald appears to have expressed some disappointment regarding the response to his series of lectures in June 1927. However, Gropius, writing from Berlin, sought to reassure him: "i don't think it is true that your lectures left no mark at the bauhaus. i know that herr scheper in particular went deeply into some of your ideas and is now applying them in his teaching."[361] In fact, various masters remained in contact with Ostwald, and in the winter semester of 1928 Joost Schmidt decided to run a "rigorous teaching program with exercises in color theory" in the workshop for printing and advertising. As he wrote to Ostwald: "We now have a number of students who were not at your lectures. Like a violinist doing daily exercises, our students will have to produce daily color studies."[362] And in April 1929 Josef Albers wrote to Ostwald and sent him a catalogue: "I enclose the catalogue of the Bauhaus touring exhibition, now opening in Basel; you will find in it illustrations of some of the latest products from Bauhaus workshops. Conveying our great esteem, Albers."[363]

The exhibition *Bauhaus in Dessau,* mentioned by Albers in his letter, was presented at the Gewerbemuseum Basel from 21 April to 20 May 1929. Even if Bill was no longer at the Bauhaus by then, he presumably would not have missed it—no doubt traveling to Basel on a free SBB ticket begged from his father.

In Berlin

Contrary to Lucia's hopes, she and László Moholy-Nagy did not "find each other" again; instead they separated in spring 1929 and ultimately decided to divorce. After his departure from the Bauhaus, László Moholy-Nagy initially designed stage sets (photographed by Lucia Moholy) for a production of *Hoffmanns Erzählungen* at the Kroll Opera in Berlin in 1929 and for the avant-garde Piscator-Bühne, both of which closed in 1931. Moholy-Nagy's former colleague from the Bauhaus, Oskar Schlemmer, was also able to bring his stage experience to bear at the Kroll Opera—for instance, in his design for Arnold Schoenberg's *Verklärte Nacht.* And Marianne Brandt, another former colleague, also went to Berlin after she left the Bauhaus in 1929 and worked "for a short time at Gropius's architectural practice in Berlin."[364]

It seems that Max Bill spent some time in Berlin in spring 1929, however, there is no knowing whether he saw any of the productions at the Kroll Opera that former Bauhaus masters had worked on. On the other hand, there are suggestions that he did enjoy the delights of free love—witness *hermafrodit* (1929, see p. 268), the subtly exposed body of a woman in *Frau* (1929, see p. 217), and the deep violet-washed drawing of naked lovers in *Violette Nacht* (1929, see p. 217). In 1929 Bill signed and named these works using conventional upper- and lowercase.

Following his return from Germany in November 1929, Bill included a subtly erotic drawing, *frau,* in the exhibition he presented at his studio and apartment at Stadelhoferstrasse 27 in Zurich. This exhibition, *malerei und grafik,* was reviewed as "Atelierausstellung Max Bill Zürich" in *Werk* 16:11 (November 1929), p. XV.

In the same way that Bill left no records of the names of people he spent time with at this point in his life, he also left no hints as to where he was. And although he does refer to places in general terms—as in the watercolor *Dorf im Vor-Frühling* (1929, no. 17, "Village in very early spring")—that period of his life remains shrouded in mystery. Another watercolor, also done in 1929 (no. 23), with a reduced, geometric group of architectural structures is simply titled *Alter Stadtteil* ("Old part of town").

Bill's watercolor *dorf im vor-frühling* (35 × 50.5 cm) was in the estate left to me; on 29 June 1995 I gave it to Teddy Kollek, mayor of Jerusalem from 1965 to 1993 (who came to visit me in Haus Bill in Zumikon) in memory of Bill's participation in the Town Planning Subcommittee of the Jerusalem Committee during the Kollek era.

364 Weise 2002, p. 238

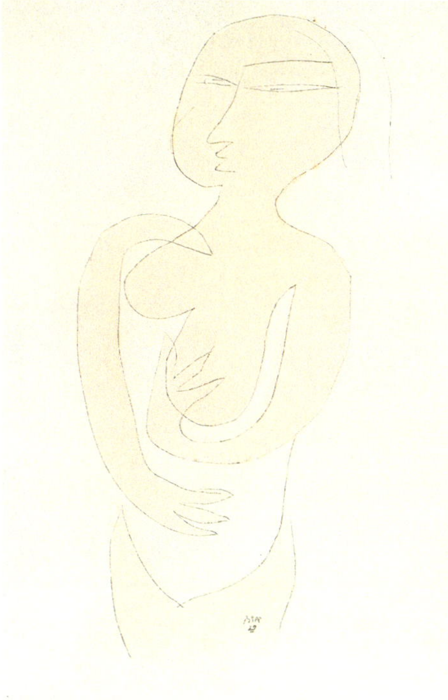

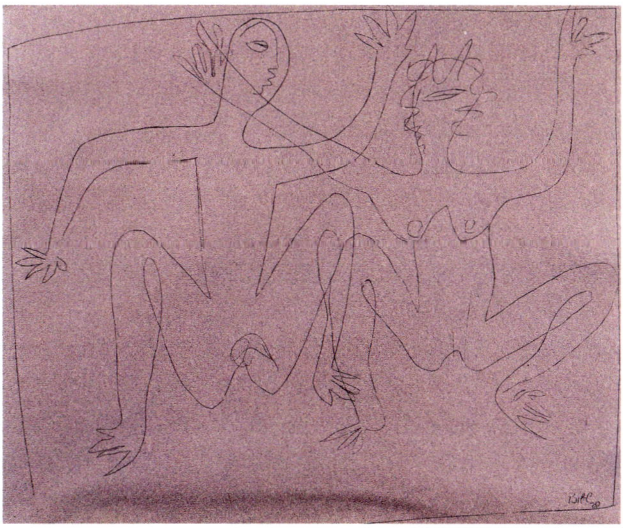

Max Bill, *Frau,* 1929, india ink on Japan paper, 60 × 44.8 cm
Max Bill, *Violette Nacht,* 1929, india ink on violet laid paper, 47 × 62.5 cm

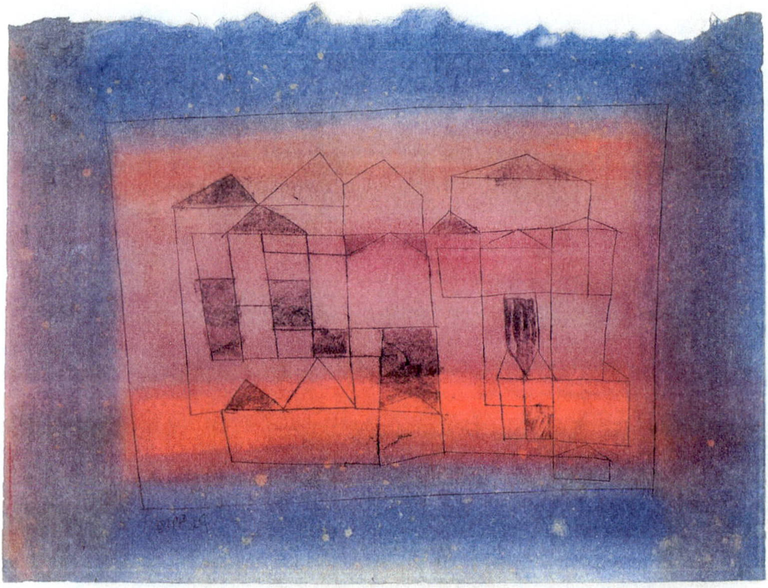

Max Bill, *Alter Stadtteil,* 1929,
watercolor on paper, 21.5 × 29.5 cm

Dark Times for the Old Masters

The machinations of the Nazi regime put a sudden end to Oskar Schlemmer's promising new start in Berlin. "At the age of 45, he was hit both by the death of his friend Otto Meyer-Amden and by artistic exclusion."[365]

Oskar Schlemmer's friend, Otto Meyer-Amden, was born in Bern in 1883 and died in 1933. In 1934 an obituary by Schlemmer was published in the journal *Das Werk,* along with a text by Sigfried Giedion on Meyer-Amden's artistic work, with numerous black-and-white illustrations (*Das Werk* 21:3 [March 1934], pp. 65–81). Giedion concludes that Meyer-Amden's work had been "a never-ending debate between the inhibitions and prohibitions within him and around him and his stubborn determination to go beyond that and achieve his own clarification of form" (p. 81). Otto Meyer-Amden only ever received one public commission in his native country: the stained glass window in the parish hall in Zürich-Wiedikon. Max Haefeli, a member of the Swiss Architects' Association (BSA) collected works by Meyer-Amden.

Humiliated and ostracized—derided by the Nazis as "degenerate"—Oskar Schlemmer had no choice but to remain in Germany, wretchedly enduring his situation. Although "he had taught at the Bauhaus in Weimar and Dessau, and had been a professor at art academies in Breslau and Berlin, he did not enjoy the status that would have enabled him to emigrate like his Bauhaus colleagues Kandinsky, Klee, and Moholy-Nagy." In company with other artists in his immediate circle, such as Willy Baumeister and Julius Bissier, Schlemmer was forced into "inner emigration and struggled to eke out a meager living at the same time as fighting to preserve his own artistic existence. With his works banned from museums—only exhibited as 'degenerate art'—he had to pursue his groundbreaking work in the most modest of circumstances. He built a simple home (with expert help from Hans Fischli) for himself and his family—and for their animals, their life-sustaining cohabitants—close to the Swiss border, looking out over the Rhine Plain."[366]

Schlemmer's home studio (1935–37) in Badenweiler, built by dipl. Ing. Hertel (an architect from Lörrach) with architectural assistance from Hans Fischli, is illustrated in Karl Jost, *Hans Fischli (1909–1989)—Architekt, Maler, Bildhauer* (Zurich: gta 1992), p. 235.

365 Bill 1980 [b]
366 Bill 1980 [b]

Born in Stuttgart in 1888 Oskar Schlemmer "was part of a generation of artists who found that not only were their careers affected by two world wars, they themselves suffered all the more because they were German nationals—in various ways, but most crucially through persecution and wasted years."[367]

Oskar Schlemmer "was the youngest of six siblings, some more than 20 years older than he was. . . . At the age of 8 he left his parental home—his mother was from Swabia—and was brought up in modest circumstances by an older sister in Göppingen. . . . Between 1909 and 1916 he met not only his teacher Hoelzel but also [Willi] Baumeister and Otto Meyer-Amden, who became his dearest, most loyal friend. . . . In Berlin in 1911 he encountered Herwarth Walden's Sturm. . . . He was called up to fight in the First World War and was wounded."[368]

At the memorial organized by Tut Schlemmer for her late husband in 1958—Oskar Schlemmer would have been seventy on 4 September 1958—Max Bill encountered his old friend and fellow-student at the Bauhaus, Katt Both; Nina Kandinsky was also present in the throng of guests.

Schlemmer did not live to see the end of the Nazi era. In April 1943 he died at the age of just fifty-four in a sanatorium in southern Germany. It seems that his heart simply gave out in those dark times. Schlemmer's ostracization had a long-term impact on the reception of his art. In 1980, following the publication of the monograph and catalogue raisonné of his work by Karin von Maur, Bill commented with regret that "Oskar Schlemmer was still far too little known, underestimated as an artist."[369]

In 1930 László Moholy-Nagy created his now world-famous *Lichtraum-Modulator;* he later noted that the play of light and shadows it produced taught him many things that he was subsequently able to use in his films.

Lucia Moholy once said to me that Schlemmer "moved in the same way as his figurines."

367 Lauterbach 1958
368 Lauterbach 1958
369 Bill 1980 [b]
370 See "L. Moholy-Nagy," *telehor* 1–2 (28 February 1936) texts in Czech, German, English, French, with numerous images, global distribution: Kommissionsverlag Dr. Hans Girsberger, Zurich
371 Max Bill, Zürich-Höngg, to Professor Moholy-Nagy, Berlin-Charlottenburg 9, Fredericastrasse 27, studio, 27 April 1933, Bibliothek Max Bill
372 Giedion 2007, p. 394

In fact, those films sometimes took him into dangerous situations, for instance, when he was shooting his silent documentary *Grossstadt-Zigeuner* (Berlin 1932, 16mm, b/w), which focused on the lives of a group of Roma who would soon be deported to concentration camps by the Nazis. As a filmmaker with an acute social conscience, he also spoke out against the fact that, as he saw it, "industrialization [had been] led astray by capitalism," which "only the ruling class" had any interest in retaining in its present form.[370] In 1933 he would like to have given some lectures in Switzerland and asked Max Bill if he could help to organize a lecture tour with assistance from the Swiss Werkbund. However, it seems that nothing came of that idea, which would have provided a much-needed source of income for Moholy, but Bill did invite Moholy to visit him and his wife Binia in Zurich: "dear moholy. . . . we moved into our brand new house at the beginning of the month and would be very pleased to see you in zurich. you are always heartily welcome here."[371]

There is no knowing for sure whether Moholy-Nagy ever came to see Max Bill's new home, which he was certainly proud of. However, it is possible, since Moholy-Nagy sometimes visited Zurich in the 1930s; there are records of him staying with the Giedion-Welckers in Doldertal: "in the 1930s Max Ernst, Moholy, Arp, and Vordemberge-Gildewart were often in Doldertal for weeks on end."[372]

In the early 1930s it was hard to secure the funds needed to build residential properties. In order to find a way around the funding crisis in the property market, a number of interested parties—including Max Bill—set up Baukredit Zürich, a mutual building society. And since Bill was one of the first to open a savings account there, he was granted a loan relatively quickly, which he then used to realize his own design for a new home for himself and Binia. The site was on the edge of the village of Höngg, a suburb of Zurich, and the house itself was constructed from prefabricated panels. Since the local building regulations did not permit a flat roof, Bill designed a very shallow pitched roof. The architect Robert Winkler, ten years older than Bill, oversaw the construction process; as a member of the team at the architectural practice Hubacher and Steiger, which had built the Zett-Haus in Zurich, he already had a wealth of experience.

Once the Nazis had seized power in 1933, Moholy-Nagy—like so many others—ultimately came to the conclusion that he had to make his escape from Germany. He left in 1934 and first made his way to Amsterdam; his new wife Sibyl initially remained in Berlin with their little daughter

Hattula. A year later Moholy-Nagy traveled on to London via Brussels to meet up with Sibyl and Hattula, who were waiting for him there; in 1937 the whole family emigrated to America, where Moholy-Nagy became the founding director of the New Bauhaus in Chicago.

"Professor Moholy-Nagy from Berlin, formerly professor at the Bauhaus in Dessau" particularly liked to talk about "the two main driving tendencies at the Bauhaus," as he had previously done in a series of lectures in March 1931 at the School of Applied Arts in Pressburg [Bratislava] on "new paths in photography," "appropriate typography," and "modern painting." Although Moholy-Nagy's German was not especially good, he delivered his lectures "in German with slides."[373]

In the same chapter, "Moholy-Nagy in Brünn und Pressburg," the author also mentions that Josef Albers, Moholy-Nagy's former fellow-master at the Bauhaus in Dessau, had applied unsuccessfully for a professorship at the same school of applied arts.[374]

Before Moholy-Nagy crossed the Atlantic, Walter Gropius (also with a stop in London) and Anni and Josef Albers had already made it to the United States.

For more on emigration, involvement in the war, and the struggle against Fascism, see the dissertation by Folke F. Dietzsch: "as the Fascist state gained strength in Germany, the persecution of modern art and artists (including members of the Bauhaus) began; it culminated in 1937 in the 'degenerate art' exhibition in Munich. . . . Documentary evidence shows that 81 former Bauhaus students left Fascist Germany for more than 20 other countries. . . . Almost a third of these émigrés already left Germany in 1933 . . . the majority of those who had left remained in exile."

"Of the former bauhaus students there is evidence that 35 were arrested (multiple times in some cases), remanded in custody, or imprisoned. Four were interned; of the 19 sent to concentration camps, ten were murdered."[375]

373 Mojzisová 1986, pp. 282–83
374 Mojzisová 1986, p. 283
375 Dietzsch 1990, pp. 51–53
376 Max Bill, Adelboden, Switzerland, to Xanti Schawinsky, United States, 17 January 1947, Schawinsky-Archiv
377 Reported by the Bauhaus student Hubert "Höbi" Hofmann in conversation with Max Bill and Angela Thomas during a Bauhaus conference in Weimar, GDR, 1984

Moholy-Nagy was a very active new arrival in the United States, always prepared to be flexible if need be. As an artist he was unmistakably his own man. Although there were of course points of contact between his work and that of other artists, such as El Lissitzky or Friedel Vordemberge-Gildewart, Moholy preferred to respect the claims that had already been staked. Not unlike Max Bill later on, he regarded his artistic work as a constructive, wide-ranging contribution to a world in need of a form of renewal that could only be achieved by many individuals working together. Some years later, Moholy-Nagy contacted Bill from the United States and asked if Bill would like to come to Chicago as a key player at the New Bauhaus—at which point Bill realized, to his great pleasure, that his former Bauhaus master now regarded him as an equal. However, Max Bill did not accept that very complimentary invitation and later on felt he had made the right decision.

"dear xanti, ... i was very sad to hear about moholy's death. i wrote a long obituary for the "neue zürcher zeitung," another one by me will appear shortly in "domus," and i am preparing an 8-page supplement on him for the "grafische mitteilungen." and yet, looking back, i am glad i didn't agree to go to work with him in chicago when he asked, i've got the feeling i would have been very fed up with the school by now. which wouldn't be ideal."[376]

Controversy and the New Director

Having taken up his new appointment as director of the Bauhaus in April 1928, Hannes Meyer restructured the teaching program so that now three days per week were devoted to theory and the other three working days were given over to practical work. This meant that there were now fewer contact hours than at traditional art academies and the students had more time for discussion and debate.[377] "The course structure introduced in 1927 stipulated that all students had to take a preliminary course in their first semester; this led into practical workshops, lectures, and exercises in the second semester. From the third to the fifth semester students specialised in one of the workshops, with the third semester taken up by workshop tasks and design tasks; these were then reduced in the fourth semester, allowing the students to concentrate on individual laboratory work from the fifth semester onward. Wall painting, carpentry, metalwork, and weaving were merged to form a new "furniture and fixtures" (*Ausbauabteilung*) department. Training in wall painting continued in other areas, although now there was no talk any more of poster painting and the application and testing of new techniques."[378]

Before introducing these changes Meyer had categorically spoken out against what he called "the bogus-hype-theatricality of the Bauhaus as it used to be."[379] He attached particular importance to focused, targeted work and gave architecture and building pride of place in the Bauhaus curriculum. In his view a stricter approach to the organization of the Bauhaus plus a more academic training would help the Bauhaus to achieve economic success and raise its status in the public eye. "Before he took over as director, free painting classes led by Paul Klee, Wassily Kandinsky, and Oskar Schlemmer had been introduced. However, Meyer now made greater use of these artists in the curriculum for the first four semesters; he also appointed scientists, technicians, psychologists, and others as visiting professors and employed various experts in the architecture department."[380]

It was only in a text written many years later that Bill touched on the economics of the Bauhaus: "Hannes Meyer tried to increase the output from the Bauhaus workshops, above all as a way of making it possible for impoverished students to study at the Bauhaus."[381]

Mart Stam, for instance, arrived in Dessau in mid-1928 as a visiting professor of town planning and elementary building theory and taught there until 1929.

In a meticulously researched publication, Renate Scheper, onetime daughter-in-law to Hinnerk Scheper (master of wall painting at the Bauhaus in Dessau), discusses the restructuring undertaken by Meyer. Whereas Gropius had yielded to "pressure from the students," Meyer felt that "the ideal training consisted of practical planning and building."[382]

378 Scheper 2005, p. 28
379 Hannes Meyer to Adolf Behne, 28 January 1928, Bauhaus-Archiv
380 Scheper 2005, p. 28
381 Bill 1953, p. 59
382 Scheper 2005, p. 28
383 Wingler 1974, p. 53
384 Statement filmed in 1988 by Thomas Grimm in Dessau, during the exhibition *experiment bauhaus.*
385 Kandinsky 1976, p. 145
386 Gunta Stölzl, cited in Kandinsky 1976, p. 145

An ardent believer in collective creativity rather than individualistic production, Meyer seriously considered terminating the contracts of all the artists at the Bauhaus. In view of that, it may in fact be true that Kandinsky (or his wife Nina?)—hoping to prevent his own dismissal—entered the ideological power struggle and denounced Meyer for donating money to Rote Hilfe, the German branch of International Red Aid. The leftist students at the Bauhaus certainly raised that issue in their newspaper. Regardless of who in fact denounced Meyer, he was removed from his post on 1 August 1930.

In his little "bauhaus primer," Hans M. Wingler states dryly: "Hannes Meyer. 1927 Dessau bauhaus head of the architecture section; 1928 director; 1930 dismissed due to the increasing politicization of the school."[383]

An eyewitness to those events, Gertrud Arndt, whose husband Alfred Arndt was appointed head of the new furniture and fixtures department in 1929, lent weight to the leftist students' suspicions. She remembered that her husband had complained to Fritz Hesse, the mayor in Dessau, about Meyer's removal. However, when Arndt pointed out to Hesse that issuing letters of dismissal was the sole preserve of the Bauhaus masters' council, the mayor merely replied that Kandinsky had been the only master in Dessau at the time and that he had agreed Meyer should be dismissed.[384]

Nina Kandinsky gave a different account of those events: "In my view Gunta Stölzl went too far when she implied that Kandinsky more or less ousted Hannes Meyer because of his Communist sympathies.... Once the wider public had got wind of political activities at the Bauhaus, the mayor, Fritz Hesse, paid a visit to Kandinsky and Klee. Hesse, a clever, energetic man, presented them with just one option: 'Either you see to it that all political activity at the Bauhaus ceases immediately or the school will be shut down.' Kandinsky realized how serious the situation was ... he suggested that Hesse should talk face to face with Meyer. Hesse did that, but found it impossible to make any headway with Meyer. He therefore asked Meyer to leave the school. Meyer refused. However, since he was a Swiss citizen, it was easy enough for the Anhalt government to remove him from office. That forcible intervention created a sense of crisis at the Bauhaus."[385] And according to Gunta Stölzl, it was Kandinsky who proposed that Mies van der Rohe should replace Hannes Meyer as director: "In the summer of 1930, during the Bauhaus vacation, I received a telegram from Kandinsky that read: 'Hannes Meyer has been dismissed. We presume you agree with this.' And then I was informed, in similarly succinct terms, that Mies van der Rohe had been named as the new director."[386]

"... Europe's most advanced cultural institution"

Many years later Bill put that sequence of events in a wider political context: "In that era of growing political tension, when the black spectre of 'cultural Bolshevism' first loomed into view in the skies above Germany, the newly elected town council in Dessau removed Hannes Meyer and replaced him with the architect Ludwig Mies van der Rohe. And when the National Socialists gained the majority in Dessau in 1932, they ordered the Bauhaus to close. An attempt to run the school as a private institution in Berlin foundered within a few months. Teachers and students alike were labeled enemies of the state, persecuted, and condemned to inactivity. Thus, after just fifteen years in operation, in 1933 Europe's most advanced cultural institution sank into deep oblivion."[387] When the Bauhaus in Berlin was shut down by the Nazis, Josef Albers was assistant director to Mies van der Rohe. Albers, who left Germany with his wife Anni that year, was the first Bauhaus master to emigrate to the United States, four years before Gropius and Moholy-Nagy, "with whom he largely avoided contact."[388]

Achim Borchardt-Hume, curator of the exhibition *Albers and Moholy-Nagy: From the Bauhaus to the New World,* at Tate Modern in London in 2006, writes in his catalogue that Albers managed to save his wife's family but he provides no detail as to how this happened: "[Josef Albers] ... had witnessed the destruction of cultural values in his homeland and [had] rescued his wife's Jewish family from Nazi persecution ..."[389]

Borchardt-Hume then adds that "at the invitation of Ted Dreier, the philanthropist founder of the liberal Black Mountain College, Albers and Anni crossed the Atlantic Ocean en route to North Carolina. Their arrival did not go unnoticed in the East Coast press, which enthusiastically welcomed the arrival of 'A Teacher from the Bauhaus.'"[390]

In 1963, ten years after Max Bill wrote the text that I have cited here, a booklet was published in the German Democratic Republic (GDR), which described the dismissal of Hannes Meyer in the following terms: "In 1930 the Social Democratic council of the town of Dessau fired

387 Bill 1953, p. 59
388 Borchardt-Hume 2006, p. 76
389 Borchardt-Hume 2006, pp. 76–77
390 Borchardt-Hume 2006, p. 76
391 Pazitnov 1963, p. 31
392 Faber, "Das Bauhaus in Dessau vor Torschluss," *information* 1:3 (August/September 1932)

H. Meyer as director of the Bauhaus for pursuing 'Marxist teaching methods, which undermine civic concepts of building and architecture and infect young people.' The real trigger for his dismissal was the voluntary contribution that H. Meyer made to the international workers' support fund for the striking miners in Mansfeld. This expression of solidarity with the working class on the part of the Bauhaus director was the last straw for the Social Democratic councillors. The police carried out search warrants at the Bauhaus and any foreign student leaders were ordered to leave the country. Hannes Meyer and a group of Bauhaus architects traveled to the Soviet Union, where they formed a shock brigade known as the Red Front (*Rotfront*). Before his departure, H. Meyer stated in an interview: 'I am traveling to the USSR to work in a place where a truly proletarian culture is being forged, where socialism is on the rise, where the social structures still endure that we have attacked here in the name of capitalism.'"[391]

"In 1930, even before the Nazis had a numerical majority, Hannes Meyer was summarily dismissed. He was banished because of his 'Marxist mindset' by the then still-democratic social democrats who were in the majority at the time. That's how effective the de facto power of the National Socialists already was by then."[392] An editorial note is appended to this text in *information:* "This article had already been typeset when we read the following report from Dessau in the German press: 'The municipal council in the town of Dessau has recorded a majority vote in favor of a National Socialist proposal to close the Bauhaus on 1 October and to dismiss the teaching staff. The Social Democrats abstained.'"

More information may be had from a short biography of Hannes Meyer in Walter Scheiffele's *Bauhaus, Junkers, Sozialdemokratie* (Berlin: Form+Zweck, 2003): "In August 1930 Meyer was dismissed without notice. In October 1930, under the auspices of the Supreme Economic Council of the USSR, he took up a post as head architect for Giprovtus and as a professor at the Institute of Architecture and Building (WASI)" (p. 281). In 1936–39 he was in Switzerland again. Scheiffele's book also contains a short biography of the same Fritz Hesse (a social democrat born in Dessau) who dismissed Meyer "without notice"; it seems that as the mayor of Dessau he had played a "crucial part in the relocation of the Bauhaus from Weimar to Dessau." After the war, in July 1945 he was"reappointed mayor of Dessau by the American authorities" (p. 279).

The Bauhaus Stage

Clemens Röseler, a friend of Max Bill's, had already joined the Bauhaus stage workshop in 1927 and may have encouraged Bill to follow suit, which Bill then did in January 1928.

Clemens Röseler was studying under Kandinsky, having previously gained experience in the wall-painting workshop. Like Xanti Schawinsky, who was also very active on stage, he lived in the Prellerhaus—the accommodation block for Bauhaus students. Röseler, who was friends with Max Bill and T. Lux Feininger, was a busy multi-talent, for instance giving T. Lux banjo lessons in his free time. During the course of 1928 Röseler concentrated on devising color schemes for the Bauhaus wallpapers that the firm of Gebr. Rasch & Co sold on the open market.

T. Lux Feininger took "a double portrait of Max Bill and a female student on the terrace outside the Bauhaus cafeteria": "this photograph is now in the photographic collection of the Metropolitan Museum in New York" (T. Lux Feininger, 22 Arlington Street, Cambridge, Massachusetts, 29 September 2004, to Angela Thomas Schmid, Zumikon).

As a prospective member, he was required to provide not only examples of drawings or craft pieces he had made but also a clean bill of health and a certificate of good character from the police. Schlemmer accepted Bill on condition that he passed a month's trial. Once again Bill found himself in an educational test bed. The official program for the stage department was described in the Bauhaus quarterly:

> (a) The stage department delivers practical and theoretical training for those with stage-related talents, promoting a collaborative effort toward the common goal of a new stage form.
>
> (b) The stage department is divided into the stage workshop for painters and technicians and the experimental stage for dancers, actors, directors.
>
> (c) Since the work in this department is predominantly experimental, there are no teaching contracts and no guarantee of a training with a final exam for a particular area of expertise.[393]

The statement in paragraph (c), with its reference to experimentation, was especially appealing to Max Bill. But then, as if echoing the warning that there was "no guarantee of a training with a final exam," toward the end of 1928 Bill found himself obliged to leave the Bauhaus for personal reasons, without graduating.

393 Oskar Schlemmer in *bauhaus* 1:3 (1927), p. 6

394 Schlemmer, p. 6

The Bauhaus stage—in a room that was originally only intended as a lecture theater—could be opened out on both sides (toward the main hall and the kitchens). And although the students and staff in the stage department were the underdogs at the Bauhaus—the stage was the worst- funded department—Oskar Schlemmer still had high ambitions for it:

> Mission:
> (a) In the stage department, students solve problems set by the departmental staff. Depending on the aptitudes of the individual, those problems are either ideational-creative or artisanal-practical.
> (b) Above all they relate to aspects of stagecraft, namely form, color, space, and movement.
> (c) They also relate to language and tone as well as to theatrical ideas and composition.
>
> All these areas, in their fundamental forms and manifestations, are to be investigated, tested, and applied with the aim of arriving at a new stageworthy presentation mode.
>
> Performances:
> The results of these studies are to be presented in loose sequences, initially in performances at the Bauhaus and later on at other venues.
>
> Fields of activity:
> (a) Construction of masks and costumes
> (b) Construction of instruments, apparatuses, props
> (c) Scenography, stage design
> (d) Producing stage models
> (e–g) Gymnastic, dance-based, musical, linguistic studies and productions
> (h) Improvisation, extemporization, dramatic composition
> (i) Choreographic presentations, diagrams. scores.[394]

By the time Bill joined the stage workshop, Oskar Schlemmer had already been in close contact with the musician and conductor Hermann Scherchen for several months. They were working on a production of Igor Stravinsky's *Les Noces* with colored slide projections that was due to be performed in

Berlin in January 1928, and Schlemmer was utterly absorbed in his slide designs when Bill arrived.[395]

From mid-August until the end of September 1927 Schlemmer was with his wife and children in Ascona in the Ticino, "the summer refuge for numerous Bauhauslers and other illustrious visitors from the art world"; there he had met up with "Scherchen and his wife, the actress Gerda Müller, whom he knew from productions they had both been involved in at the Volksbühne in Berlin."[396] The two men, Scherchen and Schlemmer—the latter slim and delicately built "with a shaven head, slightly protruding ears, and bright, clear eyes ... always amiable, modest, respectful toward others"[397]—explored the idea of a "music-dance-numbers theory." And soon they started to contemplate a future collaboration of some kind. Scherchen felt that Schlemmer should move on from his *Triadic Ballet* and venture into entirely new territory, that he should try working "with mechanical forms" rather than human beings. The two men discussed "forms as such—their colors, their numbers" and Scherchen came up with the idea of "a spatial configuration of forms and colors, mechanically operated, that functioned in the same way as a fugue."[398] But then Scherchen and Schlemmer evolved a very different plan and abandoned the idea of matching the movements of an elaborate stage mechanism to music. They now decided to try to realize Igor Stravinsky's *Les Noces* as a sequence of dance scenes "with colored slide projections instead of dancers."[399]

Schlemmer was so absorbed by his discussions with Scherchen that he extended his vacation in Ascona (without permission from the Bauhaus, as Paul Klee had once done before him) and did not return in time for the beginning of new term—praise be to the creatives with minds of their own! Between October 1927 and January 1928 Schlemmer created "nine smaller designs in colored inks" for the planned production of *Les Noces* and "twenty-five sections of the painted projection frieze in tempera paints on black photocard."

Max Bill had vivid memories of Schlemmer's three-dimensional, light-and-shadow designs: "The 'figural cabinet' of flat, colorful, geometric figurines was worn by actors in black leotards who moved around on the black stage and seemed to be alive thanks to changing lighting effects, when their various colors were seen in the glow of other colors. Dances with sticks, metal dances, and other stage effects were

395 One of these sketches, in colored inks and titled *Das Brautbett,* is illustrated in black and white in Scheper 1986, p. 100
396 Scheper 1986
397 Lauterbach 1958
398 Scheper 1986
399 Scheper 1986

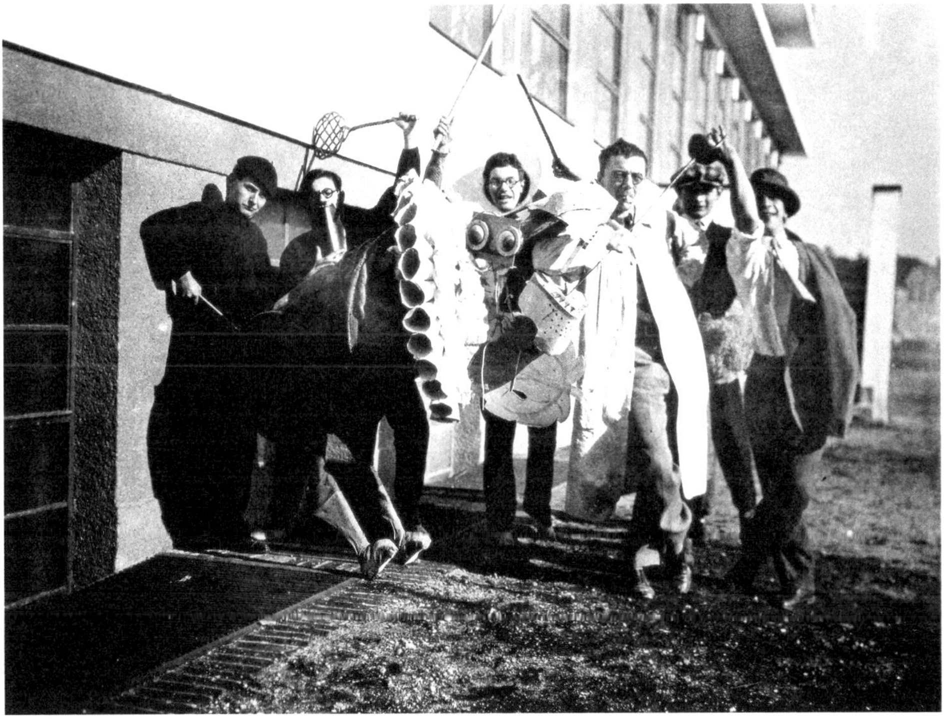

T. Lux Feininger, "The old stage crew." Students from the Bauhaus stage workshop outside the Bauhaus building, Dessau. From left: Clemens Röseler, T. Lux Feininger, Max Bill, Joost Schmidt, Roman Clemens, Xanti Schawinsky, 1927–28

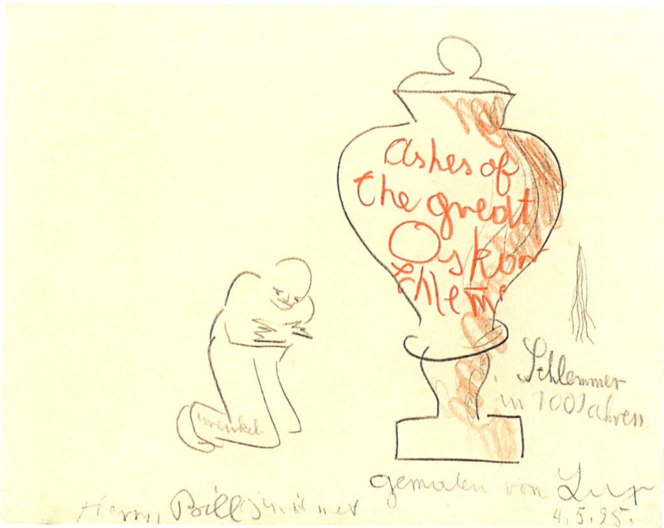

T. Lux Feininger, Caricature: "Ashes of the great Oskar Schlemmer," 4 May 1928, graphite and colored pencil on paper, 21.5 × 27.4 cm

devised at the Bauhaus stage, extemporized with Schlemmer, we also crafted costumes for them." The chance to express ideas through movement had a powerful appeal for Bill. "The *Triadic Ballet,* the figural cabinet, the sticks dance ... were partly created there.... Afterward, at the performances we students even tried to dance, too. Schlemmer himself composed the music for those performances, for the metal dance, for instance."[400]

Elsewhere, in a later interview about Schlemmer, Bill returned to the topic of the *Triadic Ballet:* Schlemmer "was rather remarkable, he was actually very reserved. take the *triadic ballet* for instance, the figures always pass by each other, they have very little to do with each other. they only have spatial relationships, very isolated relationships. there are very few direct-human forms of expression in it."[401]

The exercises involved in creating a piece were a group activity. For the rest of the time the students at the Bauhaus stage could do whatever they wanted; as Bill remembered it, there was no fixed timetable or schedule. That perfectly suited his mindset.

"Objective and Professional"— Oskar Schlemmer's Mantra

When Max Bill joined the Bauhaus stage he walked into a hive of activity fueled by Schlemmer as he developed his ideas for *Les Noces.* Bill may well have enjoyed that atmosphere, that sense of experimentation, or did it unsettle him, did it knock him off balance? All too soon, however, Schlemmer discovered—to his great disappointment—that the performance of *Les Noces* in Berlin had been postponed. When no new date was fixed for a performance, Schlemmer and Scherchen lost contact. Was it that Scherchen's commitments elsewhere prevented him from pursuing their plans? Was his diary just too full? Certainly, a month later he was working in Winterthur, in Max's native town: on 19 February 1928 he conducted the Swiss premiere of an orchestral version of Bach's *Die Kunst der Fuge,* arranged by Wolfgang Graeser. This was followed by a series of performances of *Die Kunst der Fuge,* all conducted by Scherchen—in

400 Max Bill in an interview about Oskar Schlemmer

401 Max Bill in a TV film about Oskar Schlemmer, SW3, aired 19 May 1984, 10 p.m., with excerpts from the reconstruction of the *Triadic Ballet*

Zurich, Lausanne, Geneva, and Frankfurt am Main in March and April 1928. That same year the tireless Scherchen also took over as head of music at the Ostmark Rundfunk (radio station) in Königsberg in the Free State of Prussia.

Did Max Bill have a chance to go to any of those concerts? Maybe he went with his mother, who complained in her petition for divorce of her husband's lack of cultural curiosity.

Bill kept in contact with Hermann Scherchen and later created a logo and a cover design for the scores released by Scherchen's music publishing company, Ars Viva. Bill's radically pared-back design is seen on the cover of Wladimir Vogel's *Tripartita* (1933–34, see p. 520). In 1933, when Scherchen organized a month-long working conference for new music (*Arbeitstagung für moderne Musik*) in Strasbourg, the composers he invited to participate included Vogel.

Hermann Scherchen first became friends with Wladimir Vogel in Berlin after the First World War. "Scherchen—as both conductor and publisher—championed Vogel's music whenever he could. Two premieres instigated by Scherchen in the 1930s especially helped to advance Vogel's career: *Zwei Etüden für Orchester* (1930) in Königsberg in 1931, and a brand new *Ritmica Ostinata* [for brass and percussion] in Berlin in 1932."[402]

Scherchen also wrote from Riva to the author Elias Canetti, inviting him to come to Strasbourg after 23 July 1933.

There were two concerts per day—"by no means light music"—and lectures, as Canetti recalls, who has plenty to say about Scherchen the "conductor."[403]

When Vogel emigrated to Switzerland in 1933 Max Bill was one of the first artists he met there. They had a mutual acquaintance: Robert Blum. Bill had worked with Blum at the cabaret theater, "Der Krater," in Zurich after March 1930 and Vogel knew him from Busoni's composition class at the Prussian Academy of the Arts in Berlin, where they had both been master students.

"I contacted Busoni when I heard that he was to take over the master class from Richard Strauss but would only accept five students. He had already brought three with him from Switzerland where he had spent the First World War, that is to say, my Swiss colleagues Luc Balmer

402 See Hansjörg Pauli and Dagmar Wünsche, *Hermann Scherchen: Musiker, 1891–1966* (Berlin: Hentrich, 1986)

403 See Canetti 1985

404 Vogel 1977, p. 174

405 Wladimir Vogel, Zurich, to Walter Labhart, 7 May 1974, in Vogel 1977, p. 252

(Bern), Robert Blum (Zurich), and Walther Geiser (Basel), who—besides their various gifts—had one thing in common: hard Swiss currency."[404] Among the other students who joined Busoni's class (which ultimately numbered more than just five) was Kurt Weill from Dessau, who later achieved global fame. Vogel once commented that, since he was born in Moscow to a German father and a Russian mother, he had German nationality on paper. "When I had left Germany and was living in Switzerland with a German passport, I was treated as a German."[405]

A copy of *Schriften und Aufzeichnungen über Musik* by Wladmir Vogel, in the Bibliothek Max Bill, has a dedication from the editor: "To Max Bill, who is better informed about developments in new music than any other visual artist, with best wishes from the editor on 22 December 1977, Walter Labhart"; and the composer added his own signature in red pencil a few years later, again on Bill's birthday: "Wladimir Vogel 22 December 80."

Another score published by Scherchen's Ars Viva, this time in Brussels but still with Bill's cover design, was *Joh. Seb. Bach, Musikalisches Opfer, Version Roger Vuataz* (1937). In December 1940 Bill attended a lecture given by Scherchen in Zurich on "The Musical Interpretation and Future Development of Music," and in 1950 Scherchen published *Joh. Seb. Bach: Die Kunst der Fuge.*

In the Bibliothek Max Bill there is a copy of *Joh. Seb. Bach: Die Kunst der Fuge,* arranged for orchestra by Roger Vuataz in 1950 (dedicated to his friend Hermann Scherchen), copyrighted to Hermann Scherchen's publishing company (Ars Viva, Zurich), with the standard black-and-white Ars Viva cover designed by Max Bill; the dedication, in red pencil, reads: "To Mr. Bill with friendly gratitude Hermann Scherchen Zürich 7.V.50." Roger Vuataz (born in Geneva in 1898), who arranged the *Kunst der Fuge,* became head of the music section at Radio Geneva in 1942.

By now the Cold War was already well under way and soon, after almost thirty years of dedicated work, Scherchen would lose his job in Winterthur —all of a sudden—because of "incompatible political views."

The Law-Abiding Nature of Bach's Fugues

At the Bauhaus some students developed a special interest in Bach's fugues. "Inspired by Klee's teaching" a collective of Bauhaus students in Dessau—Püschel, Neugeboren, and Marx—decided to create a "graphic, three-dimensional version of a fugue by Bach."[406] And Thomas Flake, son of the poet Otto Flake, set himself the task of "creating a graphic scheme of the laws governing a fugue by Johann Sebastian Bach by studying the score and playing a record of the piece."[407]

A work by Heinrich Neugeboren, his *Stereometrische Darstellung von vier Takten einer Fuge aus dem "Wohltemperierten Klavier" von J. S. Bach*—intended as a proposal for a Bach monument, which he first modeled in 1928—is illustrated in Klaus-Jürgen Winkler, "Die Werkstätten für Wandmalerei und Bildhauerei" (1974), p. 19.

Xanti Schawinsky

Alexander "Xanti" Schawinsky, from Basel, enrolled in Dessau with the matriculation number 16, soon after Katt Both (no. 4) and well before Max Bill (no. 151). Xanti, who was four years older than Max, had previously worked as a set designer at the Stadttheater in Zwickau and at the Bauhaus he was able to build on the skills he had already acquired. From the start he was an enthusiastic, very active member of the Bauhaus stage workshop. Xanti also played in the Bauhaus band, which Bill sometimes joined as a banjo player.

For one semester Xanti Schawinsky gave Clemens Röseler, T. Lux Feininger, and Roman Clemens private tuition based on his own experience of practical stagecraft. As the political atmosphere worsened, Roman Clemens, a German student in the stage department and fellow student of Max Bill's, decided to leave Nazi Germany; Max Bill—already back in Switzerland by that time—made Clemens welcome in his small apartment in Zurich.

In the late 1940s Xanti once asked Bill to describe what he had expected of the Bauhaus and what he had actually found there, to which Max replied: "It felt as if you just suddenly arrived there one day, following an irresistible urge—not expecting anything in particular but hoping to find

406 Winkler 2003, p. 106
407 Fischli 1968, p. 56

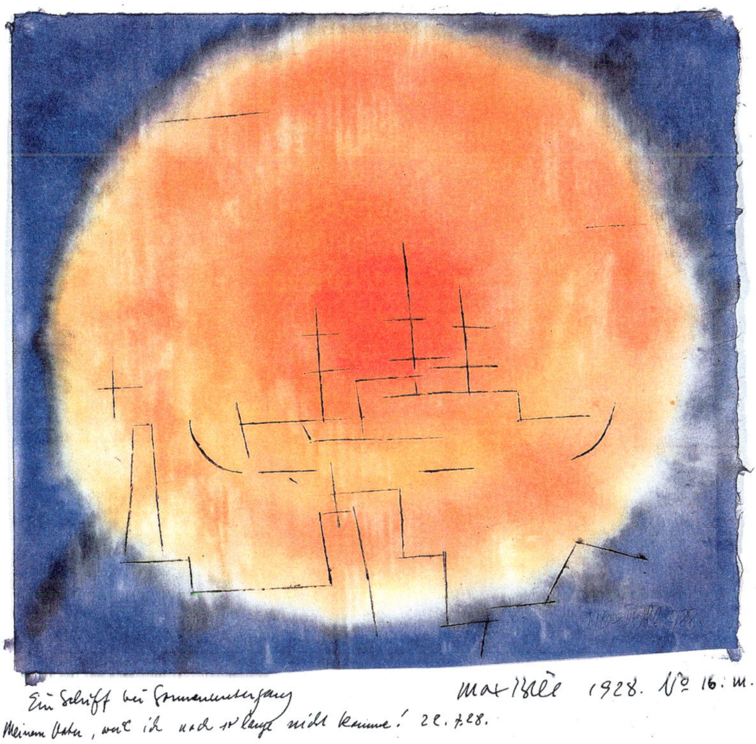

Max Bill, *Ein Schiff bei Sonnenuntergang,* 1928, watercolor and india ink on paper, inscribed with a dedication to Bill's father: "Meinem Vater, weil ich noch so lange nicht komme! 28.7.28"

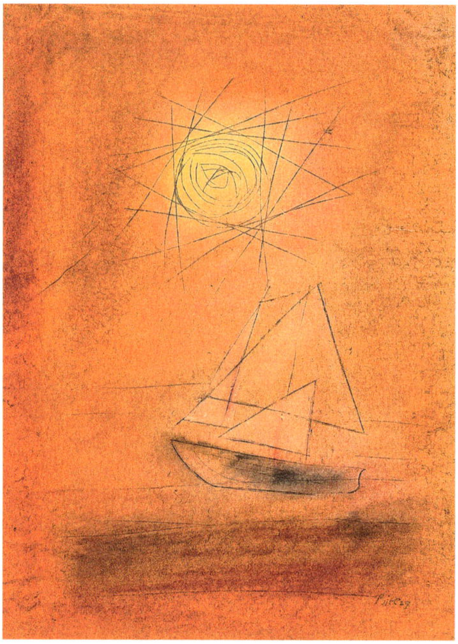

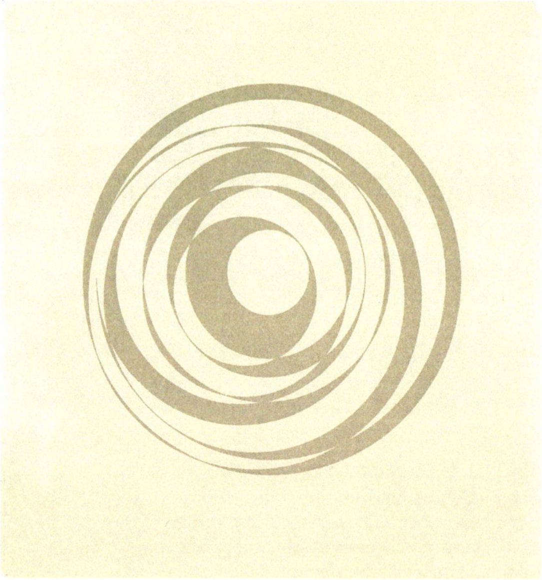

Max Bill, *Ein Schiff unter der Sonne,* 1929, watercolor and india ink on paper, 44×32 cm
Max Bill, Sheet from the series *fünfzehn variationen über ein thema,* 1935–38

the essence of the modern spirit: a combination of education, knowledge, experimentation, youthful high spirits, and cultural awareness. Once you were at the Bauhaus, you were no longer aware that you were searching for something. You worked, experimented, debated. Life outside the Bauhaus ceased to be of interest because you were part of a community where everyone was united, from the most important artists of our time to random, repellent careerists who had somehow washed up at the Bauhaus. We found friends and even dearer lady-friends, sometimes studying seemed superfluous, but we never forgot to work."[408]

T. Lux Feininger may perhaps have been jealous of Max, who was friends with Clemens Röseler. Röseler taught T. Lux to play the banjo and the latter once declared that he would always vouch for Röseler "through thick and thin." At any rate, one day T. Lux's creative urge was kindled by the figure of Max Bill. In May 1928 he drew a caricature showing "*urenkel*" (great-grandson) Bill kneeling devoutly before an urn containing the "ashes of the great Oskar Schlemmer," with an ironic dedication to "Herr Bill"—"gemalen von Lux 4.5.28" (painted by Lux) (see p. 232). The mix of English and German adds to the drawing's comic effect. Theodore Lux Feininger later recounted in his autobiography (*Zwei Welten: Mein Künstlerleben zwischen Bauhaus und Amerika* [Halle, Saale: Mitteldeutscher Verlag, 2006]) that when he and his father had been to the cinema, they used to discuss the movie in English, which filled him with pride.

Lyonel Feininger's Ship Motifs

T. Lux and his parents lived in one of the Bauhaus masters' houses. It may be that Bill visited him there—he certainly seems to have seen works by Lyonel Feininger. There are suggestions in Bill's work that he was influenced by Feininger's style, even if only in passing. Lyonel Feininger's interest in ship motifs certainly informs two of Max Bill's works on paper. *Ein Schiff bei Sonnenuntergang* (1928, no. 16), a watercolor done in July 1928 during the summer vacation when Bill was in Italy for the second time, is dedicated to "my Father because it will still be a while before I'm there! 28.7.28." The other work, *Ein Schiff unter der Sonne* (1929, no. 33), was done the following year.

As a student Max Bill was not as self-analytical as Lyonel Feininger, who memorably once asked, "What exactly am I doing when I paint a picture? I dismember nature and think I am creating a life in art.

408 Bill 1947

I pick up a razor blade and dissect the corpse, hoping to find the soul but not finding it. I torment myself looking for my own soul. And what is left in the painting? Cut after cut. A network of sharp or uncertain cuts. You may think they are construction lines. You may even think they are the energy lines of life, which I have discovered. Sadly no, they are quandaries. They are signs that I am coming from the outside, trying to seek out the secret of the soul. And yet I know that that is impossible."[409] Meanwhile, Bill was most definitely searching for "construction lines" and adapted one aspect of Feininger's methods to that end. His depiction of the sun with a linear overlay in *ein schiff unter der sonne* (1929, see p. 238) can be seen as an early precursor of his series of *fünfzehn variationen über ein thema* (1935–38) (see pp. 24, 238, 672).

Feininger felt something of an affinity with German Romanticism, particularly with the Romantics' love of landscapes by the Baltic Sea. In 1931 the Nationalgalerie in Berlin presented a retrospective exhibition to mark his sixtieth birthday. Once the Nazis had seized power Feininger still could not initially bring himself to return to the United States, despite the fact that his wife's Jewish heritage and his own involvement in modern art meant that he would more than likely be targeted by the Nazis. It was only after their house was searched by the Gestapo, "around 378 of his paintings were removed from German museums," and his work was shown in the exhibition *Entartete Kunst* that he and his wife, Julia, "left Germany, with America as their destination, on 11 June 1937."[410]

Multitalented Bauhauslers

"On the invitation of Gebrüder Rasch work started on wallpaper designs; anyone was allowed to submit a design. A selection was made from the submissions and each participant received a small fee. A smaller working group finalized the collective's ideas and these became the basis for the

409 Lyonel Feininger, cited in Schreyer 1956, p. 139
410 See Eckmann 1997
411 Schawinsky 1927
412 Thümmler 1999
413 Thümmler 1999
414 Thümmler 1999
415 Information kindly supplied by Burckhard Kieselbach, who had access to the archives of the Rasch wallpaper factory, Kieselbach Design, Bramsche 2007

products made at the Rasch factory, which were then sold on the open market as 'Bauhaus wallpapers.' Although the designers remained anonymous, the company paid fees for their designs and royalties to Bauhaus G.m.b.H., which the school had created as a vehicle for doing business with industrial partners."[411] The committee of four masters set up to oversee the design work for the wallpapers consisted of Josef Albers, Ludwig Hilberseimer, Hinnerk Scheper, and Joost Schmidt.

The contract between the Bauhaus and the manufacturers, Gebr. Rasch & Co., for products with the trade name *Bauhaus-Tapete* (Bauhaus wallpaper) was signed in March 1929, at a time when Bill had not yet finally decided whether he would stay in Dessau or return to Zurich.

In April 1929 Bill was still placing small ads in *Letzte Politik* seeking work in Dessau.

This contract stipulated that "all designs and colors must be expressly approved by the Bauhaus."

The colors were decided by Hinnerk Scheper "and his students, standing over the machines in the factory in Bramsche. The bauhauslers seem to have taken such delight in this task that Hannes Meyer once joked that now the last disciples of art had gone off to mix wallpaper colors."[412]

Moreover, "the Bauhaus retained the right to design and produce publicity materials, such as posters, advertisements, and so on, in order to ensure that the public image of the Bauhaus conformed to its own aesthetic guidelines. This contract also stated that five per cent of the revenue from sales was to be spent on advertising.... The Bauhaus wallpapers were designed in the wall painting workshop, which was run by Hinnerk Scheper in Dessau."[413]

Max Bill's friends Clemens Röseler, Hanns Fischli, and Margaret Camilla Leiteritz were all among the participants in the open competition for wallpaper designs.

"One of the competition winners, Hanns Fischli, took the method Josef Albers taught in the foundation course and applied it to wallpaper.... The other winner was Leiteritz, who had devised patterns with lines and dot grids."[414] Margaret Leiteritz and Fischli won "most of the prizes for bauhaus wallpaper designs."[415]

Bill seems to have been in close contact with Margaret Leiteritz; she and Fischli took all the prizes in that competition between them. In 1929, after Bill had returned to Switzerland, he received a letter from Hilde Rantzsch in Dessau reporting on Margaret Leiteritz's latest news—evidently Rantzsch was confident that Bill would be interested: "Leiteritz is in Kassel, working at the Staatstheater as a set painter, but ... she doesn't write."

Burckhard Kieselbach confirmed that Margaret Leiteritz was in Kassel: "In 1929–30 Frau Leiteritz spent a semester as an intern at the Staats-theater in Kassel, where she worked on stage sets in the paint studio."

Rantzsch also reports, a little caustically, on Lou Scheper, who was "stuck in Moscow with her husband, writing brainy articles and playing the female intellectual."[416]

Meanwhile, Lou Scheper herself was enthusiastic about the opportunities she was enjoying in Moscow: "The commission to work as a 'specialist' on color in the Moscow cityscape, made possible by a leave of absence [from the Bauhaus], opened up a huge testing ground and provided experiences that benefitted the Bauhaus and Bauhauslers."[417]

Bauhaus student Lou Scheper-Berkenkamp, who married Hinnerk Scheper in 1922, was involved in the activities of the stage workshop led by Oskar Schlemmer. She also painted and participated in the touring exhibitions of works by "Junge Maler am Bauhaus" ("Young painters at the Bauhaus"). Hinnerk Scheper was given leave of absence from the Bauhaus to take up a position in Moscow "as a color consultant for architecture and town planning," after which he and his family returned to the Bauhaus in Dessau.[418]

"It should not be forgotten that besides giving members of the wall painting workshop at the Bauhaus direct practical experience, the work they did on major commissions also provided a vital source of income. And the fact that the wall painting workshop was commercially viable—by way of an exception for an educational institution—was in no way detrimental to our teaching."[419]

Bill's own attitude to political events in the Soviet Union at that time is seen in his cover design for *Nebelspalter,* a satirical Swiss weekly. He mocks the current situation in the USSR where "a batch of Soviet leaders is for sale at well below cost price," as the wall poster tells us. In the image a Soviet soldier holds a flyer that looks like a wanted poster with a

416 [Probably Hilde Rantzsch], Dessau, to Max Bill, [November or December 1929], Bibliothek Max Bill

417 On connections between Bauhauslers and Soviet artists, see Larissa A. Shadowa, "Hinnerk Scheper und Boris Ender im Maljarstroj," *Wissenschaftliche Zeitschrift der Hochschule Architektur und Bauwesen, Weimar,* 26:4–5 (1979), pp. 323–27

418 Neumann 1971, p. 91

419 Lou Scheper, cited in Neumann 1971, p. 95

420 Scheper, cited in Neumann 1971, p. 95

stenciled image but no name on it as yet—although the bespectacled face is clearly that of Leo Trotsky. The suggestion is that Josef Stalin, suspecting Trotsky of involvement in a conspiracy, now wants to sell him off as quickly as possible.

Progressive Color Schemes versus Burnt Nazi Red

"Clear light and clear dark tones, pure white and pure black, graduated grays without impurities—that was the color world that the ugly browns and burnt reds of the Third Reich broke into. Everything that was there before 1934 was buried and now has to be painstakingly retrieved and brought to light again."[420] When Max Bill—particularly in the 1940s—used "pure white and pure black" in his paintings, he was referencing the clarity of the color spectrum that had been nurtured at the Bauhaus.

Lou Scheper, a remarkable woman, designed the color scheme for Hans Scharoun's Berliner Philharmonie (1962–63). Sadly, I never met her face to face; she died very suddenly in 1976, shortly before she and her son Dirk Scheper were expected at the *Max-Bill-Retrospektive* that Max Bill and I had installed at the Akademie der Künste in Berlin. Ever since their time together at the Bauhaus—their "home," as Lou Scheper called it—there had been a strong tie between Max Bill and Lou Scheper.

Membership of the Bauhaus family naturally extended to Hinnerk Scheper's son. And so it was that, on my request, Dirk Scheper delivered what proved to be a very moving address at the memorial for Max Bill at Schauspielhaus Zürich. He described the day before Max's death, when the two of them had worked together for many hours in the Bauhaus-Archiv in Berlin.

Who Did What on the Bauhaus Wallpapers

A critical comment by Max Bill (as he told me) regarding an image in a book of Bauhaus wallpaper samples brought the wrath of Dr. Emil Rasch, director of Gebr. Rasch & Co., down on his head. The sample book, which was published by Rasch in 1932, included a portrait photograph of Walter Gropius. Bill pointed this out in a review, mockingly remarking that it was much more refined to use a photograph of Gropius, who had gone to the United States, than a photograph of Hannes Meyer, who had admittedly overseen the wallpaper competition in Dessau but who had then gone over to the Soviet Union—the wrong side. Bill was later sure that when he presented his proposals for the Hochschule für Gestaltung in Ulm, Emil Rasch had stirred up opposition to the project in Germany because of his lingering resentment at that jibe.[421]

I cannot say whether Bill's view was justified—it may have been no more than a suspicion. At any rate, no documents have emerged that would support it. On the other hand, there is no doubt that during the planning phase of the Hochschule für Gestaltung Bill had to overcome various obstacles placed in his path by German industrialists.

The question as to who did or did not do what at the Bauhaus reverberates throughout the history of the Bauhaus. It seems that Bill, for his part, was always keen to be as historically accurate as possible in his accounts of what happened and who was involved. Nevertheless, in the mid-to-late 1940s, when Hannes Meyer read Max Bill's recollections of the Bauhaus in Dessau he expressed some astonishment that Bill now "suddenly" sympathised with him.

In April 1947 Hannes Meyer wrote: "Max Bill, architect and printmaker [was a] very effective businessman and manager. Has a hand in everything that counts as modern art . . . [and] gave a lecture on the Bauhaus last year in Milan and was suddenly on my side. Boom time?"[422]

The wallpaper catalogue that Bill was referring to in that conversation with me was designed by Joost Schmidt in the summer of 1932; it was the last commission that Schmidt took on at the Bauhaus in Berlin.

"In the photoplastic on the cover, besides a silver sphere reflecting part of Schmidt's studio in one of the master houses, there is also a piece of Bauhaus wallpaper with a typical example of classic Bauhaus wallpaper patterns. The large silver glass sphere was suspended from the studio ceiling, the roll of wallpaper was laid on a table and was photographed with the hand-written banderole.

In this charmingly grotesque, rounded reflection of wallpaper, typography, and the surrounding space, factual representation is

421 Max Bill, looking back at his time at the HfG in Ulm, in conversation with Angela Thomas, 1 October 1975

422 Hannes Meyer, Mexico, to Waldemar Adler, 28 April 1947, Archiv Stiftung Bauhaus Dessau

423 Nonne-Schmidt 1984 [c], pp. 21–22, 116, and fig. 40, p. 36

424 Rasch 1971, p. 183

transformed into an artistic composition. The writing below the picture provides an indication of the specific nature of the wallpapers, which can be confirmed by perusing the original pattern samples in the catalogue."[423]

The client was Gebr. Rasch & Co. in Bramsche, north of Osnabrück. Emil Rasch's sister, Maria Rasch, had studied at the Bauhaus in Weimar at the same time as Hinnerk Scheper, and it was through that connection with Scheper that Emil Rasch was able to personally call on Hannes Meyer in 1928 in his office at the Bauhaus in Dessau.

Rasch later described that meeting. Meyer, showing some "resistance to the idea of wallpaper," had initially been distant and aloof: "In that meeting at the Bauhaus in Dessau, which Hinnerk Scheper set up for me, it did not at all come as a surprise to me that the then director, Hannes Meyer, was rather reserved at first when I proposed the idea of producing Bauhaus wallpapers. However, since he was in principle keen to work with manufacturers as a way of improving the school's finances and also wanted to introduce new practical training routes for the students, Hannes Meyer did then warm to my idea and our subsequent collaboration was very harmonious. Once, when I complimented him on the precise, timely execution of our plans and on his reliable, businesslike attitude, he replied, 'You needn't be surprised, I'm from a family of entrepreneurs in Basel.' ... It was not until after the war that I was compensated for not having had the chance to get to know Walter Gropius back then."[424] That last comment confirms the implication in Max Bill's mocking criticism, namely that Rasch had no connection with Walter Gropius in 1932.

Gret Palucca: Part of the Bauhaus

As a rule, Bill's work on the Bauhaus stage was challenging and satisfying; on one occasion, however, there was an incident that was both extremely painful and life changing. In 1924 Gret Palucca, who had studied dance with Mary Wigman, launched her career as solo artist and married Friedrich Bienert, an industrialist's son from one of the wealthiest families in Dresden. Both Kandinsky and Moholy-Nagy were welcome visitors in his parents' home. Moholy-Nagy designed the cover for a book about the Bienerts' notable art collection, and in 1925 Friedrich Bienert's mother, Ida, commissioned Piet Mondrian to redesign an interior in the family home, which became known as the *Salon de Madame B..., á Dresden.*

Gret Palucca subsequently founded a school of her own; however, this was then closed down by the Nazis, with the "reason" being that she was a "half-Jew of the first degree through the maternal line."[425] Many years later in the autumn of 1988, when Bill and I were in Leipzig, in the then GDR, to install an exhibition of his works on paper in the museum there, I was present when he telephoned Palucca, by now a world-famous dancer, in Dresden and inquired after her health and well being in the friendliest of terms. She died in 1993—one year before Bill.

Gret Palucca, who founded her own dance school in Dresden, was credited with guiding "modern dance out of its expressionist phase and into the realm of the spirit and abstraction ... until it became buoyant and immaterial. She rightly saw Klee and Kandinsky as the fathers of her great art." On her visits to the Bauhaus Palucca showed the students "not only her dances but also her exercises, which gave an insight into the way she created her choreographies."[426] Palucca's skin was pale and her weightless, technical perfection was subtly alluring. People were struck by her immense energy and those who saw her dance described her style as abstract and absolute.

Palucca was only six years older than Bill, who greatly admired her. On 6 May 1928 she demonstrated a series of technical exercises and improvisations at the Bauhaus. However, when Bill subsequently tried to recall one of those exercises and attempted to recreate Palucca's circular movements, a serious accident occurred. Ironically enough, having had to provide a medical certificate just a few months earlier when he applied to join the stage workshop in January 1928, it was on that same stage that he was severely injured. "Gret Palucca, she was an outstanding dancer, had been doing exercises, her own training.... One of those exercises, which I asked her about, especially impressed me.... I then decided to try those exercises myself on the Bauhaus stage. I had started on one of them, not noticing that someone was doing something up above me on the trapeze; when he descended we hit our heads together, knocking over half of my teeth out.... That was pretty much the end of me spinning round on that spot."[427]

Bill's injury meant that he had to have a curved steel plate fitted into his upper palate. The dentist's bills must have severely depleted his funds. And then, later that same year, there was yet another setback,

425 Ralf Stabel, "Tanz Durch die Regime des 20. Jahrhunderts," in *Neue Zürcher Zeitung*, 8 January 2002

426 Grote 1959, p. 8

427 Max Bill in Scheidegger 1998

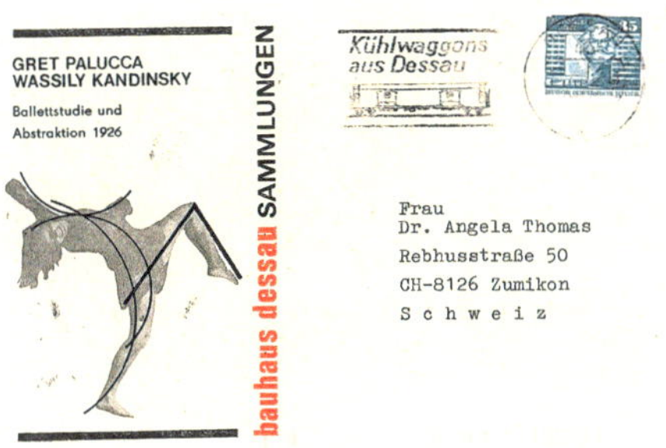

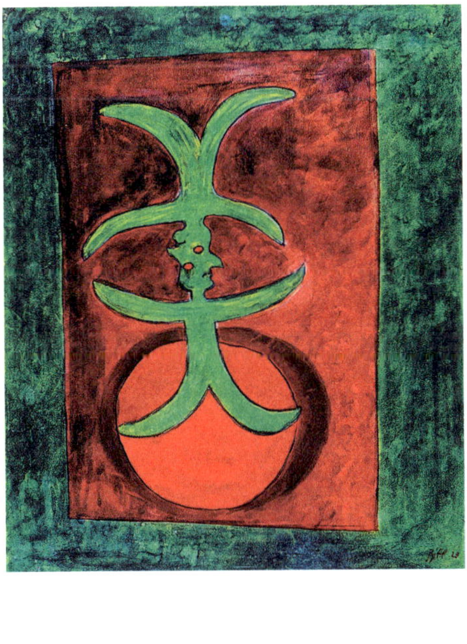

Postcard "Gret Palucca, Wassily Kandinsky: Ballettstudie und Abstraktion 1926," Bauhaus Dessau Sammlungen, GDR, Late 1980s

Max Bill, *Siamesische Zwillingsakrobaten,* 1929, oil on card, 66.4×56cm

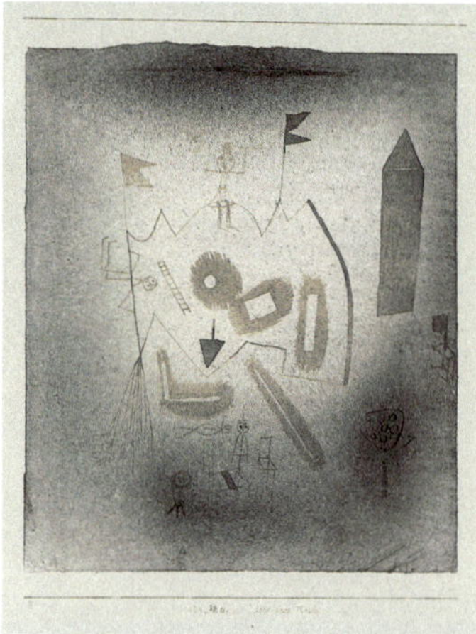

Paul Klee, *seltsames Theater, 1929, 316*, 1929, pen and watercolor on paper on cardboard, 31.7×26.7 cm

Oskar Schlemmer, *Reihenfolge 1–11*, ca. 1928, Sequence of scenes with *Triadic Ballet* figurines and props used in "Bauhaus dances," Bauhaus stage, Dessau, colored pencil on paper, 28.3×22 cm

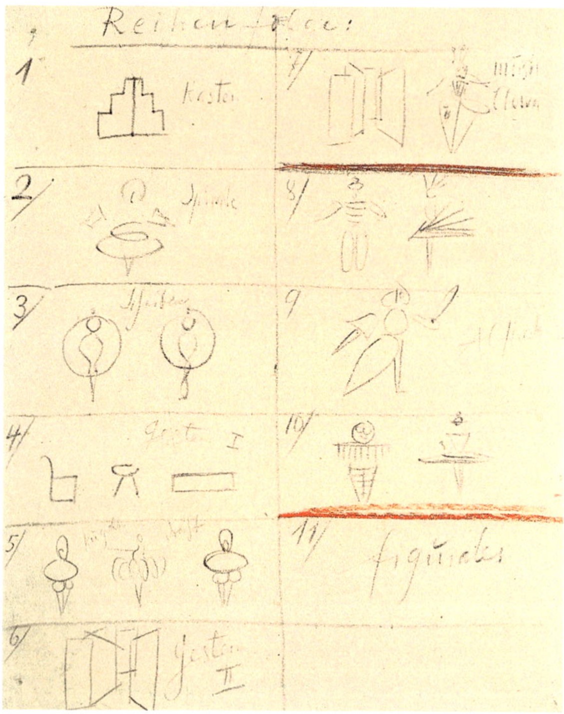

albeit much more banal. When Bill was absent from Dessau during the summer vacation Hanns Fischli sold off the latter's belongings, as Bill had asked him to do, but then kept some of the money for himself, contrary to Bill's expectations. As a result Bill's financial difficulties were now insurmountable and he had no choice but to leave the Bauhaus because he could no longer afford to continue his studies.

In 1929 Bill processed that life-changing accident in an oil painting, translating it into a garish red-and-green figurative composition entitled *siamesische zwillingsakrobaten* (see p. 247). The very distinct circular shape in the lower half of the composition recalls the circular movements executed by Gret Palucca that Bill was trying to replicate on the Bauhaus stage. As a boy at the Waldheim in Oetwil am See it was Bill's ski bindings that tore. And now, at the Bauhaus, news of that freak accident would have immediately have spread throughout the school. It may even be that Paul Klee's painting *Seltsames Theater* (1929; Strange Theater) was a response to that dramatic moment on the Bauhaus stage.

Max Bill noted that that performance at the Bauhaus was "probably on 7 July 1928," and in the list of recent events at the Bauhaus in *bauhaus* 2:4 (1928), p. 24, there is indeed a listing for 7 July 1928: "new performance by the Bauhaus stage: sticks dance, musical clowning, games after texts by Jean Arp etc. Performers: Manda v. Kreibig, Carla Grosch, E. Siedhoff, and others."

Interestingly, a program for a "ballett- und pantomimenabend" (ballet and pantomime evening) one year earlier on 9 July 1927, which is illustrated in Dirk Scheper, *Oskar Schlemmer: Das Triadische Ballett und die Bauhausbühne* (Berlin: Arsenal, 1988), fig. no. 178, p. 159, names Max Bill not only as cellist but also as a performer in a "figurale pantomime."

Hanns Fischli, who arrived at the Bauhaus at the start of the summer semester in 1928, a year after Bill, was intrigued by the special aura surrounding the members of the stage workshop: "Because we knew that they dwelled in the cellar and had no money, the Schlemmer group had a strange importance. Whether they were running around or sitting at a table in the canteen, you would always look twice—it was always theater first for them, they only ever came back down to earth when they were finished. Of all the masters, Schlemmer had the most contact with the students. Tut, his wife, who only sporadically appeared at parties, was a legendary figure to us."[428]

Besides running the stage department, Schlemmer also delivered a course—two hours per week—on *Der Mensch* (The Human Being). It was

428 Fischli 1968, p. 60

obligatory for students in their third semester, which included Max Bill in 1928. "Each week's teaching on 'Der Mensch' is preceded by an evening of life drawing. If no good models are available, the students fall back on their own resources and take turns to sit for the others. Then the life drawing sessions are relocated to the stage, where ... sets, props, spotlights, and sometimes gramophone music provide inspiration and variety."[429]

"Hitherto life drawing had been restricted to nudes. In the winter of 1927–28 figure drawing was introduced (the schematic representation of the human body as a line, plane, body, according to numbers, dimensions and proportions, as a skeleton, as musculature, and so on) and was complemented by classes on the human being."[430]

Once again Bill was not keen to submit to external discipline. He preferred to interact with his fellow human beings on his own terms. He, Röseler, and sometimes Annemarie Hennings, too, attended the free painting classes run by Klee and by Kandinsky. "I joined Schlemmer's stage, painted, made music, and studied theory.... In the spring of 1928, after the departure of Gropius, Moholy, Breuer and Bayer, I joined Kandinsky's free painting class, I also went to Klee and did theoretical work relating to painting and architecture."[431]

Paul Klee: Bauhaus Master

Halfway through the First World War, Paul Klee was conscripted into the German army. His father, who lived in Switzerland, had German nationality, which automatically passed to his son. Fortunately for Paul Klee he was not sent to fight on the front line. In fact, works by Klee were still being exhibited during the war at Der Sturm in Berlin, and in 1917 he achieved the most lucrative sales of his career so far.

"During the war Klee already increasingly engaged with issues concerning the theory of pictorial composition. In 1918–19 he wrote his first essay on art theory, which was published in the anthology *Schöpferische Konfession,* ed. Kasimir Edschmid (Berlin: Erich Reiss, 1920).

Having been released from military service in late 1918, Klee was finally discharged in February 1919, after which he rented a studio in Suresnes Castle in Munich. He now became intensely preoccupied

429 Oskar Schlemmer, "Unterrichtsgebiete," *bauhaus* 2:2/3 (1928), p. 23
430 Schlemmer, "Unterrichtsgebiete"
431 Bill [ca. 1930]

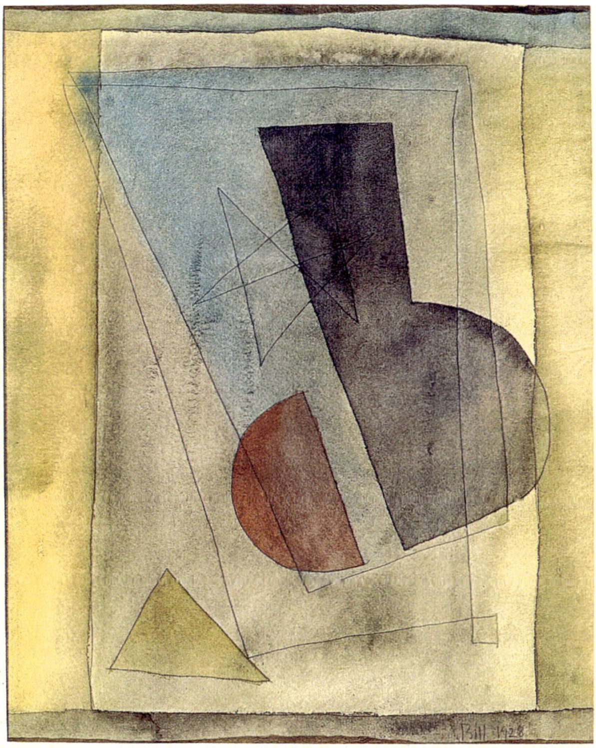

Max Bill, *Düstere Bewegungen,* 1928, gouache and ink over watercolor on laid paper, 27.4 × 23.2 cm

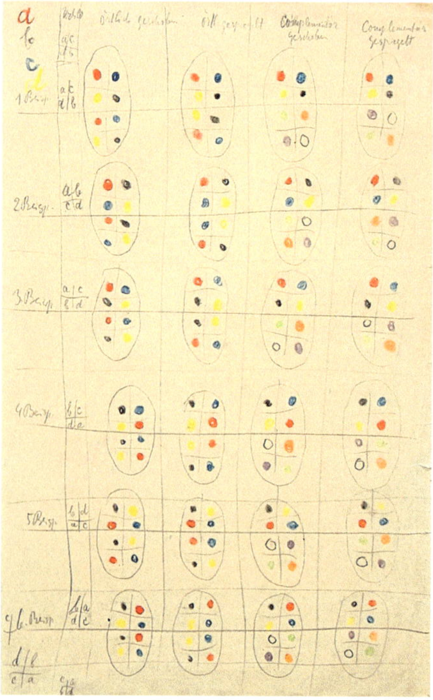

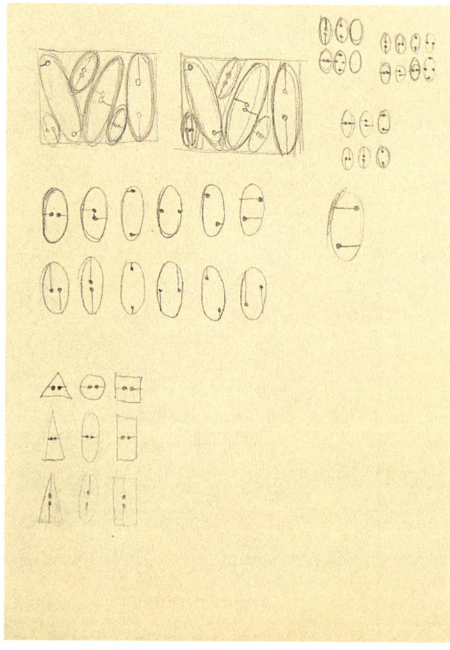

Paul Klee, *Bildnerische Gestaltungslehre: I.3 Specielle Ordnung,* ca. 1928, colored pencil and graphite on paper, 33×21 cm

Max Bill, Untitled, ca. 1928, graphite on paper

with oil painting for the first time. . . . In spring 1919 Klee became involved in the cultural politics of the Bavarian Soviet Republic. Following the Republic's collapse in June, he fled to Switzerland to escape the military regime. There he met Hans Arp and became acquainted with Tristan Tzara and other members of the Dada movement in Zurich."[432]

There is no knowing whether Paul Klee told his students in Dessau about his involvement in the short-lived Bavarian Councils Republic in spring 1919 in Munich, but if he did, it would be fair to assume that Bill would have been glad to hear that Klee had been on the side of the progressive thinkers.

As it happens, unlike Schlemmer, Klee never ever named any of his students in his diaries.

When the military regime put an end to the Councils Republic, Klee was immediately in danger and could only escape the murderous clamp down in Munich by fleeing the country. During the Bavarian Councils Republic, the free economist Silvio Gesell had been named People's Deputy for Finances. Max Bill later acquired a booklet on economics by Gesell (see p. 102).

Even before Gropius appointed the forty-year-old Klee as a master at the Bauhaus in Weimar in December 1920, Klee had already gained public recognition (in May 1920) with an exhibition of 363 works at Galerie Neue Kunst—Hans Goltz in Munich.[433]

The first two monographs on Paul Klee (by Leopold Zahn and Hans von Wedderkop) appeared around this time in collaboration with Klee himself.

And following his first solo exhibition in the United States, organized by Katherine Dreier under the auspices of the Société Anonyme in 1924, Klee also established his reputation outside Europe.

"Katherine S. Dreier began to acquire works by Klee. Dreier was an American artist, collector, and educator of German ancestry who spoke German and traveled annually to Germany to visit relatives. In New York in January 1920, together with Marcel Duchamp and Man Ray, she founded the Société Anonyme, Inc., subtitled Museum of Modern Art. . . . Through the Société Anonyme, Dreier organized Klee's first one-person show in America. The exhibition took place at the society's new galleries at 44 West 57th Street in New York from January 7 until February 9, 1924."[434]

432 Helfenstein 2000, pp. 74–75
433 Helfenstein 2000, p. 75
434 Endicott Barnett 2006, pp. 31 and 33

In October 1925, having achieved success in the United States, Klee also had his first solo exhibition in Paris, at the Galerie Vavin-Raspail.

"In November, in their first group show at the Galerie Pierre in Paris, the Surrealists presented two works by Klee.... The Surrealists, most notably René Crevel, Paul Éluard, Louis Aragon and Max Ernst, greatly admired Klee's art."[435]

In autumn 1925, some time before Bill arrived at the Bauhaus, Paul Klee's *Pädagogisches Skizzenbuch*—a short version of his lectures for first semester students—was published as volume 2 of the Bauhaus books series. And a few years later, when Bill was among the students in Klee's free painting class, Klee wrote the text "Exacte Versuche im Bereich der Kunst," which was published in the Bauhaus quarterly (*bauhaus* 2:2–3, 1928, p. 17). In that text Klee defended his own views on art against the more rationalist approach of the new Bauhaus director, Hannes Meyer. And that difference between the two men partly explains why Klee was already starting to think about leaving the Bauhaus by 1928.

"Klee increasingly felt that his teaching position in Dessau was an obligation that he could not bring himself to abandon because of the financial consequences of leaving. In 1928 he entered into fruitless negotiations regarding a professorship at the Städelschule in Frankfurt; in 1929 he contacted the Staatliche Kunstakademie in Düsseldorf."[436]

Might the students have picked up on his unease when he was teaching?

At the Bauhaus the female students had their own physical education teacher—Karla Grosch—who had trained with Gret Palucca. Grosch was particularly close to the Klee family, and her sister, Ju Aichinger-Grosch, remembered Klee telling her that in Dessau he had seen and heard Karla "marching past singing 'Siegreich woll'n wir Frankreich schlagen' (In triumph we will quell the French)."[437] By 1933 Klee—unable to suppress his anxiety—openly feared for himself and others and, that same year, he drew a bitterly sad drawing entitled *Auswandern* (Emigration), which is illustrated in Lothar Lang, *Das Bauhaus 1919–1933: Idee und Wirklichkeit* (Berlin: Zentralinstitut für Formgestaltung, 1965), p. 138.

435 Helfenstein 2000, p. 109
436 Helfenstein 2000, pp. 109–10
437 Report by Ju Aichingergrosch in Grote 1959, p. 50
438 Retrospective report by Eva Weininger, New York, 1991, in Weininger 1994, pp. 379–80
439 Weininger 1994, pp. 379–80

Eastern versus Western

The change in the atmosphere at the Bauhaus—following the departure of Gropius, Moholy-Nagy, Breuer, and other "old" Bauhauslers such as Andor Weininger—also unsettled Max Bill. After "refounding" the defunct Bauhaus band at the beginning of the summer vacation in 1928, he left for Italy where he could drink in the sunshine and contemplate all that had happened in Dessau. As was the norm for any Bauhaus activity, there were heated ideological debates among the members of the Bauhaus band, and it may be that Bill somewhat exaggerated his own role in refounding the band, considering that its membership was in any case constantly in flux.

"As Andor recounted, at first he mainly played the Hungarian folk music he had grown up with, but he also played cabaret and revue items. He was very aware of Bartók and his research. Andor's sister studied at the Liszt Academy in Budapest, where her teachers included Bartók and Kodàly. On his travels Andor also got to know the beautiful songs of Dalmatia and Yugoslavia. . . . In 1923 he spent five months at the Jungfrau cabaret in Hamburg, and took a lot of ideas away from there. At the Weimar Bauhaus there was a group of Hassidic Jews, who liked to sing together, and Andor learned three of their songs. As well as that there were Russian and German songs, and so on, until he had a repertoire of over 80 numbers. . . . Andor also always went to Berlin whenever there was a chance to hear Josephine Baker or some other first-rate group. Those were the influences."[438]

As it happens, on 9 December 1994, when Max Bill collapsed at Berlin-Tegel airport and was pronounced dead by the doctor on call, he had with him the several-hundred-page catalogue *Das frühe Bauhaus und Johannes Itten,* which contains the text by Eva Weininger cited here—despite the fact that he had been diagnosed with angina and advised not to carry any heavy weights.

It seems there were two main phases in the band's life. In the early days of the Bauhaus band it played melodies with a life-affirming, bohemian feel. This phase was largely dominated by the pianist Andor ("Andreas" or "Andie") Weininger, who then left the Bauhaus in April 1928. When Weininger was in the band, he devised the programs, "but Schlemmer and Hirschfeld also each contributed a march. Ludwig Hirschfeld's march was originally called *Soviet Marsch,* only later on he cut out the word 'Soviet.' Our copy, printed on the Bauhaus printing press, has a hole at the relevant spot."[439]

After Weininger and other older members had left the band in 1928, it entered its second phase. The arrival of Xanti Schawinsky soon led to the "Americanization" of the band, which—according to Eva Weininger—would not at all have been to Andor Weininger's taste. The new band members included Eddie Collein, Ernst Igeler, and Roman Clemens.[440] "The amateur musicians in the Bauhaus jazz band threw themselves into what they were doing with an intensity that no professional musician could have contemplated—a professional would have been finished after fifteen years of that."[441] The music sounded "metallic" because the band stood on a metal dais.[442]

Whereas Höbi Hofmann remembered Schawinsky as the leader of the band, T. Lux Feininger had a different recollection of that time: "After the performance Xanti Schawinsky returned to his base, the Bauhaus ... he was an outstanding member of the band (albeit not its leader, as he sometimes seemed to think) so I respected what he did at our rehearsals." It seems Xanti also had a "talent for securing donations and used it to such good effect that the band was able to buy two saxophones, which he wanted to learn to play over the summer. And there was still enough money in the kitty for a trombone, which Röseler volunteered for."[443] In Hans Fischli's memories of the band, Xanti—the "black-maned tiger"—learned the saxophone in no time at all and transported the girls "into ecstasies" at the Saturday-evening dances in the Bauhaus canteen.[444] It is striking that T. Lux does not list Max Bill as a member of the newly formed band, whereas he does name Roman Clemens, who used to appear at that time along with T. Lux, Xanti, and Max Bill on the Bauhaus stage under the direction of Oskar Schlemmer.

Meanwhile, T. Lux asked his family to buy him a clarinet. His mother was against the idea; his father was in favor. His father won the day and even paid for T. Lux to have lessons with the principal clarinetist at the Staatsoper in Dessau, with the result that toward the end of the summer of 1928 he was already ready to give of his best "as a full member" of the "reformed" Bauhaus band.[445] The fact that T. Lux only joined the new Bauhaus band in the late summer may explain why Max Bill does not feature in T. Lux's memories of the band. According to Bill's own account, he refounded the band before the summer vacation in 1928, as it were on

440 Feininger 1994, p. 378
441 Statement by Hubert "Höbi" Hofmann, filmed by Thomas Grimm in Dessau in 1988, during the exhibition *experiment bauhaus*
442 Statement by Hofmann, 1988
443 Feininger 2006, pp. 85–86
444 Fischli 1968, p. 57
445 Feininger 2006, pp. 86–87

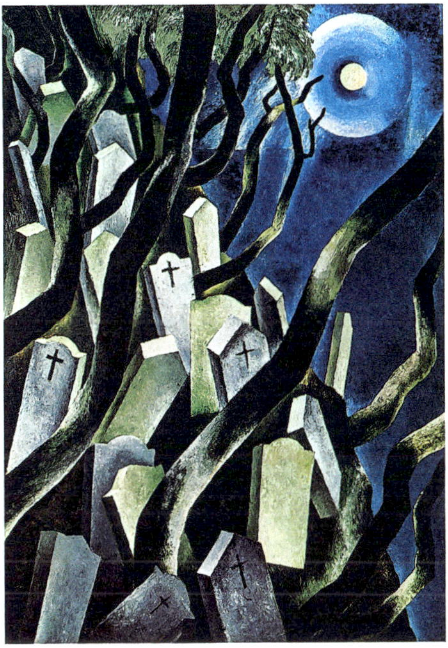

Otto Morach, *Verlassener Friedhof bei Positano*, ca. 1926–28, oil on canvas, 100×72cm

Max Bill, *einheit aus kugel und endloser spirale*, 1978–83, granite, diameter 50cm

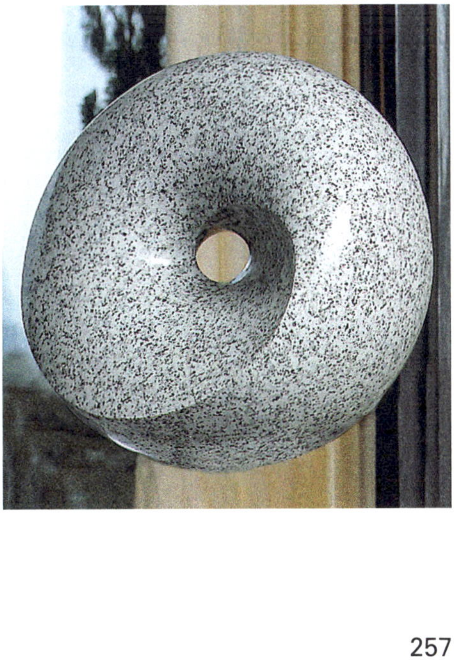

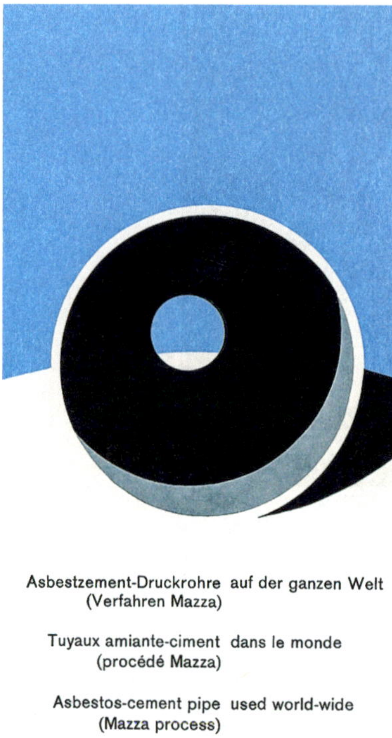

Max Bill, "Asbestzement-Druckrohre auf der ganzen Welt (Verfahren Mazza)," advertising brochure, 1961

an interim basis—sometimes playing the banjo himself—at any rate, before Xanti Schawinsky took over and embarked on the "Americanisation" of the band.

This view is supported by a photograph of the Bauhaus band playing for an event in Dessau, in or around 1928; this image has been reprinted in *Bauhaus und Bauhäusler: Erinnerungen und Bekenntnisse*, ed. Eckhard Neumann (Cologne: Dumont Taschenbücher, 1985), fig. 43, p. 57.

Max Bill in Positano

During the summer vacation of 1928 the nineteen-year-old Max Bill made his second trip to Italy. This time he traveled via Salerno to Positano to see his friend Arnold "Arne" Mehl, who was on a leave of absence from the Bauhaus; Arne had sent Max a postcard from Positano with a cross marking the house where he was staying.

As Max told me, he knew Arnold "Arne" Mehl, who was four years his senior, "from the Bauhaus." Although Mehl does not feature in the list of students at the Bauhaus in Dessau published by Wingler, a later letter from Bill to Josef Albers refers to a close friendship between Bill and Mehl: "dear albers . . . i was very interested to find that you have arnold mehl's address. we were especially close friends at the bauhaus . . ."[446] In the Archiv Stiftung Bauhaus Dessau, there is just one extremely sparse record of Mehl, which indicates that he was enrolled there between 1927 and 1929, and that he took the "foundation course, print workshop, free painting classes."

Erwin Bill had expected that Max would pay him a visit during the vacation in order to report in person on what he had achieved in his studies so far, but Max had other plans and in July 1928 he sent his father a watercolor, *Ein Schiff bei Sonnenuntergang* (see p. 237), by way of an apology of sorts.

Positano was also the summer vacation destination for Otto Morach, the teacher who had accompanied the Kunstgewerbe students to *the Exposition Internationale des Arts Décoratifs* in Paris in 1925 and who had visited Max Bill at the Bauhaus. It was in Positano that Morach painted his expressionist *Verlassener Friedhof bei Positano* (see p. 257), with a strangely three-dimensional sun pierced by a circular hole.

446 Max Bill to Josef Albers, 8 North Forest Circle, New Haven Connecticut, 5 June 1952, Archiv Max Bill.

Years later Otto Morach's painting *Verlassener Friedhof bei Positano* (ca. 1926–28) was exhibited in Zurich and illustrated in the exhibition catalogue *GSMBA Sektion Zürich,* Kunsthaus Zürich, 27 November 1969 to 4 January 1970, fig. 6.

The sun in this painting looks to me like a precursor to Max Bill's very much later granite sculpture *einheit aus kugel und endloser spirale* (1978–83), which also has a circular hole at its center. Bill's sculpture is now on public view outside the building that used to be home to IBM Schweiz at no. 26 General-Guisan-Quai in Zurich. Elsewhere, Bill's cover design for a brochure advertising pressure pipes made from asbestos cement is also reminiscent of that sun in Morach's impression of a cemetery. That brochure was produced in 1961 by the Eternit Aktiengesellschaft Berlin "on behalf of thirty-five asbestos-cement pipe manufacturers" who had exhibition stands at the fifth international water supply congress (*Internationaler Wasserversorgungs-Kongress*) in Berlin (29 May–3 June 1961).

Bill arrived in Salerno late one evening and rented a donkey cart to take him to Positano, which then traveled through the night with a stop in Amalfi for coffee. As they pressed on by the light of the full moon Max was taken aback by the sight of the gigantic cathedral in Amalfi. However, when the donkey cart arrived in Positano early the next morning, Max realized that he had forgotten to bring the marked postcard with him and he now discovered to his bemusement that one house looked very much like the next. So he walked through the streets whistling the Bauhaus song. The refrain, sung to an old march tune, started with the words "Itten—Muche—Mazdaznan—Mazdaznan—Mazdaznan" and, wherever they were, Bauhauslers used the first seven notes of that refrain as a call signal to attract the attention of fellow students or masters.

The first person named in the song was the legendary Swiss artist Johannes Itten, who had previously been the guru of a small Mazdaznan community in Herrliberg am Zürisee; during his time as a master at the Bauhaus in Weimar his teaching was also underpinned by his Mazdaznan beliefs; the song also names the painter Georg Muche, another Mazdaznan follower, who designed the Haus am Horn during his time in Weimar.

The Bauhaus whistle had been "started" by Andor Weininger. It consisted of the "first seven notes of a song sung in Hungary by marching soldiers. Andor knew it from his home village, where it was sung by [Danube] Swabians in their own dialect with very funny words: 'Wenn die Pelzkapp wiedig wird, wiedig wird [when your fur

447 Weininger 1994, p. 380
448 Bill 1966, p. 4
449 Posener 1990, p. 266

hat's filled with bugs]'... But what he did with that banal melody, which he liked to play at the beginning of a set, had nothing to do with marching or fur hats or Mazdaznan; it was a starter, an 'invitation to the dance,' fiery, exuberant, rousing."[447]

On this occasion the Bauhauslers' whistle was not enough to track Arnold Mehl down, so in the end Max found a postman who was able to point him in the right direction. Then he and Arne, who liked to think of himself as a Romantic wanderer, set off for Paestum to see the three early Greek temples there: the Temple of Poseidon, the Temple of Demeter, and the Basilica, with its columns that narrow very noticeably toward wide capitals. Bill already knew the Basilica from an illustration.

His great role model, the architect Le Corbusier, had included a photograph of the Basilica at Paestum (built between 600 and 550 BCE) in his book *Vers une architecture*—on p. 108 in the German translation, *Kommende Baukunst,* which Bill had received as an achievement prize from the Kunstgewerbeschule in Zurich in December 1926.

Bill examined the Poseidon temple with the greatest of care, as if he were on a scientific expedition. "It was in the morning, on a day that was going to get hot, and I felt I understood why the Greeks had left Paestum—it was swampy and had mosquitoes. So that was Paestum: the Basilica, the Temple of Poseidon. I remember regretting that the temples did not have roofs. But what particularly surprised me was the coherence of those built structures. Not just their geometric definition, but also their dimensions, the way the material was used. From the Renaissance through classicism to the concrete classicism of Auguste Perret, people were accustomed to buildings becoming ever lighter. And now, here were columns placed flat on a concrete base, terminating after a cursory bulge in a powerful, wide abacus. That takes the weight. Most astonishing of all were the proportions. Seen from the front, the relationship of interstice to column is 6 to 5. And, even more astonishing ... the relation of abacus to interstice is 3 to 2. These measurements and the overall coherence of the building was an entirely new, alien experience for me. It seemed to me like an excessive use of materials. Beautiful in and of itself, impressive, but futile."[448]

Julius Posener, a German-Jewish architect and architectural critic, found that his service as a volunteer in the British Army took him to Paestum, years after Bill had been there, and he later wrote enthusiastically of that visit in his autobiography: "Southern Italy, which is full of Greek towns, was called 'magna graecia'—great Greece—by the Romans. The Poseidon temple is the great miracle of architecture. I have never seen anything like it, before or since, not even in Egypt."[449]

Arne and Max enjoyed the next few days—swimming in the sea, eating in trattorias by the harbor, and venturing out at night with the fishing boats. After a short stopover in Vietri, Max then took the train back to Dessau. He may, of course, have made a detour to Winterthur to visit his parents, who had now been living apart for over a year. Back at the Bauhaus, Bill and his friends reported on their holidays: Clemens Röseler had visited his grandfather, who lived by the Rhine, and he imitated the old man's shuffling gait and tired voice; Erich Consemüller—who would soon make his name as a self-taught photographer—had ridden through Lapland with a friend; and Vladas Svipas had tales to tell of his homeland, Lithuania.

Erich Consemüller was an old hand who had previously studied at the Bauhaus in Weimar and enrolled (with matriculation number 19) in Dessau to continue his studies.

Vladas Svipas, who had also first studied at the Bauhaus in Weimar, subsequently enrolled twice in Dessau: first with matriculation number 9 and then again in the summer semester of 1928 (with matriculation number 273), after the arrival of Hanns Fischli and Annemarie Hennings.

In the Bauhaus canteen there were magazines lying out, and it was there that Max Bill first saw black-and-white reproductions of Constructivist works from the USSR; however, he was not able to read the accompanying texts. "Contact with the outside world came in the form of magazines, Russian or Polish avant-garde publications or maybe also something in French. But it was mainly Russian magazines ... and Czech magazines like *Stavba;* a lot from the East. That handful of magazines, they were our dietary supplements." In the Bauhaus canteen, besides reading magazines, the students also "ate with the young masters, sat with them, and talked through all kinds of issues."[450]

Stavba, the architectural magazine mentioned by Bill in the Scheidegger film, was a Czechoslovakian publication, not Russian. Two *Stavba* covers (3:2, 1924, and 10:5, 1932) are illustrated in an essay by Alena Kubova, "A Construction of Relations: Establishing the Centers of the Architectural Avant-Garde in Czechoslovakia," in *The Art of the Avant-Garde in Czechoslovakia 1918–1938,* IVAM Center Julio Gonzalez, exh. cat. (Valencia, 1993), p. 234.

450 **Max Bill in conversation with the former HfG student Hans Roericht, notes taken by Angela Thomas, 1983**

451 In CIAM—*Internationale Kongresse für Neues Bauen* 1979, pp. 218–20

In the early 1920s there had been a series of lectures on modern architecture in Prague and Brno (Brünn). In 1924 the speakers included Walter Gropius, Le Corbusier, J. J. P. Oud—in other words, elite figures in the world of New Building (Kubova, p. 232).

In 1929, a number of functionalist Czech artists founded the Léva Fronta (Left Front) and presented their plans for collective living at CIAM III (Kubova, p. 235). The planning committee for CIAM III met in Paris in 1930; the full international congress on "Rational Land Development" then took place on 27–29 November 1930 in Brussels. Contributors included figures such as Gropius, Le Corbusier and Rudolf Steiger. There were also reports from European groups "on housing issues," including a "15-page report, written by Teige and submitted by the Czech group, on housing issues in Czechoslovakia."[451]

Analyzing Painting: Point and Line to Plane

In 1927 Max Bill bought a copy of Wassily Kandinsky's *Punkt und Linie zu Fläche: Beitrag zur Analyse der malerischen Elemente,* which was later translated into English by Howard Dearstyne and Hilla Rebay as *Point and Line to Plane* (New York: Guggenheim, 1947). As Kandinsky explains in his introduction, he first systematized the ideas that led to this book during the three months he spent in Goldach on Lake Constance at the beginning of the First World War.

When a new edition with an introduction by Max Bill was published by Gerd Hatje in 1955, Bill reworked and modernized Herbert Bayer's typography.

László Moholy-Nagy's cover design for no. 11 in the series *Bauhausbücher* is illustrated, in color, in *Albers and Moholy-Nagy from the Bauhaus to the New World* (Tate, 2006) p. 70, fig. 10 and p. 31, fig. 34.

Of particular interest here are, first, figures 9 and 10 in Kandinsky's book—a photograph of Gret Palucca leaping into the air and a schematic, analytical drawing of her leap by Kandinsky—and, secondly, a view of a room in the Constructivist exhibition in Moscow in 1921 (fig. 70). Besides studying the magazines in the Bauhaus canteen, Bill was now also able to learn more about Constructivism from Kandinsky's book: "The 'constructivist' works of recent years are, for the most part and especially in their original form, 'pure' or abstract constructions in space, without practical application, which distinguishes these works from the art of the engineer and compels us to assign them to the field of absolute art. The vigorous use and strong accentuation of the line by point connections are striking in these works (fig. 70)."[452]

When Kasimir Malevich visited the Bauhaus in Dessau in 1927, he may have brought some Russian art magazines with him. Malevich's book *Die gegenstandslose Welt* (The non-objective world) was published in German in 1927 as volume 11 of the Bauhaus books series, with the typography, the front cover, and the jacket designed by Moholy-Nagy. As Max Bill put it, "Kasimir Malevich was one of the first to attempt to organize what he himself called non-objective forces on a plane. He in fact envisaged a world of remarkable, aesthetic satellite configurations. In so doing, he created new kinds of imaginary objects, as we see in his drawing from around 1915–16."[453] Bill also discussed Alexander Rodchenko's achievements: "Rodchenko objectivized the idea of expressive constructivism in a series of circle constructions. Here, like Malevich, he was searching for the floating state that is typical of Russian Constructivism, especially compared to Dutch Neoplasticism."[454]

Bill's intense perusal of magazines with images of contemporary art from the Soviet Union convinced him that artists there were producing much more advanced work than anyone at the Bauhaus. That in itself raises the question as to why Bill, as a student, was drawn to the paintings of Paul Klee rather than to Moholy-Nagy's art, which was certainly the most avant-garde at the Bauhaus. In fact, Klee's work spoke to him because of its combination of the unconscious and the conscious, of intuition and knowledge. Bearing in mind that Paul Klee's work was very warmly received by the Surrealists in Paris, including Max Ernst, it is not so very surprising that for a while around 1930 Bill—as it were following in Klee's footsteps and of course hoping for artistic success—described his own work as "surreal," that is, up until 1936 when he started applying the term Concrete art to his own work.

An example of Bill using the term *Surrealist* to describe his own work is seen in a letter to Fischli, in which he mentions that he has the chance to write an essay for Individualität, a Basel publisher. "steiner is a possibility (you know him from dessau, willi eidenbenz, he is in

452 Kandinsky 1926, p. 97
453 Bill 1976 [b], p. 41
454 Bill 1976 [b], p. 41
455 Max Bill, Zurich, Stadelhoferstrasse 27, to Hans Fischli, 28 January 1930, Archiv SIK
456 Cited in Hahn 2008, p. 82

magdeburg at the moment, he produces completely abstract paintings, based on mathematics, and of course you and i. steiner and the two of us are surrealists."[455] Willi Eidenbenz's son Florian told me in 2008 that his father settled in Basel in 1933.

Dashed Hopes of Studying Architecture

Although Bill had not only created proposals for a Swiss national library (1927, see p. 301) and for a high-rise building in Osaka (1927, see pp. 175, 176), entirely on his own initiative, but had also collaborated on a design with Hanns Fischli, his dream of studying architecture at the Bauhaus never became a reality, much to his regret. Nevertheless, as he later pointed out, he took the opportunity to attend guest lectures at the Bauhaus by the Dutch architect Mart Stam, who would actually have been Walter Gropius's preferred successor. Stam had declined that offer but he did take up the invitation to become a visiting professor of town planning and elementary building theory, and lectured at the Bauhaus from mid-1928 to 1929.

In late 1928 Bill found himself obliged to leave the Bauhaus for financial reasons. However, he may have visited the Bauhaus from time to time in 1929 unofficially, having already exmatriculated.

Later on, when Bill provided details of his own biography, he often described his time at the Bauhaus as lasting "until 1929" rather than 1928, which was his official departing date. In a questionnaire that he filled out in 1965 for the Bauhaus archive, which was still in Darmstadt at that time, he states that he attended the Bauhaus in "spring 1927–winter 1929." In the same questionnaire, in addition to the masters I have already named here (Albers, Kandinsky, Klee, Moholy-Nagy and Schlemmer), he also names "building engineer Köhn" as one of his teachers.[456]

Since Bill had no difficulty dealing with numbers (unlike his occasional problems with spelling), his reference to "winter 1929" can hardly have been an error or a careless slip.

Where exactly Max Bill did spend his time in 1929 is something of a mystery. It seems that in January 1929 he occasionally stayed overnight with his father in Winterthur; he also looked for somewhere to live in Zurich and moved into lodgings in Mühlegasse; in early February he moved to Stadelhoferstrasse. Looking back, however, he also mentioned an otherwise unspecified stay "in Germany." This might have been a reference to a possible visit to the Bauhaus touring exhibition in Breslau (presented in connection with the Werkbund exhibition *Wohnung und Werkraum*), which included a stand with a Junkers gas radiator in a display designed by Bauhaus master Joost Schmidt, whom Max Bill knew from rehearsals for the Bauhaus stage (see p. 231).[457] That time "in Germany" could also have referred to a possible visit to the *Film und Foto* exhibition in Stuttgart, where El Lissitzky was in charge of the Soviet display. If Bill did in fact return to Dessau in 1929, he may well have attended more guest lectures by Mart Stam. Whatever the case, in later years Max Bill remarked more than once that, as an architect, he had made extremely good use of what he had learned from Mart Stam's lectures on structures.

These talks and lectures at the Bauhaus by El Lissitzky and Naum Gabo in early October and early November 1928 are listed in the recent events in *bauhaus* 3:1 (1929), p. 25. Since Max Bill only officially left the Bauhaus in October/November 1928, and was definitely in Dessau in "Nov.–Dec. 28" and later talked of lectures by El Lissitzky and Naum Gabo, it is very possible that he was present at those events.

In 1938 Bill was invited to participate in the exhibition *Abstracte Kunst* in Amsterdam. Mart Stam, whom Bill would dearly like to have worked with in the USSR some years earlier, was not only a member of the exhibition committee in Amsterdam, he also helped to install the exhibition, which opened at the Stedelijk Museum in April 1938. Bill showed two works: *konstruktion* (1937, see p. 671) and *vier constructies: variaties over een thema* (1935–38) (four variations on a theme: two brass reliefs and two paintings on glass, 102×122 cm). These two works are illustrated together in a photograph in the catalogue (p. 15). Bill's work was seen here in the company of other outstanding exhibits, including four compositions by Piet Mondrian and three works by Moholy-Nagy, who was living in exile in London at the time.

Mart Stam seems to have been well disposed toward his former student at the Bauhaus, the ambitiously independent Max Bill. In August 1946, after the Second World War, he made a private visit to Bill in Switzerland. Following that meeting, Bill commented that Stam was one of the few who, in the political controversy and turmoil of the 1930s and 1940s, never descended into reactionary thinking. It pleased Bill that Stam, like Bill himself, always took a stand against

457 Joost Schmidt's stand with a "Junkers gasiator" is illustrated in Joost Schmidt, *Lehre und Arbeit am Bauhaus 1919–32* (Düsseldorf: Edition Marzona, 1984), p. 116

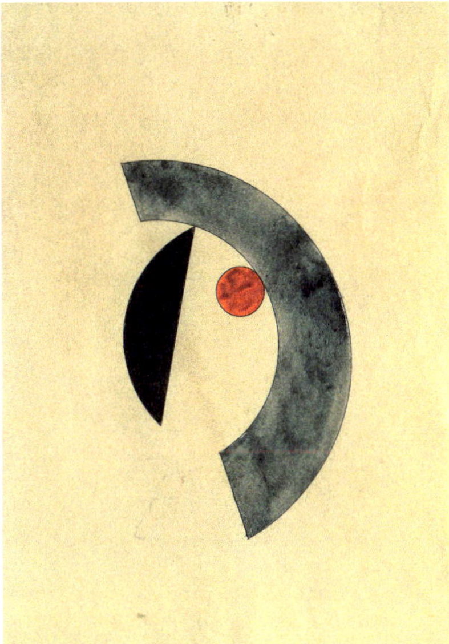

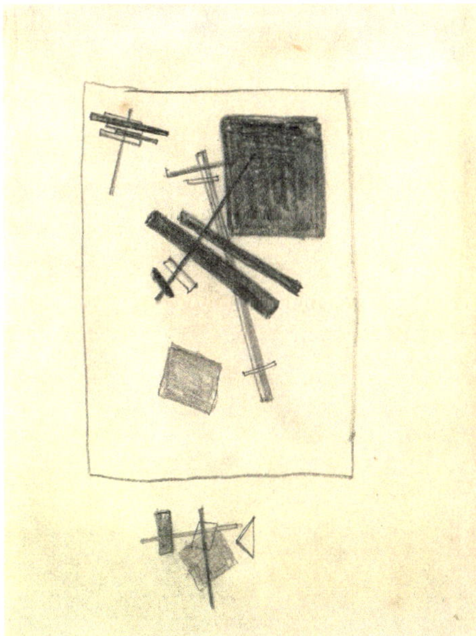

Alexander Rodchenko, Untitled,
ca. 1918, gouache on paper, 30×20.7 cm

Kasimir Malevich, Untitled,
ca. 1915, graphite on paper,
21.5×16.5 cm

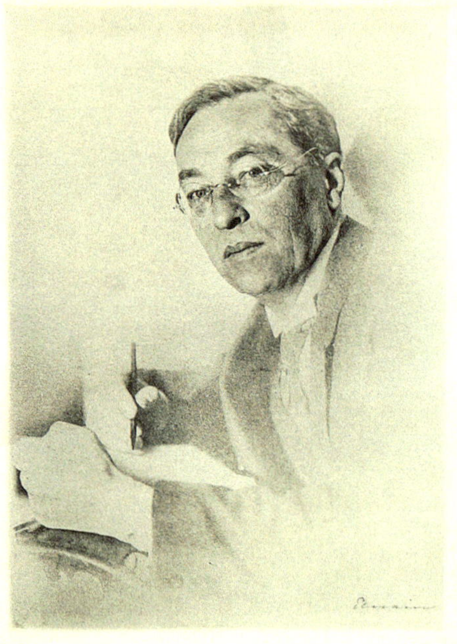

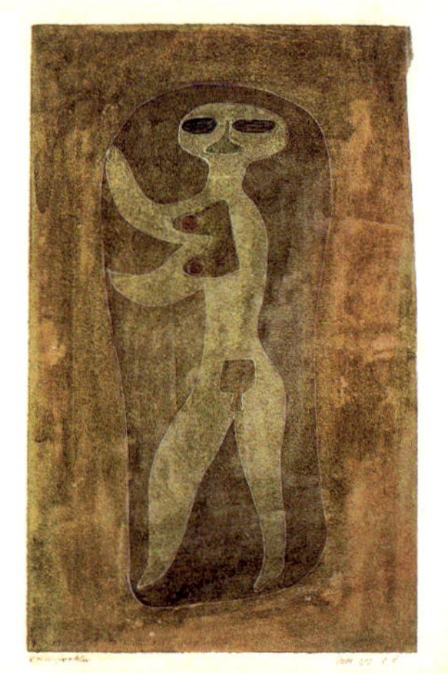

Wassily Kandinsky, 1925
Max Bill, *hermafrodit,* 1929, oil paints and varnish on paper on card, 63.5×40.5 cm

any attitude (or form) that was merely "representative and empty": "he's one of the only men i've ever met who didn't react. i was pleased he took a stand ... against everything that is merely representative and empty."[458]

In one version of his curriculum vitae he notes rather enigmatically: "I collected my worldly goods in Dessau, traveled around in Germany, and ended up in Zurich."[459] He provides no details as to where exactly he went in Germany before finally returning to Switzerland, nor as to anyone he might have been traveling with. He gives very little away. It is possible he was in Frankfurt am Main, because a year later, in a letter to his father, he refers to "huge housing estates" in Frankfurt: "In Germany there are huge housing estates (possibly some 1200 houses in Frankfurt), in Dessau ca. 400 etc., there is almost no need to discuss the form, in practice it has proved to be pleasing and functional, and not at all crazy, the state financed the housing association and, in so doing, approved the direction of travel."[460]

In conversation with me about this period in his life, he once remarked that "under the influence of German free economists I radicalized my political view." In fact, it would be odd if he had not developed radical ideas and had not taken a political stance in those harsh times.

Might Max Bill also have visited Berlin in 1929, specifically the architectural practice of Walter Gropius, who was still the director at the Bauhaus when Max arrived? Might he have seen Gropius's drawings for a high-rise housing estate in Berlin-Haselhorst? Whatever the case, not long afterward, in 1931, when Bill designed a jacket for the remaining stock of the book *Rationelle Bebauungsweisen,* published following CIAM III, the image he chose was one of Gropius's drawings of the twelve-story apartment blocks that he had designed for Berlin-Haselhorst in 1929 (see p. 567)—more on this will follow in due course.

458 Max Bill, Zurich, to Georges Vantongerloo, Paris, 11 August 1946, Vantongerloo-Archiv

459 Bill [ca. 1930]

460 Max Bill, Zurich, to Erwin Bill, Winterthur, 15 September 1930, Archiv Max Bill

New Ambitions as an Ad Man

In Dessau Max Bill was impressed not only by Mart Stam's lectures but also by his political integrity. In the summer of 1930, by which time Bill was back in Zurich, he wrote to Stam in the hope of traveling to the Soviet Union with Stam and the May Brigade, where they would be joining the effort to rebuild the country. Bill was seeking employment in advertising: "I wanted to get into some business as an ad man, I felt advertising had something that I could work on in a new diversified way, drawing on all my various skills."[461]

In 1929 Bill placed advertisements in the free-economy magazine *Letzte Politik,* in Berlin. I was alerted to this by the antiquarian bookseller Peter Petrej in Zurich, following which I bought a large set of issues of *Letzte Politik* from him for my archive.

Hard Times

Over the course of its history the Bauhaus was closed down three times: in Weimar in 1925, in Dessau in 1932, and in Berlin in 1933. In August 1930 the Bauhaus director, Hannes Meyer, was dismissed by the municipal authorities in Dessau because of his "Marxist teaching methods."

The Communist students at the Bauhaus in Dessau used their paper, *Sprachrohr der Studierenden,* to ask who had denounced Meyer: "Mr. Kandinsky, is it true that you or your wife Nina spread the news about the drawing Hannes Meyer did in support of Red Aid to the relevant parties, with the result that it would come out in the press?"[462]

In October 1930 the architect Mies van der Rohe took over as director. Paul Klee left the Bauhaus in 1931. At a meeting of the Dessau town council on 22 August 1932, the reactionaries prevailed and the motion to close the Bauhaus was passed. A new Bauhaus, a private institution, subsequently opened in Berlin-Steglitz with Mies van der Rohe as director, only to be

461 Bill [ca. 1930]
462 In *bauhaus: sprachrohr der studierenden: organ der kostufra* 3 [1930]
463 In *Berliner Lokalanzeiger,* 24 August 1932
464 Huggler 1969, p. 110

closed by the SA (Hitler's paramilitary *Sturmabteilung*) and the police in April 1933. A few months later, in July 1933, the teaching staff voted to "officially dissolve" the Bauhaus; the signatories included Mies van der Rohe, Albers, Kandinsky, Hilberseimer, and Walter Peterhans.

"The closure is merely the logical outcome for an enterprise that was at its core sickly and alien to both our race and our culture. . . . With its insipid, anti-national stance it was only ever an irritant."[463]

The art historian Max Huggler has described the trip Klee made to Egypt at the age of forty-nine around the turn of the year in 1928–29. He notes that "the first thirty-eight works Klee listed in 1929 all seem to have been processing impressions from that trip" and goes on to suggest that "even without that trip to the Nile, Klee would still have tackled the most important problem that was still waiting to be addressed by him—light."[464] However, Huggler's claim that it was only in 1929 that Klee turned his attention to light, as such, is hard to justify—one need only recall his trip to Tunisia in 1914 and the importance of light in the watercolors he did on that trip.

By way of an aside—some decades later Klee's onetime student, Max Bill, took the opportunity to follow in the master's footsteps in Egypt. Years before his trip to Egypt (1985) Bill had already purchased a book by a member of the Institut de France on the mosques of Cairo (Gaston Wiet, *Les Mosquées du caire,* photographies de Albert Shoucair [Paris: Librairie Hachette, 1966]). Following the inauguration of his *four cubes cut into halves which makes eight elements* (1973–85) at a site close to the King David Hotel in Jerusalem, he and his first wife, Binia Bill, traveled on from Israel to Egypt. Like Klee all those years before him, Bill was particularly impressed by their trip on the Nile.

After Binia Bill's death in April 1988, Bill resolved that he and I should go on a world tour. He was especially keen to return to Egypt, to show me the Nile landscape that he had been so taken with. But we never did make that trip. Just a few days before his sudden death in December 1994, I was with him in Paris when he met up again with gallerist Denise René and told her he was sure he had "another ten years of creative work" ahead of him.

On 18 December 1929, two months after the Wall Street crash, Paul Klee celebrated his fiftieth birthday at the Bauhaus in Dessau. On the back of the composition that Max Bill gave to Klee as a birthday present—titled *hermafrodit* [*sic*] in Bill's hand, there is a dedication: "To my dear master Klee on the day that he can look back on half a century, on his own life, which has been crucial to my work in particular and to art in general.

On 18 December 1929, dear Mr. Klee, all the very best and warmest congratulations and greetings! Yours, Bill."[465]

It seems that Max put a much greater effort into wording his good wishes to Klee on his fiftieth birthday than he put into the small postcard that he drew for his father, Erwin Bill, when he turned fifty (see p. 115).

At this point Bill had not yet adopted the exclusive use of lowercase that was the norm at the Bauhaus and his dedication to Klee is written using conventional lowercase and uppercase. It was only in 1930 that Bill started to consistently use the "more economical" lowercase.

While the orthography in his birthday greetings was conventional, the motif of a hermaphrodite was wholly unconventional. Indeed, there is a touching intimacy in this work. Bill never normally wore his heart on his sleeve like this—never in his dealings with his father and not even in communications with his favorite uncle, Ernst Geiger. This very unprudish work, dedicated to Klee, conveys a sense of Bill's special, trusting affection for him. A few days later Klee, who had been showered with good wishes, thanked Max Bill in writing, briefly but with sensitivity:

"Dear Herr Bill,

Your composition is gently strong and serious. Warm thanks in this regretfully short form. These are hard times and for days I have been expressing my thanks for greetings from all sides. The form you found deserves more. Yours, Klee."[466]

It is not impossible that Bill's choice of a hermaphrodite as a motif had something to do with the formation of his own attitudes to sexuality, or could it be that, when Bill was thinking about his present for Klee, he concentrated primarily on his perception of Klee as a person—or was it a combination of the two? Bill also created a technical variant on this composition in another *hermaphrodit* (1929) done in black ink on Japan paper, in which the figure is not a painfully touching, physical misfit but instead has a wittily playful air.

In a later letter to Siegfried Salzmann, Bill described the technique of that work differently to the way it is now labeled at the Zentrum

465 The exact wording of the dedication was kindly given to me in 2007 by Stefan Frey, Nachlassverwaltung Paul Klee, Bern

466 Paul Klee, card postmarked in Dessau, to Max Bill, Stadelhoferstrasse 27, Zurich, 26 December 1929, Bibliothek Max Bill

467 Max Bill, Zurich, to Dr. Siegfried Salzmann, 18 March 1971, cited in *Paul Klee* 1971, p. 124

468 Max Pulver, cited in Grote 1959, p. 18

Paul Klee: "*hermafrodit* is a tempera painting glazed with a transparent varnish."[467] This letter is not reprinted in the Winterthur catalogue for the same exhibition, *Paul Klee und seine Malerfreunde. Die Sammlung Felix Klee,* Kunstmuseum Winterthur, 7 February–18 April 1971.

Looking back, the Swiss writer Max Pulver tried to capture the impression that Paul Klee (a classmate of his brother's) had made on him: "He seemed to me like a creature from a half-way world, fluctuating between the poles of male and female, a dual being with an ever fluid internal interchange, a magnetic field with no fixed resting points." As a youth Klee had been "slight, pale, with Arabian almond eyes (his grandmother was from Southern France), calm, composed, but—for all that composure—pulsating with inner life."[468]

Free Painting Classes with Paul Klee and Wassily Kandinsky

The young Bill pursed his own "liberal" path (as he put it) in Dessau; he often took an interest in things that were not in fact on the teaching program at the Bauhaus. Having left the metal workshop for Oskar Schlemmer's stage workshop during his third semester in January 1928, in his fourth and final semester he also attended the free (that is to say, optional) painting classes run by Paul Klee and Wassily Kandinsky. Klee's classes were very popular, much more so than Kandinsky's. It seems the students found it harder to connect with Kandinsky's art.

"When I arrived at the Bauhaus in 1927, Kandinsky had just turned 60. I had already been wondering what all those painters were doing at the Bauhaus, after all, besides Kandinsky there was also Klee, Feininger, Schlemmer, Moholy, Muche, and Albers. And yet officially no one was painting at the Bauhaus. However, I soon realized that these important artists were also teaching subjects that in some cases were only loosely connected to their own work as painters. Kandinsky, for instance, taught a kind of 'history of recent art,' in combination with that, and following that, he also taught a form of composition theory founded on advances in the development of art. In Kandinsky's drawing classes, diverse objects would be combined to create a still life of sorts, which the students then drew—concentrating on the structure of the arrangement as a whole, creating studies that might contain only horizontals, verticals, or diagonals, accentuated or not depending on their importance. Rounded and angular forms were contrasted. Overall, these studies were not about 'composition' as such, but rather about analyzing what was there in front of us. After a while, however, I discovered that, for all the official 'rejection' of painting there was still painting going on at the Bauhaus. There were even some students who did nothing but paint pictures. We poured scorn on that. We insisted on practical outcomes, social products. But lurking in the background there was that *maladie de la peinture,* a stealthy yearning for forbidden fruits. And I, too, one day found myself enquiring about the 'free painting classes,' asking what went on there and if I could enroll. So I joined Kandinsky's (and Klee's) free painting classes, which entailed taking one's latest 'inventions' to Kandinsky or Klee once a week.... It was only then that I got to know Kandinsky."[469]

As Bill himself said, looking back, he only attended "Klee's obligatory course very sparingly." That must have been around the time when he preferred spending time on the banks of the Elbe to going to classes. Nevertheless, "later on, once a week I went to his studio, where he welcomed students from his free painting class and discussed the fruits of their labors."[470]

During those visits to Klee's studio, in the masters' house he shared in Dessau, Max might have seen two works that Klee did in quick succession in 1927: *Pastorale* and *Junger Garten.* In each case, Klee added the word *Rhythmen* (rhythms) in brackets, to the titles. Those works by Klee were "detailed, finely drawn and largely made up of abstract motifs, creating an even, mirrored repeat pattern."[471] As to the contents of those works, Max Huggler has suggested that Klee's mind was now turning "to the laws that govern existence and co-existence.... He discovered the spiritual principle by studying nature. In 1927 he engaged intensely with blossoms and seeds ... which have the most detailed, most highly differentiated forms."[472] Klee's artistic investigations into the world of plants

469 Bill 1951, p. 97
470 Max Bill, Zurich, to Dr. Siegfried Salzmann, 18 March 1971, cited in *Paul Klee* 1971, p. 124
471 Huggler 1969, p. 102
472 See Huggler 1969, pp. 151–62
473 Huggler 1969, pp. 104–5
474 Stefan Frey has researched the topics in the courses that Paul Klee taught at the Bauhaus in Dessau and has published these in his text "Paul Klee—chronologische Biografie 1920–1931" in *Paul Klee Lehrer am Bauhaus,* exh. cat. Kunsthalle Bremen 2003, p. 239; however, it is no longer possible to establish which courses Max Bill attended, even if only—as he himself put it—"very intermittently"
475 Max Bill, Zurich, to Dr. Siegfried Salzmann, 18 March 1971, cited in *Paul Klee* 1971, p. 124

may have reminded Max Bill of his own childhood and of his mother, far away in Winterthur, who had introduced him to the plant world.

Marie Bill-Geiger benefited from her brother Ernst's knowledge of botany. He passed on to her both the German and Latin names of numerous trees and plants, which she avidly absorbed. Her parents had never granted Marie and her sisters the privilege of any further or higher education.

The catalogue raisonné of Paul Klee's work dates the oil painting *Zeit der Pflanzen* (also known as *Zeit und Pflanzen*—"time and plants") to late 1927.

Huggler has also suggested that Klee's works from that period are not merely "inventions with poetic contents"; on the contrary, they raise important questions "concerning the objectivity of our concept of time."[473] As it happens, the student, Max Bill, and the master, Paul Klee—both of them free spirits—had a similar tendency to not always appear at what they knew was the appointed time. In 1927, much to the other masters' irritation, Klee was even late for the start of the winter semester.

During the period when Bill was attending Klee's weekly painting class[474] he was "greatly influenced by the contents and look of the works of Paul Klee."[475] He was particularly struck by a fascinating motif in Klee's *Vorort von Beride, 1927.04.,* in which there is "a mighty, oval heavenly body ... dense black-and-white, with rays circling round and round." It may be that this drawing triggered something in Max Bill, it may be that it was somewhere in the back of his mind in 1935 when he embarked on a set of variations on a theme—variations "in motion"—which became his later renowned *fünfzehn variationen über ein thema* (1935–38, see pp. 24, 238, 672).[476]

476 Paul Klee's *Vorort von Beride 1927.04.* is illustrated in Max Huggler, *Paul Klee* (Frauenfeld and Stuttgart: Huber, 1969), p. 107; Huggler also describes the painting: "The ground zone has 'bar lines'—above the tower, wall and trees is the mighty oval star.... The formal opposition of a translucent architectural drawing and the compact roundedness of a celestial body up above it is seen in a number of Klee's works." Huggler goes on to suggest that this compositional method, with "diverse, separate elements that give the viewer the feeling of needing to somehow create a 'union' between them," had been taken up by younger painters and used to create an "internal pictorial tension comprising both order and chaos."

Max Bill's comment that "it was only then that I got to know Kandinsky" should perhaps read "got to know Kandinsky properly." In conversation with the American art historian and Kandinsky specialist Vivian Endicott Barnett, Bill mentioned that he first studied under Kandinsky as a first-semester student in 1927, when he took the obligatory preliminary course. Students taking the preliminary course had to execute analytical drawings and compositions, assembling "a kind of still life from highly diverse objects." The course consisted "solely of theory" and the "structural analysis" of items—furniture or objects—placed together on a table. "I was very lazy in those days. It didn't interest me at all." However, in his second year at the Bauhaus, Max Bill voluntarily enrolled in Kandinsky's free painting class: "There were just a few students, seven or eight," and they could paint "whatever they wanted." At that time Max Bill's style was "semi-constructive naturalistic," for instance he might draw "a face consisting solely of a line, a small square, and a rhombus."[477]

Bill also told Vivian Endicott Barnett how it was that Kandinsky once visited him in his loft in 1928: "I had painted a large composition. I couldn't take it on the bus with me, so I said, I couldn't bring it, it was too big. But Kandinsky was going to put on a little exhibition with his students, in the museum, so he wanted to see their works." That was why Kandinsky climbed the stairs up to Bill's loft. Bill felt it was a "huge honor." When Kandinsky saw Bill's large-format painting of a stylized dancing girl, *tanzendes mädchen* (1927–28), he "rather liked it and it was included in that exhibition."[478]

The catalogue for the exhibition *Max Bill. Maler, Bildhauer, Architekt, Designer,* ed. Thomas Buchsteiner and Otto Letze, Kunstmuseum Stuttgart 2005, contains a report by Vivian Endicott Barnett, "Hommage an Max Bill und Wassily Kandinsky" (pp. 22–24), in which she describes her visit to Haus Bill in Zumikon on 20 November 1994 when she had lunch with Max Bill and Angela Thomas Bill, and Bill talked about his memories of Kandinsky's teaching at the Bauhaus and their lifelong contact. This catalogue also has a black-and-white reproduction of Bill's *tanzendes mädchen,* 1927–28, oil on canvas, 146.5×110.5cm (p. 22), estate of Max Bill left to Jakob Bill.

477 Max Bill, recorded in Endicott Barnett 2005, p. 22

478 Endicott Barnett 2005, p. 22

479 Christof Hertel, "Genesis der Formen oder über die Formentheorie von Klee," in *bauhaus, zeitschrift für gestaltung* 4:3 (1931), [p. 7]. Wassily Kandinsky was the editor-in-chief of the journal

Another painting by Max Bill, *räumliche komposition no. 9,* which he dated 1928, may well also have been made in connection with Kandinsky's classes. At any rate, in some respects it recalls Kandinsky's *Offenes Grün* (1923), particularly the black-and-white stripes and the superimposed white disc in the lower right corner of Kandinsky's composition. Might Bill have seen *Offenes Grün* at the Bauhaus in Dessau? Or might he have seen it in Will Grohmann's book *Wassily Kandinsky,* which was published in 1924? Another potential source of inspiration for Bill's *räumliche komposition no. 9* could be Josef Albers's *Tectonische Gruppe,* 1925 (see fig. p. 118)—although Bill's composition is ultimately also very much his own.

When Bill had left the Bauhaus and was first able to exhibit in Switzerland, in a group show at Kunsthalle Bern that opened on 15 June 1930, his carefully worked oil painting, *räumliche komposition nr. 9* (1928), did not appear in the list of exhibits. After Max Bill's death in 1994 this painting went to his son Jakob Bill.

Learning to See One's Own Paintings

In Klee's teaching at the Bauhaus he mainly concentrated on "demonstrating his theory of forms" to second- and third-semester students and on pictorial analysis in his free painting class. There is no knowing if Bill, now in his fourth semester, attended Klee's lectures on form, be it sporadically or otherwise. Klee's free painting classes were held in his own studio at home, and it was always his wife, Lily Klee, who opened the door to the students. Christof Hertel, one of those students, described those classes: "In the painting class Klee had his own method, although he never stuck rigidly to it. Usually he started by discussing the format. Next he would move on to the actual scene and then to everything ... that was happening in that scene. Up to that point the discussion focused solely on forms. After that the focus was on the expressive qualities of those forms. The quite incredible thing—it must have been entirely intuitive—was the way that Klee taught the painters to see their own pictures properly for the first time."[479]

Bill and his friend Clemens Röseler both attended the free painting classes offered by Klee and Kandinsky. In 1928 the art historian Ludwig Grote reported on his visit to an exhibition of works by students in Kandinsky's painting class: "The absence of any kind of dogma in this exhibition is clear evidence of Kandinsky's gifts as a pedagogue.... All the works on display have a sense of law and order. These young people favor law-based forming over genius-inspired gesture."[480]

Klee had a very personal relationship with his painting utensils and gave them nicknames—as Bill later did with some of his own sculptures; the family's names for some of his sculptures were very different to the published titles: *unendliche fläche in form einer säule* (1953) was known as "the sword"; *konstruktion aus 30 gleichen elementen* (1938–39, see p. 665) was "the dachshund"; *fünfeckfläche im raum mit vollem kreisumfang* (1977) was "the bishop's miter." Klee's "main tools, his sharp pencils and etching needles had wonderful nicknames, 'Lupus [wolf], Fünfzhart [five too hard], Chrüttli [little herb], Nero, Judas, Rigoletto und Robert der Teufel [Robert the Devil].' The paint pots, which Klee modeled himself and decorated with found objects such as shells, were not merely functional utensils, they are still objects in their own right."[481]

An untitled, undated oil painting shown in that exhibition by one "Hermann Röseler" (presumably Clemens Röseler), with a central star motif (a star of David?), is illustrated in black and white in an issue of *Der Kunstnarr* (edited by Ernst Kállai, Dessau, April 1929, p. 21). It accompanies a text written by Kandinsky at the Bauhaus in January 1929 (by which time Bill had already left). Kandinsky's text gives an insight into the escalating disagreements around painting at the Bauhaus:

"Depending on 'tendency' and disposition, quite different things are demanded of the painter today. Especially the 'abstract' painter. Some people insist that we should only paint walls. And only inside. Some wish us to paint the outside of their houses. And only the outside. Some demand that we should serve industry, that we should supply patterns for materials, ties, socks, crockery, parasols, ash trays, carpets. Just applied art. Only we should leave off painting pictures once and for all.... While there are some who mourn, others rejoice that painting is practiced at the Bauhaus, not only by the masters but also by the young people, that for two years now the Bauhaus has been giving regular instruction in painting— besides being taught in the practical 'wall-painting workshop' painting is now also cultivated in non-practical 'free painting classes.' There are also Bauhaus students who are to be found neither in the practical departments nor in

480 In *bauhaus, zeitschrift für gestaltung* 2:2/3 (1928), p. 31, Schriftleitung Ernst Kállai
481 Bäschlin et al. 2000, p. 199
482 Wassily Kandinsky, "Die kahle Wand," *Der Kunstnarr* 1 (1929), pp. 20, 22
483 Bill [1944]

the non-practical painting classes but who nonetheless work in a 'free-painterly' manner —carpenters, metalworkers, weavers, even architects are painting.... The obsolete word Art has been ... resurrected at the Bauhaus, of all places."[482]

Klee and Kandinsky, who lived in the two halves of one of the masters' duplexes in Dessau, were friends. Following a suggestion from Klee, Walter Gropius had appointed Kandinsky as a professor at the Bauhaus in Weimar in 1922. When the Bauhaus relocated to Dessau, where it received support from the town as a school of design, Kandinsky moved with it.

"... masterpieces of painterly skill"

Wassily Kandinsky was born into a wealthy, bourgeois family with a very European outlook. He studied law and economics in Moscow and became an attaché to the Russian embassy in Syria. In 1895, at the age of twenty-nine, he completely changed direction and soon moved to Munich to study painting; in 1922 he readily grasped the opportunity to teach at the Bauhaus in Weimar.

Max Bill described Kandinsky, a widely traveled man, as someone with "an unmistakably mystic attitude and faith, someone who resisted the spiritual hierarchies of his time and constantly sought the means to overcome them (he did then find those means in the individual achievements of artists such as Wagner, Debussy, and Schoenberg, in the poetry of Maeterlinck, in paintings by Cézanne and Picasso).... And there were other outstanding members of the Russian avant-garde who had the same response as Kandinsky: Marc Chagall, Naum Gabo and his brother Antoine Pevsner, Pavel Mansurov, and El Lissitzky (temporarily) all moved abroad, while their compatriots who remained behind—including Tatlin, Rodchenko, and Malevich (initially)—started to change their ways."[483]

Bill greatly admired Kandinsky's great skills "as a dialectician and teacher," his "captivating lectures," his lively way of "taking old and the very newest art back to its essential spiritual and artistic foundations and revealing its underlying principles," all of which gave his students hours of "deepest insight and profound pleasure." "At the Bauhaus, besides teaching first-semester students, which gave him a decisive influence on the overall direction of the institute, Kandinsky had also gathered together a number of individual students in a free painting class. However, since the Bauhaus was not set up as an art academy but as a school teaching practical skills, any interest in painting and the status of painting was highly controversial."[484] As a young man Bill thus already became acquainted with a highly divisive issue that he would encounter again many years later in his capacity as rector of the Hochschule für Gestaltung in Ulm, which he co-founded and designed, and where he also taught.

In his homage to Kandinsky, which is both emotional and admiring, Bill continues: "The relationships that Kandinsky had with his students were particularly warm. On visits to his home they saw that his studio was as clean as if no one ever did a stroke of work there. And yet his paintings were masterpieces of painterly skill. He ground his pigments himself, there were stands with beautifully ordered jars of paint powders, the space and the human being radiated the tranquillity of a steady, natural harmony, with no hint of disquiet in a highly personal discipline. Despite having produced such complex theoretical and pedagogical texts, Kandinsky remained a supreme artist and his oeuvre grew day by day."[485]

Print Media

The October 1928 issue of *bauhaus* lists (under the rubric "events at the Bauhaus") an exhibition of watercolors by Max Bill and Albert Braun that had taken place on 5–13 July in 1928.[486] The same issue also alerts its readers to a lecture series planned for the coming winter. A lecture by Ignaz Jezower "on the sociology and aesthetics of film" is listed for 5 October; other speakers include the Marxist writer "Lu Märten, author of groundbreaking historical materialist works on the form arts" and the anarchist writer Erich Mühsam, who had been actively involved with the Bavarian Councils Republic. All the invited speakers were clearly on the political left.

There is no knowing if Max Bill attended Erich Mühsam's lecture in October 1928, but he certainly did read Mühsam's work and he kept up

484 Bill [1944]
485 Bill [1944]
486 In *bauhaus, zeitschrift für gestaltung* 2:4 (1928), p. 24
487 In Ralf G. Hoerig and Hajo Schmück, Datenbank des deutschsprachigen Anarchismus, http://dadaweb.de/wiki/Willkommen_im_neuen_DadAWeb_!
488 "Max Bill: The Early Years. An Interview by Angela Thomas," in *Journal of Decorative and Propaganda Arts* 19, Swiss Theme Issue (1993) pp. 98–119, here p. 104

with the latest developments in politics and culture by subscribing to a weekly paper, *Die Weltbühne: Wochenschrift für Politik, Kunst, Wissenschaft,* founded by Siegfried Jacobsohn with assistance from Kurt Tucholsky, now under the direction of Carl von Ossietzky. Another weekly for readers with an interest in politics and culture, *Die schwarze Fahne,* was edited by Ernst Friedrich, who also owned Freie Jugend, the company that published the paper in Berlin and Vienna. Besides texts by Leo Tolstoy and Kurt Tucholsky, this anarchist weekly also included portraits of critical artists such as Käthe Kollwitz, George Grosz, Frans Masareel, and Carl Meffert.

A few years later Carl Meffert was one of the first to leave Germany for Switzerland, where he adopted the pseudonym Clément Moreau. Max Bill and Moreau became personally acquainted in Switzerland.

According to Ernst Friedrich, *Die schwarze Fahne* sometimes had a circulation of forty thousand.[487]

Even if I cannot say whether Bill only subscribed to *Die schwarze Fahne* after Mühsam's talk or whether he was already a reader by then, I do know that during his time as a student at the Bauhaus he had a private subscription to this anarchist, anti-militarist weekly. Max Bill mentioned this to me himself, and I included this information in a text that was published in 1993, before his untimely death.[488]

The October 1928 issue of *bauhaus* would also have been of particular interest to Bill for another reason. On page 10 there is a reproduction of an architectural study project—"a terraced housing project for Tel Aviv"—by Bill's classmate Philipp Tolziner who, on a trip from Moscow, would visit us in Zumikon many years later. And with wider historical ramifications, in the same issue there is a report (pp. 8–9) on the "Vorbereitender internationaler Kongress für neues Bauen" (Preparatory international congress for new architecture) that was held in Switzerland on 25–29 June 1928 at Château de La Sarraz, which was owned by the notable patron of the arts Hélène de Mandrot. The report reprints the "official declaration" that was agreed at the congress and signed by leading architects, including H. Häring (Berlin), P. Jeanneret (Paris), Le Corbusier (Paris), E. May (Frankfurt), G. Rietveld (Utrecht), Mart Stam (Rotterdam), and the Swiss architects M. E. Haefeli (Zurich), W. M. Moser (Zurich), Hans Schmidt (Basel), and Hannes Meyer from the Bauhaus in Dessau.

This planning meeting prepared the way for the first meeting of CIAM (Congrès Internationaux des Architectes Modernes), which took place soon afterward. A good many years after that "official declaration" had been drawn up in the summer of 1928, the young Bill attended a meeting of CIRPAC (the executive body of CIAM) with the Swiss, leftist architect Hans Schmidt (one of the first signatories to that declaration); it was during that CIRPAC meeting in Zurich on 8–11 July 1939 that Max Bill became a member of CIAM.

Max Bill's Search for Clarity

As a student Max Bill remained true to the idea of a free economy, which he had first heard about in Winterthur through his friendship with the somewhat older Hans Hinterreiter. In 1928 the *Bauhaus* editorial team invited students to respond to a questionnaire on their reasons for coming to the Bauhaus and what their initial impressions were. Bill was among those whose answers were published in the paper:

"Max Bill:

I initially wanted to study architecture at the Bauhaus because Corbusier had turned my head.

My impression of the Bauhaus was not what I had expected, I was somewhat disappointed. But little by little I did then find what had actually attracted me to the Bauhaus: clarity.

I haven't acquired a new attitude to life, I have found my old attitude increasingly affirmed.... The most important requirement for humans as social beings is personal freedom ([Silvio] Gesell: physiocracy through free land and free money). That's why technology is so important.

Technology is supposed to liberate people, but due to the capitalist system it has only enslaved people all the more."[489]

Bill, young and rebellious, unfortunately does not specify why he was initially "disappointed" at the Bauhaus. But he does convey the importance the Bauhaus now has for him by concluding his response to the questionnaire with an imaginary superstructure of outstanding personalities. Remembering his experience in Paris in 1925, when he first saw the Eiffel Tower, he gives Gustave Eiffel a place on his personal Olympus; Chaplin is also there, as are Picasso and Stravinsky—maybe influenced by Kandinsky, who particularly admired both. To my surprise, he also includes Sigmund Freud (later in life Bill had little respect for psychoanalysis). "I imagine the Bauhaus bigger than it is in reality: Picasso,

489 Bill 1928, p. 25

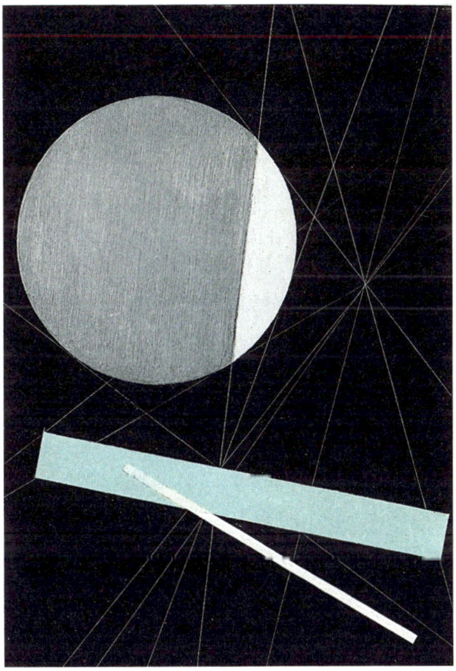

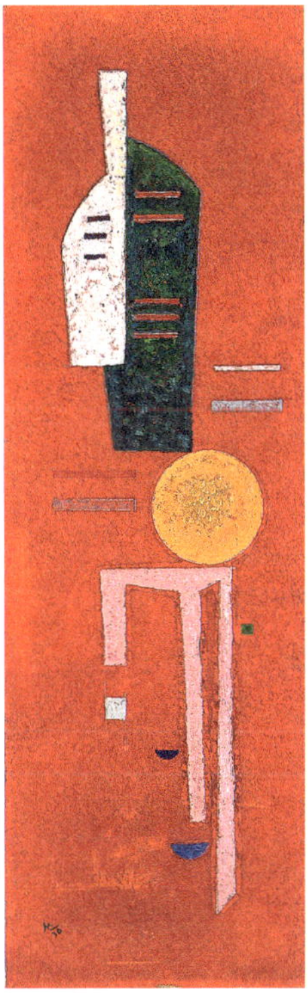

László Moholy-Nagy, *Composition TP5,* 1930, oil and incised lines on galalith, 29.5×21.5 cm

Wassily Kandinsky, *Streifen,* 1930, oil on card, 48.5×16 cm

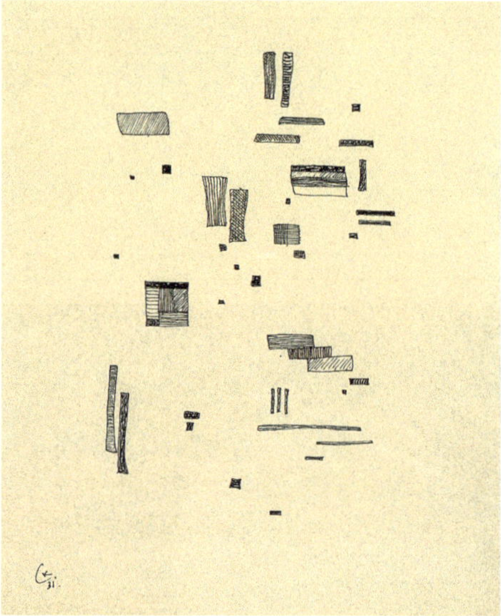

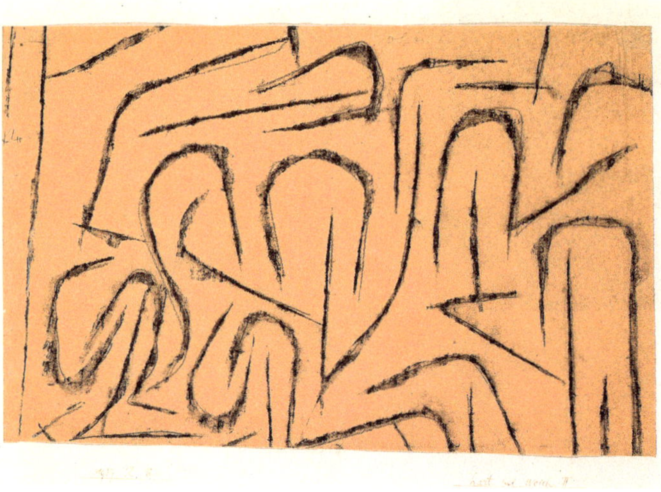

Wassily Kandinsky, *Dessin no. 26,* 1931, india ink and ink on paper, 22×18cm

Paul Klee, *hart und weich II, 1937, 158,* 1937, charcoal on paper on cardboard, 22.2×35.3cm

Jacobi, Chaplin, Eiffel, Freud, Stravinsky, Edison etc. also actually all belong to the Bauhaus."[490]

His selection of important personas suggests that Bill must often have gone to the cinema back then in Dessau, like master Feininger, who was a keen cinemagoer—in later years Bill only rarely went to the cinema.

It is striking that Bill's list of major artists and thinkers starts with Picasso. Bill had first been introduced to Picasso's work by Moholy-Nagy when he and Annemarie Hennings were invited to dine at home with the Moholy-Nagys. Why Bill, as a Bauhaus student, was drawn to the paintings of Klee and Kandinsky rather than the work of Moholy-Nagy—which positively radiates clarity—will forever remain a mystery.

In 1933 Kandinsky's work, like that of so many others, was derided by the Nazi regime as "degenerate" and in 1934 he left Germany and settled in Paris, but Bill remained in touch with him. "In the last ten years of his life, which were overshadowed by the war and the occupation, Kandinsky created entirely new, astoundingly diverse works. And without his ever-new world of forms suffering neglect, color grew increasingly important in his art."[491]

After Kandinsky's death in 1944, Max Bill acquired several of his works. In response to the question as to which was "his favorite . . . Bill thought for a moment and said, the one with the red ground, *streifen* [see p. 283], was his 'favorite painting.'"[492]

Paul Klee Flees Germany for a Second Time

In October 1931 Klee arrived in Düsseldorf to take up a teaching post at the art academy. Initially only four students attended his course in painting techniques. He "rented lodgings in Düsseldorf but retained his home in Dessau until April 1933."[493] Directly after Hitler seized power, having been appointed Chancellor of Germany by President Paul von Hindenburg on 30 January 1933, "the National Socialists ramped up their campaign against modern art. Klee now became one of the main targets in public attacks on exponents of 'degenerate art.' In 1933 works by Klee were pilloried by the National Socialists in three *Schandausstellungen* [disgrace exhibitions] in Mannheim, Chemnitz, and Dresden."[494]

490 Bill 1928, p. 26
491 Bill [1944]
492 Endicott Barnett 2005, p. 23
493 Helfenstein 2000, pp. 139–40
494 Helfenstein 2000, pp. 139–40

On 17 March 1933, while the Klees were away from their home in Dessau, the police and Nazi paramilitaries forced their way in, searched the house, and removed numerous documents—enough to fill three laundry baskets. Klee temporarily took refuge in Switzerland. This was the second time he had fled Germany, with the first being after the demise of the Bavarian Councils Republic in 1919. "In the display of 'degenerate art,' organized at the behest of a totalitarian dilettante, Klee's masterpieces were the main attractions, decried as changelings spawned by a racial alien 'with roots in the Orient.'"[495] On 6 April 1933 Paul Klee wrote to his wife Lily: "Because, even if it were the case that I am a Jew from Galicia, that would still not change one iota of my persona and my achievements. I cannot voluntarily . . . abandon my standpoint, otherwise I would be creating a comic monument to myself for all time. I would rather face trials and tribulations than play the tragi-comic part of someone currying favor with the ruling powers."[496] Paul Klee reiterated that same argument to his son Felix, who remained in Germany.

The writer Walter Mehring later discussed Klee's "painterly commentaries" on his decision to turn his back on a humanly demeaning career in Nazi Germany. He picks out *Von der Liste gestrichen* (Struck off the list), "a 'negroid' coffee-brown self-portrait with a large black × scrawled on his head, and the watercolor *Protzige Wehr* [Showy resistance]. Klee—by no means a Jew but very much an artist—came to a decision, which demonstrated a strength of character that anyone who has lived in such corrupt times will recognize."[497]

". . . his open-minded 'humanity' rebelled against the systems established by the Bolsheviks and the Nazis."[498]

"Publicly branded a 'degenerate artist,' having lost his most important art dealer due to the closure of Galerie Alfred Flechtheim, and having been removed 'with immediate effect' from his teaching post at the state academy of art in Düsseldorf on 21 April 1933, Paul Klee was compelled to find a completely new source of income."[499] In late October 1933, after a vacation in the south of France, Klee met Kandinsky in Paris: "Kandinsky was planning to move to France and, like Klee, reshaping his plans for his professional future."[500]

495 Mehring 1965, p. 87
496 Grohmann 1954, pp. 77–78
497 Mehring 1965, p. 87
498 See Di San Lazzaro 1966, p. 564
499 Frey 2000, p. 201
500 Helfenstein 2000, p. 139
501 Helfenstein 2000, p. 151
502 Helfenstein 2000, p. 151

Kandinsky and his wife Nina—who was thirty years younger than him—subsequently settled in Neuilly-sur-Seine, where they received a visit from Gualtieri di San Lazzaro, who lived in Paris and published the outstanding art periodical *XXe Siècle.* San Lazzaro later recalled Nina Kandinsky's "strong Russian accent" and the ideological rigor of Wassily Kandinsky, who had been vehemently opposed to both the Bolsheviks in his homeland and the Nazi regime in Germany.

The Most Devastating Time in Klee's Life

A few months after Klee's temporary escape to Switzerland in March 1933, he fled Germany again, for the third time, never to go back; he and his wife Lily finally returned to Switzerland in December 1933. Rolf Bürgi, the son of Hanni Bürgi-Bigler in Bern, who had consistently collected Klee's work, applied for a residence permit for Paul and Lily Klee, which was granted in December 1933.

"Klee's return to Bern, a combination of emigration and escape, was the worst setback of his life. At a stroke the internationally renowned artist found himself increasingly isolated in a provincial town with little in the way of inspiring culture."[501]

However, in 1934 Paul Klee was overcome by a severe artistic crisis that lasted well into 1936. Various factors exacerbated the situation. Firstly, Will Grohmann's catalogue raisonné of Klee's drawings, *Paul Klee: Handzeichnungen 1921–1930,* which was published in Germany in autumn 1934, was confiscated by the Nazi regime in 1935. Secondly, in February and March 1935 Kunsthalle Bern presented an overview of Klee's work since 1919 "which was also shown ... at Kunsthalle Basel," but the sales at both exhibitions were "relatively modest," and, thirdly, in autumn 1935 Klee contracted systemic sclerosis, which meant that in 1936 he was only able to produce twenty-five works in total, an unusually small number for him.[502]

In 1937 Klee's health stabilized somewhat and during the course of the year he produced 264 works—despite the National Socialists' touring exhibition *Entartete Kunst* (Degenerate art) opening in July of that year in Munich, with fifteen of Klee's works being "subjected to defamatory comment," which could have had a severely detrimental effect on his state of mind. "Among other things his paintings were reviled as 'psychopathic art.' During the mass confiscation of examples of 'degenerate art' in the summer and autumn of 1937, over 100 works by Klee were removed from German museums."[503]

Klee lived a very reclusive life in Bern due to his illness, but he was not forgotten. In 1937 Kandinsky visited him there for the last time and Picasso also visited him that same year. Other visitors included Jawlensky, Georges Braque, and Max Bill, who was now able to re-establish contact with the former Bauhaus master whose work he so greatly admired. Among the works by Klee in Max Bill's estate there was one from 1937—the year when the exhibition *Entartete Kunst* was shown—entitled *Hart und Weich II.* Bill discussed it in a short text: "At times at the Bauhaus I was very much under Klee's influence. In my view he is one of our most important artists, particularly with regard to art theory. Many of his works explore the idea of variations, as in this case, in *Hart und Weich II.*"[504]

During this period Hanni Bürgi-Bigler's daughter-in-law, Käthi Bürgi, who had already started collecting Klee's work at a young age, would sometimes take him to an exhibition by car: "In early June 1939, for instance, they went to the preview in the Galerie Fischer in Lucerne for an auction of works confiscated by Nazis from German museums."[505] It is hard to imagine what kind of an effort it must have taken for Klee to view those works removed from German museums—and how demoralising that occasion must have been for him.

Lotte Beese

Lotte Beese, a very motivated student, enrolled at the Bauhaus in Dessau some time before Max Bill and she was still there when Max arrived. She had developed a vehemently anti-national political stance in the aftermath of the First World War. At the Bauhaus she at last found kindred spirits and, for the first time in her life, felt she fitted in. Having initially enrolled for Gunta Stölzl's weaving class, she was later accepted onto Hannes Meyer's building theory course.

The architecture department at the Bauhaus, led by Hannes Meyer, comprised two sections: building theory and the practical, hands-on building section.

503 Helfenstein 2000, p. 158
504 Bill 1976, p. 36
505 Frey 2000, p. 202
506 See Tolziner 1989
507 Borngräber 1977, p. 115

Lotte Beese was ultimately hired by Meyer to work in his practice in Berlin and they became romantically involved. She took a deeply intimate photograph of him, and he took similarly loving photographs of her. In their professional work their aim was to bring applied art and "free" art together under the canopy of architecture—demonstrating their own intrinsically hierarchical attitude, which deemed architecture superior to all other forms of art. Above all they wanted to design, develop, and build contemporary, modern architecture that would be a powerful force for good. From time to time when Meyer won a major commission, such as the training center for the Allgemeiner Deutscher Gewerkschaftsbund (ADGB) in Bernau, he would invite architecture students from the Bauhaus to work on it with him as members of a collective.

The Hannes Meyer Brigade

In early 1931 Philipp Tolziner, a Bauhaus student, traveled to the USSR and joined the Hannes Meyer Brigade in Moscow (sometimes referred to as the Red Bauhaus Brigade).

Philipp Tolziner, a Jewish student from Munich, who enrolled at the Bauhaus at the start of the new semester in the summer of 1927 (matriculation number 132), joined the same building theory class as Lotte Beese. He later recalled the way that they were met with a deluge of technical facts relating to building and construction engineering. Added to which, Hannes Meyer, who designed the ADGB building in Bernau (which was realized by Bauhaus students) advised them to read not only specialist literature but also modern literature. Tolziner felt that in the Bauhaus power struggles probably all the students in the building section were on Hannes Meyer's side: "we were enthused both by his determination to provide us with a scientific basis for problem solving and by his maxims: 'serving the people,' 'the people's needs not the needs of luxury,' 'everything we make must be high-quality and inexpensive.'"[506]

Architects were urgently needed in Moscow because of the severe housing shortage. "At that time the population of Moscow was around 2.8 million, that is 250% more than in 1920 after the Revolution and the Civil War. Over half of the buildings were not connected to the sewage system. 5,000 new houses had been built by 1930, but that still only allowed four square meters living space per resident."[507]

Max Bill and I met Philipp Tolziner at a Bauhaus conference in Weimar on 30 June 1989, not long before the demise of the GDR. After that, having traveled from the USSR to see the exhibition *Hannes Meyer—Urbanist, Architekt, Lehrer* at the Museum für Gestaltung in Zurich (March to May 1990), Tolziner came to see us at Haus Bill in Zumikon. Among other things, he told us that he had spent time interned in one of Stalin's Gulag prisons.

In November 1930, before Tolziner went to Moscow, Lotte Beese had already joined Hannes Meyer there; on 31 July 1931 she gave birth to their son Peter in Brno. As an unmarried mother she was unable to find new work there when her contract came to an end. Perhaps feeling unjustly treated by Meyer, she commented that the once so dapper Bauhaus director now wore worker's togs like an imitation proletarian. Meanwhile Meyer had already embarked on a new relationship with Lena Bergner, another former Bauhaus student.[508]

Temporarily leaving her son with friends in Prague, in April 1932 Lotte set off for the Ukraine and a job in Kharkov, where there was a terrible famine as a result of the state's compulsory collectivisation of farms and farming. The official, ideological line was that the famine was a "historic necessity," "the lot of the peasant class," and since Lotte was fundamentally sympathetic to Communism, she initially accepted that official line without question. She contacted Hannes Meyer from Kharkov, but the final rupture between the ex-lovers was now an inevitability. Lotte had to go to court to secure child support for their son and although Meyer tried to undermine her case by presenting her as a typical Western woman who could not cope with life in the Soviet Union, a people's court in Moscow decreed that Meyer should pay child support of 250 roubles per month. Lotte Beese was profoundly affected by the end of her relationship with Hannes Meyer. As if to add insult to injury, at times she was suspected of being a spy because she was still a German national. Undeterred, she now started designing kindergartens and schools for the city of Orsk in the Ural region.[509] Then one day, completely by chance, she ran into the Dutch architect Mart Stam in a street in Kharkov; she had attended his lectures at the Bauhaus in 1928, like Max Bill. Now her life took a very different—no less complicated—turn, given that Stam was a married man with a wife (Lenie Lebeau) and daughter (Jettie) in Moscow.

508 See Schilt and Selier 1993

509 A highly lucid design by Lotte Beese for a day nursery for 90 children in Orsk has survived from this period (Lotte Beese, axonometry, "Standardgor project," ca. 1934, illustrated in Schilt and Selier 1993, p. 19)

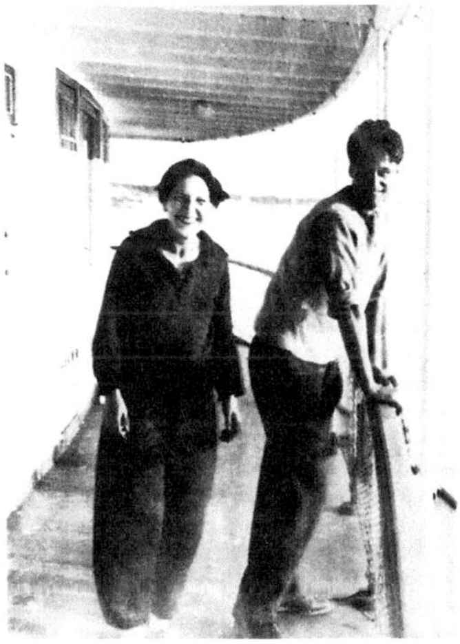

Lotte Beese and Mart Stam on a boat on the Volga, 1933

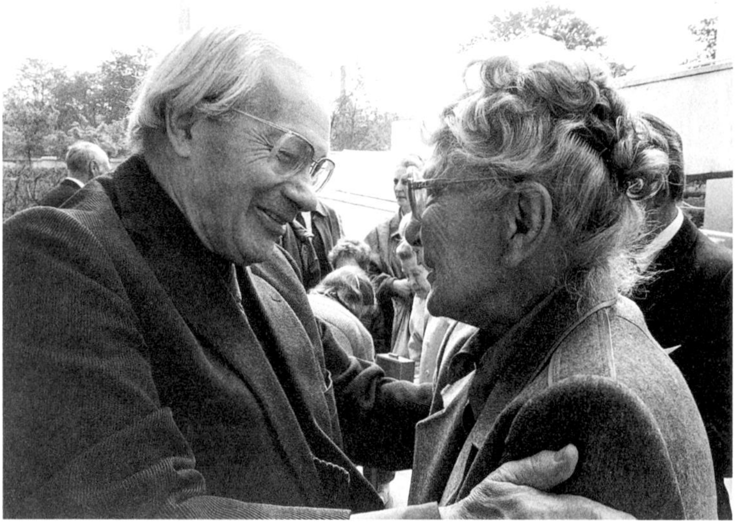

Angela Thomas, Max Bill and Lotte Stam-Beese at the Bauhaus-Archiv, Berlin, May 1985

The May Brigade

Mart Stam had gone to the USSR with Ernst May, who had previously been the city architect in Frankfurt am Main. The first task the Soviet authorities gave May and his team—the May Brigade—was to create a master plan for Magnitogorsk, an industrial city with 200,000 inhabitants. The brigade developed various projects; in the end Stam's ideas were approved and became the basis for the new city. Even before the completion of the first apartment blocks in Magnitogorsk, Stam received a new commission, namely to draw up a master plan for the city of Makeevka —an industrial center with 250,000 inhabitants in the Donetsk region of Ukraine, 250 kilometers away from Kharkov where Lotte was.[510]

In August 1933 Lotte left Kharkov to join Mart, and in the autumn of that year they set out on the 300-kilometer journey, partly by road, partly by boat on the Volga, from Magnitogorsk to Orsk in the Urals, where the May Brigade was to design a new industrial city as part of the Standardgor Project. Mart Stam and Lotte Beese subsequently traveled to Moscow, probably in late 1933, to continue their work on the project, which was now led by the Swiss architect Hans Schmidt; other members of the team in Moscow were Grete Schütte-Lihotzky, Werner Hebebrand, and Ernst Zeman (from the original May Brigade). The finished design was to be delivered during the course of 1934. At this point more former Bauhaus students—Konrad Püschel, Tibor Weiner, and Philipp Tolziner, all members of the Hannes Meyer Brigade—joined the May Brigade as reinforcements.

Hans Schmidt—who would later call on Max Bill's services as an architect in Switzerland and who would support Bill as a prospective member of CIAM—had left for the USSR with the May Brigade on 1 September 1930. Comprising around twenty people altogether, including the Dutch architect Mart Stam, that group mainly consisted of

510 "The Ernst May group, of which he is a member, and which has been hired for five years by the Soviet government, started working as an autonomous group, only to be integrated into the 'Standardgor project,' which began in 1932.... In the 'Standardgor project' there were nearly 150 foreign specialists, mostly German, as well as some American industrial specialists.... Hans Schmidt, having collaborated with Ernst May on the plans for Magnitogorsk and 'greater Moscow,' drew up the master plan for the city of Orsk, with Mart Stam, in 1934." Françoise Very, "Hans Schmidt et la construction de la 'ville socialiste' d'Orsk," in *VH 101: L'architecture et l'avant-garde artistique en URSS de 1917 à 1934,* Revue Trimestrielle, Paris 1972, pp. 147–55, with illustrations

German architects and engineers. Schmidt was invited to take on this work in the USSR because of his track record as co-editor (along with Mart Stam, El Lissitzky, and Emil Roth) of the architectural journal *ABC* from 1924 to 1928.

Stam and Beese subsequently left for Kazakhstan, where Stam had been planning to work on what was to be his last project in the USSR: the construction of a new town on Lake Balkhash, 200 kilometers away from Alma-Ata (now Almaty). But, when Stam realized what that project entailed, he immediately withdrew from it.

The Human Cost of Each Kilo of Copper

The government's plan was that between sixty and seventy thousand forced laborers, housed in pitiable conditions in the new town, would work in the region's copper mines. When Mart Stam returned to Moscow to report to the authorities, he explained that he was unable to fulfill the contract because, as he put it, each kilo of copper was paid for with a human life.[511] Since any refusal to work could be treated as sabotage and punished with deportation, Stam and Beese applied preemptively for exit visas. They were on tenterhooks as the authorities kept them waiting for months for a response, which did ultimately go in their favor.

In October 1934, before leaving the USSR for the Netherlands, Lotte Beese and Mart Stam married in Moscow. Part of their thinking was that Lotte might more easily be granted a residence permit in the Netherlands as the wife of a Dutch citizen. However, since the Soviet Union was not yet recognized by the Netherlands, the marriage ceremony conducted in Moscow was declared null and void. Lotte and Mart thus married again, in Amsterdam, in August 1935.

In 1943, during the Second World War, the architects Mart Stam and Lotte Stam-Beese divorced in the Netherlands. I was present in 1985 when Lotte Beese and Max Bill met by chance—to their immense delight—and greeted each other with great warmth. Lotte Stam-Beese lived until the age of 85 and was cremated in Rotterdam on 21 November 1988.

511 See Schilt and Selier 1993
512 Wingler 1962, p. 558

The Bauhaus Melting Pot

The matriculation lists of students at the Bauhaus in Dessau reveal just how international the student body was. While there was a remarkable "frequency of names of Slavic and Jewish origin, there were also all sorts of English-American, Scandinavian, Italian, even Japanese names."[512]

In the previously cited issue of *bauhaus* (2: 2/3 [1 July 1928]), with Max Bill's responses to the student questionnaire, there are also statistics relating to the students currently enrolled at the Bauhaus: out of a total of 166 students, 45 were women and 37 were "foreigners" (that last group is not subdivided into men and women). We can add here that there were of course a number of Swiss students among the "foreigners." Max Bill told me that in his day there were around six Swiss Bauhauslers in total, including Paul Klee (born in the schoolhouse in Münchenbuchsee), with whom he could converse in Swiss German.

Klee's father, Hans Klee, came from Lower Franconia in southern Germany, but from 1878 to 1932 he lived and worked in Switzerland as a music teacher at the Bernese teacher training seminar in Hofwil. Klee's mother Ida, née Frick, was born (as a Swiss national) in Besançon and trained as a singer in Stuttgart. She was a musician, like Klee's future wife Lily Stumpf, who was born in Munich in 1876. Lily Stumpf and Klee met in 1900 and she married him against her father's wishes in mid-September 1906. Their son Felix, their only child, was born in late November 1907.

A year after Bill's arrival, the new intake for the summer semester of 1928 included the Swiss students Hanns Fischli (matriculation no. 247) and Annemarie Hennings (matriculation no. 265).

Before Hanns Fischli arrived at the Bauhaus (when he still spelled his first name with a double *n*), he had been in contact with the "religious socialist" professor Leonhard Ragaz in Gartenhofstrasse in Zurich, and, as a member of a circle of young people that gathered around Ragaz, he had read works by authors such as Tolstoy, Gogol, Gorky, Romain Rolland, Henri Barbusse, and Leonhard Frank. Another member of that circle was an odd fellow by the name of Albert Ehrismann. Albert lived in Badenerstrasse, in his parents' fourth-story rented apartment, where Hanns Fischli painted deer on the walls for him.

Around 1930 Max Bill designed the cover for Albert Ehrismann's book of poems with the captivating title *Lächeln auf dem Asphalt* [Smiling on the Asphalt] (Zurich: Orell Füssli, 1930) (see p. 410); meanwhile, in the summer of 1930 Albert Ehrismann wrote a favorable review of the program at the Krater cabaret theater ("with sets that are a joy in themselves. The Krater has got painters!"[513]); Max Bill had been an active member of the theater since April of that year.

Hanns Fischli's father was a craftsman who lived in the canton of Thurgau in east Switzerland before moving with his wife to Zurich, her native city, where he became a land registry surveyor; he and two assistants surveyed the Uetliberg. As it happens, Hanns Fischli was the father of Peter Fischli, one half of the artists' duo Fischli & Weiss.

The young people in the group around Ragaz produced their own monthly paper, *Nie Wieder Krieg* (Never again war). As a believer in the group's anti-war aims and the associated ideology, Fischli now ate no meat and "avoided every narcotic toxin," as he put it.[514] He was soon seriously undernourished and when he was in the last year of an apprenticeship in construction drawing in Zurich, he fell ill with double pneumonia. After six weeks confined to bed, Fischli traveled to Stuttgart to see the Weissenhof Estate and later declared, "I had only ever seen flat roofs in illustrations. It was miraculous!"

In the spirit of New Building, Hanns Fischli, ironically enough, designed a flat-roofed shed for the conservative Entlisberg section of the garden allotment association—for which he was paid fifty Swiss francs.

Fischli did not take his final apprentice's examination and falsified the date when he had to be at the Bauhaus, "advancing it by ten days, so that after bidding farewell in the office I had to leave the next day in order to be at the Bauhaus in time.... Construction drawing, I'd done that, now I wanted to move on and become an architect."[515]

513 Albert Ehrismann, "Der Krater," in *Tages-Anzeiger*, 18 June 1930
514 See Fischli 1968, p. 12
515 Fischli 1968, p. 17
516 Fischli 1968, p. 18
517 Fischli 1968, p. 18
518 Huggler 1969, p. 92 (in the chapter "Die klassische Schau der Natur")

Fischli and Bill Meet for the First Time

"On the eleventh of April 1928 at seven o'clock in the morning . . . having traveled through the night, I alighted from the third-class, non-smoking carriage in the Zurich–Stuttgart–Berlin express and stepped out onto the station platform in Dessau. The Bauhaus was deserted, the staff and students were not yet back from their spring vacation. I was of course too early. A young lady in the office added my name to a list. Two students had stayed behind, Swiss, as it happened. I went to find them, one was called Bill. . . . They thought it was clever of me to come so early, I could find a room before the hustle and bustle. . . . Bill, with scruffy hair, lived in the outskirts on the other side of the town. . . . There was an endless wheat field, as flat as a pancake all the way to the horizon. Although it was far away from the school, the route there went through a pine forest. . . . We collected my luggage from the school janitor. Before I moved into my room, two houses away from Bill's, he showed me his lodgings. Three times as big, a single space stretching the full length of the attic, a hanging bookcase, two divan beds, easels and tables, and a huge blue velvet curtain concealing the kitchen area."[516] Although Fischli had been traveling all night, Max still showed him his work that same day. "I had never been in a painter's studio before. He showed me his works at some length. I, the boy from the sticks, thought they were just as good as real Klees. And then I had to admit I was exhausted."[517]

Parallelism in Paintings by Hodler and Klee

Klee's biographer, Max Huggler, has suggested that there may be an important stylistic affinity between the work of Ferdinand Hodler and that of Paul Klee: "As we know, the underlying structural principle in Hodler's art was parallelism, which he regarded as the fundamental, all-embracing law of nature. Given the close connections between his work and Art Nouveau, there is no question as to the source of his parallelism, and it may be that the parallel figurations in the work of Paul Klee were influenced by the same stylistic context."[518]

It is hardly surprising that an early role model for Bill was Ferdinand Hodler, the Swiss artist his mother admired most—after all, he wanted to please his mother. Paul Klee became his next role model. Bill could converse with him in Swiss German, which most of the other students could not understand—almost as if master and student had a secret language.

When Hanns Fischli arrived at the Bauhaus, Bill already had a reputation: he was that Swiss student causing a stir. And Fischli was now only too happy to stoke the rumors that Bill had arrived "as a rich man" and "ate live fish." Looking back later Fischli reported that when he was first at the Bauhaus he had paired up with a "pure" young woman in his class, who went in for Mazdaznan exercises, which Fischli soon felt were not for him. He attended Josef Albers's preliminary course—which he reported on articulately and precisely—and, like other students, found that he was not immune to the famous Bauhaus hangover: "We skipped classes and three of us, including Bill, who was at least over his hangover, roamed around on the banks of the Elbe."

One day Bill happened to mention that he had heard there was a competition in Zurich for a design for a new kindergarten complex. Applications were invited from architects in and from Zurich. "An express letter—ten days later we had the necessary documentation. After all, we had both come with the same aim—we wanted to be architects!"[519] So Hanns Fischli and Max Bill started to work together on a proposal for the competition for a "Kindergarten and Community Center in Zurich" (1928).

Standing Out but Losing Out

"Three weeks later we sent our plans for the jury to review, that's to say, so that the jury could award us the prize. There could be only one solution—ours. In order to be ready for the ensuing correspondence and not to look like complete novices, our 'architectural practice'—Bill & Fischli—had its own writing paper in a DIN format, the kind commonly used in German manufacturing. Bill was favored by the alphabet, but—considering that I was the only more or less accredited professional in our practice—I felt that my name should be on the top line. I also drew accurately and knew how costs should be calculated and on what basis. But there was no arguing against the fact that B comes before F in the alphabet."[520] Fischli felt that he was the construction draftsman and knew what he was doing. Bill, on the other hand, had singlehandedly prepared a proposal (in Dessau in 1927) for the Swiss National Library competition (see

519 Fischli 1968, p. 31
520 Fischli 1968, p. 31
521 Fischli 1968, p. 31

p. 301) and therefore took the view that his name should come first—in recognition of his skills, not just because of alphabetical order.

Max Bill told me that his first design for a building for the Swiss National Library, which he later reworked, had been exhibited at the Bauhaus in Dessau, where Hannes Meyer also saw it. Max Bill only saw that original 1927 design again on 15 January 1994, during the exhibition *Max Bill* at Fondation Saner, Studen bei Biel; a visitor had brought it with her to the exhibition. In 2002 Max's son Jakob Bill purchased it for his collection at the Kornfeld auction house.

Bill had not been admitted to the building theory course, but that did not stop him from attending lectures in the building department from time to time. In 1927, when he was working on his design for a Swiss National Library, he daringly applied some of his newly acquired knowledge. Submissions to the competition had to be posted by a certain date, which could be verified from the postmark. Unfortunately Bill took his entry to the post office in Dessau one day late and although he tried his best to charm the clerk behind the counter, she punctiliously refused to backdate the postmark.

Around this time Josef Albers noticed that Fischli's attendance at the preliminary course was somewhat erratic. Hanns explained what was keeping him away and Albers then took an approving look at Bill & Fischli's plans for a kindergarten, to be constructed from steel, glass, and concrete (see p. 301). Albers, much admired at the Bauhaus, wished them good luck, and their imaginations ran riot—"once we had won the competition (as we thought) we would draw up all the plans in Dessau; every so often one of us would travel to the occasional meeting. After all, we felt everything was perfectly clear from our drawings. In order that members of my family back home in Switzerland should not receive too sudden a shock when they read in the papers that we had won first prize, from then on whenever I posted items to them, I named the sender as 'Hanns F. Maler + Architekt [painter + architect], Bauhaus in Dessau'—not yet quite nineteen years old, barely trained, broadly speaking gifted, and already with two occupations to my name! . . . And yet, we were already eliminated in the first round; the jury cited an unbalanced built volume. In our eyes the design was very good, despite perhaps not having the characteristic features of an infant school, the classrooms had glass walls on three sides, we wanted openness, never mind the trams passing by. . . ."

Fischli looked back at that experience in some amusement: "We worked very well together; Bill cleverly explained our thinking to visitors and made tea. While I transposed our sketches into legible drawings on a scale of 1:200, he saw the ladies safely home."[521] In retrospect Max was not at all bothered by the jury's negative response and commented, with a dry smile, that in that kindergarten competition Bill & Fischli "didn't just stand out, they also lost out." And as Fischli later remarked, "through our work together on the competition Bill and I became good friends. Working under the sloping ceilings in his big room was inspiring. And then he made a space for me to work and live in. We pooled our households in the hope of saving money. His funds were slowly diminishing, so he became more active. It was his *Gründerzeit*—he was starting to make a name for himself."[522]

Bill's *Gründerzeit*

As Fischli recounts, Max Bill "wanted to bring together a group of young Bauhaus painters and organize touring exhibitions in Europe so that we would become famous and our paintings would be in demand. When we drew up a list of participants, we first put down Klee and Kandinsky and then ourselves. When the list was arranged in alphabetical order, Bill came first because there wasn't anyone whose name started with A. Group Z. The *dernier cri*—never to be surpassed!"[523] Bill, by now good friends with Fischli, had full confidence in his compatriot and the two of them drew up the statutes for the newly founded Group Z. Not yet twenty years of age, Bill became "director and secretary" of Group Z and designed a special letterhead and a visiting card. He also made a visiting card for his own personal use.

Annemarie Hennings and Hilde Rantzsch also became members of Group Z, as did Bill's friends Clemens Röseler and Alfredo "Freddo" Bortoluzzi. In a letter sent to Bill in late 1929 and signed "H" (presumably Hilde Rantzsch), there is news of Bortoluzzi: "Botoluzzi [*sic*] is in Karlsruhe, at Schützenstr. 12. Six months ago he was dancing ballet." And in the same letter there is also news of another Group Z member, Clemens Röseler, who T. Lux Feininger especially looked up to: "as to Röseler, he is designing stage sets in Stralsund. The same job that handsome Hildebrand (Katt's blond Schorsch) used to have."[524] Writing to Bill after he had

522 Fischli 1968, p. 49
523 Fischli 1968, p. 49
524 A photograph of Max's friend Clemens Röseler, whom he played with in the Bauhaus band, is illustrated in Fiedler and Feierabend 1999, p. 149; "Katt" is Katja Both, seen in the double portrait *zwei freundinnen* (1927, see p. 161); it has not been possible to identify Katt Both's "blonder schorsch" ["blond George"]

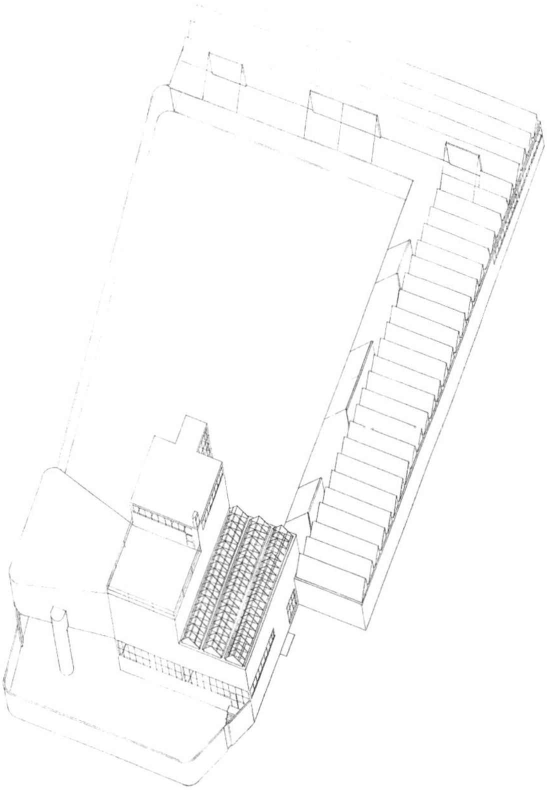

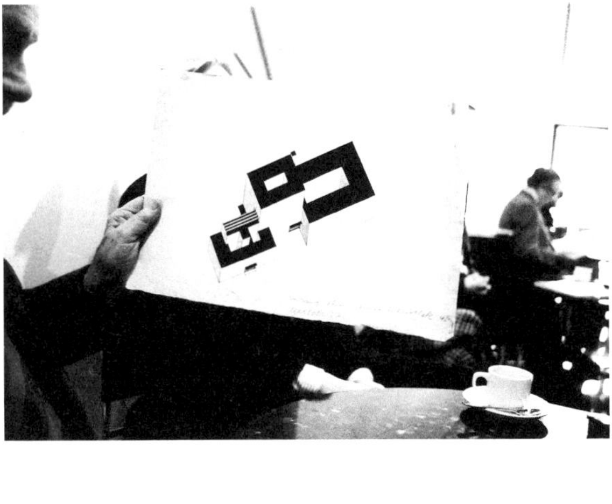

Max Bill and Hanns Fischli, Design for a kindergarten and community center in Zurich, 1928
Max Bill, Design for the Schweizerische Landesbibliothek, 1927

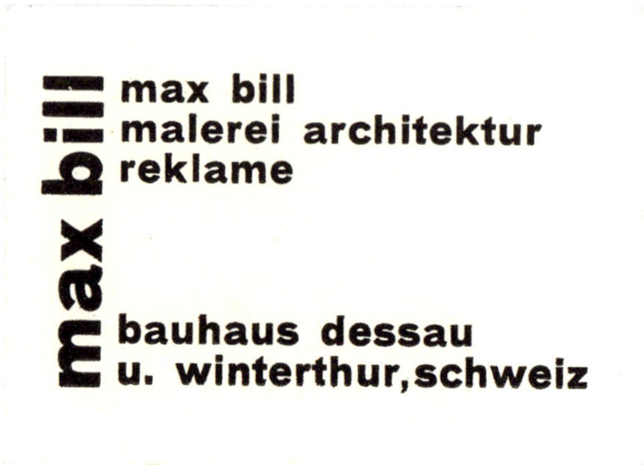

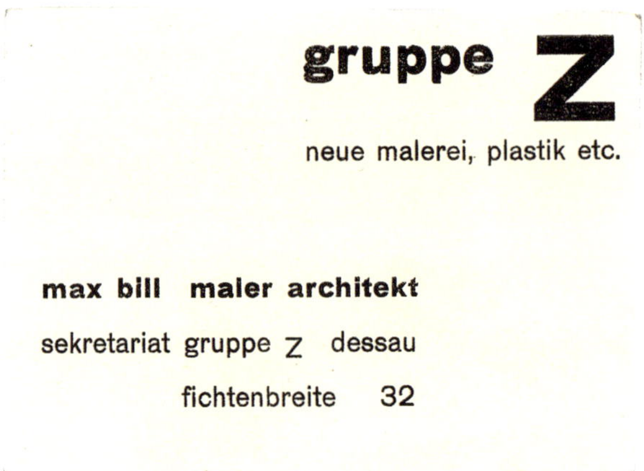

Max Bill, Personal business card, ca. 1929
Max Bill, Gruppe Z business card, 1928

left the Bauhaus, "H" also reports on the whereabouts of other members of Group Z—Janosch, Margaret Leiteritz, and Lou Scheper.[525] Although the leaders of Group Z in Dessau, namely Bill and Fischli, had specifically had a "stack of writing paper with a letterhead" printed, in the end there were no exhibitions and no paintings were sold.[526]

Since Hanns Fischli's dress-sense and style were not deemed Bauhaus-worthy by some of the other students when he first arrived in Dessau, they decided he needed a makeover. Hilde Rantzsch (see p. 161), a Group Z member who attended free painting classes in the summer semester of 1928 and joined the weaving workshop in the winter semester of 1928, took Hanns under her wing and revamped his wardrobe. She also suggested he should wear a beret to hide his protruding ears. Once Hilde's work was done, Liesl Träger decided to teach the new boy how to dance. "One day after a party, when dawn was already breaking, she stood me up in front of her door, made me whistle the beat of the main song and didn't let go of me until I'd got the dance steps. . . . Smile, boy, you'll soon be one of the best dancers . . . with rhythm in your loins and a girl in your arms, you'll be both expert and master."[527]

The first name of the student Liesl Träger (matriculation number 211), who worked with Max Bill on the bauhaus stage, was sometimes also spelled "Liesel." After her time at the bauhaus, when she married in Switzerland and became Liesl Steiner-Träger, she remained a close friend of Max Bill's.

Fischli on Klee at Home

We know from Hanns Fischli's account of visiting Klee at home that the students never saw him in his work clothes and that, although there were plenty of paintings in his studio, either upright or lying flat, he never made a point of showing them to the students. "On the table there were large clay vases filled with clean brushes, bottles with solvents and binding agents, varnishes and lacquers. We saw what kinds and makes of paints he used; he also didn't hide away the many kinds of fine paper. . . . We were allowed to look at the fish in the aquarium with him; he would switch the light on and off, carefully shooing certain fish away so that we could see

525 (Probably) Hilde Rantzsch, Dessau, to Max Bill, [November or December 1929], Bibliothek Max Bill

526 Fischli 1968, p. 50

527 Fischli 1968, p. 58

other ones hidden behind them.... He would bid us farewell with a handshake at the studio door; his wife, Lily, solid but light-footed, with an apple face, would accompany us to the front door, where she had greeted our little group as we arrived and now let us out again."[528]

Petty Crooks

At the Bauhaus in Dessau Hanns Fischli was friends with a young woman called Sascha.

Fischli's friend, a young woman named Sascha, whose surname is not mentioned anywhere, once visited Bill in Zurich after his return to Switzerland.

Hanns, Sascha, and Max were all struggling to make ends meet: "For a while we three could only count on the 105 marks that my father punctually transferred on his pay day.... We missed having fruit to eat."[529] However, one day they came up with a way of perhaps alleviating their extreme lack of funds, as Hanns Fischli once explained: "On a walk by the Elbe we passed a field of rhubarb and on the way back took a few lovely stems home with us. We cooked them in our little kitchen—they made a nice meal with some semolina pudding. At last we had something sweet again, the jam in the canteen had long been far too expensive.... So we immediately set up a rhubarb-jam factory. That would provide the income we needed.... We now started pilfering on a grand scale, not always from the same field, we ventured far and wide. We had helpers, but were very picky about who we employed. Sascha was never allowed to come with us, she was too distinguished, but we'd take Hilde Rantzsch at the drop of a hat, she was made for work like that.

Hanns Fischli's platonic friend, "gracious" Sascha, was allowed to buy stoneware pots at the market, at least the small and middle-sized ones; we bought the five-kilo pots ourselves because of the weight."

The helpers had to be able, early risers because we worked an early shift, leaving Fichtenbreite at 2.30 a.m., it was already starting to get light by 4.30, we had to have the harvest in by then.... However, we bought the sugar—in big lumps—you had to crush it—we bought it in bulk because

528 Fischli 1968, p. 48
529 Fischli 1968, p. 50
530 Fischli 1968, pp. 50–51

it was cheaper that way . . . and we bought paraffin in the form of candles that we melted down; the paraffin, in its liquid state, was poured onto the full pots of jam to create an air-tight seal."

A huge, borrowed pan "stood on the little gas cooker, comfortingly hissing and glugging for hours on end. The three of us formed a production line, one washing the rhubarb, one peeling, one chopping. A sweet aroma, mingled with gas, filled the room. We were becoming increasingly choosy when we went out pilfering, only taking very thick stems because they filled the growing number of stoneware crocks more quickly. And we were also becoming increasingly miserly when we added the sugar: reduce the cost price, charge the usual price, bigger profit. . . . We decided our main customer should be the cook at the Bauhaus canteen, our fellow students should benefit from the vitamins. Now we'll get through the winter, no bother. And if we sell some paintings too, all the better. The gas meter was whirring. . . . But then there was an interruption to our foraging. One morning a rhubarb grower spotted us harvesting and we only managed to escape by the skin of our teeth. . . . running in all directions. . . . we got back to Fichtenbreite, gasping, at different times and from opposite ends. We pictured ourselves arrested, convicted, outcast. We had been lucky, but the rhubarb raids were over. Just convert the stock into cash as effectively and quickly as possible, then see about building up a new existence."

Only one night Fischli and Bill suddenly heard "a strange noise in the kitchen. . . . In the morning we found the mess. A paraffin seal lay in pieces on the floor next to a three-kilo crock, there were pretty little bubbles on the jam, and it smelled sour. Each night more burst, the next one started to stink, in exactly the order they had been made. . . . Each night one of us dragged the fermenting stuff, reeking of stupefying sour alcohol, down through the house to the outdoor privy; the other one took a shovel and stole soil—instead of rhubarb—not to create the finest compost but to tip into the pit for olfactory reasons. Once again, this had to be done judiciously, one night a shovelful from here, the next night one from another corner of the garden. . . . And as for the stoneware crocks, we washed them out, filled them with meadow flowers and gave them to the girls in our neighborhood as the latest interior décor idea. And the moral of the story? Boys, never be miserly with sugar!"[530]

Bill never mentioned the rhubarb field story to me himself. In a sense it was a sequel to the petty pilfering at the kiosk in Winterthur, when Bill had to keep a lookout. Although he did once try to commit that story to paper, he ended up putting it off for another time, as he told Xanti in a letter: "in the end i threw the whole thing into the wastepaper bin and decided to return to my autobiography later on ... perhaps on pius's 100th birthday."[531]

The name "Pius" (Latin for "the pious one") was a reference to the Bauhaus director, Walter Gropius; at the Bauhaus people dropped the first half of his surname—it saved time, in the same way as only using lower-case letters. Accordingly, Gropius's second wife, Ise, was known as "Pia," the feminine form of "Pius."

Housemates No More

When the gasman came Fischli and Bill ran off or laid low because all the jam making had left them with huge gas bills. Then, in late July 1928 during the summer vacation, Bill's landlord gave them notice to leave by 1 October of that year. Since Bill was planning to be in Italy by August, he knew he would not be able to deal personally with his household effects. "Before I left, my tenancy was terminated; the leaving date was when I would be abroad. We knew that in advance, Fischli and I, and made suitable arrangements. In my room there was a built-in stove, which the caretaker was going to buy, so I gave Fischli written permission to sell it on my behalf for 80 marks, only he sold it for 70 marks. He was supposed to use the money to settle my debts: 25 marks to repay a loan from him, 15 marks to pay my tab at the Bauhaus canteen, and 40 marks for a coal bill. The tab at the canteen was paid, but the coal bill is still outstanding."[532]
At the time Hanns Fischli was still not of age, so Bill tried to recover the profits from the sale of his household effects in Dessau from Hanns's father, Emil Fischli; however, his efforts were thwarted when "Emil Fischli lodged a challenge regarding the legality of the order to pay."[533]

The Bauhaus director, Hannes Meyer, a fair man with a strong social conscience, gave the students their share of "the gross profit from any models they designed for manufacture.... In 1929 32,000 marks were paid out to the students."[534] Max Bill did not receive any such benefits because, during his time at the Bauhaus, he did not create any designs

531 Max Bill, Zurich, to Xanti Schawinsky, United States, 1 March 1947, Schawinsky-Archiv
532 Max Bill, Zurich, 1 August 1929: compilation for the lawyer Dr. Hans Duttweiler, Bahnhofstr. 65, Zurich 1, copy in Bibliothek Max Bill
533 Bill, 1 August 1929 for Duttweiler
534 Lang 1965, p. 79
535 Lang 1965, p. 79

(such as furniture) that were suitable for commercial manufacture. His activities of a more liberal kind on the Bauhaus stage, which he valued so highly, gave him a form of freedom of movement, but they did not improve his finances.

Hannes Meyer reported on the students' financial situations: "The average living costs for a student in those days amounted to 75 marks per month, that is to say 900 marks per annum. The annual income of the students (around 100 students in total), who benefited financially from working in the workshops, was on average 320 marks, which equated to a student grant of about thirty-five percent of the total they needed."[535]

Unpaid Invoices

At this point in his life, Max Bill was still repeatedly rebuked by his father for not yet having learned how to handle money. Nevertheless, since Erwin Bill was now making preparations to marry his second wife, he asked Max to design an announcement card. Max fulfilled his father's request and five years later also designed a visiting card for Lina Bill-Wolf and his father. Erwin Bill and Lina Wolf, daughter of Jakob Wolf and Lina Wolf, née Flückinger, married in autumn 1928 and remained in Winterthur until the end of December 1931, at which point they moved to the municipality of Ligerz on Lake Biel, where Ernst Geiger lived. Erwin Bill was appointed parish clerk in Ligerz on 9 January 1932, and his wife Lina became conductor of a local ladies' choir.

Although Max Bill had provided the typographic design for the visiting cards for "Lina Bill-Wolf, Ligerz" and "Erwin Bill, Ligerz," for decades he was unable to recall the surname of his father's second wife. It was only in his later years when I read a text to him by the writer Christa Wolf (on Inge Scholl and Otl Aicher), that he suddenly remembered that Wolf was also the maiden name of the Lina that he had addressed as "Aunt Lina."

As he had previously done in Winterthur, after the move to Ligerz Erwin Bill continued to fulfill his duties as the *Turnus* secretary for the Schweizerischer Kunstverein, at least until 1940. There are records showing that in this capacity he took delivery of written applications from artists hoping to participate in the *Turnusausstellung, the Exposition de la société suisse des beaux-arts 1932.* In 1932 Max Bill, by then living in Goldbrunnenstrasse in Zurich, sent the necessary application forms to his father, but in vain—his name does not appear in the catalogue for 1932.[536] It seems Max was not able to profit—in terms of exhibition participation—from his father's official role as *Turnus* secretary. In Ernst Geiger's visitors' books there are entries by both Max Bill's father and his second with Lina Bill-Wolf. It seems they attended the *Herbstausstellungen* (autumn exhibitions) year after year, only never together.[537]

Bill's time at the Bauhaus was thus bookended by two major events. When he arrived there, Erwin Bill and Max's mother Marie had just divorced, and now, when he was considering leaving the Bauhaus due to a lack of funds and a 40-mark debt for coal (which was a little over half of his monthly budget), his father had married a new wife. Their wedding—which Max may or may not have attended—took place on 1 October 1928. And at the end of that month, Bill decided not to continue with his studies at the Bauhaus.

Removed from the List

Despite already having decided to withdraw from the Bauhaus, in late November 1928 Max Bill traveled back to Dessau—presumably in order to retrieve the money owed to him by Fischli, which in fact proved impossible. On 26 November 1928, with Dessau as his sender's address, Bill wrote "to the Bauhaus in Dessau. I hereby wish to inform you that I have to leave the Bauhaus for financial reasons. . . . I politely request that you issue me with a statement of the work I did at the Bauhaus. I would like to express my heartfelt gratitude for all that the Bauhaus offered me. With the greatest respect, Bill."[538] Bill cited financial reasons for his departure; he expressed his thanks—albeit rather concisely and in general terms, without naming any masters in particular, and ended his letter with a standard pleasantry. The director replied, with similar brevity: "We have taken note of your communication of 26th inst. and, in compliance with your request, your name has been removed from the list of students at the Bauhaus. . . .

536 Information kindly supplied by Gabrielle Schaad, documentation by the Schweizerisches Institut für Kunstwissenschaft, SIK

537 Ernst Geiger's visitors' books, Museum Neuhaus, Biel

538 Max Bill, Dessau to the directorate at the Bauhaus, 26 November 1928, copy in Bibliothek Max Bill

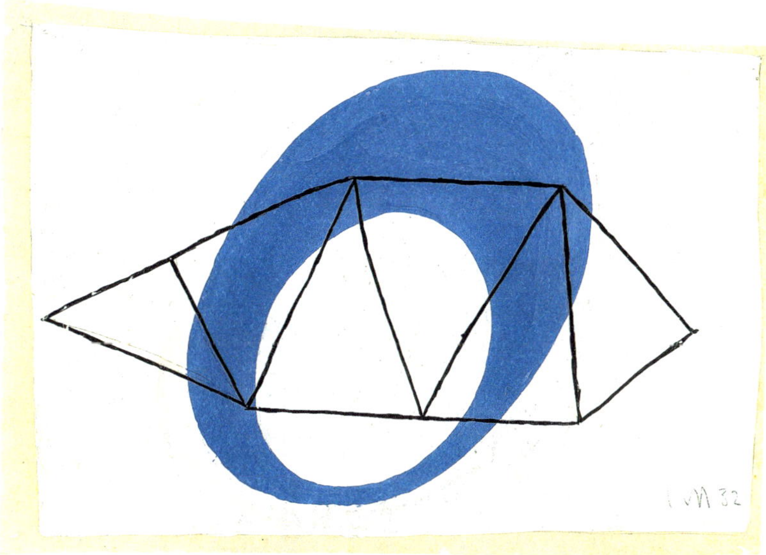

Max Bill, Design for a mural with a large O, 1932, gouache on tracing paper, 21.6×30.9 cm

Max Bill, Wedding announcement for Lina Wolf and Erwin Bill, 1928

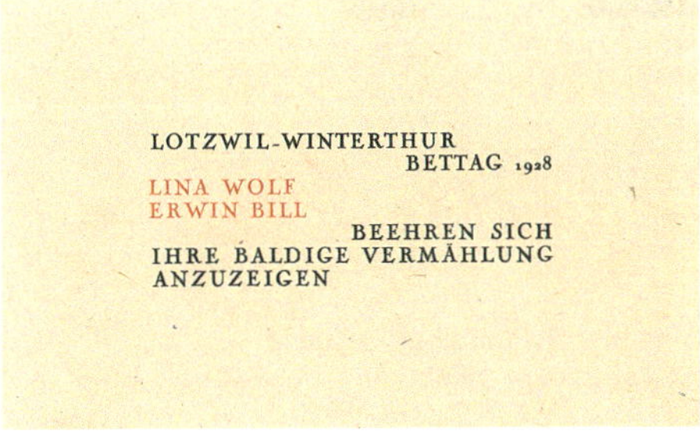
LOTZWIL-WINTERTHUR
BETTAG 1928
LINA WOLF
ERWIN BILL
BEEHREN SICH
IHRE BALDIGE VERMÄHLUNG
ANZUZEIGEN

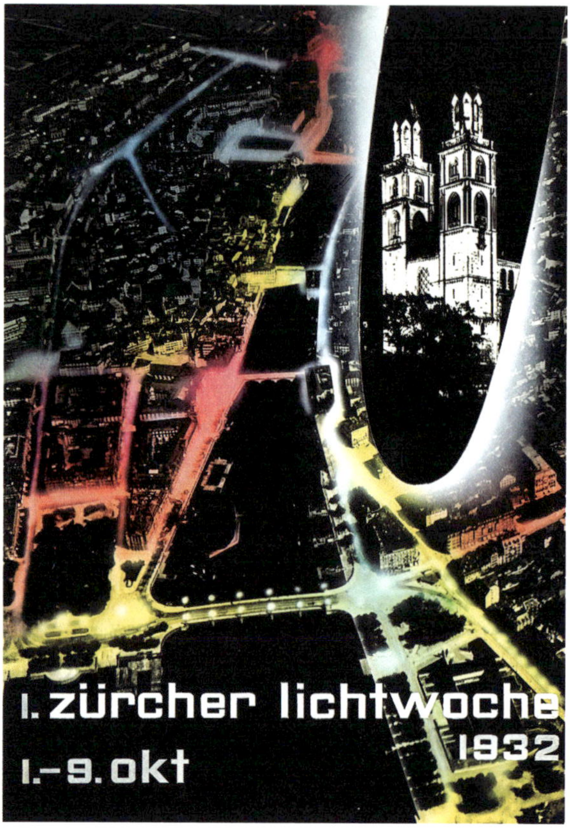

Max Bill, *1. Zürcher Lichtwoche,*
Poster design, 1932, photo collage and gouache on cardboard, 50 × 34.5 cm

Hannes Meyer, Bauhaus in Dessau, 26.11.28."[539] Bill then received his notice of exmatriculation: "We herewith certify that Herr Max Bill was a student at the Bauhaus in Dessau from 20.4.1927 to 30.10.1928. . . . Following completion of the preliminary course in the Bauhaus metal workshop [Max Bill] transferred into the stage department and attended the free painting class in his last semester. Dessau, 27 November 1928, Hannes Meyer, Director."[540]

"Then one day it was time to leave again and the whole thing was behind one like a dream receding into the distance because now one was in the midst of society, filled with Bauhaus ideals—fundamental principles—that had become a daily necessity. And the further that time ebbed away, the clearer its essence became. It started with the feelings returning that one had had on first leafing through Bauhaus publications. Then there was the memory of first encountering that audacious Bauhaus building, the good fortune of coming into contact with the great painters Kandinsky and Klee and all the other Bauhaus masters and students that one soon grew close to. And then one's memories of all the discussions about architecture and town planning, colors and forms, social issues. One had gathered together all those experiences, and now the aim was to carry them out into the world, in as pure a form as possible, and to perfect them through new experiences of one's own . . . with the sole aim of helping to construct a truly progressive culture."[541]

Looking back Bill described his time at the Bauhaus as a "way station" that had given him "the certainty of what it is to act in a straightforward manner"—a certainty that he had needed and that his parents had not been able to pass on to him. His time at the Bauhaus had put him on a more even keel and had stabilized his thinking.

Light and Photography

For the young Max Bill it was as though he had "seen the light" in Dessau. The Bauhaus master Joost Schmidt, known to all as "Schmidtchen," based his color-theory teaching on the scientific color theory developed by Wilhelm Ostwald, whose talks Bill had attended. In 1928 Schmidt decided that in the winter semester he would run a "rigorous teaching

539 Hannes Meyer, Dessau, to Max Bill, Dessau, 26 November 1928, Bibliothek Max Bill

540 Meyer to Bill, 27 November 1928, Bibliothek Max Bill

541 Bill 1947

program with exercises in color theory" in the workshop for printing and advertising, because, as he wrote to Ostwald, "We now have a number of students who were not at your lectures. Like a violinist doing daily exercises, our students will have to produce daily color studies."[542]

As it happens, all the "technically sophisticated" lighting schemes for the Bauhaus building (with the exception of the vestibule and the main lecture hall) were designed by Marianne Brandt, "or in collaboration with her"[543]—that is to say, the same Marianne Brandt whose designs Max Bill had not wanted to execute in the metal workshop.

Following his return to Switzerland Bill actively engaged with light as such.

When Schmidt was commissioned to work on "Berlin im Licht" (a festival of light put on by electricity suppliers in 1928), he and students from his sculpture workshop used photography as a "design tool," as Bill's classmate Heinz Loew remembered it.

"Models of neon signs were photographed in various combinations, to give the impression of illuminated streets, squares, kiosks, and buildings."[544]

Since the interaction between staff and students at the Bauhaus was much like that of an extended family "with a lively exchange of ideas directed by goal-oriented individuals,"[545] Max Bill would no doubt have been aware of the work Schmidt was doing, even if he was not personally involved in it.

Joost Schmidt had at least one character trait in common with Ernst Keller, Max Bill's teacher at the Kunstgewerbeschule in Zurich. As Loew later put it, Schmidt's works "could be compared with those of the old masters, in the sense that they combined a high level of craft skills with creative inspiration. Of course that way of working was extremely time consuming." But there was also an additional factor in Schmidt's approach, namely that his "teaching theories had a mathematical basis."[546] Moreover, "thanks to his innate thoroughness, after engaging with the

542 Joost Schmidt, Bauhaus, Dessau, to Wilhelm Ostwald, 3 October 1928, Wilhelm Ostwald Archiv
543 Weise 2002, p. 235
544 Loew 1984 [b], p. 8
545 Loew 1984 [b], p. 9
546 Loew 1984 [b], pp. 9, 7
547 Loew 1984 [b], p. 7
548 Joost Schmidt's cover for the special Bauhaus issue of the magazine *Junge Menschen: Monatshefte für Politik, Kunst, Literatur und Leben aus dem Geiste der jungen Generation* 5:8, *Bauhaus Weimar* (November 1924), is reproduced in Loew 1984 [b], p. 25, fig. 20
549 Nonne-Schmidt 1984 [c], p. 20

material at great length he would arrive at a constructive, rational solution without ever neglecting aesthetic, formal, and artistic considerations.... As a teacher at the Bauhaus, Joost Schmidt could probably be described as unique. He tried to foster the students' awareness of their own emotions and unconsciousness and to help them to find a rational solution for the given task, albeit never at the expense of their own individual judgment.... He always had time for the Bauhauslers and their problems. In a community like the Bauhaus, where work is life, there were often personal conflicts, which could only be resolved by dialogue. For most Bauhauslers, Schmidtchen was the person they could confide in.... He was a good listener and his analytical skills usually led to a solution."[547]
In November 1924 Joost Schmidt had designed the entire typographic layout for the special Bauhaus issue of *Junge Menschen*.[548]

In October 1925 Walter Gropius asked Joost Schmidt, who had an intense interest in "lettering of various kinds," to provide "obligatory calligraphy teaching for both foundation courses," which Schmidt then carried out until 1932.[549]

Schmidtchen's course in lettering and typography will thus also have been obligatory for Max Bill when he took the foundation course in his first year at the Bauhaus in 1927.

The cover design has a striking motif: a black disc with a white hole at its center, which may or may not have played into Bill's design for his *wandmalerei mit grossem "o"* (1932, see p. 309). During Max Bill's time at the Bauhaus, Joost Schmidt also published an essay, "Schrift?," in *bauhaus* (2: 2/3, 1928).

Just a few years later Max Bill would again come across the idea of grappling with mathematical principles—albeit now in conjunction with the creation of an artistic oeuvre—in the thinking of the pioneering Belgian modernist, Georges Vantongerloo, when the two men met in Paris in the mid-1930s. Bill found he was able to tap into something he already knew from Schmidtchen's theories and not only engage in the ensuing debate but also develop his own position, which ultimately bore fruit in his text "Die mathematische Denkweise in der Kunst unserer Zeit" (1949 [b]). The knowledge he gained at the Bauhaus proved to be a firm foundation for the future.

There is no knowing how often Bill in fact attended the obligatory classes on his timetable, or how often he succumbed to the Bauhaus hangover and just failed to turn up. However, we do know for certain that he came into contact with Joost Schmidt in the experimental stage workshops: witness the photograph taken in 1928, where Bill is flanked by Alexander Schawinsky, Andor Weininger, Joost Schmidt, T. Lux

Feininger, and Clemens Röseler (see. p. 231). Joost Schmidt remained in Dessau until early 1933. "On 17 March 1933 the SS, the SA, the police, and detectives searched the masters' houses for weapons and explosives—in vain.... The new authorities have come up with yet more attacks, that's to say, they are applying a new law retrospectively; payments of the agreed compensation have been halted (the contracts run until 1935) and they are freezing bank accounts. And they say that, because Joost Schmidt was at the Bauhaus, he is a cultural Bolshevist."[550]

Despite being derided by the Nazis as a "cultural Bolshevist," Joost Schmidt remained in Germany during the Second World War; he died from malaria in Nuremberg on 2 December 1948. His widow, the former Bauhaus student Helene Nonne (who had married Schmidt in September 1925), was invited as a guest lecturer by Max Bill to the Hochschule für Gestaltung in Ulm in the 1950s.

In 1932, a few years after Max Bill returned to Switzerland from the Bauhaus, he created a poster design for the first Zürcher Lichtwoche (Zurich lights week) in which he included a photocollage that is immediately reminiscent of Joost Schmidt's use of photographic elements for the "Berlin im Licht" commission realized at the Bauhaus in 1928.

Ostwald's Theory of Forms

Back in Zurich, Max Bill longed to continue to debate artistic issues as he had done at the Bauhaus and decided to visit his old friend Hans Hinterreiter from Winterthur, specifically to discuss Wilhelm Ostwald's theory of forms. At the time Hinterreiter and his partner Mina Salm, who had "some capital," were living quietly in an Alpine cabin near the town of Seelisberg in the canton of Uri, where they would remain until 1935. In his cabin high up above Lake Lucerne Hinterreiter showed Bill some color tests that

550 Nonne-Schmidt 1984 [a], pp. 116–17

551 Cited in Hans Hinterreiter's attempt at a short autobiography drawn up for the Spanish art magazine *El Cobalto*, 8 June 1949, estate of Hans Hinterreiter

552 "Aufgabe und Verwirklichung der Minimalwohnung: Entwurf zu Thesen zum 2. Kongress der CIAM Frankfurt am Main 1929" is reprinted in Hans Schmidt, *Beiträge zur Architektur 1924–1964* (Zurich: gta, 1993), pp. 50–52 and 194 note 16 (first published by VEB Verlag für Bauwesen, Berlin, GDR, and Pfalz Verlag, Basel in 1965)

he had dried in the sun. Outside in the Alpine air the colors had become "too harsh" and Hinterreiter's sensitive eyes wanted their hues to be softened. Having trained as a scientist, he was keen to address the color problem in a suitably scientific manner. He explained to Bill that he had found little that was of any use to him until, luckily, he came across Ostwald's color theory. That marked a turning point in his painting and "revolutionised" his artistic approach.

Hans Hinterreiter adopted certain terms and ideas promoted by Ostwald: "nets," "rotators," "reflectors," repetitions through rotation, reflection and shifting. Hinterreiter now felt that "the ascribing of color to a form" was the artist's most important action and that it decided the artistic value of a work.[551]

A few practical experiments were enough to convince Hinterreiter that Ostwald had discovered the basic laws of color harmony and had formulated them with great acumen. However, he also felt that color harmony was something spiritual, abstract, and needed forms to become visible. In Hinterreiter's opinion what Ostwald achieved in his set of four folios, *Die Welt der Formen,* was inspired but still only a minor foray into that field. Following that visit it would be some years before Bill and his very reclusive friend met again.

Ernst May

It may be that Bill was less attracted by the avant-garde Suprematist, Constructivist art production cultivated in the USSR around the time of the Revolution in 1917 and seen in Western Europe some years later in black-and-white reproductions than by the utopian notion of revolutionary Soviet architecture. At any rate, around 1930 Bill became very interested in the idea of going to the *terra incognita* of the USSR as an "ad man" with an architectural brigade, designing texts and typographies—not with the former Bauhaus director Hannes Meyer but with the May Brigade, which included Mart Stam. However, his plans did not come to fruition. Like many others, it seems that Bill had little real knowledge of the situation in the USSR at that time nor of the disastrous consequences of Josef Stalin's policies.

Ernst May had been appointed city architect in Frankfurt am Main in 1925. He was also one of the two keynote speakers at CIAM II in Frankfurt am Main in 1929, where the focus was on "minimum dwelling."[552] The other keynote speaker was Walter Gropius, first director of the

Bauhaus and co-founder of CIAM. The Swiss architect Hans Schmidt, who would employ Max Bill's services ten years later for the Swiss National Exhibition (*Schweizerische Landesausstellung*, Zurich 1939), had prepared a position paper for the congress on "The Purpose and Realisation of Minimum Dwelling." This paper, in a somewhat revised form, was presented to the congress by Walter Gropius, with the title "Sociological Premises for the Minimum Dwelling of Urban Industrial Populations." That same year Ernst May gave lectures in Moscow, Leningrad, and Kharkhov, in which he discussed new towns, housing in Germany, and the rationalisation of housing construction. This prompted the Russian government to invite May to relocate to the USSR with a team of experts. May took up the offer and on 8 October 1930 he and his brigade set off for Moscow: "The idea of playing a part in this huge, unique task—even at the risk of failing—seems much more meaningful to me than fearfully trying to secure my own existence."[553]

In Germany—after the Great Depression—"in the building industry alone [there were] over 500,000 workers without employment and in the early 1930s 90% of architects were unemployed." In Frankfurt am Main it was said that "1,400 architects" applied to emigrate to Moscow.[554]

Our young, post-Bauhaus Bill would also dearly have loved to join that brigade and in the summer of 1930 asked Mart Stam (whom he knew from the Bauhaus) to put in a word for him, since Stam was already planning to become part of the May Brigade.

When the May Brigade—consisting of Ernst May and a team of just twenty—arrived in Moscow, the new-build apartments they had been promised were not yet ready, so they had to find accommodation in a number of hotels; however, soon after that all the members of the brigade were allocated more or less identical apartments in a newly built five-story block. There was an economic gulf between the Meyer Brigade and the May Brigade: Meyer and his team did not accept any privileges and only allowed themselves to be paid the same meager wages as their Russian comrades (300 rubles for novices, 400 rubles for experienced

553 Ernst May, "Bekenntnisse des Städtebauers," in *Das neue Russland* 5/6 (1930), p. 55

554 Borngräber 1977, pp. 116–17

555 Walter Schwagenscheidt, "Glückliche Jahre der Arbeit mit Ernst May," in *Baukunst und Werkform* 9 (1956), p. 477

556 Konrad Püschel, "Die Tätigkeit der Gruppe Hannes Meyer in der UdSSR in den Jahren 1930 bis 1937," in *Wissenschaftliche Zeitschrift der Hochschule für Architektur und Bauwesen* 5/6 (1976), p. 468

workers). By contrast, May—emphasizing his specialist skills—had negotiated foreign currency contracts for himself and his team, so that their earnings were paid into a bank abroad. Mart Stam—who had worked with May's team on the master plan for Magnitogorsk—gave a lecture at the German Club in Moscow on "The Construction of the Socialist City of Magnitogorsk."

Constructing Magnitogorsk

Bill, ever alert to the latest trends, was looking for a job where he could work as a cool, uncompromising ad man, designing letterings and fonts. However, as it happened it was the Basel architect Hans Schmidt, who emphatically warned him not to go to the USSR, explaining that that was not a good time for foreigners to go to Moscow if—like Bill—they were not members of the Communist Party. At one time around a thousand foreign architects were working in the Soviet Union, including three from Basel: Hans Schmidt, Hannes Meyer, and René Mensch, none of whom played down the immense difficulties they had to contend with. Meyer and Schmidt at least had a Marxist outlook, but René Mensch was certainly not a Communist—he had been brought up in the Catholic faith. Between 1930 and 1937 Hans Schmidt, with his wife Lili Imboden and their child in tow, worked as an architect in Magnitogorsk. During those early years the population had to contend with famine, food rationing, collectivization, and, starting in December 1934, a wave of purges, trials and executions.

Ernst May commented, unsentimentally: "Building in the USSR is not some romantic game, it is a matter of life and death."[555]

After Hannes Meyer was expelled from the Bauhaus, he took up an invitation to teach at WASI (Higher institute for architecture and building) in Moscow. In 1930 he and Béla Scheffler arrived in Moscow. By 1931 the members of Hannes Meyer Brigade included (among others) Klaus Meumann, Konrad Püschel, Anton Urban, Tibor Weiner, Philipp Tolziner—whom Max Bill knew well from the Bauhaus—and René Mensch. They lived cheek-by-jowl with Russian families in an uncomfortable old building on the Arbat. "There was a terrible shortage of building supplies; factory buildings took priority for cement and steel, which could only be used for residential construction in urgent cases. There was an almost complete lack of trained bricklayers, plasterers, carpenters, joiners, and plumbers."[556]

Hannes Meyer, former director of the Bauhaus in Dessau, gave a sober account of the situation when he was working in the USSR: "In 1931, when I was asked to work on one of the eight brigade designs for the Greater Moscow competition, I had no idea as yet how paltry my knowledge and experience were compared to the gigantic task facing us. The training that we had gained in Western European town planning was wholly incompatible and entirely at odds with the social system of the USSR."[557]

As it happens, most of the research on this topic has been conducted in the West, mainly drawing on the few documents that Meyer and Schmidt were able to bring with them from the USSR.[558]

The Swiss architects arrived in the Soviet Union when it was already two years into its first five-year plan. Stalin summed up the broad direction now pursued by the Party and the government; the aim was to "turn our agrarian nation into an industrial nation that would be capable, using its own resources, of producing all the armaments it needed." Initially "the USSR was obliged to import machinery and to recruit foreign technicians. Hugh L. Cooper, who supervised the construction of the hydroelectric power plant at Niagara Falls, was retained by the Soviet Union to construct the Dneprostroi Dam, American engineers were working in Magnitogorsk, Henry Ford and engineers from the Austin Motor Company set up the car plant in Gorki, and J. K. Calder supervised the building of the Stalingrad tractor plant. These specialists withdrew again in 1933 and 1934."[559]

Lotte Beese also reported that Hannes Meyer, unlike other foreigners working on these projects, did not take accept the privileges they were offered. He himself described the food he and his team ate in Birobidzhan: "600 grams of bread per day, fish, tiny portions of course, and cabbage or barley soup—that was our midday meal. No evening meal. In the office we were meant to save paper and the telephone connections were unreliable. The distance between construction sites, the slow trains, and the simultaneous construction of the same types of project in

557 Hannes Meyer, "La Realidad Sovietica: Los Arquitectos," in *Arquitectura* 9 (Mexico 1942)
558 Schnaidt 1990
559 Schnaidt 1990
560 Schnaidt 1990
561 El Lissitzky, Lugano, to Sophie Lissitzky-Küppers (13 February 1924), in El Lissitzky 1976, p. 35
562 Schmidt 1976, p. 399
563 El Lissitzky, Lugano, to Sophie Lissitzky-Küppers, 13 February 1924, in El Lissitzky 1976, p. 34

different locations hindered the plan's author from supervising the construction process." Many of the foreign architects found it hard to cope with the culture shock of their work in the Soviet Union: "These men, who might at best have designed urban settlements in the past, were now expected to draw up plans for whole cities."[560]

Mart Stam, El Lissitzky, Hans Schmidt, and Lotte Stam-Beese

In 1924—the same year when Max Bill enrolled at the Kunstgewerbeschule in Zurich—Mart Stam spent some time in Zurich. In February of that year, Mart Stam, Sophie Taeuber-Arp, and Jean Arp all went to collect the "Proun" artist El Lissitzky when he arrived in Zurich by train. El Lissitzky, who was suffering from pulmonary tuberculosis, had come to Switzerland for medical treatment, initially in a sanatorium in Agra in southern Switzerland.

Lissitzky and Stam had originally met in Berlin when Stam was working in Max Taut's architectural practice. Following a period in Amsterdam, Lissitzky spent some considerable time in Switzerland where he met Mart Stam again and got to know the Basel architect Hans Schmidt. Lissitzky described his arrival in Zurich to his wife Sophie: "At the station I was met by 1½-kilometer-tall Stam and big Pra [Arp written backward] with his white curls. Stam is revolutionizing architecture here, too.... In the very near future Stam and some other young architects (Hans Schmidt, Wittwer, Emil Roth) will be publishing a newspaper similar to *G.*"[561]

The magazine in question was *ABC: Beiträge zum Bauen.* The first issue was published in Basel in 1924, edited by Emil Roth, Hans Schmidt and Mart Stam: a total of ten issues of came out between 1924 and 1928. According to Hans Schmidt, who was very active at *ABC,* it was Lissitzky who had come up with the idea. The magazine *G* ("Gestaltung," meaning "design"), mentioned by Lissitzky in his letter to his wife Sophie Küppers, was produced in Germany by Lissitzky and Mies van der Rohe around this time.[562]

Lissitzky was booked into a small hotel because the Arps only had a very small apartment. "Arp is a very good, decent fellow. Not even the slightest whiff of profiteering."[563]

Lissitzky's relieved conclusion that there was no hint of profiteering about Arp may have been an allusion to a comment about the city of Zurich by Richard Huelsenbeck, the co-founder of Cabaret Voltaire, who once described it as a "luxuriant idyll" where "international profiteers" congregated. Huelsenbeck, who subsequently co-founded the Dada group in Berlin, had made that comment during the First World War, comparing "luxuriant" Zurich to Berlin, the city "where hunger rolls louder and louder."[564]

Boosted by the events of the Russian Revolution, which had remarkably little effect on politics in Zurich, El Lissitzky noted that "Switzerland is very busy with its own 'federal art,' people here need a dose of dynamite."[565] Clearly he was thinking not of acts of terrorism but of cultural explosives to shake people out of their torpor. Mart Stam admired El Lissitzky for his passion and described him as someone brimming with ideas: everything he did was geared toward creating a meaningful world for the good of the next generation.[566] After Lissitzky's visit to Zurich, he went to stay with Margarethe Hardegger—once one of the most sought-after, rousing activists who had progressed from a social democrat working with trade unions to an outright anarchist; Lissitzky "was suffering from tuberculosis, lonely, and in financial straits" and she cared for him in her own home, the Villino Graziella as she called it. Her villa was down below Brione, in the municipality of Minusio, "in the midst of an overgrown garden by a small stream with a waterfall."[567]

Anyone standing on the top-floor balcony of the Villino Graziella had a wonderful view of Lake Maggiore, the wooded slopes above Lake Locarno, and Italy in the distance. Lissitzky, very touched by Margarethe Hardegger's kindness, wrote to his friend Sophie Küppers that he "had found some people, who were human beings . . . a couple, he's a good carpenter, his wife has already been through a lot, they have 57 white hens." However, when Sophie Küppers visited El in the Ticino, she was rather less enthusiastic: "when it rained the water ran down the walls inside this romantic dwelling. And that's where my unpractical, too clever friend was lying—looked after somehow or other by his hostess." Lissitzky, for his part, felt that "these people deserve my respect."[568]

564 Huelsenbeck 1920, pp. 34–35
565 El Lissitzky, Lugano, to Sophie Lissitzky-Küppers, 13 February 1924, in El Lissitzky 1976, p. 35
566 See Stam 1976
567 Bochsler 2004, p. 345
568 Bochsler 2004, p. 345
569 Jean Arp, in Adriani 1980, p. 41

ABC, Beiträge zum Bauen

The new magazine *ABC, Beiträge zum Bauen* was intended to blaze a trail for revolutionary writing on architecture. It was launched in Basel in 1924, edited by Hans Schmidt, Hans Wittwer and Emil Roth, and published contributions from Mart Stam, Hannes Meyer, and El Lissitzky.

Mart Stam and Hans Schmidt had already met in the Netherlands, where Hans Schmidt worked from 1920 to 1922.

In 1924 El Lissitzky was working on his idea for a book to be named *Die Kunstismen,* and Jean Arp and the publisher Eugen Rentsch liked the concept. In the summer of 1924, the Arps traveled to Ambrì-Sotto to work there, in the Upper Ticino, where El Lissitzky and his wife Sophie Lissitzky-Küppers were already staying. Jean Arp wrote a short text on Dadaism for *Die Kunstismen.*

In 1929 Max Bill bought the book *Die Kunstismen 1914–1924,* published by Eugen Rentsch Verlag in Zurich in 1925, as his signature (with conventional upper and lower case) and year date confirm (Bibliothek Max Bill).

El Lissitzky versus Jean Arp

However, during that summer in the Upper Ticino a major dispute flared up between the Proun artist Lissitzky and the post-Dadaist Arp. Sophie Lissitzky-Küppers tried to calm tempers and—in the hope of defusing the situation with a pleasant diversion—the Lissitzkys and the Arps made an expedition across the mountains and down into the Valle Maggia. They came across an artists' colony by Lake Maggiore, which "was home to the strangest saints and sects. We were happy to get back to the cooler, purer air of the Gotthard."

Arp, in a mock complaint, hinted at one aspect of the dispute in a letter to his Dada-friend Hannah Höch in Berlin: "Dear Haha, your and Segal's immortalizations [in *Die Kunstismen 1914–1924*] almost led to Eli-Aas [Lissitzky's first name Elias + "Aas," as in "devil" or "swine"] Lissitzky bumping me off with a lukewarm Proun bone."[569]

During the Second World War Hannah Höch kept a low profile in the outskirts of Berlin. After the war a group of members of the Akademie der Künste (West Berlin), including Max Bill, visited the elderly Dada pioneer in her studio. That was the first and last encounter between Bill and Höch.

Saved from Disillusion in the USSR

In August 1930 Mart Stam wrote to Max Bill turning down Bill's request to travel to the USSR with his brigade: "Herr Bill, Advertising Technician, Stadelhoferstrasse 27, Zurich. Dear Bill, You are correct in all that you wrote about Russia. However, I have to disappoint you, because I myself have no influence on the selection of the team members, and someone has already been given responsibility for any lettering or signage. And even apart from that, I am sure that we will have to make at least some concessions there."[570] As it turned out the foreign "barefoot architects on Siberian construction sites" had to sign up for ribbon developments and open spaces that facilitated the equal distribution of sun, air, and greenery. The functionalism of the audacious *Neues Bauen* (New architecture) practiced in Europe was not (or no longer) really welcome in the Soviet Union.

According to Claude Schnaidt's analysis of the situation, the Germans applied that principle with particular rigor: "They created their rows of north-south blocks regardless of the topography of the site or its size, and at the people's assemblies they were plied with questions: 'Where is the boulevard where a lad can go walking and window-shopping with his girl in the evening?'"[571]

According to decisions taken at the Plenary Session of the Central Committee of the Communist Party in June 1931, the aim for Soviet architecture was to develop new ideological contents—but rather than new contents receiving approval, old-school Russian architects found favor and were encouraged by the party. In August 1932 the first polemical articles were published, denouncing the "inadmissible rubber-stamp solutions" proposed by the German architects working in the Soviet Union, and by the end of that year the majority of the May Brigade had returned home. The Swiss architects stayed a few years longer until the Great Purge, which took hold in 1936. Now all foreigners were barred "for reasons of security" from participating in any urban planning projects; all such foreigners either had to leave the country or become Soviet citizens. Hannes Meyer left the Soviet Union in June 1936; Hans Schmidt left in 1937.

Schmidt had specifically advised Bill not to travel to the Soviet Union for work, and in 1930, when Mart Stam had had to turn Bill's request

570 Mart Stam, Stam u. Moser, Architekten, Frankfurt Am Main, to Max Bill, Stadelhoferstrasse 27, Zurich, 5 August 1930, Bibliothek Max Bill

571 Schnaidt 1990

572 Winkler 2003, p. 102

down, despite knowing how much the young Bill wanted to gain experience abroad, Bill will surely have been both angry and upset. But maybe his two older colleagues had in fact saved him from disillusion and disenchantment.

Post-Bauhaus in Switzerland

After Bill had left the Bauhaus and settled in Zurich, two of his former classmates in the stage workshop—Liesel Träger and Roman Clemens—also moved to Zurich. Roman Clemens became the lead set designer at the Stadttheater (now the opera house) in Zurich (1923–43), after which he concentrated on painting. Liesel Träger soon married and became Liesel Steiner-Träger. In Zurich Liesel lived for a while in a corner house at the top end of Kirchgasse, which still has figurative decorations painted on its façade.

Liesel Steiner-Träger remained a close friend of Max Bill's. She taught for many years in the Werkseminar at the Kunstgewerbeschule Zürich. After she died on 1 May 1980, Max kept the announcement of her death. "This evening, in the 77th year of her life, our dear friend Liesel Träger-Steiner was released from her suffering. We remember her with love and gratitude. In quiet grief: friends and acquaintances." Max Bill wrote an obituary for her, which was published in the *Neue Zürcher Zeitung,* 6–7 September 1980, p. 67.

The Bauhaus master Gunta Sharon-Stölzl also emigrated to Switzerland; she set up a workshop in Zurich where Hilde Rantzsch worked for a while around 1933–34—of course that was the same Hilde Rantzsch who had studied at the Bauhaus, who had been drawn by Max Bill (see p. 161), and who had been one of Bill's rhubarb thieves in 1928.

Pre-emigration

In May 1928 Gunta Stölzl, Arieh Sharon, and another Bauhausler, Peer Bücking, traveled to Moscow for an international architecture conference. The "little Bauhaus delegation" was sent there "to find out more about *VKhUTEIN, the advanced institute of technology and the arts.*"[572] "At the end of their trip to Russia Sharon gave a lecture at Moscow University on the Bauhaus and its aims. And on their return to Germany Arieh Sharon and Peer Bücking's reports were received with great interest at the Bauhaus."[573]

Gunta sent a postcard to Oskar Schlemmer from Moscow, also signed by Arieh Sharon: "Moscow—magnificent city—always sunny.—where is your comradely heart?—mine finds nourishment in the streets here. It's very international—Eastern—not at all Western. We are given a warmer welcome than the King of Afghanistan. Constantly rubbing shoulders with famous architects—am I still a weaver-girl? Not in the slightest longing for Germany."[574]

However, there was one member of the masters' council who not only took no interest in those reports but who was openly dismissive, namely Kandinsky: "When we were back in Dessau we were surprised to find that Kandinsky did not express any interest in our impressions and experiences. He didn't want to hear anything about the situation in Russia.... He was convinced that the Russian people would never accept the Communist system."[575] And it was against this backdrop that Kandinsky's wife Nina reported that it was "all too understandable that Kandinsky was categorically opposed to any radical activities at the Bauhaus. Once bitten, twice shy, he tried to prevent the worst from happening at the Bauhaus."[576]

Nevertheless, other staff and students at the Bauhaus were glad to see Sharon and Bücking at the Bauhaus in early June 1928, and their report was followed by a lively debate. Bill will hardly have missed that event, and it may even have been their report that not only convinced Bill that architecture and art in the USSR were more advanced, more progressive than at the Bauhaus but also persuaded him to try to find work in the USSR.

In 1928 Arieh Sharon independently drew up plans for a center for the Worker's Council in Jerusalem: *Entwurf für das Haus des Arbeiterrates in Jerusalem.* The following year it was illustrated in *bauhaus* (3:1, Dessau 1929). After their time at the Bauhaus Bill and Sharon

573 In Stiftung Bauhaus Dessau 1997, p. 52

574 Gunta Stölzl, Moscow, to Oskar Schlemmer, Bauhaus, Dessau, 30 April 1928, in Stiftung Bauhaus Dessau 1997, p. 52

575 Stölzl cited in Kandinsky 1976, pp. 144–45

576 Kandinsky 1976, p. 145

577 *See The Jerusalem Committee,* pamphlet ed. Yissakhar Ben-Yaacov, Jerusalem 1978, p. 24 and p. 29

578 Winkler 2003, p. 102

579 Stölzl to her brother Erwin (5 December 1928), in Stiftung Bauhaus Dessau 1997, p. 53

remained friends and kept in touch by letter. In the early 1930s Sharon, by now living in Tel Aviv, invited Bill to work on the design of a Swiss section at the Levant Fair in Tel Aviv (1932). And many years later, in 1978, during the era of Teddy Kollek, the Socialist mayor of the city of Jerusalem, both Arieh Sharon (born in Poland) and Max Bill would be co-opted onto the Town Planning Subcommittee of the Jerusalem Committee.[577]

Arieh Sharon, born in Jarosław, Galicia, was eight years older than Bill. He had been in a kibbutz in Palestine since 1920 where he had trained as a carpenter and a farmer. In Dessau, as a highly motivated student (who was granted some special exemptions), he had very rapidly acquired a wide knowledge of architecture and building in the class of Hannes Meyer. "Sharon was a student on the first proper architectural course, which began in the summer semester of 1927 and, according to his account, had only seven students. Besides his studies Sharon also had to help to maintain the masters' houses. Work on some practical proposals filled the next phase. The most important of those was the competition entry, led by Meyer and Wittwer, for the ADGB trade union school in Bernau."[578]

Gunta Stölzl and Arieh Sharon, who would become a renowned architect, had grown close during their trip to the Soviet Union. Gunta wrote to her brother about this, telling him of her love for Arieh: "It's fine for me now, things are almost going too well, in personal matters. . . . I like him and there are really no problems. . . . And I gladly admit that things are rather easier here at the Bauhaus than in a parlour in an apartment block. We don't need to hide behind a certificate, and if we do have to—then that's what we'll do."[579]

In that last remark Gunta was of course referring to the free love that was tolerated and practiced at the Bauhaus. But when she became pregnant—as an unmarried woman—the need for a "certificate" became more urgent. She was a master, but did not live in one of the masters' houses and would now have to find lodgings for herself and her child. So Arieh and Gunta married in August 1929; financial constraints meant that they just had a plain civil ceremony with no grand wedding celebrations—oddly enough no one at the party-loving Bauhaus organized anything for the newlyweds. When Gunta Stölzl married, she had to relinquish her German citizenship and take her husband's nationality and become a Palestinian citizen.

This all happened two years after the National Socialists had announced their "race laws" at the first Nuremberg Rally, claiming that there was "one superior Nordic race and other variously inferior races." And it would not be so very long before the Nazis—trumpeting the misogynistic mantra "back to your kitchens!"—declared that married women were no longer allowed to work as civil servants.

In October 1929, when the Nazis were demanding that all areas of political life in Germany be "cleansed," Gunta and Arieh's daughter Yael was born. Six weeks after the birth of Yael, a major conflict erupted at the Bauhaus between students on the right and on the left. "At the Bauhaus there is nothing but trouble and all sorts of intrigues seem to be in play."[580]

Gunta's parents, who were not as unconventional as their daughter, looked into Arieh Sharon's background and Tut Schlemmer tried to allay their anxiety by reassuring them that Sharon was "very talented." Gunta hoped to move into the Schlemmers' masters' house after they left the Bauhaus, but in vain, as it turned out. While Gunta was on maternity leave from the Bauhaus weaving workshop, she was temporarily replaced (until 1 November 1929) by Anni Albers.

Gunta Stölzl had been promised the lower floor in the Schepers's house (Hinnerk Scheper was a young master at the Bauhaus). Initially, however, she spent some time living at her studio. "We're living in the studio—because the apartment is not ready yet, I'm not going to Schlemmers, upstairs, but to Schepers, on the ground floor—for the moment that's not bad, because there's already some furniture there and, apart from a wardrobe, I won't need to look for anything else."[581]

For a while Gunta and the baby lived on the lower ground floor at the Schepers' home, but when she returned to work she still had to look after the baby on her own during the week because Arieh Sharon, who was working in Bernau near Berlin, only spent the weekends at home in Dessau. "We're a happy family! But I've no idea what's going to happen with my work at the Bauhaus, at the moment it's just eating me up."[582] It was not until the autumn of 1930 that their "weekend marriage" came to an end; Arieh was back in Dessau, but now he had no work.

It was only much later that Gunta Sharon-Stölzl discovered that the "intrigues" at the Bauhaus that affected her were partly stirred up

580 Sharon-Stölzl to Benita Otte, Autumn 1929, Stiftung Bauhaus Dessau 1997, p. 57
581 Gunta Stölzl to her brother Erwin, 9 December 1928, Stiftung Bauhaus Dessau 1997, p. 56
582 Sharon-Stölzl, Dessau, to her brother Erwin, 11 November 1929, Stiftung Bauhaus Dessau 1997, p. 56
583 Stiftung Bauhaus Dessau 1997, p. 57
584 Stiftung Bauhaus Dessau 1997, p. 57
585 Sharon-Stölzl, Dessau, to her brother Erwin, 5 July 1930, Stiftung Bauhaus Dessau 1997, p. 57
586 Stiftung Bauhaus Dessau 1997, p. 57

by "the national-socialist weaving master Kurt Wanke, whom she had once admired, but who had turned a number of students against her. Naturally trusting, she discovered too late that he was the 'rat' in her workshop." She now found that she was opposed by "the students Herbert von Arend, Ilse Voigt, and Margaretha Reichardt, who were busily creating trouble with support from the Bauhaus teacher Walter Peterhans, who—first covertly, then openly—criticized Gunta Stölzl for her private life and her teaching, without ever specifying his complaints."[583]

Walter Peterhans had in fact been offered the post teaching photography at the Bauhaus that Lucia Moholy, despite her major achievements, was never offered.

Intrigues against Gunta Sharon-Stölzl

"Another crucial factor was Klee's departure from the Bauhaus. He had taught in the workshop for years.... Like Gunta Stölzl, Klee took Hannes Meyer's side against the growing reactionary forces."[584] Gunta Stölzl described the situation to her brother Erwin: "Yesterday we found out that Klee is going to Düsseldorf. It's a massive blow—it could hardly be worse.... Klee is a huge loss."[585]

It was no longer possible to ignore the crisis at the Bauhaus and in Germany. Given the destabilizing impact of Klee's decision to leave, the drastic political situation in Germany, and Arieh Sharon's poor employment prospects, he and Gunta started to discuss emigrating. A little over a month before Hannes Meyer was dismissed from the Bauhaus, Gunta and Arieh were seriously considering emigrating to the USSR. Sharon already had a contact in the Soviet Union, the Bauhausler Hinnerk Scheper, who was working there. And the likelihood of Sharon finding work in Germany was rapidly diminishing, partly because of his close connection with Hannes Meyer, who was seen by right-wing extremists as a "red" with suspicious contacts in the Soviet Union.

On 1 August—National Day in Switzerland—Hannes Meyer was dismissed "without notice" as director of the Bauhaus because of "his political stance." "The Bauhaus remained closed until 21 October, when Mies van der Rohe took up his post; he was soon followed by Lilly Reich—the 'woman at his side'—who later took over the textile department."[586]

Following the appointment of Mies van der Rohe as the new director of the Bauhaus, the attacks on Gunta Sharon-Stölzl—who was married to a Jew—only increased. Some people did speak up in her defense, including Grete Leischner, Gret Preiswerk (who later worked with Gunta in exile in Zurich), and Anni Albers; these three asked former weaving students to step up in support of Gunta Stölzl.[587] But a determined, internal campaign was now being waged against Gunta Sharon-Stölzl—the only woman who had made a career at the Bauhaus as a master. She was accused of "misdemeanors." She wrote to her brother saying that she liked the new director Mies, but he was "only there two days a week."

"Everything is so uncertain here ... maybe Russia after all—but don't say anything to our parents. The crisis just goes on and on here ..."[588]

Meanwhile, she herself was "in a difficult position, firstly, because of Sharon–H. Meyer, secondly, because I am on a friendly footing with the members of my workshop, thirdly, because six of the older ones have gone and the younger ones are stirred up by people who are supported by certain masters."[589] Gunta did not specify exactly which masters were party to that campaign.

"One of Gunta Stölzl's main adversaries among the masters appears to have been Wassily Kandinsky.... One reason would have been the fact that Klee and Stölzl took Meyer's side.... Gunta Stölzl's position as the only female master at the Bauhaus certainly would have been a thorn in Kandinsky's side, because he regarded women as inferior beings, in every sense."[590]

Three female students in Gunta's workshop hatched a plot against her and complained about her to the new director. Confronted with untenable accusations filled with sexual innuendo—and having found a swastika painted on her door—Gunta had to admit that Joost Schmidt and Alfred Arndt were the only two masters still on her side.

"I was right," she wrote to her brother Erwin; the father of one of the female students in her workshop had "not calmed down" and had lodged a complaint against her with the local authority, above all "attacking her for her private life ... The mayor doesn't want to deal

587 Stiftung Bauhaus Dessau 1997
588 Sharon-Stölzl, Dessau, to her brother Erwin, 26 June 1930, Stiftung Bauhaus Dessau 1997, p. 56
589 Sharon-Stölzl to her brother Erwin, 14 December 1930, Stiftung Bauhaus Dessau 1997, p. 58
590 Stiftung Bauhaus Dessau 1997, p. 58
591 Sharon-Stölzl to her brother Erwin, 19 March 1931, Stiftung Bauhaus Dessau 1997, p. 59
592 Sharon-Stölzl to her brother Erwin, 3 April 1931, Stiftung Bauhaus Dessau 1997, pp. 57–62
593 Sharon-Stölzl, Dessau, to Benita Otte, 26 March 1931, Stiftung Bauhaus Dessau 1997, p. 58

with the complaint, because it will create a fuss around the Bauhaus again and things are already touch and go here at the Bauhaus, he wants to dismiss me . . .

Mies and Klee and others are saying I should resign, because that would make it easier for me to move on. Whatever the case, Mies is not taking action, he doesn't want to keep me."[591]

Convinced that she had no alternative, she handed in her notice.

"I have resigned . . . the Bauhaus is internally and externally on such thin ice . . ."[592]

Gunta Sharon-Stölzl then writes to her friend Benita Otte: "I have resigned—you know about all the dirt that has been thrown at me, but things are even worse and more devious than I had suspected. Wa Ka [Wassily Kandinsky] is also behind it, and when the fox bites it's not worth trying to defend yourself—he is biting because he is afraid of my Bolshevist husband, who poisons the students' minds. Albers believes that, too, and even claims Sharon staged the coup against Schmidtchen [Joost Schmidt] and Mies doesn't value that kind of a colleague if that's what the movers and shakers feel. And of course Pe Ha [Walter Peterhans] fanned the flames hardest of all . . ."[593]

Some leftist students did still stand up for Gunta and resisted the campaign against her: "Two of the rabble-rousers against me have been excluded by the student body and, in the face of that pressure, have also been excluded by the director. Schmidtchen is making every effort on my behalf. The students are split into two camps, right and left. As of now the left is still stronger. It's more or less the opposite among the teaching staff!"[594] However, the political balance soon tipped to the right. The story of the dismissal of Gunta Sharon-Stölzl perfectly exemplifies the wider situation in Germany: after the "rabble-rousers" had been thrown out and Mies van der Rohe had voiced his approval, "the mayor of Dessau came with a German nationalist—and—they were reinstated! That is the power of politics and I just happen to have fallen victim to it. . . . I'm afraid that in this political situation it's hard to put up any resistance anywhere."[595] Mies van der Rohe told Gunta Sharon-Stölzl that the complaint against her, which "above all impugned her private life," had been "lodged with the government by a town councillor" on the insistence of the father of Ilse Voigt, a Bauhaus student. However, Gunta was never given a copy of that complaint to read for herself.

594 Sharon-Stölzl to her brother Erwin, 21 May 1931, Stiftung Bauhaus Dessau 1997, pp. 57–62

595 Sharon-Stölzl to her brother Erwin, 15 June 1931, Stiftung Bauhaus Dessau 1997, pp. 57–62

Although the new Bauhaus director, the third and last director, was a "fabulous architect ... as a person and specifically as a director, he [was] very reactionary," to quote a Swiss architecture student at the Bauhaus. He or she only signed the article with the initial "m.," in a bid to avoid reprisals. This person backed up their assessment of the situation with the fact that Mies van der Rohe had responded to the actions of the student representatives, most of whom were Communists, by "sending in the riot squad and having the people in question arrested."[596]

By November 1928—a little over a year after the first Nuremberg Rally in August 1927—Adolf Hitler was in Berlin, where he made a speech at the Sportpalast. On 1 May 1929, in the Berlin districts of Mitte, Wedding, and Neukölln, there were violent clashes during which over thirty people lost their lives and many others were injured. Erich Weinert's play, *Der rote Wedding,* set to music by Hanns Eisler, recalls those events.[597] When elections were held in September 1930, 6.5 million people voted for the National Socialists.

Max Bill was no longer at the Bauhaus to witness the Gunta Sharon-Stölzl "case." He had officially left the Bauhaus in late 1928—although it is likely that he finally left Dessau in 1929, after returning once or twice. One of the contributing factors to Bill's departure was his deep unease at the worsening friction between the political left and right. And now, even as an ex-student, he found himself caught between the two sides; on one hand he loyally maintained contact with Albers and Kandinsky, and with Klee, too; on the other hand he also remained friends with the "seditious, Bolshevist Jew" Arieh Sharon.

Gunta Sharon-Stölzl in Zurich

In April 1931 Gunta Sharon-Stölzl and Arieh Sharon visited Gunta's friend Benita Koch-Otte in Prague; Arieh Sharon traveled on from there to Palestine in May 1931, and Gunta went to Switzerland where she was granted entry on the strength of her Palestinian passport. She now started to build a new life for herself there. In November 1931 she established a small

596 "m." in *information* 1:3 (August/September 1932), Zurich, typographic design by Max Bill

597 See Müller 2000, p. 63

598 As described by Egidio Marzona, previously a publisher and collector of Bauhaus objects

textiles studio in Zurich and set up the handweaving company S-P-H-Stoffe together with two former Bauhaus students, Gertrud Preiswerk and Heinrich-Otto Hürlimann.

In Zurich Max Bill met up with Gunta again, in exile after she had been harassed out of her job, and designed visiting cards and a business letterhead for her. Other women, active at the Bauhaus and later murdered by the Nazis, included Friedl Dicker and Otti Berger.

Otti Berger (born into a Hungarian Jewish family in Vörösmet in 1898 and murdered in Auschwitz in 1944) was at the Bauhaus with Max Bill; in 1927 she joined the textile department led by Gunta Stölzl and Anni Albers.

Gertrud Preiswerk, who would later become Gertrud Weiss, remembered very well how popular Max Bill was with other students at the Bauhaus.[598] Rather surprisingly, Gunta Sharon-Stölzl—a foreigner—managed to obtain a work permit in Switzerland (albeit a time-limited permit that she had to re-apply for every six months). However, she suffered a severe personal blow in January 1932 when Arieh Sharon told her, on a visit to Zurich, that he had fallen in love with another woman in Palestine. In spring 1932 fabrics made at S-P-H-Stoffe went on sale at the newly opened Wohnbedarf shop in Zurich, which, as it happens, commissioned its advertising from Max Bill (see p. 513). Regrettably, S-P-H-Stoffe had to close again in the summer of 1933 following a loss-making business transaction with Wohnbedarf AG.

At Easter 1933 Gunta Sharon-Stölzl made a short trip to Sicily. It may seem surprising that, as an exile, she would choose to travel to Italy with its Fascist regime, but a lot of Bauhauslers had a particular fondness for Italy: Max and Binia Bill spent their honeymoon there in 1931, and Paul Klee visited Sicily in the summer vacation of 1931. On her return to Switzerland Gunta Sharon-Stölzl set to work on a curtain fabric for the Corso theater in Zurich at the same time as Max Bill was designing the lettering for the theater's name sign—which still stands resplendent today (see p. 484).

At the Corso theater Gunta Sharon-Stölzl's fellow contractors included the Xanti Schawinsky, who had studied at the Bauhaus, and the Surrealist painter Max Ernst, who had traveled from France and was already on the Gestapo's black list.

Was this a brotherly work-creation initiative for creative artists fleeing for their lives from the Nazis? Whatever the case, these three figures were certainly not primarily engaged by the Corso for social reasons, but above all because of their outstanding creative skills.

Despite quickly finding her feet in Zurich Gunta Sharon-Stölzl, very much an exile, was not at all at ease in her new surroundings: "I'm so depressed here sometimes—I know so few people here—we were very spoiled in that respect at the Bauhaus."[599] Three months later, things took a dramatic turn for the worse, as it did for many immigrants from Germany: "I have absolutely no idea where I can go if Switzerland is off the cards —France, Paris is already saturated with émigrés who have no idea how to make a living."[600] However, in September 1934 Gunta won a large contract for wall fabrics and a stage curtain for Kino Urban in Zurich. Max Bill was impressed by her fabrics and would later exhibit some of them when he curated the Swiss pavilion at the Milan Triennial in 1936. In the exhibition catalogue, those exhibits are credited to Sharon & Hürlimann, Stoffe, the new company founded by Gunta Sharon-Stölzl and Heinrich-Otto Hürlimann.[601] At that point she was still using the surname "Sharon," but a few months after the Triennial she and Arieh divorced, leaving her afraid that she would now become stateless. Gunta Stölzl in fact spent the next fifty years living in Küsnacht on Lake Zurich. Not long before she died on 22 April 1983 at the age of eighty-five, I ran into her in Kirchgasse in Zurich, and she told me that she "just wanted to die." In 1987 I included one of her tapestries in the exhibition *Angelica, Anna und andere Schwestern von Gestern,* which I curated at Kunsthaus Zürich.

Max Bill and I once ran into the architect Arieh Sharon at the Hotel am Zoo on the Kurfürstendamm in Berlin, where he told us that Walter Gropius had always stayed there when he was in Berlin. This is confirmed by Gropius's biographer, Reginald R. Isaacs in Cambridge, Massachusetts. In 1955 Gropius was invited to Berlin to participate "in the redesign of the Hansa district." In August 1955, after he arrived at Tempelhof Airport in Berlin, he was welcomed by former Bauhausler Hinnerk Scheper. "Walter Gropius always took a room in the Hotel am Zoo, at 25 Kurfürstendamm, in the now rebuilt house where he had lived with his parents between 1895 and 1902. The building had been gutted by fire following a direct hit during an air raid in the war; only the grand old façade had more or less survived the fire storm. On his many visits to Berlin in his later years, Gropius always stayed there, and if possible he took a room behind one of the windows that had once belonged to his parents' apartment."[602]

599 Droste 1987, p. 34

600 Sharon-Stölzl, Zurich, to her brother Erwin, 22 July 1933, in Stiftung Bauhaus Dessau 1997, p. 67

601 In *Guida della VI Triennale,* Milan 1936 (without illustrations of the works in question), p. 95, however, not mentioned in the short biography by Yael Aloni in Stiftung Bauhaus Dessau 1997

602 See Isaacs 1984

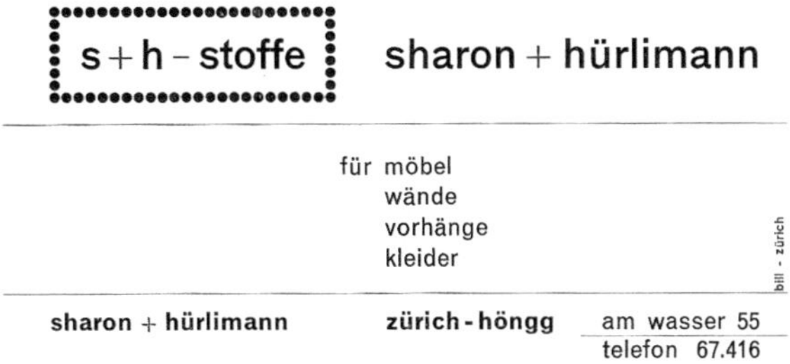

Max Bill, Letterhead for S + H—
Stoffe, Sharon + Hürlimann, 1933

Max Bill, Letterhead for S-P-H-Stoffe, founded by Gunta Sharon-Stölzl, Gertrud Preiswerk, and Heinrich-Otto Hürlimann in 1931

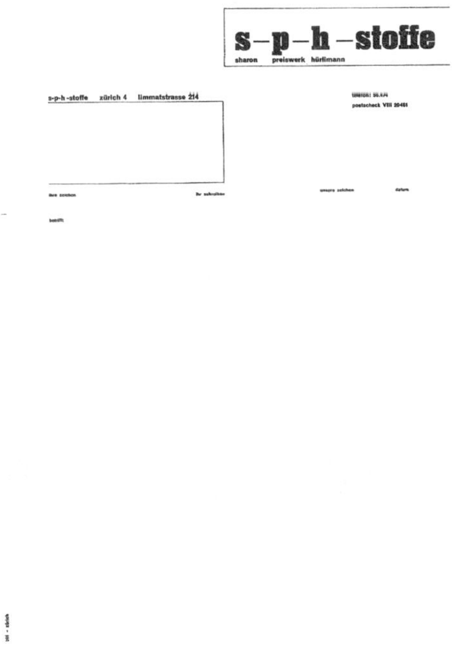

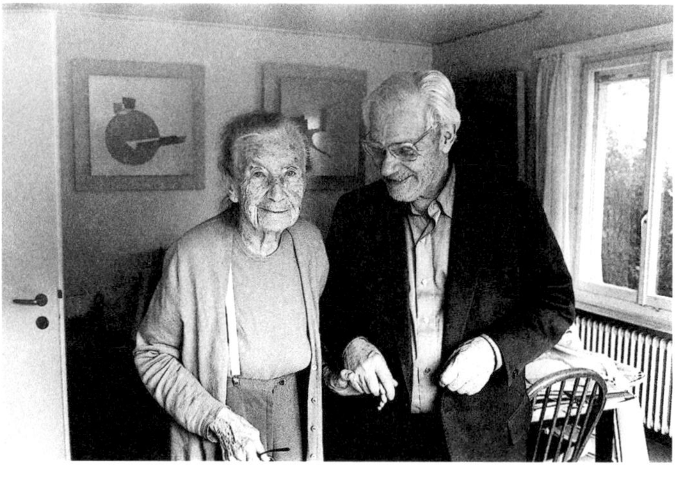

Angela Thomas, Max Bill with
Lucia Moholy in her apartment, 1988

"Photographs are in our lives, as our lives are in them"

After Lucia Moholy and László Moholy-Nagy separated in autumn 1930, Lucia became course leader for the photography class (until summer 1933) at the Itten-Schule in Berlin, which had been founded in 1926 by Johannes Itten—onetime Bauhaus master in Weimar. Having left the Bauhaus in spring 1923 because his teaching methods did not fit in there, Itten had initially returned to Switzerland. In Herrliberg (canton of Zürich) he studied Eastern philosophies and became a member of the Mazdaznan community. By the time he moved to Berlin, he had already made numerous lecture tours abroad, talking about Mazdaznan. "In Berlin he re-established contact with Herwarth Walden, who had presented two solo exhibitions of Itten's paintings at his gallery in 1916 and 1923."[603]

As so often, there are conflicting accounts of the relevant dates. Whereas Magdalena Droste writes that Lucia Moholy taught at the Itten-Schule from autumn 1930 onward, Lucia Moholy's biographer Rolf Sachsse states that she started teaching there in "spring 1930": "the Moholy-Nagys' acquaintanceship with Johannes Itten went back to the time when Itten was teaching at the Bauhaus, but during the 1920s there was no real contact between them—their characters and temperaments were just too different for that, as were their approaches to art and teaching."[604] Whatever the case, at the time when Lucia was teaching there, the Itten-Schule was housed in a modern, flat-roofed building at Konstanzerstrasse 14 in Berlin-Wilmersdorf: "The roof terrace was intended for the daily Mazdaznan physical exercises in the mornings, but it was also used by the photography department."[605]

Lucia's new lover in Berlin, Theodor Neubauer—a married man (with children) and a Communist Party politician—who had spoken up in favor of the Bauhaus at the legislative assembly in Thuringia, was arrested by the Gestapo in Lucia's Berlin apartment in 1933. Lucia now had no option but to emigrate, like so many others in those inhuman times. She traveled to London via Prague and Paris. Somber landscape photographs that she took on that journey are signed with the name Lucia Neubauer-Moholy, signaling her commitment to Theodor Neubauer. On her arrival in Great Britain Lucia vainly attempted—with help from British Quakers—to have Neubauer released from the concentration camp where he was held.

603 See Droste 1984
604 Sachsse 1985, p. 49
605 Droste 1984, p. 5

Lucia now started to work with the British intelligence services in their fight against the Nazis; at the same time she was also researching the history of photography. In 1939 her book *A Hundred Years of Photography* was published in London with an impressive first print run of 40,000. In the epilogue to what would become a standard work, Lucia Moholy summed up what she had learned: "Photographs are in our lives, as our lives are in them." Twenty years later, in 1959, Lucia Moholy settled in Zurich, where she would always remain a foreigner but where she would also see Max Bill from time to time—and where I happily visited her on many occasions during the last years of her life. She died in Zurich at the age of ninety-five on 17 May 1989.[606]

Learning to See

One of Lucia's first students—for a short time in the summer or autumn of 1930—was the young Binia Mathilde Spoerri from Switzerland, who would marry Max Bill in January 1931.

It is clear from Binia Spoerri's diary that she spent three months at the Ittenschule in Berlin (information kindly supplied by her son Jakob Bill, born in 1942).

Might Binia also have participated in the Mazdaznan exercises on the flat roof of the Itten-Schule? "Lucia taught a foundation course.... She was less concerned with mediating the practice of photography and routine technical processes than with introducing students to the business of learning to see on the basis of this technique."[607] As it turned out Binia did not stay at the Itten-Schule for long; she was not happy with the course because there was only one camera to be shared by all the members of the photography class—and, as Bill later told me, that was the last straw for Binia. In Zurich in the summer or early autumn of 1930 Binia Spoerri and Max Bill (four years her junior) met for the first time. At that point Bill was doing his best to cope with the devastating blow of losing Nusch (Maria Benz)—which we will return to in due course.

606 See Angela Thomas, "Unser Bild vom Bauhaus geprägt" [obituary for Lucia Moholy], in *Tages-Anzeiger,* 22 May 1989
607 Sachsse 1985, p. 51
608 Hahn 1977, p. 62
609 Grohmann 1958, p. 203
610 Engemann 1977, p. 5

Looking Back at Dessau

On 4 April 1928 a performance of Kurt Weill's opera *Der Zar lässt sich photographieren* was presented at the theater in Dessau. The young Max Bill was in the audience, because Weill's one-act opera was preceded by Mussorgsky's *Pictures from an Exhibition* in an avant-garde production by Bill's teacher, Kandinsky, who also designed the sets.

A few months later, toward the end of August 1928 the *Dreigroschenoper,* with music by Kurt Weill, was premiered in Berlin, not Dessau. It was a sensational success. "Suddenly Kurt Weill was world famous.... Having written the music for Bertolt Brecht's *Dreigroschenoper* and for his *Aufstieg und Fall der Stadt Mahagonny,* he was now known and admired not only in Germany but in the entire world of new music—or derided, because of the trouble caused by these topical, socio-critical works."[608]

That performance of *Pictures from an Exhibition* was a memorable experience for all those present, and it impressed both Max Bill and Paul Klee. The original score was based on "sixteen pictures, probably realistic watercolors, which Mussorgsky translated into pure music, not program music but Kandinsky created stage designs stemming from the same root, that is to say, he devised pictorial counterparts to the music by replicating the movement of the musical phrases in colorful forms and animated plays of light. Dancers appear in only two scenes.... At the first *espressivo* three long vertical strips appear in the background. They vanish. At the next *espressivo* red is introduced from the right (double color). Then, from the left, green. The middle figure emerges from a recess. It is illuminated with an intense colored light."[609]

On 13 March 1993 Max Bill and I attended a reconstruction of that performance of *Bilder einer Ausstellung* with replicas of Wassily Kandinsky's sets, presented by the ensemble Der rote Kreis at the Theaterhaus Gessnerallee in Zurich; we both liked it a lot.

As a student at the Bauhaus, Bill occasionally visited Berlin, but he never went to Weimar, although he was aware that this was where Walter Gropius's *Märzgefallenen-Denkmal* had been built. It is illustrated and described in a *Bauhaus* booklet published in May 1922: "The *Märzgefallenen-Denkmal* at the cemetery in Weimar was constructed in memory of workers in Weimar who lost their lives during the attempted coup in March 1920; it was designed by Walter Gropius and unveiled on 1 May 1922." At the time Gropius was "one of the most active members of the revolutionary Worker's Council for Art and vigorously promoted his reformist ideas."[610]

Gropius was in part inspired by the architect, industrial designer and commercial artist Peter Behrens, one of the outstanding co-founders of the Deutscher Werkbund (1907); in 1907 Behrens was retained as an artistic consultant by AEG, where he worked with students and assistants such as Le Corbusier, Mies van der Rohe, and Gropius (1908–10).

Fame had come quickly to Gropius. After leaving Peter Behrens's architecture practice in 1910 and opening his own practice in Berlin (with Adolf Meyer on his staff) in 1911—when he was just twenty-eight years old—he was commissioned to design the façade of the Fagus shoe-last factory in Alfeld an der Leine in Lower Saxony. And Gropius "secured his place in the history of architecture with an inspired innovation" for the office building in Alfeld: "He opened up the solid brick wall and introduced attenuated brick piers with full-height iron frames and glazing suspended between them. The three stories are separated by two continuous, horizontal bands of metal inserts."[611]

In Weimar, as everywhere, there were also reactionary forces, who directed their venom at Gropius. Some of those negative voices were also heard in Dessau. Once home to princes and counts, Dessau now had a population of 70,000, but in some ways it was still behind the times—which considerably complicated the implementation of the town's decision to support the Bauhaus.

Reconciliation with Hanns Fischli

When Max Bill returned to Dessau in late November 1928 he hoped to retrieve the funds he felt Fischli still owed him from the arranged the sale of his household effects. Bill reckoned he was due "Fr. 372.–' and instructed a lawyer to act for him in this matter, but he soon lost patience with the process.

"To Herr. Dr. Hans Duttweiler, lawyer, Zürich 1, Bahnhofstr. 65 . . .
re: Fischli, your letters of 30.9 + 9.10 + 17.10.

I am taking it upon myself to inform you that all your efforts to discover Fischli's address have been completely in vain, since I have

611 Nerdinger 1985, p. 34–35
612 Max Bill, Stadelhoferstr. 27, Zurich, "in sachen fischli" to Dr. Hans Duttweiler, Bahnhfostr. 65, Zurich 1, [late October 1929], Bibliothek Max Bill
613 Max Bill to Hanns Fischli, 28 January 1930, Archiv SIK

already given your office his address, that is to say, Fischli is living with his father and is not yet of age, he is working for the architect Steiger-Crawford. . . . If Fischli is not registered at this address, then that is for military reasons."[612]

The lawyer repeatedly demanded an advance on his fee but Bill was not prepared to pay anything until the matter was resolved and he had received the sum owed to him either from Hanns Fischli or Fischli's father. In the end Bill decided not to go to court and to resolve the conflict with Fischli instead, so that they could turn their attention to more pressing matters and work together on publicising and promoting important cultural-political issues. After leaving the Bauhaus Fischli was taken on at Rudolf Steiger's architectural practice in Zurich, where he worked as a construction draftsman on the Neubühl housing settlement, for which Bill would later design a poster (see p. 483).

"Max Bill, Zurich, Stadelhoferstr. 27, 28.1.1930

Hanns Fischli, I am writing to you today not because I feel I have done you an injustice but because I know that—given the situation here in Zurich—there is no point in just ignoring each other. . . . A few months ago I was considering taking you to court, but then I decided there was nothing to be gained by throwing money out of the window, when there isn't even any there in the first place. Your attitude to me was not comradely, so there was no reason for me to be comradely to you. Let's just forget the whole sorry story . . . and you can tell your Papa he should calm down again. When Sascha was here she told me about your new paintings. I'd be very interested to see what you are doing, because people here are starting to promote truly worthless modern art and it would be good to form a bloc to resist the abstract grandfathers (Lüthy–Welti [presumably Oscar Lüthy and Albert Welti] and Arp, who is good, but not Swiss). At the moment I have an opportunity to write a text about myself for Individualität (a publishing house in Basel) . . . but if one has a chance to write something, it is of course silly to only write about oneself because basically a number of people working together can achieve the same end and that forces the others to retreat because they are trumped by sheer quality. I have every faith that you will be part of this and that you can be part of it, or would Steigers be against it? In the past they were pretty much against everything that was not purely industrial?"[613]

In his rather blunt comments Bill makes no secret of his intentions: he wanted—by dint of high-quality work—to outdo and "disqualify" all those artists whose work he felt had no particular merit.

Once Bill had decided to forget the money owed to him, relations between himself and Fischli immediately improved and they started writing to each other again: "Dear Hanns. . . . Liesl Träger has married Steiner (just so you know), living in Zurich." Bill also included some information about his own private life—"At any rate I'm getting married at the end of the month, my father is furious, but that won't last"—and about his work situation—"I'm working in advertising and now have a large contract for the lettering, logos, and all the publicity for the biggest and most modern cement factory in France (see p. 395); the managing director is my patron and buys paintings of mine."[614]

Oddly, in this letter Bill makes no further reference to the woman he was intending to marry in late February 1930. It seems that for Max the overriding emotion in that situation was his father's "blind fury"; however, things turned out rather differently, not with regard to his father's fury but regarding the upcoming wedding: it never took place.

In the same way that, in his letter to Fischli, Bill did not name the woman he loved—the woman he was living with in Stadelhoferstrasse—he also did not tell Fischli the name of his patron. In fact, Max Bill's patron at the time was Max Wassmer, an influential businessman who, in April 1929, had promised the ambitious young artist that he would try to secure an exhibition for him at Kunsthalle Bern.

A Digression on Béla Bartók

Bill's time at the Bauhaus was highly productive for him. The Bauhauslers engaged with all kinds of issues—social and otherwise—and the Bauhaus put on a wide range of events. On 14 October 1927 there was a piano recital by the Hungarian composer and music ethnologist Béla Bartók, who played compositions of his own and by Zoltan Kodály. Max Bill may have been at that concert, but there is no knowing for sure.

Through his work as a music ethnologist, by the outbreak of the First World War, Bartók had collected "nearly 3,500 examples of Romanian folk music, around 3,000 Slovakian, about 2,700 Hungarian and numerous Ruthenian, Serbian and Bulgarian folk songs and tunes."[615]

614 Max Bill to Hanns Fischli, 3 February 1930, Archiv SIK

615 Richard Butz, "Auf Bartóks und Kodálys Spuren," in *Die Wochenzeitung—WOZ* 21, 23 May 2002

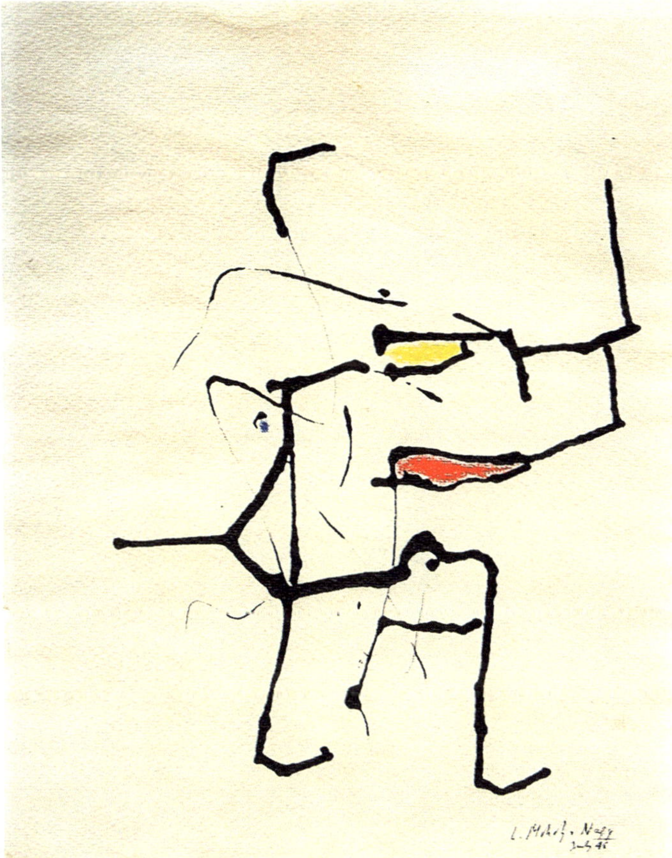

László Moholy-Nagy, *After a Bartók Theme,* 1946, watercolor and india ink on paper, 44×35cm

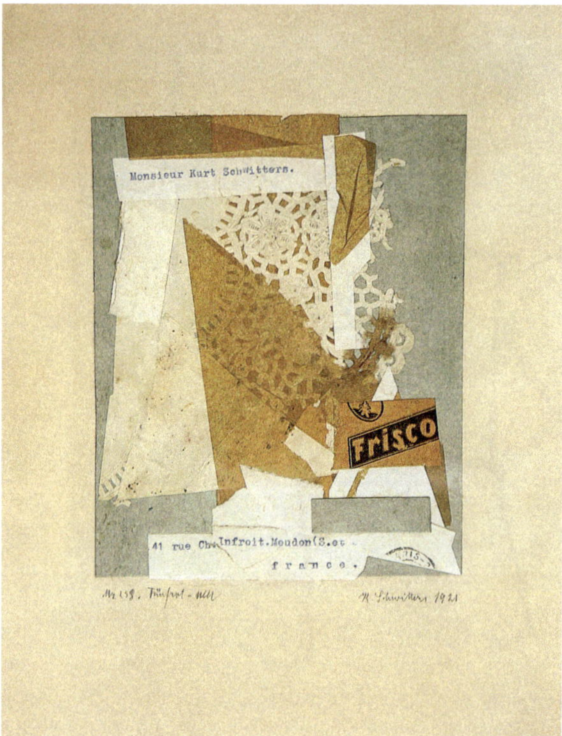

Kurt Schwitters, *MZ 258. Fünfrot-Neu,*
1921, collage, 17.4×14.1cm

Bartók later fell in love with the Hungarian violinist Stefi Geyer. They had first performed together in Basel on 30 January 1929 (playing Bartók's Second Violin Sonata), but his love was unrequited and in 1930 Geyer married the Zurich composer Walter Schulthess. Nevertheless, she and Bartók remained close friends. In the audience at that concert in Basel was the young Paul Sacher, just twenty-two years old at the time. He was deeply moved by Bartók's music and in the early summer of 1936 he wrote to Bartók asking if he would consider writing a piece for the strings of the Basler Kammerorchester, or for strings and one or two other instruments. Bartók replied that he had in mind "a piece for strings and percussion (that is to say, strings, piano, celesta, harp, xylophone and percussion)." And by the end of August 1936 Sacher already received the news that Bartók had almost finished the score.[616] On 21 January 1937 Bartók's *Music for Strings, Percussion and Celesta* was premiered in Basel by the Basler Kammerorchester, conducted by Paul Sacher.

Bartók arrived in Basel a few days before the concert. Sacher asked him about some aspects of the composition and it seemed to him that Bartók was "particularly proud of the fugue in the first movement ... which is indeed a miraculous feat. He attended the last rehearsals. His presence was immensely stimulating, even if he said very little." The premiere "was a triumph for the performers and the composer alike; the last movement was played again as an encore. Bartók's *Music for Strings,* a masterpiece from the most outstanding period in his creative career, is now a fixture in the repertoire all across the world."[617]

That exceptional success prompted Sacher to ask Bartók to write a piece of chamber music and by early September 1937 Bartók had "almost finished" the new composition. He announced that he would arrive in Basel in January 1938 and asked to be provided with two "bright-sounding" pianos. He had decided to write for two pianos because he felt "that it is impossible to achieve a satisfying balance with just one piano up against the often very incisive sound of percussion instruments."[618] On 16 January 1938, in the Konservatoriumssaal in Basel, the *Sonata for Two Pianos and Percussion* was premiered by Béla Bartók, his wife Ditta, and two percussionists based in Basel, Fritz Schiesser and Philipp Rühlig. Max Bill was present at that concert (presented by the International Society for Contemporary Music), which proved to be "another great triumph for the Hungarian master."[619]

616 See Sacher 1995
617 Sacher 1995
618 *In National-Zeitung,* 13 January 1938
619 See Sacher 1995

Bill also met Bartók himself in Basel at the home of the collectors Annie and Oskar Müller-Widmann. "On his trips to Basel the composer often stayed with the Müllers, where his Fifth String Quartet also had its Swiss premiere in 1936."[620]

Ever loyal to Bartók, it was the violinist Stefi Geyer who accompanied Béla Bartók and his wife Ditta to Geneva on 14 October 1940 when they set off for the United States, "leaving Europe behind them forever. She and other friends had made it possible for them to take that journey into exile."[621] Bartók wrote to Sacher, bidding him farewell, expressing his profound hope that "your country [Switzerland] will not be trampled underfoot."[622] Barely five years later, Bartók died in poverty in New York on 26 September 1945. The news of Bartók's death prompted his friend and compatriot Moholy-Nagy, who was now living in Chicago, to embark on a small group of works on themes inspired by Bartók's music.

László Moholy-Nagy, *Diary of a Fly (dedicated to Bartók),* 1946, was inspired by Béla Bartók's *From the Diary of a Fly,* i.e., no. 142 of his cycle *Mikrokosmos: 153 Progressive Piano Pieces* (1936–39) in six books, published in London in 1940; books one and two are dedicated to Bartók's son Péter.

Moholy-Nagy died from leukemia in Chicago on 24 November 1946 and Max Bill was later glad to express his admiration for both Bartók and Moholy-Nagy by acquiring one of the works from that group.

Special Events in Dessau

In Dessau the young Max Bill was present when Kurt Schwitters performed parts of the latest version of his sound poem *Ursonate* and engaged in discussions with the students.

"kurt schwitters made his name with his activities in hanover. he published the journal *merz*.... schwitters had a gift for creating compositions by pasting together the most unremarkable scraps and leftovers, which—for all their fragility—have remained astonishingly fresh."[623]

620 See Danuser 1995
621 Danuser 1995
622 See Sacher 1995
623 Bill 1976, p. 42
624 Max Bill, Zurich, to Josef Albers, 8 North Forest Circle, New Haven 15, Connecticut, 15 August 1952, Archiv Max Bill
625 Heinze-Greenberg et al. 2004, p. 169
626 Heinze-Greenberg et al. 2004, p. 93

Later on, when Josef Albers was trying to track down original vinyl recordings of Schwitters's voice, Bill—who had been very impressed by Schwitters at the Bauhaus—wrote to Albers, offering to help in the search: "Janis has been looking for Schwitters here. There are in fact gramophone recordings of Schwitters from a radio talk by him. It would be wonderful if Harriet Janis could get hold of that recording for Circle Records and create a new master. That would certainly be of interest. I know someone who has copies of those records, so I will ask him, he's a student of mine, we're working on a Werkbund house project at the moment."[624] And when Schwitters and Arp appeared together in Zurich on 30 October 1929, Bill made sure not to miss that "Schwitters event." Later on, when Bill started to collect art, Kurt Schwitters of course had to be represented in his collection.

On 23 November 1927 Prof. Dr. Erwin Finlay Freundlich of the Einstein Institute in Vienna gave a lecture at the Bauhaus in Dessau on the "Origins and the Age of the World." In March 1928 the architect Erich Mendelsohn presented a slide lecture on "Russia and America: An Architectural Cross-Section." Mendelsohn's architectural practice, where the team often worked to the sound of music by J. S. Bach, was one of the largest practices in Europe at the time, and Erich Mendelsohn was able to draw on his own experience for his talk at the Bauhaus.

"Important works by Mendelsohn include the Einstein Tower in Potsdam, the Mossehaus in Berlin, the hat factory in Luckenwalde, and numerous department stores—including the Schocken department stores in Nuremberg, Stuttgart, and Chemnitz."[625]

In 1924 Mendelsohn had spent several weeks in the United States, where he met Frank Lloyd Wright in person; in 1925, a year after the death of Lenin, Mendelsohn and his wife Luise (née Maas) traveled to the Soviet Union on the invitation of the Leningrad Textile Trust, for whom Erich Mendelsohn had designed a factory complex. They then traveled on from there to Moscow, where they were received in the Kremlin by President Kalinin and Trotsky's sister, Olga Kameneva, in her capacity as chairperson of VOKS, the All-Union Society for Cultural Relations with Foreign Countries.

"Leningrad looked like the abandoned shell of a life already lived: the window to Europe was firmly shut . . . whereas Moscow pulsated with vitality. The government and all areas of intellectual life fully embodied the revolution and its aims. . . . Our days in Moscow were filled with appointments, with lectures, visits, endless discussions, evenings at the theater—the performances at the Meyerhold theater were sensational back then."[626]

The Art of Fugue

Max Bill and Erich Mendelsohn had a particular experience in common. When Mendelsohn delivered his lecture at the Bauhaus, he only had the use of his right eye. He had previously had his left eye removed due to cancer; it was replaced with a glass eye in 1921.

In the 1970s Max Bill was diagnosed with a tumor in one eye, and he, too, had his left eye removed; rather than complaining when he had a glass eye fitted, he asked with interest how many people were living with just one eye in Switzerland at the time. Shortly after the operation on his eye, when Max Bill was still in a ward in the cantonal hospital in Zurich, he drew the sequential states of his series of prints *7 twins,* which was published by Marc Hostettler (Éditions Média, Neuchâtel) in November 1977.

Erich Mendelsohn and his wife Louise, who was a talented cellist and later changed the spelling of her name to "Luise," both loved the music of Johann Sebastian Bach above all else. In the same year that Mendelsohn gave his talk at the Bauhaus (1927) they traveled to the Thomaskirche in Leipzig specifically to attend the first performance in modern times of Bach's last great masterpiece, *Die Kunst der Fuge,* which he left unfinished on his death. Bach's autograph manuscript gives no indication as to whether he wrote it as a purely pedagogical work or for performance and artistic interpretation. Wolfgang Graeser, "a young German,"[627] became intensely preoccupied with this set of pieces when he was still only a young teenager. He orchestrated the score and the modern premiere of *Die Kunst der Fuge* in 1927 proved to be of huge importance for music and musicians.

In his article (which is still a wonderful read today) Felix Stössinger discusses the premiere with great understanding, pointing out that "the papers only mentioned it in passing, or not at all." "Graeser's achievement is twofold. Graeser has devised a new logical order for the piece, and has used the surviving remains to form a convincing whole; secondly, Graeser was the first person to properly hear the piece; he then gave the parts to suitable instruments and thus rendered it playable."[628]

627 Heinze-Greenberg et al. 2004

628 Felix Stössinger, "Bachs Letztes Werk," in *Die Weltbühne,* Wochenschrift für Politik, Kunst, Wirtschaft, 23, vol. 2 (1927), Reprint Athenäum Verlag, Königstein im Taunus, 1978, pp. 59–62, here pp. 60–61

629 Stossinger, "Bachs Letztes Werk," pp. 60–61

There is no knowing if Max Bill also made the journey to Leipzig for that premiere. Although this composition, which Bach regarded as his "most important" work, "consists of 18 fully worked out contrapuntal movements, it is nevertheless a fragment since the 19th movement—and thus the whole set—is missing its last 150 bars.... The story of its publication is one of the most hair-raising in German cultural history. Bach had only proofed the first 11 movements. His corrections were ignored, the printer mixed up the plates for the second half of the work ... and it was repeatedly reprinted in that meaningless muddle, which only gradually came to light! ... It was not until Graeser created order from the chaos that it could be seen as a single entity. The very first edition [in Bach's own time] was a commercial catastrophe. Six years after its publication only 30 copies had been sold. His gifted sons regarded their father's music as passé (and it is true, his work was Gothic and Baroque, it loomed like a piece of the past into the new Age of Enlightenment and lightsome Rococo). They regarded *Die Kunst der Fuge* as some kind of a teaching manual and, since it did so poorly, they sold off the plates as scrap metal. It would take another 177 years before this work, one of the most sublime of all musical compositions, would first be performed in its entirety.... There has been no more important event in German artistic life for decades. Having so often had to seem almost like enemies of the German people in our fight against false nationalism, we [*Die Weltbühne*] now rejoice."[629]

Even if Bill were not present in the Thomaskirche, as a subscriber to *Die Weltbühne* that event will not have escaped his notice. A year after that first performance the young Wolfgang Graeser, who had uncovered that masterpiece, took his own life at the age of just twenty-one.

"... bringing light into the harsh order of this world"

As I know from my own experience, in his later years Bill repeatedly listened with immense concentration to Glenn Gould's interpretation of Bach's *Kunst der Fuge.* The fascinating thing about that work, as Felix Stössinger already noted in 1927, is that "in this sequence of musical compositions, which are structured like mathematical formulas and seem to be cast from eternal crystals, with several movements capable of being played from the end to the beginning and from the beginning to the end (mirror fugues)—art ceases to be art. It is the voice of another being, bringing light into the harsh order of this world.... The music has become entirely abstract, but it is not earthly abstraction, it is other-worldly musical abstraction.... For the very first time, in large legible writing, Bach incorporates his own name as a theme into his music: BACH [the German letter names for the notes B flat–A–C–B natural].... Now completely blind, the dying Bach—struggling for breath—dictated it to Altnikol, his son-in-law.... A note on the manuscript, in another hand, states that 'the author died ... over this manuscript.'"[630] In a recent study on Bach's *Kunst der Fuge* the author suggests that it contains within it a "hidden Pythagorean tradition."[631]

After his time at the Bauhaus Bill engaged deeply with the music of J. S. Bach; he also made reference to Pythagoras and even dedicated a "monument" to him (see p. 351).

Color and Space and Sound

In a pensive phase, when Bill once asked himself the question, "How does one actually make a work of art?," he turned to the music of J. S. Bach for an answer. Bill, who played the cello and the banjo, now started to listen to Bach's music more closely: "I concentrated on Bach and saw how it was structured ... and I said to myself, we have to handle our material—color and space—the same way that Bach handled his material—sound. Bach ordered his material and discovered very particular relationships, he discovered very particular sequences that unite in harmony and become one whole.... So in music the sounds, the physics of music, approximate to what we (visual artists) have in our material, in color. And to what sculptors have in theirs, in space. So, if you identify these elements in music and, independently of the music, use them in a different way—that then equates to geometry in our field, to mathematics, which is also used in musical rhythm; we have geometry, which also exists in music, in proportions. We have colors, we have space, we have our materials. And then it came to me that I am in fact working with geometry."[632]

Bill goes on to explain that in his view people are "dependent on the relationships between things." I regard this statement as a vital key to his work. As he himself put it: "I in fact believe that mathematics is a

630 Stossinger, "Bachs Letztes Werk," pp. 60–61
631 See Dentler 2006
632 Max Bill in conversation with Werner Krüger, in Krüger 1990
633 Kruger 1990
634 See Bill 1951

component in our thinking. We are actually dependent on the relationships between things—visible or tactile relationships. We think in distances, even when we are flying, we think in distances. Those are just things that are intrinsic to us, we somehow come to an accommodation with geometries and numbers in our world. We don't even realize we're doing it."[633]

Bill's *denkmal für pythagoras* (1939–41) is an airy apparition with no solid planes, but we are fooled into imagining planes because of its outlines. It is also visually astounding because it stands, perfectly balanced, on just two narrow edges.

Wassily Kandinsky: a Father Figure

"Kandinsky, with his customary concern for us, tried to convince us that things had to keep on progressing. And, very importantly for us, often the main topic of conversation was not painting at all, but other major issues, including personal issues. Kandinsky was the sort of person who tried to guide young people, he didn't assuage their doubts, but he did awaken in them a capacity to form their own opinions, to always be critical and self-critical. His humanity, his fine feel for any situation and his paternal kindness were the secret of his pedagogical success."[634] In his encounters with Kandinsky, Bill felt a "paternal kindness" that he had never known before, a level of interest and attention that his own father had never shown him.

Bill later remained in contact with Kandinsky, who emigrated to Paris after leaving the Bauhaus. After Kandinsky's death in 1944, Bill selected and introduced various texts by the latter, which he published with Benteli in Bern; he also selected and introduced *Wassily Kandinsky: Zehn Farbenlichtdrucke nach Aquarellen und Gouachen* (Basel: Holbein 1949).

The Influence of Paul Klee

In his classes with Paul Klee, the young Max Bill developed a particular interest in certain themes in Klee's art that were to have a powerful influence on him and his own works in the coming months. In 1929 and 1930, even after Bill had returned to Switzerland, his works still showed the influence of Paul Klee. One practical technique that the young Max Bill clearly learned from Klee was the way that he painted vases. As a student Bill was not yet aware of the "theoretical backdrop" that Klee had worked out in his teaching. But in later life he attached the greatest importance to Klee's theoretical works. Bill felt that anyone taking their lead from Klee's ideas would be able to learn how to develop constructive concepts, and that Klee's writings would prove to be a veritable treasure trove for whole generations of future artists.

Useful comparisons, relating to this topic, could be Paul Klee's *Around the Fish,* 1926 (in *Paul Klee*, the Museum of Modern Art, New York, 1941, cat. no. 33) and Max Bill's *blumen,* 1929 no. 47 (ink on watercolor on ribbed paper, 41 × 28.2 cm, estate of Max Bill left to Angela Thomas, since 2004 in the collection of Alioscha Klee).

There were of course also other very significant figures teaching at the Bauhaus.[635] One such was Friedrich Koehn, an outstanding mathematician from the Einstein Institute, who taught courses in structures and building construction, which Max Bill attended. Another was Hans Wittwer, who worked for Hannes Meyer and who taught *Bauentwurfslehre* (theory of building design) from 1927 to early 1929, and yet another was Mart Stam, who first taught at the Bauhaus as a visiting professor in mid-1928.

Bauhaus 2:2/3 (1928), p. 32, which came out on 1 July 1928, informed its readers that Mart Stam, a guest lecturer from Rotterdam, delivered "one week of lectures per month on elementary building theory and town planning." Max Bill was among those who attended these lectures by the leftist Dutchman.

However, by the time Ludwig Hilberseimer started teaching building theory and constructive design at the Bauhaus in early 1929, Bill had already officially exmatriculated—although he may of course have returned "unofficially" to Dessau in 1929, without leaving any trace of his visit.

635 The information as to when particular guest lecturers delivered their lectures is cited according to Klaus-Jürgen Winkler, *Der Architekt Hannes Meyer. Anschauungen und Werk* (Berlin: VEB, Verlag für Bauwesen, 1989)

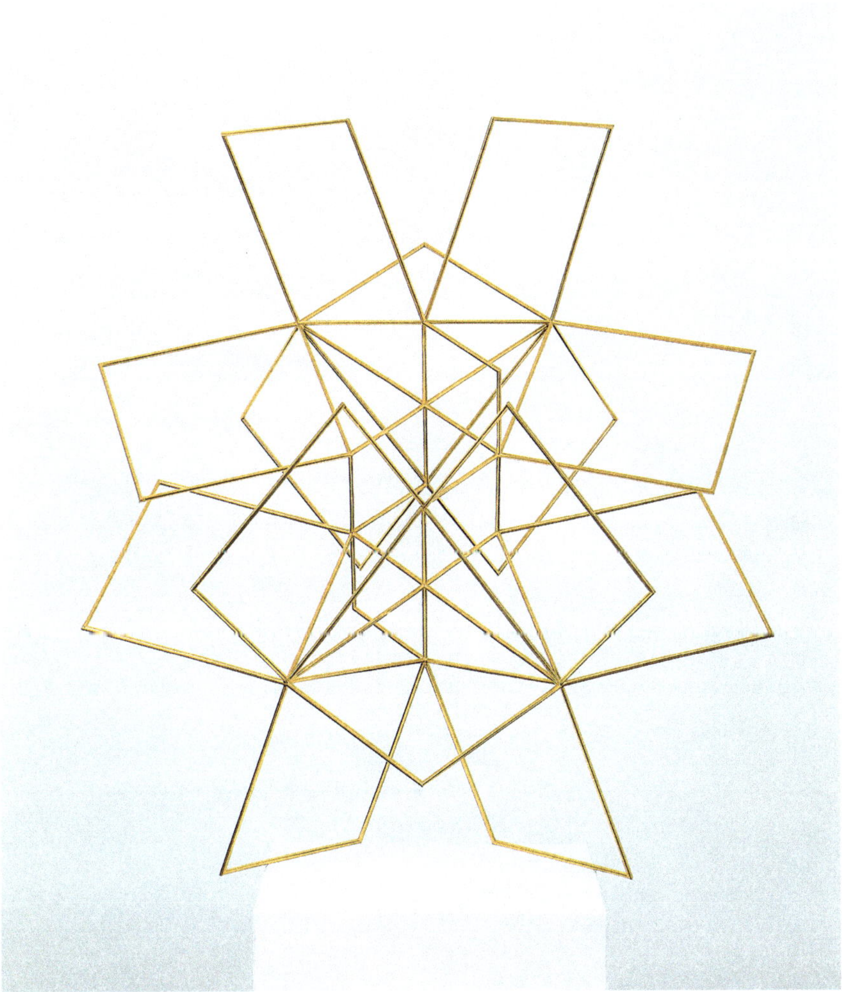

Max Bill, *konstruktion aus drei quadrat-grössen—denkmal für pythagoras,* 1939–41/1978, gold-plated brass, 90×90×80 cm

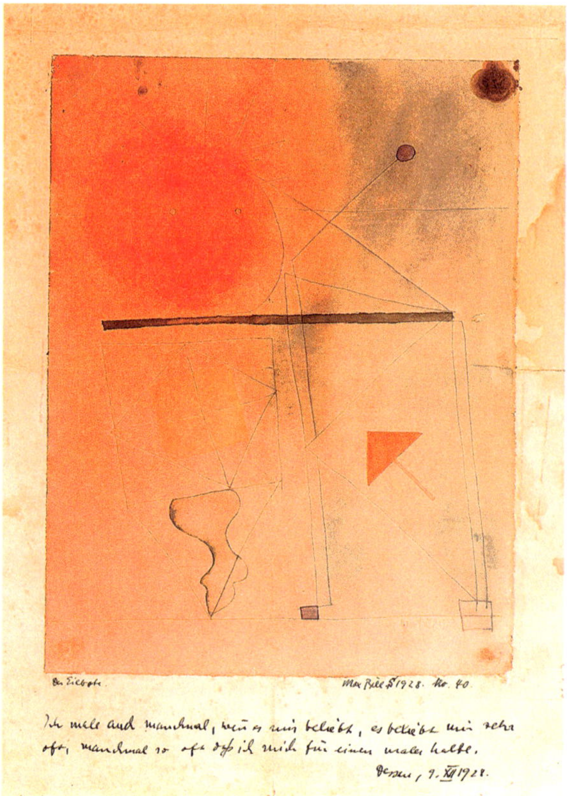

Max Bill, *Der Eilbote,* 1928, watercolor and ink on handmade paper, 30.4×23 cm

The Changing Atmosphere at the Bauhaus

It was only years later that Max Bill described the difficult situation at the Bauhaus: "In 1928 Prof. Dr. Walter Gropius, the founder of the Bauhaus, stepped down as director and was replaced by Hannes Meyer (Basel). The next phase was used as a chance to propagandize political views in an unbearable manner, and there was no shortage of efforts to cast doubt on and sideline artistic issues, so now only social issues counted.... I had had enough of that bewildering situation."[636] Having been drawn to the Bauhaus in Dessau by the charismatic architect Hannes Meyer and his architectural department, Bill now found himself taking sides with the artists, Klee and Kandinsky.

Who did what at the Bauhaus fills a whole chapter in the history of the reception of the Bauhaus, and Bill always seems to have been at pains to give as accurate an account as possible of what actually happened and who was involved—as in the case of the aforementioned production of Bauhaus wallpapers. As for the political disputes between the left and the right, not only at the Bauhaus but also in the town of Dessau, Max felt at the time that they were conducted "too fiercely and bluntly"—as he told me. He could not help worrying that everything was going to become even worse, even more brutal.

Arnold Mehl, a "particularly close friend of Bill's at the Bauhaus,"[637] returned to the Bauhaus in 1929 after spending some time "on leave" in Positano, where Bill had visited him in 1928. Of all Bill's friends, it was Mehl who was now drawn to the National Socialists' ideologies. For Bill, on a personal and political level, that was an especially disheartening turn of events. After the Second World War, he wrote to Albers, explaining what had happened: "So I wanted nothing to do with Mehl after that. He was still an incurable romantic bird of passage, he told me he was now consorting with writers and, using a pseudonym, was cooking up futuristic National Socialist novels, at which point I decided there was no need to continue our correspondence." Somewhat softening the blow, he added—in his erstwhile friend's favor—"of course it is also possible that he soon saw the error of his ways and has become normal again by now."[638]

636 Max Bill in one of his handwritten drafts of a curriculum vita

637 Max Bill to Josef Albers, 8 North Forest Circle, New Haven 15, Connecticut, 5 June 1952, Archiv Max Bill

638 Bill to Albers, June 1952

It has not been possible to establish whether Arnold Mehl, who was four years older than Max Bill, also joined Gruppe Z in Dessau. Albers gave Bill Arnold Mehl's address after the war: Ludwigsburg Württemberg, Seestrasse 65; Albers mentioned that Mehl had written "very nicely" to him and was planning "to go to Italy" (again).[639]

The Old Law

The young Max Bill would dearly have loved to own a work by his much revered teacher Paul Klee. However, lacking the funds to buy anything, he blithely suggested a swap. Klee's response was friendly, subtle, and although he declined in a very carefully worded letter, he naturally took pleasure in the fact that Bill felt so strongly about his work: "As to the implementation and realization of your wish, there are some quite considerable difficulties according to the old law. In the past, in the same situation as yours now, we would turn to friends in our own generation whose paintings we admired, with the older one always approaching the younger one. That was how I received works from Franz Marc, Kandinsky etc., by way of exchange. I will adhere to the old ways and propose an exchange with you when you have developed your fine, graceful talent to the point that the scales will be perfectly balanced when we pit one weight against the other on this side and that. Perhaps your star will soon reappear on the Bauhaus horizon, that would give me great pleasure, yours, Klee."[640]

639 Josef Albers, United States, to Max Bill, before 11 May 1952, Archiv Max Bill

640 Paul Klee, Bauhaus, Dessau, to Max Bill, undated, probably after November 1928, Bibliothek Max Bill

641 Paul Klee, card postmarked in Dessau, to Max Bill, Stadelhoferstrasse 27, Zurich, 26 December 1929, Bibliothek Max Bill

642 *Rhythmie Herbstlicher Bäume*, 1920, oil on plaster, 49 × 42 cm is illustrated in black and white in Carola Giedion-Welcker, *Paul Klee* (1961, (Hamburg: Rororo Bildmonografien, 2002), p. 58. Carola Giedion-Welcker comments on Klee's intentions, suggesting that in his works with parallel layers, "gently undulating horizontal fields often gain rhythm from verticals and circles"—as in the painting *Rhythmie Herbstlicher Bäume;* he preferred "not to pin anything down, but evidently wanted space and forms to fluctuate" (p. 56)

"Soft-strong and serious"

Some of the watercolors Bill painted at the Bauhaus were described by Paul Klee in his free painting classes as "graceful," whereas others—such as Bill's *hermafrodit* (1929, see p. 268)—were, in his view, "soft-strong and serious."[641] Bill's style was not what might traditionally have been regarded as masculine. And the aspect of his work that Klee defined as "soft-strong" would later either go one way—becoming gentle, almost lyrical—or the other—highly structured, tough or even aggressive. Bill's love for Paul Klee's work never waned, and when Klee returned to Bern in 1933 Bill re-established contact with him.

In 1942, when Max and Binia Bill's only child, Jakob, was born, after eleven years of marriage, Max gave his wife a present to which he had a strong, deeply emotional connection: *Rhythmie herbstlicher Bäume,* painted in oils by Paul Klee in 1920.[642] However, as Bill later told me, Binia was disappointed. She had expected a "personal" present from her husband, that is to say, one of his own works.

As far as starting a family went, Bill had privately not "pinned himself down," knowing that his life would go on "fluctuating."

"Berlin thinks it is already beyond abstract art"

According to Max Bill's exmatriculation certificate, he was in Dessau until the end of October 1928. However, he returned at least once to deal with the troubling sale of his household effects. On 9 December 1928, wherever he was, he painted a watercolor titled *Der Eilbote* (The express messenger); he was certainly back in Switzerland in time for Christmas.

Beneath the image in *Der Eilbote,* which is largely geometrical, with the only figuration in the head, there is a note by Bill, as it were giving account of himself: "I also sometimes paint because I feel like it, I very often feel like it, sometimes so often that I think I must be a painter. Dessau, 9. XII. 1928."

He visited the exhibition presented by the GSMBA (Society of Swiss painters, sculptors and architects) in Zurich and went to see his mother in Winterthur, who still lived in the family home at Brühlbergstrasse 8 but had reverted to her maiden name (Geiger) following her divorce in April 1927. Max may even have celebrated his twentieth birthday with her on 22 December 1928. His Christmas present for her was a work with delicately muted colors. By this time Max's father and his new wife Lina Wolf had moved to Stadthausstrasse 131 in Winterthur. Erwin Bill was still giving his elder son a certain amount of financial support.

A "promissory note" dated 1 February 1929 reveals that Max owed his father exactly 7,525 Swiss francs.

Max was keen to leave Winterthur, to escape the provincial, social, and parental constraints of living there, so he looked for lodgings in Zurich. However, as he later told me, before finally settling in Zurich he first traveled "around in Germany." The first Bauhaus quarterly for 1929 notes (p. 24) that the *Ausstellung junger Bauhausmaler* was shown in December 1928 at the Kunstverein in Halle an der Saale; the exhibitors included not only Max's friends Hilde Rantzsch, Clemens Röseler, Alexander Schawinsky, and Lou Scheper but also the same Albert Braun who had exhibited with Max Bill earlier that year in Dessau.[643] Max Bill was presumably not among the exhibitors because he had already officially left the Bauhaus by the time of the opening, although he may of course have gone to Halle to celebrate the occasion with the others.

Whereas one of Max Bill's close friends, Arne Mehl, was drawn to National Socialism, another of his Bauhaus friends, Clemens Röseler, appears to have been on the far left—at least it seems fair to assume so because his review of the exhibition in Halle was published in a Communist student paper (*Bauhaus: Organ Der kommunistischen Studierenden am Bauhaus,* 1:2, June 1930).[644]

One name that Bill was familiar with from his time in Dessau was that of the art critic Ernst "Ern" Kállai. Moholy-Nagy had designed a cover for one of Kállai's books with a four-color collage, which so impressed Bill that he kept hold of his copy for as long as he lived. In addition to that, Bill also knew the one and only issue, of the small-format art magazine *Der Kunstnarr,* edited by Kállai, which came out in April 1929. Among the refreshingly informative exhibition news in that issue, there was a note on Kandinsky: "Paris. After Paul Klee's successful entrance, now Kandinsky

643 Albert Braun was taught by Klee, Kandinsky and Schlemmer at the Bauhaus. "1927: [Braun] photographed Schlemmer's hoop dance. After 1945: fashion studio and milliners in Stuttgart. Also painting ... [died] 1984 in Stuttgart." Droste and Fiedler 1988, p. 417. No mention is made of Albert Braun's whereabouts or activities during the Second World War

644 The cover is illustrated in Gerd Fleischmann, ed., *Bauhaus: Drucksachen, Typografie, Reklame* (Düsseldorf: Edition Marzona, 1984), p. 194

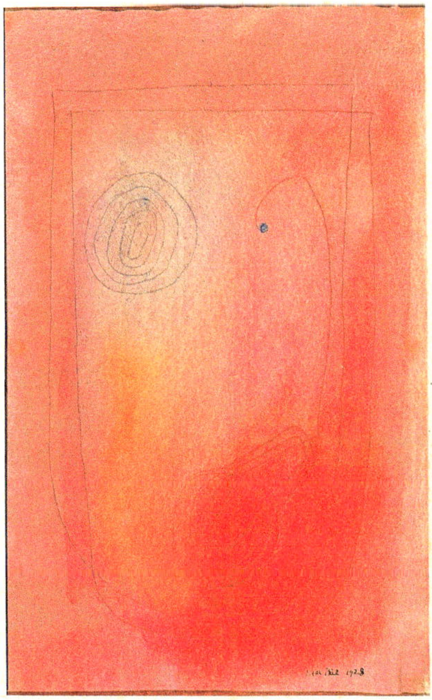

Max Bill, *Tiefer Gesang,* 1928,
gouache and ink over watercolor
on laid paper, 28.3×18.1 cm

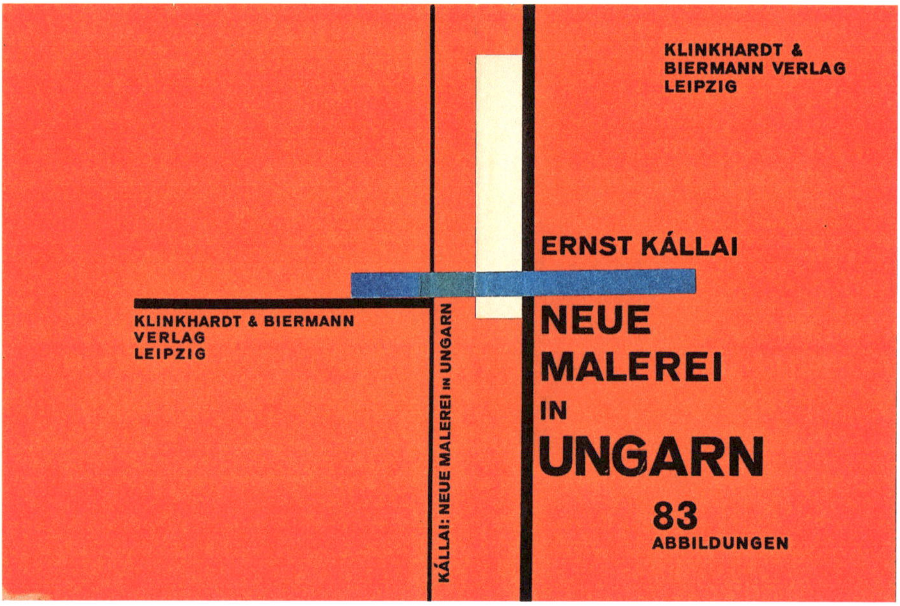

László Moholy-Nagy, Design for a book cover for Ernst Kállai, *Neue Malerei in Ungarn,* Leipzig, 1925, four-color collage, 24.7 × 18.3 cm

has also found his way into French modern art. The splendid watercolors that Möller put on display last autumn [Galerie Ferdinand Möller, Berlin] have now been a major success for the artist at Galerie Zack [in Paris]. Berlin thinks it is already beyond abstract art. Perhaps a detour via Paris would help to open its eyes."[645]

If Bill did visit Berlin around then, he may well have gone to two solo exhibitions (Willi Baumeister and Max Ernst) at Galerie Alfred Flechtheim that were warmly recommended by Ernst Kállai: "New exhibitions of particular note: at Flechtheim (of course, where else?), Max Ernst, the most gifted of the Parisian Surrealists."[646] Rather intriguingly, Kállai describes Max Ernst, a German by birth, as the leading "Parisian" Surrealist.

Just a few years later, in the 1930s, Max Ernst—on the Gestapo's wanted list—would be staying with Max Bill in Switzerland.

It seems likely that Bill was in Berlin at that time, given that in March and April 1929 he placed small ads in the free economists' paper *Letzte Politik,* which was published in Berlin. He placed two more very similar advertisements in the same paper, seeking work, later that same year—in August and September. Interestingly, in the advertisement published in March 1929 Bill only names his location as Dessau, without providing any more details. Did he still have lodgings in Dessau, which he had officially left in late 1928, or was he using a friend's postal address?

By way of an aside, this advertisement put in the paper by Max Bill with the heading "Dessau," seeking work in Dessau and the surroundings, confirms that his claims of having been at the Bauhaus "until 1929" were not mere fabrication.

In 1929 *Letzte Politik* devoted many column inches to introducing and promoting the Wära (1 Wära = 100 cents = 1 Reichsmark) in articles that range from dry to tedious. However, there are also interesting pointers to new, leftist publications, with a number of advertisements for "sexually enlightening" texts and an advertisement for *Die Frau als Künstlerin* by Hans Hildebrandt.

The same Hans Hildebrandt translated Le Corbusier's *Vers une architecture* into German and published it as *Kommende Baukunst* (Stuttgart: Deutsche Verlagsanstalt, 1926). In Stuttgart, in July 1948, Hildebrandt delivered the opening address at an exhibition of works by Max Bill and two older colleagues, Josef Albers and Jean Arp.

Elsewhere readers were informed that Felix Fechenbach's book *Der Revolutionär Kurt Eisner,* recently published in Berlin by Dietz (64 pages), was for sale at just one mark twenty, a price that even younger readers could

645 *Der Kunstnarr,* 1 April 1929, p. 38

646 *Der Kunstnarr,* 1 April 1929, p. 40

afford. Felix Fechenbach, who exhorted his compatriots to take a stand against the Nazis' inhumane practices, became one of their first victims. He was murdered or "shot while attempting to escape" as he was being transported to Dachau.

At the age of 24 the Social Democratic, Jewish journalist Felix Fechenbach became secretary to Kurt Eisner.

The failure of the Soviet Republic [Räterepublik] in Munich marked the beginning of the persecution and ostracization of Eisner, which ultimately led to his murder. Eisner's most important political thinking was grounded in the idea of dynamic grass-roots democracy that was always in contact with the people. "People from all walks of life should elect their own councils at every political level. Besides safeguarding the powers and the rights of the people, above all the councils should serve the cause of ongoing intellectual and political education. In Eisner's view, only a politically enlightened population would be in a position to shape democracy."[647]

Seeking Work in Dessau and Zurich

In his search for work in April 1929, Bill again listed his wide-ranging skills in *Letzte Politik,* only now one advertisement appeared under the rubric "Dessau" and the other under "Schweiz Zürich."[648] These texts were not yet written in lowercase, although it would not be long before Bill adopted that practice.

"Dessau: Max Bill, Designer, Bauhaus, Dessau. Designs for architecture, advertising, graphics, interiors (metal, painting, wood, textiles) all entirely modern." His other advertisement, on the same page under "Schweiz Zürich," appeared first in the list (arranged alphabetically) because Bill had cleverly placed the word *Architektur* right at the beginning: "Architecture: Max Bill, Stadelhoferstr. 27. Design: modern architecture, advertising, instruction in all areas of modern design (colors, forms, space)."

In the lead article in that Wära supplement in April 1929, with the slogan "Advertise with Wära: Join the Fight," the word *Wära* is flanked

647 See Pohl 1994

648 The two advertisements by Bill were printed under the headings "Dessau" and "Zürich" in *Letzte Politik* 8:14, "Wära" supplement (1929)

649 Max Bill in conversation with Angela Thomas, 29 August 1975

on either side by three increasingly large black dots. They are used as a graphic device but there is no mention of whose idea they were. Could it have been Bill's, who had worked with the basic forms—circle, triangle, square—on a daily basis at the Bauhaus? Or if not, did he have that solid disc in mind when he came up with the idea of a "blue dot" (as he called it)—the solid blue dot that shops in Zurich would later display in their windows as a quality mark?

The "Blue Dot" in Zurich

When he had returned to Switzerland from the Bauhaus, Bill—who was a strict vegetarian for many years—used to shop for food at Egli in Zurich. And it was through Herr Egli, the owner, that Bill suffered his "first real shock." When Max told me this story he seemed somehow diffident, almost as if he had turned back into that young man. Herr Egli had invited him to a meal with a group of successful retailers in Zurich, who were keen to create their own quality mark. The main dish was chicken, which Bill of course did not touch. He then spontaneously suggested that the businessmen should just "put a blue dot in their windows." He never heard from those gentlemen again—but before long he started to see blue dots appearing in shop windows in Zurich. Without making any attempt to seek permission they had taken his idea and had implemented it. And it came to Max Bill as a nasty shock that it never even occurred to those businessmen to recompense him for his idea.[649]

The Vagabonds' Congress

The legendary Vagabonds' Congress was held in Stuttgart in the late spring of 1929; around 500 "vagabonds" gathered there, but there were also "others sympathetic to their cause, that is to say, writers and artists, determined to alert society to the plight of those without no fixed abode, the so-called vagrants." During that congress there was also an art exhibition, which included a number of works by Jo Mihaly.

At the time Jo Mihaly and her husband, the actor and director Leonard Steckel, were living in Berlin in the artists' colony at Breitenbachplatz. "When the National Socialists came to power, Steckel immediately had to leave Germany as a 'racially' endangered Jew. In July 1933, when he was in Germany illegally, he was able to flee Berlin with his wife and new-born daughter Anja and go into exile in Zurich. . . . Compared to the deprivation and difficulties suffered by many other émigrés, life was relatively tolerable for the Mihaly-Steckels, since Leonard Steckel was invited to join the ensemble at the later renowned Schauspielhaus Zürich by the dramaturg Kurt Hirschfeld, another émigré. At that point the ensemble at the Schauspielhaus was largely sustained by German émigrés, actors and directors alike."[650]

Since Bill, by his own account, had "radicalized" his political thinking in Germany, it is possible that he, too, made the trip to Stuttgart. Jo Mihaly and her husband Leonard Steckel, who had fled to Zurich, played an important part in the cultural life of the city and moved in the same circles as Bill. From 1934 to 1938 Jo Mihaly "directed the social democratic workers and youth choir, 'the new choir.' The fact that the choir members were mainly Swiss nationals worked in its favor, that is to say, the choir could raise and critique current political and social issues in its concerts, whereas any émigrés engaged in activities of that sort would certainly have risked expulsion."[651]

In Switzerland in the 1940s Jo Mihaly and another émigré, Hans Mayer, would edit *Über die Grenzen—von Flüchtlingen für Flüchtlinge,* a magazine for exiles. Hans Mayer, who mainly worked on Georg Büchner and Walter Benjamin during his time in Switzerland, took up a chair at Leipzig University in the GDR in 1948 and remained there until 1963. His students included Christa Wolf and Uwe Johnson, both of whom would go on to become internationally renowned writers.[652]

After the fall of the Berlin Wall, Max Bill and Hans Mayer championed the same cause. As members of the Akademie der Künste they persistently argued in favor of improving the integration of colleagues from the former GDR into the academy. Some reactionary artists

650 See Schumann 2002

651 See Schumann 2002

652 Hans Mayer described his Leipzig years in his moving autobiography, *Der Turm zu Babel: Erinnerung an eine Deutsche Demokratische Republik* (Frankfurt am Main: Suhrkamp, 1991). Like Max Bill, Hans Mayer—a supreme intellect—was a member of the Akademie der Künste in West Berlin, where the two often ran into each other. The Akademie marked Mayer's 70th birthday with a festschrift: *Hans Mayer zu Ehren* (Frankfurt am Main: Suhrkamp, 1977). A series of homages by various writers is preceded by a screenprint for Hans Mayer by Max Bill

653 Koelbl 1989

654 Christa Wolf, "Am Grab," in *Neue Zürcher Zeitung,* arts supplement, 3 October 2006

spoke out against the idea, notably Heinz Mack and Gotthard Graubner, and tried to boycott it. A few years before he died, Hans Mayer visited Bill and me in Zumikon. With his sight slowly failing, he told us that he had decided not to speak in public any more, in order not "to sink below his own niveau." Like Ernst Bloch a quarter of a century earlier, Hans Mayer spent his last years in Tübingen.

In *Jüdische Portraits,* which includes a photograph of the literary historian Hans Mayer, the author and photographer Herlinde Koelbl explored the question as to who the Germans had actually driven out and what the German nation had lost as a result. The most pessimistic of her subjects was Hans Mayer, who talked of the way that anti-Semitism was flaring up again in Germany and who wondered if it had not been a mistake to return from exile to this country where almost nothing had changed.[653]

As Hans Mayer put it, he had returned from exile "to a foreign Germany"; the title of his two-volume memoir is *Ein Deutscher auf Widerruf: Erinnerungen* (Frankfurt am Main: Suhrkamp, 2 vols, 1982–84).

"It was a Monday, Monday the 28th of May 2001, the Suhrkamp Verlag—in an extensive obituary—and the Akademie der Künste had both announced that Hans Mayer would be laid to rest at 11 o'clock at the Dorotheenstadt Cemetery.... At the cemetery the first person I met was Adolf Muschg, who had come from Zurich. Grass was there.... Irina Hermlin had cut a peony from Stephan Hermlin's grave, which is directly next to Hans Mayer's grave. Volker Braun was there, Christoph Hein, Inge and Walter Jens and their son Tilman, Rainer Kirsch, of course Siegfried Unseld, the mayors of Leipzig and Cologne—around 200 people, with a good 70 percent from the East. Georg Girardet, the director of culture in Leipzig, now has to prepare a posthumous honorary citizenship for Hans Mayer.... If only Mayer had been able to be present at that act of reconciliation. I took a rose out of the bouquet for Hans Mayer and laid it on Anna Seghers's grave."[654]

"... the superiority of money over goods"

Max once told me that the physiocrats in Germany were ideologically "more radical" than the friends in Switzerland who had introduced to him the beliefs of the free economists; he also said that he had radicalized his own ideas through his contact with physiocrats in Germany.

The Wära, introduced as a medium of exchange by young campaigners (first in Germany and then in Switzerland), needed to be explained to the general public for it to be accepted by individuals and businesses. An article in *Letzte Politik* by a certain Batalanto, with the headline "Wära, a radical means," attempted to alert readers to its advantages: "Always get to the root of things. Getting to the roots, that is what it means to be 'radical.' Radical is an accolade.... Those who only like superficial remedies, who only want to gloss over things, who only seek to stamp things out for today as opposed to forever, who only tackle results and effects, they are not radical. And they will berate us, the radicals.... Let us also be happy that our money, our Wära, is a radical medium that is designed to do away with interest payments. Our Wära changes the nature of money: hitherto, if we put our money away in a cupboard, it retained its value. But if we kept bread, milk, or potatoes for a year, they would go off, they would lose their value. All goods are constantly depreciating, turning bad, decaying, rusting.... By definition money was thus superior to every kind of goods because it retained its full value, whereas goods went down in value. We have changed that aspect of money: our Wära, worth 100 marks today for instance, will only be worth 95 marks in a year's time; it loses 5% of its value annually, it dwindles away; it is a dwindling currency. We have removed the basis of monetary interest—namely the superiority of money over goods—by virtue of the fact that the Wära depreciates in the same way as goods."[655]

That first sentence, meaning "always get to the bottom of things," would have been familiar to Max Bill, because this was same method that Josef Albers always recommended to his students at the Bauhaus.

The Wära was introduced in Switzerland that same year, in 1929, albeit against the wishes of Fritz Schwarz, a leading member of the free economists' federal council in Bern. The first issue of *Letzte Politik* in 1929 announced that the Wära was now accepted at certain locations in Switzerland: "The Swiss Wära is here!"[656] There were three Wära exchange offices, one each in Basel, Bern, and Zurich. The main exchange office was at Münsterhof 18 in the center of Zurich, at Fritz Engelhardt's address.

In the enthusiastic community of physiocrats in Zurich there was a certain Lori de Rigo, who placed an advertisement in *Letzte Politik* for her artisanal book-binding business at Weierstrasse 50; in the same

655 Batalanto, "Wära, ein radikales Mittel," *Letzte Politik* 8:6 (1929)
656 *Letzte Politik* 8:1 (1929)

paper there was also an advertisement for the Zurich whole-foods retailer Wohlfahrt Müller & Co. at Oetenbachgasse 26 and at Untere Kirchgasse 4. Untere Kirchgasse in Zurich was also where the revolutionary young physiocrats met after May 1930, at the Karl der Grosse restaurant close to the Grossmünster.

Max already had good memories of Kirchgasse, because Girsberger's bookshop, in Kirchgasse, was where he had discovered certain books that would be important to him—inspiring and encouraging him to make his way to the Bauhaus in Dessau.

Women seem to have been very active in these circles; at the Swiss physiocrats' parliamentary meeting, which took place in Zurich on 3 February 1929, Lori de Rigo was voted in as chief executive and Lilli Hinterreiter was voted in as auditor.

Lilli Hinterreiter's brother was Hans Hinterreiter, Max Bill's friend from his youth in Winterthur, with whom Max discussed Ostwald's color theory in an isolated Alpine cabin after his return from Dessau. It was Hans and Lilli who introduced Max to the idea of a free economy.

From June to November 1929 the Zurich free economists met every Monday evening at Stadelhoferstrasse 34, no more than a stone's throw from Bill's lodgings. Perhaps surprisingly, a glance at the free economists' publications reveals that their typography was not at all modern—and the contents were certainly not as intellectually stimulating as those in *Die Weltbühne,* which Max Bill also read. Did Bill not feel the urge to intervene and improve the design? Given that he was seeking work, did he not offer his services—or was his offer declined?

Barely had I asked myself those questions in October 2006 than I received a telephone call from Ruth Binde in Zurich, whose late father was the free economist Fritz Schwarz. She had come across letters from Max Bill in her father's estate, and in one of those letters Max Bill addresses the very issue that had puzzled me: "Dear Fritz Schwarz, I see from the most recent issue of the F-Z [*Freiwirtschaftliche Zeitung,* the free economists' newspaper] that the S.F.B. [Schweizer Freiwirtschaftsbund, the Swiss free economists' association] has registered to participate in HYSPA [*Schweizerische Ausstellung für Hygiene und Sport,* Swiss exhibition for hygiene and sport, held in Bern in 1931] and plans to have a stand there. I know that there must only be limited funds available for this and that it is crucial that the display should be as striking and impressive as possible, also very objective and persuasive. In any case, I imagine that it will be essential to present a modern look, thereby winning over the people who are already modern in their thinking, since in due course the rest will of necessity die out. I would very much like to take charge of the design of the S-F-B stand."[657] So Bill did offer his services, albeit rather presumptuously, or, to put it rather more sympathetically, with a certain youthfully eager chutzpah—but to no avail.

Many members of the younger generation were averse to the state as such and—often pursuing their own personal anarchies—were very much in favor of free love, naked bathing, *joie de vivre,* and intellectual nourishment. Bill's reading matter included novels by Jack London (whose books were regularly recommended in *Letzte Politik*), Joseph Conrad, and Upton Sinclair.

A song that the physiocrats used to sing in Germany reflects the adventurousness and zest for life that characterized that era: "Junge physiocrats stürmen voran, jauchzen der Freiheit entgegen ... wir wollen frei sein, frei ohne Staat, ohne Gesetz, ungebunden ..." (Young physiocrats storm ahead, exultantly heading for freedom ... we want to be free, free with no state, no laws at all, unshackled ...)[658]

Good Connections

Every so often Ernst Geiger hosted a party for the teetotallers at his home in Ligerz. Those outdoor events, where Max was sometimes present, also attracted young people from Brugg, where Bill's mother Marie Geiger had been born. Geiger used to put up decorations for those nocturnal gatherings: "glowing, colored lanterns, like pillars, almost a meter long. He used to make them by rolling up cardboard into tubes ... and cutting random shapes into the tubes, which he would then cover over with colored paper."[659]

In 1929 Ernst Geiger, who had always encouraged and supported Max's art, wrote a text, "Die Radierung" [The etching], for an art journal in Geneva; it was published with just three illustrations, all of them etchings done by Max Bill in 1927 and 1929: *Selbstbildnis* (1927), *Das Mädchen mit den schönen Augen—Kattja* (1927), and *zwiegespräch* (1929). Max well may have delivered those etchings to Ligerz himself. Taking advantage of his reputation and his many connections, Geiger was clearly seeking to

657 Max Bill, letter to the office of the Schweizerischer Freiwirtschaftsbund Bern, Fritz Schwarz (3 September 30), private archives of Fritz and Elly Schwarz

658 In "Jugend am Feuer," *Letzte Politik* 8:28 (1929)

659 Information kindly supplied by Christoph Geiger in 2007

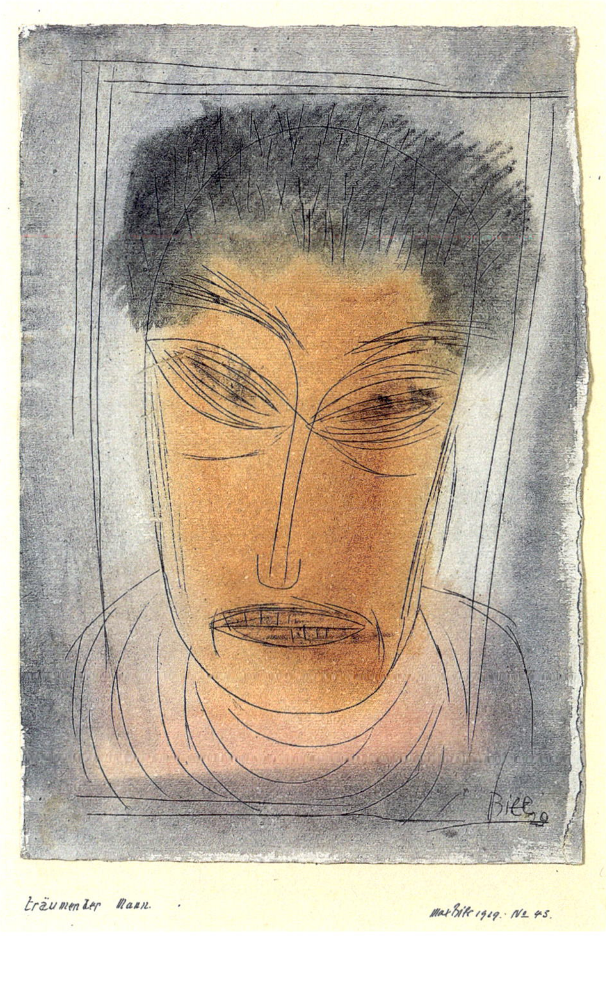

Max Bill, *träumender Mann,* 1929,
india ink over watercolor on laid paper,
41 × 28 cm

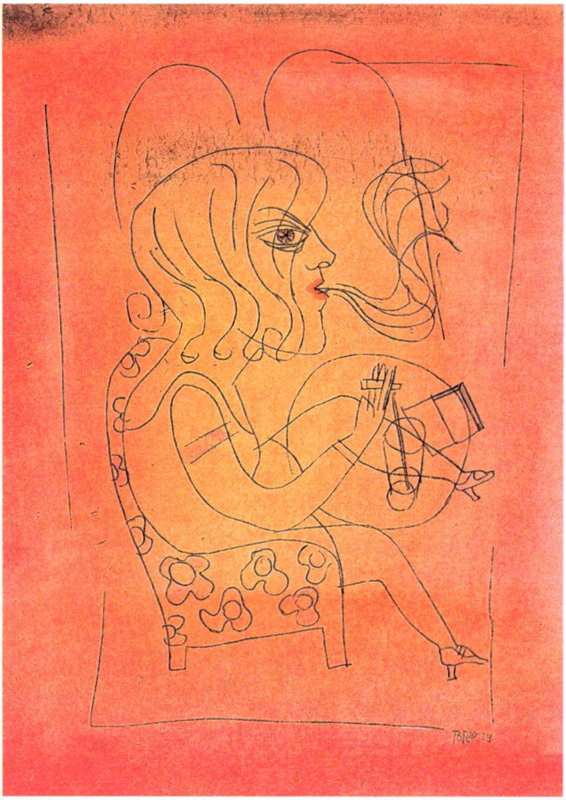

Max Bill, *Mädchen im Café,* 1929,
india ink over watercolor on Japan paper,
43×31 cm

raise his nephew's public profile—in the same way that Ferdinand Hodler had once championed Geiger's work.

"Since etching is a form of expression used by artists who otherwise work in quite different areas, we have chosen works by Max Bill, a young Zurich artist who unites the most diverse areas of art. First a silversmith, then a poster artist and painter, a Bauhausler in Dessau, now an architect and commercial artist in Zurich."[660]

Nusch: Bill's First Great Love

When Bill once again placed advertisements in *Letzte Politik* in August and September 1929, Zurich is the only named location. It seems he had finally given up on any hopes he might have had of finding employment in Dessau. The advertisement in the September issue of *Letzte Politik* was the last one Bill placed in his search for work.

"Schweiz. Zürich. Architektur: Max Bill, Stadelhoferstrasse 27. Gestaltung: moderne Architektur, Reklame, Unterricht auf allen modernen Gestaltungsgebieten (Farbe, Form, Raum)" (*Letzte Politik*, 8:30 [1929]) (Switz. Zurich. Architecture: Max Bill, Stadelhoferstrasse 27. Design: modern architecture, advertising, teacher in all areas of modern design [color, form, space]).

A month later, in September, Bill made minimal changes to the wording; under the rubric "Zürich," his advertisement now reads "Max Bill, Stadelhoferstr. 27, Gestaltung: mod. Architektur, Reklame, Unterricht auf allen mod. Gestaltungsgebieten (Farbe, Form, Raum)" (*Letzte Politik*, 8:34, 1929).

It was "through a strange chance"—which Max Bill never elaborated upon to me—that he met a fragile, capricious young woman called Maria Benz in the summer or early autumn of 1929. Did they perhaps encounter each other in Café Odéon, one of Bill's favorite haunts? Whatever the case, she was the first woman Bill lived with. They "cohabited," as the authorities put it, for six months, despite cohabitation still being illegal at that time. Maria Benz, whom Max affectionately called "Nusch," moved into his lodgings at Stadelhoferstrasse 27, where Bill had also set up his first "advertising agency."

660 Ernst Geiger, "Die Radierung," *Die Kunst in der Schweiz, illustrierte Monatsschrift*, July 1929, pp. 153–55, Archiv Christoph Geiger

Nusch, who was born in Mulhouse, was able to use her French to ease negotiations between Bill and his clients in France and West Switzerland, and her charm certainly helped him to secure advertising contracts. Extremely graceful in her movements, Nusch also occasionally worked as a model for the wealthy clientele at Grieder—a leading fashion house in Zurich. However, as a foreigner living in Switzerland without a work permit, she was in a very precarious situation.

A copy of the art journal *Cahiers d'art* (no. 7), still in the Max Bill library with Bill's name and the year "29" in his hand on the upper right of the cover, suggests that he—and Nusch?—may have been in Paris in the autumn of 1929. That issue has a full-page advertisement for "Galerie Jeanne Bucher 5, rue du Cherche-Midi, Paris 6e," which mentions "éditions des gravures modernes" (editions of modern prints) and the *"Histoires naturelles de Max Ernst."* Max Bill certainly visited Jeanne Bucher's gallery in 1930, and it seems he may also have been there in autumn 1929.[661]

"What use was Liebknecht's martyrdom?"

From November 1929 onward the Zurich free economists and their friends no longer met in Stadelhoferstrasse: "From now on the free economists' meetings will be held on Monday evenings at 8 o'clock at Bahnhofplatz 2, on the second floor of Tess-A.G."[662] And the next issue of *Letzte Politik* specified that the meetings would be led by Professor Bernoulli. That arrangement only remained in place for a few months, until May 1930, when the location and the day of the week for the meetings changed

661 In *Cahiers d'art,* no. 7 (1929), p. 17 there is a review of the exhibition *Abstrakte und Surrealistische Malerei und Plastik* (Kunsthaus Zürich, 6 October–3 November 1929)—which Bill, much to his regret, had not been able to participate in. The review is positive, full of praise: "The Zurich exhibition of abstract and surrealist art (Kunsthaus) ... which we had the pleasure of seeing ... must be the most important exhibition the Kunsthaus has ever had the honor to present.... Germany was notably represented by Kandinsky, whose works happen to be reproduced in this *Cahier.* Klee occupies a small room ... and then there are the *papiers collés* of Kurt Schwitters, constructed with a deep sense of balance and exquisite taste ... neo-plasticism, a special niche has been carved out where Mondrian dominates in all his fine tenacity.... and the Constructivists, with beautiful *papiers collés* by Lissitzky and constructions by Pevsner." This issue also contains an article by

again: "Zurich. As of now regular meetings will be held on the first Tuesday of each month at the alcohol-free restaurant Karl der Grosse, Kirchgasse 14, at 8 o'clock."[663] There is no knowing if Bill attended those meetings regularly or not, but the fact that they were chaired by Hans Bernoulli would certainly have added to their appeal for him. And, when he did attend, he may well have taken the opportunity to invite his comrades to an exhibition (curated by himself) of his own works.

Hans Bernoulli, from a line of scholars in Basel, is still remembered in Zurich; between 1914 and 1929 he built the Bernoulli Houses along Hardturmstrasse. Yet it is not widely known that, specifically because of his involvement in the Free Economy movement and his public critiques as a Free Economist (his opponents described these as "your attacks against the most important Federal Offices"), in 1938 Professor Bernoulli was forced to resign from his position as a faculty member at the ETH in Zurich.

The exact wording of the letter signed by the president of the Swiss School Council on 23 December 1938 detailing the employment ban for "Herrn Titularprofessor H. Bernoulli, Riehen-Basel, Bettingerweg 22" is given in Werner Schmid, *Hans Bernoulli Städtebauer Politiker Weltbürger* (Schaffhausen: Peter Meili, 1974), pp. 43–44.

In autumn 1928 "Bernoulli, Basel," like "Wiemken," a Surrealist artist from Basel, and "Otto Morach, Zürich," visited the *Herbstausstellung* organized by Ernst Geiger at the Ligerz "farm." Bill's father Erwin Bill and his new wife Lina Bill-Wolf also saw the exhibition and signed Ernst Geiger's visitors' book at the time.

Bernoulli seems to have liked the ambience at the "farm." In 1930 Geiger put his premises at the disposal of the Schweizer Freiwirtschaftsbund (the Swiss Free Economists' Association) for its delegates meeting, and the first person to sign the visitors' book on that occasion was "Hans Bernoulli, Basel"; other signatories include "Magda Kümmerly, Bern" (from the company Kümmerly & Frey), "Elsi Giauque, Festi" (a Taeuber student living in Ligerz) and—by way of an exception—Max's brother "Hugo Bill, Winterthur." This suggests

Will Grohmann on Wassily Kandinsky (pp. 322–29, with numerous black-and-white illustrations). The first image in the catalogue *Abstrakte und Surrealistische Malerei und Plastik* (Kunsthaus Zürich, 6 October–3 November 1929)—at odds with alphabetical order—illustrates a sculpture made in 1924 by Georges Vantongerloo (plate I), that Bill would see firsthand in Paris in the mid-1930s; the next image illustrates a *Torso* by Brancusi (plate II)

662 In "Aus der Bewegung," *Letzte Politik* 8:41 (1929)

663 In "Versammlungsanzeiger," *Letzte Politik* 9:19 (1930)

that Max's younger brother had some interest at least in the idea of a free economy. Max Bill was either not present at that meeting at the "farm" or he did not sign his uncle's visitors' book on that occasion.

In early 1929 the leader writer at *Letzte Politik* addressed the fact that life was becoming much harsher than before and informed readers that if the paper "did not appear due to *force majeure,* operational disruption, a strike, or proscription" there would be "no entitlement to replacement copies." Bill also described having seen for himself that political disputes between the left and the right in Germany were becoming increasingly violent, and that certainly played a part in his decision to leave Dessau and to return to Switzerland.

On the title page of *Letzte Politik* in April 1929 the leader writer, Arthur Bohn, reflected on the ideological differences between Communists and physiocrats: "What use was Liebknecht's martyrdom? If . . . he had dispassionately assessed his enemy—the then state, with its infinitely superior powers—a great force for good would not have been extinguished for nothing."[664]

Let us take a closer look at that newspaper article from April 1929: Bohn describes physiocrats as opponents of the present-day state. But he also goes on to say that "when the need arises" the physiocrat, "as an opponent of the state, also uses the state for his own ends. . . . The physiocrat is not embittered or disturbed by the terrible situation today, nor does he attempt to step in, offering help here and there; he pays no heed to charities and welfare institutions, because he knows that sticking plasters only perpetuate the situation by obscuring the causes of these phenomena." Moreover, a physiocrat is not out to topple the state, instead he "cuts away the foundations so that one day it will topple of its own accord."

Bohn continues: the work of the physiocrat is "thus in fact the most dangerous, despite also being the most unremarkable, quietest and generally least noticed by the enemy." Whatever the case, his aim is to "eradicate the causes of the present situation" by using "free money and free land" to create "new conditions." And finally, there is a difference between physiocrats and fanatics: the physiocrats see themselves as "scientific technicians acting according to the laws of existence."[665]

664 Arthur Bohn, "Die Kampfmethode der Fysiokraten," *Letzte Politik* 8:14 (1929)
665 Bohn, "Die Kampfmethode der Fysiokraten"
666 Bohn, "Die Kampfmethode der Fysiokraten"
667 Geiger 1969, pp. 23–24
668 Bill 1979 [b], p. 66

One cannot help but be struck by Arthur Bohn's use of the term "scientific technician" in his lead article, given that in 1930 Bill—in his search for work—described himself, rather unusually, as an "advertising technician." And, as we have seen, when Mart Stam had to dash Bill's hopes of traveling to the Soviet Union with the May Brigade, he addressed his letter to "Herr Bill, Advertising Technician."

Bohn regarded the physiocrats as the group that would in future "shape the world," whose members would be expected to undergo training "like that of a boxer"—"only that their training would lead to the mental mastery of all their powers, not only their physical powers but also their mental, intellectual, and spiritual powers ... that 'nothing is beyond me' has to become flesh and blood."[666]

Joost Schmidt

Although there are many baffling gaps in Bill's biography for the year 1929, we do know for sure that his interest in Constructivist art from the Soviet Union greatly increased around then. In all likelihood he attended not only Lissitzky's talk on modern architecture at the Bauhaus in Dessau on 1 October 1928 but also the lectures Naum Gabo gave at the Bauhaus between 2 and 9 November 1928. At the first of those lectures in November the audience learned about the "Constructivist sculptures of N. Gabo, their basis and aims."

Max yearned to visit the Soviet Union, and his uncle Ernst Geiger had had the same rose-tinted dream before him. Geiger—as we have seen—was in close contact with Russian students not only in Zurich but also in Paris, so much so that the police kept him under observation. Unlike Max, his Uncle Ernst had also made a "serious" study of Russian and tried to find employment as a forester in the Caucasus. But his hopes, like Max's, came to nothing.[667]

In his later years, when the conversation turned to speakers who visited the Bauhaus to give public lectures (which were always followed by discussions), he named the two Russian artists El Lissitzky and Naum Gabo and the Marxist art historian Lu Märten; but he did not specifically state whether he himself had been present at those talks.[668]

In 1937, at the exhibition *Konstruktivisten* in Basel, Max Bill met Antoine Pevsner, the brother of the Russian Constructivist artist Naum Gabo. In 1949 Bill, Pevsner and Georges Vantongerloo had a joint exhibition at Kunsthaus Zürich.

One of the masters in Dessau, Joost Schmidt, was in personal contact with El Lissitzky. After Oskar Schlemmer had left the Bauhaus for the art academy in Breslau, Schmidt took over the obligatory life drawing classes from him. Schmidt was also often called on to design stands for trade exhibitions, as he did for the firm of Junkers at the *Gas und Wasser* exhibition in Berlin in 1929. In 1930, when Schmidt designed the display for the food canning industry at the *Internationale Hygiene-Ausstellung* in Dresden, the stand "was constructed under his supervision in the Bauhaus workshops."[669] At that same exhibition in Dresden Schmidt ran into Lissitzky, who was overseeing the construction of "the huge Russian pavilion. Unlike the Bauhaus, he has the support of numerous assistants, fully qualified experts, not just students, like we have for the Bauhaus stand."[670] Looking back, Schmidt's wife, Helene Nonne-Schmidt, later described El Lissitzky and her husband continuing their Dresden conversation in Schmidt's master-house studio in Dessau, "when Lissitzky paid a short visit to the Bauhaus." And it was that second conversation which "reinforced Joost Schmidt's desire to hand in his notice."

Schmidt "makes an appointment with Gropius to tell him that he is revoking the promise he made in February 1928 that he would stay at the Bauhaus, and will be resigning at the next opportunity, because of the constant overload of work for commissions and the ensuing reduction in teaching. Once again he is asked to stay, because, for the second time, there is going to be a leadership change. Gropius is asked to return to Dessau, which he declines to do. After Gropius has conferred with Werkbund members, it is suggested that Mies van der Rohe take over, and he agrees to go to Dessau [starting in August 1930]."[671]

In 1930 El Lissitzky oversaw the design of the spacious Soviet hall at the *Internationale Hygiene-Ausstellung* in Dresden. His wife Sophie Küppers reported at the time: "... when I went into our hall and asked after our young assistant, I was told that he had been killed during the night by Fascists brandishing a weight fixed to a rope."[672]

669 Nonne-Schmidt 1984 [a], p. 116
670 Nonne-Schmidt 1984 [c], p. 95
671 Nonne-Schmidt 1984 [c], p. 95
672 Lissitzky-Küppers, 1976, p. 87
673 Bill 1987, p. 34
674 Ernst Kállai, in *Der Kunstnarr* 1 (April 1929), p. 40
675 Max Bill to Erwin Bill, 15 September 1930, Archiv Max Bill
676 Information kindly supplied by Dr. Robert Dünki, Stadtarchiv Zürich, 13 December 2007

Frankfurt's Mega-Estates

It seems highly probable that Max—determined to become an architect—might well have "traveled around in Germany" in 1929 (as he put it) in order to broaden his knowledge of modern architecture. Two years earlier, in 1927, he had already made a pilgrimage from Dessau to Stuttgart to visit the Weissenhof Estate where, "as well as buildings by the best known pioneers of *Neues Bauen,* there were two houses by Le Corbusier, which had been realized in situ by my future friend Alfred Roth."[673]

"Stuttgart is pulling out all the stops! After the major exhibition of modern architecture two years ago, which gave us the Weissenhof Estate, this spring it will host an international photography exhibition and a film week (Deutscher Werkbund). This exhibition also promises to be of importance."[674]

In a letter written by Max to his father in 1930 there is a sense of his growing expertise. He refers to a "huge estate" in Frankfurt—albeit not to the Weissenhof Estate in Stuttgart: "In Germany there are huge housing estates (possibly some 1200 houses in Frankfurt) in Dessau ca. 400 etc., there is almost no need to discuss the form, in practice it has proved to be pleasing and functional, and not at all crazy, the state has financed the housing association and, in so doing, approved the direction of travel."[675] It is not clear from Bill's letter whether he had seen that "huge estate" in Frankfurt for himself or only in illustrations. However, it is certainly fair to assume that when he was back in Switzerland he would certainly not have missed the *bauhaus dessau* exhibition at the Gewerbemuseum in Basel in 1929.

During the time when Max was still trying to find an apartment of his own in Switzerland, he would occasionally stay with his father in Winterthur; his father had of course been given custody of Max after he and Max's mother divorced. Bill once told me that on his return to Zurich from the Bauhaus, before he moved into his lodgings in Stadelhoferstrasse, he "first had a sublet room at Mühlegasse 5, above Kino Radium."

There are no official records of Bill registering at Mühlegasse 5—"not in the files." But this has been described by the record keepers as not so surprising, because "creative artists often didn't fulfill their official duty to register." Only that particular creative artist did register at his next address: "architect, painter and graphic artist" at "Stadelhoferstrasse 27" on "2 February 1929." This entry also records that at that time, like his father and his Uncle Ernst, Bill had no "religious affiliation." He remained at this address until 10 March 1931.[676]

Zur schwarzen Stege

The cinema, Kino Radium, below Max's spartan digs in the Niederdorf district of Zurich was in fact the city's first permanent picture house. The chances are that Bill moved in around January 1929, but we cannot be sure since, as we know, he did not register at that address as he ought to have done according to Swiss law.

As it happens, the Concrete artist Fritz Glarner, who would play a part later on in Bill's life, was born in the same street, on 20 July 1899. Bill first met Glarner in Zurich in 1932 and in 1956 Bill exhibited works by Glarner, Albers, and Vordemberge-Gildewart at Kunsthaus Zürich; Bill later tried—in vain—to persuade the authorities in Zurich to put up a memorial plaque to Fritz Glarner on the house at 31 Obere Mühlegasse.

Mühlegasse originally provided a narrow link from Niederdorfstrasse to the mills on the upper Mühlesteg. In 1912, after Oetenbachgasse had been opened up and the Rudolf Brun Bridge had been built, Mühlegasse was widened and extended as far as Seilergraben. The building that housed Kino Radium, known as the "Haus zur schwarzen Stege," still stands at Mühlegasse 5. In fact, a glance at the roof line with its two distinct gable ends, facing the river in the traditional manner, reveals that this was originally two adjoining buildings. The oldest parts of the building, which originally had stables for mill horses on the ground floor, date to the sixteenth and seventeenth centuries. In 1907 the stables were removed and the windows on the first floor were bricked up to create a shell for the new cinema. The full-length ornamental frieze on the façade, which is still in place today, was painted in 1928.

In a recent publication by Jakob Bill, it is said that it was Max Bill who "painted the façade decorations on Kino Radium."[677] Jakob Bill has since informed me that while he has no documentation to support this, the information came from Max Bill himself in conversation. However, records held by the City Council in Zurich state that the painted, geometric pattern on the façade was done by an artist named "E. Morf" in "1928."[678]

677 Jakob Bill 2008, p. 171

678 In "Auszug aus dem Protokoll des Stadtrates von Zürich," Baugeschichtliches Archiv der Stadt Zürich

679 Mebold 2008, p. 206

680 Max Bill, Zurich, 1 August 1929, compilation for the lawyer Dr. Hans Duttweiler, Bahnhofstr. 65, Zurich 1, Bibliothek Max Bill

Because of the bricked-up windows Max Bill's room had no daylight on the Mühlegasse side at least, and, as he told me, instead of paying monetary rent, he designed materials for Kino Radium—in an ideal free-economy "barter."

It has not been possible to establish the locations of any extant film posters by Max Bill.

Not long after that Max Bill moved into sublet lodgings at Stadelhoferstrasse 27, within easy walking distance of the lake and the opera house. And he registered there, in compliance with the law, on 2 February 1929. In an effort to resolve his dire financial difficulties he wrote to Georg Reinhart, an important patron of the arts in Winterthur, in January and again in early April 1929; he even sent some of his works to Reinhart, only to have them returned "with no comment."[679]

As I have previously indicated, Georg Reinhart's interest in more recent art came to a halt at the work of Ernst Ludwig Kirchner. That is most likely one of the reasons why he did not respond at all to Bill's request for support.

In the summer of 1929 Bill prepared a typewritten memorandum for his lawyer: ". . . 40.– mk. to settle an invoice for coal. . . . This sum, which is still owed to the coal merchant, was communicated to me when I was in Dessau in Nov.–Dec. 28." Bill summarizes the situation: "Conclusion: Hanns Fischli sold my household goods and furniture without my knowledge and without compensating me; he is thus liable for the losses I have suffered."[680]

Meanwhile Max Bill was again frequenting his favorite bookshop, Girsberger's, in Kirchgasse, which was just a few minutes walk away from Stadelhoferstrasse. And it was at Girsberger's, in 1929, that he bought *Die Kunstismen 1914–1924,* edited by El Lissitzky and Jean Arp, not only to further his own self-education but also because the topic was of course of the greatest interest to him.

"... you are not working, just idling in Zurich"

In May 1929 Max received an irate letter from his father. Erwin Bill, who read the newspapers and certainly some of the German classics,[681] started his letter by unrelentingly berating Max for his spelling mistakes: "People cannot put their trust in you if you self-evidently make no effort to maintain the most basic standards of decency. For as long as you fail to take life more seriously—the same reproach I have made for years—nothing worthwhile will become of you. Deeming yourself to be above opposing views, behaving in a loud-mouthed manner, using highly uncultured expletives ... your parents did not teach you any of that. You are far too wasteful in the way you work, you also take no care of your clothes. And you often appear here in garb that you know very well will annoy me.... Nevertheless, I do not deny your talents and continue to renew my trust in you, despite the fact that in the space of one-and-a-quarter years you have frittered away the funds that should have seen you through three years of study, living decently for those three years.... First and foremost you must 'become a man'.... Decide, once and for all, on a particular occupation.... People chide me for still supporting you, and they point out that you are not working, just idling in Zurich.... I have never yet seen one serious, finished work by you. Perfunctory, slipshod, time after time you appear with at least one more new, half-baked project.... And as soon as any money comes your way, it is futilely squandered.... I need to hear from you how much longer my assistance should continue and the amount you require. I want very specific details. Everything that accrues to you from elsewhere is to be transferred into my safekeeping. In the case of any infringements on your part, or if you adopt a frivolous lifestyle or do not engage in serious work, my assistance will be withdrawn forthwith.... warm regards, your Father."[682]

681 As a youth Max Bill was able to borrow books from his father's shelves, including two by Gotthold Ephraim Lessing, one of which contained his renowned drama *Nathan der Weise* (*Lessings Werke,* Leipzig: Buchhandlung Gustav Fock [1919]), bought in Winterthur at Vogel's bookshop, with a label pasted inside the front cover, "Ex Libris Alfred Erwin Bill," designed by "MG" (Marie Geiger, see p. 54). Max Bill later inherited these volumes from his father

682 Erwin Bill, Winterthur, to Max Bill, Zurich (27 May 1929), Archiv Max Bill

683 Max Bill, Zurich I, Stadelhoferstrasse 27, to Sigfried Gidion [*sic*], Zurich 7, Dolderstrasse 7, 18 June 1929, gta Archiv

684 Bill 1942 [b]

Given this very strained situation, the young hothead had no option but to take action and redouble his efforts to find work. Could he find an exhibition curator who would select his work? With that in mind, Max turned to Dr. Wilhelm Wartmann, director of Kunsthaus Zürich. Evidently he did not strike quite the right tone in their conversation, which was also the problem with a letter he wrote to Sigfried Giedion, in which he even misspelled Giedion's surname:

"Respected sir, it has come to my notice that you are supervising the organization of the Surrealist exhibition at Kunsthaus Zürich. Since I regard myself as a surrealist painter and have little chance of exhibiting anywhere else in Switzerland, and since you as yet know nothing of my works, I would like to ask if you might care to visit me in my studio, where one could discuss this matter. If you would like to know more about my work, Walter Kern may be able to speak on my behalf, it was from him that I learned that you are in charge of this exhibition, he told me so after I had attempted to come to an agreement with Dr. Wartmann, but he does not at all understand this whole matter.... If you decide to pay me a visit, it is best if you first send a card, so that I can be sure to be at home. In the hope that something can be done, with the greatest respect, yours, Bill."[683]

Max Bill no doubt assumed that if his Bauhaus master, Kandinsky, had paid him a personal visit in his student lodgings in Dessau to look at a somewhat larger composition by Bill, then the art historian Sigfried Giedion would not hesitate to seek him out in his studio apartment at Stadelhoferstrasse 27.

Looking back at that year, Bill summed up his situation as follows: "In 1929 I returned to Zurich from the Bauhaus. I now had to find a source of income. There was little to be done regarding my architectural projects because I did not want a permanent job. So I decided to earn my living as a commercial artist. I had made friends with various modern architects and I now started designing signage for their buildings, worked with them on their exhibitions, devised color schemes for painted interiors, and so on. After a time I reached the point where I was designing posters, brochures, and advertisements for numerous firms ... which allowed me to separate earning a crust from pursuing my own artistic ideas."[684]

". . . the experience of art"

The letter Max wrote to Sigfried Giedion—bearing in mind his father's ultimatum—clearly did not tempt Giedion to visit him in his studio. Bill's hope of participating in the exhibition *Surrealistische und abstrakte Malerei und Plastik* at Kunsthaus Zürich in 1929 came to nothing. A few months after that disappointment the young artist's dented self-esteem was at least somewhat restored by the art critic Walter Kern—mentioned in Bill's letter to Giedion—who reviewed Bill's studio exhibition *Malerei und Grafik.* Although Bill defined his own work as "surreal," Kern described the exhibits in *Malerei und Grafik* as "grotesque" and commented, rather aptly, that they conveyed a much greater sense of "the experience of art" than of the experience of nature.[685]

The God of Desire

Oskar Schlemmer once very entertainingly told his Bauhaus stage company about his paternal grandfather, a pastry chef in Mainz, who made a marzipan relief of the Battle of Waterloo that the family then kept for many years. And it may have been Bill's contact with Schlemmer that led him to come up with the pet name "Nusch" for his girlfriend Maria Benz, because it was Schlemmer who had designed the stage set and costumes for the premiere (in 1921) of Hindemith's one-act opera *Das Nusch-Nuschi,* which is based on a play by Franz Blei.[686] Schlemmer may well have talked about Hindemith's opera in 1928 when Bill was a member of the stage workshop at the Bauhaus—although it is also perfectly possible that Bill read *Das Nusch-Nuschi* himself, given that Blei was very highly regarded in the early twentieth century. The story of the Nusch-Nuschi—an anarchic, erotic tale—displays the author's incendiary knowledge of the power of human drives. As it happens it came out just as the third impression of Sigmund Freud's *Interpretation of Dreams* was being published in Vienna (in spring

685 Notice for, "Atelierausstellung Max Bill Zürich," *Das Werk* 16:11 (November 1929), p. XV

686 In Franz Blei, *Vermischte Schriften,* vol. 4: *Das Schwere Herz. Zwiesprachen und Gedichte,* (Munich and Leipzig, Georg Müller, 1911, pp. 149–76

687 Blei, *Das Schwere Herz, Zwiesprachen und Gedichte,* p. 160

688 Max Bill, Zurich, to Erwin Bill, 3 February 1930, Archiv Max Bill

1911). The Nusch-Nuschi of the title only appears once in the narrative. It is a mythological beast, "half large rat, half caiman, wheezing as it creeps slowly forward. Sitting on its back is the smiling figure of Kamadeva, the god of desire."[687]

In the months Bill spent with the ever fragile Nusch, he experienced his first great love, which he then alluded to with tender restraint in his portrayal of two naked lovers in *Violette Nacht* (see p. 217).

A line from Franz Blei's libretto in *Das Nusch-Nuschi* could serve as a description (from Nusch's perspective) of the progress of the love affair between Max Bill and herself: "All you have left me is this little pearl of sweat between my breasts. Come."

". . . I also lack the courage"

After living together with Nusch for some months, Max Bill wrote to his father, addressing the letter to the "Turnussekretär des Schweiz. Kunstverein": "Over the last few months Nusch has been working for me, first in France, for ZIKA, and now in Zurich. . . . At the moment I have so many things on the go that I need someone to look out for me and take over certain tasks. . . . I cannot deal with business people and I also lack the courage to just walk into a company and make a suggestion, I can come up with fabulous designs, but to no avail if there is no one to promote them for me. . . . Wherever Nusch goes everyone likes her and that is after all the main thing if you are hoping to do business."[688] But Erwin Bill wanted nothing to do with Maria Benz, without even having met her. Despite his own past—as a divorced man who had initially cohabited (illegally) with Lina Wolf—he castigated Max for his loose morals, particularly with regard to his partner, Maria Benz.

The truth of Bill's admission that he was not easily able to deal with business people was already evident in the incident when he suggested to a group of merchants in Zurich that a "blue dot" in their shop windows could stand as a mark of quality, only to find that just such a dot started to appear in the shops, but not one of the businessmen thought to offer him any payment for his idea. However, Max Bill learned his lesson, and before too long he received an official contract from Egli & Co to design a display stand for their campaign "Kraft und Frische durch gesunde Ernährung" (Strength and freshness through healthy nutrition). As it happens, that commission came when Nusch was no longer there to use her charming communication skills to support Max in his work.

In late January 1977, when Bill and I were perusing a copy of *Album Éluard* (Paris: Gallimard, 1968), he showed me that it contains several photographs of Nusch, who became Paul Éluard's second wife. One of the picture captions suggested that the photograph in question was of Nusch in Germany, acting in a play by Strindberg ("Nusch ... jouant en Allemagne une pièce de Strindberg"), but Bill immediately refuted that: "That's not true, she never acted in a Strindberg play, but she did work with her father who was a circus showman."[689] Maria Benz, who later lived in Paris, always kept the name Nusch—Bill's name for her—and in 1946 it even appeared in the announcement of her death that was placed in the papers by Paul Éluard.

"... the mechanisms by which money increases and decreases"

In early September 1929—as we have seen—Max was attempting to win the contract for the S.F.B. (free economists') display stand at HYSPA. He set out his ideas in a detailed letter to Fritz Schwarz, the director at the regional office:

"I would very much like to take charge of the design of the S-F-B stand, however, I would require your specifications very soon, so that I could complete it during the time when I have little else to do. At HYSPA I will have quite a number of things to see to and this could work out well for me, I presume that charts will need to be made, which could possibly be used again for a similar purpose at a later date.... I can imagine that there is very little or almost no money to pay for this and, as long I could have a free hand, I would do the work for what would otherwise be described as a poor fee. If my suggestion should prove to be of interest, I could work out more precise details, in the meantime I look forward to hearing from you one way or another and send my best regards, Bill."[690]

In his reply Fritz Schwarz merely asked Max Bill for "suggestions," without directly offering him a contract: "Esteemed Herr Bill, many thanks for your letter. This is our plan: we would like to commission a

689 Max Bill in conversation with Angela Thomas, 30 January 1977

690 Max Bill to the office of the Schweizerischer Freiwirtschaftsbund Bern, Fritz Schwarz (3 September 1930), private archives of Fritz and Elly Schwarz

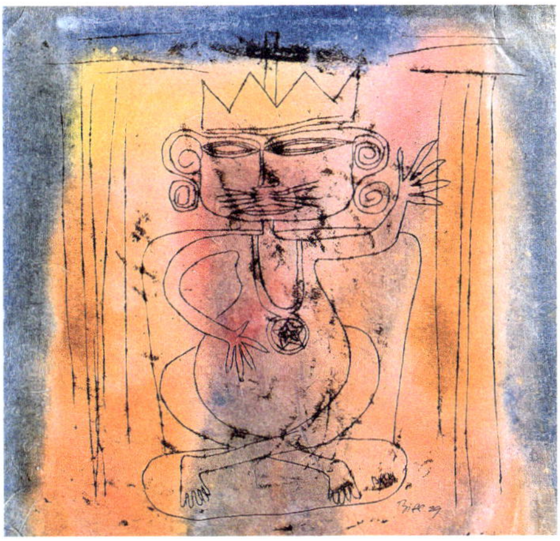

Max Bill, *Der kleine Jammer König,* 1929, india ink over watercolor on Japan paper, 33×34.5 cm

Maria Benz, known as Nusch, ca. 1930

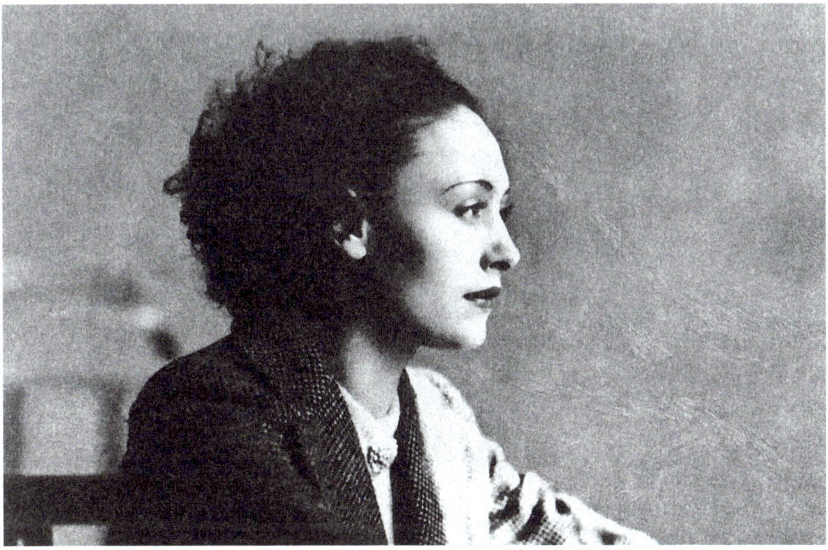

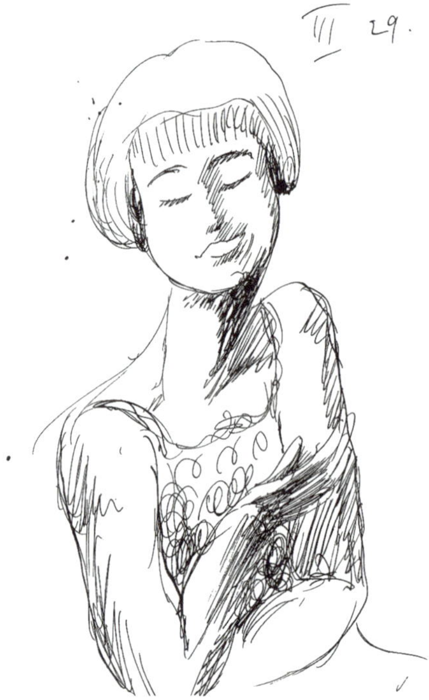

Hanns R. Welti, Untitled (Portrait of Binia Spoerri), March 1929, india ink on paper

Hanns R. Welti, Untitled (Surrealist composition with seven-branch menorah), undated, oil on canvas, 66×72cm

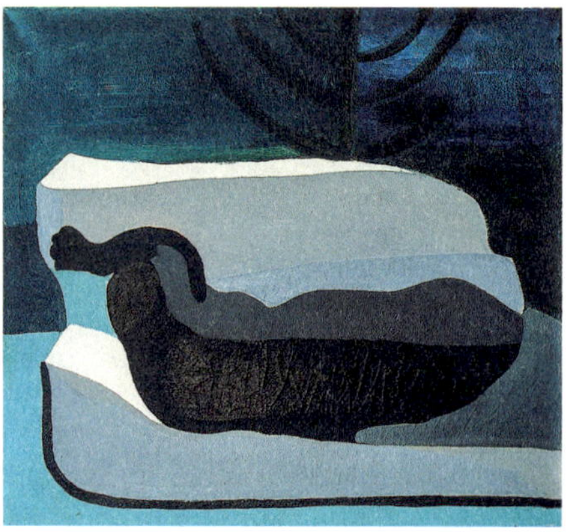

number of devices, which would represent the mechanisms by which money increases and decreases, and the effects of higher or lower interest rates. The idea is that a lever could be used to set interest rates ranging from 0% to 5%. A system of levers would then adjust rents, etc., accordingly.... We have a highly skilled watchmaker here, who will probably help me. If you have any relevant suggestions I would of course be very grateful."[691]

Fritz Schwarz's idea that members of the public could position "the lever" reminds me of Max Bill's later idea of a "millions column" outside the Deutsche Bank headquarters in Frankfurt am Main; he wanted to catch the eye of passers-by and render one million visible—"no one can really imagine a million"—in the form of a column with a million small, colored pieces of enamel. However, the bank decided to install a granite version of Bill's *kontinuität* instead.

Hanns R. Welti and Die Augen

One day in autumn 1929, when preparations were already well under way at Kunsthaus Zürich for the exhibition *Abstrakte und surrealistische Malerei und Plastik,* Max became acquainted with Hanns Welti, a Swiss artist, at Café Odéon in Zurich. It turned out that they were both smarting at not having been invited to participate in that exhibition.

"not only had the pioneers from abroad been invited to participate in the exhibition, they were rounded up to a total of 40 by second-generation pioneers. switzerland was represented, not exactly in keeping with the program, by meyer-amden. they didn't want us."[692]

After closing time Welti—"blond, tall, very eloquent"—and Bill walked back to Bill's lodgings nearby in Stadelhoferstrasse, in what had been the St. Urban monastery.

As it happened, Welti was also a lawyer, "so one evening we sat down together and founded a society"—named Die Augen [The Eyes]. "As far as I recall there were 6 members; besides Hanns Welti and myself I know for sure that they included Willi Eidenbenz, Heiri Steiner, and someone who Hanns Welti always called 'Schwarz' [Black] because—as a

691 Fritz Schwarz, Bern, to Max Bill, Stadelhoferstr. 27, Zurich 1, 11 September 1930, private archives of Fritz and Elly Schwarz

692 Bill 1971, unpaginated

German living in Zurich—he was burdened (and still is) with the name Anton Stankowski, too alien for a Swiss society."[693] Sadly Bill lost his new friend, Hanns Welti, just a few years later, when Welti died at the age of forty in 1934.

The exhibition *Zeitprobleme in der Schweizer Malerei und Plastik* at Kunsthaus Zürich in 1936 only included one stone sculpture (1931) by the late Hanns Welti.

Many years later, in 1960, Bill included Welti's relief *Umschnürtes Holz* (ca. 1928–30) in the exhibition *konkrete kunst 50 jahre entwicklung* that he organized at Helmhaus Zürich; after Max Bill's death this work went to his son Jakob Bill.

Bill designed headed notepaper for one of the society's members, Willi Eidenbenz, with the wording: "atelier hermann reinhold willy eidenbenz, auberg 1 (an der heuwage), basel, telefon 3 04 64, für schrift werbegrafik ausstellungen werbeaktionen reklamefotos industrieaufnahmen architekturaufnahmen reproduktionen portraits reportagen."[694] Clearly Eidenbenz was a man of many talents; his areas of expertise are listed as "typography, advertisement design, exhibitions, advertising campaigns, publicity photographs, industrial photography, reprographics, portraits, reportage." For some reason this business notepaper created by Max Bill for Eidenbenz—presumably in the 1930s, since Eidenbenz moved to Basel in 1933—is not included in *Max Bill: Typography, Advertising, Book Design* (Zurich: Niggli, 1999). In 2008 Willi Eidenbenz's son Florian mentioned that his father had never in fact used the notepaper designed by Max Bill, since he was himself a commercial artist capable of creating his own design.

Another member of the society, Heiri Steiner was married to Bill's former Bauhaus classmate Liesel Träger. And Anton "Schwarz" Stankowski gave his account of the founding of the new society in an interview: "At the time we were planning an exhibition with Bill and six or seven others who wanted to form an artists' group of some kind. I was a member, only not as Stankowski, but as Braun [Brown] because they were Swiss artists. We called ourselves 'Das Auge' [*sic;* 'The eye']. It was only later that the Concretes emerged from that group."[695]

According to Max Bill the group's name was not Das Auge but Die Augen, it was only somewhat later, in the early 1930s, that Anton Stankowski's pseudonym changed to Brun.

693 Bill 1971, unpaginated
694 In the typography estate of Max Bill, collection of Angela Thomas
695 Roth 1991, p. 29
696 Bill 1971, unpaginated

The intention behind the founding of Die Augen—in protest at so many artists not being included in the exhibition *Abstrakte und surrealistische Malerei und Plastik*—was "to bore a hole through the locked Zurich culture wall. But we didn't get anywhere. It soon became clear that our interests were too diverse and our impact was too meager. So there was nothing after the founders' meeting."[696]

It so happens that in March 1929—a few months before Hanns Welti met Max Bill in that autumn of 1929 (when Max Bill and Nusch were already a couple)—Welti had drawn an ink portrait of Binia Spoerri.

This ink portrait (dated "III 29.") is also illustrated in *Hanns R. Welti,* 1971. It was Bill who pointed out to me in 1975 that the girl depicted in this untitled drawing by Welti is in fact Binia Spoerri (see p. 384).

Binia was a good friend of Hanns Welti's sister Lucie, who had studied under Sophie Taeuber at the Kunstgewerbeschule in Zurich. Lucie later married the anarchist writer Adrien Turel, who managed to flee to Switzerland from Berlin in the summer of 1934.

Bill also met Adrien Turel later on.

Hanns and Lucie Welti's father was a long-time member of the Zurich City Council.

Could it be that Bill, still deeply in love with Nusch, crossed paths with Binia in 1929 in Welti's studio? In conversation with me Max only mentioned Binia first really catching his eye some months after he and Nusch had separated; it was "in the summer of 1930" that he saw Binia in the audience at the Krater, the cabaret theater, which he had been associated with since March 1930.

Abstract and Surrealist Paintings and Sculptures

The forty artists selected for the exhibition *Abstrakte und surrealistische Malerei und Plastik* at Kunsthaus Zürich (6 October–3 November 1929) included figures such as Schwitters, Arp, Vantongerloo, Vordemberge-Gildewart, J. Torres-García, Picasso, Pevsner, Mondrian, Moholy-Nagy, Malevich, Lissitzky, Léger, Klee, Kandinsky, Otto Freundlich, Max Ernst, Theo van Doesburg, Brancusi, and Josef Albers. Although Bill, much to his chagrin, was not among their number, he will certainly have gone to see the exhibition.

It may be that Bill knew of Albers's disdain for the work of his fellow-participant in that exhibition in Zurich in 1929, the Dutch artist and De Stijl founder Theo van Doesburg; Albers regarded his work "mechanical decoration." This disdain went back to the period in Weimar when Van Doesburg set up a studio and spoke out against the Bauhaus, which in turn led to a conflict between Van Doesburg and Albers, who later commented: "Van Doesburg wanted to set himself up as the Antichrist. We had right away a clash ... that cruel insistence on just straight lines and right angles. It was for me just mechanical decoration."[697]

In early 1931, not long after that exhibition in Zürich, Van Doesburg died at the age of just 47 in Davos, where he was taking a cure.

Carola Giedion-Welcker described three works by the Romanian sculptor Constantin Brancusi in that exhibition; Brancusi—a man with a rustic, rough hewn demeanor—made his career in Paris. His exhibits in Zurich in 1929 included the smooth, polished bronze *Torse de jeune homme* (1925).[698] Giedion-Welcker, who was present at the exhibition, remembered certain Swiss sculptors mocking Brancusi's work as "kitchen stove magic."[699] One wonders if Bill was drawn to it? Did that gleaming bronze—unbeknownst to Bill—inspire his own use of similarly reflective materials just a few years later in his polished brass *konstruktion mit schwebenden kubus* (1935–36)?

On 30 October 1929 the two "older" artists in the exhibition, Schwitters and Arp—who never stood on ceremony—put on a soirée at the Kunsthaus, which Max made sure not to miss. Schwitters performed part of his formidable *Ursonate* and Arp declaimed some of his own poems. That evening, sensationally, there was also a screening of *Un Chien Andalou,* by Luis Buñuel and Salvador Dalí. Schwitters later described that exhibition at the Kunsthaus as "the first comprehensive, most perfect exhibition." Whenever Kurt Schwitters visited Switzerland he was always a welcome guest in the home of Carola Giedion-Welcker and Sigfried Giedion in Doldertal in Zurich. "Sitting at the head of the table, he would come up with variations on his *Ursonate* for younger

697 Borchardt-Hume 2006, p. 68
698 The sculpture *Torse d'un jeune homme* is illustrated in Giedion-Welcker 1958, fig. 36, p. 95
699 Giedion-Welcker 1958, p. 16
700 Bruderer-Oswald 2004, p. 24
701 See Klaus Völker, "Zürich, wo kein frischer Wind weht ... Carola Giedion-Welcker und die gelebte Historie," *Gazzetta Prolitteris* 2 (Zurich, 2003)
702 Bruderer-Oswald 2004, p. 25

members of the family, or, without further ado, he would repair his fragile *Huthbild* at the dining table."[700] The Giedions had bought Schwitters's *Huthbild* after the exhibition at Kunsthaus Zürich.

Carola Welcker was born in Cologne in 1893. While she was still at university in Munich, studying under the art historian Heinrich Wölfflin, she married Sigfried Giedion, born in Prague in 1888. They both gained their doctorates under Wölfflin's supervision; first Carola with a dissertation on an oddly uncontemporary topic—Bavarian Rococo sculpture—and then a few months later Sigfried (who had only decided to study art history in 1915, having first trained as a mechanical engineer) with a dissertation on Late Baroque and Romantic Classicism. Both dissertations were published in 1922.[701]

This is the same Heinrich Wölfflin who rejected Max Raphael's dissertation "Von Monet zu Picasso." Despite that, it was subsequently published as a book (1919); moreover, at the Bauhaus in Dessau Moholy-Nagy showed the young Bill illustrations of works by Picasso in Raphael's book and took the opportunity to point out to Bill that he should not just be transposing his drawings into larger formats and turning them into paintings; he should also study scale and proportion in Picasso's compositions and learn from that.

On his return to Hanover in 1929 after the Zurich exhibition, Schwitters wrote to the Giedions thanking them for their hospitality: "It is a pity we live so far apart. There is only one single Giedion in the world, and he lives 14 hours away by express train. In all of Germany there is no one who has such an understanding of Merz, with the same degree of love and initiative, as Giedion. Is that not astonishing in a population of 60 million? . . . That exhibition in Zurich was the first comprehensive, most perfect exhibition, and it shows what important things grow on art in our world."[702]

In later years Bill would occasionally come into contact with the Giedions, who lived in Zurich at 7 Doldertal, albeit he saw them only in passing because the Giedions, who became Swiss citizens in 1937, moved in rather different social circles to Bill.

"Maybe when there is individual freedom, each person will be his own artist"

In November 1929, not long before his twenty-first birthday, Bill showed works of his own for a month in his lodgings in Stadelhoferstrasse. Somewhat surprisingly, there were no works by Hanns Welti included in that exhibition, although the two friends had so recently shared their annoyance at not having been invited to participate in the exhibition *Abstrakte und surrealistische Malerei und Plastik* at Kunsthaus Zürich. In taking the initiative and putting on his first-ever solo exhibition in Switzerland, Max Bill, like his uncle Ernst Geiger before him, was following in the old tradition of artists inviting interested parties to their studios.

Bill's first studio exhibition, *malerei und grafik,* at Stadelhoferstrasse 27 in Zurich, ran from 1 November to 1 December 1929 and was open daily between 10–12 a.m. and 2–4 p.m (see *Das Werk* 16:11 [1929], p. XI).

Having already realized the importance of light and sources of light as a student at the Bauhaus, Max only showed his work in daylight. He of course designed his own invitation cards: an idiosyncratic typographic design on monochrome gray with an eye-catching profile of a woman with shoulder-length hair. Bill sent one of those invitation cards to Hilde Rantzsch—his former classmate at the Bauhaus—who had also been a member of Group Z, which Bill and Fischli founded in Dessau. Hilde thanked him with an eight-page letter written in a variety of colored pencils: "Your invitation card looks good. Was it a success?"[703]

Might Hilde's letter have arrived on 22 December 1929, on Max's twenty-first birthday? Hilde, who was urgently seeking work, asked Max if he knew of anything for her. She mentioned paintings of her own and told him about what she herself and her friend Myriam Manuckiam had been doing; she also passed on the latest news about other former members of Group Z in Dessau. Her letter is thus a useful source of information as to the make-up of that group, which in fact never achieved financial success.

The companion named as Manoukian in Rantzch's letter was in fact Myriam Manuckiam. A photograph by Grit Kallin-Fischer shows Hilde and Myriam, with their heads close together, in or around 1927

703 Hilde Rantzsch, Dessau, to Max Bill [November or December 1929], Bibliothek Max Bill

704 Hilde Rantzsch, Dessau, to Max Bill [November or December 1929], Bibliothek Max Bill

(the original is in the Bauhaus-Archiv, Berlin; illustrated in Fiedler and Feierabend 1999, p. 518).

"Bill, I spent three months in Switzerland in the Valais with Manoukian [*sic*]. We lived like savages. Now Manoukian has gone to Palukka [*sic*]. . . . I've come back to the Bauhaus. There have been cuts since here. I've worked piles of new pictures into two beautiful tapestries and am living on other people's kindness. . . . I showed my work at the non-selective exhibition in Berlin but not a single sucker bought anything. Merde. . . . Bill, I will send you some paintings in early January. By then I will have them back from a selling exhibition in Nuremberg. Are you also thinking about doing oil paintings? I've sent various watercolors—tweaked to look like applied-arts designs—to companies that I am naïve enough to imagine employing me. I can't get round to painting anything new because I'm entirely taken up looking for a job, making embroidered evening bags and bric-a-brac of that sort. Throwing up three times a day is the most I can do. Such a shitty attitude as in this institute [the Bauhaus], where according to the brochure things are supposed to be so *menschlich,* so social. Merde . . ."

In that same letter—parts of which have already been quoted earlier here—Hilde also gives detailed accounts of other former Bauhaus students: "Janosch is in Stuttgart designing evening wear. Address: Stuttgartkannstadt, Olgastrasse 37. . . . Schawinsky is in Berlin studying to be a film director. . . . Sepp sends greetings. He's in a poor way again because he believes he has to play the Communist. That's all for Group Z."

Bill may have asked for this information in view of an exhibition that he wanted to organize. It has not been possible to establish who the names "Janosch" and "Sepp" refer to.

But she also exhorts Bill: "Keep busy. You can be sure I'll send my paintings. When is [Willi] Eidenbenz coming to Dessau?"[704] After her "savage" time in the Valais, Hilde Rantzsch—having almost despaired of ever finding employment—did then work in Gunta Stölzl's studio in Zurich in 1933–34—possibly with Bill's help, or possibly having made direct contact with her former teacher at the Bauhaus. There is no trace of her anywhere after that.

In the winter semester of 1929 Hilde Rantzsch attended the weaving workshop at the Bauhaus in Dessau and in 1930, along with other weaving students, participated in the *Ausstellung moderner Bildwirkereien* (a touring exhibition of modern weaving and tapestry) curated by Dr. Ludwig Grote.

There is no more information on Hilde Rantzsch in the Bauhaus-Archiv, Berlin, or the Archiv Stiftung Bauhaus Dessau.

Years later, on a visit to Leipzig (Rantzsch's place of birth) in August 1988, I was present when Bill asked if anyone knew if Hilde Rantzsch had survived the Second World War. But once again no one had any information. However, during that same visit, when Bill's *grafische reihen* were being exhibited at the Leipzig museum, he was able to make contact again after many years with the dancer Gret Palucca, with whom he chatted delightedly on the telephone.

In late 1929 Max Bill was not as accomplished an artist as he imagined and in reality his work was not yet on a par with that of the great abstract and Surrealist works on show at Kunsthaus Zürich. It seems that he was known to his friends as a surrealist at that time, and in his letter to Sigfried Giedion he described himself—possibly somewhat opportunistically—as "a Surrealist painter." And there is an interesting note from a friend who visited his studio exhibition at Stadelhoferstrasse: "Dear Bill, So, your exhibition is lovely, and you are also a nice fellow. As long as your heart never turns as surrealist as your paintings, I will always be as fond of you as I am now. With best wishes ..." Unfortunately the pencil signature on the back of Bill's invitation card is illegible.[705]

The Surrealists' depictions of "chance encounters between two totally unrelated objects in an improbable location" drew inspiration from the Comte de Lautréamont's prose poem *Les Chants de Maldoror* (1869). Although there is no saying whether Bill himself ever saw that book, there is evidence that it was read by Félix Vallotton; before long Bill would be able to measure his work against that of Vallotton in the exhibition that opened at Kunsthalle Bern on 15 June 1930.

Vallotton suffered from long bouts of depression and it was his friend and mentor Charles Maurin (ten years older than Vallotton) who alerted him to the *Chants de Maldoror* with its "vision of the bourgeois interiors as a place of terror." This, at least, was the conclusion drawn by the literary scholar Peter Bürger, who—as he himself put it—had "the intuition" to see Vallotton as a "proto-Surrealist artist."[706]

705 The invitation card is in the typography estate of Max Bill, collection of Angela Thomas

706 Peter Bürger, "Verfremdung des Schreckens—wie Félix Vallotton vom detailversessenen Realisten zum boshaften Kritiker der bürgerlichen Welt wurde," in *Neue Zürcher Zeitung*, 12–13 April 2008

707 "Atelierausstellung Max Bill Zürich," *Das Werk* 16:11 (November 1929), p. XV

708 In Schaub and Teubner 2003, p. 462

It may be that Bill's sense of injustice at not being included in the Kunsthaus exhibition in fact made him mature faster than hitherto, as he became ever more determined to "belong' in that group of leading artists—and to face the artistic competition on the international stage. His studio exhibition *Malerei und Grafik* was in fact reviewed by Walter Kern: "Klee and Arp are notable influences. Lucid invention, taking no account of nature, is captured emblematically." And Kern quotes an astonishing statement by the young Max Bill: "He himself says that 'maybe when there is individual freedom, each person will be his own artist.'"[707] Having spent his time at the Bauhaus seeking "clarity," now—thrown back on his own resources—Bill had a sudden flash of inspiration and articulated an idea that Joseph Beuys would formulate in very similar terms four decades later in connection with his notion of "social plastic." And as to Bill's own struggle for individual freedom—above all with regard to his father—it only became all the more intense in the coming months. But after that extreme conflict, Max Bill did in fact start to carve out a path to his own, entirely individual art.

"That's life"—Patron of the Arts: Max Wassmer

It was around 1929 that Max Bill met Max Wassmer, who lived at Schloss Bremgarten near Bern. As it happens, Wassmer had been among the small circle of friends—which also included Emmy Ball-Hennings and Hugo Ball—who were invited to celebrate the writer Hermann Hesse's birthday in Montagnola on 2 July 1927.

"Agnuzzo, 11 June 1927, Emmy, my darling, . . . I have to say Hesse is a little concerned whether you will be back for his birthday—you know what he is like. Emmy has to be there. He just wants a small circle around him. Mrs. Dolbin is coming . . . it's just three weeks away, and sister Adele is coming. And maybe also the Wassmers from Schloss Bremgarten. He himself, Hesse, has often talked about a book lately, the two heroes will be called Goldmund and Narziss. He wants to set it in the legendary era of Byzantium . . ."[708]

Ball had recently compiled and published an illustrated biography of Hermann Hesse. The two men were good friends and used the familiar "Du" in conversation and letters, whereas Ball and his former Dada colleague, Jean Arp, maintained a certain distance at that time and addressed each other using the more formal "Sie." Sadly, Hugo Ball was not able to attend that party; he fell ill before Hesse's birthday and died in September 1927 in hospital in Zurich.

Was it through his patron Max Wassmer that Max Bill met the writer Hermann Hesse? They did certainly get to know each other. Bill once told me that Hesse had asked him for advice regarding the kind of education his son Heiner Hesse should receive. Bill and Heiner Hesse were in touch later on, as sponsors for the Longo Maï cooperative in Provence.

In April 1929 Wassmer promised the young Max Bill that he would find an opportunity for him to exhibit his work. He told Bill that he would put the idea to Kunsthalle Bern first, and continued, "if I do manage that, you must of course come here & and naturally we would hope you stay with us." He also had some words of comfort for the impatient, young artist: "That's life: one day of Bauhaus, one night at a joyous masked ball & many weeks struggle for one's ideals & daily bread.... with warm regards, yours, Max Wassmer."[709]

The potential exhibition at Kunsthalle Bern did indeed take place, only a year later, from 15 June–13 July 1930. A personal invitation card that Bill sent out for this exhibition had the same motif (a female head) that he had used for his solo exhibition at Stadelhoferstrasse, albeit now printed in green rather than gray.

Max Wassmer, Bill's first real patron, was not only an art collector, he was also the general manager of France's largest and most modern cement factory. In Max Bill's typography estate there is a flyer publicising the construction of the cement factory in Héming (Alsace, France), which started in late 1928 and is seen in a photograph taken a year later in November 1929. The caption under the image reads notes that this is a view of the Héming factory under construction: "partie de l'usine à Héming en construction (novembre 1929)."

Since Bill's efforts to secure advertising contracts were greatly helped by his girlfriend Nusch at the time, who had a charming manner with potential clients, and since she also provided any translations into French—as in this case for the flyer for the cement factory—it is fair to assume that Bill's patron Wassmer will also have met Nusch. And no doubt the Wassmers were well aware of Bill's turbulent love story. With his services as a commercial artist increasingly in demand, Max Bill was starting to feel more optimistic; this particularly comes through in a letter to his father in late January 1930: "Thanks to my work for Wassmer I feel that I will soon be in a position to live independently, if I am supported by 'Nusch,'

709 Max Wassmer to Max Bill, Zurich, 15 April 1929, Bibliothek Max Bill

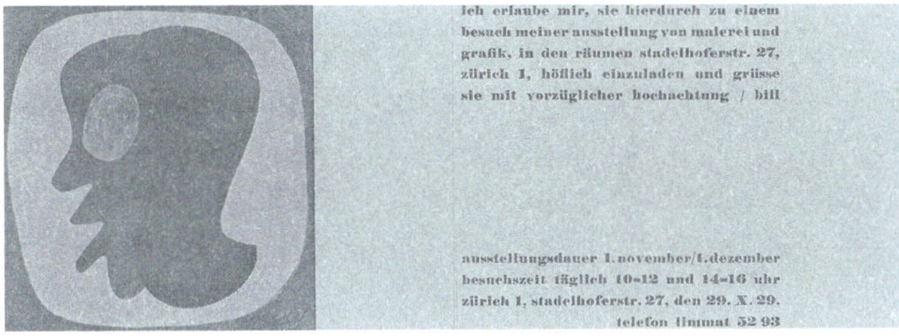

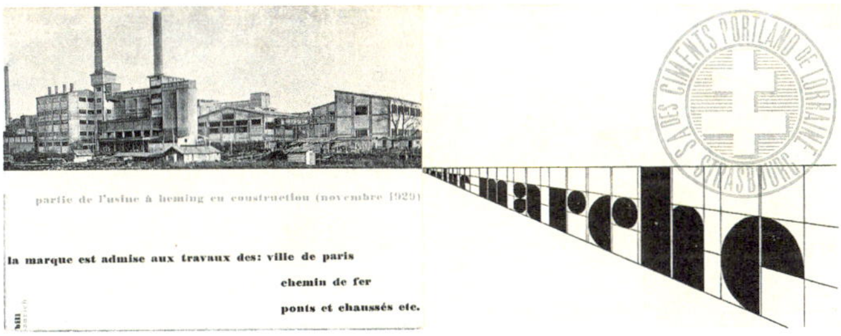

Max Bill, Invitation card for the exhibition *malerei und grafik,* 1 November–1 December 1929, 1929

Max Bill, "l'usine marche," 1929, Pamphlet for SA des Ciments Portland de Lorraine, Strasbourg, 13.8 × 20.8 cm (opened out)

Ernst Geiger, *Dame im Wald,* 1913, oil on canvas, 46 × 38 cm

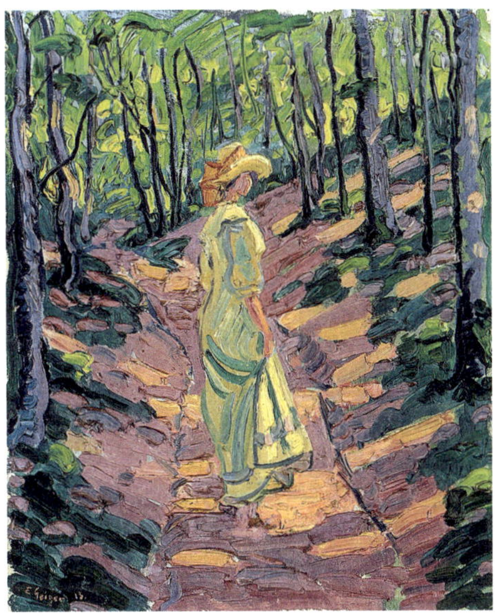

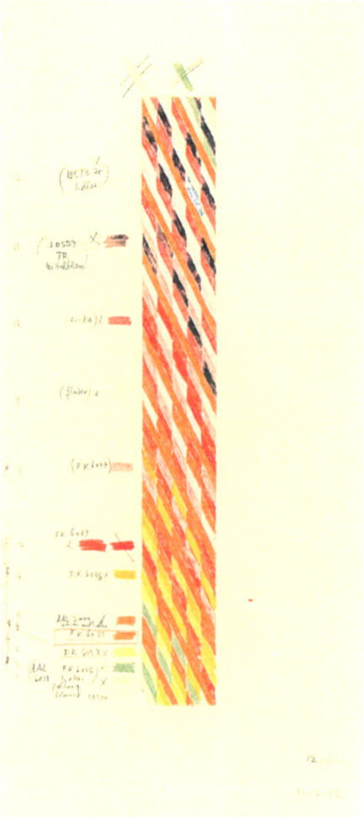

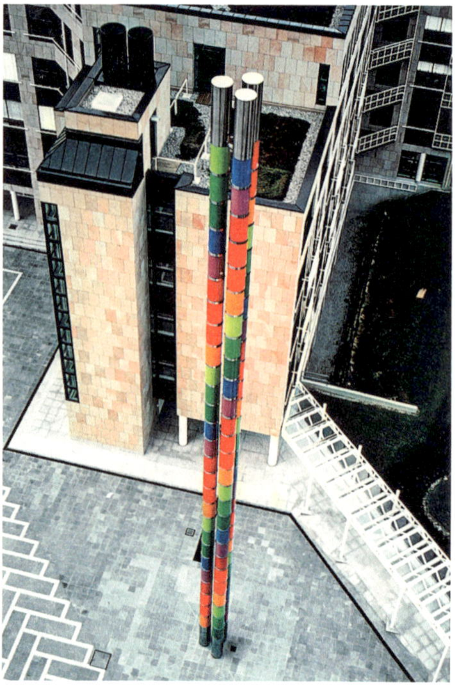

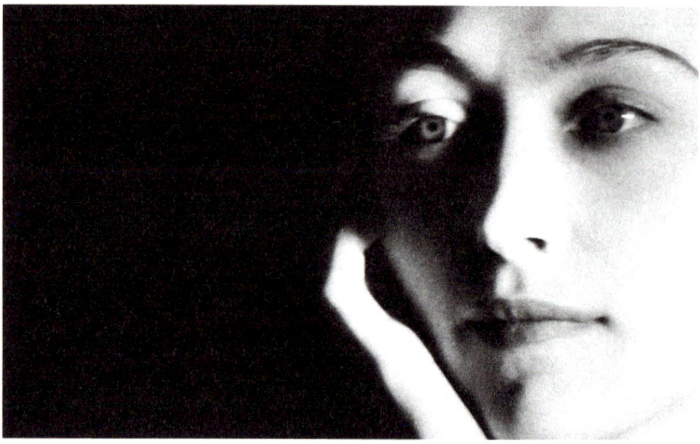

Max Bill, Sketch for *farbsäule,* 1982, colored pencil on paper, 59.5 × 26 cm

Angela Thomas, Max Bill, *gruppe von drei farbsäulen,* 1987–89, enamel and chrome steel mounted on a steel core, height 32 m

Maria Benz, known as Nusch

as I have christened my future wife, things will also soon work elsewhere, and in any case living together is cheaper than living alone."[710]

À propos saving money: In early 1930 Max received an ironically droll letter from the architect Hans Schmidt in Basel, who maybe knew of his financial straits: "Dear Max Bill, these days people only become famous (and poss. rich) through books. So grasp the following opportunity: the Stuttgart architects—perhaps known to you—the Rasch brothers, Paulinenstr. 3, Stuttgart, are publishing a book on modern typography. . . . If you've got anything suitable, please send it directly to the above address . . . with a note of your approximate age (!), . . . Yours, Hans Schmidt."[711]

Ernst Geiger Steps in Again

Bill's uncle, Ernst Geiger, was also always prepared to step in on Max's behalf. As we have already seen, in July 1929, when his nephew was back from the Bauhaus, he selected just three illustrations—all by Max Bill—for his text "Die Radierung." Perhaps Geiger wanted to assist his nephew's re-entry into Switzerland and Swiss society. Before long, however, Bill would no longer need such affectionately well-meaning gestures; and it would soon become clear that his artistic talent far outstripped that of his beloved uncle.

In the paintings dating to the first phase of Ernst Geiger's creative life, the trunks of the trees are strikingly nuanced in their coloration. It may be that Bill—consciously or subconsciously recalling those subtleties in his uncle's paintings—in fact paraphrased that feature later on. If we were to isolate one of Geiger's polychromatic tree trunks, we would be left with a three-dimensional object painted in a variety of colors—an object that in fact looks very much as if it is "related" (in both senses of the word) to Max Bill's multicolored *bild-säule* sculptures.

710 Max Bill, Zurich, to Erwin Bill, Winterthur, 31 January 1930, Archiv Max Bill

711 Hans Schmidt, Artaria & Schmidt Architekten Basel, Bureau Grenzacherstr. 32, to Max Bill, Zurich, Stadelhoferstrasse 27, 17 January 1930, Bibliothek Max Bill

"... for the purpose of their imminent wedding"

In early 1930 decisions taken by the local authorities put Max Bill under pressure and he had to react swiftly and responsibly. On 31 January 1930 Maria Benz—Nusch—received an "urgent" communication from the cantonal aliens office (issued on 27 January 1930) ordering her to "collect her passport" and leave the country by 3 February 1930; the reasons for her expulsion were that "Fräulein Maria Benz" could not demonstrate "any proper reason for her stay ... and the unlawful circumstances of her presence in Zurich cannot be tolerated."

In those days, and for many years to come, cohabitation was prohibited by law in Zurich.

The official papers of the Magistrates Court state that Maria Benz, "actress," had been living with Max Bill at Stadelhoferstrasse 27 in Zurich 1 "since December 1929." In view of the fact that she had not immediately registered and lodged her papers "in keeping with the law" at the relevant district office but had waited until January 1930, the young foreigner was "charged" and received notice from the Magistrates Court that she had to pay a fine of "twenty francs ... which, on non-receipt, will become 2 days imprisonment."[712] On the registration document stamped by District Office 1 of the City of Zurich, the young woman had given her occupation as "artiste."

That same day Max Bill and Nusch submitted a joint written appeal against her expulsion to the Zurich office of the canton of Zürich council, with a copy to the cantonal aliens office, on the grounds that "Maria Benz is currently visiting the co-signatory Max Bill for the purpose of their imminent wedding, and the necessary marriage papers will be submitted to the relevant authority within the next few days."[713]

As a foreigner Nusch would only receive a Swiss passport and work permit if she married a Swiss citizen.

712 Office of the Police Magistracy of the City of Zurich, 27 January 1930

713 Letter sent on 31 January 1930 to the "Tit. Regierungsrat" of the canton of Zürich, hand-signed by Bill and Maria Benz, Bibliothek Max Bill

714 Max Bill, Zurich, to Erwin Bill, Winterthur, 31 January 1930, Archiv Max Bill

715 Erwin Bill, Winterthur, to Max Bill, Zurich, 4 February 1930, Archiv Max Bill

716 Erwin Bill to Max Bill, 4 February 1930

So Max Bill and Maria Benz, born on 21 June 1906 in Mulhouse, wanted to marry. That same day, Max also wrote in some haste to his father: "Dear Father, on Sunday I will come to visit you in Winterthur with my bride and hope you will not be too surprised ... since we have known each other for six months now [which would mean they met in late July or early August] and have always got on very well.... She has also worked for me and will only be able to continue to do so in Switzerland if she becomes a Swiss citizen."[714]

Erwin Bill Turns Off the Money Tap

In the midst of the turmoil of officialese and impossible deadlines, an unyielding reply came from Erwin Bill, dated 4 February 1930, in which he in effect blamed Max for demonstrating the same "weakness of character" as his mother: "You ought to have seen in your mother a cautionary example of how not to behave if you do not wish to fall out with the entire world." And there were more rebukes to come: "In neither of your letters do you happen to mention the name of your bride-to-be, what she is, where she comes from, her age, etc., as one ought to do! Make no mistake, I will address your wife by her correct name, not as 'Nusch.'"[715]

Toward the end of this harsh letter, Erwin Bill addressed the awkward subject of his son's finances: "Last year, when I yet again allowed myself to be persuaded to provide substantial support for you until March of this year, I hoped that this would allow you to establish a good existence and that if you were thrifty and reliable, you would be able to pay back the capital. Once again, the warning voices were right. I cannot imagine that this business with your marriage etc. will end well. It is a regrettable, sorry tale ... and the fact that you have absolutely no idea how to live frugally is evident from the latest invoice from Gebr. Scholl. I have suspended your account there & will only reinstate it, if at all, once I have heard from you to my satisfaction."[716]

The circumstances of Nusch's expulsion strongly suggest that she and Bill were denounced. Things moved very quickly: when Erwin Bill's letter arrived, Nusch was evidently no longer in Switzerland. The documentation confirming that "Benz, Maria, Artiste" had moved out of Stadelhoferstrasse on 3 February 1930 also indicates that she moved to Strasbourg. And it seems she really did leave the country, as Max informed his enraged father by return of post: "Dear Father, ... since you will not now see Nusch before we marry because she has been expelled by the immigration authorities, because she worked for me ... I am enclosing a photograph, although she does look somewhat younger on the photograph because she is laughing and because of the artificial lighting, the photograph was taken for a Grieder advertising campaign ..."[717]

Rather oddly, in that same letter he gives Nusch's occupation as "nurse"; he also lets his father know that he would potentially be in Strasbourg during the coming week "because of the cement"—when, as we may assume, he would be able to see Nusch again. He goes on to say that he is "sure" now that his "plans will work" ... "because Wassmer is completely on my side. We regularly take lunch together when he is here in Zurich, and we address each other as 'Du,' although he is well over forty, at least that's what I would say.... I also do believe that I can and will return the capital to you that you have always put at my disposal, albeit not immediately from the first funds that come into my hands because money only accrues where there is already money, but I would gladly add interest to the capital until such time as I pay.... It would greatly ease my work if you could allow me the Scholl account and living expenses up until March."[718]

But then his already complicated situation took a turn for the worse: "Dear Max, once again you have succeeded in deceiving me and pulling the wool over my eyes in your own wretched way. The cruellest name for that would not be enough. You are driving me to despair and into an early grave.... The photograph of the soubrette, the harlot Maria Benz, whom you have chosen as your wife, is herewith returned. I now understand that you of course intentionally sought to keep her name from me ... I would at the very least be justified in calling you a common scoundrel and in ordering you to keep out of my sight for ever more."[719]

Erwin Bill had evidently made inquiries regarding Max's bride-to-be Maria Benz and, even after some time had passed, was still openly aggressive. When a man wants to slander a woman, what is more effective than to call her a "strumpet"?

However, Erwin Bill also added that if he were to "pick up the pieces" for his son again, then it would only be on the following "conditions": that "you immediately give up your present lodgings and rent a room for no more than 60–65 francs per month.... If your room is found

717 Max Bill, Zurich, to Erwin Bill, Winterthur, 4 February 1930, Archiv Max Bill
718 Max Bill to Erwin Bill, 4 February 1930
719 Erwin Bill, Winterthur, to Max Bill, Zurich, 16 March 1930, Archiv Max Bill
720 Max Bill to Erwin Bill, 16 March 1930

by me or anyone else to be in a state of disorder, you can expect the worst. You should only enter inns in entirely exceptional circumstances and you should no longer frequent the Odéon in Zurich at all."[720]

Bill's considerable financial difficulties were thus exacerbated by this extreme conflict with his father. Max was still a very young man, still finding out about himself, and now had to decide whether to marry Nusch or not. And it was not only his father who was opposed to the idea, Max Wassmer—Max's mentor and patron—was also against it.

A Meeting with Nusch in Café Aubette

When Max Bill traveled to Strasbourg with Max Wassmer in March 1930 (he had already designed a "cement logo" for Wassmer's firm), he soon headed for Café Aubette to see the interiors that Sophie Taeuber-Arp and her husband Jean Arp had worked on there from January 1927 to January 1929.

By this point the Arps had acquired French citizenship, so Hans Arp now used the first name Jean.

However, on his arrival Bill was horrified to discover that just a year after its completion the interior of the café was already seriously neglected: the stylized figures that Jean Arp had painted on the walls of the cabaret dance hall were now adorned with kitschy decorations painted on paper, and the spacious "ciné-dancing" designed by Theo van Doesburg was no longer in use.

It was also here in the Aubette—in this dispiriting shadow of what had so recently been an avant-garde interior—that Max and Nusch met again. They finally abandoned the idea of marriage, and Max gave Nusch "a financial settlement from Wassmer." Nusch, who had in any case found Zurich too straitlaced, now moved to Paris where she sat for leading artists. Dora Maar and Man Ray photographed her, and she became friends with Dora Maar; she modeled for Greta Knutson-Tzara (the Swedish wife of the former Dadaist Tristan Tzara) and posed several times for Pablo Picasso, who was very taken with her (see p. 430).

"You must immediately abandon your boastful, loud-mouthed attitude ..."

Erwin Bill now decided not to transfer money directly to his son any longer, but to have it administered for him in Zurich by a certain Gotthard Schuh: "I will, for the moment, still provide funds for your room and for the thrifty use of the necessary work materials; however, in future you will only have access to these funds with the agreement of Herr Schuh and following his scrutiny of your invoices." Just a few years older than Max and a highly skilled photographer, Schuh was from one of the families that had created the company Sprecher & Schuh in the canton of Aargau.

Erwin Bill may have met Gotthard Schuh through his brother-in-law, Ernst Geiger, or through Adolf Weibel, given that Schuh himself was a member of the Aarau section of the GSMBA at the time and "had repeatedly exhibited in Aarau between 1925 and 1930"; initially active as a painter, Schuh only "later became a leading Swiss photographer." Heiny Widmer describes Schuh's paintings as "dark-toned interiors with strongly planar figures."[721]

Max later told me that his newly appointed "financial administrator" Gotthard Schuh mainly painted at that time and was not yet very involved in photography, and he quite candidly added that Schuh had "influenced his style, albeit only for a short time."

As if appointing a financial guardian for his son were not enough, Erwin Bill still continued to chivvy him: "In the evenings you must go to bed at a reasonable hour and rise early the next morning, so that you can diligently and strenuously work for at least 8 hours per day. And if you lack the contracts to fill this time, you still have more than enough to achieve in your own self-education. You must, broadly speaking, become a decent man again, and you must not be conspicuous in your attire. I want to hear nothing more of you consorting with dubious women folk. You must immediately abandon your boastful, loud-mouthed attitude both in private and in your business dealings."[722]

721 Widmer 1974, p. 123
722 Erwin Bill to Max Bill, 16 March 1930
723 Erwin Bill, Winterthur, to Max Bill, Zurich, 18 March 1930, Archiv Max Bill
724 Max Bill, Zurich, to Erwin Bill, Winterthur 21 March 1930, Archiv Max Bill
725 Erwin Bill, Winterthur, to Max Bill, Zurich 26 March 1930, Archiv Max Bill
726 See Thomas 1983, p. 40

Max, who must have felt humiliated by this, did try to resist certain conditions but Erwin Bill refused to negotiate and merely reiterated his demands, loud and clear: "Dear Max! I will not tolerate any objections. You are no longer to frequent the Odéon and that is final."[723] Ever since the First World War, making an appearance in Café Odéon was a must for any self-respecting political émigrés and artists living in Zurich. Besides a pastry counter and six "precision billiards tables" on the first floor, anyone reading the local and foreign newspapers that were laid out so invitingly in the Odéon might also glance past them to see some of the most beautiful women in the city. The Odéon had the kind of ambience that was otherwise only found in Paris. Since Max was now at a financial disadvantage, he remorsefully gave in and drew up a list, as requested by his father, in which he restated the latter's demands, including "3. Cessation of visits to the Odéon" and "4. Submission of a cash book for inspection by Gotthard Schuh."[724]

And yet his father's reproaches and threats still came thick and fast: "If you do not at last completely and enduringly cast off your old ways, your perfunctory, unreliable demeanor, your rash behavior, and your intermittent sheer idleness ... then I have no option other than to refuse to cover your numerous debts." In addition, Max's father was "in despair" at the "slipshod, slovenly way" his son worked: "What kind of an impression must it make on any reputable businessman when your correspondence is so flawed?"[725]

A similar tale of financial intervention by an artist's father occurred in the Schwitters family. In 1923 Kurt Schwitters and his family spent their summer holidays on the Baltic island of Rügen, where they were joined by Sophie Taeuber-Arp and Jean Arp (who had married in October 1922 in Pura in the Ticino) and the Dada artist Hannah Höch from Berlin. Sophie was very taken by "Merz-Schwitters"—a large, fantastic figure chasing through the woods on the hunt for mushrooms and bellowing his sound poems like a sea monster. She also wrote to her sister that old Mr. Schwitters always bought the provisions, with the result "that we have to be very frugal." Indeed, the artist's very authoritarian father had taken charge of everyone's money, because he thought artists couldn't manage money. Even Jean Arp had submitted to this humiliation, probably out of solidarity with the "Merz-Schwitters."[726]

Despite his father's treating him like a child and despite the emotional strain of having had to part with Nusch, Max did also have moments of triumph. Some weeks after Gotthard Schuh had become a member of the Rot-Blau artists' association in Basel, Max Bill was also accepted as a member—as he reported to his father: "Yesterday I was officially accepted into Rot-Blau (after Schuh, a few weeks ago) and will now have certain exhibition opportunities that are very advantageous for me, for instance I am now a member of the Salon des surindépendants in Paris and can exhibit there without going through the selection committee. At the moment I am working on an exhibition stand to promote trade and on a cover design for the Swiss Export Address Book in 4 languages. It's nice work ... warm regards, also to Aunt Lina."[727]

Max later told me that Gotthard Schuh had invited him to his home for lunch several times and that Schuh had often taken him as a pillion passenger on bike trips through Switzerland. And soon the two of them could both be seen on the cabaret stage at the Krater in Zurich. Schuh and Bill, both fun-loving and ready to enjoy themselves, evidently had quite a relaxed relationship, which of course did little to instil the kind of self-discipline into Max that his father had evidently hoped for.

Mounting Debts

It seems that Max Bill had amassed very considerable debts by this time, because at least some of his effects were seized in lieu of payment. Despite his displeasure, Erwin Bill again sought to find a way out of the situation: "You must, in writing, transfer into my ownership the items that were seized and anything else that could be seized, including the typewriter ... so that these cannot be seized again.... As repayment for the 50 francs that Aunt Lina paid to redeem those items from the Kunstgewerbeschule, she would like to have the brass jug [made by Max Bill] or, if it is no longer in your possession, the copper jug. Make the necessary arrangements for this with Aunt Lina on your next visit. I hope you will always work hard now and be a man in every respect, even if Schuh is not there. When you come, bring your cash book with you. Warm regards Aunt Lina & y. Father."[728] Going to see his father would not have cost Max anything because he still had free travel on Swiss trains as the son of a former railway official.

727 Max Bill, Zurich, to Erwin Bill, Winterthur, 21 March 1930
728 Erwin Bill, Winterthur, to Max Bill, Zurich, 12 April 1930, Archiv Max Bill
729 Erwin Bill, Winterthur, to Max Bill, Zurich, 15 May 1930, Archiv Max Bill
730 Erwin Bill, Winterthur, to Max Bill, Zurich, 23 May 1930, Archiv Max Bill
731 Hausenstein 1921, pp. 83, 88

In mid-May 1930 Erwin Bill wrote to Max to let him know that "the debt certificate dated 1 February 1929, to the value of 7,525 francs"[729] was now null and void. A note, in Max's hand, next to those figures, reads "now: 11455.– fr."; his father had evidently cleared a very substantial debt for Max. Despite everything, it seems that Erwin and Lina still wanted to see Max in Winterthur, only he rarely visited them, as Erwin Bill pointed out in yet another letter: "In the last three months you have not once found the time to come here."[730]

Despite his financial travails, in 1930 Bill purchased Wilhelm Hausenstein's book on Paul Klee (published in 1929): *Kairuan oder eine Geschichte vom Maler Klee und von der Kunst dieses Zeitalters* (Munich: Kurt-Wolff). Kairouan (Tunisia) was "founded in 670 by Oqba ibn Nafi. The Muslims regarded Kairouan as one of the four gates to Paradise. Europeans had always been prohibited from entering the city, until it was entered in 1881 by French conquistadors exercising their rights of conquest. Since then the flag fluttering above the battlements in Kairouan had been the most fiery of all European flags: the blue, white, and red tricolor. The artist Klee painted it glowing brightly amid rust reds and pale mustard yellows, cutting into the endlessness of the Orient."

Paul Klee made his legendary trip to Tunisia in 1914 with two fellow painters, Louis Moilliet and August Macke. "In March 1916 Marc, the painter, was killed in action. A week later Klee was called up. On his return from Kairouan he was recruited into the infantry."[731]

It is almost impossible to imagine the full extent of the stark cultural shock that awaited Paul Klee when he returned from the bright sunlight of Tunisia to the darkness of Germany in the First World War and to the suffering of the war-wounded.

Like his role model, the "draftsman-painter" and violinist Klee, Bill—who played cello and banjo—also especially admired the music of J. S. Bach and Handel.

The Krater in Zurich

The Krater—a cabaret theater—was founded in Zurich in 1928. The architects Ernst F. Burckhardt and his wife Elsa Burckhardt-Blum, and Elsa's twin brother, the musician Robert Blum were among its most active members. The Krater, which Bill described as having a "semi-political program," was the precursor to two more cabaret theaters—the Pfeffermühle in Munich and Cabaret Cornichon in Zurich.

The Krater was a combination of cabaret and studio theater. The aims and ethos were somewhat idealistic: "The set up was not in the slightest commercial. It was only after Cornichon that cabaret artists started to make money; at the Krater people lost money. Let alone not being paid, the main players were even expected to make considerable financial sacrifices. It was very much an experimental, avant-garde theater, which gaily proceeded from one daring experiment to the next."[732]

The very first Krater evening took place on 3 November 1928 in an attic studio at Freiestrasse 56 in Zürich-Hottingen. Among the performers on that occasion were the composer Robert Blum (who had studied under Ferruccio Busoni in Berlin, along with the composer Wladimir Vogel), the actor Emil Hegetschweiler, and the dancer Suzanne Perrottet, a free-thinking, very modern woman who had already performed at Cabaret Voltaire when Zurich was going through its Dada phase. The review in the *Tages-Anzeiger* described the Krater event as a "production with social implications."[733] At a Krater evening in 1929 the French writer Jean-Paul Samson—a Krater member living in Zurich, who would subsequently become an ally of Bill's—presented "some poets writing in the French language." The reviews were very favorable.

Although there is no knowing if Max Bill looked in on that first Krater evening, the timing means it is perfectly possible. He had recently left the Bauhaus and only returned to Dessau "toward the end of November 1928," where he remained until December 1928, and where there were still invoices to be settled.

Suzanne Perrottet later described being asked by the composer Robert Blum if she would like to take part in a cabaret evening. "They were setting up a studio theater and wanted to have me on the artistic advisory panel, but I was also to be on stage. There were people there would became famous later on, above all Emil Hegetschweiler (actor and cabaret artiste), Jakob Bührer (writer) and Trudi Schoop, who had a special gift for mime.

732 Paul Lang, "Die Kleinkunstbühne 'Der Krater' (Zurich 1928–30)," 1 December 1955, Schweizerisches Cabaret-, Chanson- und Pantomimen-Archiv (SCCPA)
733 *Tages-Anzeiger,* 8 November 1928
734 Suzanne Perrottet [1989/90], p. 203
735 EH., in *Tages-Anzeiger,* 27 June 1929
736 In *Neue Zürcher Zeitung,* 4 July 1929
737 Letter to the members of the programming committee, signed by Dr. Paul Lang, president of Der Krater, 16 March 1930, estate of Ernst F. Burckhardt

The first show was on 3 November; in one number, it was called *The Bear,* I had to play a strumpet—just mime and dance. I had to do two dances . . . in the second dance I had to entice a swain, simulating subtle physical excitement to beguile him, flatter him—never letting him out of my eyes—capture him. I enter deeper and deeper into a trance, steadily intensifying my actions, until he stands up. Filled with wild desire I leap on him with my claws bared. That second dance in particular was a huge success."[734]

"J. P. Samson is known as fine communicator of French poetry, so there was a small but very attentive audience for his evening recital at the Krater. . . . This intimate event was graced with a sophisticated musical framework supplied by the elegant pianism of Milly Schweizer, who put her artistry at the service of Ravel, Debussy, and Honegger."[735] "Samson's reading, in its utter simplicity and poetic tone, was moving and impressive."[736]

Jean-Paul Samson had already emigrated to Switzerland during the First World War and initially stayed with the Dadaist Hans Richter, who was in Zurich at the time. André Breton, the Surrealist, and Samson had been friends since they attended the same school in France, the Collège Chaptal, in 1911–12. Breton was happy to endorse Samson as a politically upright, morally impeccable figure: "I have known Jean-Paul Samson for a very long time. . . . I greatly respect his integrity: one of a very rare breed." (André Breton cited on the back cover of Jean-Paul Samson, *Journal de l'an quarante* [Geneva: M. Boujut and Montreuil-sous-Bois: R. Proix, 1967]).

Bill, who soon became aware of the Krater and joined the ensemble in mid-March 1930, was able to bring to bear the skills he had acquired at the Bauhaus. He created stage decor and sometimes also appeared on stage himself. In a circular sent to the program committee on 16 March 1930 with a list of people currently at the Krater, whose participation might fluctuate quite considerably, Max Bill is named as a "co-opted member of the program committee."[737]

In that circular, which lists the elected members of the board and the "elected members of the program committee"(namely Elsa Burckhardt, Ernst F. Burckhardt, Emil Hegetschweiler, Dr. Arthur Mojonnier and Egidius Streiff), Bill heads the list of a total of five "co-opted" members of the program committee: 1. Max Bill, Stadelhoferstr. 27, 2. Paul Jecklin, 3. Dr. W. Lesch, 4. Maria Münch, 5. J. P. Samson, Seilergraben 31.

The fact that there was no money to be earned at the Krater will no doubt have irked Erwin Bill. But Max enthusiastically threw himself into activities there, keen to be part of the "passionate" efforts to resolve "problems of form" in a "cabaretistic Gesamtkunstwerk."[738] That same circular also informed members that when the program committee met for the second time (in Büro Burckhardt on Wednesday 19 March) Ernst F. Burckhardt would outline his proposed program for the evening of 3 May 1930.

"You are hereby invited to the second meeting of the program committee on Wednesday, 19 March 1930 at 8 p.m. at Büro Burckhardt, Münsterhof 12 (next to Waag). Presentation of the program for 3 May by program director Burckhardt. Reading and discussion of the following works: Vaucher ..."

Around that time, Max Bill designed the letterhead for Burckhardt's architectural practice. And in 1932 he did the same for the architectural and engineering firm of Hubacher and Steiger, who were moving into their new offices in the Zett-Haus. In both cases Bill consistently used only lowercase in his typographic design.

Other performers at the Krater included the writer C. F. Vaucher and, from time to time, the dancer Katja Wulff, who had been a close friend of Sophie Taeuber-Arp's ever since the days of Cabaret Voltaire.

"It has not been possible to establish exactly when Vaucher and Katja Wulff met. They lived and worked closely together for a decade.... There are unfortunately no personal notes relating to that time in the estate of Katja Wulff, which is held in the dance archive in Cologne.

C. F. Vaucher joined Katja Wulff's dance ensemble in the late 1920s.... Born in Hamburg on 31 August 1890, Katja, his first wife, was eleven and a half years his elder."[739]

Like Sophie Taeuber, who was both a visual artist and a talented dancer, Katja Wulff had trained at the Rudolf von Laban dance school.

In 1913, on the Monte Verità in the Ticino, Rudolf von Laban (a native of Bratislava) opened a summer subsidiary of his Munich school of Expressionist dance. During, and because of, the First World War he relocated his school from Munich to Zurich. "Katja Wulff joined the school in October 1916 and was immediately swept into the heart of the Dada scene. The Dada artist Sophie Taeuber was studying with Laban;

738 Paul Lang, "Die Kleinkunstbühne 'Der Krater' (Zurich 1928–30)" (see note 732)

739 Peter Kamber in Vaucher 1996, p. 223, p. 109

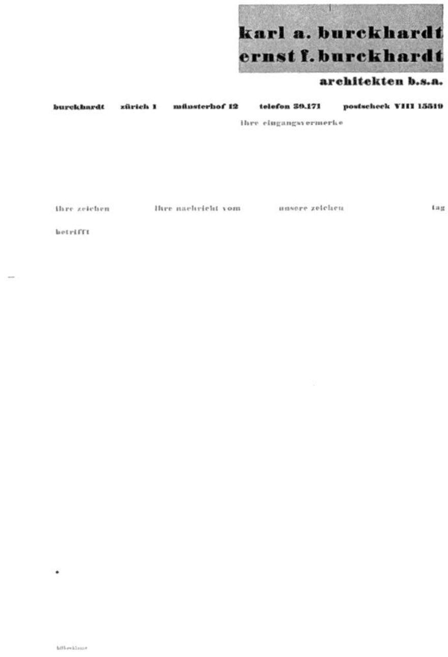

karl a. burckhardt
ernst f. burckhardt
architekten b.s.a.

burckhardt zürich 1 münsterhof 12 telefon 30.171 postscheck VIII 15519

ihre eingangsvermerke

ihre zeichen ihre nachricht vom unsere zeichen tag

betrifft

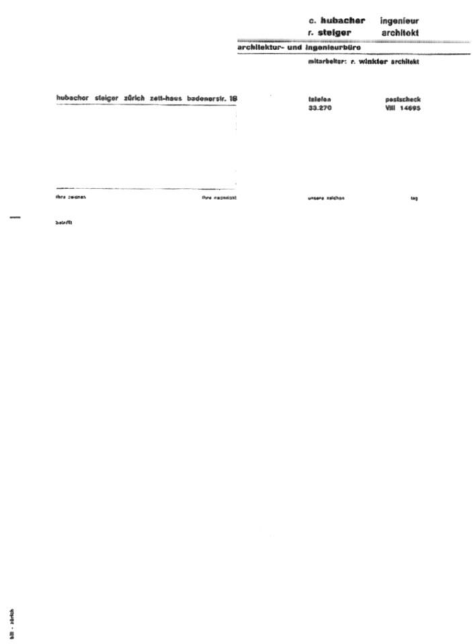

c. hubacher ingenieur
r. steiger architekt
architektur- und ingenieurbüro
mitarbeiter: r. winkler architekt

hubacher steiger zürich zett-haus badenerstr. 18

telefon 33.270

postscheck VIII 14695

ihre zeichen ihre nachricht unsere zeichen tag

betrifft

Max Bill, Letterhead for architects Karl A. Burckhardt and Ernst F. Burckhardt in Zurich, 1930

Max Bill, Letterhead for C. Hubacher (engineer) and R. Steiger (architect), 1932

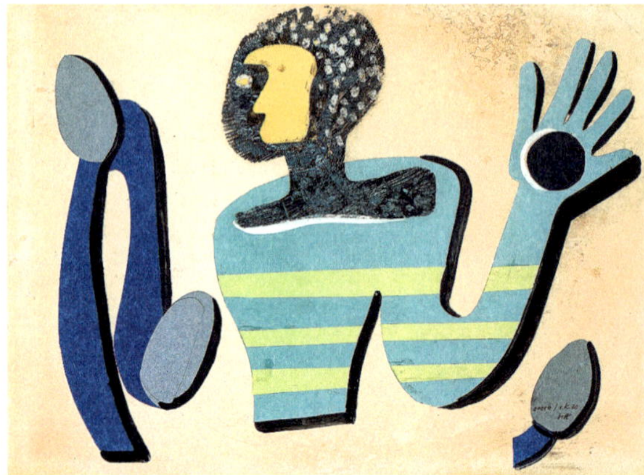

Max Bill, *œuvre/1.k.30,*
1930, collage on cardboard,
50.2×70.5 cm

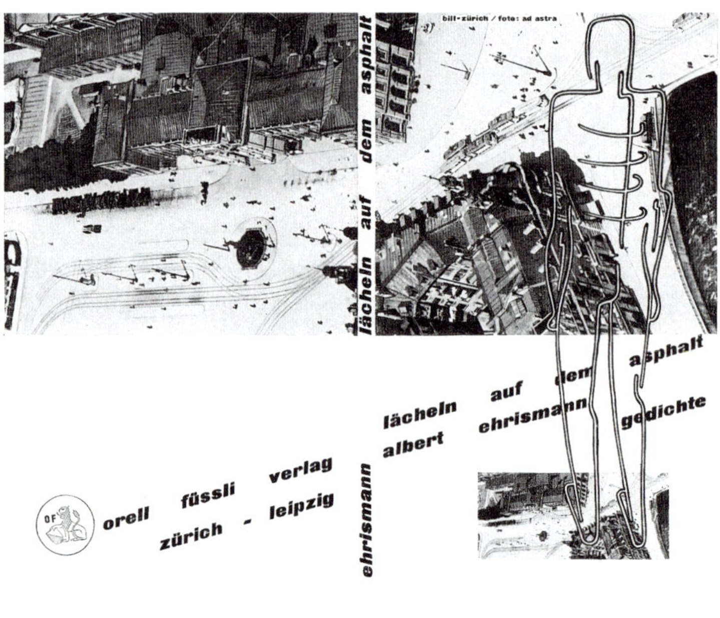

Max Bill, Book cover for Albert
Ehrismann's collection of poems
Lächeln auf dem Asphalt, 1930

Jean Arp designed 'letterheads and posters for the school,' as Katja Wulff wrote in an obituary for Laban; and the male Dadaists—'I couldn't say which appealed to me more, the beauty of the girls or the novelty of the dance' (Richard Huelsenbeck)—were always very keen to be invited to the parties at Seegartenstrasse 2 put on by Laban and his dancers Mary Wigman and Suzanne Perrottet: 'Laban and Wigman and all the rest of us loved having parties, so we invited the Dadaists to join us,' as Katja Wulff put it.... When the First World War was over Laban returned to Germany, and Suzanne Perrottet and Katja Wulff took over the Laban school in Zurich."

Mary Wigman went to Dresden and in October 1923 Katja Wulff set up her own Laban school in Basel. From 1926 Katja Wulff and her master student Marietta von Meyenburg, "who did the choreography ... presented public performances." In 1927 they put on Vittorio Rieti's *Barrabau,* with Paul Sacher conducting the Basel Chamber Orchestra. "It was a huge success."[740]

In 1917, when Max Bill was still a schoolboy in Winterthur, Katja and Sophie —brave women—were already performing at Dada events in Zurich. As Katja Wulff once told me when I visited her at home in Basel, for one of those performances she wore "a tube costume" that she could only see out of downward, so she marked out her choreography on the floor in chalk.

When asked in 1976, Katja Wulff recalled as many names as possible of performers at the Krater: "former members included Mme Suzanne Perrottet ... Marie-Eve Kreis ... Marietta von Meyenburg was also at the Krater.... There was a very good Krater program; presumably designed by Max Bill."[741] As can be seen from items in Bill's typography estate, Katja Wulff was correct to assume that the program design was by Max Bill.

As Vaucher reported, around 1928–29 the Wulff dance studio in Basel presented three ballets: *Parade* by Jean Cocteau, with music by Erik Satie; *Relâche* by Francis Picabia, also with music by Satie, and *Ariadne* by Marietta von Meyenburg (see p. 467). And it was these three ballets that established Katja Wulff's dance studio as an artistic force to be reckoned with.

Bill was an enthusiastic, enduring Satie fan; later in his life he and I attended a Satie recital in Zurich, given by the pianist Werner Bärtschi.

740 Vaucher 1996, pp. 110–11

741 Katja Wulff, Augustinergasse 3, 4051 Basel, to H.-U. von Allmen, Gwatt (Thun), 1 June 1976, SCCPA

The Krater Moves to Pianohaus Jecklin

In 1930, after its early days in an attic studio, the Krater found a new temporary home in a room at Jecklin's music shop. Bill, who quickly became a very active member of the ensemble, designed the program sheets for the first performance of the new season in April 1930 and was also responsible for the stage decor, as we can see from the flyer: "dekorationen: bill." His décor even received a special mention in two reviews in the *Neue Zürcher Zeitung.*

"Space for a hundred had been found in a room at Pianohaus Jecklin and for three hours the brilliant super-jazz of the Varsity Boys created a lively, convivial atmosphere ... *Generaldirektor Sutter,* a comical picture-sequence for which a young architect [Ernst F. Burckhardt] took the applause, provided amusing dialect entertainment. A herald in an old-style military cap recited the Californian adventures of the daredevil J. Suter—with night watchman's cries of moral outrage; meanwhile the business career of the blameless Hans Suter from Bünzlikon unfolded on stage. Emil Hegetschweiler played a valiant merchant without trotting out the usual dialect-drama catch phrases.... Max Bill's décor enhanced the surrealist ambience of the evening.... The program also boasted two surrealist films, refreshing to the eye with their optical conundrums."[742]
One of the Surrealist films referred to in the review (and named in the program) was "*Rien ne va plus,* film by 2 Burckhardts," jointly conceived by Elsa and Ernst F. Burckhardt.

Another review was published a day later: "With the cozy attic room in Freiestrasse replaced by an elegant room in Pianohaus Jecklin on Pfauen, the second season ... has begun with new verve. Emil Hegetschweiler scattered the most delightful witticisms into his *conférence....*

742 E.B., "Aufführung im 'Krater,'" in *Neue Zürcher Zeitung,* 9 April 1930
743 R., "Das Krater-Kabarett," in *Neue Zürcher Zeitung,* 10 April 1930
744 E.Br., "Die Krater-Bühne in Zürich," in *Der Bund,* 10 April 1930, estate of Ernst F. Burckhardt in SCCPA
745 E.Br., "Theaterrundschau. Das 'Krater'-Kabarett in Zürich," in *National-Zeitung,* April 1930 (day not specified), estate of Ernst F. Burckhardt in SCCPA
746 E.Br., "Theaterrundschau. Das 'Krater'"
747 Hans Marti, "Nekrolog Ernst F. Burckhardt," gta Archivs

The spirited atmosphere of two inventively produced one-act dramas (with good décor by Max Bill)—premieres, like most of the productions on this stage—went down particularly well."[743]

The same critic, with the initials "E.Br.," also wrote a few lines in the Bernese *Bund* about the "entertaining image sequences" in *Generaldirektor Suter.* It created a "very witty effect by juxtaposing different worlds: a quaint herald reads out loud—with bourgeois outrage—an account of John August Suter's adventures in California while, next to him, the blameless office career of one Hans Suter unfolds in a series of bright flashes.—Surrealist films, of which there are not many as yet, brilliant jazz music, conférence, and interludes in French filled out this inventively structured program."[744]

The first of those premieres, *Generaldirektor Sutter,* was by Bill's new friend Burckhardt, who was only credited on the program sheet as "E.F.," which explains why the reviewer does not name him: "A young architect, the author of *Generaldirektor Sutter,* had transcribed the rash Californian drama of the tragedy of gold into correct business language and also presented a short series of images outlining the career of the valiant Hans Suter, who nobly and with growing prosperity rises to the blessed realms of widespread respect and admiration, while an old-fashioned herald reads out loud the horror story of the tempestuous career of J. Suter. The contrasts are so sharp yet drawn with such a light touch that the author had no need of the clumsy, bourgeois satire that so many writers resort to."[745]

The second premiere of the evening, named on the program sheet as *Gretchen oder Vive la France,* was by Goldschmied, another writer from Basel, and received a similarly complimentary review: "The sketch *Gretchen* by Goldschmied (Basel) has a distinctly literary air.... All kinds of tangled truths shone through in these dialogues. The authors of these two fresh new dramas deservedly savoured their curtain calls in the midst of Max Bill's surrealist scenario."[746]

Known to his friends as "E.F.," Ernst Friedrich Burckhardt was born and raised in Zurich, but he actually came from a very prominent family in Basel. In Zurich the local colloquialism "ck-dt"—derived from the name Burckhardt—is still verbal shorthand for "wealthy and from Basel." Ernst F. Burckhardt, who studied architecture in London and opened his own practice in Zurich in 1924, was a nephew of the renowned Swiss sculptor Carl Burckhardt.

In Burckhardt's obituary there is no information as to what his wealthy family's interests were. It merely states, somewhat enigmatically, that Burckhardt realized "various buildings for his father's company."[747]

In 1936, thanks to his "connections" in Basel, Max Bill was commissioned to design a tourist leaflet for the Verkehrsverein Basel; he included in it an illustration of a sculpture, *Amazone,* by Carl Burckhardt (Max Bill, *Basel,* folded leaflet, ten sides, 1936, typography estate of Max Bill, collection of Angela Thomas).

Decades later, in 1974, Bill returned to that same sculpture when he was commissioned to design two special-issue Europa stamps for the Swiss postal service. One features Burckhardt's *Amazone,* the other features his own sculpture, *kontinuität.*

According to the plans set out by the program committee, led by Ernst F. Burckhardt, there were two Krater events scheduled for 3 and 4 May 1930. However, these were postponed until 24 and 25 May; that then provided an opportunity to screen some Surrealist films, which were to be collected in Paris by E.F. and Max. The records show that the program committee met on 26 April, so if E.F. and Max left soon after that meeting, they could well have been in Paris anytime from 27 April onward. That date is significant because an exhibition by the artists' group Cercle et Carré was on show in Paris from 18 April to 1 May 1930. Max certainly stayed in Paris for some time, maybe even for two or three weeks.

Materials in the estate of Ernst F. Burckhardt in the gta Archiv shed no light on when Burckhardt and Bill were in Paris; the archive contains neither journals nor diaries used by Burckhardt.[748]

It seems highly likely that he and E.F. would have left Paris again by 16 May because Dr. Paul Lang, the Krater president, had arranged an internal scratch night (followed by a board meeting) at the Helmhaus in Zurich "for members and co-opted members" on 16 May. Since the latter applied to Max Bill, he would have been expected to attend. The writers who had submitted texts to be tried out that evening included Albert Ehrismann; when Ehrismann's collection of poems, *Lächeln auf dem Asphalt,* appeared later that year, the jacket design was by Max Bill. The next public event at the Krater—a matinée with the writer Albin Zollinger—was scheduled for 18 May. Burckhardt and Bill, high-spirited yet responsible

748 Information kindly supplied by Alex Winiger, gta Archiv, 2004

749 Krater announcement, 2nd season 1930, President, Dr. Paul Lang, 25 March 1930, SCCPA

750 Dr. Paul Lang, Kilchberg, 3rd president's announcement, SCCPA

751 Erwin Bill, Winterthur, an Max Bill, Zurich (23 May 1930), Archiv Max Bill

members of the Krater team, would no doubt also have been in Zurich for that event.

The program for the matinée was to include "dances by members of the Wulff-Basel dance studio, Suite for Small Orchestra composed by Robert Blum and played by an ensemble from Baden. Premiere of the drama *Man Kann Doch Nicht Einfach Mutter Sagen* by C. F. Vaucher."[749]

"The next program has been postponed until 24/25 May. Dances by members of the Wulff studio, composition by Blum, surrealist films that are being brought from Paris . . ."[750]

My suggestion that E.F. and Max could have been in Paris for any length of time between 27 April and 16 May 1930, is in fact lent weight by yet another exasperated letter from Erwin Bill to Max, dated 23 May:

"Dear Max!

I clearly need hardly tell you that you have flouted almost all the conditions, the preconditions for my continued support. You knew very well that settling your debts would put me under financial pressure, and yet you traveled to Paris where the harlot Maria Benz resides, and, despite your father's purse being empty . . . you squandered hundreds of francs and have frittered away a great deal of time."[751]

Having identified the films they wanted, Max and E.F. did not take them back to Switzerland themselves, as they had intended; instead the copies were sent by post to the Krater from the Société parisienne d'exploitations cinématographiques.

On the invitation of the Krater, these films by Germaine Dulac were screened in Zürich on 31 May and 1 June 1930. Correspondence regarding the rental fee for these copies from the Société Parisienne d'exploitations cinématographiques, Paris, 23 May 1930, and E. Burckhardt, Münsterhof 12, Zurich, is held in the Schweizerisches Cabaret-, Chanson- und Pantomimen Archiv.

Inspiration in Paris

In Paris Burckhardt and Bill went to "movie palaces" and partly used their time there to seek inspiration for Krater events in Zurich. They also specifically wanted to hire three films by the French director Germaine Dulac: *La coquille et le clergyman* (1928), *Étude cinégraphique sur une arabesque* (1929), and *Thème et variations* (1928).

Étude cinégraphique sur une arabesque (1929), with the Surrealist Antonin Artaud as co-author, established Germaine Dulac's reputation in the 1920s as an avant-garde filmmaker. There are no records of any meetings in Paris between Bill and Burckhardt and the feminist director (born in Amiens in 1882).

In the summer of 1930, on the invitation of the Société des artistes décorateurs, the German Werkbund presented an exhibition at the Grand Palais in Paris, which ran from 14 May to 13 July 1930.

When Max Bill and Ernst F. Burckhardt were in Paris, did they have a chance to visit that exhibition, which included Moholy-Nagy's now renowned *Licht-Raum-Modulator* (1930)? Or had they already returned to Switzerland before it opened? There is also the question as to whether Ernst F. Burckhardt participated on 17 May in the planning event, in Paris, for CIAM III. It seems not, since his name does not appear in the minutes of the Paris meetings (now in the gta Archiv).

The German architect Julius Posener published a review of that Werkbund exhibition "which Walter Gropius and other architects—shall we say, of the Bauhaus kind—installed at the Salon des arts décoratifs.... There was a very interesting modern room, designed in the Bauhaus manner—down to the last detail." Posener's response to that room was ambivalent; he described it as "modern" and "interesting" but took exception to its supposedly "doctrinaire nature." As a whole the display looked "modern-German provincial" to him and he particularly objected to its "preachy" atmosphere. And he pointed out one especially "unbearable" feature: "There were whole pages printed with a single sentence, over and over:

wir schreiben alles klein, denn wir sparen damit zeit
wir schreiben alles klein, denn wir sparen damit zeit
wir schreiben alles klein, denn wir sparen damit zeit
wir schreiben alles klein, denn wir sparen damit zeit
[we always write in lowercase because it saves us time]."[752]

Posener's review, which appeared in the trade magazine *Baugilde,* was of course written in the usual manner, using upper and lower case. In 2007 Bauhaus-Archive celebrated that Paris exhibition by presenting a special exhibition in Berlin: *Werkbund-Ausstellung Paris 1930—Leben im Hochhaus / Werkbund-Exhibition Paris 1930—Living in a High-Rise,* with a slim accompanying publication, Bauhaus-Archiv, Museum für Gestaltung, Berlin, November 2007–April 2008.

752 Posener 1990, pp. 204–5
753 Carola Giedion-Welcker, cited in Bignens 1985, p. 61

Erwin Bill once again remonstrated with Max after that trip because he felt his son had simply been shirking—which may in part have been true. But for the young Bill that trip to Paris was a chance to recharge his batteries and it gave him a foretaste of a promising future. In Paris Burckhardt and Bill visited various galleries—where Max saw original works by Pablo Picasso for the first time—and of course they went to nightclubs, too. Max also told me that—once they had sobered up again—they went to see "works by Max Ernst," presumably at Galerie Jeanne Bucher.

I had to search long and hard in the many books about Max Ernst that Bill collected over the years before I at last came across a reference to Max Ernst's exhibition activities in 1930; a book published by the Museum of Modern Art, New York, reports that Max Ernst participated in exhibitions in two Paris galleries in 1930 (without specifying the months): in Galerie Jeanne Bucher and in Galerie Vignon (see Alfred H. Barr, *Fantastic Art, Dada, Surrealism,* New York, 1936, p. 18).

A Max Ernst exhibition in 1930, at Galerie Vignon in Paris, is also mentioned in the exhibition catalogue *Arte abstracto arte concreto. Cercle et carré, Paris 1930,* IVAM center Julio Gonzalez, Valencia 1990, p. 329, again without specifying the month.

Max Ernst's *Rêve d'une petite fille qui voulut entrer au Carmel* was published in Paris by Editions du Carrefour in 1930.

In 1938 Bill bought a book about Picasso by the American art collector and writer Gertrude Stein (domiciled in Paris): *Anciens et modernes Picasso par Gertrude Stein. 63 Reproductions dont 8 en couleurs* (Paris: Librairie Floury, 1938); inside there is a pencil marking by Max Bill: "bill 1938." Over the years his collection of books on Picasso grew until he about as many books on Picasso as on individual Bauhaus masters.

A few years later Ernst F. Burckhardt (in collaboration with Karl Knell) oversaw the refurbishment of the Corso theater. In one of her articles, Carola Giedion-Welcker points out that, had her husband not intervened—Sigfried Giedion was a shareholder at the Corso and a consultant for the refurbishment—"there would never have been a mural by Max Ernst in the Corso bar"; instead there would have been a photo-montage proposed by Ernst F. Burckhardt.[753]

Max Ernst's wall painting *Pétales et jardin de la nymphe Ancolie,* 1934, oil on plaster 415 × 531 cm, was later removed from the Corso, transferred onto wooden panels and relocated to Kunsthaus Zürich. In 2007–8 it was temporarily on display at Museum Tinguely in Basel.

That exhibition was accompanied by a very informative publication: Werner Spies and Anja Müller-Alsbach, *Max Ernst im Garten der Nymphe Ancolie,* ed. Museum Tinguely (Ostfildern-Ruit: Hatje Cantz, 2007).

The *Cercle et carré* Exhibition

Max Bill—whose stage décor for the Krater had been described as surreal in two reviews—found himself on an ideological knife edge in Paris when he made contact with a number of artists who specifically opposed the Surrealists. Bill's witty traveling companion, Ernst F. Burckhardt, was in a similar position, having previously made a surrealist film with his wife Elsa, which had been screened at a Krater event.

In his obituary E.F. is described as a multifaceted, well-read man who "unrelentingly battled against mediocrity and lazy compromises."[754] But he was also generous and known for his big heart, which led to various romances—not mentioned in his obituary, but which I heard about from Elsa Burckhardt-Blum's nephew Rudolf in Zumikon. Rudolf Blum, a patent attorney, laughed out loud with delight when he learned that, as it were maintaining a proper balance, his Aunt Elsa had had an affair with Max Bill.

Nusch, whom Max saw again in Paris, was now moving in Surrealist circles, but he was also drawn to the artists' group Cercle et Carré, which had been set up in opposition to Surrealism. The core of that group comprised around a dozen artists, including Piet Mondrian, Florence Henri, Georges Vantongerloo, Sophie Taeuber-Arp, Jean Arp, and Antoine Pevsner, "the most idealistic of the Russian Constructivists."[755] The group had organized an exhibition, which was still on in Paris when Bill was there.

The exhibition *Cercle et carré* was on display at Galerie 23 from 17 April to 1 May 1930, 23, rue la Boëtie, Paris. Although it was described on the poster as the group's first international exhibition—"1ère exposition internationale du groupe ○ et □, peinture sculpture architecture théâtre"—there were no subsequent exhibitions.

The poster design was by Georges Vantongerloo, who also participated in the exhibition.

The Flemish artist Georges Vantongerloo (who was born in Antwerp in 1886 and died in Paris in 1965) had been living in Paris for some years

754 Hans Marti, "Nekrolog Ernst F. Burckhardt," gta Archiv

755 Prat 1980, p. 213

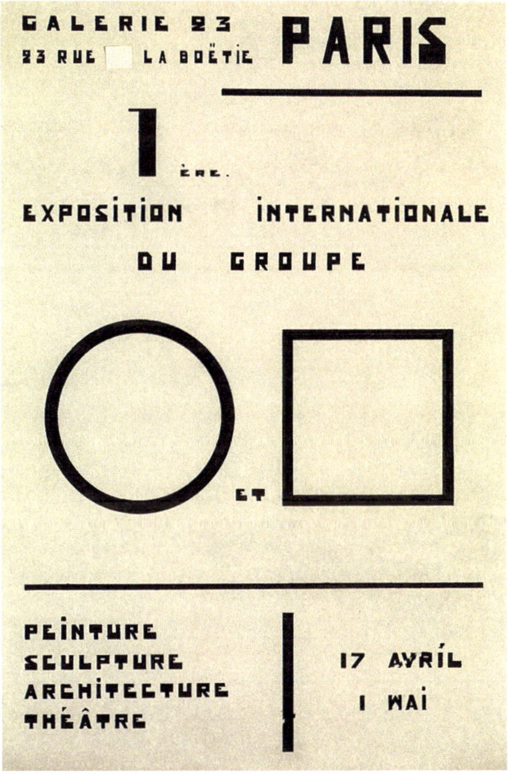

Georges Vantongerloo, Poster for the exhibition *Cercle et carré*, 1930

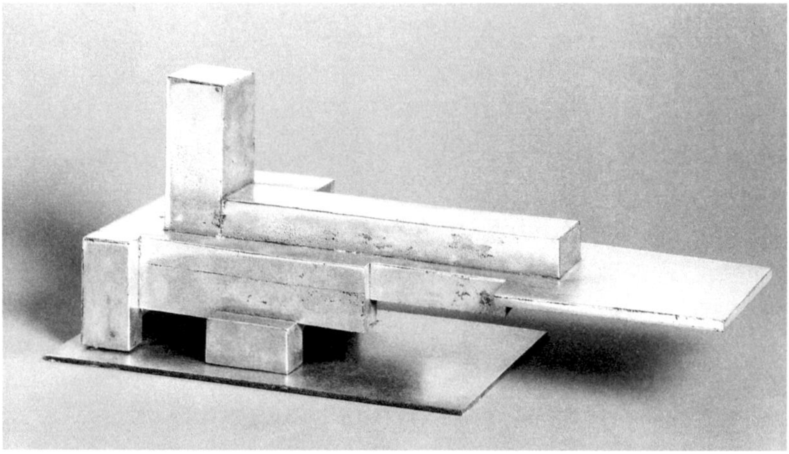

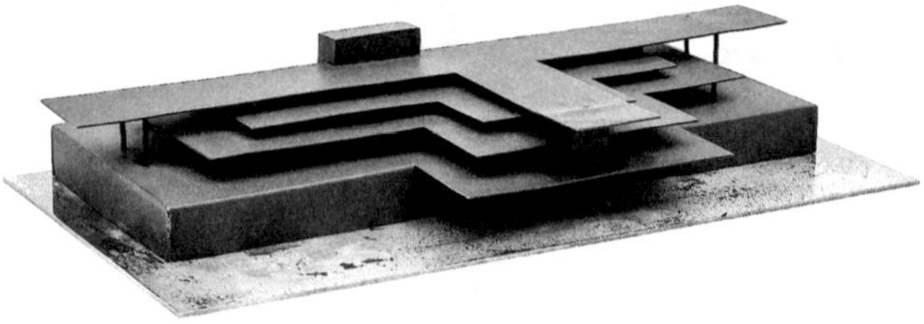

Georges Vantongerloo, *Aéroport type A, série A,* 1928, metal, 22×45×100cm, proposed length: 370m

Georges Vantongerloo, *Aéroport type B, série A,* 1928, metal, 6.5×37.5×20cm

by then. He was a generation younger than the famous Henry van de Velde, whom Max Bill would get to know in person in his later years. During the First World War Vantongerloo initially found refuge in the Netherlands, where he evolved his own concept of painting and sculpture around 1917; his reflections were published in the magazine *De Stijl* from 1918 onward. His life was one long intellectual adventure, a one-man expedition that was reflected in his art. Bill attached great importance to the work produced by the ever-curious Vantongerloo.

That visit to Paris in 1930, which Bill's father so sorely resented, was to have a major impact on the young Max Bill. What he saw and heard in Paris prompted him to change course and to bid farewell to his brief "surreal" phase. The ideas he developed in Paris, under the influence of Cercle et Carré, changed his perspective forever and led Bill to his own independent artistic work—to new, more rational solutions, which he would later describe (in 1936) as "concrete forming" and "Concrete art."

In the as yet rather distant future (1949)—thanks to his own active efforts—Bill would share an exhibition at Kunsthaus Zürich with two artists from the generation before his who had exhibited with Cercle et Carré in 1930. That gave him the chance to measure his own creative powers against that of his older fellow artists, as well as to test (through comparison) his concepts and the Concrete works he had produced so far. In this exhibition Bill's works were shown alongside sculptures by the Russian artist Antoine Pevsner and works by the Flemish artist Georges Vantongerloo, who was by now a close friend of Bill's.

The proposal for this exhibition (submitted to the Zurich Art Committee), the exhibition poster, the catalogue design and the exhibition architecture and design were all the work of Max Bill (see *Antoine Pevsner, Georges Vantongerloo, Max Bill,* exh. cat., Kunsthaus Zürich, 15 October–13 November 1949).

While most of the artists participating in the *Cercle et carré* exhibition showed paintings, Georges Vantongerloo exhibited speculative models of airports that bridged the divide between architecture and sculpture—archisculpture, as it is called today.

Of the three airport objects shown by Vantongerloo, one is now in the collection of the Wilhelm Lehmbruck Museum in Duisburg, another is in my own collection.

Vantongerloo was far ahead of his time, ahead of his fellow artists in Cercle et Carré, who struggled to understand his work. He was also keenly interested in mathematical issues, which he had engaged with for years as an autodidact. But since no one wanted or was able to discuss his ideas with him, he had to resort to monologues.

In a dissertation submitted at the Sorbonne in Paris a decade later the art historian Marie-Aline Prat described his approach as mathematical delirium ("délire mathématique"), which in my view unjustifiably suggests that the artist was something of a scatterbrain.

The original impetus that led to the founding of Cercle et Carré came from Joaquín Torres-García, whom Bill had heard about—as he told me later—from Hanns Welti.
The *Cercle et carré* exhibition in Paris included two works by Hanns Welti.
In May 1930 Bill visited Torres-García (born in Montevideo) in his studio in Montmartre, in Rue Marcel Sembat. Torres-García had moved into his studio in 1929 and partly used it for conversations with other artists.[756]
In 1928 the painter Jean Hélion organized an exhibition with five artists at the Galerie Marck in Paris, including himself and Torrès Garcia. At this "événement" Theo van Doesburg met Torrès Garcia. According to Marie-Aline Prat, Torrès suggested to Van Doesburg that they should do something together to combat Surrealism ("contre le surréalisme"). Following an invitation to Van Doesburg's studio, Torrès wrote two articles on the latter's art. However, Torrès subsequently decided to work with Michel Seuphor—whom he visited in Vannes in late 1929.[757]
Among the guests who regularly dropped into Torres-García's studio in Montmartre were artists such as Georges Vantongerloo, Sophie Taeuber-Arp, Jean Arp, Antoine Pevsner, and Piet Mondrian. Photographs of Torres-García from that time show a somber figure; like so many artists, he was greatly troubled with financial worries.

Bill learned from Torres-García that Cercle et Carré had neither a manifesto nor a constitution of any kind. The only formality was a membership fee of 25 French francs. The artists' ideological common denominator was an international outlook and a strong sense of being "anti-sur," that is to say, they specifically distanced themselves from the Surrealists.
15 March 1930 saw the publication of the first issue of the journal *Cercle et carré*. Van Doesburg took umbrage and wrote to Seuphor: "You will of course understand that that journal—the product of a vulgar spirit—obliges me to take action, and I am sure to find some friends 'on the other side' with the same intentions." This letter was

756 Schipper 1974
757 Prat 1980, pp. 32, 34
758 Prat 1980, p. 54
759 Grohmann 1958, p. 202

then published in the second issue of *Cercle et carré,* which came out on 15 April 1930, just a few days before Bill arrived in Paris; no doubt Torrès Garcia told him all about Van Doesburg's response.

Jeanne Bucher—
a Leading Gallerist

Most of the artists actively associated with Cercle et Carré were from outside France and many had found the atmosphere in Paris distinctly unwelcoming, even hostile. The group thus had both an artistic and a social function: "it lent moral support in the widest sense: people went there to meet up, to dine together."[758] The group's meetings were held in the early evenings in a quiet first-floor room at Café Voltaire. Wassily Kandinsky, who had been granted a German passport for himself and his wife in March 1928, showed two works at the *Cercle et carré* exhibition. Unusually, Communist and anti-Communist views co-existed in Cercle et Carré, with Otto Freundlich and Jean Gorin on the Communist side and Torres-García and Michel Seuphor among the anti-Communists. Piet Mondrian also exhibited with Cercle et Carré, whereas Theo van Doesburg held back from that group, and although both these former De Stijl artists frequented the same restaurant in Paris—Le Dôme—they never sat together.
We will meet Gorin and Freundlich again at the Paris-based artists' association Abstraction-Création; Max Bill, now twenty-five years old, would become a member in December 1933.

In September 1932 "calamity" befell the Bauhaus and it was "closed by the Anhalt government, where the Nazis were now in the majority.... In view of these political developments Kandinsky decided to leave Germany; a last attempt to maintain the Bauhaus in Berlin failed, because the Nazi government intervened there, too." It is worth adding here that it would be some months before Kandinsky finally left Germany. "By Christmas of 1933 he was in Paris, having spent October there in order to see if he could indeed live and work in Paris."[759]

In April 1930, just a few days after the second issue of the journal *Cercle et carré,* a rival magazine, *AC* (Art Concret), edited by Van Doesburg, also came out in Paris; as it happens, *AC* never progressed beyond that first issue. Max Bill stumbled across it quite by chance in Paris and read it when he was there with Ernst F. Burckhardt. In a comparison of the two periodicals, *Cercle et carré* and *AC,* art historian Marie-Aline Prat has concluded that the latter advocated a more rad-ical, leftist position. That one and only issue of *AC* left its mark on Max Bill's subsequent intellectual development and on his own evolving concept of Concrete art.

Jan Brzekowski, who founded the magazine *L'Art contemporain* in April 1929 together with Nadia Grabowska (who would later marry her teacher Fernand Léger), looked back at that time later on: "Mondrian and Doesburg both used to frequent Le Dôme—only not without presenting their mutual friends with some small problems of diplomacy. With Doesburg always seated close to the door or on the terrace and Mondrian always deep inside, friends had to greet Doesburg before they could join the Mondrian/Seuphor group."[760]

Those days in Paris, which Erwin Bill was sure Max had just "frittered away," in fact proved to have an exceptionally important impact on his future theoretical and practical output. He was in the right place at the right time. There was no other city where he could have so intensely engaged with and processed the artistic ideas that were currently ricocheting between surrealism and rationalism in Europe. And in May 1930 Max Bill noticed an advertisement in *Cahiers d'art* for Galerie Jeanne Bucher, which had been showing avant-garde work since 1925.

In her very first exhibitions in 1925, Jeanne Bucher presented sculptures by Lipchitz and works on paper by Picasso; in 1926 she showed Max Ernst's *36 Dessins pour une Histoire Naturelle.* In 1927 she presented an exhibition with works by both Lipchitz and Picasso, and toward the end of 1927 Max Ernst again stepped into the limelight, this time together with Jean Arp. Jeanne Bucher continued her series of avant-garde events in May 1928 with a group show that included works by Braque, Léger and, once again, Ernst and Picasso. She thus made her mark with the leading art connoisseurs of the day.

In March 1929 Bucher relocated from her first premises at 3, rue du Cherche-Midi, to the Ancienne Librairie Sacre du Printemps at no. 5 on the same street. In April to May 1929—a year before Bill and Burckhardt arrived in Paris—she presented an exhibition in her new gallery with work not only by her regular artists (Picasso, Léger, Lipchitz, Braque, Gris and Ernst) but also, for the first time, Joan Miró and Paul Klee.

760 Jan Brzekowski, cited in Prat 1980, p. 42

761 Serge Brignoni, cited in Billeter 1997, p. 19

762 André Breton, cited in Billeter 1997, p. 25

He decided to visit Madame Bucher at her gallery. Since she had been born in the Alsace, visitors whose French was not very fluent could converse with her in German. She was an outstanding gallerist with an unerring eye for art, which she did not just sell—she loved the works she handled. In December 1929 Max Ernst had had another solo exhibition at Galerie Jeanne Bucher and I imagine that some of his works may still have been at the gallery, where Burckhardt and Bill would have been able to see them in May 1930.

Bill had taken a considerable number of watercolors with him to Paris—works he had produced as a student in Dessau (1927–28), when the Bauhaus was on vacation, and after that in Zurich (1929–early 1930); he was hoping that a gallery in Paris might be interested in his watercolors and took them with him when he went to see Jeanne Bucher.

Two days after the Cercle et Carré exhibition ended (1 May 1930), a solo exhibition opened at Galerie Jeanne Bucher with works by the young Swiss artist Serge Brignoni (3–17 May 1930), and when Max Bill visited the gallery, he met not only Brignoni but also Joan Miró and Jacques Lipchitz.

"One of the few gallerists who held out was Jeanne Bucher, and I was lucky enough to be able to show my work at her gallery."[761]

Cycladic Idols in the Louvre

At that first meeting Brignoni introduced himself to Max Bill as "Swiss-Italian." Born in San Simone in the Ticino, Brignoni was three years older than Bill and, having studied in Berlin for a while, had now been living in Paris for some time. In 1926, four years before that chance encounter with Max Bill, Brignoni had shown his work at Odette Luce in a joint exhibition with Joan Miró, who had just transitioned from realism into surrealism in his paintings. Brignoni read the magazine *La Révolution surréaliste* and kept company with Surrealists. Yet he was not a "partisan," he merely "sympathised" with the Surrealists who increasingly leaned toward the French Communist Party in the 1930s.

One of them, André Breton, described Brignoni's style as "vicérale" and "animal-végétal."[762]

The Swiss sculptor Alberto Giacometti was also living in Paris at that time, and he and Brignoni explored the treasures in the Louvre. Brignoni recalled their expeditions: "As we wandered through the Louvre, Alberto Giacometti and I discovered Cycladic sculptures in dusty, out-of-the-way display cases. We were fascinated by their abstraction, their symbolism, which has nothing to do with Classical Greek sculpture."[763] Max Bill was also very struck by those (mostly female) Cycladic figures and later on he started to collect examples for himself. Bill clearly appreciated the elemental nature of these "ideally" formed idols, yet they had no direct influence on his own later sculptural thinking—unlike Giacometti, who spontaneously reacted to his discovery of these Cycladic pieces by creating a flat head (*Tête qui regarde,* 1927–29, marble).

When Max and I first met, he once remarked, "your figure reminds me of a Cycladic idol."

A few years after that first meeting, Bill and Brignoni—both from Switzerland—became active members of the international artists' association Abstraction-Création in Paris. On 22 December 1933 Bill also started exhibiting his work there. In the late 1930s both men also became members of the artists' group Allianz in Switzerland (founded in 1937, albeit with less impact than Abstraction-Création). However, Brignoni felt ever more lost as a member of Allianz; he even described himself as a "loser."

In spring 1930 the world had still not recovered from the Wall Street Crash just a few months earlier; numerous galleries had had no choice but to terminate their artists' contracts. And the wide-awake individuals who met at Galerie Jeanne Bucher would soon also become aware of the imminent threat emanating from the Nazis, which would clearly affect them, given that the Nazis' declared political aim was to destroy "modern" artists and their works.

Another regular visitor at Galerie Jeanne Bucher was Piet Mondrian, and Serge Brignoni recalled an incident from that period: "I remember meeting a tall, gaunt man at Jeanne Bucher's gallery, dressed very correctly, but with an impoverished look." When he had left again Jeanne Bucher told Brignoni that she was "touched by the man's dignity, his decency, he had barely enough to eat. Each time he comes I take one of his paintings out of sympathy and give him 500 French francs. The

763 Serge Brignoni, cited in Billeter 1997, p. 24
764 Billeter 1997, pp. 21–22
765 Serge Brignoni, cited in Billeter 1997, p. 22
766 See *Jeanne Bucher,* 1994, p. 56
767 Lipchitz 1972, p. 230
768 In *Cahiers d'art,* no. 2, 1928, p. 94
769 Françoise Gilot, cited in Klepsch 2007, p. 181

basement is full of them, and I haven't yet been able to sell a single one." Brignoni then of course added that "the tall man was Piet Mondrian."[764] While Moholy-Nagy and others admired Mondrian as the "purest" painter of that time, not in moral terms but in terms of his painterly style, there were also anti-Mondrianists, and Brignoni not only counted himself among the latter, he also repeated a mean-spirited quip by Picasso.

"One of Picasso's deadly comments—about Mondrian—was doing the rounds: "How bored he must get, he's spending his whole life painting the same picture." A sentiment that I in fact shared."[765]

It was also Moholy-Nagy who designed the typography and cover for Piet Mondrian's book *Neue Gestaltung: Neoplastizismus: Nieuwe Beelding,* which appeared as no. 5 in the series *Bauhausbücher,* published by Albert Langen Verlag in Munich (n.d.)—and Max Bill acquired a copy, which he marked inside with "bill."

When Max Bill visited the ever-enterprising Madame Bucher she was preparing a solo exhibition of works by Lipchitz, who had shown works at her gallery since 1925; it was to open on 13 June 1930 with no less than a hundred sculptures in rooms specially rented for the occasion in the Galerie de la Renaissance in Rue Royale.[766] Looking back later on Lipchitz recalled that exhibition with Jeanne Bucher in 1930 as a major event in his career.[767]

This perfectly demonstrates how myths are born. Jeanne Bucher will certainly not have merely been acting "out of sympathy"; after all she had already exhibited *Des Peintures de Piet Mondrian* two years earlier. A favorable review of the exhibition appeared in *Cahiers d'art:* "... neoplasticism and its leader [Mondrian] occupy a very prestigious position among advanced artists in Holland. J. J. Oud, the director of the school of architecture in Rotterdam regards Mondrian as the most remarkable painter in the current generation of European artists."[768]

At that time the name of the sculptor Lipchitz had at least two associations for Bill.

Chaim Jacob Lipchitz, born in Lithuania in 1891, arrived in Paris in 1909, where he took the name Jacques Lipchitz. From 1913 onward he was in contact with Picasso and other artists committed to Cubism. Having managed to leave France and escape the Nazi regime in 1940, he settled in New York. Although the Nazis were fully aware of his location, during their occupation of Paris they used his name as an excuse to search Picasso's home, as the latter's partner Françoise Gilot recalled: "More or less once a week or a fortnight a group of uniformed Germans would arrive and ask, menacingly, 'This is where monsieur Lipchitz lives, isn't it?'—'No, monsieur Picasso lives here.'"[769] Her descriptions of the threatening events of that time have informed certain recent publications. See, in particular, Michael Carlo Klepsch's highly informative *Picasso und der Nationalsozialismus* (Düsseldorf: Patmos, 2007).

Firstly, he knew it from a reproduction in *Die Kunstismen 1914–1924* (edited by El Lissitzky and Jean Arp), which he had only recently purchased —the image in question, in the section on Cubism, was of a reduced, understated sculpture made by Lipchitz in 1916 (p. 41, fig. 39). Secondly, as Bill later told me (if I remember correctly), he had seen paintings by Fernand Léger and sculptures by Lipchitz in Le Corbusier's *Pavillon de l'Esprit Nouveau* in Paris in 1925.

Lipchitz had had a house designed and built in Boulogne-sur-Seine by Le Corbusier, whom Max Bill greatly admired. Lipchitz moved into his house in 1925, five years before he and Max Bill met at Jeanne Bucher's gallery.

Le Corbusier also designed L'Artaude, a villa in Le Pradet, near Toulon, France, for Hélène de Mandrot—a patron of the arts and the owner of La Sarraz, the castle in Switzerland where CIAM was founded. He then advised Hélène de Mandrot to commission Lipchitz to create two outdoor sculptures for the villa. Two sculptures by Lipchitz, *Femme couchée à la guitarre* (1928) and *Le Chant des voyelles* (1931–32)—now recognized as masterpieces—were then indeed installed in the garden in Le Pradet in 1932.[770] Lipchitz's *Le Chant des voyelles,* which Hélène de Mandrot donated to Kunsthaus Zürich in the late 1950s, now stands close to the entrance to the Kunsthaus.

Thirteen years after Bill met Miró, Lipchitz, and Brignoni at Galerie Jeanne Bucher, works by Joan Miró would be destroyed by the Nazis. "The campaign against leading exponents of 'degenerate art' in France became ever more ruthless in 1943. In March of that year six hundred paintings and drawings by modern artists were annihilated in the grounds of the Jeu de Paume—besides works by Picasso and so many others, there were also works by Paul Klee, Joan Miró, and Max Ernst."[771]

770 See Baudin 1998, pp. 317–18

771 R. Vallard, *Le Front de l'art, défense des collections françaises 1939–1945* (Paris, 1997), cited in Klepsch 2007, p. 180 note 217

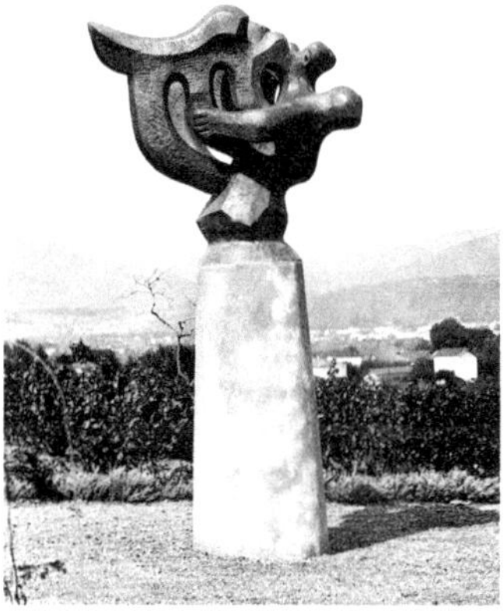

Jacques Lipchitz, *Le chant des voyelles,* 1931–32, bronze, edition of 7, 129.5×121.9×215.9cm (with base)

Paul and Nusch Éluard

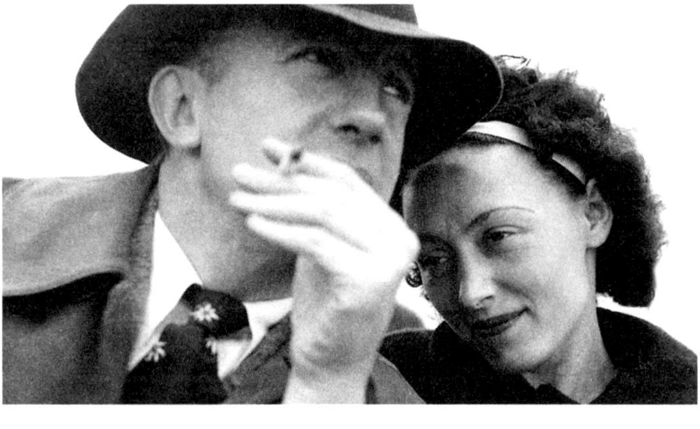

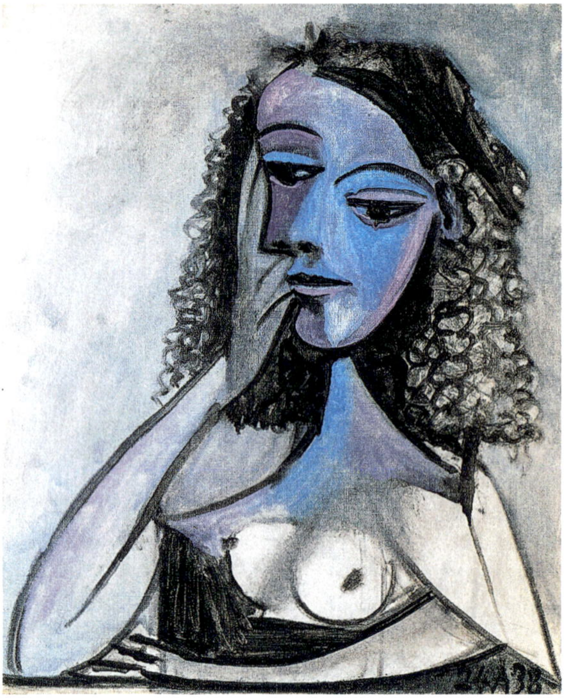

Pablo Picasso, *Portrait de Nusch Éluard,* 1938, oil on canvas, 55×46cm

"... we all love Paul Klee"

Having reviewed Bill's sheaf of watercolors, Jeanne Bucher returned them to him with the words, *"nous aimons tous Paul Klee"*—"we all love Paul Klee." But she also had some advice for Bill: "Start to work independently, and in a year's time I will exhibit your work." Well aware that he was a capable, talented young man, she urged him to free himself from Klee's influence and to produce something new, something of his own. And if he truly felt he had done that, he was free to return in a year and she would keep her word. Having stepped across the gallery's threshold with such high hopes, Bill may have found her comments quite mortifying—a bucket of cold water. But on reflection he must have realized that this was very carefully targeted advice given by an experienced gallerist to a young artist. And, having learned his lesson from that shock, Bill did indeed very soon strike out on his own with works that mark the true beginning of his oeuvre.

Bill was not only—rightly and with good reason—turned down in Paris by Jeanne Bucher, he was also turned away by Nusch. When he went to visit the woman he had almost married, it seems she had just met the poet Paul Éluard, her new lover and future husband. Looking back, Max could no longer remember if Nusch had let him into her apartment or not, nor could he remember what he did for the rest of that night, because he had been completely drunk.
This was the only time that Bill, a progressive teetotaller—thanks to the influence of his uncle Ernst Geiger—ever told me of an occasion when he had been drunk.

Paul Éluard and Nusch

It was one evening in May 1930 that Paul Éluard, in the company of René Char and Louis Aragon, encountered Nusch for the first time.
In 1941 René Char took up arms in his own homeland and fought against the German occupying forces. "Both respected and much admired as 'Capitaine Alexandre,' the leader of a resistance cell in Vaucluse ... he quietly produced an outstanding, enduring account of that time in his *Feuillets d'Hypnos.* Albert Camus published *Hypnos* in 1946 and became a friend of Char's; Paul Celan translated

it into German [*Aufzeichnungen aus dem Maquis*], which has now come out in a new edition."[772]

René Char, a tall young poet, was leading an exuberant, ebullient life in Paris with his Surrealist friends, and the three of them ran into Nusch outside the Parisian department store Galeries Lafayette; at the time she was a "pretty little extra" at the Grand Guignol theater.

"One evening in May 1930, on the sidewalk outside the Galeries Lafayette, Paul was walking along with Louis Aragon and René Char. Nusch, the pretty little extra from the Grand Guignol had been frightened by the three friends. It took some time to calm her down again ..."[773]

At least that is the account given by a good friend of Éluard's, the photographer Dora Maar. Éluard and Maar were both members of a revolutionary group of Surrealists, and since Dora Maar later became a close friend of Nusch's, I am happy to accept her version of the story. According to the writer Unda Hörner—not mincing her words—Éluard "picked Nusch up" when he was out and about with his friend René Char.[774] The two sources cited here do at least agree that René Char was there with Éluard on that occasion in May 1930 and that Nusch was performing at the Grand Guignol.

The Grand Guignol first opened its doors in 1897 and finally closed again in 1962; its speciality was high drama.

The Grand Guignol was named after its founder, Monsieur Guignol. It dated back to the eighteenth century. In those days, in Lyon, whole families would go to the Grand Guignol. There was a touching naïveté to the performances, and parents did not hesitate to take their children there (see "Grand Guignol, d'origine lyonnaise ... en lutte contre les agents d'autorité," in *Petit Larousse illustré* [Paris: Librairie Larousse, 1979], p. 1387).

If Nusch was on her way either to or from work, preoccupied with her role, when she suddenly encountered the three men—including Char with his unusual height and broad shoulders—it is hardly surprising that she was startled and that it took the men some time to calm her down again. Unda Hörner has described the relationship that then developed between Nusch and Éluard as "a form of mutual dependence": "When they met, they were both seeking support of some kind. Nusch, born in Mulhouse into a family

772 Horst Wernicke, "'Einen Blitz bewohnen,' zum 100. Geburtstag des französischen Dichters René Char," in *Neue Zürcher Zeitung,* 14 June 2007
773 Dora Maar, cited in Avril 2001, p. 13
774 See Hörner 1996, pp. 142–43
775 See Hörner 1996

of circus artists, had posed for nostalgia postcards in Berlin before becoming a performer at the Grand Guignol.... Well used to poverty and an unstable existence, when she got to know Éluard (who had come into a small fortune following the death of his father in 1927) she found someone to care for her and a partner who would do anything for her. Meanwhile, Éluard seems to have found in Nusch a devoted, gentle companion, who—like Gala [Éluard's first wife] in the past—would do whatever he wanted. And given Nusch's history, she was not unused to moving in artistic circles; she became a favorite model of Man Ray's and participated in Surrealist activities.... Gala, who now only came to visit in the company of her new partner (the Surrealist artist Salvador Dalí), was not a real rival for Nusch."[775]

Having parted from Max Bill—who receives no mention in either of those two publications on Nusch and Paul Éluard, aside from the indirectly ironic fact that Nusch named her dog Billy—Nusch now had to make a new start in Paris. But it was fraught with difficulty and she soon found that she had gone from the frying pan into the fire, into the undertow of yet another kind of turbulence. Nusch's new lover was in fact still married to Gala, although Gala was openly living with Salvador Dalí by now. In early July 1930, within a few weeks of meeting Nusch, Éluard mentioned her in a letter to Gala, asking if it would be convenient for him to come to see Gala for a few days together with Nusch, or for them possibly to stay somewhere near Cadaqués, where Gala and Dalí lived.

All the protagonists in this emotional tangle are seen together in a photograph taken in Cadaqués (Spain) in 1930: Gala, beside her husband Paul Éluard, behind them the poet René Char and, beneath Éluard's navel, lying on a lounger, his lover and future wife, the delicate Nusch (illustrated in Unda Hörner, *Die realen Frauen der Surrealisten* [Mannheim: Bollman, 1996], p. 142). The cover image of the first paperback edition of this book (Suhrkamp Taschenbuch, 1998) is a photograph of Nusch taken by Man Ray—even if the sitter is erroneously identified as Gala in the book.

In the autumn of 1930 Gala and Paul Éluard decided to divorce. Gala and Dalí married in 1933 and, barely a year later, in August 1934—despite Éluard having assured Gala that he could never imagine living with any other woman—he and Nusch married. And although, as Hörner puts it, Gala was "not a real rival" for Nusch in 1930, Nusch now found that she had to share Éluard's feelings with her predecessor.

Although Éluard sought security in Nusch, he told Gala that he believed he would never be able to live with Nusch nor with any other woman. "The fact that I had Nusch with me when you and I decided to divorce prevented me, in that moment, from seeing clearly how alone I would be in future. Because I do not believe I will ever be able to live with another person, neither with Nusch nor anyone else."[776]

That same year Éluard wrote to Nusch, his "little child": "My dear little one ... I will be back on Tuesday 8th at the latest and will hold you in my arms again, tender and pure. I hope you are well, that you are waiting for me like a good girl, that you are certain of my love, my dear little child, my beautiful Nusch." Just a day after that, however, he wrote to Gala, the women he had elevated into an all-powerful, all-embracing dream figure: "I think only of you, I worship your sex, your eyes, your breasts, your hands, your feet, your mouth, and your thoughts, all my Gala."[777]

Even after marrying Nusch, Éluard—still consumed with the idea of Gala—continued to write to his first wife in letters filled with obsessive, erotic, sexual fantasies. "Why did you not have any prints made of those nude photographs? I would like to have had some of you making love. And I would make love to you in front of Nusch, and she would just stroke herself—whatever you wish."[778]

Paul Éluard was not averse to sexual experimentation; he, his first wife Gala and Max Ernst lived in a turbulent three-way relationship for a while.

When Nusch—a foreigner without a work permit—was living with Max Bill in Zurich, she had modeled at the Grieder fashion house. But what must it have done to her self-esteem in Paris when Max Bill, who loved her and had wanted to marry her, broke off their relationship because his father, who held the purse strings, was so adamantly opposed to her? Nusch was as pretty and delicately attractive as ever but now she also appeared vulnerable and brittle. And it was this special aura that inspired so many artists to photograph her and to make portraits of her. Man Ray photographed her, sometimes nude, leaving us a clear picture of her silhouette, and Nusch often modeled together with the stunningly beautiful Lee Miller or her friend Dora Maar, Picasso's lover. The Swedish artist Greta Knutson-Tzara painted her, as did Pablo Picasso—several times—

776 Paul Éluard to Gala, 21 October 1930, in Éluard 1987, p. 120
777 Paul Éluard, cited in Hörner 1996, p. 143
778 Paul Éluard, Paris, to Gala, February 1931, in Éluard 1987, p. 135
779 Caws 2002, p. 185

who also had a short affair with her. Far from raising any objections, her husband Paul Éluard positively condoned the affair—proud and flattered that Picasso coveted his wife.

Max Bill, at that very young age, was certainly guilty of emotional betrayal when he abandoned Nusch. One wonders if Nusch ever managed to live on her own terms after that. Or was she reduced to an erotic plaything for Éluard and Picasso? There appear to be similarities here with the situation of the psychoanalyst Sabina Spielrein, another woman who found herself caught between two men—in her case she was "objectified" by C. G. Jung and Sigmund Freud, worn down by them, "sacrificed." In later life Bill told me that, on the contrary, Nusch had been "well off" with Éluard—but maybe that was no more than a fond hope as he sought to assuage a lingering sense of guilt.

Nusch suffered from sleeplessness and various psychosomatic disorders; on the advice of a therapist she started creating collages when she was unable to sleep.

One of these collages by Nusch Éluard was shown in the exhibition 1937 at Kunsthalle Bielefeld in 2007. (Nusch Éluard, *Untitled,* ca. 1936, photomontage, 13.7×8.6cm, collection of Karen Amiel Baum, illustrated in 1937. *Perfektion und Zerstörung*, ed. Thomas Kellein, Kunsthalle Bielefeld [Tübingen: Ernst Wasmuth Verlag, 2007], p. 419.)

However, I would certainly not want to portray Nusch merely as a "victim"—I feel deeply sympathetic toward her, although I never met her myself. A "victim" could never have been active in the Resistance, as she was, transporting secret information across Paris in bonbon jars.

After the Second World War Nusch and Paul Éluard once visited Max Bill in Zurich, as he told me. Not long afterward, in November 1946, having telephoned with her friend Dora Maar to arrange to meet for a meal, Nusch suddenly collapsed. At the age of just forty, when Paul Éluard was away in Switzerland, she died alone from a brain haemorrhage in her Paris apartment, utterly unexpectedly.[779]

Albin Zollinger at the Krater

Assuming that Bill and Burckhardt were back in Zurich by 16 May 1930, they would then also have been there in time for the next Krater event, a matinée on Sunday, 18 May, at "precisely 11 o'clock," as we learn from the invitation card, which was most probably designed by Bill. The matinée was at Galerie Aktuaryus, Bahnhofstrasse 16; Albin Zollinger, author of *Der halbe Mensch,* read from as yet unpublished poems and prose, and the pianist Irma Schaichet played pieces by Kodály and Scriabin.

In a letter to a certain Fräulein Forrer, Ernst F. Burckhardt referred to his time in Paris with Max Bill. It seems the two young men had met her in Paris—and that she may have bought a watercolor from Bill: "Dear Fräulein Forrer ... are you still enjoying your Bill? We greatly enjoyed our sojourn in Paris and will draw strength from it for a long time to come. Did you see Max Ernst at Rosenberg's? Do call on us as soon as you arrive in Zurich. With very best wishes."[780]

Max later told me that "Fräulein Forrer" was one of his first collectors; it seems she is the same collector later named by Bill in exhibition catalogues as Anita Hug-Forrer of St. Gallen. Once, when he I and were staying in a hotel in Sils-Baselgia, Bill mentioned that the director of the library diagonally opposite the hotel—the Biblioteca Engiadinaisa—was in fact Anita Hug-Forrer, now quite elderly. He would like to have visited her there, but the opportunity did not arise. A library brochure notes that the Biblioteca Engiadinaisa opened in 1962 with support from "the foundation established by Anita Forrer's friend Louise Silverberg"; "Anita Forrer, who provided the land where the library was built," had "a holiday apartment on the upper floor of the building ... where she spent the summer months until well into her old age."[781]

In April 1938 Anita Forrer met Annemarie Schwarzenbach, who fell "head over heels in love" with her. "Since the writer was in one of the worst of her drugs crises, she clung to her new friend—'from that first day in Sils when I saw you standing next to your blue car'—hoping that Anita Forrer would help her to break free from her morphine addiction. Over 160 letters, almost all from Annemarie Schwarzenbach to Anita Forrer, reflect their extraordinarily intense relationship,

780 Ernst F. Burckhardt, Zurich, Münsterhof 12, to "Fräulein Forrer," [no address], 20 May 1930, SCCPA

781 Alexis Schwarzenbach, "Annemarie Schwarzenbach und Anita Forrer," pamphlet for the eponymous exhibition at the Biblioteca Engiadinaisa, 7 July–31 October 2008, Sils 2008

782 Schwarzenbach, "Annemarie Schwarzenbach und Anita Forrer"

783 BJ., "Matinée des 'Kraters,'" in *Neue Zürcher Zeitung,* 20 May 1930, SCCPA

784 EM., "Matinée des 'Kraters,'" in *Tages-Anzeiger,* 21 May 1930, SCCPA

785 SCCPA

which would be fraught with setbacks. It started as passionate love, turned into friendship—albeit seriously hampered by Annemarie Schwarzenbach's vain struggles with morphine—and ultimately ended in separation in June 1939 when Annemarie Schwarzenbach left for Afghanistan with Ella Maillart."[782]

Whereas previous events at the Krater had been very well received in the press, the critics at the matinée with Albin Zollinger were more divided in their opinions.

"Albin Zollinger, author of the troublesome book *Der halbe Mensch,* read a novella, a fragmentary account of the life of a publisher ... inorganic in its effect and disjointed in the mismatch between action and motivation. Somehow even his living breath was not enough to lend credibility to the problematics of these events"[783]—to quote a review in *Neue Zürcher Zeitung.*

The review in the more liberal *Tages-Anzeiger* is very different, even poetic: "but sometimes the skies turn a wonderful calm blue above a Krater opening. Then a quiet figure at the margins may talk of things that travel out beyond the abyss. Albin Zollinger never shouts out loud; at the first of this year's Krater matinées he read from his own poems.

Zollinger looks deep into things and thus does not need the external shell of their noise. It is as if he taps on people's shoulders and they open their souls at the touch of his fingers. It might initially seem that his novella *Halberstein* is a psychological dissection of a human being, but the pleasing moment in the story comes when one realizes that Zollinger has not become embroiled in the analysis of a soul.... Something like the simple sobriety of a mountain-clear autumn day surrounds the figure and the path of Halberstein, the human being who became a publisher by dint of chance and opportunity ..."[784]

During the weekend of 31 May–1 June 1930 the Krater presented a comprehensive program (devised by Ernst F. Burckhardt) at Pianohaus Jecklin. On two evenings, starting at 8.45 pm, there were, among other things, screenings of the three films by Germaine Dulac that Max Bill and Burckhardt had gone to Paris to seek out on behalf of the Krater. The program sheet included a short note about the director: "Germaine Dulac is regarded as the leader of a small group of avant-garde directors in Paris. The first two films, *Arabesque* and *Thème et variations* are short experiments, interesting forays into the technical potential of film. However, *La coquille et le clergyman* is more than just a visual experiment. It probes the subconscious thoughts and dreams of the human spirit and as such recalls the Surrealist film *Un chien andalou,* which was shown at the Kunsthaus last autumn ..."[785]

Un chien andalou by Luis Buñuel and Salvador Dalí was, as we have said, screened at Kunsthaus Zürich on 30 October 1929 during a soirée with Kurt Schwitters and Jean Arp that was presented in connection with the exhibition *Abstrakte und surrealistische Malerei und Plastik.*

The Surrealist director Germaine Dulac described her own films as "visual music" (*musique visuelle*), and a distinctly double-edged review declared that that was "the correct term for her cinematographic experiments because they amount to little more than captivatingly photographed pictorial impressions and rapidly dissipating, atmospheric scraps."[786]

"People were particularly excited to see the three films by Germaine Dulac that the program director, Ernst F. Burckhardt, had brought from Paris. In these films Dulac took shifting photographic images and wrested from them quiet, reflective effects with a force of expression that is reminiscent of incoherent dreams. At times there was a sense of things secretly heard and felt.... The captivating inscrutability of these mysterious pictorial games has to come from a highly active artistic imagination for it to have a lasting impact."[787]

Another critic, in the *Neue Zürcher Zeitung,* came to the conclusion that Dulac's work was not on the same level as Buñuel's *Un chien andalou.* However, the *National-Zeitung* in Basel published a much longer, more favorable review—possibly somewhat in its own interest given that the films had been secured by Burckhardt, the son of a well-known family in Basel. That review names Ernst F. Burckhardt but—perhaps naturally enough—makes no mention of his co-opted assistant, Max Bill, who had no connections with Basel.

"... the Surrealist films that are included in the cinema program at the moment are especially innovative.... The two short pictorial experiments by Germaine Dulac reveal the new intensity of photography; but they are too self-aware to qualify as 'musique visuelle,' with steps by a dancer on points pedantically juxtaposed with similar movements by precision machines merely creating the effect of contrived association-seeking.

786 Carl Seelig, "Premiere im 'Krater,'" in *Tages-Anzeiger,* 5 June 1930, SCCPA

787 E.Br., "Theaterrundschau," in *National-Zeitung,* 3 June 1930, SCCPA

788 EB., "Aufführung im 'Krater,'" in *Neue Zürcher Zeitung,* 2 June 30, SCCPA

789 Carl Seelig, "Premiere im 'Krater,'" in *Tages-Anzeiger,* 5 June 1930, SCCPA

790 EB., "Aufführung im 'Krater,'" in *Neue Zürcher Zeitung,* 2 June 1930, SCCPA

791 E.Br., "Theaterrundschau"

792 EB., "Aufführung im 'Krater'"

793 Carl Seelig, "Premiere im 'Krater'"

The more broadly drawn, irreally evocative film *La Coquille et le clergyman* strives to achieve the intensity of tangled nightmares, but it lacks the powerful fantasy and variety of *Un chien andalou,* which was shown a year earlier."[788]

The next event put on by the Krater after the Germaine Dulac screenings was a performance at Jecklin's by Marietta von Meyenburg and Marie-Eve Kreis—two dancers "from the Katja Wulff Studio in Basel." In fact, as we know from press reports, there were in fact three dancers, because Katja Wulff spontaneously joined the other two.

"Three slim dancers from Basel appeared: Katja Wulff performing a parody of a popular song from *Der blaue Engel,* with Marietta von Meyenburg and Marie-Eve Kreis as eager students in similar pastiches of diverse contemporary topics."[789] "The dances by Katja Wulff, M. von Meyenburg, and M. E. Kreis, which were met with warm applause, convey something of the mood of our own time . . ."[790]

"The dances presented by Katja Wulff, Marietta von Meyenburg, and Marie-Eve Kreis were especially full of life. The public has already had an opportunity to get to know the future-oriented work that is led by Katja Wulff in the Basel dance studio. This time the audience saw new, subtle nuances."[791]

The conservative *Neue Zürcher Zeitung* published a very positive review of the "slim dancers" and the Basel *National-Zeitung* reported on the performance with pride. Elsa Burckhardt-Blum's brother, Robert Blum, composed a suite of short pieces (*Suite kleiner Stücke*) specially for that evening, and the program sheet announced that "the amiable artist" would himself be at the piano.

Blum's suite of short pieces was "distributed throughout the program so to speak; it was a refreshing pleasure to hear the individual movements of this 'divertimento,' with the complex sonority of trumpet, saxophone, harmonium, and piano creating a piquant blend of tonal colors."[792]

A review in the *Tages-Anzeiger* reported that Blum's "compositions driven by dissonances and contemporary rhythms" had set the atmosphere "alight,"[793] and the critic in the *Neue Zürcher Zeitung* also spoke well of the "new compositions by Robert Blum."

During that second season the members of the press were very well disposed toward the Krater, and after the shows "friends of the Krater" regularly met at the Jecklin Keller.

Sacrilege and Provocation

In a book about Max Ernst, published as recently as 2008, the very first illustration is a film still from *La coquille et le clergyman* with the caption: "Films such as Luis Buñuel's *Un chien andalou* and *L'âge d'or* (Max Ernst acted in the latter) and *La coquille et le clergyman* (1927) by Antonin Artaud and Germaine Dulac show how enduringly sacrilege and provocation informed the phantasms of Surrealism."[794]

A still from *La Coquille et le clergyman* is illustrated in *Max Ernst: Une semaine de bonté,* ed. Werner Spies, Albertina (Vienna), Max Ernst Museum (Brühl) and Hamburger Kunsthalle (Dumont, 2008), p. 10, fig. 1.

Binia and Max Meet at the Krater

In summer of 1930, as Max Bill told me, during one of those unconventional Krater events where everything seemed to have been touched by "the Surrealist mood of the time,"[795] he suddenly noticed a young woman —Binia Spoerri—and immediately tried to find out more about her. The architect Elsa Burckhardt-Blum was able to tell him more about the woman who had caught his eye, because Binia was a friend of hers. So it was at one of those events, when there was "a real Krater mood ... and the atmosphere was fanned by high spirits, lively conversation, and loud music from the ever spinning turntable,"[796] that Binia Spoerri and Max Bill first connected—be it in May, in June or not until September 1930, there is no saying exactly when. Binia, a sophisticated young woman born on 18 August 1904 in Zürich-Fluntern, was four years older than Max.

Following the shows on 30 May and 1 June, on 14 and 15 June there were two more public performances at the Krater. In addition, according to a communication from the president, Paul Lang, at the end of June there was an end-of-season ball with cabaret interludes "by invitation only." Besides members of the Krater, this in-house celebration was also

794 Spies 2008, p. 10, fig. 1
795 EB., "Auffuhrung im 'Krater,'" in *Neue Zürcher Zeitung,* 2 June 1930
796 H.S.S., "'Krater'-Soirée," in *Zürcher Volkszeitung,* 12 June 1930, SCCPA
797 Fischer 1969, p. 69

for "Krater friends" (the list of names does not include Binia Spoerri); each person was allowed a "maximum of two registered guests." The next Krater event was on 27 September 1930.

Binia Spoerri did, however, photograph Max Bill working on the decorations for the November Ball at Kunstmuseum Winterthur in 1930 (illustrated in *Max Bill: Aspekte seines Werkes,* ed. Kunstmuseum Winterthur and Gewerbemuseum Winterthur [Sulgen and Zurich: Niggli, 2008], p. 208).

Max Ernst: Reliable Friends and Destructive Foes

Max Ernst spent some uncertain "surreal" years in Paris. And then the time came when the friction within the Surrealists' group was compounded by external pressures: Max Ernst fled after the French police interrogated him—the brutal methods used by the French police in interrogations were common knowledge.

"Animosities, intrigue, and misunderstandings pervaded the Surrealist group. There was no clarity as to the role painting should play. . . . The Rif War, which the Surrealists had opposed in a manifesto, forced Ernst to flee the police. The manifesto had created a huge stir; Ernst had been interrogated and his name was on the blacklist, along with those of his friends. So he traveled to Bretagne, to the ocean, under a false name and with a fake passport."[797]

Max Ernst's passions and desires were often overshadowed by tragedy. He and his first wife Luise Straus separated in 1922, a year after he and Paul Éluard had become friends. And although Éluard was providing Ernst with long-term financial support, Max embarked on a passionate affair with Éluard's wife Gala. In 1924, in the midst of all that, Paul Éluard suddenly disappeared; he was nowhere to be found. He had left Europe in a state of deep depression and his disappearance was widely regarded as little short of scandalous.

"Using money that he was supposed to pay into a bank for his father" Éluard purchased a passage to Indochina. When he sent a telegram from Saigon, Gala and Max Ernst followed him there, hoping to persuade him to return to Paris. "When Max Ernst and Gala met up with the escapee in Saigon, Paul Éluard had already come to the conclusion that it would be better to regard his attempted break with his old life as a mere lapse and to go back to Paris. However, Max Ernst did not go back with his friend, instead he and Gala went traveling and only returned to France, via Marseilles, three months later."[798]

In 1925, when that episode was over, Ernst rented his first studio in Montmartre.

The events leading up to Ernst's second marriage would be no less tumultuous. Jean Aurenche, a well-known film director happened to tell Ernst about his younger sister Marie-Berthe Aurenche, who had "received a strict education in a girls' boarding school on an island" and was now to due to return to Paris "in order to marry a certain lawyer, in accordance with her parents' wishes."[799] Max Ernst immediately suggested that Jean Aurenche should "bring his sister to one of the Surrealists' meetings." At their very first meeting Max Ernst and Marie-Berthe were instantly enraptured by each other and decided to become a couple. All set to leave Paris by the night train, they were at an inn eating supper with Paul Éluard when Marie-Berthe's tyrannical father burst in with a number of police officers in pursuit of "the German who had abducted his daughter." The lovers managed to hide, "and Éluard claimed that he was Max Ernst and allowed himself to be arrested. By the time the mistaken identity came to light, Max and Marie-Berthe had already left Paris."[800]

The political reaction in the early 1930s to *L'âge d'or*—Luis Buñuel's second Surrealist film, which Max Ernst and Salvador Dalí both worked on in 1930—has largely been forgotten: "The screening at Studio 28, an avant-garde movie theater in Paris, triggered a fierce contest between pro and anti. *L'âge d'or* was shown from 12 November until 3 December when members of a young, right-wing organization wrecked the seating. The police stepped in and banned any more screenings."[801]

This act of vandalism has been researched in some detail by Jürgen Pech: "Not long after the premiere in late 1930 at Studio 28 in Paris, one of the first non-profit cinemas, members of two radical right-wing groups—the Camelots du Roi and the Ligue Antijuive—stormed into a screening, smashing furniture and destroying paintings by Salvador

798 Fischer 1969, p. 67
799 Fischer 1969, p. 83
800 Fischer 1969, p. 83
801 Fischer 1969, p. 131
802 Pech 1991, p. 73
803 Frau Wassmer, Schloss Bremgarten bei Bern, to Max Bill, [ca. May/June 1930], Bibliothek Max Bill
804 Estate of Ernst F. Burckhardt relating to the cabaret association *Der Krater,* in SCCPA

Dalí, Max Ernst, Joan Miró, Man Ray, and Yves Tanguy that were on display in the foyer. The film was banned after that."[802]

In 1933, Max Ernst, who had long been harassed by the French police, was blacklisted by the Nazis. A year later, Max and Binia Bill invited him to stay with them in Zürich-Höngg.

The time Max Ernst spent at the home of Max and Binia Bill in 1934 is not mentioned in Lothar Fischer's illustrated monograph *Max Ernst* (Hamburg: Rororo Bildmonografien, 1969).

"Or did it rekindle your love?"

Max Wassmer—keen to help the young Bill to earn a living—not only commissioned him to design publicity materials for his cement manufacturing business, he also bought two of Max's watercolors, both done in 1928: *filosof* [*sic*] and *mondanbellender hund.* Perhaps even more importantly, he helped to ensure that Bill participated in the exhibition that opened at Kunsthalle Bern on 15 June 1930.

Looking forward to that event, Wassmer's wife, Tilli, invited Bill to stay with them in Schloss Bremgarten near Bern. She assumed that he would arrive in Bern some time before the opening: "You will of course come to us at Bremgarten and then stay for a while. . . . Perhaps you might like to bring some materials with you to work on. . . . The tower will be at your disposal." Word had evidently reached the Wassmers of Bill's trip to Paris in April/May, and Tilli was curious to find out how his meeting with Nusch in Paris had gone: "No doubt it was good for you to see your Nusch in Paris! Or did it rekindle your love? We can talk about all of that when you are here."[803]

Bill and his patron Max Wassmer naturally also met in other circumstances. In one instance Wassmer's name is on the guest list for the Krater cabaret theater.

"Wassmer, Max A., Schloss Bremgarten bei Bern," is listed as no. 87 in an index of "members of the visitors' organization, Friends of the Krater, drawn up on 12 Sept. 1930"; no. 39 on the same list of Friends of the Krater is the writer "Humm, R. J., Adlisbergstr. 88, Zürich," who will reappear in the present context in due course.[804]

Wassmer was always a staunch supporter of Max Bill's and the exhibition at Kunsthalle Bern came just a few months after Bill had told Hanns Fischli that he now had a patron. That exhibition included two other works by Max Bill from Wassmer's own collection: *tanzendes mädchen* (1927–28) and *sitzende* (1929). Two more works by Max Bill in the same exhibition—*rauchbläser* (1929, see p. 445) and *hermafrodit* (1929, see p. 268)—were bequeathed to me by Max and are now in my collection. The horizontal-vertical structure in the oil painting *rauchbläser* is distantly reminiscent of *Tectonische Gruppe* (see p. 152), painted at the Bauhaus in 1925 by Bill's preliminary course teacher, Josef Albers.

A New Quality Mark: bill

As if he had set himself the task of coming up with a publicity campaign for his own work, Max now decided to use the name "bill" as his own distinctive quality mark. The newcomer thus set himself apart from the other four artists participating in the exhibition at Kunsthalle Bern, all of whom were referred to, in the usual manner, by their first and last names: Jakob Probst, Leo Steck, Walo von May, and Félix Vallotton.

Max had known works by Félix Vallotton since he was a boy—his female nudes, sometimes quite bizarre, and his unmistakable landscapes. Soon after Vallotton's death in Paris in December 1925, Swiss art collectors loaned around a hundred paintings by Vallotton for a memorial exhibition at Kunstmuseum Winterthur, which opened in May 1926. By that time Max was a silversmith apprentice at the Kunstgewerbeschule in Zurich. However, he was still living with his parents in Winterthur, so it is fair to assume that he would not have missed that major exhibition in his own home town. And when he saw some of his own early works on display at Kunsthalle Bern in June 1930, he will surely have felt honored that they were in the company of works by the late Félix Vallotton, who had helped him to "learn to see" as a child in Kunstmuseum Winterthur.

Bill, who had clear memories of Vallotton's work from his childhood and youth, actively campaigned to persuade Kunsthaus Zürich to buy Vallotton's *Le Bain au soir d'été* (1892), which is now in the Kunsthaus collection.[805] And on 2 November 1975 he brought me a catalogue from a Vallotton exhibition that was then on display at Galerie Nathan in Zurich. Of the paintings illustrated in the catalogue, he was fascinated by *Les feux* (1911); I liked *Dôme de l'hôpital aux Andelys* (1924), and Bill drew my attention to the colors at the edge of the path, the way that the yellow turns into green (exh. cat. *Exposition Félix Vallotton, Gemälde und Zeichnungen,* Galerie Nathan, Zurich, 26 September–13 December 1975, figs. 9, 25).

805 Max Bill in conversation with Angela Thomas, 23 June 1975

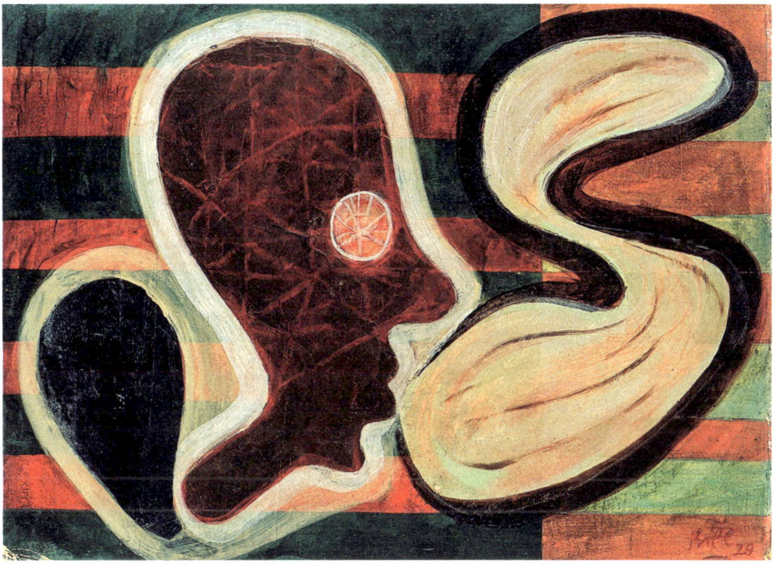

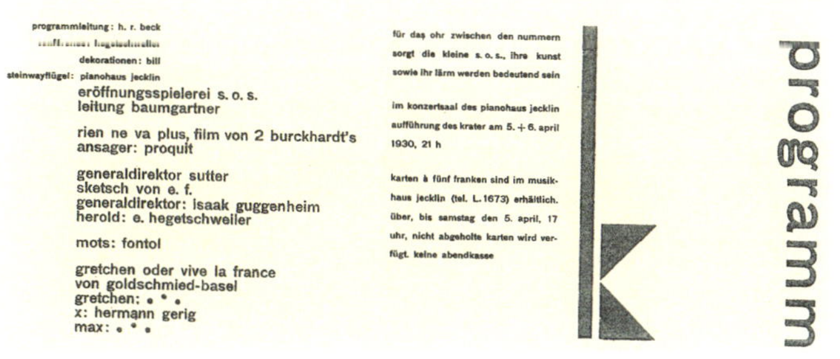

programmleitung: h. r. beck
dekorationen: bill
steinwayflügel: pianohaus jecklin

eröffnungsspielerei s. o. s.
leitung baumgartner

rien ne va plus, film von 2 burckhardt's
ansager: proquit

generaldirektor sutter
sketsch von e. f.
generaldirektor: isaak guggenheim
herold: e. hegetschweiler

mots: fontol

gretchen oder vive la france
von goldschmied-basel
gretchen: • • •
x: hermann gerig
max: • • •

für das ohr zwischen den nummern sorgt die kleine s. o. s., ihre kunst sowie ihr lärm werden bedeutend sein

im konzertsaal des pianohaus jecklin aufführung des krater am 5. + 6. april 1930, 21 h

karten à fünf franken sind im musikhaus jecklin (tel. L. 1673) erhältlich. über, bis samstag den 5. april, 17 uhr, nicht abgeholte karten wird verfügt. keine abendkasse

k

programm

Max Bill, *rauchbläser*, 1929,
oil on hardboard, 30 × 42 cm
Max Bill, Invitation to a soirée presented
by the Krater on 5 and 6 April 1930, 1930

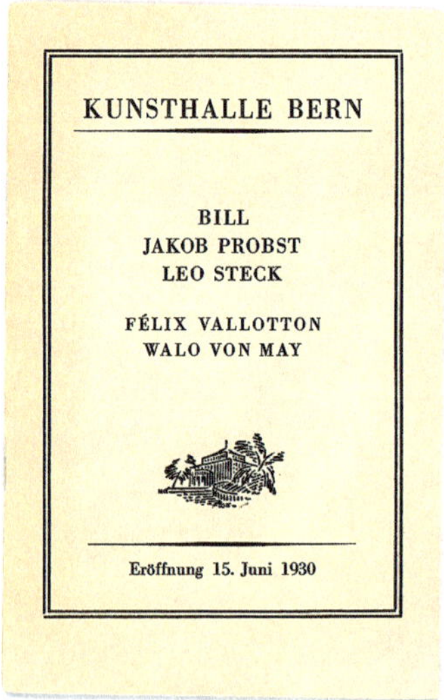

KUNSTHALLE BERN

BILL
JAKOB PROBST
LEO STECK

FÉLIX VALLOTTON
WALO VON MAY

Eröffnung 15. Juni 1930

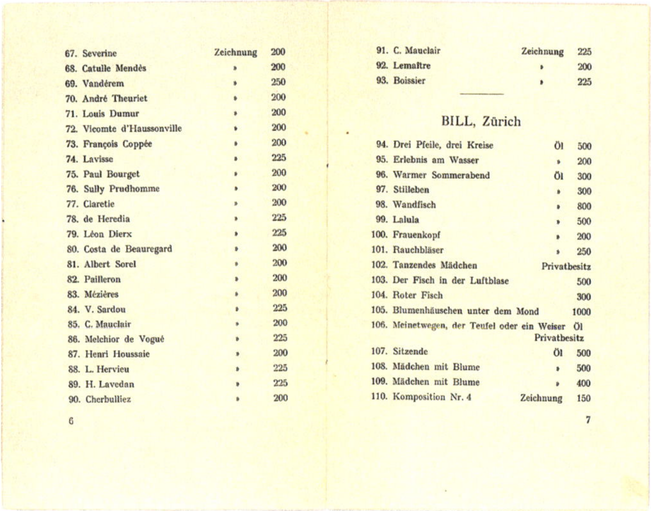

67. Severine	Zeichnung	200
68. Catulle Mendès	»	200
69. Vandérem	»	250
70. André Theuriet	»	200
71. Louis Dumur	»	200
72. Vicomte d'Haussonville	»	200
73. François Coppée	»	200
74. Lavisse	»	225
75. Paul Bourget	»	200
76. Sully Prudhomme	»	200
77. Claretie	»	200
78. de Heredia	»	225
79. Léon Dierx	»	225
80. Costa de Beauregard	»	200
81. Albert Sorel	»	200
82. Pailleron	»	200
83. Mézières	»	200
84. V. Sardou	»	225
85. C. Mauclair	»	200
86. Melchior de Vogué	»	225
87. Henri Houssaie	»	200
88. L. Hervieu	»	225
89. H. Lavedan	»	225
90. Cherbulliez	»	200

6

91. C. Mauclair	Zeichnung	225
92. Lemaître	»	200
93. Boissier	»	225

BILL, Zürich

94. Drei Pfeile, drei Kreise	Öl	500
95. Erlebnis am Wasser	»	200
96. Warmer Sommerabend	Öl	300
97. Stilleben	»	300
98. Wandfisch	»	800
99. Lalula	»	500
100. Frauenkopf	»	200
101. Rauchbläser	»	250
102. Tanzendes Mädchen		Privatbesitz
103. Der Fisch in der Luftblase		500
104. Roter Fisch		300
105. Blumenhäuschen unter dem Mond		1000
106. Meinetwegen, der Teufel oder ein Weiser	Öl	Privatbesitz
107. Sitzende	Öl	500
108. Mädchen mit Blume	»	500
109. Mädchen mit Blume	»	400
110. Komposition Nr. 4	Zeichnung	150

7

Program for the exhibition *Bill, Jakob Probst, Leo Steck, Félix Vallotton, Walo von May,* which opened on 15 June 1930 at Kunsthalle Bern

Max Bill price list, from the program for the Bern exhibition

There is a possibility that Bill may have traveled back to Zurich from Bremgarten or Bern a day before the exhibition opened—at any rate, there were events at the Krater on Saturday, 14 June, and Sunday, 15 June 1930, both starting at 8.30 p.m. As ever, they were reviewed in the papers. The premiere of the drama *Langlois* was presented by J. P. Samson and R. Wolfsohn, and there was a grotesquerie, *Mensch zwischen Rad und Wad,* by the Krater president Paul Lang; a "film of vehicular hurly-burly," shot by Gotthard Schuh, was also shown. This was reviewed in the *Neue Zürcher Zeitung,* albeit with no mention of Schuh: "In satirical ecstasy Paul Lang swings up into his satire of the world.... The car demon is seated on his throne and an old-style ruminating pedestrian is dispatched in an instant. Running concurrently there is film of vehicular hurly-burly. We are given a glimpse of a new epoch." However, the critic, "BJ," was sure that no one in the audience had understood a word of Samson's story and BJ was also not impressed with the program sheet: "the name of the director is given as "the director." So very informative."[806]

Meanwhile another critic was not at all bothered by that little joke: "The Krater was full of life.... the pink program with the (extinct!) lunar crater had attracted a large number of Krater friends.... It was all entirely up to the minute: jocular-grotesque episodes, sketches rejigged for a cabaret evening, brief intermezzos ... harmlessly impish satire, epigrammatic chansons, much anonymous modesty, much merry collaboration, chicly perfumed collectivity, intellectually appreciative delight, and—entertainment."[807]

There is no sign of the pink program in Max Bill's typography estate, which came to me in its entirety.

The writer Albert Ehrismann was also larking about in the audience and penned a review: "Paul Lang writes a play—*Mensch zwischen Rad und Wad*—calls it a grotesquerie and in it rails honestly and eloquently against the omnipotence of the automobile. And he hits the mark, sparking off flashes of insight that are deft, poetic, and bold. And for that very reason his piece is proper Krater comedy, new, experimental, and plays very well on the rough wooden boards of this cabaret stage. Production: Gotthard Schuh, who has also made a top-notch background film with automobile wheels and white policeman's gloves, which sets things rolling

806 BJ., "Veranstaltung des 'Kraters'" in *Neue Zürcher Zeitung,* 17 June 1930, SCCPA

807 H.S.S., "'Krater'-Soirée," in *Zürcher Volkszeitung,* 18 June 1930, SCCPA

à la Piscator ... and, 'last but not least,' Emil Hegetschweiler in a mime study as an unlicensed fisherman on the Quai bridge at midnight. How he pulled that off!—You should have seen it! Bravo, Hegi!"[808]

The humoresque by the left-leaning, French writer Samson (who lived in Zurich), which the *NZZ* critic did not understand at all, was discussed more sympathetically in the *National-Zeitung* in Basel: "*Langlois,* a humoresque by J. P. Samson and R. Wolfsohn was very nimbly translated by Dr. Paul Lang, the intellectual leader at the Krater; the pliability of the French dialogue was not lost.... Without doubt the most inventive presentation was Paul Lang's *Mensch zwischen Rad und Wad,* a grotesque staged by Gotthard Schuh. Two devices simultaneously projected films of contemporary street scenes with traffic onto the walls, in front of which a pedestrian faced legal action in the semi-darkness. This emotional figure tried in vain to defend the lyricism of the passer-by against the tyranny of the traffic. Hermann Gerig (Basel) added fresh accents to the dialogue."[809]

Bill, who may or may not have managed to be in Zurich for that Krater event on the evening before the opening in Bern, was certainly personally acquainted with the rebellious, non-conformist writer Albert Ehrismann. As it happens, just a few days after the exhibition in Bern opened, an internal Krater evening was planned, during which the company would read "manuscripts by Ehrismann." According to a circular, dated 22 June 1930, from the Krater president, Paul Lang, that meeting, which Max Bill would also be expected to attend, was scheduled for 25 June 1930. The venue was the home of one Maria Münch, at Böcklinstrasse 17, Zurich. Maria Münch, like Max Bill, sometimes designed stage sets for the Krater. The same circular also announces that Gotthard Schuh had been voted onto the program committee at the most recent meeting—the same Gotthard Schuh chosen by Erwin Bill to oversee his son's finances.

Bill was extremely active at the Krater, and in June 1930 the rest of the company approved his proposal to put on a whole evening himself in February 1931.

"In June" the Krater decided on "a general program," with three shows per month "in November (Lang), in January (Burckhardt), in February (Bill) and in March (Schuh)." However, given that they would not have a

808 Albert Ehrismann, "Der Krater" in *Tages-Anzeiger,* 18 June 1930, SCCPA

809 E.Br. "Theaterrundschau. Die Krater-Bühne in Zürich," in *National-Zeitung,* 21 June 1930, SCCPA

810 In "Der Krater," Jahresbericht Saison 1930, Dr. Paul Lang, 4 October 1930, SCCPA

new performance space until the beginning of October, "the prospect was rather uncertain"; moreover the Krater president, Dr. Paul Lang, stepped down, "exhausted," at the beginning of October 1930. His duties were taken on by Ernst F. Burckhardt.[810]

Binia Visits Bill in His Studio

On 9 August 1930 the registrar for the city of Zurich wrote to "Herr Max Bill, architect" at Stadelhoferstr. 27: "We acknowledge your withdrawal of your intent to be joined in marriage with Maria Benz in Strasbourg. We hereby return to you, as requested, your birth certificate and your proof of residence."

After his painful separation from Nusch, Bill felt the urge to travel abroad, to go east. He wanted to leave Switzerland (and his father) far behind him. So he wrote to Mart Stam, to ask whether he could become part of the team led by Stam and Ernst May, whether there might be work for him in the Soviet Union, if not as an architect then possibly at least providing lettering and signage, or as an "advertising technician." However, as we have already seen, on 5 August 1930, Mart Stam replied from Frankfurt, politely declining Bill's hopeful request.

It may be that it was only really after his hopes of traveling to the Soviet Union came to nothing that Max Bill fully registered Binia Spoerri. Did they become aware of each other at the "experimental" Krater ball on 27 September 1930? Or had they already met face to face at the Krater in June—without Binia imagining their meeting might lead to anything because Bill was already hoping to leave for the Soviet Union?

Whatever the case, Bill later told me that, following their initial meeting in the Krater, Binia visited him in his studio at Stadelhoferstrasse 27 in the autumn of 1930. On 20 September 1930 the Krater issued a "polite" invitation to an "experimental ball" at the Belvoir in Zurich (see fig. p. 342). Bill designed the invitation and painted the décor for the evening; he is also named as one of the performers in a "13 minute cabaret." Other company members listed for that event include Gotthard Schuh and the composer Robert Blum. However, when the ball was postponed, another notice designed by Bill followed. It pokes fun at the Calvinist attitude of the Zurich police and assures the reader that the postponed ball "will be all the more wonderful."

"The Krater Ball experiment has been postponed to Saturday, 27 Sept. at 9 p.m., since a police license has not been granted due to the next day being a day of repentance when there should be prayer (not dancing) from the early hours onward. So, given the long time that now stretches out before us, it will be all the more wonderful. Tickets are already on sale at Blumenstump, Bleicherweg 6" (typography estate of Max Bill, collection of Angela Thomas).

"participants are altendorf. beck. bill. blum. fontol. grau. guggenheim. hegetschweiler. pfister. proquit. schuh. silander. wolfensberger. master of ceremonies beck. decor bill."

Binia Spoerri was from a "good family," as people used to say. She was the youngest of three daughters born to Ferdinand Jakob Spoerri and Elise Spoerri-Gross in Zürich-Fluntern. Before Binia met Bill she had already studied cello in Paris with Diran Alexanian and Pablo Casals and had graduated from the École normale de musique in 1926. In the autumn of 1930 she had just returned from Berlin, where she had briefly attended a photography course taught by Lucia Moholy at the Itten-Schule at Potsdamerstrasse 75—a design school founded by Johannes Itten. According to Bill, Binia visited him in his studio in the hope of "learning more about current art and typography." Soon after Binia's visit she and Bill started working together on design commissions for various clients.

At the same time Bill was still an active member at the Krater. The next annual general meeting for the Krater was held at the splendid Hotel Baur en Ville in Zurich. Paul Lang stepped down as president and Ernst F. Burckhardt was elected to take over from him. Besides Paul Lang and Ernst F. Burckhardt (who was accompanied by his wife Elsa), the members with voting rights present on that evening also included Max Bill and his "financial manager," Gotthard Schuh. The architect Egidius Streiff was voted in as treasurer.

Egidius Streiff was born in Glarus in 1897 and studied at the ETH under Professor Moser, whom he admired. He already lost his mother as a child; his father, who owned the Trümpy & Co. cloth mill in Glarus, was, from time to time, also a member of the cantonal council.

Although Streiff was described as a "Glarner [man from Glarus], Glarner and yet again Glarner" by Herr Prof. Dr. H. C. Hans Hofmann, with whom he collaborated on various development plans,

811 In *Zum Andenken an Egidius Streiff* [1952?]

812 In the supplement to the April issue of *Letzte Politik* 8:14, (1929)

813 "Der Krater," list of members in October 1930, estate of Ernst F. Burckhardt on the cabaret association "Der Krater," in SCCPA

he accepted a position in Hans Streuli's architectural practice in Wädenswil (canton of Zürich) and moved to Zürich-Enge. "He kept his wealth quiet, almost fretfully, like a secret."[811]

In the future Max Bill would often come into contact with Egidius Streiff, who was eleven years his senior and would always be associated in Bill's mind with that carefree time at the Krater cabaret. One important point of contact arose when Streiff became Secretary of the Swiss Werkbund in 1931 and, as such, was later involved in the organization of the Swiss pavilion—designed by Max Bill—at the Milan Triennial in 1936.

In 1949 Bill would design the topography and layout for his own documentary overview *Moderne Schweizer Architektur (1925–1945)*, edited by Egidius Streiff (together with Professor Dr. Linus Birchler, Dr. Giedion, Werner Jegher [engineer], Peter Meyer [architect] and Dr. Georg Schmidt). Three years after the publication of this compendium—which features no buildings by Streiff but does include designs by Bernoulli, Bill, and Fischli—Egidius Streiff died at the age of fifty-four. In March 1952 he was cremated in Zurich.

In the minutes of that annual general meeting Max Bill is (still) listed under the heading "Co-opted Members of the Program Committee: 1. Max Bill, designer, Stadelhoferstrasse 27; 2. Robert Blum, music director, Staadhof, Baden, Aargau; 3. Frau Maria Münch, Boecklinstr. 17; 4. J. P. Samson, Seilergraben 21."

This self-identification by Bill echoes the advertisement, seeking work, that he put in *Letzte Politik* in April 1929: "Switzerland Zurich. Architecture: Max Bill, Stadelhoferstrasse 27. Design: modern architecture, advertising, teacher of all areas of modern design (color, form, space)."[812]

During that same meeting Elsa Burckhardt-Blum and Gotthard Schuh were voted onto the program committee as full members.

In October 1930 the full list of Krater members was set out in (almost) alphabetical order: "H. R. Beck, architect; Max Bühler, printer; E. F. Burckhardt, architect; Karl Egender, architect; Dr. G. Guggenheim, lawyer; Isaak Guggenheim, entrepreneur; Emil Hegetschweiler, actor; Paul Hürlimann, entrep.; Dr. Paul Lang, writer; Emil Mauser, entrep.; Dr. Arthur Mojonnier; Gotthard Schuh, painter; Egidius Streiff, architect; Konrad Falke, writer."[813]

Konrad Falke was considerably older than Max Bill. Three years after Bill was born, Falke published *Kainz als Hamlet, ein Abend im Theater* (Zurich and Leipzig: Rascher, 1911) in honor of the actor Josef Kainz, whom he had seen playing Hamlet at the Neues Schauspielhaus in Berlin in early 1900. Kainz died of cancer in Vienna on 20 September 1910.

The architect Karl Egender had come to the Krater through his contact with both Emil Hegetschweiler and Albert Ehrismann. Egender had recently won a prestigious commission to design new buildings for the Kunstgewerbeschule and the Kunstgewerbemuseum in Zurich. Work began on this complex in 1930 and was completed in 1933; at this point, in 1930, Egender's building for the lido in Küsnacht on Lake Zurich had just opened. He himself was a keen swimmer and a fan of competitive cycling, and he commissioned his cabaret colleague Max Bill to design the signage for the lido. Max would dearly have loved to be designing buildings by now but still had to content himself with small signage contracts. Also in 1930 Karl Egender married the painter Trudy Wintsch, and Max Bill subsequently designed the jacket for *Kleine Reise ins Elsass* (Zurich: Girsberger, 1937) by Trudy Egender-Wintsch.

Karl Egender was born in 1890 in Burzwiler in Alsace. When he was seven his family moved to Zurich, where his father set up his own plasterer's business. Egender did an apprenticeship as a structural engineering draftsman in the Wassmer brothers' architectural practice in Zurich; in 1921 he opened his own architectural practice in Zurich. In 1930–39 Bruno Giacometti (brother of the artist Alberto Giacometti) was an important member of Egender's practice. Later on Ernst F. Burckhardt periodically worked in his practice.

Karl Egender became a member of BSA, of SIA, of CIAM and of the GSMBA (president of the Zurich section in 1950–56). Egender's designs include the terrace restaurant and fashion section at the *Schweizerische Landesausstellung* in Zurich (1939), the indoor stadium at Zürich-Oerlikon (1939), and the theater Stadthof 11 in Zürich-Oerlikon (1956–59); his last major work, the Globus department store on Bahnhofstrasse in Zurich, was opened in 1969.[814]

The Krater at the ETH

In October 1930 the students' union at the ETH (Swiss Federal Institute of Technology) in Zurich contacted the Krater to ask if the company would like to take part in an ETH party in November. The Krater ensemble decided to accept the invitation and Bill volunteered for the planning team along with Samson, Burckhardt, Maria Münch, and Gotthard Schuh.

The ETH party was the culmination of celebrations marking the seventy-fifth anniversary of the founding of the ETH, and the invitations

814 See Dosch 1979–80

der **krater**

lädt sie zu seinem

ball-
versuch

im belvoir, samstag, den 20. sept., abends 21 uhr

eingang seestr. strassenbahn brunaustr.

höflich ein

wenn sie sich amüsieren wollen, tanzen wollen, gemütlich in ungezwungener, lustiger toilette --- dann kommen sie an den krater-ball ---

es gibt dort musik von elektr. verstärktem grammofon aus dem pianohaus jecklin, zum tanzen, schiessbude, ballenwerfen, 13-minuten-kabarette -

mitwirkende sind: altendorf, beck, bill, blum, fontol, grau, guggenheim, hegetschweiler, pfister, proquit, schuh, silander, wolfensberger
leitung des abends: beck. dekorationen: bill
kabarette: silander und proquit.

eintritt beträgt: kraterfreunde fr. 5
eingeführte fr. 10
(einladung=eingeführt)
vorverkauf bei blumenstump, bleicherweg 6, telefon 36.117

also

samstag, den 20. september, 21 uhr im belvoir, in ausgezeichneter laune.

Max Bill, Invitation to an "experimental ball" put on by the Krater, 1930
Max Bill, *Binia Bill-Spoerri,* ca. 1931

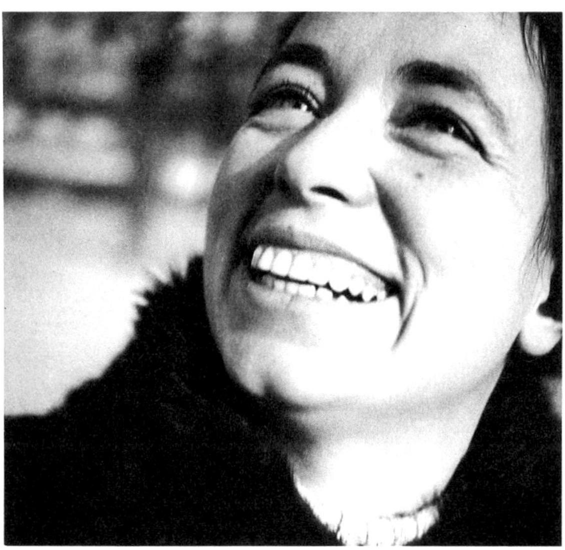

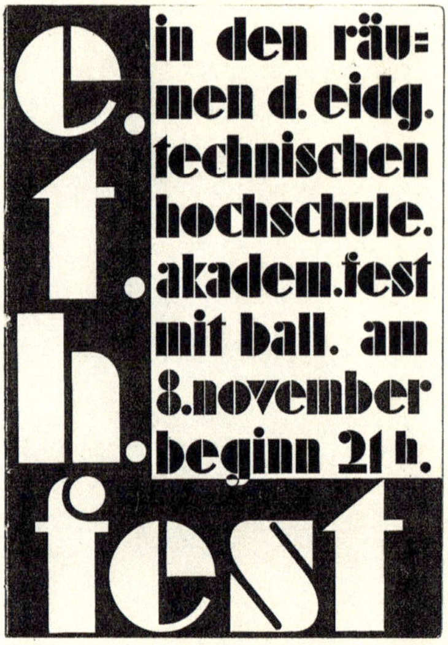

Max Bill (presumably), Invitation to a party and ball at the ETH on 8 November, starting at 9 p.m., 1930

Erwin Bill in his SBB uniform, photo montage from Erich Schmid's film *Bill—Das absolute Augenmass,* 2008

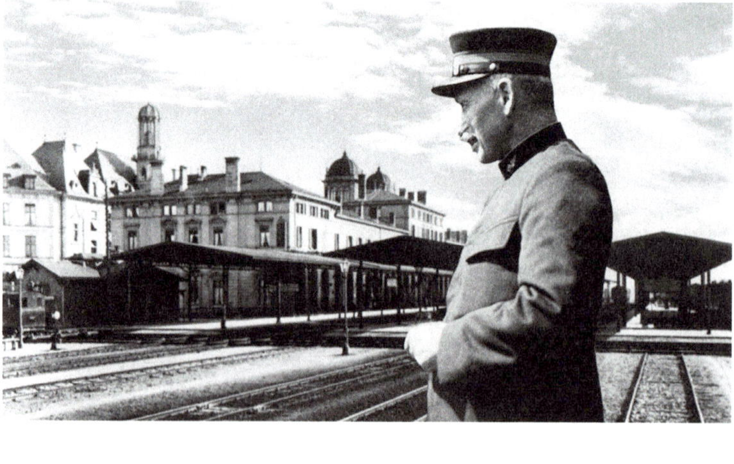

may well have been designed by Max Bill. Although there are no specimen copies of it in his typography estate, the striking design and the use of lowercase lettering do point in his direction. In the list of "associations participating" in the ETH party on 8 November 1930, the "Künstlerbühne Der Krater" is named first, although the Krater members who took part on that occasion are not named individually.

During the course of the preparations for that event, Max Bill discovered that there was a darkroom at the ETH. And after Binia Spoerri visited Bill at his studio in Stadelhoferstrasse, she embarked on exploratory work in the ETH darkroom on his advice. Later on Max could no longer recall the name of the professor in charge of the darkroom at the time, however, he did remember that Binia worked there for several months, maybe even for a year. At that time the ETH did not have a photography department, as such, but it did have a darkroom.

"Bill specified: there was no photographic department; Binia stayed in the photographic laboratory of the ETH, experimenting, doing photographic-technical research with a professor in charge (whose name Bill couldn't recall). She stayed there for a couple of months, for about one year."[815]

"In 1931 I married Binia Spoerri from Zurich. She had studied cello with Stutschewsky, Alexanian, and Casals, but after graduating she switched from music to photography, which she learned at the Eidg. Politechnikum [ETH]."[816]

". . . to improve the quality of life"

Many writers were eager to have their works premiered at the Krater and in October 1930, alone, "around 60 manuscripts" were submitted. The members who volunteered to read those texts and make a stageworthy selection included Elsa Burckhardt-Blum, Samson, and Schuh—but not Max Bill because he was currently preoccupied with anthroposophical texts.

815 In "Max Bill: The Early Years. An Interview by Angela Thomas," trans. Susan Ernst-Peters, *Journal of Decorative and Propaganda Arts,* 19, Swiss Theme Issue (1993)

816 Bill 1942 [b]

One wonders if Bill decided for himself to explore anthroposophy, or did the idea come from elsewhere, perhaps from Binia Spoerri? Or could he have been inspired to do so by a lingering memory of books Wassily Kandinsky recommended to his students at the Bauhaus?

In the same way that Jean Arp was "probably" introduced to theosophical ideas by Kandinsky (see *Das Auge des Eros: Kandinsky, Klee, Arp, Miró, Calder,* exh. cat. Munich: Haus der Kunst, 1994, p. 537).

At that time—as Max Bill told me—he read various things to further his own education and had a special interest in fundamental research. As he once explained to me, although people in those days were already living in a "post-Einstein" era, the wider impact of Einstein's thinking was not yet well publicised. After his time at the Bauhaus, Bill had read various books by anthroposophists, such as Paul Schatz and Hermann Baravalle von Brackenburg, which were "certainly important ideologically" for him. Bearing in mind the sums that Erwin Bill was still expecting his son to pay back, it seems most likely that in those days, around 1930, he borrowed the books he was reading, rather than buying them.

The Bibliothek Max Bill contains a copy of Hermann Baravalle von Brackenburg's *Das Reich geometrischer Formen* (Stuttgart: Freie Waldorfschule, 1935). According to a handwritten note in the book, Max Bill read it in 1941.

Later on, in the 1950s, when Max Bill became founding-rector of the Hochschule für Gestaltung in Ulm, he appointed both of those anthroposophists—Paul Schatz and Hermann Baravalle von Brackenburg—to the teaching staff, which infuriated some other faculty members, notably Tomás Maldonado.

Max Bill told me this on 31 March 1993 in Zumikon, following a trip together to Paris, when he came across a reference to the artist Joseph Beuys in connection with Rudolf Steiner in an article in the *Neue Zürcher Zeitung.* Prof. Dr. Hermann Baravalle von Brackenburg taught foundation level "constr. geometry" as a guest lecturer at the Hochschule für Gestaltung in Ulm in 1954–59; the engineer Paul Schatz arrived at the HfG as a guest lecturer for constructive geometry in 1955 (see Hartmut Seeling, "Geschichte der Hochschule für Gestaltung Ulm, 1953–1968," diss. Universität Köln, 1985, pp. 689, 709; Bibliothek Max Bill).

Anyone reading Max Bill's writings has to search long and hard before finding any indication of his own personal views on anthroposophy. Did

817 Max Bill, "Der Gesamtkunstwerkkreuzweg," *Züriwoche,* 24 March 1983, p. 49

818 Giedion 2007, p. 392

he intentionally keep them to himself? In the end I found what I was looking for in an exhibition review by Bill, in which he commented that he took a favorable view of anthroposophy since, like the Bauhaus (which he refers to in the same breath), its aim was "to improve the quality of life."

This quotation is taken from an article by Max Bill on the exhibition *Der Hang zum Gesamtkunstwerk,* conceived by Harald Szeemann and shown at Kunsthaus Zürich in 1983. Bill criticized what he sees as the "arbitrariness" of Szeemann's concept: "the exhibition certainly does not solely present fixed ideas à la Richard Wagner or Gabriele D'Annunzio, on the contrary, these mingle—entirely arbitrarily—with notions aiming at improving the quality of life, of the kind found in anthroposophy or the Bauhaus movement, for instance, or in the force field of Antoni Gaudí's cathedral."[817]

In the late autumn of 1930, Binia and Max's friends Elsa Burckhardt-Blum and Carola Giedion-Welcker set off for Moscow via Berlin. As a student in Munich, Giedion-Welcker had been drawn to the ideals of the Bavarian Councils Republic, and that "orientation toward the political left," which she and her husband Sigfried Giedion shared, endured as long as they both lived. As their son Andres later recounted, it endured despite Giedion-Welcker recognizing the "catastrophic nature of the developments" in the Soviet Union that she saw for herself on that trip to Moscow. Part of her reason for visiting Moscow was to find out, on her husband's behalf, if it might be possible to hold a CIAM Congress there. With that in mind, when she was in Moscow she "made contact with the architects' team led by the German architect Ernst May. She also attempted to make contact with Mart Stam and El Lissitzky." On her return to Switzerland she told Sigfried Giedion, who held the position of Secretary at CIAM, that he would be best advised to go to Moscow himself in May 1931 and "definitely head for the Grandhôtel, where May is living."[818]

"At some point I have to build my first house . . ."

After years of conflict with his father, the young Max Bill decided to approach him in a very different guise. In September 1930, keener than ever to design and build a house, he presented himself as a well informed judge of architecture with a special expertise in *Neues Bauen* and proposed a construction project for his father to consider. Erwin Bill thanked him for his proposal in mid-September.[819]

Erwin Bill had a potential construction budget of 28,000 Swiss francs. However, for all Max's eagerness to sign a construction contract with his father, the total cost of his proposal was 35,000 Swiss francs. But now, having been unable to get on top of his own debts for so long, Max suddenly set out very careful calculations for his father, in the hope of persuading him to increase his budget and build a larger house. Erwin Bill had never before received such a well-considered letter from his son.

"Dear Father ... please find enclosed a brochure with KOBAG's terms and conditions. Although you feel that the construction cost should not exceed 28,000 fr., I believe that is not right, if you really want to have a comfortable, well constructed house. Of course I don't know how much you can raise for the construction without taking out a mortgage ... but if you were to build with KOBAG, paying 35,000 francs ... in monthly installments ... funds would be released to you ... and from these calculations [not included here] you can see that, with the monies available to you, it would be possible for you to have a larger, better house than you thought, and that it would automatically pay itself off at the same time.... And as to the design ... the house fits so well into this area because it will be built without pomp and eye-catching superstructures, such as a pitched roof ..."

With regard to the two different building costs mentioned in this exchange of letters, I would like to include a relevant quotation, by way of comparison. A few years before this, Le Corbusier and Pierre Jeanneret drew up plans for two dwelling houses "Am Weissenhof" (1927) in Stuttgart, which were built by Alfred Roth. "The construction costs alone for the duplexes were 28,800 deutsch marks for the smaller one and 33,600 deutsch marks for the larger one ... I remember that cost projections for our buildings were very considerably exceeded."[820]

Max did not try to sway his father with arguments alone but rather to convince him with hard facts, extolling the virtues of flat roofs and of the new possibilities open to him: "We now use different means to build with, we have steel-frame constructions and poured concrete, which

819 Erwin Bill, Winterthur crossed out and replaced with "gyrenbad b. turbenthal," to Max Bill, [13?] September 1930, Archiv Max Bill

820 Roth 1977, unpaginated

821 Max Bill, 15 September 1930 to Erwin Bill, Archiv Max Bill

822 Max Bill to Erwin Bill, 15 September 1930

removes the need for wood as the main load-bearing element combined with stone (it is different for fully timber-built houses). Window frames are made from reliable materials that don't swell up in the rain, develop cracks, etc. and that don't make the inside dark and spoil the beautiful view. . . .Every era has built in its own way. And we have our way. . . . In Zurich 3 estates are currently being built with over 400 dwellings constructed in this way, some villas are still under construction, others in the environs of Zurich are finished, lakeside houses on Lake Zurich, also in Mürren, Montana. . . . In Zurich a synagogue, the Gewerbeschule, and the cantonal hospital . . . are all being built like that. In Basel Professor Moser has built a concrete church and the landscape conservation authorities are no longer in any doubt that it is better to build modern houses than to paper over the Swiss landscape with imitations of old styles. . . . And there is another thing. You feel that your furniture would not fit into this house. But my proposed house has larger rooms than yours, so there is enough space. . . . You have an Empire table, a matching sideboard and small table, a cupboard that can also be described as Empire. And you have Stabelle chairs that you place round the Empire table, and it doesn't perturb you." Max Bill pursues his point by citing Kandinsky's home in Dessau as an example: "In Dessau Kandinsky mainly furnished his home with Russian Baroque . . . good pieces from one era will always go well with good pieces from another era. . . . They will certainly fit, there just has to be enough space, because cluttered houses are unpleasant to be in."[821]

Later on, Bill stayed true to his precept that "overloaded apartments are unpleasant," notably when he built his own studio-and-home in Zumikon (1967–68). Its dimensions are very generous—as Bill himself said, you can always fill it (not to be mistaken for "overloading") later on.

His conclusion reveals how urgently he wanted to find work as an architect: "I would be very happy if you liked the proposal and if you decided to let me build it. At some point I have to build my first house, if I want to be asked to build more . . . with warm regards, to Aunt Lina, too."[822]

Erwin Bill was possibly already thinking of moving away from Winterthur with his second wife, Lina—which could be why Max came up with his proposal for a new house.

"Max didn't like" the house designed by his father, as Dora Nyfeler (parish clerk for Ligerz) told me in 2008. After his father died, Max "actually wanted to have it demolished." But "because he couldn't have built a new house on the same spot, he sold it in the early 1960s."

In the end, on 31 December 1931, Erwin and Lina Bill moved to Ligerz by Lake Biel, where they would indeed have a new home (called "In der Baume') built for them, but to a design by Erwin Bill. When Erwin Bill registered in Ligerz, his new place of residence—having retired from his position with Swiss railways—he gave his status as a "man of private means" and, very soon afterward, on 9 January 1932, he embarked on his duties as the new parish clerk for the village. Erwin Bill was also still the *Turnus* secretary for the Schweizerischer Kunstverein, which meant that he took delivery of written submissions from artists applying to participate in *Turnus* exhibitions.

Registration forms had to be "returned by 15 March 1932 to Mr. Erwin Bill, Turnus Secretary, Ligerz. Veuillez réexpedier ce bulletin à M. Erwin Bill, secrétaire du Turnus, à Gléresse, d'ici au 15 mars 1932." And the works registered by the artists had to be in Zurich by 2 April 1932 at the latest. In 2007 Christoph Geiger kindly sent me a copy of a registration form of that type.

With these contributions to the social fabric, Erwin Bill in effect improved his own status and on 18 December 1937 he was elected president of the parish council in Ligerz and remained in office until early May 1943.

Group Z, Zurich

Bill's new friend Hanns Welti had shown two works at the *Cercle et carré* exhibition in Paris in 1930—the exhibition that Max Bill and Ernst F. Burckhardt may well have seen when they were there. In the autumn of 1930 Jean Arp visited studios in Paris to seek out suitable items for an exhibition to be held in Zurich. When that exhibition opened as *Produktion Paris 1930* at Kunstsalon Wolfsberg, the opening address was given by Carola Giedion-Welcker. The introduction to the catalogue was written by Sigfried Giedion.

Hanns Welti's work was also selected for *Produktion Paris 1930,* which suggests that he may have had studios in both Zurich and Paris. Other participants included Ernst, Léger, Van Doesburg, Mondrian, Vantongerloo, the Arps, and the Delaunays. Since this was a selling exhibition Arp

823 Jean Arp to Carola Giedion-Welcker, 25 October 1930, in Bruderer-Oswald 2007, pp. 68–69
824 "Produktion Paris," in *Neue Zürcher Zeitung,* 31 October 1930, late edition
825 Jean Arp to Sigfried Giedion, 14 November 1930, in Bruderer-Oswald 2007, p. 69
826 In SCCPA
827 Founding protocol of Gruppe Z, Zurich, Bibliothek Max Bill

proposed that "a fixed price of 5,000 French francs be charged for works by Mondrian, Arp, and Vantongerloo because they are basically all equally hard up."[823]

The critic writing in the *Neue Zürcher Zeitung* was not at all impressed by this exhibition, as unimpressed as he had been by *Abstrakte und surrealistische Malerei und Plastik* at Kunsthaus Zürich in 1929: "that these dayflies ... want to live forever and that abstraction all too easily descends into stagnation and *ennui* was already observed and deplored in the Surrealists' exhibition at Kunsthaus Zürich."[824]

Arp's response to this scathing review, which had yet more jibes, was that "of course it's tedious when things that go without question elsewhere are just grunted at with bloodshot eyes in Switzerland."[825]

On 9 December 1930 the last Krater program committee meeting was held "at Burckhardt, Münsterhof" in Zurich—but Bill did not put in an appearance on that occasion. According to the minutes the members present were E. F. Burckhardt, Schuh, and Samson: "It was decided that all members will read André Gide's *Prométhée mal enchainé* with a view to adapting it for a full-length evening program overseen by G. Schuh."[826] There is no knowing if Bill read that book by Gide, but we do know that it was around then that he and Hanns Welti set up a new Group Z, based in Zurich.

An *earlier* Gruppe Z had of course previously been formed in Dessau in the late 1920s. Its members had included—besides Max Bill, who acted as secretary for the group—Hilde Rantzsch, Annemarie Hennings, and Hanns Fischli, among others.

The relationship between Bill and Hanns Fischli, which had suffered a few dents, was now mended, improved, and in excellent working order, so in December 1930, sitting amiably side by side, those two members of the first Group Z in Dessau now put their names, in alphabetical order, to "the Zurich minutes recording the foundation and constitution of 'Group Z Painting and Sculpture': Group Z is a union of designers formed for the mutual promotion of their interests.—Planned activities—Group Z will present exhibitions in Zurich, Switzerland, and abroad.... The following sign this constitution, thereby founding Group Z December 1930 Zurich—Bill Fischli Leuppi Steiner Welti."[827] The typewritten name "Schwarz" was added to that list, only to be crossed out and replaced by hand with "Brun."

Anton Stankowski's original pseudonym "Schwarz" (black) was changed to "Brun" (brown) in the Zurich Group Z.

The announcement of the opening of the memorial exhibition *Hans Fischli (1909–1989)* at Ortsmuseum Meilen, with the title "Wer Nur Musik Versteht, Versteht Auch Davon Nichts—Werke von Hans Fischli im Ortsmuseum Meilen," was published in Tages-Anzeiger, 1 October 1990.

". . . Bill presumably has no money"

Besides books on music and anthroposophy, in early the 1930s Max Bill also read a book by Paul Niggli on structural crystallography and a book by Andreas Speiser on mathematical thinking.

Looking back, Bill could not say for sure if the title of Andreas Speiser's book *Die mathematische Denkweise* (Zurich: Rascher, 1932) had influenced his choice of title for his own text "Über die mathematische Denkweise" (*Werk* 36:3 [March 1949], pp. 86–91).

Around 1931, having immersed himself in these various disciplines and having heeded Jeanne Bucher's heartfelt advice to shake off the artistic influence of Paul Klee, Bill started to develop a new concept entirely of his own.

On 22 December 1930 he turned twenty-two and just one month later, on 22 January 1931, he and Binia Spoerri married in a civil ceremony with Elsa Burckhardt-Blum as one of their two witnesses.

After working as an intern in the office of architect Karl Egender, Elsa Burckhardt-Blum—a friend of Binia and Max's who was studying art history at the time—decided to concentrate solely on architecture. Elsa, who was eight years older than Max Bill, was both a friend and a lover for a time. He told me this unprompted, although without saying when that liaison was—before or after his marriage to Binia Spoerri.

Besides Binia and Max and their witnesses, there was no one else at the ceremony—not even their parents. Binia's mother, Ida Elise Spoerri, née Gross, had sent the young couple "20 Swiss francs . . . because Bill presumably has no money to pay for a wedding breakfast'—as Max told me. However, Binia's parents did also send a gift of one thousand Swiss francs.

Binia Bill took a portrait photograph (undated) of her mother Ida Spoerri. Her mother's face is distinctly careworn (illustrated in *Binia Bill—Fotografien,* Aargauer Kunsthaus [Zurich: Scheidegger & Spiess 2004], p. 77).

Binia's father, Ferdinand Jakob Spoerri, who began life as a farmer's boy in the Töss Valley in the canton of Zürich, later became the representative in Japan for Gebrüder Volkart, a global company that traded coffee and cotton worldwide. Having been orphaned at a young age, Ferdinand Jakob had "risen astonishingly high," as Max told me, and now had "a large Japanese collection in Switzerland." Meanwhile, Ferdinand Jakob's brother stayed on the farm, often lost at cards, and ran up debts, which Binia's father paid off from time to time. Another uncle, Henry D. Gross—Ida Elise's brother—freely admitted that the news of his niece's marriage to Max Bill had come as a shock; but as soon as he had recovered he transferred some funds into their post office account.

Although Binia and Bill were ideologically opposed to the social circles that Binia's parents moved in, they did occasionally accept an invitation to visit the Spoerris. Perhaps frustratingly, no commissions came Bill's way from the Spoerris' contacts. On the contrary, when a friend of Max's father-in-law needed an architect, the contract did not go to Bill, as he had hoped, but to Karl Egender, whom Bill had worked with at the Krater in 1930. There is no knowing if that project was realized or not. Although architects came and went in Egender's practice, it seems he never called on Max Bill's services.

Many years later, when we were talking, Max suddenly recalled meeting Anna and Rudolf Baumann-Kienast at his parents-in-law's house when he and Binia had been invited for a meal. As far as Bill he remembered that meeting must have been in the early 1930s—presumably before Seidenfirma Baumann had gone into liquidation in the first half of the 1930s. Looking back Max could not imagine that his father-in-law would ever have invited a guest embroiled in a failed company.

In the year before Annemarie Hennings arrived at the Bauhaus—where Max Bill "fell for her"—she had painted the *King David* frieze in the home of Anna Baumann-Kienast in Lugano. And Binia had read, and recommended to Max, Rudolf Baumann's book *Der Tropenspiegel* (Zurich: Orell Füssli, 1925).

Honeymoon

Bill's third trip to Italy, which took him all the way to Sicily, was his honeymoon with Binia in February 1931. Binia was four years older than he and had more experience of the world, which still mattered at his young age. Their choice of destination may seem surprising, considering that by then Italy was already in the grip of a Fascist regime. However, as Max Bill told me, Binia had already been to Sicily twice—once with her parents and once with a dance group led by Suzanne Perrottet, whom Bill also knew from the Krater. The newlyweds stayed in a hotel and—in the true spirit of the free economists—suggested to the hotelier that instead of paying their bill in cash, they could design a photo-brochure for his hotel.

Binia and Max also traveled to the south of the island to see the temples at Agrigento. Bill's lasting impression of the Temple of Concordia was of a magnificent structure, both in its technical concept and architectural rigor. From there they went on to Porto Empedocle.

The Sicilian author Andrea Camilleri was born in this little town. Nowadays Porto Empedocle—with the fictive name Vigàta—is known to millions of readers and television viewers across the world as the setting for Camilleri's novels featuring the maverick detective Inspector Montalbano, who voices Camilleri's trenchant opposition to the Mafia and critical view of politics in Sicily (see Saverio Lodato and Andrea Camilleri, *La linea della palma: Saverio Lodato fa raccontare Andrea Camilleri* [Milan: Rizzoli, 2002]).

"A tiny tank engine with a proud plume of black smoke.... Two little coaches were coupled to it, each with a pretty, cast-iron, open-air platform, with fluttering orange curtains to protect travelers from the sun and the rain. Each coach had two compartments: first class with red velvet seats and third class with wooden benches.... There was no second class. The people traveling on the Porto Empedocle-Castelvetrano line were either rich or poor.

And since—be it from a sense of modesty or because you can never know or because the tax collector is always lurking somewhere—naturally no one wanted to openly admit to their wealth, so no one ever sat in the first class compartment....

Things were still in full swing at the pier, workers shouting, neighing horses pulling carts with sulfur and rock salt

828 Andrea Camilleri, "Der Bummelzug," *du* 771 (November 2006), p. 28

that had been unloaded from the train. They took their cargo to large, open storage areas, huge sulfur-yellow and salt-white patches, and returned to the pier station."[828]

The sound of that name so pleased Bill that he would gladly have lived there for that reason alone. He was thrilled with the pier with its sulfur and rock-salt warehouses. The sight of the strange, luminescent yellow of the sulfur was no doubt a delight to Bill, but—true to nature—he was particularly attracted by certain architectural details. In particular, he found it "astonishing and practical that the pier was constructed from sections of columns and walls from nearby temples, giving them a practical purpose." He was all in favor of this unfussy "recycling," as we would call it today.

Earning a Living

Back in Zurich, Binia and Max worked together on commercial contracts, mainly designing typographies for advertising and books, with Binia often providing photographs and Bill concentrating on the typographic design.

Bill also continued to read free economist publications such as *Kampf der Absatzkrise und der Arbeitslosigkeit!* by Fritz Schwarz (Bern: Pestalozzi-Fellenberg-Haus, 1931) and also Schwarz's *Vorwärts zur festen Kaufkraft des Geldes und zur zinsbefreiten Wirtschaft!* (Bern: Genossenschaft Verlag Freiwirtschaftlicher Schriften, 1931), which he wrote his own name on—"bill." Did Bill possibly design that slim volume? Inside it there is no mention of any designer.

In 1930 Katja Wulff, who sometimes performed at the Krater, like Bill, commissioned him to design a program sheet for a performance by members of her school for expressive dance (as taught by Rudolf von Laban) on "3 December in the Blue Room at the Mustermesse, 8.15 p.m."; he also designed a flyer for her school (brown on pale green paper) and a poster for a performance at the Stadttheater on 19 April 1932 (see fig. p. 354). That poster is particularly striking—a rainbow print in red, orange, yellow, light green, green, blue, violet, and black on a white ground. This commission shows that Bill was still in contact with friends in Basel. He and Katja Wulff had worked well together at the Krater, and Binia photographed her "around 1931" (see *Binia Bill: Fotografien,* Aargauer Kunsthaus [Zurich: Scheidegger & Spiess, 2004], p. 75).

Binia also made a portrait photograph of the dancer Marie-Eve Kreis from Katja Wulff's dance studio in Basel. Although there is no reproduction of the portrait of Marie-Eve Kreis in *Binia Bill—Fotografien* (published to accompany the exhibition at Aargauer Kunsthaus in 2004), in the catalogue of a selling exhibition, the *Werkbund-Ausstellung Ortsgruppe Bern SWB,* held at Kunsthalle Bern on 24 August–22 September 1935, the entry no. 78 reads "Bill, Binia, SWB, Zurich 10, Limmattalstrasse 253" and is illustrated with seven photographs, including her "Portrait Marie-Eve" priced at "15.fr."

Max Bill would certainly not have missed that performance in April by Tanzstudio Wulff, because the program was also of interest to him. The type of dance practiced at the Wulff dance studio could best be described as Surrealist. A review in the Basel newspaper (the *National-Zeitung*) of the ballet *Mercure* with music by Erik Satie, described it as a "drastic mix of the various talents available at the Wulff studio" Elsewhere, in *information,* it was said that "things start in a distinctly classical style and end amid black-lacquered palm stands and padded sofas. And Prosperina is abducted on a motorcycle."[829]

The photographs illustrating the article in information were taken by Gotthard Schuh; Bill designed the typography for *information.*

Relâche, one of the three pieces to be performed that evening, had been premiered in Paris by a Swedish company in November 1924. It was an "instantanéiste" ballet in two acts "with a cinematographic entr'acte by René Clair."[830]

Bill's interest in film continued. He purchased a copy of the book *René Clair, Entr'acte,* ed. Glauco Viazzi (Milan: Poligono Società Editrice, 1945) about this work by the filmmaker René Clair, and added it to his library, having marked it inside in pencil with "bill."

In 1933 Bill again worked for Katja Wulff; this time he designed a six-page leaflet for the "Wulff Schule Labanschule, staatlich anerkannt [officially certified]."

In 1983, when I told Bill about my visit to see Katja Wulff, who had been able to tell me more about her friendship with Sophie Taeuber, he pointed out that Katja—whom he knew very well—had been married to a Communist by the name of C. F. Vaucher, or "Fauchi," as Bill called him. When I went back to see Katja Wulff again and remarked that she had made no mention of having been married to a Communist, which would certainly have been something of an exception in Switzerland in those days, she just said, "Oh you know, anyone who reaches my age has seen

829 "Neuer Tanz und Neues Theater in Basel, Tanzstudio Wulff," *information* 1:7 (Zurich, January 1933)

830 See Viazzi 1945

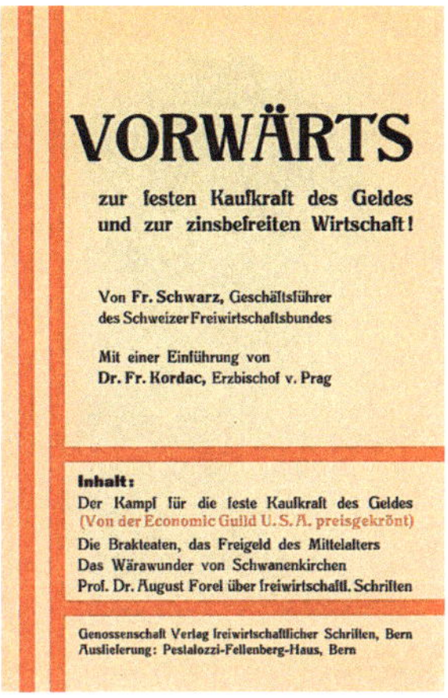

VORWÄRTS

zur festen Kaufkraft des Geldes und zur zinsbefreiten Wirtschaft!

Von Fr. Schwarz, Geschäftsführer des Schweizer Freiwirtschaftsbundes

Mit einer Einführung von Dr. Fr. Kordac, Erzbischof v. Prag

Inhalt:
Der Kampf für die feste Kaufkraft des Geldes
(Von der Economic Guild U. S. A. preisgekrönt)
Die Brakteaten, das Freigeld des Mittelalters
Das Wärawunder von Schwanenkirchen
Prof. Dr. August Forel über freiwirtschaftl. Schriften

Genossenschaft Verlag freiwirtschaftlicher Schriften, Bern
Auslieferung: Pestalozzi-Fellenberg-Haus, Bern

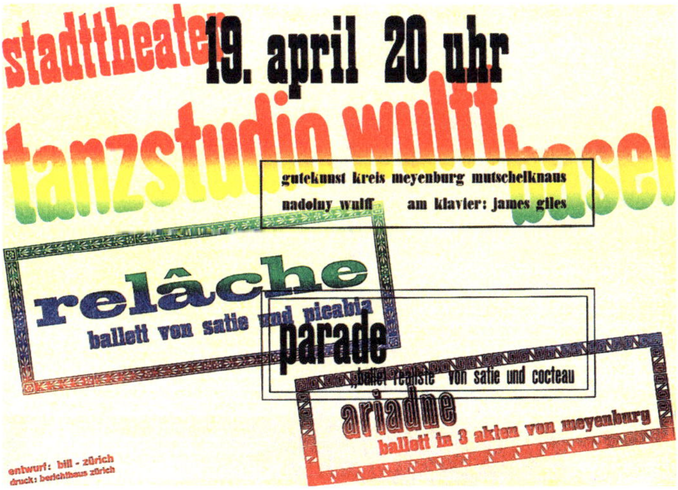

Fritz Schwarz, *Vorwärts zur festen Kaufkraft des Geldes und zur zinsbefreiten Wirtschaft!*, 1931

Max Bill, *stadttheater, tanzstudio wulff basel, 19. april 20 uhr*, Poster design, 1932

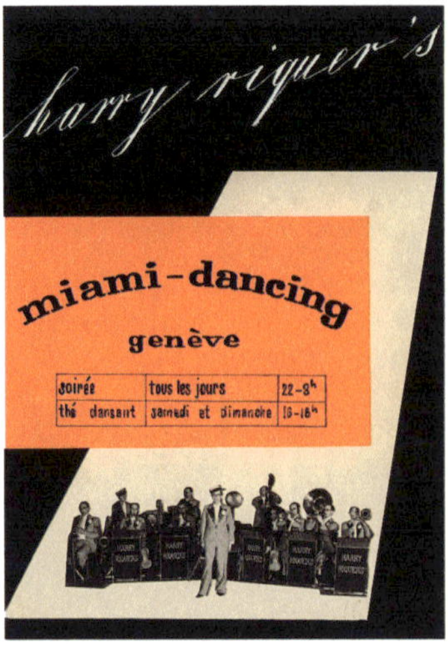

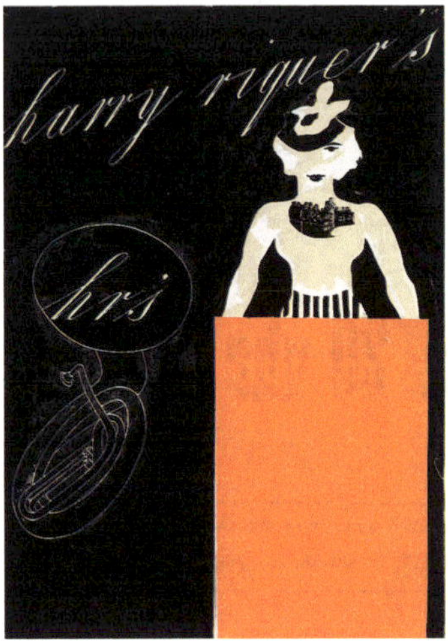

Max Bill, *harry riquer's, miami-dancing, Genève,* Poster design, 1932, collage and photograph on paper, 28.7 × 20.5 cm

Max Bill, *harry riquer's hr's,* Poster design, 1932, collage and tempera on paper, 129 × 95 cm

Max Bill, Catalogue for the Swiss section at the *Deutsche Bauausstellung* in Berlin, 1931

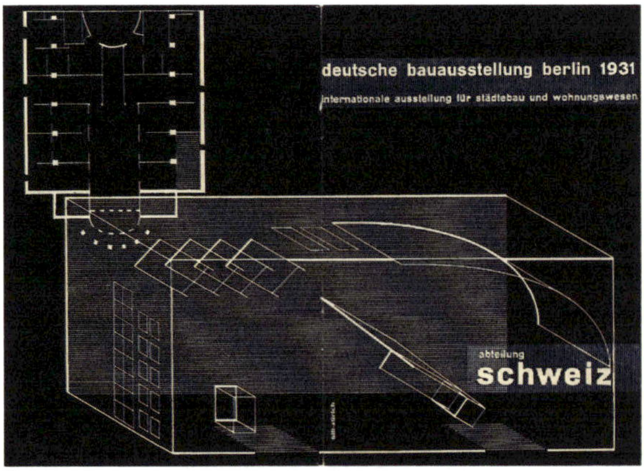

and done so much!" When Katja Wulff died in Basel some years later, in June 1992, she was not far short of her 102nd birthday.

"One or two people from the Krater," whom Bill did not specifically name, later went over to the Frontists—Frontism in Switzerland equated to National Socialism in Germany. And it was because of that split that the Krater cabaret disbanded in the early 1930s.[831]

With the unemployment rate reaching alarming levels not only in Germany but also in Switzerland, Bill continued to engage with the political issues of the day. He read Silvio Gesell's booklet *Die Ausbeutung, ihre Ursachen und ihre Bekämpfung,* in which Gesell pitted his own theory of capital against that of Karl Marx. That publication was in fact the text of a lecture on financial exploitation that Gesell had given in Dresden in 1922 to a "socialist association for mutual continuing education" and that had now been published—ten years later, in 1932—by Pestalozzi-Fellenberg in Bern.

In October 1932, when Binia and Max Bill were commissioned to design a poster for Harry Riquer's "Soirée et thé dansant" at Miami-Dancing in Geneva, Bill took a black-and-white photograph of the band shot by Binia, cut away the background, and added orange to convey a sense of optimism (see p. 468). Harry Riquer and his Modern Orchestra also appeared in Zurich at the Corso, which opened again on 1 August 1934 after its refurbishment by Ernst F. Burckhardt. The Corso presented "various light orchestras and jazz bands. And Max and Binia Bill took the opportunity to strike up business arrangements with some of them. Max Bill created a letterhead for Harry Riquer's Modern Orchestra (playing at the Corso) and he also designed their music stands and banners.... So the Corso in Zurich temporarily became a client for Max and Binia Bill and the center of their lives."[832]

On 1 and 2 November 1930, free economists, physiocrats, and "related associations" met in Dessau for a conference on land reform. The program included "Visits: Bauhaus, Junkers factory, and other landmarks in Dessau." Did Bill—who already knew all those landmarks very well—decide to return to Dessau for that conference? As it turned out the visit to the Bauhaus had to be curtailed because the conference members were not granted access. The "report on the Dessau meeting" describes

831 Max Bill in an interview with Peter Kamber, according to handwritten notes kindly made available to me by the author

832 Jakob Bill 2008, p. 174

the incident: "The Bauhaus was unfortunately inaccessible for a closer, internal viewing, and what we learned about the work there in conversation was hardly encouraging, that is to say, a climb down back to old teaching methods."[833]

One wonders if Bill—now in love with Binia—still regularly participated in events put on by the free economists.

In 1930, on 1 and 8 December, the architect Hans Bernoulli delivered two lectures in Zürich, "at the Waag" (the lecture titles are not mentioned); a meeting was also announced in the same issue of *Letzte Politik,* to be held at Karl der Grosse, a restaurant in Kirchgasse, on 15 December.[834]

The Swiss physiocrats issued a notice announcing a skiing trip to the sparsely populated canton of Appenzell over Christmas with a rented ski cabin to stay in. More information was to be had from "Hans Forrer, Zürich, im Sydefädeli 20."[835]

In 1931, the year when Julius Posener's review of the Werkbund Exhibition at the Grand Palais in Paris had so enraged Walter Gropius, Posener was working, without pay, in Erich Mendelsohn's architectural practice in Berlin; after that he worked "as an assistant site agent at the Columbushaus construction site at Potsdamer Platz." The Columbushaus, designed by Erich Mendelsohn, was a steel-frame building. Posener, a German Jew in Berlin, noted how the situation in Germany "rapidly worsened" from summer of 1931 onward: "it was a dictatorship run by Chancellor Brüning, who governed by means of 'emergency legislation.' The unemployment figures were in their millions, by late 1932 they had risen to seven million. The mood in the office was correspondingly despairing. Everyone knew that there would be no more projects of that size."[836] Although Posener started to hear terrible accounts of torture, he could not believe them at the time: "As to the entirely true stories of torture in the basement of the Columbushaus (yes, the building where I had been a site agent), I just didn't believe them."[837]

In 1933 Posener managed to find work in Paris as an architecture critic for *L'Architecture d'Aujourd'hui.* As such his life in exile was comparatively comfortable, certainly infinitely more comfortable than the lives of the many émigrés arriving in France from Germany who had to

833 L.H.H., "Aus der Bewegung," *Letzte Politik* 9:43 (1930)
834 In "Versammlungs-Anzeiger," *Letzte Politik* 9:45 (1930)
835 "Versammlungs-Anzeiger," Letzte Politik 9:45 (1930)
836 Posener 1990, pp. 209–10
837 Posener 1990, p. 214
838 Hans Marti, "Nekrolog Ernst F. Burckhardt," gta Archiv

eke out an existence without any form of employment. In Paris Posener met Mendelsohn, who had also had to leave Berlin and was now doing work in London and Jerusalem. Mendelsohn offered Posener a job in his Jerusalem office—and so it was that Posener moved from France to Palestine, the second country he emigrated to. Mendelsohn's Jerusalem office was in a windmill in the district of Rehaviah. In 1941, Julius Posener voluntarily enlisted in the British Army; once the war was over he returned to Germany as a keenly observant member of the British intelligence service. He subsequently settled in Jerusalem and it was not until 1961 that he saw Berlin again.

Later on Max Bill and I met Julius Posener—the author of the critical review of Gropius and others at the *Werkbund* exhibition in Paris in 1930—at the Akademie der Künste in Berlin, where he and Bill were both members.

Poznan, Poland

In 1930, the same year when Bill was first able to participate in an exhibition at Kunsthalle Bern, his friend Ernst F. Burckhardt commissioned him (the "advertising technician," as he called himself) to design signage and lettering for the Swiss section of the international exhibition for travel and tourism in Poznan, Poland. Part of his work on that commission involved creating signage for the display stand for the Swiss company, Adolph Saurer AG.

Max Bill designed the typography for the Swiss section of the *Internationale Ausstellung für Verkehr & Touristik* in Poznan, Poland 1930 (architect E. F. Burckhardt); typography estate of Max Bill, plates 10 and 11.

Burckhardt was happy with Bill's designs and in 1931 ensured that another contract went to Bill, this time in connection with the *Deutsche Bauausstellung Berlin 1931—Internationale Ausstellung für Städtebau und Wohnungswesen.* Bill designed the catalogue for the Swiss section and, whereas Burckhardt devised the exhibition architecture for the Swiss section in his office in Berlin, Bill worked on signage and lettering in situ.

In his obituary for Ernst F. Burckhardt, Hans Marti wrote that "exhibition-making was his passion and he had many exhibitions to his name.... He understood better than anyone how to communicate the essence succinctly and pithily; despite positively bubbling over with ideas and initiatives, everything he said was clear and made sense. He made great demands on all those who worked with him."[838]

Rather surprisingly, just a few months after his wedding in January 1931, Bill traveled to Berlin and checked into Hotel am Knie in Berlin-Charlottenburg without Binia—all the more surprisingly perhaps, given that Binia had attended Lucia Moholy's photography course at the Itten-Schule for a while and would have known her way around the metropolis.

"... on monday evening there will be a lecture here by ozenfant, everyone's going and afterward moholy is going to do something."[839]

Other former Bauhauslers were also involved in that exhibition and Bill soon ran into not only Moholy-Nagy and Herbert Bayer but also Kandinsky, who had created a "ceramic wall piece" for the exhibition. A contemporary photograph shows Kandinsky at the exhibition with a client—a certain Frau Körting—inspecting the "music room" he had designed for her.

A photograph showing the stand by Moholy-Nagy, Gropius, and Bayer ("Exhibition of Building Worker's Unions, Berlin, 1931 in collaboration with Walter Gropius and Moholy-Nagy"), is illustrated in Alexander Dorner, *The Way Beyond "Art"—The Work of Herbert Bayer* (New York: Wittenborn, Schultz, 1947), p. 204.

An architectural drawing done by the former Bauhaus director Walter Gropius for the *Deutsche Bauausstellung 1931* is illustrated in G. C. Argan, *Walter Gropius e la Bauhaus* (Turin: Giulio Einaudi, 1951), fig. 101.

The wall design is illustrated in Will Grohmann, *Wassily Kandinsky* (Cologne: M. Dumont Schauberg, 1958), p. 202; the music room is illustrated in Eckhard Neumann, ed., *Bauhaus und Bauhäusler, Erinnerungen und Bekenntnisse* (Cologne: Dumont Taschenbücher, 1985), p. 62, fig. 51; in 2006 I saw a reconstruction of the music room on display at the Musée d'art moderne et contemporain de Strasbourg.

Katt Both—another former Bauhausler who is seen with Hilde Rantzsch in the double portrait Max Bill drew in Dessau (see p. 161)—also played an active part at that trade fair in Berlin. She had joined the otherwise all-male team at Otto Haesler's architectural practice in Celle in 1929 and now she and Haesler had created comfortable interiors for "a single-level apartment for the 'Family of a Blue-Collar Worker' and for a duplex apartment for the 'Family of a White-Collar Worker' with generous washing facilities and dressing rooms," which were shown at the exhibition in 1931.[840]

839 Max Bill, Berlin, to Binia Bill, Zurich, 9 May 1931, Archiv Max Bill
840 Maasberg and Prinz 2004, p. 78
841 Gatje 2000, p. 17
842 Gatje 2000, p. 17

After the Second World War, Max Bill and Katt Both met again at the memorial for Oskar Schlemmer on 6 September 1958.

One wonders, might Bill also have seen Marcel Breuer, there, another Bauhausler?

When Marcel (actually Lajko) Breuer was still a student at the Bauhaus in Weimar, he was chosen by Gropius to create the interior design for the Haus am Horn, the Bauhaus model house for the first ever Bauhaus exhibition, held in Weimar in 1923. Breuer subsequently spent 1924 and 1925 in Paris. In 1926 Gropius appointed him as a master at the newly opened Bauhaus in Dessau, where Breuer remained during the time that Bill was studying there, until—in connection with Walter Gropius's departure—he left for Berlin in 1928. With encouragement and active support from Gropius, Breuer set up his own architectural practice in Berlin, having left the Bauhaus (like Bill) without a diploma in architecture.

"Several key members of the faculty had left the Bauhaus with Gropius in 1928, or shortly thereafter, and Breuer decided it was time to open his own architectural office in Berlin. Gropius again lent a hand in the attempt which was ultimately successful, to persuade the authorities of the German Association of Architects to admit Lajko as a member despite his absent diploma."[841]

In the late 1920s, when Mies van der Rohe had not included Breuer among the architects selected to propose designs for the Weissenhof Estate in Stuttgart (1927), Walter Gropius had ensured that Breuer was nevertheless involved in the project as the interior designer for the buildings designed by himself and by Mart Stam. However, in 1931, with no work coming in, Marcel Breuer concluded that he had no option but to close his Berlin practice and to leave Germany.

Robert F. Gatje has raised the question as to whether Mies van der Rohe was jealous of Breuer because the latter, despite being Hungarian, had participated in the German Werkbund exhibition in Paris in 1930 on the invitation of Gropius, whereas Mies van der Rohe, a German by birth, had not been invited to participate. When it came to the exhibition in Berlin in 1931, Mies van der Rohe only invited Breuer at the last minute.[842]

Walter Gropius left Germany in 1933; having made it to London in 1934, he found an apartment in Hampstead in the newly opened Lawn Road Flats (now known as the Isokon Building) designed by Wells Coates. Marcel Breuer and Moholy-Nagy also emigrated to London and took apartments in the same block as Gropius. Soon all three were working for the Isokon Furniture Company—Breuer's renowned plywood Long Chair was of course produced by Isokon. Gropius, who became Isokon's first "controller of design," remained in the Lawn Road Flats until 1937, when he emigrated to the United States and was appointed to a chair at Harvard.

Wohnbedarf AG

It was Bill's friend Ernst F. Burckhardt who designed the interior of Wohnbedarf AG's first, relatively modest showroom (in Claridenstrasse, Zurich). Max Bill was commissioned to design the company logo. "I designed it so that it could still be easily read from a side view—severely foreshortened." His design is still the company logo today. At the time Bill was so unusually satisfied with the letter "o" in his Wohnbedarf logo that he used it again that same year "on the poster for the rock-paintings exhibition at the Kunstgewerbemuseum in Zurich."[843]

Since 1933 the shop has occupied a larger premises at Talstrasse 11, very close to its first location.

In the exhibition catalogue *Um 1930 in Zürich: Neues Denken, Neues Wohnen, Neues Bauen* (1977) there is an illustration of the first Wohnbedarf shop, with signage by Bill (p. 187).

The exhibition *Negerkunst: Prähistorische Felsbilder Südafrikas* ran from 2 to 30 August 1931. Max later recalled that when he was "producing a set of metal letters, [he] also commissioned a corrugated-iron relief with an off-center O shape. In those days that was so extreme that it elicited no response at all."[844] Nowadays that *wellrelief* (1931–32, see p. 476) is regarded as one of Bill's most important works, which certainly anticipated Minimal Art.

"... his search for a way out"

Since Bill was often in Basel, which is just an hour away from Zurich by train, it is fair to assume that he will not have missed the very impressive Jean Arp exhibition installed in Kunsthalle Basel by Dr. Georg Schmidt in 1932 (see p. 476). It was Arp who had suggested to the young Bill that he should become a member of the international artist's association Abstraction-Création in Paris: "... it was like this, there was an exhibition in Zurich

843 Bill 1977 [b], pp. 186–87
844 Bill 1977 [b], pp. 186–87

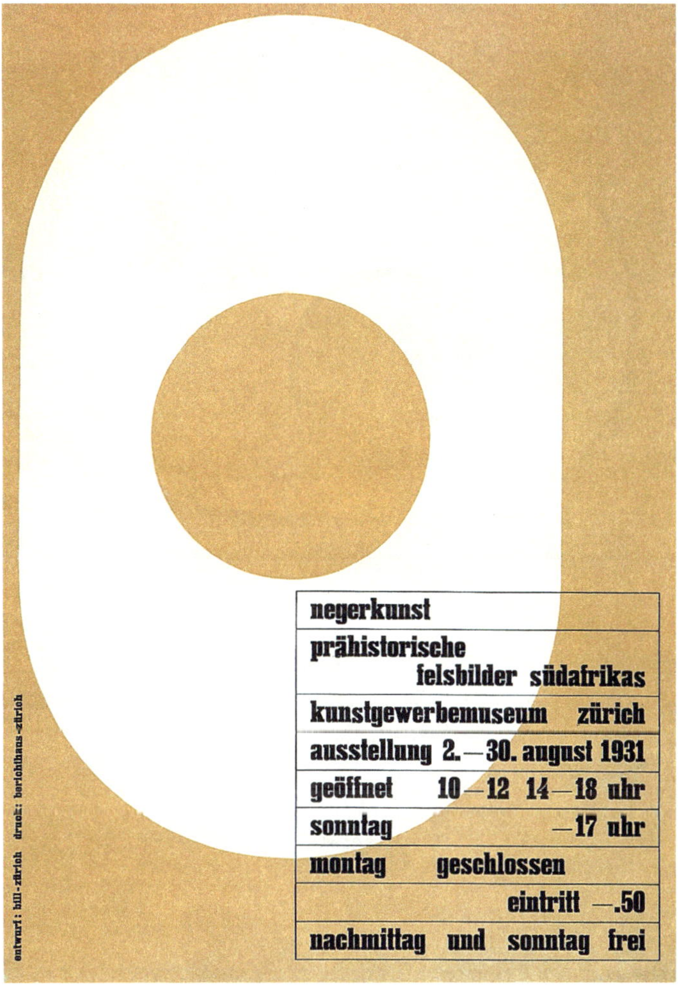

Max Bill, Poster for the exhibition *Negerkunst: Prähistorische Felsbilder Südafrikas* at the Kunstgewerbe-museum in Zurich, 1931, letterpress, linocut, and layout, 128×90.5 cm

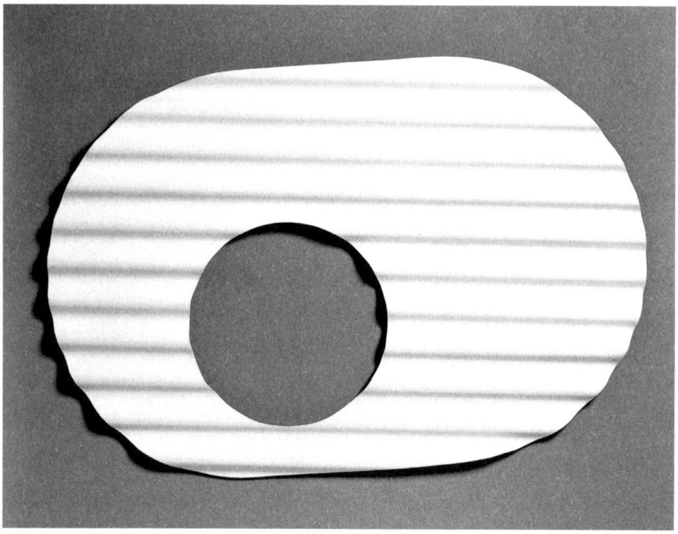

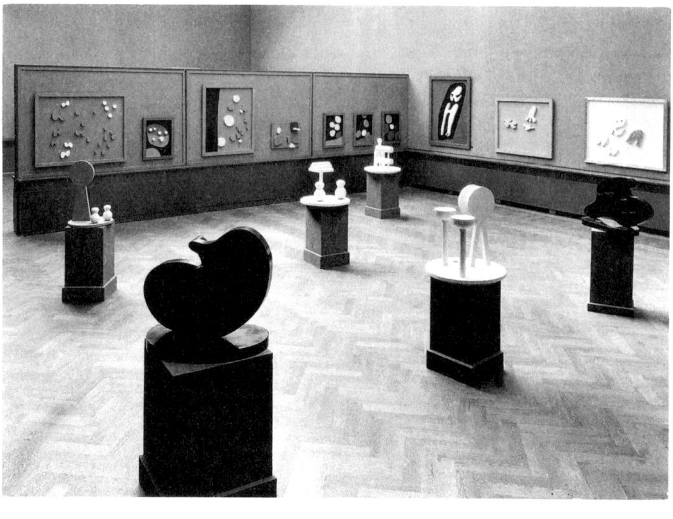

Max Bill, *wellrelief,* 1931–32, iron, synthetic resin varnish, 80×120cm

View of the Jean Arp solo exhibition at Kunsthalle Basel, 1932

that we younger artists were not admitted to. We were very put out. But it was actually because of that incident that I came into contact with Arp … and he immediately said that I should exhibit with Abstraction-Création and become a member. That was in late 1931, I'd say."[845]

The exhibition Bill was referring to in the interview with Doris Schmidt, that he had not been invited to participate in—much to his regret—was *Abstrakte und surrealistische Malerei und Plastik* at Kunsthaus Zürich (6 October–3 November 1929).

Bill's comment that he "actually had already met Arp on a visit to Paris" is a reference to his visit to Paris in 1925 as a young silversmith apprentice when two of his pieces had been selected by Sophie Taeuber-Arp to be shown at the *Exposition international des arts décoratifs.*

Bill made that statement during a television portrait and also went on to explain why he did not follow up on Arp's suggestion until two years later in December 1933: he felt he still had to do a lot of work, on his own, to fully free himself from the influence of his Bauhaus teachers. He called it his search for a way out: "My teachers ranged from Klee and Kandinsky to Schlemmer and Moholy and in those early years, 1930, 1931, things were still all mixed up together for me, and I had to somehow find myself in the midst of all of that … I had a whole conglomerate of teachers behind me—all of whom interested me one way or the other, but now I first had to find a way out, somehow. In fact I found it relatively quickly. And that was also the reason why Arp noticed me, and then I received an invitation from Abstraction-Création; I didn't actually discover new things there, just things that I had already taken as read."[846]

After he had successfully found a "way out" and could see his way forward to his own art production—and had something of his own to show—Bill gladly took up Arp's suggestion (despite having described him not so long ago as an "abstract grandfather" in a letter to Fischli) and joined Abstraction-Création. In Paris Arp introduced Bill to Piet Mondrian, who was also a member of the group. They visited Mondrian in his studio in connection with preparations for an Abstraction-Création exhibition. That particular exhibition, which Bill was also able to participate in, opened on 22 December 1933, Bill's twenty-fifth birthday. "At the time I was very interested in what Vantongerloo and Mondrian were doing … that didn't lead to actual similarities, it led to very different things—but it did have some influence. For instance, I'd say that was when the white ground appeared in my work. Actually very typical of that time. The white

845 Max Bill in Schmidt 1983
846 Schmidt 1983

ground was not there before. And it disappeared again afterward. But for a while white was the basis of everything I did. And, very broadly speaking, it arose from those circumstances. Only to a very limited extent from drawings I'd done for Klee. Or for Kandinsky."[847]

In the 1930s Max Bill designed newspaper advertisements for businesses such as Egli & Co., an advertising display (1931) for the same company (all in lowercase), and a publicity stand "Schweizer Baukatalog" (1932)—with traditional uppercase and lowercase. These were followed, among other things, by an exhibition stand—"Schweizer Wein"—for an agricultural trade fair in Zurich in 1934.

These two commissions are documented in black-and-white photographs in the typography estate of Max Bill.

Meanwhile Binia Bill was making her name as an avant-garde photographer. Up until the early 1940s she also photographed the majority of Max Bill's works.

Bill's First Home-and-Studio

Between October 1932 and March 1933 a new home for Bill and Binia was built to Max Bill's own design on the edge of the village of Höngg just outside the city of Zurich; it mainly consisted of a two-story studio-lounge-bedroom.[848]

In 1933 the architect Elsa Burkhardt-Blum—one of the Bills' marriage witnesses and a good friend—was commissioned by Gotthard Schuh to design her first house; Schuh was of course Bill's erstwhile financial manager.

Elsa Burckhardt-Blum: studio-home for Gotthard Schuh, Zollikon, built in 1933, demolished in the 1970s. "Whereas the ceilings in Max Bill's

847 Max Bill in Schmidt 1983

848 Since much has already been published about this house, I will merely alert readers here to the relevant sources: Max Bill "Vom Bauhaus bis Ulm," *du* 424:7 (July 1976), pp. 12–24, particularly p. 14; Eva Bechstein, "Die Häuser von Max Bill in Zürich-Höngg und Zumikon," in *Künstlerhäuser von der Renaissance bis zur Gegenwart,* ed. Eduard Hüttinger (Zurich: Waser, 1985), pp. 255–67; Das Atelierhaus Max Bill 1932/33: *Ein wohn-und atelierhaus in Zürich-Höngg von Max Bill und Robert Winkler,* ed. Arthur Rüegg (Zurich: Niggli, 1997). The ownership of the house in Höngg was transferred to Jakob Bill on 1 January 1979

studio-and-home had to be concrete, as stipulated by building regulations, Gotthard Schuh's house was entirely timber-built" (quotation and image in *Das Atelierhaus Max Bill 1932/33: Ein wohn-und atelierhaus in Zürich-Höngg von Max Bill und Robert Winkler,* ed. Arthur Rüegg [Zurich: Niggli, 1997],p. 68).

With one building already to his name by that time, Bill would no doubt have been keen to win that contract for Schuh, who had also worked with him at the Krater cabaret. Elsa Burckhardt-Blum and her husband Ernst F. Burckhardt would later design the Oberer Letten river-swimming pool in Zurich; in the late 1940s, some years after Max Bill, Elsa increasingly turned her attention to Concrete art. She signed her Concrete paintings—which were shown at Galerie Suzanne Bollag in Zurich—with the initials "E.B.B." In 1958 Ernst F. Burckhardt was killed in a car crash in England. Elsa, who was in the passenger seat and heard the terrible sound of his neck breaking, survived despite fracturing sixty-three bones. The Burckhardts' son Christoph later told me that after that accident Binia had done all she could to help his mother.

Binia and Max Bill remained close friends with Elsa Burckhardt-Blum. Elsa was one of a small number of people who were especially important to Max Bill—most were in fact men—people that he always remained faithful to, and after Elsa's death he wrote her obituary for the *Neue Zürcher Zeitung* (8 April 1974), the same paper for which he also wrote obituaries for Paul Klee, Wassily Kandinsky, and Josef Albers.

The Circle around Wladimir Rosenbaum and Aline Valangin

It was around this time that Bill came into contact with Wladimir "Ro" Rosenbaum and his wife Aline Valangin. Rosenbaum, a left-leaning, highly cultured lawyer in Zurich, had founded the "co-operative for literary publications" that published the periodical *information* (with Ernst F. Burckhardt on its editorial team). Bill first met Rosenbaum through his own work for *information* and he strongly suspected that Rosenbaum had provided the start-up finances for *information.*[849] In conversation with me he once remarked that "*information* only had a print run of 500. Rosenbaum and Georg Schmidt's brother funded it."[850]

849 Max Bill in conversation with Peter Kamber, in Kamber 1990, p. 92

850 Max Bill in conversation with Angela Thomas, 25 August 1975

Peter Kamber has written a highly recommendable, very well-researched book about the fascinating personas and activities of Aline Valangin and Wladimir Rosenbaum and their circle: *Geschichte zweier Leben. Wladimir Rosenbaum und Aline Valangin* (Zurich: Limmat, 2000).

Wladimir Rosenbaum and the writer Aline Valangin lived in a large, welcoming house—called the Baumwollhof—at Stadelhoferstrasse 26 in Zurich, where Sophie Taeuber-Arp was a frequent visitor. Before the Bills moved to Goldbrunnenstrasse they were of course close neighbors of Rosenbaum and Valangin, and from the early 1930s onward the Bills were also invited to the Baumwollhof from time to time.

"We met in Zurich during the First World War and always remained in friendly contact, be it in Zurich in the 1920s or in Paris in the 1930s." However, Sophie was never invited to Aline Valagin's house La Barca in the Val Onsernone, near the Italian border—for which Max Bill would design a brochure.[851]

Aline Valangin, Rosenbaum's first wife, had known Sophie Taeuber-Arp since the First World War and, looking back, remembered always being on friendly terms with her. However, Sophie Taeuber-Arp's recollection was rather different. She remembered Aline being jealous of her "in a very primitive way." In the 1920s, communications between Sophie and her husband were difficult and very unsettling for Sophie. In May 1926 she wrote to Jean Arp summing up the situation: "... it has been rather a while since I last wrote. I don't even really know if I should write about how I am and what I'm doing. You don't like people saying too much about themselves, but what's left of the marriage then?"[852]

She had succumbed to a sad apathy, but then Rosenbaum had turned up on her doorstep, which lifted her spirits: "Rosenbaum was here yesterday. There is something in his heart that strongly attracts me. He was asking about you and what you had said about the road trip we went on before Easter." But at the same time Sophie also tried to placate her husband: "Don't be uneasy, I barely see him, it's just that my relationship with him is another way of connecting more closely with life.... I didn't

851 Aline Valangin, La Villerna, Via Signor in Croce 24, Ascona, to Monsieur Beretta, Ascona (1 October 1981), kindly made available by Ra Efrem Beretta, Ascona

852 Sophie Taeuber-Arp to Hans Arp, in dossier "Lettres de Sophie," 22 May 1926, Stiftung Hans Arp und Sophie Taeuber-Arp

853 Taeuber-Arp to Arp, 22 May 1926

854 Sophie Taeuber-Arp to Hans Arp, n.d., Stiftung Hans Arp und Sophie Taeuber-Arp

go because she is jealous, in a very primitive way and I don't want to be treated badly again, but that will all be over soon. As it happens, your mother has a very good opinion of him."[853]

"... I find it such a struggle to live ... there's a dance at the Rosenbaums' tomorrow, maybe I'll go. It's just a shame that you're not here ..."[854]

Neues Bauen— New Architecture

Rosenbaum, a brilliant man, advised the leading architects involved with *Neues Bauen* on legal matters, for instance in connection with the Werkbund estate in Neubühl (Zurich 1930–32), for which Bill designed the poster (see p. 483). The Neubühl estate was the most important construction project in Switzerland at the time.

There is no doubt that Bill would rather have had architectural commissions of his own, but he was still a young man who simply had to be patient. However, many of the established *Neues Bauen* architects did call on his services in connection with buildings such as the Zett-Haus (1931–32) in Zurich, where Bill designed the lettering for the "Zett Restaurant" and the "Roxy Bar" (see p. 483); he also designed the business letterhead for the architect Rudolf Steiger and his professional partner, the engineer Carl Hubacher.

In the early 2000s Evelyne Lang Jakob published a study on the Zett-Haus, which also explores the part played by Flora Steiger-Crawford in its design. In 1924 Rudolf Steiger married Flora Crawford, the first woman to graduate from the ETH with a diploma in architecture (1923). According to Lang Jakob, up until 1928 Rudolf Steiger's office was "mainly" run by Flora, after which he took over. "Their early collaborative work fell into that first period: the realization of the first stage of the Neubühl Estate and the planning for the Zett-Haus in Zurich. The first rupture in their teamwork came in 1931, when the Steigers, now a family of three, moved into the newly finished section of the Neubühl Estate.... On completion of the Zett-Haus, Rudolf and Flora Steiger-Crawford moved their office into the new building....

Flora Steiger-Crawford significantly contributed to a number of buildings and was responsible for the Eckbau (corner building) of the Zett-Haus (1930–32) at the junction of Rebgasse and Müllergasse. Rudolf and Flora Steiger-Crawford, in collaboration with the engineer Carl Hubacher, were able to build the Zett-Haus in Aussersihl—an avant-garde office block with apartments, an underground garage, and a cinema with a sliding roof —thanks to the fact that the site was owned by Hubacher's father. Flora Steiger-Crawford designed the Eckbau at the rear of the site, which adjoins one side of the main building.... the Eckbau has one restaurant entered from the street and another restaurant looking out to the garden at the back. The upper floors accommodate small, extremely functional apartments and studio flats. Steiger-Crawford, making a virtue out of necessity, extended the restaurant across three floors, and the curved ribbon windows in the very compact corner apartments create a sense of space.... The Zett-Haus is regarded as one of the earliest and purest examples of *Neues Bauen* in Zurich. In the magazine *Das Werk,* Peter Meyer wrote admiringly of the skilled exploitation of this corner site, albeit without mentioning Flora Steiger-Crawford's part in it."[855]

After Easter 1933, the former Bauhaus master Gunta Sharon-Stölzl started work on a curtain fabric for the Corso theater in Zurich (refurbished by Ernst F. Burckhardt, together with Karl Knell), and Max Bill designed the roof-level sign up above the façade. Another figure from the Bauhaus—the "black-maned tiger" Alexander "Xanti" Schawinsky—was also working for the Corso, designing stage décor.[856]

Xanti and Bill had both been involved with the Bauhaus stage and had played in the Bauhaus band. Schawinsky, who had also spent some time in Berlin, was well acquainted with Karola Piotrkowska, the partner (and future third wife) of the philosopher Ernst Bloch. On Bloch's arrival as an émigré in Switzerland, he paid a visit to the Bills in Höngg—possibly on Xanti's recommendation?

In the obituary for Ernst F. Burckhardt he is credited with having saved the idiosyncratic Jugendstil façade of the multi-purpose Corso theater.[857]

Christoph Bignens has written about the connections between the two Zurich theaters, the Roxy and the Corso, and the then theater-reform movement: "Hans Curjel, the art historian and friend of Sigfried Giedion, had played a major part as director in the experiments at the Kroll Opera in Berlin. After his arrival in Switzerland in 1934 Curjel was appointed director and head of programs at the newly opened Corso. Dr. Hans Curjel and Otto Klemperer jointly led the Kroll Opera

855 Lang Jakob 2003, pp. 111, 122
856 See Bignens 1985, p. 36
857 Hans Marti, "Nekrolog Ernst F. Burckhardt," gta Archiv, ETH Zürich

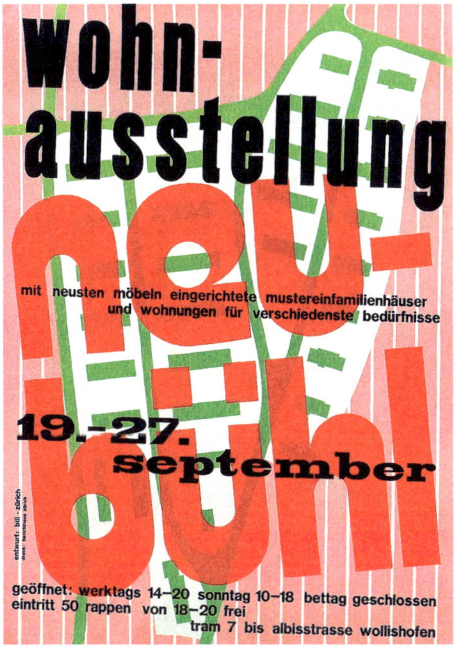

Max Bill, Poster for *Wohnausstellung Neubühl,* 1931, letterpress, linocut, and layout, 128×90.5 cm

Binia Bill, Max Bill's Lettering for the Zett Restaurant and the Roxy Bar, 1932

Max Bill, Cover design for *information* 2 (July 1932)

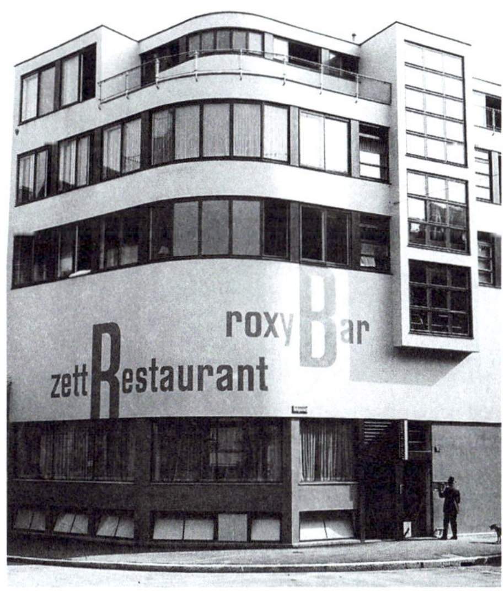

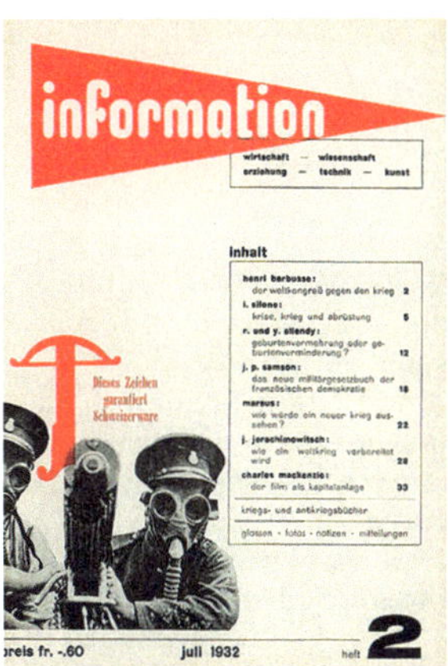

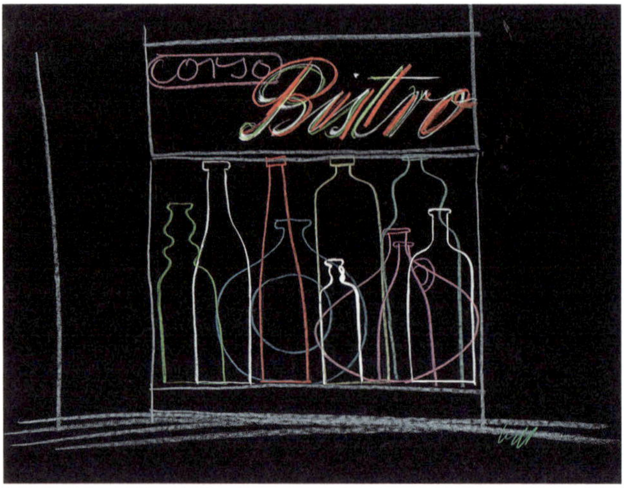

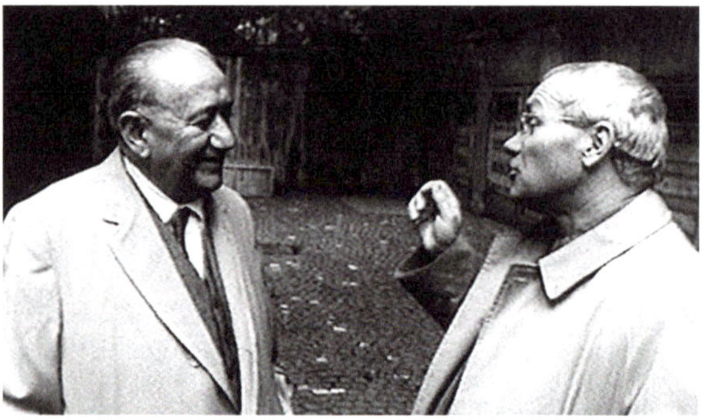

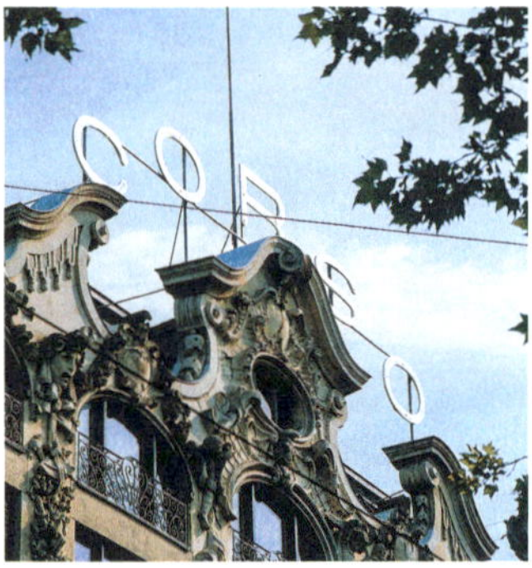

Max Bill, Sketch for lettering for the Corso Bistro, ca. 1934, colored pencil on black paper

Max Bill and Ignazio Silone in Zurich outside the house that was once home to to Rosenbaum and Valangin, 1970s

Max Bill, "Corso" sign on the Corso-Haus in Zurich, photographed in 2007

in Berlin. And it was thanks to Curjel that Schlemmer and Moholy-Nagy were commissioned to create stage designs for the Kroll Opera. In exile in Zurich Curjel did much to promote the Corso, where Max Bill met him when he was designing the lettering for the Corso sign. Alexander 'Xanti' Schawinsky, another former Bauhausler, later designed sets for the Corso stage."[858]

A Friendly Welcome

When Roman "Clemi" Clemens, a native of Dessau and a fully qualified electrician, first stepped into the Bauhaus, it was to install the electrical wiring in the new buildings; but he was so taken with Gropius's designs that he immediately enrolled as a student.

Roman Clemens, the son of a clockmaker in Dessau, was a set designer and Concrete painter. In 1932, following his studies at the Bauhaus, he arrived in Switzerland, reputedly "a little crazy but also very capable" (Max Bill). In 1932–43 Clemens was the first set designer and head of décor at the Stadttheater in Zurich, where he created sets for around two hundred productions. In 1948–49 he and the architect Werner Frey carried out a commission to design and finish the interior of Studio4, a cinema in Zurich that is now home to the municipal Filmpodium (see Marianne Herold, *Roman Clemens* [Zurich: ABC, 1991]).

Like Bill, Clemens attended the free painting classes taught by Klee and Kandinsky. Like Bill, Clemi played the banjo and—like Bill—joined Oskar Schlemmer's stage workshop.

"The stage class was a small, steady group consisting of Xanti Schawinsky—whom Roman Clemens was particularly impressed by because of his glittering imagination—Lux Feininger, Fritz Winter, Georg Hartmann, Hermann Röseler, Andor Weininger, Albert Mentzel and sometimes also Max Bill. In reality, no distinctions were made between students in different semesters, nor was there any systematic, fixed syllabus. . . . The members of that little team usually got on well with each other; their enthusiasm for their work together . . . and Schlemmer's collaborative approach fostered mutual inspiration. Day and night there were endless discussions and people never stopped asking, 'How could we do it differently?'"[859]

858 See Bignens 1985, p. 36
859 Herold 1991, p. 22

In 1932 Roman Clemens left Germany for Switzerland, where he was immediately taken in by Binia and Max Bill, although the apartment they had temporarily rented in Goldbrunnenstrasse 141 was already rather small for two people.

From 10 March 1931 to April 1933 Binia and Max Bill lived at Goldbrunnenstrasse 141. In April 1933 they moved to Limmattalstrasse 253 in Höngg, to their new studio-and-home designed by Max Bill. In 1934 the district of Höngg was absorbed into the City of Zurich and in 1953 the house was renumbered as Limmattalstrasse 383 (information kindly supplied by Dr. Robert Dünki, Stadtarchiv Zürich, 13 December 2007).

There was a very active network of progressive thinkers in Zurich in those days. And so it was that the dancer Suzanne Perrottet (Binia's traveling companion on a trip to Sicily before she married Bill) met Romans Clemens through the Bills, by which time Clemens had already found employment at the Stadttheater as a stage designer. Perrottet believed in free love and had had a child with Rudolf von Laban—a son born out of wedlock, as many would have disapprovingly said at the time. She was now trying to find a suitable vocational course for her son, André, and turned to Clemens for help: "Make a stage designer out of him!"

André Perrottet's wife Julia takes up the tale: That was how "he started to work with Roman Clemens in early 1934. He watched everything the master did and built models of individual sets according to Clemens's designs. But when it came to the pond in the palace garden in *Die Entführung aus dem Serail,* Clemens wanted to have real water lilies. They asked Roland von Wyss, the city gardener, if he could supply anything of that kind. The gardener liked the idea and said they could cut water lilies in the pond in Belvoir Park, as many as they needed! So Clemens and André went there themselves and cut water lilies with meter-long stems and took them back to the theater on a tricycle. And the water lilies—tenderly cared for—lasted for over a month and successfully played their part in each performance."[860] Over a decade after arriving in Switzerland as an exile, Clemens, who barely features in any emigration histories of that time despite his very considerable contribution to Swiss society, was interned in Lyss, canton of Bern, from May to August 1945.[861]

860 Julia Perrottet in Perrottet [1989–90], p. 233
861 Bruns 2007, p. 179
862 Postcard from Will Grohmann, Dresden, Regerstr. 31, postmarked St. Blasien, [6 March 1931–1933], to Herrn Max Bill, Zurich 3, Goldbrunnenstr. 141, Bibliothek Max Bill
863 Bill 1977 [b], p. 187

Having gone to no little trouble to discover Max Bill's address, in the early 1930s the art historian Dr. Will Grohmann in Dresden wrote to Bill at Goldbrunnenstrasse to inquire if Bill could send photographs of two of his own works for a "special issue [of *Neues Frankfurt*] on young European painters" and also to ask if Bill could tell him "which of the former Bauhaus people were Swiss? With best regards, yours, Will Grohmann."[862] Although it had been some time since Bill had left the Bauhaus, Grohmann—an authority on Bill's teachers Kandinsky and Klee—clearly still remembered the young Max Bill and evidently regarded him as a "young European painter."

Max Bill: Designing *information*

Erstwhile Krater activists—Burckhardt, Bill, and Samson—sought and found a new platform in Zurich with other like-minded individuals, notably Georg Schmidt, Max Raphael, and Ignazio Silone. That new venture, which Silone particularly threw himself into, was the anti-Fascist periodical *information* (publisher: Oprecht & Helbling AG Verlag; editor: Ignazio Silone; typography: Max Bill). It first came out in June 1932 and its stated aim was to publish analytical texts "on economics, science, education, technology, and art" that would inform and shake up the general public.

"during that period they came up with a plan to publish a critical periodical, which would be called *information* and provide exactly that. ignazio silone was in charge. a circle of left-leaning intellectuals merged there with ciam people. i was asked to see to the design" (see p. 483).[863]

Bill took the design of the small-format *information* into his own hands. The paper's avowed intention was to initiate an anti-Fascist movement. Although it never achieved that aim, it was nevertheless sophisticated in its arguments, speaking out against monopoly capitalism and against the Swiss "Frontists" who were propagating Hitler's disastrous ideas to loud applause in certain quarters in Switzerland. Although the paper was published by Oprecht, Bill later commented that "Oprecht himself never did much for it. It was too far to the left for him." The last issue of *information* came out in February 1934, by which time its original circulation had more than halved.

Jean-Paul Samson was in close personal touch with Fritz Brupbacher, a well known anarchist physician who devoted his time and skills to the poor in Zurich. Samson edited and translated *Socialisme et liberté,* a selection of texts by Brupbacher (Neuchâtel: La Baconnière, 1955).

Moving in the same leftist circles as Samson, Max Bill also met Brupbacher, whose political analyses Ernst Geiger—Max's uncle—had already heard about decades earlier as a student in Zurich, and Max of course also met Brupbacher's third wife Paula, known as Paulette, because she wrote for *information.*

Bill's friendship with François Bondy was well known in Zurich. In his later years the relationship between the Bondys and Bill was so close that the Bondys would even tell him very personal things.

Since Paulette—a very direct, temperamental person, who spoke "German with a French accent"[864]—had studied philosophy in Bern and (presumably later) medicine in Geneva, she might perhaps have been one of the Russians that Ernst Geiger had associated with as a younger man.

The Brupbachers' guest book opens with an inscription: "A very singular book of friends of the supranational Brupbacher-Raygrodski inn for geniuses"—that seems to be very much in keeping with Jean-Paul Samson's observation that Brupbacher had a special interest in "*les gens hors série,*" in special outsiders. Paula Brupbacher-Raygrodski—a physician with a practice at Kasernenstrasse 17, who was particularly known for the help she gave to workers' wives in Zürich-Aussersihl—was also the president of the Communist organization, Rote Hilfe, and actively advocated for émigrés. In the 1930s there were regular meetings of locals and refugees in the Brupbachers' private residence on the Zürichberg. Their "supranational genius" guests included the émigré writers Ignazio Silone and Hans Sahl. Paulette, who was born into a cultured, Russian-Jewish family in Pinsk (Belarus), had herself arrived in Switzerland as a foreigner. As a Jew who was not allowed to study in Tsarist Russia, she became one of the many Russian women who "captured Switzerland with their intelligence and charm."[865]

864 Verena Thalmann, "An Ihrem Schicksal hat sich mein Mitleid entzündet—die Zürcher Armenärztin Paulette Brupbacher (1880–1967) und die Aussersihler Arbeiterfrauen," in *Tages-Anzeiger,* 30 July 1988

865 Obituary for Paula Brupbacher in *Volksrecht,* 24 January 1968

866 See Frei 1987

The Brupbachers, to many people's surprise, were not at all interested in conventional gender roles: "In practice most revolutionaries lead extremely bourgeois lives with self-sacrificing wives in the background.... A striking exception among those pasha-revolutionaries in Switzerland was seen in Paulette and Fritz Brupbacher, a married couple—both workers and physicians—who accepted neither gender traits nor a division of roles in their professional and private lives."[866]

Fritz Brupbacher died in 1945. After his death Paulette documented her experiences treating women from working families (*Meine Patientinnen: Aus dem Sprechzimmer einer Frauenärztin* [Zurich: Büchergilde Gutenberg, 1953]). Having herself done so much to help others, Paulette Brupbacher died in relative isolation in a home in Unterengstringen (canton of Zürich) on 31 December 1967.

"... all in all, modern human beings"

At this point Max Bill was still in contact with the free economists and corresponded with their chief executive, Fritz Schwarz, in Bern, sending him letters filled with detailed analyses and new ideas. In September 1932, for instance, he wrote: "Because of my basic stance regarding art, architecture, the law, etc., most of the people I interact with regard me as a Communist. I don't at all object to that since Communism is also an opposition movement (in Europe). Through my daily work (I design brochures, advertisements, signage for buildings, advertising campaigns) I am constantly coming into contact with people, with architects and businessmen, whose own stance—even if often not obviously Communist—is nevertheless largely tolerant. Typically, these people sometimes have very large fortunes, a high level of intellectual education, and are, all in all, modern human beings. I know that waffling about collectivity and Communism goes down particularly well with those sorts of people, that in a sense, having given up Christianity, they now feel the need for a new religion, 'Communism.' But that's by the by. The main point is, how can we exert any influence on those people, how do we persuade them even to consider our demands?

We have now published the third issue of a monthly paper, *information;* I'm obliged to play a part in it because of my connections with these people, although I am using my skills on behalf of a paper whose contents I cannot sign up to ... which cannot pay me a fee, but it does give me complete freedom in its design. That appeals to me, any task without constraints has to be appealing.

I now have two requests: take a look at that paper. If you have time, write an article on 'Fascism and Economics' or something along those lines, social democracy could easily come in for criticism in it (there is no fee). I would, however, like to read the article before you submit it, so that any points that might cause it to be rejected could be removed. After that you would send it to the editorial committee, referring to the issue you have read. If it is rejected, I will try to find out why. I personally don't yet want to engage in politicking with these people, who are pretty well funded, that's why I'm not doing anything myself yet. An article about 'Crisis and Morgan' could also be of interest, if there are numerous sources cited (as in dissertations), as academic as possible, with as little as possible tending toward free economics, that's for later. I do believe that by this means it would be possible to reach some of the people that could be important to us. And, when the time comes, we could get address lists from 'information' and send out brochures to those people....

My second request is: a critique of various points to do with editing free economist texts. Also, I have the feeling that we haven't addressed the fact that brochures and books on a modern topic, like ours, should not have cover designs that are a poor second to what you see on Protestant news sheets and tracts. Every time I get a new text I see with the same shock that the cover image has still not been improved.

'Morgan,' a publication that would have endless possibilities if it were presented properly, also perhaps if it were not marked 'Verl. Freiwirtsch.' [published by the free economists], is currently impossible to give to anyone who has a modern sensibility. I don't think that can be the intention, so I have a suggestion. My input, my contribution to advancing our ideas would be to come up with covers, with designs for flyers, posters, etc. It's not that I have too little to do, if anyone is not suffering the pain of unemployment, it is me, but something has to be done, our publications should be bought and read ... of course [my input would be] gratis with the exception of immediate expenses.

867 Max Bill, Goldbrunnenstrasse, Zurich, to Fritz Schwarz, Schwarztorstrasse 76, Bern, 18 September 1932, Fritz and Elly Schwarz archive

868 Max Bill, Zurich 3, Goldbrunnenstrasse 141, to Fritz Schwarz, Bern, Schwarztorstrasse 76, 26 November 1932, Fritz and Elly Schwarz archive

869 François Bondy, "Silone in der Schweiz," in *Neue Zürcher Zeitung,* 5 November 1987

Finally, on a personal note: Is it necessary to make so much of religion as in recent issues of the F-Z [*Freiwirtschaftliche Zeitung*], in fact in all the free-economist publications? Is 'attacking' the Soviet Union so very essential, if the same thing could be achieved differently? We should be aware that in Zurich large numbers of intellectuals may be Communists and that it is as important to persuade those people as it is to persuade miners to revolt and to refuse to pay interest.... with very best regards Bill."[867]

This letter provides an insight into Bill's political views, which were tied in with his hope of a revolution of a very particular kind—a free economy revolution. Not generally known for his restraint, Bill had so far kept out of the ideological firing line. But in November 1932 he did have the self-confidence to stand up "to a number of Communists," to defend his free economist stance—it is not impossible that those "Communists" were working on *information.* He described the situation in another letter to Fritz Schwarz:

"Re: F.Z. [*Freiwirtschaftliche Zeitung*], no. 46

In the issue of the F.Z. cited above, in the article "Die Arbeiterschaft und ihre Führer," there is a passage about the Russian monetary system. In a recent discussion I took it upon myself to outline my interpretation of this passage to a number of Communists and to polemicize on it. Of course they treated the whole thing as a complete fabrication and dismissed it as absolutely impossible. So I offered to try to obtain the best possible proof, whereupon the Communists said they would write to their 'information center' in Berlin (where they may perhaps discover the opposite to what they think). I would therefore be most grateful if you could supply the documents I need.... with best regards Bill."[868]

Texts and Images in *information*

The founding and survival of *information* for almost two years was largely down to Ignazio Silone, who had been expelled from the Italian Communist Party in 1931 because of a "Trotskyite conspiracy." As an émigré he was in severe financial difficulties, so he alone received a fee for his work on *information.*

In 1936 Max Raphael and Ignazio Silone would both stay at the home of the patron of the arts and collector Marcel Fleischmann, who owned a number of works by Picasso.[869]

The other contributors, mostly men, included Sigfried Giedion, Jean-Paul Samson, Dr. Georg Schmidt, Max Raphael, Hans Schmidt, and Rudolf Steiger (both architects), Rudolf Jakob Humm and Jakob Bührer (two Swiss writers).

Bill greatly appreciated the work of Jakob Bührer, who wrote with great commitment and a certain pathos that might perhaps be compared to that of Anna Seghers; one of his titles is *Im roten Feld, Roman von der Geburt einer Nation* (3 vols., Zurich: Büchergilde Gutenberg, 1938–51). In his later years Bill would also come into contact with Bührer's daughter, the social democrat politician, Selma Gessner-Bührer.

Bührer also wrote an obituary poem for the artist Otto Meyer-Amden (*information* 1:8, March 1933), a close friend of Bill's onetime Bauhaus master, Oskar Schlemmer.

Hans Mühlestein—in whose home in the Engadine Bill would later meet the philosopher Ernst Bloch, before Bloch's expulsion from Switzerland—also occasionally contributed articles, for instance "Vae Victis!" and "Die neue Hure Babylon."

Mühlestein also had a particular interest in Hodler; in 1914 he published *Ferdinand Hodler. Ein Deutungsversuch.* Later on, he and Georg Schmidt, a colleague at *information,* jointly published *Ferdinand Hodler 1853–1918* (Zurich: Rentsch, 1942), which came out with the same publisher that had published Lissitzky and Arp's now famous book *Die Kunstismen 1914–1924.*

The only reproduction of a work of art that appeared in *information* was a woodcut by Carl Meffert—under the heading "Proletarian Art"; it was from a folio of woodcuts by Meffert, which Georg Schmidt reviewed in that same issue (no. 8). Carl Meffert was the son of a German civil servant. With painful personal experience of orphanages and prisons, he had frequented intellectual and Communist circles in Berlin before fleeing to Switzerland, where he adopted the pseudonym Clément Moreau. Since Moreau and Secondo Tranquilli (the pseudonym adopted by Ignazio Silone) were among the first émigrés to arrive in Switzerland, they were sometimes seen as model exiles and pampered like mascots. Those who followed in the flood of émigrés that arrived after the Nazis had seized power in early 1933 were generally not met with the same warm welcome, prompting certain groups in Switzerland to seek out and implement new ways of showing solidarity with them.

870 Magnaguagno 1980
871 Magnaguagno 1980

Before Moreau and Silone became involved with *information,* they had already encountered each other in the Ticino at the agricultural commune Fontana Martina, where Moreau was a member.

It is worth mentioning here that in the late 1920s the young Max Bill and his uncle Ernst Geiger went hiking in the Ticino and—before Silone and Meffert were on the scene—sought out the Fontana Martina commune. Geiger and Bill wanted to form their own opinion of the alternative lifestyle that was being tried out at the commune. They stayed for a while, and Geiger captured the view from there, looking toward Italy, in a painting titled *Fontana Martina Richtung Italien.*

When they met again in Zurich in 1932, it was not only in connection with *information* but also as political activists who were "working with the unions, the publisher Emil Oprecht, and bourgeois families to help German émigrés. The ban on political activities did not prevent them from launching a flyer campaign supporting farm workers in their fight against wage cuts."[870]

Silone, the son of a laborer from Abruzzo, was said to have smuggled illegal flyers from the Ticino to Italy; Moreau then used the same hand press that these flyers had been printed on to make his linocuts for Fritz Jordi's periodical *Fontana Martina.*[871]

In Zurich Silone was friends with Fernando Schiavetti, who had also fled Italy and Mussolini. Schiavetti's daughter, Annarella Rotter-Schiavetti, later told me that in their family her father's nickname had been "*cavallo di cartone*" (cardboard horse). In Clément Moreau's folio, *Linolschnitte zu Ignazio Silone* (Berlin: Litpol, 1980), there is a reproduction of a pencil portrait of Ignazio Silone done by Moreau in 1933.

Max Bill supported the campaign against wage cuts by designing a poster; he also drew a caricature for *information* (no. 5, November 1932, p. 29) showing "morality snoopers at work" and signed "bill-Zürich." That same issue contains a text on "proletarian theater in Basel" by a certain "V.C.F." (p. 27), most probably Charles Ferdinand Vaucher.

Vaucher's surname should have been pronounced in the French manner, but his friends in Basel called him "Faucher" or "Fauchi" ("with a strong 'f' and a really rough 'ch'"). ["Fauchen" in German describes the hissing sound made by cats.] In Zurich Max Bill also called him "Fauchi," accentuating the first syllable like a hissing cat.

In 1933 Fauchi, a brave man, started taking refugees across the border to Switzerland in his car. His first marriage was to the dancer Katja Wulff, who had performed in Zurich at the short-lived cabaret, the Krater, along with Max Bill and others, including Marie-Eve Kreis and the Expressionist dancer Trudi Schoop (see also the illustrations in

C. F. Vaucher, *"Aus meiner linken Schublade." Erzählungen eines Lebens, mit Zwischentexten von Peter Kamber* [Zurich: Rotpunktverlag, 1996], in the picture section [unpaginated], "C. F. Vaucher und Katja Wulff" and "Tanzstudio Wulff" in the Stadttheater in Zurich, 13 April 1932, with Katja Wulff, Marie-Eve Kreis and C. F. Vaucher).

Bill also placed advertisements in *information* on behalf of Wohnbedarf and others, and notices of new publications from "Verlag Dr. Oprecht & Helbling AG, Zürich Rämistrasse 1," for instance, "Coming soon: Elisabeth Thommen, *Blitzfahrt durch Sowjetrussland* . . . Elisabeth Thommen, a prominent member of the Swiss women's movement, has recently returned from a trip through Russia. Her descriptions of her experiences and impressions are pithy and lively. Price: boxed, ca. 2 francs" (*information,* no. 5, November 1932). What this notice fails to mention is that Max Bill designed the typography for *Blitzfahrt durch Sowjetrussland.*

Elisabeth Thommen was married for a time to the author Jakob Bührer, meaning that for a time she was also step-mother to Selma Bührer; on this see Selma Gessner-Bührer, *Fräulein, Sie sind vielseitig. Die Lebensgeschichte der Selma Gessner-Bührer* (Zurich: Realotopia, 1993).

One of the most informative texts published in *information* is a detailed discussion by Dr. Alfred Kantorowicz of the *Braunbuch über Reichstagsbrand und Hitlerterror* (*information,* no. 2, September 1933). Anyone who read that book could never later claim not to have known what the Nazis were already doing in Germany. And as to wider political attitudes at *information,* it was not attached to either the Social Democratic Party or the Communist Party in Switzerland; it deplored Stalin's paranoia but it was not hostile to the Soviet Union.

". . . wonderful that the ground is at a slant"

Using the new notepaper he had designed after moving to Goldbrunnenstrasse 141, Bill wrote to an old Bauhaus friend, Arieh Sharon, who was now in Tel Aviv. By the same post he also sent Sharon materials for the design and organization of the Swiss Section in the General Foreign Pavilion at the Levant Fair in Tel Aviv in 1932.

In 1932 Sharon was thirty-two years old and had opened his own architectural practice in Tel Aviv. The authorities now decided that

872 Davidi Kuna 2001, pp. 108–9

the Levant Fair needed permanent pavilions, and Sharon was awarded first prize in the design competition for a pavilion for Histadrut (the General Federation of Labor). This was his first major commission in Palestine and he subsequently described his group of four pavilions, which was constructed in time for the Levant Fair in 1934, as the "first avant-garde construction" in Tel Aviv.

Sharon's daughter Yael Aloni sent Bill's original letter to me with an accompanying note describing the circumstances. Yael Aloni's research has shown that in Tel Aviv in 1932, after her father had left the Bauhaus in 1931, he received "his first contract" to participate in the Levant Fair. "The second time was in 1934. In both exhibitions the work was for the Histradut pavilion. The Histadrut was a general workers' union"; Yael Aloni added in her note that in Arieh Sharon's *Kibbutz + Bauhaus* (Stuttgart: Krämer, 1976), the two pavilions, which are illustrated on pp. 52 and 53, are incorrectly dated 1933.

Looking back years later he described those pavilions as his "most successful" project, "the most important" to him: "It was the pride of my life. Working with the various sections of Histadrut, which was still idealistic and credible in those days ... we built four pavilions with echoes of the Bauhaus. When I arrived at the Bauhaus in 1926 the three banners in the primary colors red, blue, and yellow made a deep impression on me, no one could come up with a color for the fourth banner, so it was left white, maybe as a symbol of peace. The four pavilions, in a range of different sizes, were constructed from modules. The roofs had jute coverings: red for the unions' pavilion, blue for the cooperatives, green for the agriculture workers, and orange for the smallest pavilion, which represented citrus fruit production.

Unlike the other buildings at the Fair, solid structures, the Histadrut pavilions were open on all sides. The exhibition areas inside them were visible from far away and conveyed a sense of openness and lightness. While they were all the same width, they were not the same height. Because the roofs were sloping, the module became more open as the height (and length) of the roof increased. The same construction method was used throughout, but the differences in their proportions and colors gave each pavilion and its displays a unique identity."[872]

In his letter Bill wrote: "Dear Sharon ... sweating as I toiled, I have fulfilled your requests to the best of my ability.... You will receive, by the same post ... a number of sheets of paper, which I hope will serve their purpose for you. Firstly 2 alphabets, one capital letters, one small letters, with matching proportions. I have drawn them so that with the help of not too dim assistants they can be enlarged or reduced as needed. The proportions are the same in the capitals and in the small letters and are noted on the capital S. Capital letters have to be used at the beginnings of words on the signage in the Swiss section.... I thought that there could be a poster wall of some kind opposite the entrance. And on the adjoining wall 'Switzerland,' as big as possible, but still legible ... possibly a narrow partition, floor to ceiling, with travel posters, to give the space some structure. Information, a table and chairs.... I think it's wonderful that the ground is at a slant, so everything will be at a slant, the pumps will be at a slant, everything, that will be a great effect, the vertical slatted wall with travel posters could be placed at a slant on the other side. In case you need it, I am also sending you the proportions of the Swiss cross (white on a red ground), it always looks good, is decorative and you can make it very big, for example on the wall above 'information'...."

After various technical details, Bill adds a note on what he and Binia are currently working on: "We have an awful lot to do. Next week I'm also making an exhibition stand at the Mustermesse in Basel and I'm doing the buildings catalogue for the Bund Schweizer Architekten (Association of Swiss architects), an entertaining task. And otherwise I'm working for Wohnbedarf ... we're here, there, and everywhere. With very best wishes from both of us. Bill."[873]

In his letter to Arieh Sharon on 25 March, Bill mistyped the year as "34" and corrected it to "32." In both 1932 and 1934 there was a Levant Fair in Tel Aviv. However, this letter was most probably written in 1932, since the sender's address is Goldbrunnenstrasse 141—by 1934 Max and Binia Bill were already in their own house in Höngg. This argument of course only holds water if Bill—already at Höngg—was not using up old writing paper left over from Goldbrunnenstrasse. However, I think that is unlikely, since as a graphic artist and typographer, Bill always designed new writing paper with his current address after any move.

Bill's proposals were therefore most probably intended for the Fair in 1932. As yet it has not been possible to establish if his package arrived in Tel Aviv in time and/or whether a "Swiss section" as Bill

873 Max Bill, Zurich 3, Goldbrunnenstrasse 141, to Arieh Sharon, Tel Aviv, Palestine, 78 Yarkan Street, 25 March 34 [corrected to "32"] Bibliothek Max Bill

874 Georg Schmidt to Secondo Tranquilli and Ernst F. Burckhardt, 9 March 1933, Ignazio Silone sent a copy to R. J. Humm, 12 March 1933, Zentralbibliothek Zürich / estate of R. J. Humm, cited in Holmes 2005, pp. 77–78 and p. 90 note 75

envisaged it was in fact realized. Sigal Davidi Kuna, an architect who wrote her master's thesis on the 1934 Levant Fair, has undertaken further research into the 1932 Levant Fair.

A Serious Anti-Fascist

The driving force behind *information* was Ignazio Silone, who was taken in by Wladimir Rosenbaum and Aline Valangin at their home, Baumwollhof, in Zurich and by the art historian Georg Schmidt in Basel.

Silone and Aline Valangin were lovers from 1931 to early 1933; for more on this see Peter Kamber, *Geschichte zweier Leben. Wladimir Rosenbaum und Aline Valangin* (Zurich: Limmat Verlag, 1990, enlarged ed., 2000), see also Eveline Hasler's novel *Aline und die Erfindung der Liebe* (Zurich: Nagel & Kimche, 2000).

Silone also sometimes stayed with Max Bill's friend Ernst F. Burckhardt, and, as we know from a letter written by Georg Schmidt, it was Burckhardt who was the "link man" between Silone and Bill, who then went together to the printers' cooperative in Aarau where *information* was to be printed. In Erich Schmid's film *Bill—Das absolute Augenmass* there is a very touching clip of Silone and Bill meeting again after many years (see p. 484) and recalling that trip.

Georg Schmidt described the division of labor at *information:* "Tranquilli is de facto editor-in-chief, i.e., he does the most important cerebral work: getting hold of the articles. That, to a large extent, determines the character of the periodical. And, in that regard, too, we have almost always been in agreement, i.e., E.F. [Burckhardt] and I have accepted Tranquilli's suggestions without further ado. While Tr. [Silone] was living with E.F., it was E.F.'s job to act as a link man, helping to source images, (partly) setting up the connection with Bill, etc. My job was to take care of the Swiss bits and pieces, copyedit all the articles, read corrections and galley proofs. Has this division of labor proved to be viable, or not? In my view it has been entirely viable because it reflects our strengths and capabilities."[874]

The historian Deborah Holmes, who has published a study on Silone's exile in Switzerland, has also investigated the work done at *information* and the various personal interconnections. She describes how a group of recent émigrés from Germany and "six Swiss" (not named) planned a new weekly paper: "In an attempt to prevent Silone from gaining as much influence over any new journal as he has over *information*, the leader of the

Swiss Communist Party, Humbert-Droz, tries to turn Humm against him by elaborating on the official version of his expulsion from the PCI for Trotskyite conspiracy. Humm has, however, already been sufficiently impressed by Silone's contribution to *information* to be inured to party gossip ... he particularly stresses *information's* status as opinion-leader rather than opinion-led."[875]

However disturbing the fact that Jules Humbert-Droz—co-founder and strong man of the Communist Party of Switzerland—tried to sideline Ignazio Silone, it is not as shocking as the deep prejudice he displayed (as told by Humm): Humbert-Droz "says that all Italians are like that."

R. J. Humm wrote to Aline Valangin "it seems you have to be lenient with Tranquilli. His penchant for intrigue is known in official party circles, he was eliminated from the Italian party for something of exactly that sort. HD [Humbert-Droz] says that all Italians are like that—enough said. Tranquilli's latest article in inf. [*information*] is very good. . . ."[876]

The situation as a whole was further complicated by the fact that R. J. Humm embarked on an affair with Aline Valangin, whose relationship with Silone now came to an end. "Another contributing factor to the crisis [at *information*], of which Humm, understandably, seems to have been entirely ignorant, was the traumatic end of Silone's relationship with Aline Valangin, motivated in part by the beginning of her affair with the very same Humm. At this point, as their correspondence shows, Silone and Humm were already, if not friends, then good acquaintances at the very least."[877] It seems that Silone mainly blamed Valangin for their break-up: "Silone was particularly horrified by what he presented in a bitter letter to Valangin as her evil seduction" of Humm.[878]

Deeply shaken by the end of that affair, Silone formally broke off contact with Valangin and Rosenbaum, as we learn from a letter sent by Silone on 6 April 1933 and titled "Liquidation des résidus." Holmes concludes that this all had dire consequences for the daily life and the

875 Holmes 2005, p. 79

876 R. J. Humm to Aline Valangin, 26 April 1933, bcl / Fondo Aline Valangin, cited in Holmes 2005

877 Holmes 2005, p. 79

878 Ignazio Silone to Aline Valangin, 3 April 1933, Schweizer. Sozialarchiv, cited in Holmes 2005, pp. 79–80

879 Holmes 2005, p. 80

880 Hendrick Feindt, "Die Filmkritik und das Nichts der Oberflächen" in *Neue Zürcher Zeitung*, 7–8 August 2004

881 Holmes 2005, p. 69

finances of the cooperative that published *information.* Nevertheless, Silone continued his work as editor and on 12 July 1933 wrote to the author Bernard von Brentano: "there are several novelties at *information:* Burckhardt is leaving, and the editorial staff and the board of the cooperative will also be changed."[879]

Bernard von Brentano, who Silone wrote to, was a fellow author who had come to Switzerland from Germany. He had previously worked in Germany at the *Frankfurter Zeitung,* where he and Bernhard Diebold were both film critics. "When it came to films such as *Woman in the Moon, the Blue Angel* [with Marlene Dietrich], *Metropolis, Faust and the Nibelungen*" those two longstanding critics had the "droit du seigneur."[880]

Bernard von Brentano's novel *Theodor Chindler* would be published in 1936 by Emil Oprecht, who supported numerous authors in exile and published over 100 titles, including Arthur Koestler's *Ein Spanisches Testament* (1938) and Willy Brandt's *Krieg in Norwegen* (1942).

Many of the texts by Silone in *information* were subsequently reprinted in his book *Der Faschismus* (1934). He sometimes published articles as "Silone"; other articles, which he wrote in French for translation into German, were published under pseudonyms. His "Einführung in eine Diskussion über den Fascismus," for instance, is credited to "Marsus."

"Fascism, even in its specific Italian incarnation, has already mutated many times and can have no single definition. The truth is to be found in an analysis of all its elements 'in the contradictory rhythm of its mutual relationships.'"

And, as Holmes reports, in his attempt to define Fascism, Silone continued by suggesting "that Fascism is not nationally specific, nor even specific to economically underdeveloped countries. He believes that it menaces any country where capitalism rules and proletarian revolution is seen as a threat, and is therefore also possible in Switzerland. The only sure defense is to take the wind out of Fascism's sails by refuting capitalism."[881]

The majority of the articles in the May 1933 issue of *information* attempted to analyze the situation in Germany. In an article on "the first phase of a Fascist dictatorship," Silone drew parallels with Italy. As Deborah Holmes puts it: "He emphasises the regime's connections to capitalist high finance in a manner typical for *information* where economic concerns outweigh psychological or cultural considerations." In her examination of the third and last phase of *information,* Holmes concludes that the group once again tried to launch a leftist attack in Switzerland with the intention of driving a wedge into the increasingly fascist middle classes.

At that point *information* regarded itself as "the only radical left-wing review in Switzerland."[882]

Although Bill contributed his skills to *information,* he was not fully signed up to its views. After *information* had folded Bill created the graphic design for Silone's book *Der Faschismus: seine Entstehung und seine Entwicklung,* which was published by Europa-Verlag Zürich in 1934.

As to the affairs that Aline Valangin sometimes engaged in alongside her relationship with her husband Wladimir Rosenbaum, Bill once remarked to Peter Kamber that "Aline was a very attractive woman, an intelligent woman. And when she was interested in what people did, she made a beeline for them. Basically I found it perfectly normal that relationships emerged from that. I always just thought that Rosenbaum would probably recoup his losses in some way or other, but whatever the case, I always had the feeling that the two of them got on very well. . . .There was no confusion, those were just temporary convergences, which then diverged again somehow."[883]

By way of an aside, Hans Bolliger (the Dada expert living in Zurich) once turned to Bill and asked him (in my presence) if he hadn't also had an affair with Aline Valangin, because the writer Rudolf Jakob Humm, who had fallen for Aline after Silone, had been jealous of Bill in those days. Bill said he had not. Later, when we were alone again, he told me that he had truly not had an affair with Aline Valangin, and that was the end of the matter.

Wladimir Vogel

In June 1934 a new man entered Aline Valangin's life, the German-Russian musician Wladimir Vogel, born to a German father and a Russian mother in 1896. He had studied in Berlin with Ferruccio Busoni and had emigrated to Zurich after spending some time in Strasbourg. "Max Bill was among the first intellectuals and artists in our country to become friends with Vogel, who had emigrated from Germany to Switzerland in 1933. Around that time Hermann Scherchen commissioned Bill to design a regular cover for *Musica Viva* [a quarterly music magazine]. . . . [Two decades later]

882 See Holmes 2005, pp. 84–85
883 Kamber 1990, p. 125
884 See Vogel 1977
885 Max Bill to Wladimir Vogel, Oetlisbergstrasse 7, 8053 Zurich, 28 March 1978, Archiv Max Bill
886 Oesch 1967, p. 61

when Bill, who had always had a keen interest in contemporary music, became co-founder and rector of the Hochschule für Gestaltung in Ulm, he contacted Vogel and commissioned him to write a piece for the ceremonial opening of the new school that had been built to his own design; the remit was a set of fanfares for brass instruments; these were later absorbed into Vogel's *Turmmusik I–IV.*"[884]

Having first designed a cover for Wladimir Vogel's *Tripartita* (Ars Viva, 1933–34, see p. 520)—composed in Strasbourg and dedicated to a certain Madame Marise Mathis—Bill then also designed a cover for Vogel's *Dai tempi più remoti, tre pezzi per pianoforte* (Eulenburg, 1977), which "greatly delighted" Vogel (illustrated in *Max Bill: Typografie, Reklame, Buchgestaltung* [Sulgen: Niggli, 1999], p. 286). Vogel responded by dedicating a composition, *Graphique,* to Bill, which Bill wittily thanked him for in March 1978: "dear wladimir vogel ... i am deeply appreciative of the honor you have bestowed on me by dedicating *graphique* to me and now hasten to thank you most warmly. all the more so, since i have in the meantime learned that beethoven later scratched out the words 'intitolata bonaparte' on the score of his symphony no. 3 in e flat, evidently no longer in agreement with the dedicatee. i of course am keen to avoid any-thing of that sort! ... with warm regards, yours, bill."[885] As he did with Silone, Bill always maintained a certain politeness with Vogel; they did not use the familiar "du" form in conversation.

Vogel had left Germany "voluntarily, legally and in a timely manner," that is to say, in keeping with the law, which was why he could never be sent to an internment camp in Switzerland. "However, according to the not exactly principled immigration regulations at the time, Vogel could not be granted either a residence permit or a work permit ... and he had to leave Switzerland every three months, even if only briefly."[886]

Initially Vogel spent one half of the week with Oskar and Annie Müller-Widmann in Basel and the other half with Rosenbaum and Valangin in Zurich, where—with his hosts' approval—he unobtrusively taught music in order to earn some money. When he first arrived in Switzerland he had his entire worldly goods in a single suitcase. "Since he then encountered certain difficulties in Basel, that same year—1935—he moved to Zurich, where, with a recommendation from the architect Erich Mendelsohn, he was kindly taken in by the lawyer W. Rosenbaum, who very effectively supported all kinds of émigrés and was forever submitting pleas to the aliens office for them. In those tumultuous times many leading figures came and went at Rosenbaum's house: Toller, Tucholsky, von Brentano, Tranquilli-Silone, Hans Curjel and his wife, Erich Mendelsohn and his wife, J. P. Samson ... and a throng of local artists, such as Hermann Haller and

Gregor Rabinovitch."[887] It is worth adding here that the locals who were seen there also included Binia and Max Bill.

It was through Vogel that Wladimir Rosenbaum and Aline Valangin met the writer Elias Canetti. And it was at their home in Stadelhoferstrasse that Canetti read, to a very select audience, a chapter from the novel that became *Die Blendung* (published in English as *Auto da Fé*). James Joyce was a member of that expert audience.

Canetti and Vogel both took part in the modern music conference that Scherchen organized in Strasbourg in 1933. There is no knowing if Bill was there, too. Whatever the case, years later he lent me his copy of Canetti's *Blendung.*

". . . the most progressive ideas in Switzerland"

Rudolf Jakob Humm, who also wrote for *information,* was active on the political left. In 1923 he had married Lili Crawford, Flora Steiger-Crawford's sister, and in 1931 he and Lili moved into an apartment at the Neubühl Estate, with its modernist, flat-roofed homes; Humm's brother-in-law Rudolf Steiger had been closely involved in the planning process for the estate. R. J. Humm was co-founder and secretary of Das neue Russland (the "New Russia" society) and had set up an anti-war committee together with Jakob Bührer and Valentin Gitermann in 1932.

From 1929 onward, Aline spent three months in La Barca every summer. At that summer residence in Comologno, in the Tichino, she also advised Humm as he was working on his novel *Die Inseln* (1932–34), which was published at Christmas 1935 by Oprecht with the year date 1936. In 1935 Humm started translating texts by Ignazio Silone and other writers into German—mainly for the Büchergilde Gutenberg in Zurich. A photograph shows Humm outside La Barca (Rudolf Jakob Humm holding a cigarette, together with Aline, 1930s, illustrated in Rudolf Jakob Humm, *Die Inseln: Roman* [Suhrkamp: Frankfurt am Main, 1990], p. 197).

887 Oesch 1967, p. 61
888 See Holmes 2005
889 R. J. Humm to Walter Roshardt, 28 October 1932, Zentralbibliothek Zürich /estate of R. J. Humm, cited in Holmes 2005, p. 90 note 70

Although there was a range of political opinions at *information,* Humm nevertheless regarded it as a platform for the most progressive ideas in Switzerland.[888] And, as Deborah Holmes recounts, after the annual general meeting of Das neue Russland in 1932, Humm wrote a concerned letter to Walter Roshardt: "I don't know if you noticed that the entire group from 'information' was missing yesterday. That absence is not without significance ... it is essential that we work with that group. We have to make sure we are worthy of their interest."[889] In 1934 R. J. Humm moved into the Rabenhaus at Hechtplatz in Zurich, and his new home soon became a favorite meeting place for artists and writers.

On 12 October 1940 Wladimir Rosenbaum and Aline Valangin divorced by mutual agreement but still remained good friends. Rosenbaum subsequently married his second wife, Anne de Montet, with whom he later had two daughters, and Aline became close to the composer Wladimir Vogel. She managed to make enough from texts she published to keep Vogel and herself afloat; Vogel was still prohibited from taking paid employment in Switzerland. Aline always remained close to Rosenbaum and in later life expressed the wish that she might be buried alongside Rosenbaum and his fourth and last wife. When she died in 1986, her wish was granted. Wladimir Rosenbaum's funeral, which I attended, had been held two years earlier in Ascona in autumn 1984; the eulogy at his funeral was given by Max Bill.

Max Raphael versus C. G. Jung

Max Raphael, a Marxist cultural historian, also contributed articles to *information;* this was of course the same Max Raphael whose book, *Von Monet zu Picasso,* Moholy-Nagy had shown to the young Max Bill at the Bauhaus just a few years earlier. And, during the course of the Picasso exhibition at Kunsthaus Zürich (11 September–30 October 1932) Max Raphael—who had visited Picasso early on in his Paris studio—gave a lecture on "Picasso as a sociological problem." Not long after that Raphael wrote a text for *information* responding to an article by C. G. Jung in the *Neue Zürcher Zeitung,* in which Jung maintained that Picasso was schizophrenic. Raphael, taking diametrically opposed class interests as his starting point, argued that ever since the unproductive petit-bourgeois class had—due to the rise of capitalism—"seemingly become the judge of intellectual production, it always defends the privileged quiescence of its own impotence with the same argument—as C. G. Jung has done in the NZZ—by pointing to the madness, the ailments of the artist."[890]

For more on Max Raphael's various visits to Switzerland, see my research: Angela Thomas Jankowski, "Max Raphael, genannt Machol," in *"Wir lassen uns die Welt nicht zerbrechen." Max Raphaels Werk in der Diskussion,* ed. Hans-Jürgen Heinrichs (Frankfurt: Suhrkamp, 1989), pp. 219–41.

Not pulling his punches, Raphael went on to compare the "solvent impotence" of one such as C. G. Jung with the "productive intellectual powers" of Pablo Picasso. However, Johannes Widmer, an art manager and collector of works by Max Bill's uncle Ernst Geiger, wrote to Geiger, taking Jung's side: "Dear Friend, ... Zurich is still vomiting Picasso. Fortunately at least Jung, the psychologist, has put him in his place."[891]

Johannes Widmer's wife had been born into the Wegelin banking family in St. Gallen. One of her brothers, Dr. Robert Widmer, still owns an important collection of works by Ernst Geiger.

The Zett-Haus: Refugee Center

Once Adolf Hitler had seized power in Germany, Georg Schmidt and other *Neues Bauen* architects set up a refugee aid committee. A committee office was opened in the Zett-Haus at Badenerstrasse 18, close to the Sihl bridge in Zurich.

The Zett-Haus was designed as a multi-purpose building "with shops, parking, a restaurant, a cinema, offices—topped by small apartments in an arcade. The glazed roof of the cinema can be opened. There is a roof terrace with a swimming pool. The construction notably has two rows of internal supports (concrete clad steel)" (see p. 483).[892]

890 Max Raphael, "C. G. Jung vergreift sich an Picasso," *information* 1:6 (December 1932), pp. 4–7

891 Johannes Widmer, Geneva, to Ernst Geiger, Ligerz, 17 November 1932, Archiv Christoph Geiger

892 Mercedes Daguerre, *Architekturführer Schweiz, 20. Jahrhundert* (Basel: Birkhäuser 1997), p. 46

893 See Bloch 2005, p. 140 note 1

894 Perrottet [1989–90], p. 227

895 Bill 1976 [b], p. 36

896 Information kindly supplied by historian Simon Erlanger

897 Ernst Bloch, Wengen, Hotel Silberhorn, to Karola Piotrkowska, 26 December 1932, in Bloch 2005, p. 149

That was where the typographer Jan Tschichold went for help, as did the philosopher Ernst Bloch, who fled from Germany to Switzerland in December 1932 and arrived in Zurich via Basel, Bern, Wengen, and Interlaken.[893] Carl Meffert, alias Clément Moreau, also found lodgings in the Zett-Haus, where a 15-square-meter room cost between 30 and 50 Swiss francs per month. And it was at the Zett-Haus that Moreau met his future wife, Nelly Guggenbühl, who was helping refugees to find accommodation.

The dancer Suzanne Perrottet opened a dance school in the Zett-Haus, where she also became friends with Richard P. Lohse. "In 1932 I moved into the Zett-Haus. It had just been completed and was very modern.... There was space on the flat roof for me to give lessons, and there was also a large pool on the roof. It was ideal, first teaching in the sun and then a dip. From up there you could look straight down onto the roof of the Roxy cinema, which was in the same building. The roof was retractable and when it was open, you could see the audience inside the cinema, but not the screen. It was very interesting to see them first laughing and then turn serious or sad, you could imagine the whole film. There was also an artist living in the Zett-Haus, Richard P. Lohse ... something very special connected me to him."[894]

By now more and more refugees were arriving in Switzerland from Germany, including the former Bauhaus master Paul Klee, who hastily returned to Bern in 1933. Max Bill was soon "in close contact" with him again.[895] Scientists from Germany mainly emigrated to Geneva, in the hope of receiving one of the few research grants that were available there.[896]

Ernst Bloch and Karola Piotrkowska

In 1933 the philosopher Ernst Bloch and Karola Piotrkowska, his partner and future third wife, visited Binia and Max Bill in their new home-and-studio in Zürich-Höngg. With the political situation in Germany now posing an existential threat to Bloch and Piotrkowska, Bloch had left Berlin for Switzerland in December 1932, several weeks before Piotrkowska, who courageously continued to act as a courier for the Communist Party. Bloch felt the benefit of the mountain air in Switzerland, and friends gave him "a free rail ticket right to the top of the mountain with the Jungfraubahn, which opens again on 28 December."[897] Bloch was so impressed by the Jungfraujoch, where everything felt so very unfamiliar to him, that he decided to write a "landscape essay about the Alps," which he then did some time later.[898]

That essay "Alpen ohne Photographie" was published in Ernst Bloch, *Literarische Aufsätze,* Gesamtausgabe, vol. 9 (Frankfurt am Main: Suhrkamp, 1965).

Bloch's first letter from Zurich to Karola Piotrkowska in Berlin was sent on 30 March 1933; in it he writes that he is trying to arrange for her to be able to study in the architecture department at the ETH.

Sensing a Future in Freedom

Bloch may have told the Bills, in glowing terms, about his trip up to the Jungfraujoch, and Max may have responded by telling Bloch that his own father, Erwin Bill, had once worked as a railwayman on the lower section of the Jungfraubahn. Did Ernst Bloch and Max Bill perhaps realize that there were certain similarities in their backgrounds? Like Erwin Bill, Bloch's father had worked for the railways (in Germany); he "was the embodiment, in an entirely negative sense, of the typical German civil-servant persona.... Max Bloch, a railways auditor, could think of nothing better than to send his unhappy son to become an apprentice in an ironmonger's shop when he left school." Ernst Bloch was ultimately only able to study philosophy thanks to his mother, who was much more sympathetic to her son than his rigid, autocratic father.[899] The dominant, widespread "educational" practice in those days—which Bloch could not escape as a boy growing up in a moderately well off, Jewish family—was authoritarian and repressive, and it was that formative experience that motivated his swift revolt against bourgeois society. Bill and Bloch (a few years older than Bill) may thus well have felt a certain political affinity.

"But the road that cuts into the mountains—all the more so the train that swiftly dissects it—leaves almost nothing of the familiar form intact."[900]

"On the Jungfraujoch" Bloch had discerned 'an area of transition that the lower world does not know at all.'" And for Bloch the sublime

898 Ernst Bloch, Interlaken, Hotel Weisses Kreuz, to Karola Piotrkowska, 15 March 1933, in Bloch 2005, p. 175 and note 10
899 Münster 2004, p. 29
900 Bloch 1965 [a], pp. 442–43
901 Bloch 1965 [a], pp. 442–43
902 Münster 2004, p. 143

nature of the mountain brought Kant to mind, who once said that "all that is sublime conveys a mere inkling of our future freedom."[901]

As it happened Karola Piotrkowska and Max Bill already had a mutual friend—Xanti Schawinsky—and it may have been Schawinsky who introduced her and Ernst Bloch to Binia and Max Bill.

Xanti and Bill knew each other from their carefree days of experimentation on the Bauhaus stage and in the Bauhaus band. They had encountered each other again in 1931 at the *Internationale Bauausstellung* in Berlin, where they were both working as exhibition designers: Bill (as we have already said) for the Swiss section and Xanti for the German section (see "Demonstration at Exhibition of Architecture, Berlin 1931, designed by Xanti Schawinsky," illustrated in Xanti Schawinsky, "Development of Form in Advertising," *Industrial Arts* 1:3 [1936], pp. 232–37).

Ultimately the good-looking Xanti arrived in Zurich, where he designed sets for the Corso stage in 1933. Thanks to their work for the Corso, Xanti and Bill re-established contact with Gunta Stölzl, the former Bauhaus master, who was making a curtain for the theater. And Xanti also made contact with another former Bauhausler in Switzerland: we see him in 1933 in a photograph with Marcel Breuer, playing boccia in Ascona (illustrated in Hans Heinz Holz, *Xanti Schawinsky* [Zurich: ABC-verlag, 1981], p. 31).

Karola Piotrkowska was from a wealthy Jewish family. Her father was the director and owner of a large textiles factory in Lodz, which had a hundred employees in 1905, the year when Karola was born. At that time the workers at the factory in Lodz were predominantly Jewish and members of a union affiliated to the Bund, the Jewish workers' party, which was active in Poland, Lithuania, and Russia. Karola's privileged background meant that "as a student she had no financial concerns."[902] Moreover, when she decided she wanted to study painting and architecture in Berlin, her family moved—for her sake—to Berlin-Charlottenburg. It was in Berlin's art world that she met Xanti Schawinsky. After emigrating to Switzerland, she enrolled in the architecture department at the ETH in Zurich.

In 1927 Ernst Bloch started work on his book *Erbschaft dieser Zeit* (later published in English as *Heritage of Our Times)*, for which Max Bill would design the cover. Up until he and Karola each left Germany, they had mainly lived in Berlin, where they were on friendly terms with figures such as Bertolt Brecht, Kurt Weill, and Otto Klemperer (director of the famously progressive Kroll Opera). In 1930 they spent a few months living in Arthur Koestler's house, after which they moved into the so-called Red Block, an artists' colony in Berlin-Wilmersdorf, where they remained until they made their separate escapes. Most of the residents in the Red Block were union members, mainly socialists and Communists, but there were also some independents. When the Nazis started to attack Social Democrats and Communists, the Red Block mustered agitprop teams "who were sent out into working-class districts to harangue the locals."[903]

It was largely the tragic political events unfolding in Germany at the time that prompted Bloch to write *Erbschaft dieser Zeit* with its detailed discussion of the failings of the Marxist party in Germany during the Weimar Republic, at a time when Fascism was on the rise.[904] Bloch specifically identifies inadequacies in the political propaganda put out by parties on the left.

". . . I will deal with four intellectual beasts: Ossietzky, Tucholsky, Kerr, and Mehring"

The catastrophic economic and political impact of the Wall Street crash in 1929 was also felt in Germany. Some observers explained the huge rise in support for the National Socialist German Workers' Party (NSDAP) at the Reichstag elections on 14 September 1930, when the NSDAP came second to the Socialist Party of Germany (SPD), as a direct consequence of the widespread deterioration in the country's economy. The political situation was now extremely precarious.

The leftists at the Red Block remained solidly united as these events unfolded, and in 1932 Karola Piotrkowska became an active member of the Communist Party of Germany. During those years in Berlin, from 1930 to 1933, Ernst Bloch became acquainted with many leading intellectuals—from Siegfried Kracauer, Bertolt Brecht, and Helene Weigel to Theodor Adorno, Walter Benjamin, and Carl von Ossietzky, the co-producer of *Die Weltbühne,* who was convicted of treason and sentenced to prison for eighteen months in 1931. After the Nazis came to power he was re-arrested and sent to a concentration camp in March 1933.

903 See Münster 2004, pp. 159–69
904 Münster 2004, pp. 179–92
905 Huonker 1985, p. 151
906 Gabriele Killert, "Stellungsloser Teufel—Alfred Kerr," in *Neue Zürcher Zeitung,* 23 June 2004
907 Kerr 2004
908 Gabriele Killert, "Stellungsloser Teufel—Alfred Kerr"

During New Year celebrations in 1932–33 Joseph Goebbels, the Nazi minister of propaganda, "venomously set his sights on his victims: 'That moment will come in spring, when I will deal with four intellectual beasts: Ossietzky, Tucholsky, Kerr, and Mehring.' In Ossietzky's case Goebbels was able to achieve his brutal goal due to the fact that, even after the burning of the Reichstag, Ossietzky still refused to flee Germany. At the time of Goebbels's speech, Tucholsky was living at Florhofgasse 1 in Zurich—he had in fact already settled permanently in Sweden in 1929. Mehring and Kerr escaped at the last minute in late February [1933], the former made it to Paris, the latter initially traveled to Zurich."[905]

Alfred Kerr, a Jewish intellectual, was one of the first to see what was on the horizon, and already issued a stark warning in 1928: "Whatever lies are told by Hitler, that man of broken promises—domination by the N.S.D.A.P. means war! Ultimate misery! Germany's disintegration!"

"One need only read Tucholsky's *Briefe aus dem Schweigen* and his *Q-Tagebücher*—the most harrowing of all the texts by that great fighting spirit—to see what it means when a visionary with the most acute sight analyzes infamy and its potential extremes with prophetic precision, all the while writing in utter isolation, unable to take action."[906]

In 1933, when his career was abruptly halted by the Nazis, Alfred Kerr left Germany in great haste, at the age of sixty-five. He had been Germany's most important, wittiest theater critic. He took his family to London, where they found accommodation in a boarding house. In London Kerr worked for some years on a semi-autobiographical novel.[907] He sent dispatches from London to the *Pariser Tageblatt,* a German-language daily paper in Paris. However, in his diary, published as *Ich kam nach England,* he writes that for all his gratitude to his hosts, he still found it hard to cope with their "obstructive lack of imagination." After the Nazi invasion of France in 1940, he was no longer even able to write for émigré newspapers in Paris.[908]

In 1936, when Carl von Ossietzky was awarded the Nobel Peace Prize for 1935 in absentia, he was in Oranienburg concentration camp. He died in 1938 after years of maltreatment in various camps.

At the Bauhaus Max Bill subscribed to Ossietzky's *Weltbühne* and read it avidly. He greatly admired it. Once, in a hotel in Paris, Bill pointed out a plaque to me that had been put up in honor of Carl von Ossietzky who had stayed there.

During Ernst Bloch's time in Berlin, von Ossietzky actively championed his cause. "In 1931, when Ernst Bloch became embroiled in the 'plagiarism affair' after the *Berliner Tageblatt* ran an article accusing him of copying a story by a certain Bohdan that had been published in the *Berliner Börsen-*

Courier, it was Ossietzky who stepped in and rejected the accusations as 'absurd.' That was also the first, important, public appraisal of Bloch's philosophy and work." Carl von Ossietzky became "the first great intellectual martyr under the Nazis. There is not the slightest doubt that Ernst Bloch would have suffered the same fate if he had not hastened to leave Germany in March 1933."[909]

The Heritage of Our Times

On 27 February 1933 the Reichstag in Berlin went up in flames, and the Nazis insisted that the fire had been set by Communists. Days later—in the early morning—SA soldiers surrounded and searched the Red Block. However, before they arrived Johannes R. Becher had managed to wake the residents and warn them of the imminent danger, giving Karola just enough time to put Bloch's manuscripts into a suitcase. That done, her only option was to hide the suitcase in the attic. Bloch himself was in southern Germany by that time, and when the SA soldiers asked Karola where he had gone, she said she had no idea.

The SA searched the apartment, rummaging through Karola's lingerie, but found nothing suspicious. As Karola later recounted, she already thought "the worst was over when an SA officer suddenly said, 'And now you can show us the attic.' Climbing the stairs was like climbing the steps to a guillotine. You're going to be arrested when they find the manuscripts. My mind was racing—how can you save yourself? But then it suddenly occurred to me that I also had the key to Peter Huchel's attic space on my keyring. He had let us store a medieval wooden sculpture, a Madonna and Child, in his attic because we had run out of space in ours. So I calmly opened the padlock to his attic door. I knew that he, entirely apolitical, would have nothing to hide—and the Madonna and Child smiled brightly as we went in. The men then immediately left, the manuscripts had been spared, and so had I."[910] Karola telephoned Bloch in southern Germany and told him he had to take the very next train to Switzerland, which he did. She remained in Berlin until mid-April, working partly for Rote Hilfe until she, too, left and arrived—unchallenged—at Zurich station with Bloch's precious manuscripts.

909 Münster 2004, p. 162
910 Karola Piotrkowska, cited in Münster 2004, pp. 166–67
911 Münster 2004, p. 168
912 Münster 2004, p. 169

In his haste to flee Germany for Zurich, Ernst Bloch left his manuscript *Erbschaft dieser Zeit* in Ludwigshafen by mistake. "Thanks to the help of a German philosophy student from Heidelberg, who brought it safely across the border to Zurich, he was reunited with his manuscript."[911]

Bloch's biographer Arno Münster describes their initial reception in Zurich as "anything but friendly." However, Ernst Bloch and Karola Piotrkowska soon found allies in Zurich—such as Binia and Max Bill—and made contact with other émigrés from Germany. "One of those allies was Theo Pinkus, a highly regarded bookseller, who founded a workers' library in Zurich's old town in 1933; another ally was the philosopher and art historian Joachim Schumacher."[912]

By way of an aside, many years later—in the summer of 1978—Theo Pinkus introduced me to Arno Münster in Paris.

When Ernst Bloch arrived in Zurich, he first had to process the stark contrast between the tragic events playing out in Berlin and the very different situation in Switzerland. Having only narrowly escaped with his life, Bloch now found himself being shown around Bill's new modernist home-and-studio, his pride and joy. According to Bill, Bloch merely remarked: "You're not at home here, you're on board. Unfortunately there's no ocean." Meanwhile Bill had his own reservations about Bloch's style as a writer; he found it "too expressionistic." But he greatly enjoyed his conversations with Bloch, who would sometimes run his hand over Bill's crew cut.

Year later, at a meal following the inauguration of Max Bill's *Monument für Ernst Bloch* (1989–90) in Bloch's native town, Ludwigshafen am Rhein, his widow Karola lent across the table to Bill and me, and said, "Switzerland is a beautiful country—but it was a prison for me."

Looking back it strikes me that Max Bill's "monuments" are almost all dedicated to individuals who had to leave Germany. The exception to the rule is his *denkmal für pythagoras* (see p. 351), but the others—to Georg Büchner, Albert Einstein, and Ernst Bloch—are all dedicated to exiles. And the same is also true of his unrealized, as yet unpublished project for a memorial to Karl Marx, intended for Marx's native town of Trier in Germany (the drawings and a model for this memorial are in the Estate of Max Bill to Angela Thomas).

Concrete and Cement

Sigfried Giedion—as Max Bill once told me—wrote a text on concrete buildings for the *Neue Zürcher Zeitung,* and Bill designed a double-page spread on the use of cement (promoted by the Swiss Cement Association) for the same issue of the *NZZ.* Among the images Bill selected for that commission were a picture of a bridge by Robert Maillart and a photograph of a concrete column resembling a plant that had been cut open. Because Bill did not know who had designed the column, he went to inquire at Maillart's studio in Bärengasse (Zurich), where he was met with a very friendly welcome.

A portrait photograph by Binia Bill shows Sigfried Giedion, albeit about ten years later, "around 1944," on a visit to the Bills, sitting in a chair with one foot pushed under the edge of a Berber rug (illustrated in *Binia Bill—Fotografien* [Zürich: Scheidegger & Spiess, 2004], p. 103).

When Bill asked outright if Maillart was the person who had designed that column, Maillart merely replied, "could be"—leaving Bill none the wiser. Following that first meeting Bill "met Robert Maillart several times, partly in connection with the Swiss National Exhibition in 1939," for which Maillart designed his Cement Hall, and Bill, "working for his friend, the leading architect Hans Schmidt, had the chance to contribute to the first Swiss exhibition on urban planning and regional development."[913]

Robert Maillart was active in Russia from 1912 onward; after the Revolution he returned—quite destitute—to Switzerland. In 1924 he opened a branch of his engineering practice in Zurich, where Bill went to see him in the early 1930s. Giedion and Mirko Roš, a professor of engineering, were the first to champion Maillart's designs.

When Maillart died in 1940, Bill felt it was only right to commemorate his life and work with a publication. But the war made it impossible to gather the necessary materials, so Bill's book, *Robert Maillart: Brücken und Konstruktionen* (Zurich: Verlag für Architektur) was delayed until 1949.

The double-page spread on Swiss cement, designed by "bill-zürich reklame," appeared in the *Neue Zürcher Zeitung* on 24 July 1934. One of the seven images shows a "daring bridge [by Robert Maillart], a masterpiece of engineering. Its light, elegant arc connects the two sides of the Prättigau valley." To the left of that image there is picture of an electricity

913 Max Bill, manuscript, October 1990; he later reworked this version for a publication issued by the Kunstgewerbemuseum Zürich, Bibliothek Max Bill

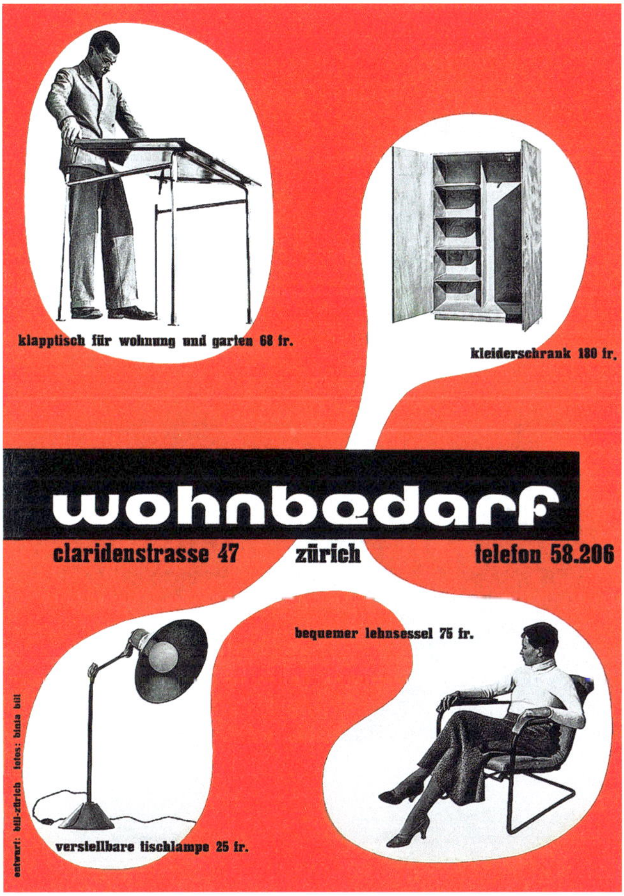

Max Bill, Poster for Wohnbedarf AG, with Max Bill standing at a folding table and Binia Bill-Spoerri seated in a cantilevered chair, 1932, 128×90.5cm

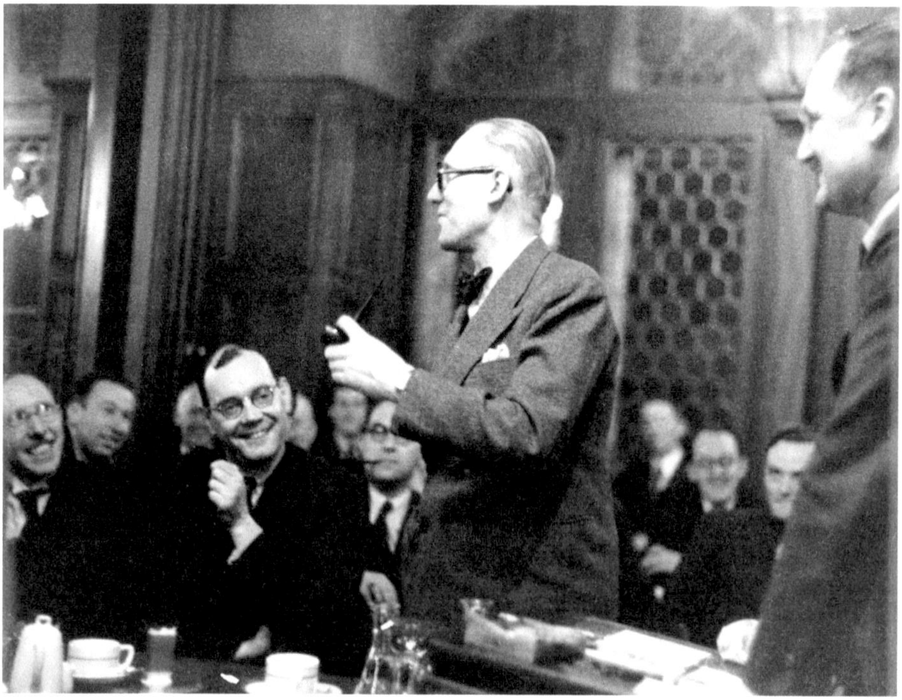

Foreground, center left, seated:
Ernst F. Burckhardt, center, standing:
Le Corbusier, 1938

pylon that used "a minimum of materials." The overall look of the spread designed by Max Bill is not sensational or deliberately arresting; on the contrary, it is informative, objective, and enlightening.

Max Bill included in it a short historical essay on "things worth knowing about cement": in 1824 a patent had been granted to an inventor in Leeds "to produce an artificial stone, which he called Portland cement because of the similarity of its color with that of stone quarried on the peninsula of that name.... It is, however, unlikely that this was Portland cement as we know it today. The fundamental importance (to the reliability of the product) of heating the chemical composition to a specific sintering temperature was only discovered by Isaac Charles Johnson in 1844, which is why many regard him as the inventor of Portland cement. From that point onward it started to be produced in all the civilized nations and it soon became the most important of all the various hydraulic binding agents.... The widespread use of Portland cement is attributable to the fact that merely mixing it with water will cause it to solidify into a rock-hard substance. Portland cement is either used on its own, mixed with sand (to make mortar) or mixed with sand and gravel (to make concrete)."

Looking back much later on, Simon Maurer summed up Max Bill's growing influence: "his one-man agency—'bill-zürich reklame'—set the tone in advertising in Zurich in the thirties and forties. Bill created campaigns for pretty much everything, promoting the architecture of the Zett-Haus (still standing—in a sorry state now—at Badenerstrasse 18), anything from Sasha dolls to Shell motor oil. Clarity and 'economy' were his watchwords as a designer—yet he used astonishingly playful means to pursue those aims. A brochure—in the obligatory lowercase text—for Wohnbedarf, which produced and sold modern furniture, states that the purpose of furniture determines its form. It tells its readers that there is no longer any need for the 'lions' heads' that adorn the candelabra on the Quai bridge; wild animals belong in the zoo or in the steppes. And yet, of all things, Bill created a whimsically reworked image of a lion to highlight the functionalism of the furniture."[914]

914 Simon Maurer, "Max Bill war auch ein gewitzter Grafiker. Dies zeigt eine Ausstellung im Zürcher Museum für Gestaltung," in *Tages-Anzeiger,* 15 January 1999

"... the limitless future"

In the early 1930s the work Bill did creating advertisements for concrete and cement earned him enough to live independently. Decades later, still grateful for those early commissions, he designed an image to mark the twenty-fifth anniversary of the Verband Schweizerischer Transport-Betonwerke (VSTB; Swiss association of ready-mixed concrete manufacturers)—an image that also provides a small yet telling insight into Max Bill's own outlook.

Bill presented his design in 1992 at a ready-mixed concrete plant in Schlieren near Zurich and explained it to his audience: "The 5×5 years of the VSTB, in groups of 5, form a field of 25 squares. The middle row of white squares, the limitless future, merges into the surrounding squares." Max Bill's pictorial realization of what he described in his talk as the "limitless" future is in part informed by the experience he gained at the outset of his career. When he designed the cover for Ernst Bloch's *Erbschaft dieser Zeit* (*Heritage of Our Times*), he was acutely aware, as he once told me, that no one could yet know what that heritage would be, so he came up with the idea of a hand with a circular void in its palm. And in his design for the VSTB the future is represented by a row of empty white squares that will only be filled in by future generations.

In the film *Un chien andalou,* directed by Luis Buñuel, there is a similar hand, with a hole in it, from which ants creep out. That particular scene was inspired by a dream that Salvador Dalí mentioned when the film was being made.

In 1932 Bloch contributed numerous articles to *Die Weltbühne,* a magazine that Max Bill had read since he was a student at the Bauhaus; he also wrote"a number of other texts analysing the rise of the Nazis and their propaganda lies, which were later included in his book *Erbschaft dieser Zeit* (first edition 1935)."[915]

915 See Münster 2004
916 Girsberger 1981, p. 40
917 Benedikt Loderer, "Zum hundertsten Geburtstag von Sigfried Giedion, Architekturschriftsteller und Geschichtsschreiber der Industrialisierung—vom Fortschritt und vom Elend der Moderne," in *Tages-Anzeiger,* 13 April 1988

Le Corbusier's Architectural Oeuvre

Bill designed a four-page brochure and the jacket for volume II of the catalogue raisonné of the work of Le Corbusier—whom Bill had already chosen as his role model in 1926, when he was still a very young student at the Kunstgewerbeschule in Zurich. Le Corbusier had steadily grown in renown as a participant in the design competition for the Palace of Nations in Geneva, as the co-founder of the Congrès international d'architecture moderne (CIAM) in 1928, and as the leading contributor to CIAM's Athens Charter, which defined the CIAM concept of a functional city, where living, working, circulation, and leisure are separated.

László Moholy-Nagy made a film documentation of the CIAM Congress in Athens. Bill may or may not already have seen that film at that time.

In order to ensure that the jacket of the second volume of Le Corbusier's catalogue raisonné (1929–34) could be produced as planned, Bill waived his fee, as the publisher later remembered with gratitude: "When it came to the publication of volume 2, Max Bill designed a detailed, four-page brochure and the attractive jacket. However, when Bill's five-color jacket design was in jeopardy because of the printing costs, he did without a fee, so that I could still go ahead and have it printed."[916] Marcel Breuer, who was living in exile in Switzerland at the time, helped to check the proofs, and Max Ernst translated Sigfried Giedion's introduction into French.

Unlike so many others, Sigfried Giedion—born into a Swiss manufacturing family in Prague in 1888—never had any real financial worries. He earned his doctorate on Late Baroque and Romantic Classicism at the University of Munich in 1922, where his supervisor was Heinrich Wölfflin. Following a visit to Weimar, Giedion wrote an article on the Bauhaus for the magazine *Das Werk.* When he read Le Corbusier's *Vers une architecture,* he traveled to Paris to seek out the author in person; Le Corbusier then took him to CIAM, and Giedion became CIAM's first general secretary.

By the time Max Bill first met Giedion, who was twenty years his senior, Giedion had settled in Zurich. He was a co-founder of Wohnbedarf. Marcel Breuer created the interior design for the showroom and Bill designed the logo, posters, and various advertisements. Giedion had also been involved with the Neubühl Estate in Zurich.[917] And it was Giedion who commissioned the architects Alfred and Emil Roth to design the Doldertal Apartments in Zurich, which they then jointly planned and constructed together with Marcel Breuer.

The Doldertal Apartments (1935–36)—which were presumably proposed by Marcel Breuer in order to secure a much-needed, steady source of income (from rent) for the Giedions—are regarded as an early example of New Building.

Many years later, on the occasion of the fortieth anniversary of the construction of the Doldertal Apartments, Carola Giedion-Welcker was keen to discover from Marcel Breuer what part he had played in the planning process: "I would be very grateful if you would write to let me know which architectural ideas came from you. Roth claims the angled position came from him. I know that the piloti were your idea, as were a lot of other things. . . . But I would like to have a few sentences, on paper, from you describing your contribution."[918] However, Marcel Breuer did not fulfill her wish, because he did not like that kind of "dividing things up"; he merely stated that he and Roth "developed this project together." And he added, "I hope, C.W., that this letter is the last chapter of the Doldertal controversy."[919]

Giedion and Bill, from very different social classes, had first met as contributors to the anti-Fascist monthly *information* (published from 1932 to 1934). They were also later both involved in the preparations for the exhibition *Zeitprobleme in der Schweizer Malerei und Plastik* at Kunsthaus Zürich (13 June–22 July 1936). Although Bill had already built his own home-and-studio in Höngg by 1933, neither Giedion nor Alfred Roth invited him to join CIAM. Bill did not become a member until the leftist architect Hans Schmidt, in Basel, proposed him as a member in 1938–39.

Volume II of Le Corbusier's catalogue raisonné (covering the period 1929–34) was published in late 1934 and includes projects such as the Tsentrosoyuz Building in Moscow, the Pavillon Suisse at Cité Internationale Universitaire in Paris, and the proposal for a Soviet palace in Moscow. As to its reception: whereas volume I had been enthusiastically received by experts and critics just a few years earlier, volume II was studiously ignored or even derided as a product of "Western decadence." Max Bill edited *Le Corbusier & P. Jeanneret: 1934–1938,* that is, volume 3 of the complete works (see p. 684); more on this will be discussed further below.

The financial crisis and the "outbreak of the Second World War . . . prevented the distribution of the Corbusier volumes, which were dependent on the export market."[920]

918 Carola Giedion-Welcker, Zurich, to Marcel Breuer, 15 March 1976, in Bruderer-Oswald 2007, pp. 361–62

919 Marcel Breuer to Carola Giedion-Welcker, 15 April 1976, in Bruderer-Oswald 2007, p. 362

920 Girsberger 1981, p. 43

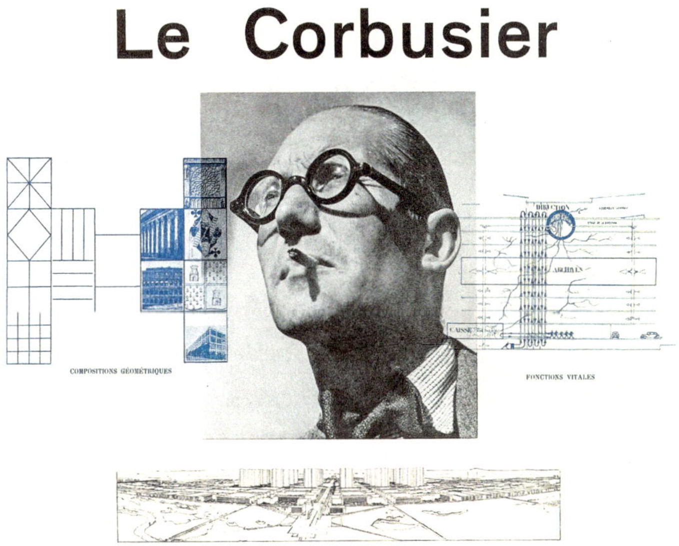

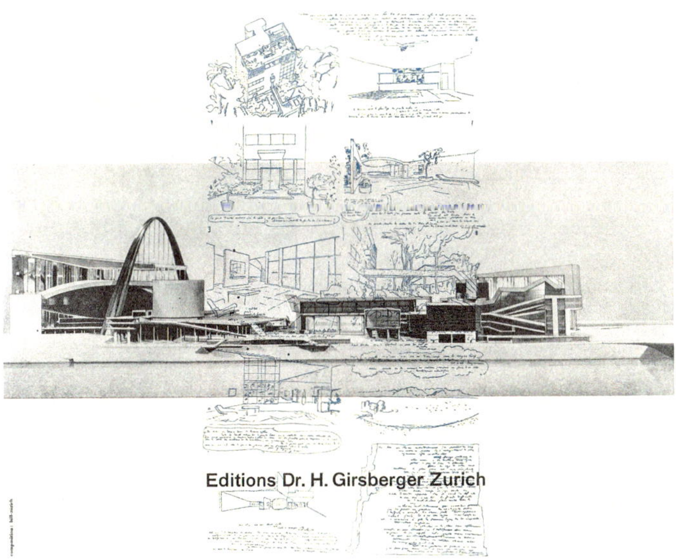

Max Bill, Brochure for vol. 2 of the catalogue raisonné of the work of Le Corbusier, front and back covers, 1934

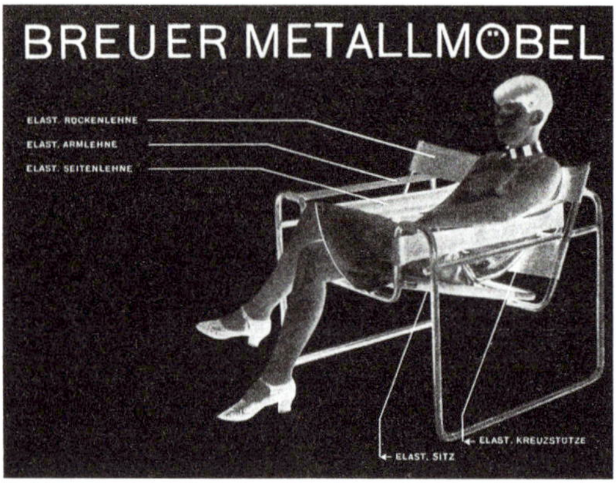

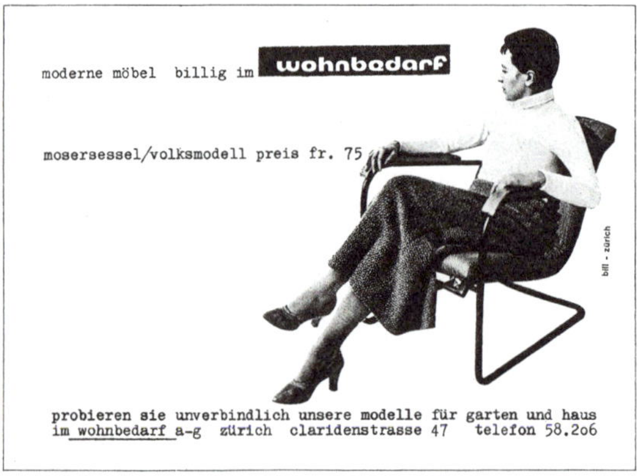

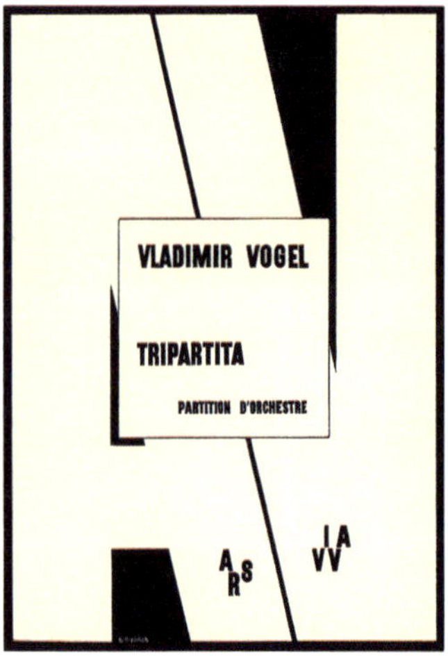

Herbert Bayer, *Breuer Metallmöbel,* catalogue cover for Marcel Breuer chair, 1925–26

Max Bill, Advertisement for the Mosersessel/Volksmodell for Wohnbedarf AG, Zurich, 1932, 13 × 19 cm

Max Bill, Cover for the orchestral score of *Tripartita* by Wladimir Vogel, Verlag Ars Viva, 1934

Cultural Bolshevism

At some point in the 1930s the Nazi term of abuse, "cultural bolshevism," started to be heard in Switzerland, too. In 1932 the leading German typographer Paul Renner attempted an informative analysis of that vile label, which was spreading so rapidly.

In the Bibliothek Max Bill there is a copy of Paul Renner's *Kulturbolschewismus?* (Erlenbach-Zürich, Munich, and Leipzig: Eugen Rentsch, 1932) marked in pencil with "bill 1932"; there is no indication in the book as to who designed the typography.

He devoted the first chapter of his book to "The Anti-Semitic Baiting of Modern Art": "For some time now—in flyers, brochures, and books, in newspaper articles and meetings—there have been calls to fight for German civilisation. It is said to be under threat from cultural Bolshevism." Renner goes on to describe the current situation in Germany, where there are particularly ferocious attacks on "everything that is suspected of coming 'from the East.' And that 'Easternness' is discerned not only in the Jews, but also in advocates of Russian Communism. Marx is the symbolic arch enemy because he embodies both Jewry and Communism." In Germany the proclaimed "task of the visual arts is to give form to the physical models that guide the development of a race. Works of art are to bring into being examples of perfect racial purity.... Consequently, the claim is that German art can only be produced and understood by racially pure Germans and that this is, by definition, impossible for all aliens."[921]

Renner also describes the brutal repression of anyone brave enough to question these edicts: "When the young Munich painter Panizza dared to object, asking 'where does that leave good modern art?,' he was shoved to the ground by Nazi security guards with knuckledusters and kicked in the stomach, and had to be taken to hospital, covered in blood, with damage to his cheekbone and a slit ear."[922] Renner reports that the ministry of education in Thuringia had removed "all works of modern art" from the state's museums on the pretext that the artists in question were tainted by "Easternness." And while there was outrage in Germany "at the architectural Bolshevism of naked walls ... the first thing that happened after the Weimar art school was taken over was the destruction of all Schlemmer's wall paintings."[923] Anyone who was familiar with the history of German art, writes Renner, "knows how much it owes to Jews. They are not only the most avid art collectors, they also have many other innate talents. The

921 Renner 1932, pp. 6–7
922 Renner 1932, p. 9
923 Renner 1932, pp. 10–11

Jew Max Liebermann is the leading painter in Berlin,"[924] and, as Renner rightly pointed out, "Every attempt to deliberately produce patriotic art has led to a form of provincialism that always ultimately falls victim to time."[925]

The second part of Renner's study is titled "The Political Baiting of *Neues Bauen.*" Renner comments, ironically: "Recent architecture is not suspected of having been imported from France by Jewish art dealers, even if its reviled avant-garde, Le Corbusier, does live and work in Paris. The fact is that his opponents regard him as a Bolshevist, so they resolutely face East as they wage their cultural battle. They behave as if it is not common knowledge that the latest developments in architecture, which arose in the West, were taken to Russia by architects from Holland, Switzerland, and Germany, and that it is called 'the German style' in Russia."[926] And he concludes: "It would be a fool's errand to try to parry the insinuations and insults that are aimed at individual modern architects. Good architects tend not to be of a nervous disposition and know how to defend themselves."[927] The latter was certainly true of Max Bill, who would often have to keep his nerve as an architect. In 1932 Renner referred to the particularly venomous attacks on Le Corbusier, which led, six years later, to an article by Fred de Diesbach—one of his most vicious enemies—that was published with the title "Le Corbusier ou le bolchevisme en architecture."

Fred de Diesbach wrote: "We accuse M. Le Corbusier of aesthetic Bolshevism . . . and want to demonstrate that, in addition to promoting his political opinions and his far-left sympathies, this architect has advanced the Marxist spirit in the world"; de Diesbach followed this with the suggestion that a cell had been formed at the CIAM Congress in 1928: "on 28 July 1928 a congress for modern architecture was founded at La Sarraz (canton of Vaud, Switzerland), where a mother cell was created, one of those organisms that are to the Communist revolution what the 'sociétés de pensée' were to the French revolution."[928]

924 Renner 1932, p. 16
925 Renner 1932, p. 22
926 Renner 1932, p. 23
927 Renner 1932, p. 27
928 Fred de Diesbach, "Le Corbusier ou le bolchevisme en architecture," *Revue Anticommuniste* 3 (April 1938), pp. 80–81
929 SS. in *Neue Zürcher Nachrichten,* 8 May 1933

Fred de Diesbach also claimed that Le Corbusier negated civilization and had a nihilistic concept. Moreover, not only was his oeuvre entirely Marxist—"purement marxiste"—his architecture was simplistic and manifested "unsound" aesthetic values.

In 1933 Binia and Max Bill both participated in the exhibition *Zürcher Werkkunst Einst und Jetzt* at the Kunstgewerbemuseum in Zurich (23 April–18 June) and were both named in the same newspaper review of the exhibition. The critic reports that furniture by Wohnbedarf AG was displayed at a "spacious stand' with "seating tailored to human beings" and "portable and collapsible tables.... Next comes the print section, which includes work by a number of alumni from the Kunstgewerbeschule. Here we find names that are widely known today, such as Max Bill and Walter Käch, both of whom are represented with outstanding graphic designs for business and advertising purposes. And then there is a series of photographs, some of which were already seen at the last Christmas exhibition put on by the Swiss Werkbund. We make special mention here of Hans Finsler (teaching at the school), H. Steiner, Max Linck, Binia Bill, Gotthard Schuh, and Anton Stankowski, who also has a number of prints in the exhibition.... *Neues Bauen,* which opens up houses to the light, the sun and fresh air, is also seen to advantage."[929]

The "H. Steiner" named in this review was Heiri Steiner, who studied at the Kunstgewerbeschule in Zurich in the 1920s and who married Liesl Träger, a fellow student from Bill's time at the Bauhaus (see Heiri Steiner, "Erinnerung an Ernst Keller 1924–27," in *Ernst Keller Graphiker 1891–1968 Gesamtwerk,* exh. cat. Kunstgewerbemuseum Zürich, 2 May–13 June 1976, pp. 21–22; there is a copy of this catalogue in the Bibliothek Max Bill).

1934

In 1934, Nusch, Bill's first great love, married the poet Paul Éluard in France. In that same year Bill lost his friend, Hanns Welti, whom he had known since 1929 and who had introduced him to Torres-García, the co-founder of Cercle et Carré. Welti was only forty years old when he died, and Bill was deeply affected by his death.

Around this time Hermann Scherchen, a musician and music publisher, commissioned Bill to create a logo for his company, Ars Viva, and a signature cover for its scores. Bill came up with a modern, radically pared back design in black and white, which greatly pleased Scherchen and which he immediately used for Wladimir Vogel's *Tripartita* ("composed in 1933–34 in Strasbourg"; see p. 520). In July–August 1933—as we have already seen—Scherchen organized a conference on modern music, where the participants included Wladimir Vogel. Scherchen and Vogel had first met in Berlin soon after the First World War.

In his capacity as both a conductor and a music publisher, Scherchen was a dedicated champion of Wladimir Vogel's work. In the early 1930s Scherchen conducted premieres of compositions by Vogel: *Zwei Etüden für Orchester* in Königsberg in 1931 and the brand new *Ritmica Ostinata* for brass and percussion in Berlin in 1932.

Scherchen also invited the writer Elias Canetti to the conference. When the Nazis began burning books in Germany, Canetti—"still worn down by the war that had finished fifteen years earlier"—felt that "it would only be a few years until the next war."

Canetti thus found himself in a city that had an important place in literary history, for that was where Lenz "encountered his idol Goethe, who was also his downfall, and Büchner, his pupil, was also here, sixty years later, who—thanks to Lenz—brought German drama to fruition in a fragment." Canetti climbed the cathedral tower in Strasbourg. From the top he gazed out toward the Vosges and the Black Forest. And a few steps later he was facing "the panel where Goethe and Lenz and their friends had written their names."[930]

The thought of Büchner's *Lenz* may have been of some comfort to him—as it was some years later to Max Bill, who bought it for himself—comfort, because it holds out the hope that progressive literature will always outlive our darkest days.

During the Second World War and in the 1950s Max Bill was at times intensely preoccupied with Büchner's ideas and thinking.

During that conference in Strasbourg, Wladimir Vogel decided to emigrate to Switzerland, He arrived in 1933 and Max Bill was one of the first to offer a friendly welcome. Vogel's professional relationship with Hermann Scherchen had had an unusual beginning. It was in a tram going down Potsdamer Strasse. Vogel showed a score to Scherchen, who rapidly looked through it, jostled by other passengers, and gave it back with the words: "Talented, but still poor!" Scherchen and a very dispirited Vogel parted outside the gallery Der Sturm. "Not precisely encouraging ... but soon my dealings with Scherchen improved and led to mutual

930 Canetti 1985, pp. 66, 70
931 Vogel 1977, p. 194
932 Vogel 1977, p. 194
933 Vogel 1977, p. 194
934 Vogel 1977, p. 192

appreciation and friendship. The *Suite für Streicher und Pauken*—the composition in question—later provided the basis for my *Tripartita,* one of the first pieces Scherchen published at Ars Viva."[931]

"... distinctly architectural forms"

Wladimir Vogel had first arrived in Berlin in 1918. As we have seen, he studied with Ferruccio Busoni, and his fellow students included Kurt Weill and Robert Blum. Since Robert Blum was the twin brother of Elsa Burckhardt-Blum, both of whom knew Bill well from their time at the Krater cabaret, there was already a point of contact for Bill and Vogel in their first conversations in Zurich.

During his time in Berlin Vogel had been in close contact with the architect, Erich Mendelsohn, and with various artists who exhibited at Herwarth Walden's gallery, Der Sturm. On one visit to the Mendelsohns' home, Vogel had taken with him the score of his *Zwei Etüden für Orchester,* which had "just been christened by Scherchen.... Mendelsohn looked at the score with me and was astonished to see distinctly architectural forms in the notation. So I explained to him—from a musical point of view—how the various instrumental groups function within the structure and the fabric of the piece as a whole. Ever since then I have been fascinated by 'common denominators' in music and architecture, which I went into in greater depth during my time in Zurich."[932]

"It was Mendelsohn's wife Louise, a music lover and an excellent cellist, who built the first bridge for me between music and architecture."[933]

The work Vogel was doing on commonalities between architectural and musical structures must have been extremely interesting for Bill, who was also sure that there were "common denominators" connecting music and the visual arts. The two men had many shared interests. They discussed fugues by J. S. Bach and Albert Einstein's theories, and they certainly saw eye to eye when the conversation turned to Kandinsky and his work.

Wladimir Vogel once had the opportunity to attend a talk by Albert Einstein, in a packed lecture hall, on his theory of relativity: "Einstein explained his theory of relativity. He used very understandable examples and presented them as if he were improvising—not in a disciplined, pedantic manner. I was very struck to hear a scholar delivering a lecture in such an 'unscientific' way."[934]

In fact, a few years before Bill first encountered Kandinsky, Vogel had come into contact with the Bauhaus and Kandinsky through his open-minded, forward-thinking teacher Busoni, who—it is worth mentioning—also had the greatest admiration for J. S. Bach.

In 1923 Busoni was invited to participate in a concert of contemporary music to be presented in connection with the Bauhaus exhibition in Weimar. And so it was that "one dull autumn day" Busoni—at his own expense—took some of his master students, including Hans Hirsch, Wladimir Vogel, and Kurt Weill (who would later compose the score for Bertolt Brecht's *Dreigroschenoper*) with him to Weimar, where Vogel then met the Kandinskys. "We left Berlin and arrived in Weimar, full of expectation. Busoni had taught there many years earlier, and while he was grandly settled into the Hotel zum Erbprinzen, we were more modestly accommodated at the Weisser Schwan. The concert was held at the Stadttheater in Weimar. The program consisted of *Fünf Polyphone Studien* by Busoni, *Marienleben* by Paul Hindemith, *Concerto Grosso* by Ernst Krenek, and, in the second half, *Die Geschichte vom Soldaten* by Ramuz and Stravinsky, in the German version by Hans Reinhart. And it was at that concert that Busoni first met Stravinsky, who had also been invited for the occasion.... After the concert there was a banquet at the Hotel zum Erbprinzen, where Gerda and Ferruccio Busoni were seated next to Stravinsky, surrounded by Kandinsky, Klee, and others."[935] Wladimir Vogel was also in that group, seated next to Wassily and Nina Kandinsky: "We were immediately drawn to each other and got on splendidly. Was it our shared Russian past or the idea of abstract painting as a form of music? Whatever the case, we were kindred spirits, and we remained close for many years to come, until Kandinsky died."[936]

Wladimir Vogel and Aline Valangin at La Barca

In Switzerland Wladimir Vogel embarked on a liaison with the writer Aline Valangin. They later married, but in the early 1930s Valangin was still married to the highly regarded lawyer Wladimir Rosenbaum. Max Bill designed two book covers for Aline Valangin and he also designed a brochure for her villa, La Barca, in the Ticino. The photographs in the brochure were most probably taken by Binia Bill.

935 Vogel 1977, pp. 179–80
936 Vogel 1977, p. 191

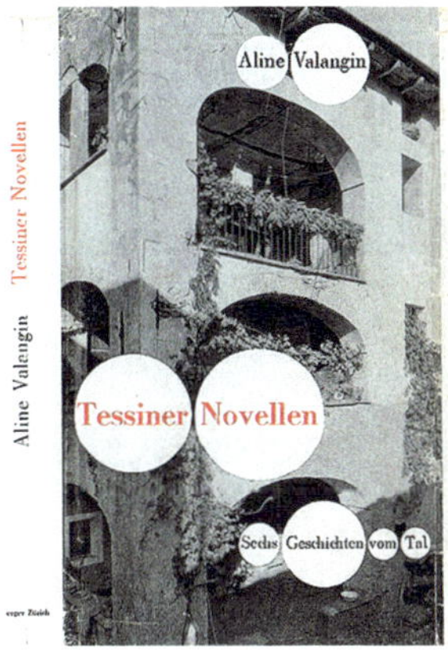

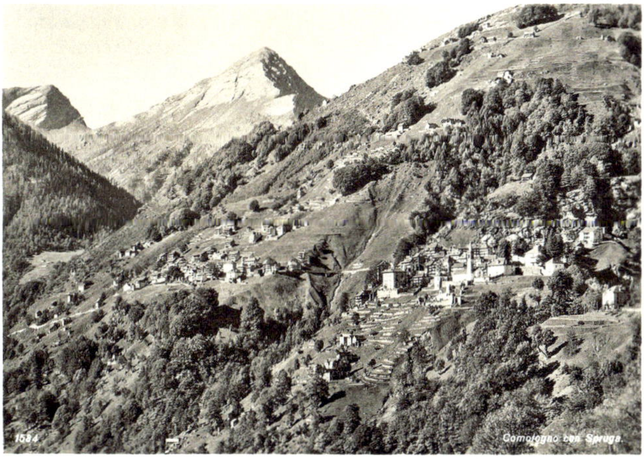

Max Bill, Book cover for Aline Valangin's *Tessiner Novellen. Sechs Geschichten vom Tal,* 1939, 11 × 18.5 cm

The village of Comologno in Valle Onsernone, below right Aline Valangin's summer residence, La Barca, Postcard

Outside Aline Valangin's house, La Barca, ca. 1934–35. Seated, from left: Max Bill, Wladimir Vogel, unidentified woman, Binia Bill-Spoerri (partly hidden), unidentified man (partly hidden), Aline Valangin (in wide-brimmed hat). Standing, rear, from left: Manfred Bukofzer (musicologist), Wladimir Vogel's father (wearing a cap). Seated on the garden wall, from left: Franziska Bosshard, Klara Bosshard-Spoerri (Binia's sister), Wladimir Rosenbaum, two unidentified women, Georg Schmidt (director of Kunstmuseum Basel, 1939–61)

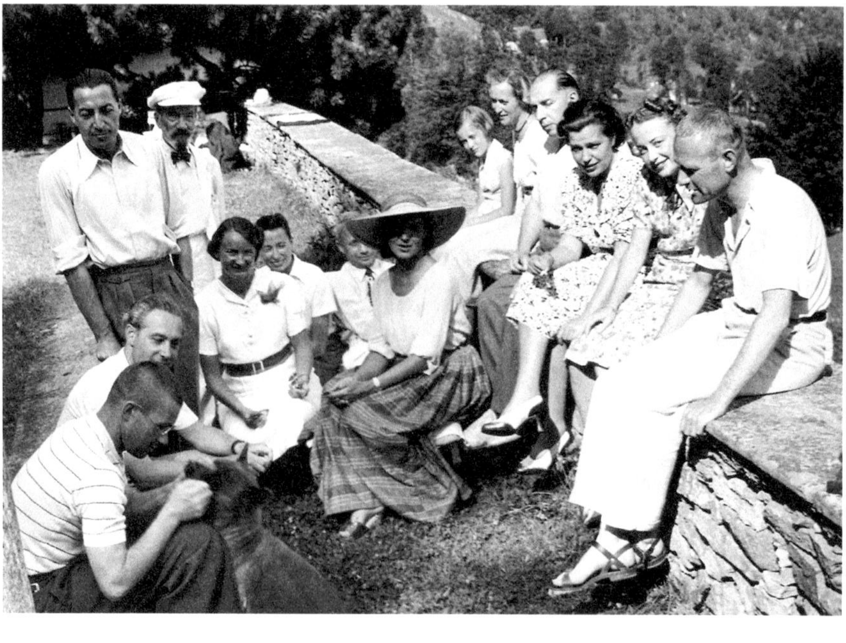

Vogel's biographer, Hans Oesch, described La Barca: "In Valle Onsernone, which runs northwest beyond Locarno toward the Italian border, Madame Aline had a summer house, La Barca, where Vogel could live and work undisturbed for months on end (aside from the irritant of having to exit the country, for however short a time, every three months). He partly lived in the company of others, partly in great isolation with only Madame Aline for company—she also had her own creative work to pursue. At that time, besides writing poems in French, she was working on a series of novellas set in the Ticino, which were published soon afterward in two volumes.... In the winter of 1935–36 Vogel wrote to Annie Müller-Widmann in Basel: 'We are snowed in. Every morning I diligently clear the snow and now my hands are rough and tremble when I'm working on a score ... but the composition is progressing ... letters keep me in touch with the outside world.'"[937]

When Valangin's poems (*Geschichten vom Tal*) and novellas (*Tessiner Novellen*) were ready to go to print, she entrusted their typographic design to Bill. They came out in 1937, published by Girsberger—Bill's old bookseller. Girsberger later wrote: "Other than that, there were a number of shorter, elegantly belletristic publications, such as *Kleine Reise ins Elsass,* a slim volume by Trudy Egender, and Aline Valangin's *Tessiner Novellen,* both designed by Max Bill, and Carola Giedion-Welcker's *Moderne Plastik,* an important book published in both German and in English, in a version translated by Morton Shand." Girsberger gladly acknowledged his debt of gratitude to Max Bill: "It was largely due to my collaboration with Max Bill, who designed many of the best jackets and brochures in those days, that my publications—always notable for their graphic design—enjoyed a special status in the international market."[938]

"It was at La Barca, that Vogel—with the approval of the canton of Ticino, which preferred not to be too rigid in its implementation of decrees from the immigration authorities—was able to put on a summer course on modern music. The participants included the renowned musicologist Manfred Bukofzer ... and the pianist Landerer. The debates were animated. Of particular interest was Willi Reich's introduction to composing using only twelve interrelated tones, which kept the friends up at nights.... For a long time La Barca in Comologno served as a place of refuge for lost souls marooned in Switzerland—Max Ernst was there, too, as was the cellist Hermann.... Others seen there from time to time included Max Bill

937 Oesch 1967, p. 62
938 Girsberger 1970, p. 31

and Max Terpis.... After that interlude in friendly company, the odyssey resumed. Following a statement by an informer, who testified that Vogel was teaching music in Zurich, the aliens office stepped in. Weary of these dealings, Vogel resolved to move to Brussels.... Since Madame Aline's marriage was now far from secure, she decided to go to Brussels with Vogel, partly to see how things would turn out and partly because she felt she could be of use to him there."[939]

After one winter in Brussels Wladimir Vogel and Aline Valangin moved on to Paris, where they re-established contact with Jean Arp, who was living not far away in Meudon. They regularly returned to La Barca for the summer months and it was there that they read in the papers that the war had been declared in September 1939. They had no radio, and even the Zurich newspapers took a day to arrive. They decided to stay where they were, in the Ticino. Some years later Max Bill designed a house for them in Ascona, also in the Ticino. Oddly enough Hans Oesch makes no mention of that house in his biography of Wladimir Vogel.

"Swiss politicians like to claim the composer Wladimir Vogel as one of our own, because he mainly lived in Switzerland after fleeing Berlin. Nevertheless, despite being persecuted by the Nazis as a 'degenerate artist,' initially he was unable to work here in Switzerland. Vogel was naturalized in 1954 but still could not find a permanent position."[940]

In the 1950s, when Max Bill decided to commission music for the ceremonial opening of the Hochschule für Gestaltung in Ulm, when many prominent guests from abroad would be present, he turned to Wladimir Vogel, to whom he had been a loyal friend since the early 1930s. Vogel's response, a composition for a brass ensemble, was then performed at the opening ceremony in Ulm—much to Bill's delight, as someone who always loved the sound of brass instruments.[941]

939 Oesch 1967, pp. 62–63
940 Thomas Schacher, "Bresche für einen Verkannten," in *Neue Zürcher Zeitung,* 7 June 2007
941 See Vogel 1977, p. 284
942 Carlepsch 2007, pp. 64–65
943 Carlepsch 2007, p. 76

Max Ernst's Mural in the Corso

In February 1934 there were violent clashes in the streets of Paris and the mounting threat facing leftist parties in France only made them close ranks; meanwhile in Germany the National Socialists' rise to power reached a highpoint.

"... emboldened by that seizure of political power in a neighboring country, militant Fascistic units in Paris attempted to stage a coup. Although the peculiarly disorganized march on the Palais Bourbon in February 1934 by members of the extreme right wing in France ended in turmoil, the dramatic side-effects of their mobilisation and the bloody street battles that left fourteen dead and at least two thousand wounded shone a sharp light on the internal endangerment of French democracy and changed the social climate for ever."[942]

"As in Spain, some months earlier, a moderate coalition of the left in Paris, led by Léon Blum, had come to power with the declared aim of introducing social and societal reforms. The union of parties supporting the coalition had only come about due to the danger posed by the increasing strength of Fascism in Europe, which the new government—not least in view of the recent internal unrest—wanted to hold in check."[943]

All political parties in Germany, with the exception of the NSDAP, had been dissolved and banned, and the unions had been destroyed. In 1936 the leftist Front Populaire in France triumphed in the parliamentary elections; their overwhelming victory filled France with new hope, and the artist Georges Vantongerloo, for one (a good friend of Max Bill's) was at his most productive during the period when the Front Populaire was in power.

In 1934, Max Ernst—who had been blacklisted by the Nazis since 1933—painted a large-scale mural in the Corso Bar in Zurich. On that visit he stayed partly with Carola and Sigfried Giedion in Doldertal and partly with Binia and Max Bill in Höngg. It may be that Nusch and Paul Éluard in Paris—Éluard was a very close friend of Max Ernst's—had given him Bill's address in Höngg. Whatever the case, in Zurich Max Bill and Max Ernst certainly met at Girsberger's office during the production of volume II of Le Corbusier's catalogue raisonné and also in connection with their separate commissions for the Corso—and they enjoyed each other's company.

Regarding the interconnections between the people Bill got to know in Zurich, it is worth adding here that the wife of the bookseller and publisher Hans Girsberger, from whom Bill bought his books—

and for whom he designed books—"joined the staff in Rosenbaum's legal practice on Stadelhoferstrasse" even before she had finished her law degree.... Later, when this preeminent Zurich law firm suddenly had to close under strange circumstances, she ran her own legal practice for several years.[944]

At that time Wladimir Rosenbaum was chair of the board of directors for the Corso society, which owned the Corso variety theater. Whenever he could, Rosenbaum found employment in Zurich for exiles who had been persecuted by the Nazis. As he recalled many years later: "We embarked on a huge construction project. We decided to have a bar on the first floor, and in that bar there was a very large blank wall. The board members were not sure what to do with it. So I asked Max Ernst if he felt able to paint a sizable mural. He said yes. I inquired what he thought he would charge for that. He asked if a thousand francs would be too much, to which I replied, 'Let's see.' At the next board meeting I conveyed this information, and the members berated me for wanting to squander the society's money on such nonsense. So I just said, 'Let's not beat about the bush: either you agree to a thousand, or I resign from the board!' At which the members agreed to the thousand, and Max Ernst painted a mural several meters wide."[945] In retrospect, it is not entirely clear exactly who—Rosenbaum or Sigfried Giedion—came up with the idea of engaging Max Ernst; some say it was Sigfried Giedion.

"Through Sigfried Giedion he was commissioned to create a large mural for the Corso Bar in Zurich. Giedion, a shareholder in the Corso, persuaded the relevant parties.... As Carola Giedion-Welcker later recalled: 'On 16 July 1934, Max Ernst sent a telegram from Paris with a positive response and announcing his arrival in Zurich. Invited for a holiday—as he put it—with his friends in Doldertal [the Giedions] ... and then going on to stay with Bruno Séguin, he set to work immediately after he arrived. It was an intense, physically demanding endeavor, all day, every day, during the hot summer months, although the lake opposite the Corso provide ample opportunity for relaxation and perfectly satisfied the artist's love of sporting activities.'"[946]

Gotthard Schuh, who had managed Max's finances a few years earlier at the request of Erwin Bill, took a number of photographs

944 Girsberger 1970, p. 26
945 Wladimir Rosenbaum in Kamber 1990, p. 190
946 Carola Giedion-Welcker, "Max Ernsts Wandbild von 1934 für die Corso-Bar in Zürich" (1966), cited in Bruderer-Oswald 2007, p. 102

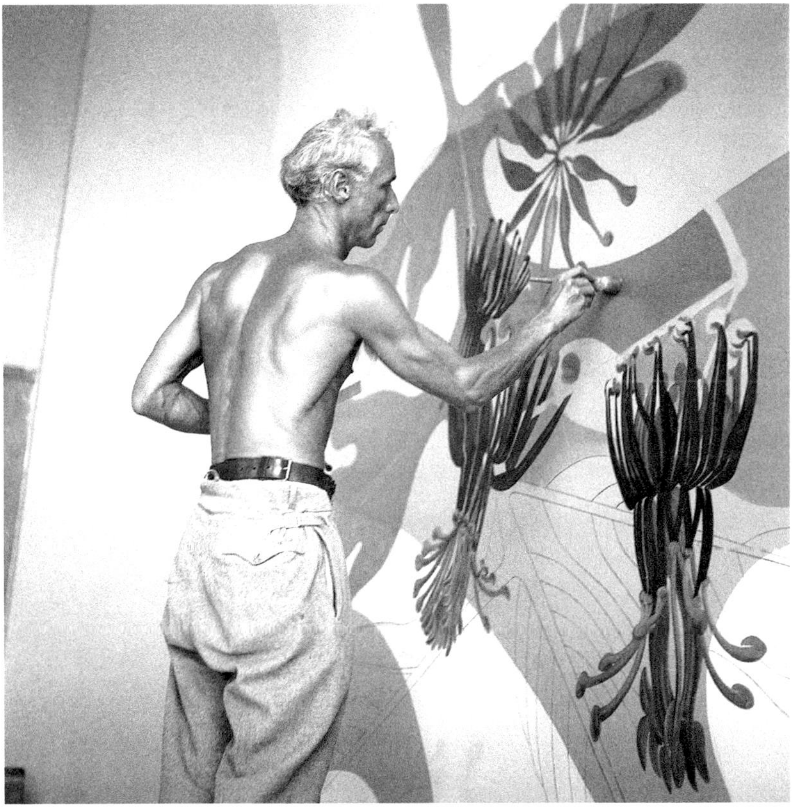

Binia Bill, Max Ernst working on his
mural for the Corso Bar in Zurich, 1934

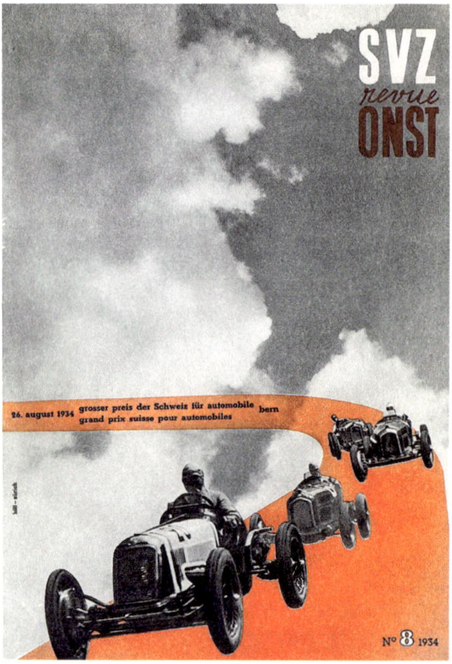

Max Bill, Cover design, "Grosser Preis der Schweiz für Automobile, Bern," for *Revue der schweizerischen Verkehrs-zentrale* 8 (1934), intaglio print, red and black

capturing the sheer panache with which Max Ernst painted his mural—over 4 by 5 meters—for the dance bar at the Corso.

A few years before that, in 1930, Gotthard Schuh—who was already known as a painter—had published the first of his photographs. Later on he looked back at that time: "1930, which was when I published my first photograph, happened to be an important year in the evolution of photography, because it was in 1930 that various individuals—quite independently—picked up a camera for the first time: Cartier-Bresson, Capa, Eisenstaedt, and Brassaï. . . . Between them they created a new aesthetic, a new form of pictorial tension, conveying hitherto unknown meaning" (in *Arche Kalender Schweiz, Literatur und Kunst,* 2008).

In this text by Schuh, there is no mention of Binia Bill, who also started taking photographs in 1930.

And Binia Bill, very struck by Max Ernst's charisma, also took several photographs. In one she concentrates on the painter in action, with strong highlights and shadows playing across his bare back (see p. 533); in another she shows Ernst F. Burckhardt and Hans Curjel watching Ernst at work.

Hans Curjel was multitalented. Having first studied music he subsequently studied art history under Heinrich Wölfflin in Munich at the same time as Carola Welcker and Sigfried Giedion, who married in 1919. The three had remained friends since their student days in Munich. Other friends from that time—fellow students—were Hans Finsler, who later became a renowned photographer, and Franz Roh, one of the few who survived imprisonment in a Nazi concentration camp. During their time at university in Munich the friends had sympathized with the Bavarian Councils Republic. As students Hans Curjel, Sigfried Giedion, Hans Finsler, and Franz Roh formed a small leftist faction that crucially helped to establish the first students' parliament in 1918–19. They all remained on the political left in later life.

Having first been appointed Kapellmeister at the Schauspielhaus in Düsseldorf (1924–25) and then deputy director of the Kunstakademie in Karlsruhe (1925–27), Curjel soon felt the pull of Berlin, the pulsating metropolis. In Berlin he became a very active player at Otto Klemperer's Kroll Opera until it closed in 1931, first as a dramaturg and then as a member of the board of directors. At the Kroll Opera he engaged both Moholy-Nagy and Oskar Schlemmer to design stage sets, at a time when both had already left the Bauhaus in Dessau. However, in view of the rapidly worsening political situation in Germany, Curjel increasingly felt he had no option but to leave and emigrated to Zurich, where he became director of the Corso theater (1933–42).

As something of an afterword on the mural by Max Ernst (now in safe-keeping at Kunsthaus Zürich): when the art historian Willi Rotzler wrote an obituary for Hans Curjel in 1974, he remarked that during the course of "the difficult task of raising the tone at a variety theater" Curjel had commissioned "the Surrealist Max Ernst to paint a primal forest backdrop for a dressage act."[947]

Max Ernst as Grandma

In 1934 Bill was commissioned to design the cover of an issue of the official magazine of the Swiss Travel Center; that particular issue was devoted to the Swiss Grand Prix in Bern, and Bill, a great fan of the automobile, pictured racing cars floating through the heavens.

Bill's interest in motor racing never waned and even later in life he would still spend hours watching motor racing on television.

In 1934, when Binia and Max Bill were invited to Comologno by the Rosenbaums, to spend their summer holiday at La Barca, they arranged that Max Ernst would take care of their house in Höngg in their absence. However, just as they were about to set off in their car, Max Ernst jumped in with them—"Max Ernst just tagged along," Bill told me later. Since they had the roof down, Max Ernst bundled himself up in a scarf, and when they gave a lift to a farmer on the way, Bill told the farmer to "take good care of Grandma in the back." Bill also described more of that trip: "Max Ernst was in the car when we collected Aline. She knew Max Ernst, but she was not that close to him and was clearly surprised to see him. We drove to Meiringen and stayed overnight there. The plan was that Rosenbaum would come from Bern to meet Aline in Meiringen, so that they could drive to La Barca together, and we would follow in our car. When we arrived in Meiringen, I said to Aline, 'Listen, about Max Ernst—he says he's coming, too,' to which she replied, 'for goodness' sake, Rosenbaum will be furious. Max Ernst cuts all the old prints out of books and makes collages from them, it'll be a disaster. Heavens above, what am I going to do about Max Ernst?' So, before Rosenbaum arrived, she went

947 Willy Rotzler, "Hans Curjel und die Synthese der Künste," in *Neue Zürcher Zeitung,* 12 January 1974

948 Max Bill in conversation with Angela Thomas

949 Max Bill in Kamber 1990, p. 171

950 Kamber 1990, pp. 176–77

for a walk with Max, and afterward said everything was fine and she told Rosenbaum that Max was coming."[948] Bill also remembered that once they were at La Barca "Rosenbaum was very pleased that Max Ernst had come, because they spent half the time playing chess and ping pong with each other."[949]

Peter Kamber's *Geschichte zweier Leben* (1990) has reproductions of photographs taken by Binia Bill in Comologno, where her subjects included Max Ernst and Wladimir Rosenbaum playing chess.

The holiday guests at La Barca were far from idle—Ernst scrubbed the swimming pool in the garden and Bill used a sickle to cut the grass around the edge of the pool.

Tarring and Feathering a Fascist

On that visit to the Ticino in 1934, Max Ernst still retained all his extraordinary, seductive appeal—that was before his flight from the Nazis took its toll on his psyche, his features, and his physique. Once muscular and toned, his body was later emaciated by hunger. But in the garden at La Barca, Aline could not help noticing "Dadamax, slender and lithe, performing all sorts of taxing gymnastics."[950]

When her guests read in the newspaper that Jakob Wilhelm Hauer would be coming to Ascona, Max Ernst and Max Bill decided to launch a political attack on him, as Bill told me. They decided to tar and feather him. They felt a deep urge to make an example of this believer in Fascist ideals, to expose him to (international) ridicule. The action they planned to take could either be described as a political, artistic performance—*avant la lettre*—or as a purely political attack. Their very real, entirely understandable hostility toward all those who chanted "Heil" (meaning both "hail" and "health or salvation") but who were already instigating the greatest calamity, would thus have been given vent creatively and wittily, without threatening the victim's life.

"A strange story connected Max Ernst and me with Rode. In those days in Germany there was a religious philosopher, an apostle, who believed in the old German religion with marriage ceremonies under oak trees. We read in the paper that he was coming to Ascona, we'd already heard about him.... His name was J. W. Hauer and the Nazis regarded him as the leading authority on old religions. So he was coming to Ascona for the Eranos conference, where he was to give a lecture.

When we read about that Max Ernst and I resolved that that should not pass off without a scandal and we hatched a plan. We decided we would go to the station, intercept him, daub him with tar, add feathers, and drive him through Ascona. That was the idea. Now we just had to find a way of carrying it out: where to get tar, how exactly to proceed, could we find someone to help us so that the police wouldn't stop us before he was covered with feathers? We wanted to have our photograph taken with him and to send the picture straight to the *New York Times.*"

Bill and Ernst were telling Rosenbaum about their plan "by the fireside in the evening" when an Austrian by the name of Walther Rode, who was also present, cried: "You can't do that to him!"—"Hauer talks rubbish and we should just take it lying down? Let him babble away in Ascona, spreading nonsense? We won't stand for that!"—"But he has formed his beliefs through scientific study, and if he articulates those beliefs, well, that's his business, and we have to let him. It may one day be shown that they don't hold good, but he should be allowed to articulate them."[951] Aline remembered the appeasing Austrian "using quaint expressions in a Viennese twang" as he tried to dissuade the two artists from executing their plan—but events then took a very different, unexpected turn.

Just a few days after that heated dispute, Aline Valangin and the young villagers put on their annual dance. Rode, after a long day playing chess with Rosenbaum, dressed for the evening, unaware that it would be his last. He danced with a pretty girl from the Ticino, who had come in traditional costume: "a wide skirt with a narrow waist, a white blouse with a lace collar ... and *zoccoli,* flat wooden shoes that are easy to slip into but that also fall off easily. Rode was instantly charmed by her. He teased her, with Austrian gallantry, saying that he was just waiting for her to lose a shoe. She gaily replied that that would never happen, they would stay on. The repartee continued, to an fro, drawing in the others, who were soon betting on it. By now it was late, nearly midnight. I called out to everyone that it was time for the last dance—put on a record, a waltz, and turned to a young man who took me in his arms. We danced well together, I was contented, but soon I was surprised to find that we were almost the only ones dancing.... I stopped, and, without fully understanding what I was looking at, saw that Rode had fallen to the ground. A neighbor was kneeling by him, saying, 'he's dead.' Rode had been standing in a corner,

951 Max Bill in Kamber 1990, pp. 176–77
952 Aline Valangin in Kamber 1990, pp. 177–78
953 Max Bill in Kamber 1990, p. 178
954 Kamber 1990, pp. 172–76
955 Oppenheim [1978] 2007, p. 196

not dancing, gazing in admiration at the pretty girl who had now slipped out of her *zoccoli* and was barefoot. He had cheered and had called out, 'Finalmente, at last,' and, with that, had sunk to the ground."[952]

Rode, the lawyer who had defended a Fascist's right to freedom of thought, died on 12 August 1934, right next to where Max Bill was standing. Ernst and Bill placed his body on a table in the library at La Barca. "I don't know where Rosenbaum had disappeared to, but we were in the library, gazing at Rode. And then Max Ernst said, 'Just look at those feet, it's strange what's left of a person when they die.'"[953]

Meret Oppenheim—Passionately in Love

Instead of intercepting J. W. Hauer in Ascona, Max Ernst had an infinitely more pleasing encounter in that little town on the shores of Lake Maggiore. He ran into Meret Oppenheim in Ascona and took her back with him to Comologno. "Little Meret," barely twenty years old when she was "scooped up" on that occasion by Max Ernst, was stunningly beautiful. Aline Valangin also found her "ravishingly beautiful and young." She gave the lovers the "two-room apartment in the tower ... and that was where they spent their time."[954] Meret Oppenheim and Dadamax, deeply attracted to each other, barely left their hide-out. Meret Oppenheim, who was considerably younger than Max Ernst, described the result of that encounter as "passionate love on both sides."[955]

"In 1978 Meret Oppenheim prepared her own written account (rectifying certain errors) of her relationship to Max Ernst," which is quoted at length in Oppenheim [1978] 2007, pp. 195–96.

Yet after that holiday in the Ticino, in October 1934, Max Ernst returned to Zurich with Max Bill but without Meret. It may be that Bill drove back via Maloja in the Bregaglia, for one last meeting with the philosopher Ernst Bloch after the authorities had decreed in September 1934 that Bloch was to be expelled from Switzerland.

Whether Bill met up with him on that occasion, which would be in keeping with Bill's preference for economically organized trips, or whether Bill made a special trip from Zurich to Maloja for a last meeting with Bloch on Swiss soil, before the latter complied with the order to leave the country—Bloch and Bill certainly met in Maloja and discussed Bill's proposed cover for Bloch's *Erbschaft dieser Zeit*, which was soon going to print, only for Bloch to reject the cover design Bill had brought with him.

"What Is Surrealism?"

In 1934 Max Ernst was commissioned to design a poster for an exhibition at Kunsthaus Zürich and Max Bill helped him to select typefaces at a local printer's workshop.

Ernst's poster with seven hands, each pointing with its index finger at the name of one of the exhibitors, is illustrated in the chronology compiled by Julia Drost in the chapter "Max Ernst in der Schweiz" in Werner Spies and Anja Müller-Alsbach 2007, p. 198.

That exhibition, *Abstrakte Malerei und Plastik: Hans Arp, Max Ernst, Alberto Giacometti, Julio González, Joan Miró* (11 October–4 November 1934) was accompanied by a catalogue priced at just 50 Rappen, with no images but with a text by Max Ernst called "Was ist Surrealismus?" In it Ernst twice cites his friend, the poet Paul Éluard, and refers to André Breton's Surrealist manifestoes. Ernst also had the largest group of works in the exhibition, over fifty, dating from 1919 to 1934.

The exhibition list indicates that there were twelve works on show by "Hans Arp, Meudon Val-Fleury." The least expensive could have been bought for 1,000 Swiss francs, with the most expensive—the plaster sculpture *Concrétion Humaine II*—costing 1,800 Swiss francs. There were also twelve works on display by Alberto Giacometti, with prices ranging from 300 to 900 Swiss francs, that is to say, none as expensive as Hans Arp's works. Meanwhile the works by the other exhibitors, Julio González and Joan Miró, were on sale for higher prices than Arp's: González was hoping for 2,000 Swiss francs at best and Joan Miró was demanding the highest price of all—3,400 Swiss francs for his oil painting *Table au coq,* done in 1920.

Looking back at that time, one is often struck by the close interconnections between so many of the artists working then. In a typical example, when Max Ernst was staying with the Bills in Höngg, preparing for that exhibition, he returned to their house one day with the sculptor Alberto Giacometti and introduced Binia and Max Bill to him.[956]

One wonders, did the forty-three year old Max Ernst influence the ideological development of the twenty-six year old Max Bill? Were Ernst and Giacometti, with their experience of the political situation in Paris, intellectual sparring partners for Bill? Just a few years earlier, in June 1929, Bill had written to Sigfried Giedion describing himself as a "surrealist painter," and in late 1929 his former classmate in Dessau, Hilde Rantzsch, had asked him if he could explain what "surreal" meant, what "Surrealism" was—clearly she believed he would have an answer. And there is no

956 Bill 1976 [b], p. 36

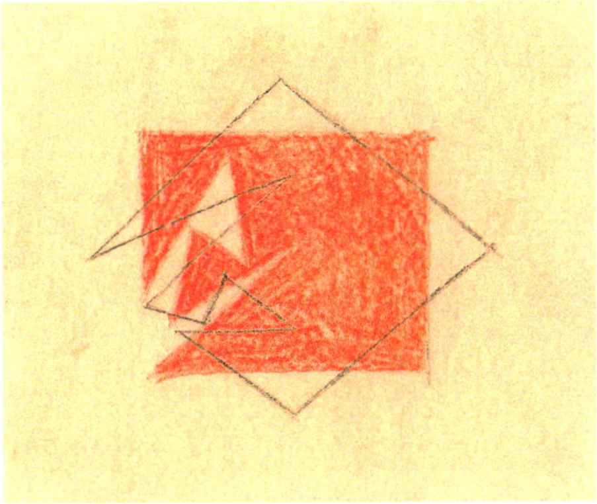

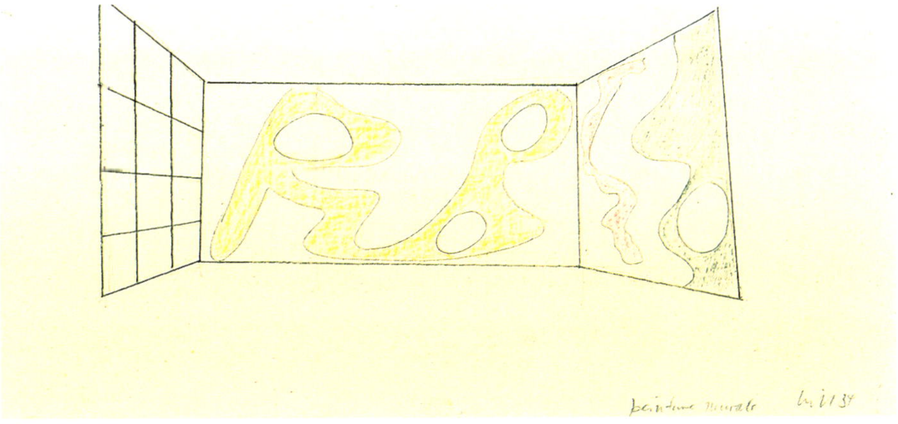

Max Bill, Untitled (Two-part construction), 1934, graphite and colored pencil on tracing paper, 12.7×10.5cm

Max Bill, *peinture murale,* 1934, color drawing, 13×29cm

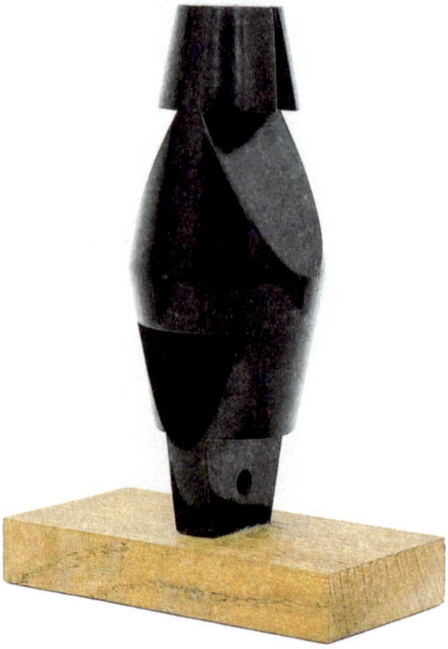

Max Bill, *schwarze plastik,* 1934, wood, 28.5×20×10cm
Max Bill, Sketch for *schwarze plastik,* 1934, graphite and colored pencil on paper, 29.7×21cm

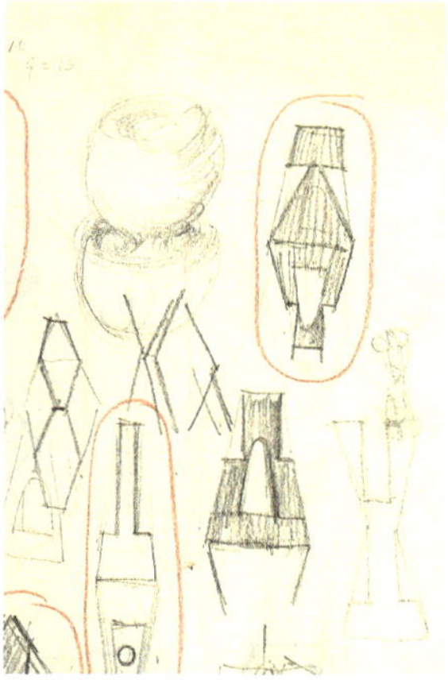

reason to assume that Bill had only described himself to Giedion as a Surrealist painter as a tactical ploy, in the hope of being invited to participate in the exhibition *Abstrakte und surrealistische Malerei und Plastik* at Kunsthaus Zürich. In fact, considering the work Bill had produced so far, he would also have been perfectly justified in describing himself as an abstract painter, since his motifs were indeed abstractions of figurative models (see, for instance, *rauchbläser,* p. 445).

This small work shows that Bill still had to decide which stylistic direction he wanted to take. Could it be that Max Ernst persuaded Max Bill into a second Surrealist phase? It seems not. However, there are clearly "organic" influences exerted by the work of Jean Arp. I have in my possession a loosely flowing, colored drawing—*peinture murale*—done by Max Bill in 1934, which is reproduced here for the first time (see p. 541). This composition clearly displays the influence that organic forms in the work of Jean Arp had on Bill. In 1932 he had avidly studied the solo exhibition of the work of Jean Arp installed by Dr. Georg Schmidt at Kunsthalle Basel (see p. 476), and his own work had been seen alongside that of Jean Arp and other members of Abstraction-Création at their exhibition in Paris (2–16 March 1934). It may even be that Bill produced *peinture murale* in connection with that exhibition in March 1934.

In the end it was neither a "surrealist" influence exerted by Max Ernst nor the "organic" influence of the work of Jean Arp that was to prove crucial to Bill's artistic and ideological development: it was the work of Piet Mondrian, whom Max Bill first met in December 1933—the "purest contemporary painter," as Moholy-Nagy had described him.

Bill must have become more closely acquainted with Mondrian when he participated in that Abstraction-Création exhibition in Paris in March 1934. He clearly fell under the spell of Mondrian's art during the course of that year and—rather than engaging with the paintings of Max Ernst, who was living at the Bill's house in Höngg—Bill turned his attention to the compositions by Mondrian that he had seen in Paris. In fact he now entered what he himself called his Mondrian phase. But that, too, for all its intensity, was only a passing phase.

First and foremost, Bill's close study of Mondrian's work sharpened his eye and helped him to achieve the clarity that he had so long been striving for. Mondrian's work also showed Bill the "way out" that he had been seeking for his own work since the early 1930s. Now, by 1934 at the latest, Bill was able to see a clear path to his own concept of art, which he would define in theoretical terms just two years later—with reference to Theo van Doesburg, Mondrian's former De Stijl colleague—and which he would first describe as Concrete art in 1936. Remarkably, he was now fulfilling the prophecy of the astrologist whom he had consulted before leaving for the Bauhaus. In conversation with me many years later Bill could no longer recall the name of the astrologist who had so encouragingly told him that he would "start a whole new direction in art."

Max Ernst used his text in the catalogue for *Abstrakte Malerei und Plastik* as a platform to set out his own personal response to the question "What is Surrealism?" However, Bill now found that the views he was currently developing were diametrically opposed to Ernst's thinking. Two years later Bill formulated his ideas in a text on Concrete design and Concrete art that was first published in the catalogue for the exhibition *Zeitprobleme in der Schweizer Malerei und Plastik* at Kunsthaus Zürich in 1936.

In 1934 Ernst wrote: "Painters and sculptors initially found it hard to banish reason, taste, and deliberate intention from the process of creating a work art."[957] Two years later Bill—specifically referring to "reason'—took the view that new works of art now had to be created by consciously deploying "ratio." Whereas Ernst specifically spoke out against the Abstraction-Création artists in Paris who saw themselves as rivals to the Parisian Surrealists, Bill had of course only recently become a member of Abstraction-Création (in December 1933). He had in fact done so on the advice of Jean Arp, the same Arp who now joined forces with the Surrealists in the Zurich exhibition—readily taking advantage of the opportunity to exhibit his work. Arp never hesitated to associate with his Surrealist colleagues in Paris.

Georges Vantongerloo pointedly commented on Arp's ideological divergence from the rest of the group Abstraction-Création: "Arp, he's everywhere."

Max Ernst was of course staying with the Bills at this point, so Max Bill now found himself in something of an ideological predicament, trying to negotiate conflicting Surrealist and rationalist ideas and notions of art. However, given that he was an open-minded individual—never, ever petty—and given Max Ernst's appealing personality, plus the fact that the two men shared the same political views, it seems safe to assume that their conversations would have been enriching for both, entertaining and life-affirming.

957 Ernst 1934, p. 4
958 Ernst 1934, pp. 5–6

Ernst and Bill: Different Opinions

In his essay Max Ernst lays out his own very differentiated concept of Surrealism: "The Surrealists are widely described as painters of a constantly mutating dream world, but this should not be taken to mean that they reproduce their dreams in painting (that would simply be descriptive, naïve realism), or that each artist uses the elements of dreams to construct a private, little world in which he can act with benevolence or malevolence (that would simply be a 'flight from time'). What it does mean is that these artists move freely, boldly, and confidently along the borderline between the inner and the outer world, a borderline that is physically and psychologically entirely real ('surreal') even if it has not yet been adequately defined and determined; it means that they register what they see and experience there and that they intervene wherever their revolutionary instincts tell them to." At this point Ernst inserts a footnote, directing a barb against Abstraction-Création: "As opposed to abstractivism, which deliberately restricts its possibilities to the purely aesthetic interaction between colors, planes, volumes, lines, and space—apparently in the hope of resuscitating the old myth of creation, as witnessed in the name *Abstraction-Création.*"[958] This attack on creation, on artists who saw themselves as creators, as geniuses, was connected with an idea that Max Ernst regarded as passé, old-fashioned. He categorically rejected the notion of the artist as hero—in the same way that Max Bill always resisted the glorification of any individual.

In a similar vein, Max Bill disdained the personality cult that later surrounded the conductor Herbert von Karajan, much to the latter's satisfaction. Bill was also averse to the idea of exhibiting "memorabilia"; in one specific case, for instance, he saw no reason for exhibiting jewelry that the writer Else Lasker-Schüler had once worn.

And since, according to Max Ernst's interpretation of Surrealism, it should never merely be naïve, descriptive naturalism (dream images should never be rendered 1:1 in a work of art), a creative act was required from the artist to ensure that the work was not naturalistic but Surrealist. This, as it happens, is very reminiscent of Bill's own thinking, namely that ratio and conscious artistic forming alone were not enough to produce Concrete art; here, too, artistic creativity also has to come into play. Or to put it very clearly: neither a viable Concrete work nor a viable Surrealist work could come about without creative input from the artist. The quality of a work of art is decisively shaped, sustained, and validated by the creativity that has gone into it.

On 12 October 1934 Max Ernst wrote a letter to his friend and occasional lover Lotte Lenya. The sender's address indicates that he was still staying with Binia and Max Bill at the time. "Dear Lotte, dearest Lenya, I am happy that you are thinking of me. You are forever flitting through my mind. Since the silly exhibition is at last opening tomorrow [according to the poster it was due to open on 11 October], I will soon be in Paris. I am so looking forward to seeing you . . . I am terribly faithful to you. And I would be even if I didn't want to because my beauty is a thing of the past. My left eye is swollen, red and blue, and hurts. I don't know what that means . . . I am sending you a thousand kisses and . . . will probably be there on Monday. Yours, Max Ernst."[959] Ernst's claim—so soon after his intense encounter with Meret Oppenheim—that he had been "terribly faithful" to Lotte Lenya, would no doubt have been understood as a running joke by those who knew him well. Max Ernst was of course still also close to his wife, Marie-Berthe Aurenche, whom he had married in 1927 and who would accompany him to Paris when he left Zurich again.

Max Ernst "has left, happily holding hands with Marie-Berthe," as Carola Giedion-Welcker put it. And, as she then added, "He departed, Arp arrived!"[960]

Jimmy Ernst, Max Ernst's son from his first marriage (to Lou Straus), later recalled that "Marie-Berthe worshiped Max and lived her uncertain existence as his wife without a word of complaint," and Marie-Berthe sometimes even managed "to add to the family's income by knitting dresses for Elsa Schiaparelli or—when things were really terrible—by asking for help from her wealthy parents, the Aurenches, conservative Catholics from the upper echelons of society who had bitterly opposed their daughter's marriage to a German, a lapsed Catholic, divorced and without a penny to his name."[961]

A year later, "in the late summer or autumn" of 1935, "Little Meret" Oppenheim would part with Max Ernst at the Rhumerie Martiniquaise in Paris. They were there together when "out of the blue" she suddenly said "I don't want to see you any more." Max was "deeply hurt."[962] But Jimmy Ernst had already seen in Paris that his father used to "examine every

959 Max Ernst, Limmattalstrasse 253, Zürich-Höngg, to Lotte Lenya, Paris, 12 October 1934, in Drost 2007, pp. 200–201
960 Carola Giedion-Welcker to Marcel Breuer, 17 October 1934, in Bruderer-Oswald 2007, p. 104
961 Ernst 1985, p. 79
962 Oppenheim [1978] 2007, pp. 195–96
963 Ernst 1985, p. 79
964 Kandinsky 1976, p. 174
965 Ernst 1985, pp. 79–80

good-looking woman in his field of vision, and he made very little effort to conceal his relationships with the many women who turned up at our apartment or who would join us for coffee at Les Deux Magots in the late afternoons."[963]

The many people Max Ernst socialized with in Paris also included Jean Arp, Alberto Giacometti—whom he called "Giaco" for short—and Paul Éluard. Max Ernst and Paul Éluard had a special bond that came from their shared experience of all kinds of troubles over the years. Éluard—no longer with his first wife Gala, who had left him for Salvador Dalí—was now seen in the company of Nusch, whose name Jimmy Ernst spelled "Nuche" in his memoirs, reflecting the French pronunciation. From time to time Pablo Picasso would also appear in the same social circle.

Nina Kandinsky mentions in her memoirs that during a reception at Tristan Tzara's home in 1933 she and her husband met the poet Paul Éluard: "At the time Éluard indicated that in some ways he sympathized with Communism. We fell into conversation with him ... he sensed that we had little time for Communism and was evidently disappointed in us. All at once he broke the conversation off."[964]

Jimmy Ernst described one such occasion: "Les Deux Magots was at the center of things for a long time.... Those afternoons spent sitting outside the café across from the Abbaye de Saint-Germain-Des-Prés were a ritual.... I remember Picasso joined us one afternoon ... he was not a member of the Surrealists' group, but was always welcome.... He was a good friend of Éluard and his new wife Nuche. While everyone else was talking ... he was busily occupied creating something from empty matchboxes. And when he had run out of matchboxes, he ordered more from the waiter, tipped the matches out and continued building his many-faceted tower. Nobody paid much attention to him, apart from the tourists, who might not have recognized Giacometti or Man Ray or Arp in those days, but who certainly knew who that other artist was. As suppertime approached, the convivial gathering broke up and we all—including Picasso—set off for Brasserie Lipp. The people at the surrounding tables were poised to snatch up the 'sculpture' ... but just as we were leaving Picasso stopped in his tracks, turned round, and went back to the table. He picked up his creation, crushed the matchboxes between his hands and stuffed the debris into his coat pocket."[965]

When Alberto Giacometti left Paris again to go home to Switzerland, Max Ernst used him as a courier and sent an explanatory note to Carola Giedion-Welcker. "Giacometti is traveling to Zurich this evening. I have entrusted the following to him: 1. For you the watercolor for Egender; 2. Cahiers 3–5 (complete) of La semaine de bonté for you; 3. Cahier 5 of the same semaine for little Binia. Giaco will give everything to Egender ... very good news of Mr. Rosenbaum from you!! ... Marie-Berthe sends *mille tendresses,* as does your honorable sincere Max Ernst."[966] So book 5 of *Une semaine de bonté* was for "little Binia." No doubt that was Binia Bill.

It is striking that Max Bill's library contains all five parts of Max Ernst's *Une semaine de bonté ou les sept éléments capitaux:* premier cahier "Le lion de Belfort," deuxième cahier "L'eau," troisième cahier "Le feu—la cour du dragon," quatrième cahier "Le sang—Œdipe," dernier cahier "Le noir—le rire ou coq l'île de paques, la vue—intérieur de la vue, inconnu—la clé des chants;" it was published by Jeanne Bucher, Paris, 1934 and all were marked by hand with the edition number: 206.

La Semaine de la Bonté is in fact the name of a charitable organization in Paris that used to put up garish posters in the city streets to attract attention to itself. "The artist [Max Ernst] adopted the formula that sought to promote human kindness in bad times and, having slightly changed the name, printed his own suggestions for kindness—a series of collage novels, that have guarded their secret to this day."[967]

"On le nomme aussi MAMAN par erreur"

The five books of *Une semaine de bonté* mainly contain collages by Max Ernst. The texts, to which Paul Éluard also contributed, are not just surreal, they are also extremely enigmatic. It was Éluard who wrote the sentence *"On le nomme aussi MAMAN par erreur"* (People also call him MAMAN by mistake) in book 4. Many of Max Ernst's collages revolve around sexual domination and repression. As an art historian, I am particularly struck by the image of a woman, with bare breasts, hanging in a tree, which

966 Max Ernst to Carola Giedion-Welcker, 30 April 1935, in Drost 2007, p. 202
967 Paul Jandl, "Die Woche der Güte. Max Ernsts Zyklus 'Une semaine de bonté' in der Wiener Albertina," in *Neue Zürcher Zeitung,* 18 April 2008
968 Jandl, "Die Woche der Gute"
969 Jandl, "Die Woche der Gute"
970 Paul Jandl, "Die Woche der Güte"
971 Spies 2008, p. 11

looks very much like a paraphrase of Giovanni Segantini's painting *Die bösen Mütter* (1894, see p. 84) with its depiction of evil mothers cursed and cast out.

Paul Jandl also pointed out in that same exhibition review in 2008 that the originals had been "shown once before, seventy years ago." The title above the last day of Max Ernst's "creation story of a horror-filled anti-world" is "L'Élément inconnu." A catalogue was published to accompany that exhibition in the Albertina in Vienna: *Max Ernst: Une semaine de bonté. Die Originalcollagen,* ed. Werner Spies (Cologne: Dumont, 2008).

Paul Jandl also describes his reaction to these graphic novels by Max Ernst, which he regarded as "shorthand for a long narrative.... No one need know what it means. It sets in motion a hermeneutics of unease that one cannot escape."[968]

"If Surrealism ever coupled horror with trivia, until one looked much like the other, then it was certainly here.... The grotesque and the infamous, the rage of malefaction and the glittering rationalism of technology converged in a vision of terror that mirrored the time when the cycle was made."[969] Max Ernst's five-part novella, published in 1934, was a visionary response to the deep Fascist shadow that was descending on Europe.

After some time Paul Éluard managed to persuade Max Ernst to exhibit his collages, and in 1936 they were shown in Madrid—albeit censored—at a major Surrealist exhibition at the Museo Nacional de Arte Moderna. Five sheets from *Une semaine de bonté* were kept under lock and key *"por razones especiales"*—"for particular reasons."[970]

The art historian Werner Spies recounts that Max Ernst told him "very appreciatively ... that the works he [Ernst] had loaned to the museum in Madrid, which Paul Éluard had delivered, had been returned to him intact, despite the turmoil of the Spanish Civil War. He was moved by such respect being shown to an artist's work in a time when life and death were at stake."[971]

In 1935 Max Ernst had still enthusiastically joined in the celebrations in Paris for 14 July, and the many events marking France's national day filled him with hope for the future. His wife was not in Paris at the time; she was staying with her parents in the Ardèche.

"... the 14th of July was a wonderful celebration. The demonstration at the Bastille was fabulous; it seemed that at least the Fascists will not force their way in here ... Marie-Berthe is in the Ardèche with Papa and Maman. As for me, I'm not allowed in there any more, because I'm such a poor beggar ... warm wishes, yours, Max Ernst."[972]

It was an understandable if misguided assumption by Ernst that the Fascists would "not force their way in" to Paris; within just a few years he would find himself in an internment camp in France along with numerous other intellectuals and artists, from where he sent an SOS card to Jeanne Bucher with a desperate cry for help.

And in that same summer Giaco—Alberto Giacometti—took Ernst back with him to his home in Switzerland. It was not long before Ernst also fell in love with the Bregaglia, that magnificent landscape that Bill's uncle Ernst Geiger had long ago studied for his doctoral dissertation. Even today the Bregaglia is still sparsely populated, but those who do live there are often on the political left, culturally aware, and loyal to each other. Two photographs of Alberto Giacometti and his guest have survived. They are dated 1934, although Giacometti's sister-in-law remembered that Max Ernst did indeed visit them in the summer of 1935, not 1934.

These photographs are reproduced in *Von Photographen Gesehen: Alberto Giacometti,* ed. Bündner Kunstmuseum Chur and Kunsthaus Zürich, Stiftung für Photographie (Chur and Zurich, 1986), p. 34.

Giacometti's sister-in-law Odette, married to the architect Bruno Giacometti, later recalled the excitement of those days at her mother-in-law's house in Maloja with Max Ernst, Alberto, and Diego Giacometti. "Max Ernst already started telling us his Surrealist dreams over breakfast. During the day we were very busy. We had hired an old horse and cart from a neighbor and searched the glacial river bed for specially shaped rocks. Max Ernst then worked on them and painted them—his main occupation at the time. And since he was very hard up, in the evenings I had to darn his pullovers—ripped by the rocks—so that he could wear them again the next day."

They made "many expeditions to the Forno Glacier. Diego was our mountain guide; Alberto came too. ... My mother-in-law, who was used to seeing her husband Giovanni painting outside in the open air when the weather was good, could not understand Max Ernst because he didn't go outside, he just worked away at his frottages on the beautiful pine floor in the studio."[973]

In *Das Bergell: Heimat der Giacometti,* ed. Ernst Scheidegger (Zurich: Ernst Scheidegger 1994) there are also photographs showing

972 Max Ernst, 26 rue des Plantes, Paris, to Carola Giedion-Welcker (19 July 1935), cited in Drost 2007, p. 202

973 Giacometti-Duperret 1994, p. 177

974 Bill 1976 [b], p. 36, fig. p. 37

Max Ernst with members of the Giacometti family in the Bregaglia, as well as some of the river-granite rocks worked by Max Ernst (pp. 176–79); a photograph showing Luciano, Odette, Diego, Bianca, Ada and Alberto Giacometti along with Max Ernst on the Forno Glacier 1935 is reproduced in Werner Spies and Anja Müller-Alsbach 2007, p. 205.

In 1962, when Alberto Giacometti was honored for his work at the Venice Biennale, he appeared—as Carola Giedion-Welcker wrote in *Die Weltwoche* on 21 January 1966—"entirely unmoved and unburdened by his 'fame.'" He died in 1966. Max Bill was among the many who traveled to the Bregaglia for Giacometti's funeral. In Ernst Scheidegger's film *Alberto Giacometti* Bill can be seen in the impressively lengthy procession of mourners who wanted to pay their last respects to a Swiss sculptor who was known throughout the world.

Max Ernst told Bill that when he and his team were passing through the Bregaglia on their way to set up the Milan Triennial in May 1936, he should collect one of those rocks as a gift and take it back home with him. "Luckily we had a very strong carpenter with us" who helped to load up the 71-centimeter-tall granite river rock—not painted but with a relief chiseled into its surface by Max Ernst and now named *Mysteriöses Ei* (*Mysterious egg,* 1935).[974]

In August 1935, as the political situation in Germany steadily worsened and grew ever more alarming, Max Ernst also managed to pay a visit to the patron of the arts Hélène de Mandrot at her country residence, Château de La Sarraz. And as a memento of his stay, he left her a severe portrait of Walter Gropius done in black and red ink on a roof tile.

(The portrait of Walter Gropius done on a roof tile is reproduced in Drost 2007, p. 206.)

On 8 June 1935 Bertolt Brecht was stripped of his German citizenship by the ministry of the interior and had no option but to emigrate. Not long after that, in the autumn of 1935, another refugee from Germany (a certain Alfred Thomas) would knock at Binia and Max Bill's door in Höngg; they took him in for several months—and Max Bill was subsequently prosecuted for harboring him and ordered to pay a fine.

We will return later to this refugee—Alfred Thomas—and his time in Zurich.

Following Max Ernst's first visit to La Sarraz, Hélène de Mandrot invited him back in 1936 on condition that he—like the other artists coming as guests—would once again express his gratitude in the form a work of art for her. During his visits to La Sarraz Max Ernst made around twenty works in total, including *La Ville entière* (1935–36), which he gave to Madame de Mandrot. She later donated it to Kunsthaus Zürich.[975]

Madame de Mandrot, who also had an apartment in Paris, was a regular visitor at Galerie Jeanne Bucher, where Max Bill had met the sculptor Jacques Lipchitz in May 1930. And in 1931 she commissioned Lipchitz to create two large-scale sculptures, which were then installed in the grounds of her villa (designed by Le Corbusier, built in 1930–31) in Le Pradet in the department of Var, around twelve kilometers from Toulon. Those two sculptures are now at Kunsthaus Zürich—extraordinarily generous gifts from Hélène de Mandrot.[976]

Madame de Mandrot, who had been widowed in 1920, continued to support Max Ernst, and in late 1936 put on a private exhibition of his work at her Paris apartment on the Champ de Mars. A visitor to that exclusive exhibition commented afterward: "the attention of the many artists who were present ... including Max Ernst himself with his beautiful countenance and long hair, was distracted from the works on display by a lavish buffet."[977]

A few years later Max Bill and his friend Georges Vantongerloo received a similarly gracious invitation from Madame de Mandrot to visit her at her castle, La Sarraz, in Switzerland; they spent their time there in 1939 together with Alfred Roth and Hans Curjel, shortly before the Second World War broke out.

Guernica 1937

In the late 1930s Max Ernst remained in close friendly contact with Nusch and Paul Éluard in Paris. Now living in an old house in Rue Jacob with his new love, the painter Leonora Carrington, he invited the Éluards home with him one day. As his son Jimmy recalled (having decided to drop in

975 Baudin 1998, pp. 321–22
976 Baudin 1998, p. 320
977 Eric Poncy, Paris, to his parents, 14 December 1936, Archives de la Maison d'artistes
978 Ernst 1985, p. 159
979 Angelo d'Orsi, "Le cri de Guernica," *Libération*, 19 October 2007
980 Ernst 1985, p. 163

on his father unannounced), "soon Max rolled up with Paul Éluard and his new wife Nuche."[978]

The Éluards and Max Ernst had come directly from the Spanish Pavilion, where they had seen Pablo Picasso's *Guernica*—a harrowing protest against barbarism that brought many viewers to tears at the time. Guernica, the old Basque capital, had been bombed on 26 April 1937 using a method that later became known as carpet bombing, that is to say, "a massive bombardment aimed at the total destruction of an entire city or certain neighborhoods, generally the city centers where the symbols of power are found and where there is also the greatest concentration of inhabitants. This is exactly what happened in Guernica when it was attacked by the German Luftwaffe with the support of the Italian air force. Mussolini and Hitler were Franco's allies. . . . On the day after the raid Franco declared that Guernica had been destroyed and burnt down by the 'Reds' (Republicans). That lie, like the bombing, was the *ante litteram* beginning of what is now called 'total war.' Anyone trying to justify these unjustifiable wars needs not only falsehoods but outright reversals of reality."[979]

Like many others at the time, Max Ernst wanted to join the international brigades in Spain to fight against Franco. But, as Max Ernst put it, Paul Éluard and André Malraux persuaded him not to go, declaring that he was more important as an artist than as a "riddled corpse."[980]

By now a similarly perverse misrepresentation of reality was being disseminated in the term "degenerate art." In 1937, at the Nazi regime's touring exhibition *Entartete Kunst* (Degenerate art) in Munich, Adolf Hitler and Joseph Goebbels saw Max Ernst's painting *La belle jardinière,* which was decried in the catalogue as a "mockery of German womanhood."

Max Ernst's *La belle jardinière* (1923) is illustrated in Jimmy Ernst 1985, p. 171.

Various works by Wassily Kandinsky were also held up to ridicule in *Entartete Kunst* (fifty-seven of his works were confiscated by the Nazis), just a few months after he had been able to prepare a retrospective for Kunsthalle Bern and had taken the opportunity—on two days in February—to see Paul Klee for the last time.

That same year Max Bill acquired a slim volume by Professor E. Kolman for his library: *Wissenschaft, Religion und Marxismus* (Basel: Universum-Bücherei, 2nd ed. Moscow: Iskra Rewoluzii, 1937), which he marked inside with "bill." In this publication Kolman discusses "intellectuals as the allies of the proletariat" and the "demise of bourgeois knowledge."

André Breton

In 1938 Max Ernst provided a contribution to a book edited by André Breton. The Surrealists drew considerable inspiration from the works of both the Marquis de Sade and Sigmund Freud. On 30 March 1938 a limited edition of André Breton's *Trajectoire du rêve. Documents recueillis par André Breton* was printed in Paris, "sur les presses G.L.M. 6 rue Huyghens." Max Ernst's contribution was his own translation of a dream once reported by Albrecht Dürer—an artist whose work Max Bill, too, greatly admired, particularly the master engraving, *Melencolia.*

Dürer not only kept a written account of his dream in 1525 of a mighty flood, he also captured it in a "fleeting watercolor" reproduced in black and white in Breton's *Trajectoire du rêve, documents recueillis par André Breton* [Paris: G.L.M., 1938]): "In 1525, during the night between Wednesday and Thursday after Whitsuntide, I had this vision in my sleep, and saw how many great waters fell from heaven. The first struck the ground about four miles away from me with such a terrible force, enormous noise and splashing that it drowned the entire countryside."[981]

It is worth mentioning here that shortly after Hitler seized power, Max Ernst painted a picture titled *Europa nach dem Regen* ("Europe after the Rain," 1933). It is now in the collection of the Staatliche Kunsthalle Karlsruhe and is illustrated in the essay by Werner Spies "Die Desaster des Jahrhunderts," in *Max Ernst: Une Semaine de bonté,* 2008, p. 11.

Breton's book also included a text by Paul Éluard, "Je rêve que je ne dors pas"—"I dream that I am not sleeping." However, that same year, in 1938, Breton and Éluard's friendship ended due to an ideological dispute. Breton had been sent to Mexico on a cultural mission by the French Ministry of Foreign Affairs. In Mexico he not only met Leo Trotsky, who was living there in exile, he also became personally acquainted with him and grew to admire him.

"The many conversations he [Breton] had with Trotsky, whose unbounded intelligence and breadth of vision amazed him, strengthened his thinking not only regarding the political order but also the regarding the way life is ordered. Despite the reservations he would later

981 Breton is citing a passage from Albrecht Dürer's *Underweysung der Messung*

982 Audoin 1970, pp. 34–35

983 *Paris 1937–Paris 1957: Créations en France,* (Paris: Le Centre, 1981), p. 74

express toward Bolshevism and even Marxism in general, he remained faithful to the memory of that great revolutionary and maintained friendships within the political organizations that he sympathized with.

It was in Mexico that Trotsky, in collaboration with Breton, would edit *Pour un art révolutionnaire indépendant,* a formulation whose spirit is the very negation of 'cultural' Stalinism."[982]

However, on Breton's return from Mexico his relationship with Éluard foundered and was destroyed forever when he learned that poems by Éluard were now being published in *Commune,* a Stalinist review. Despite having been friends for years, they never met again after that. "Max Ernst then left the group [of Surrealists] out of solidarity and moved to St. Martin d'Ardèche."[983]

In January–February 1937 the Galerie Beaux-Arts in Paris presented an international exhibition of Surrealist art. Shortly before André Breton's *Trajectoire du rêve* was to go to print, a shocking rumor that Sigmund Freud had been arrested in Vienna swept through Paris. That immediately prompted Breton to write a foreword, issuing a stark warning. However, it then turned out that the great man, already suffering from cancer, had in fact escaped from Vienna—leaving for London at the last minute.

Breton's foreword reads: "On the eve of publishing this book, we learn with immense anguish of the arrest of Sigmund Freud in Vienna. Thus a whole life of brilliant insight, of exclusive devotion to the cause of human emancipation on the largest scale ever dreamed of, is almost certain to end in a vile prison, subjected to the humiliating tortures of one of Hitler's concentration camps ..."

There are two postscripts, the first written on 17 March: "This afternoon there was an announcement that, contrary to the rampant rumors, Professor Freud, the founder of psychoanalysis, has not been arrested. He is living quietly in his home town of Vienna"; the second postscript was added by André Breton on 18 March 1938 "Freud has not been arrested but he is being 'held in custody' ..."

Breton was called up to serve in the French army in 1939–40; after he was demobilised he managed to cross the demarcation line and enter the *zone libre.* In the end, having made contact with the Emergency Rescue Committee in Marseille (an American aid organization offering assistance to persecuted intellectuals and artists), he met up again with various old acquaintances there, including Max Ernst.

Escape, Internment, Exile

In 1939 Max Ernst and Leonora Carrington moved to Saint-Martin-d'Ardèche, not far from Avignon. But their time together there was soon cut short. Rumors, fears, and terrible truths were mounting up. Like many others, Max Ernst was well aware that—for political reasons—he was in acute danger. As a German national in France he was interned in 1939, first at a camp in Largentière and then in Les Milles. He sent a postcard with a heart-rending cry for help to his gallerist Jeanne Bucher: "Chère Jeanne, S.O.S. Max." Paul Éluard made every effort to secure Max Ernst's immediate release, and although he was indeed released from Les Milles, he was soon re-arrested by the Gestapo in Saint-Martin-d'Ardèche. He managed to escape again, but he was now unable to find Leonora.

"Freed for Christmas, he returns to Saint-Martin-d'Ardèche, where he is arrested again. He escapes. He cannot find Leonora; having lost her mind, she has fled to Spain where she is interned in a mental asylum."[984]

During the Nazi reign of terror, Max Ernst was not only separated forever from Leonora, he also lost his first wife Lou Ernst, mother to his son Jimmy Ernst. Lou, born in Germany to Jewish parents, had been interned at Drancy near Paris and there was no way for Max Ernst to save her. She was subsequently transported to Auschwitz, which she did not survive.

When he fled from the Gestapo, Max Ernst took a painting with him—*Schwarzer Pfeil* (1935–36)—a response to the landscape disfigured by the threat of Hitler's expansionary ambitions. Many years later, when Klaus Völker saw that painting in Zurich in the collection of Carola and Sigfried Giedion, he described the "black arrow" as "Nazi Germany's border-changing trail of blood."[985] As Max Ernst fled south, the French and Spanish villagers he encountered immediately understood his painting; it helped him to safety. After that perilous escape from France, a severely emaciated Max Ernst arrived in the United States, where he met many acquaintances from Europe who had also been forced to leave. His subsequent marriage in New York to the collector Peggy Guggenheim was relatively short-lived. The time would come when Peggy would exchange a painting by Max Ernst for a painting by Malevich—but more of that later.

984 "Hommage à Max Ernst," *XXe siècle*, special issue, Paris (1971), last page, "une vie dans une page"

985 See Klaus Völker, "In Zürich, wo kein frischer Wind weht"

986 "Hommage à Max Ernst"

987 Max Bill in conversation with Angela Thomas

"Wanted by the Gestapo, Max Ernst managed to reach the United States where he arrived, after many tribulations, on 14 July 1941; he was immediately arrested as a 'German subject' but was released again three days later. Marries Peggy Guggenheim."[986]

At the Bauhaus in Dessau in 1928 Nina and Wassily Kandinsky celebrated their receipt of German passports—the same year that Max Bill was a student in Kandinsky's free painting class. Eleven years later, by which time the Kandinskys had moved to Neuilly-sur-Seine, the most elegant of Paris's suburbs, they had the extraordinary good fortune to be granted French citizenship. Now their new French passports prevented them from being interned in France as German citizens, which they had been up until very recently.

Max Bill: Experimentation

Max Bill, who started to play the cello as a young boy and who played both the cello and the banjo at the Bauhaus in Dessau, married the cellist Binia in 1931 and was always in contact with musicians such as Hermann Scherchen and Wladimir Vogel. In light of that, it is hardly surprising that in the early 1930s his artistic development was closely intertwined with his knowledge of music; he was convinced that the methods used to pursue, develop, and elaborate musical themes must also be applicable in the visual arts. That led him to certain outcomes, which were as yet not specifically mathematical, although he was also well aware that the laws governing musical structures are entrenched in mathematics. It was not until he encountered Georges Vantongerloo in Paris that Bill's thinking started to become more overtly mathematical. Around 1935 he began to engage intensely with the problems associated with mathematical bodies, although this is not to say that he now became consumed by mathematics. "Firstly, as I see it, I don't understand that much of it, and secondly I certainly didn't want to end up just illustrating mathematics."[987] By way of a short aside on the topic of "illustrating": as Bill once told me, he would very much liked to have illustrated "the scandalous Bible stories," but since he was no longer working figuratively at the time when that idea piqued his interest, there was never any question of him acting on it.

In 1935 Bill came up with an idea for an object—an endless loop. In an interview in 1965 Maria Wetzel asked him what had led to his *unendliche schleife* (see p. 559). Bill: "It had an odd prehistory. In 1935 my friend

Marcel Breuer was commissioned to construct a model house for an electrical trade exhibition in London, with an electric radiator instead of an open coal fire. However, since the expected "conversations by the fireplace" would lack the drama of flickering flames—there would just be anonymous, radiated warmth—Breuer asked me to think of something to alleviate that shortcoming.

Marcel Breuer and Bill had known each other since Bill's time at the Bauhaus and both had carried out commissions for Wohnbedarf in Zurich in the early 1930s. However, Breuer did not take up Bill's suggestion, since he had already decided to enliven the fireplace with a sculpture by the British artist Henry Moore.

I pondered, wondering what could be done—something for people to look at when they were sitting by the fireplace—and came up with the idea of suspending this figure, the *unendliche schleife,* above the fireplace.... Not understanding enough about mathematics at the time, I didn't yet know that it in fact embodied a mathematical principle. I had never seen a "Möbius strip" ... Möbius (who lived around 1800) took a lengthy strip and twisted it and taped the two ends together, so that there was no longer an inside and an outside, as in a ring, but just a single 'one-sided surface.' I had chanced upon the same idea: I wanted to create a form in motion. So when I first saw a Möbius strip, I was initially rather shocked. But then the match between my idea and his cleared the path for all sorts of new ideas! I was able to proceed along that path and arrived at insights and possibilities (that I had secretly long sensed), which greatly helped me to move forward. It was basically an entirely fortuitous spark."[988]

There is no saying whether Max Bill really had never seen a picture of a Möbius strip. However, of particular interest in the subsequent evolution of this sculpture (originally intended to be suspended), is Bill's willingness to experiment, even to the extent of sawing the plaster form into pieces and reassembling these in a different order.

Maria Wetzel, having received an unusually detailed answer from Bill but still not letting go, asked why Max Bill had given his *unendliche schleife* the date 1935–53.

This tale of chance—a watershed in Bill's art production—and its consequences is particularly fascinating, because it casts a revealing light on certain aspects of Bill's approach and modus operandi. Years after the interview that is cited here, he returned to that same idea—that is how important it was to him for his own development as an artist.

988 Max Bill in Maria Wetzel, "Interview mit Max Bill," *Diplomatischer Kurier* 13 (June 1965), p. 540

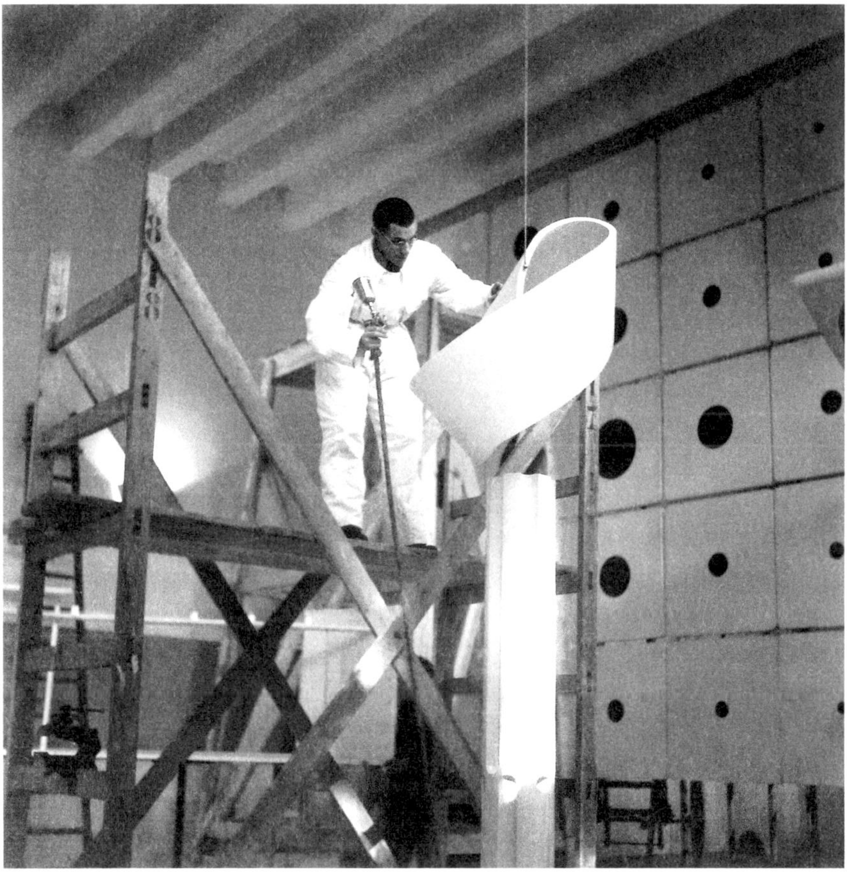

Binia Bill, Max Bill working on *unendliche schleife* in the Swiss Pavilion at the Milan Triennial, 1936

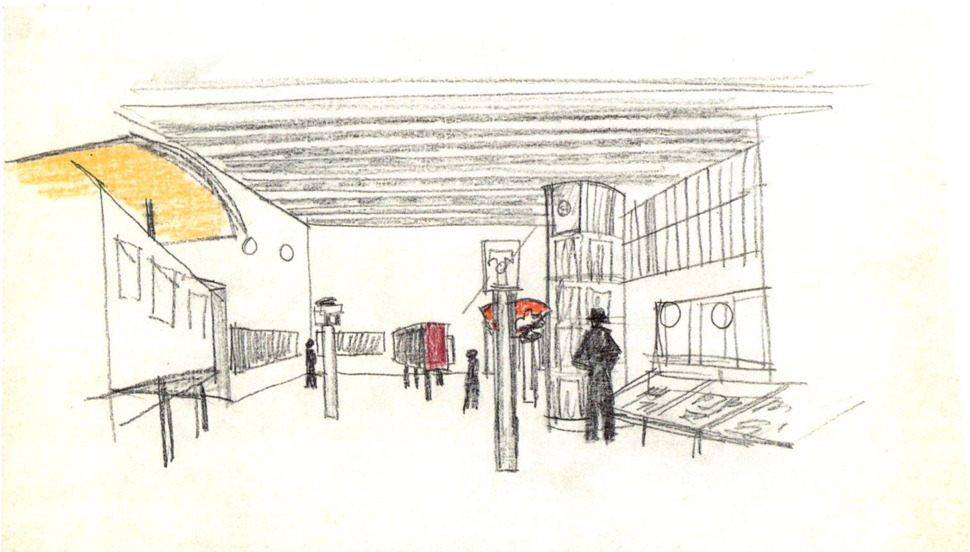

Max Bill, Drawing of the exhibition design in the Swiss Pavilion at the Milan Triennial, 1936, graphite and colored pencil on tracing paper, 22.6×41.2 cm

Once again Bill provided a careful explanation: "In 1936, when the Swiss government asked me to design the display in the Swiss Pavilion at the Milan Triennial, I decided to include three sculptures—one of which was *unendliche schleife.* But later on its shape fundamentally changed. It became larger, we sawed it into pieces, we made it shorter and then taller again.... Heaven knows how many things I did before it reached its final form. And then there was also the question of the material to be used to realize the plaster model. There is a bronze *schleife* now at Middelheimpark in Antwerp. But the material that best suited the idea was stone. I was determined to have a version of this work in proper volcanic rock, in granite. And that's when it turned out that the 'strip,' originally the same thickness throughout, now had to taper toward the outer edges and be thicker along its center line, increasing its plastic volume—but not becoming bulky. I wanted to avoid bulk, that was for sure. It also matters that despite its weight and inertia, this material, which very clearly is what it is, which—one might imagine—is better suited to kerbstones and the like—was transformed.... As soon it was finished I sent it to an international sculpture exhibition in Paris, where it was the last work that visitors came to. At the opening André Malraux [the French Minister of Culture at the time] was very taken with it and, despite having to overcome considerable (financial) difficulties managed to acquire it for the Musée d'Art Moderne [Version IV, Wassen granite, 1960]. That was a very nice success for me."[989] By way of an aside, this exhibition also included works by the English sculptor Henry Moore, whose work Marcel Breuer had selected in 1935, before he saw Max Bill's *unendliche schleife.*

Bill later returned to the same subject, not in an interview but in his text "Idee-Konzept-Werk: über ein Thema" in the catalogue for his exhibition in Berlin in 1977. He again outlined the circumstances that led to this work: "Unlike most of my sculptures (and paintings), the idea for *unendliche schleife* arose from my efforts to find a practical solution for a particular situation. In 1935 Marcel Breuer was entrusted with the project planning for a model house in a London exhibition, a house running solely on electricity. Even the traditional fireplace was to run on electricity. Marcel asked me if I had a sculpture that would enliven the fireplace. We both felt that a fireplace with no fire to sit around, no fire to gaze into, was problematic."

Bill analyzed the problem and saw its implications: if there is only a static, electric "fire," which merely glows, "you don't see any movement." But warm air rises, and the air current could set something in motion, like a windmill, of sorts. That then led Bill to the conclusion that

989 Wetzel, "Interview mit Max Bill"

"a suspended object would offer the least resistance to rotational movement." However, he rejected the idea of suspended paper spirals or of a small windmill of some kind. He felt he had to find something entirely new as a substitute for the fire. Bill's "search for a planar, almost weightless form" ultimately led him to the elemental solution that he then named *unendliche schleife:* "I made a model from layers of paper glued together. I wrote to Marcel Breuer, telling him that I had an idea for something quite new, floating, hung up above the electric fire. Only he wrote back ... saying he had already selected a sculpture by Henry Moore to stand on the electric heater.... At the time I had just won the competition to design the display in the Swiss section at the Milan Triennial in 1936. My concept was a space with three groups of exhibits, each with an accent sculpture. One of those sculptures was *unendliche schleife,* suspended from the ceiling, twisting in the air above a column. It was realized by craftsmen—according to my small model—as a plaster strip, the same thickness throughout.... I then came up with a larger version, recumbent, not suspended any more. It also had to be more stable, so that it could be rendered in stone later on. The plasterers made a model, about 180 cm in length, which I later sawed apart and used the pieces to create the final version, concentrated into 150 cm, which was subsequently hewn in different types of stone [by stonemasons employed by Max Bill]."

As he sawed the plaster model into pieces and reconfigured it, Bill made a discovery that took him by surprise: "When we were constructing the skeleton for the plaster model, I realized that you always measure it at right angles, as you do with parallels." Bill's practical work thus led him to a conclusion that would not have been unfamiliar to his role model, Georges Vantongerloo, with his background in Euclidean geometry: "So I was faced with a line that was parallel to itself! The Euclidean geometry I knew went as far as 'parallel lines intersect at infinity.' That statement had always preoccupied me and had fascinated me in its controversial foresight. It had haunted me and now, in this situation, it was no longer valid. This line was parallel to itself and flowed on infinitely without ever being able to intersect itself. I was very proud of my discovery."

In his text for the exhibition at the Akademie der Künste in Berlin, Max Bill reveals something of the workings of his mind. And he also returns to Möbius: "One day someone said to me that the way I had found a formally perfect, sculptural solution for the Möbius strip was fabulous.

990 See Bill 1977 [a], pp. 28–39
991 Münster 2004, p. 173
992 Information kindly supplied by Jürg Frischknecht, 2007
993 Hans Mühlestein on Silone's *Fontamara, information* 1:9 (April 1933)

But I had never heard of a Möbius strip. I looked in a lexicon and read that August Ferdinand Möbius (1790–1868)—astronomer, mathematician, professor, and director of the observatory—worked on analytical geometry. Later I also read that J. B. Listing had discovered the same dual surface in 1861, four years before Möbius."[990]

"Not all downward paths are necessarily gloomy"

On the same day that Karola Piotrkowska graduated from the architecture department at the ETH in Zurich, she and Ernst Bloch received an injunction from the Swiss immigration authorities ordering them to leave Switzerland by 15 September 1934 at the latest. There was no chance to appeal the decision. And since Bloch had already been blacklisted by the Nazis—as had many other leftist intellectuals—he had no choice but to resume his travels. He and Karola spent their last few weeks in Switzerland "in the Engadine, near St. Moritz, very close to Heinz Neumann, a leading figure in the German Communist Party."[991]

Bill later told me that, before they finally left, he visited Ernst Bloch "in Celerina or Maloja, together with the art historian Hans Mühlestein."

It seems that in the 1930s Hodler's biographer, Hans Mühlestein, lived in both Maloja and Zürich; in letters from Mühlestein written between "late 1932 and May 1935 the address is always Maloja, with no further details. However, it is evident from another document that from 4 April 1933 to 2 August 1938 (with a seven-month interruption in 1935) he was registered in the city of Zurich."[992] Additional research by Jürg Frischknecht has shown that the municipality of Celerina, where Mühlestein's wife, Anita Pidermann, was born, has no records relating to Mühlestein.

Mühlestein had been a contributor to the periodical *information,* which Bill had designed, and had written a favorable review of Ignazio Silone's book *Fontamara* for *information.*[993]

Ignazio Silone wrote *Fontamara* while he was in a sanatorium in Davos. Max Raphael, the Marxist cultural philosopher and contributor to *information,* also spent some time in a sanatorium in Davos. At the time Swiss sanatoriums found favor among émigrés not only because of possible improvements to their health, but also because when patients checked in on arrival their details were not passed on to the aliens section at the local police station.

Two Italian editions of Silone's *Fontamara*—the story of Ignazio Silone's native town under Fascism—had been "illegally imported into the country ... before a German translation was published in 1933 by Oprecht & Helbling in Zurich. Five thousand copies sold in just five months; it was soon translated into eleven languages and is now regarded as a classic of world literature. Max Bill designed the first German edition—there had been a plan to include illustrations in the second edition, also published in 1933, but time ran out and the book had to do without. Moreau's paper cuts were put to one side, until the Büchergilde Gutenberg brought out its edition in 1944, by which time Moreau had long been living in Argentina, his next place of exile."[994]

Hans Girsberger had in fact inadvertently let the chance to publish Fontamara slip through his fingers. One day Silone had appeared at his office in Zurich "with the suggestion that I should publish *information*—a left-leaning, campaigning periodical. Although it was largely financed by one of our young architect friends, and despite already knowing the proposed team very well, I could not bring myself to do that. For all my willingness to countenance criticism of the prevailing circumstance, I was deeply averse to the destructive undertone, the open criticism of all our institutions, all the more so since these were promulgated by a foreigner living as an émigré.... That was how I missed the opportunity to publish Silone's novel *Fontamara,* a bestseller, which was soon released by another publisher."[995]

The hostility toward foreigners and toward the periodical *information* that comes across in this statement by Girsberger, a man of some intellect, is all the more astonishing given that in 1924 he had written a dissertation on utopian socialism: "Der utopische Sozialismus des 18. Jahrhunderts in Frankreich und seine philosophischen und materiellen Grundlagen." At the same time, in Girsberger's recollection of his decision not to publish Silone's book, there are echoes of the xenophobia that was then rampant in some parts of Switzerland, where first-generation Italian immigrants who had come as workers were particularly subjected to slander.

Ernst Bloch had already published a text on "the Alps without photography" ("Alpen ohne Photographie," 1930), in which he described the Jungfrau as "this most almighty of all summits," when a visit to the Engadine again inspired him to write about his immediate surroundings. His essay "Maloja-Chiavenna-Drift" (1934) opens with the circumspect

994 Magnaguagno 1980
995 Girsberger 1970, pp. 14–15
996 Bloch 1965 [b], p. 499

pragmatism of an émigré facing an uncertain future and now trying to strengthen his own resolve: "Not all downward paths are necessarily gloomy." And he continues: "The famous road from familiar little Maloja ... is a steep descent. Turn by turn the old Maloja ravine runs down from Maloja into the Bregaglia. This descent to Italy, the steepest, the most exciting and the liveliest."[996]

Many years later I sat in the passenger seat as Bill drove down what Bloch described as the "steepest ... most exciting and liveliest" road through the Maloja pass into the Bregaglia, where we visited his onetime student Ernst Scheidegger in the latter's holiday home in the village of Bondo. Scheidegger cooked wonderfully fresh rainbow trout for us that he had caught himself; they were truly delicious and a delight to behold.

Ernst Bloch Takes Issue with CIAM

Ernst Bloch and Karola Piotrkowska both actively participated in the architectural discourse of that time; Bloch set out his ideas on architecture in various publications and was well informed about the latest topics being discussed at CIAM. It is fair to assume that Bloch and Bill would have continued those discussions, face to face, in the Bregaglia.

Bill was of course an advocate of the rationalism of *Neues Bauen.* Although he had already built his own house in Höngg, he was still not a member of CIAM, but in spring 1931—after CIAM III—he had accepted the commission to design the jacket for the remaining stock of the book *Rationelle Bebauungsweisen* (see p. 567).

The book *Rationelle Bebauungsweisen,* arising from CIAM III (held in Brussels in 1930), was issued by CIAM and edited by Sigfried Giedion, who also contributed an introduction; it was published in an edition of 2000 by Englert & Schlosser in Frankfurt. Not long afterward the publishing house folded. 1,600 unsold copies of the book went to the Julius Hoffmann publishing house in Stuttgart; with no change to the copyright but with a new dust jacket designed by Max Bill, these went on sale again in autumn 1931.

It is no longer possible to determine exactly who asked Bill to take on that task—be it Sigfried Giedion, Walter Gropius, or Rudolf Steiger. However, it could well have been Gropius (who might have approached Bill during the *Deutsche Bauausstellung* in Berlin), particularly in view of the fact that Bill's cover design features one of Gropius's drawings for the twelve-story apartment blocks he designed for the Berlin-Haselhorst housing estate in 1929.

"Gropius contributed a lot of drawings, with Giedion clearly in charge of the editing; meanwhile a lot of other things, including the cover, seem to have been coordinated by Rudolf Steiger. Unfortunately the existing documents, the correspondence relating to the book, do not indicate whether he was the person who brought Bill on board to design the cover. However, it is evident that there was general dissatisfaction regarding the print quality and the color of the cover."[997]

In a letter to the Dutch CIAM architect Cornelis van Eesteren, Sigfried Giedion indicated that he was not happy with the cover by Max Bill: "The book has just come out; apart from the cover and the lack of a proper index of the drawings, I think it's excellent."[998]

In *Erbschaft dieser Zeit* Ernst Bloch criticized "stirrings under [capitalist] cover" and "social democratic 'modernity' à la Giedion." In fact he delivers a fundamental critique of the fact that "ratio," in the form advocated by CIAM architects (Sigfried Giedion was the secretary at CIAM), was still not an "index of what is true."

Sigfried Giedion had taken his lead from a lecture by Walter Gropius, who was of the opinion that CIAM III should speak out "against the usual three or four story house." Giedion put it in a nutshell: "The high-rise requires a new, that is to say, community-based form of living."[999]

"Thus the residential apartment block was advocated by some for urban-planning reasons, while others put forward arguments proposing the collectivisation of certain tasks fulfilled by families and ultimately the 'socialisation of the family'; in other words, collectivisation ensuing from technological and economic conditions was seen as a social phenomenon."[1000]

In light of the importance of Ernst Bloch's views both at the time and far beyond that particular historical context, I would like to cite them in greater length here:

997 Information kindly supplied by Daniel Weiss, gta Archiv

998 Sigfried Giedion to Cornelis von Eesteren, 29 October 1931, gta Archiv

999 *CIAM—Internationale Kongresse für Neues Bauen,* 1979, p. 87; and Sigfried Giedion, "III. Internationaler Kongress für Neues Bauen," *Frankfurter Zeitung,* 16 December 1930

1000 CIAM—*Internationale Kongresse für Neues Bauen,* 1979, p. 87

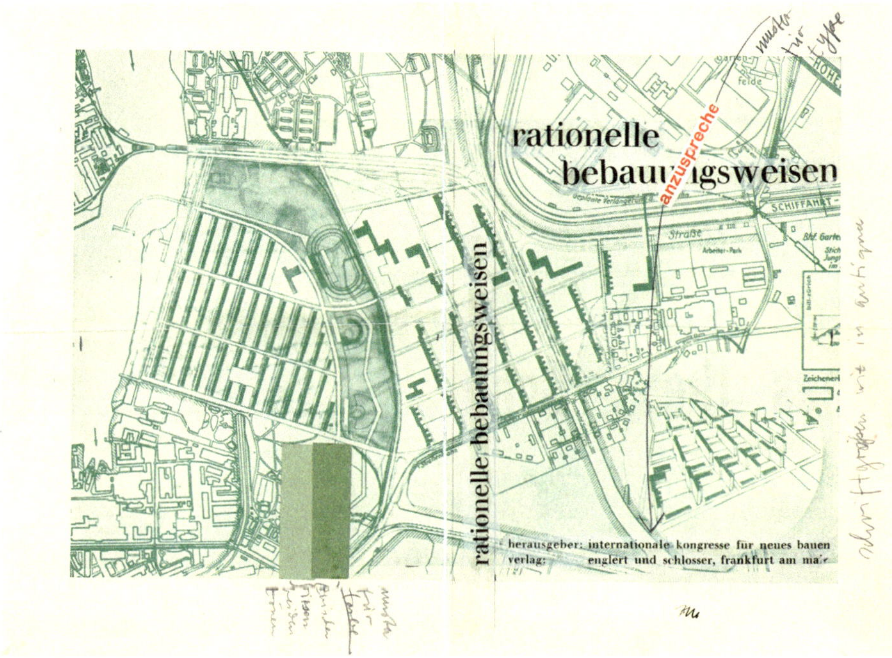

Max Bill, Cover design for the remaining stock of the book *Rationelle Bebauungsweisen,* 1931

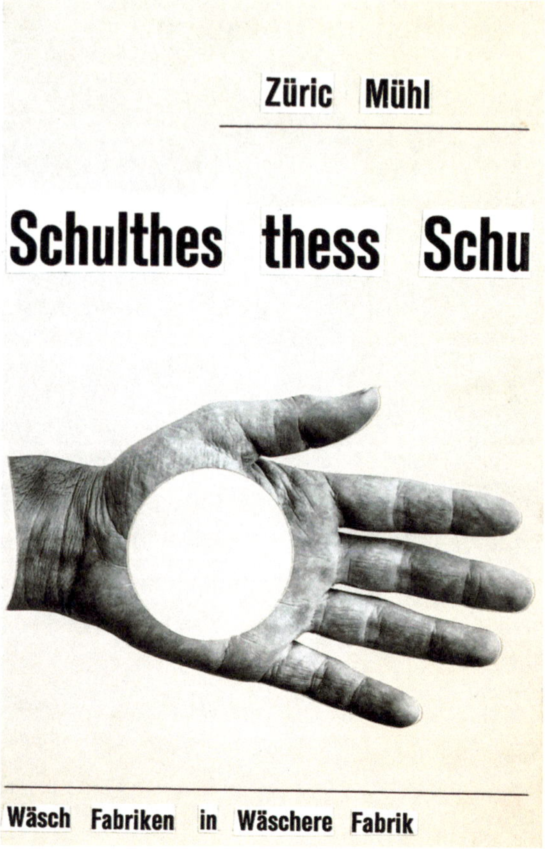

Max Bill, Design for an advertisement, ca. 1930, collage with photograph on card, 23.4×15.5 cm

"... since the Ratio occurs in capitalist objectivity only as a disjointed and abstract one, i.e. limited to a private economy, since it ultimately in fact, in Roosevelt's America, serves the planned destruction of the forces of production in the interest of the capitalist system, in short, the 'stabilization' of the crisis, it also in no way already appears as the full index of what is true or as one which only needs to be continued to the end, to be made completely 'reasonable' in order to become one. The basic condition for the concrete use of the many 'systematically arranged things' of today is rather the completed revolution [in the Soviet Union]; without this, in fact, Ratio is only the familiar—rationalization. Therefore the so-called stirrings under cover, namely the many technical-collective 'beginnings' in late capitalism, can also nowhere already directly be greeted as 'socialist.'"[1001]

Bloch vehemently chastises the (unnamed) CIAM architects led by Sigfried Giedion, accusing them of a lack of political awareness—yet he must have also seen Max Bill as one of their number, having so recently visited the Bills in Höngg.

Max Bill was not uncritical of Giedion, and that would not change in the years to come. Unfortunately there is no knowing what line Bill took in conversation with Bloch regarding the notion that without a revolution conditions in society would never in fact change.

Bloch had had to flee Berlin and arrived in Switzerland with his own bitter experience of the politics that were already threatening the lives of so many of his friends and comrades. And he mocks that supposedly "peaceful growth of capitalism into socialism": "... this seems a false indirectness, namely none at all; if it [CIAM ideology] already sees in every sliding window a piece of future state, then it obviously overrates the technical-neutral, underrates the class-biased element. It overrates the neutral cleanliness, comfort of the new architecture.... It underrates the fact that this 'uniform hygienic living' is still in no way orientated nor can be orientated even only potentially toward a classless society.... It underrates the representation which conversely modern big business produces out of its 'functionalism.'"[1002]

On that last visit to see Bloch in Maloja, Bill took with him his design for the jacket of *Erbschaft dieser Zeit.* Bill proposed a hand with a round opening in the palm—because there was as yet no knowing what the heritage of those times would look like. But Bloch was not convinced by Bill's proposal, and Mühlestein did not defend it. Bloch considered the hand with a void in its palm "too avant-garde"—as Bill later told me in conversation.

1001 Bloch 1962, pp. 218–19
1002 Bloch 1962, pp. 218–19

Bloch's book *Erbschaft dieser Zeit* was published in 1935 by Oprecht & Helbling in Zürich. "The critical reception was cool" and "in press outlets in the Soviet Union his book—which, as it happens, in no way kowtows to Stalin—was completely ignored."[1003]

And yet, maybe Bloch's response was only in keeping with his strong objections to the CIAM architects' ideas, to the way that they saw "in every sliding window a piece of future state." Or maybe his comment was intended ironically, one friend talking to another, knowing that "too avant-garde" might also be something of a comfort to Bill. It allowed Bill almost to take the rejection as a compliment because he above all wanted his work to be seen as avant-garde. That little addition of the word *too* merely indicated that—from Bloch's point of view—Bill had just overshot the mark.

When Karola Piotrkowska and Ernst Bloch finally left Switzerland, Hans Mühlestein and his wife Anita Pidermann accompanied them as far as the border where they bade farewell with heavy hearts.

This information is contained in a text by a certain Mr. Pidermann, possibly a nephew of Mühlestein's wife, Anita Pidermann: "Sein und Sollen. Aus dem Leben und Werk des autonomen Hans Mühlestein" (typewritten text in the Zentralbibliothek Zürich; information kindly supplied by Jürg Frischknecht, 2007).

Bloch's response after their expulsion does not come as a surprise. He describes the steep descent from Maloja toward Fascist Italy: "pain ... granite peaks and swastikas ... halt at the border, marked by a bridge. In the same way that today's Swiss and the Fascists are not so very far apart politically."[1004]

Friedl Dicker and the Bloch Family

Karola Piotrkowska and Ernst Bloch fled to Vienna and married in November 1934, with the result that Karola, as Bloch's wife, lost her Polish citizenship and became a citizen of reviled Nazi Germany. In 1937 the Blochs' son Jan was born in Prague.

1003 Münster 2004, p. 192
1004 Bloch 1965 [b], p. 499
1005 *Neue Zürcher Zeitung*, 12–13 January 2002, p. 60
1006 Maasberg and Prinz 2004, p. 28

During her training as an architect, Karola had worked for a while as an intern in the office of the renowned architect Auguste Perret in Paris. In Prague she met Friedl Dicker, who had once studied at the Bauhaus in Weimar and now gladly lent Karola her support.

Friedl Dicker had been the long-term partner of Franz Singer, whom Lucia Moholy so appreciated as a human being and as an architect. In the meantime, Singer had emigrated to London, like Lucia Moholy, who managed to make her way there via Prague.

The Nazis regarded Vienna as "one of the main Jew-cities" (Hermann Göring) and their plan was that within just a few months of Hitler's invasion of Austria "the whole story should be over." 17,000 businesses were to be Aryanized or put into liquidation, thousands of apartments were to be cleared and their contents monetized. March 1938 saw the first attempts to integrate this mass-expropriation into the National Socialist bureaucratic machine. The "appropriate transfer of Jewish assets" was the euphemism for this process, which is discussed in detail by Tina Walzer and Stephan Tempel in *Unser Wien. "Arisierung" auf Österreichisch* (Berlin: Aufbau-Verlag, 2001).[1005]

In 1934, before Karola's arrival in Prague, Friedl had been arrested in Vienna for "Communist machinations." However, she had managed to emigrate to Prague, where—small in stature but courageous, full of fire and energy—she again became an active member of a Communist group. Friedl Dicker felt it was vital to try to resist the growing Fascist threat. Politically aware and socially engaged, she had married her cousin Pavel Brandeis in 1936 and was now a Czech citizen. Friedl never tolerated lies and had a complete aversion to any form of mannered behavior.

When her comrade Karola Bloch arrived in Prague, Friedl Dicker was able to use her connections to find work for her. Karola had herself already carried out daring missions, at risk to her own life, as a courier for the Communist Party, even when she was already pregnant. Friedl Dicker was able to secure "small, independent commissions" for Karola, somewhat easing the exposed, uncertain situation the Blochs and their child were in as émigrés.[1006] In the end, the Blochs managed to emigrate to the United States, where Karola changed the spelling of her first name to Carola; she later retained that spelling even when they returned to Germany after the Second World War and first lived in Leipzig in the East before finally settling in Tübingen in West Germany.

However, Friedl Dicker decided to stay in Prague, despite having been granted a visa to emigrate to Palestine. After the German invasion and destruction of liberal Czechoslovakia, Friedl and her husband, Pavel Brandeis, were deported to the concentration camp at Theresienstadt. In the camp Friedl—who had trained both as an artist and as a psychoanalyst—tried to do what she could to alleviate the situation for the children in captivity by giving art lessons. On 28 September 1944 Pavel Brandeis was transferred from Theresienstadt to Auschwitz. He somehow managed to survive the war. However, Friedl Dicker-Brandeis—who volunteered to join the next transport to Auschwitz, on 6 October 1944, to be close to her husband—was killed by the Nazis in the gas chambers three days later, on 9 October 1944. Adding to the horror of all the stories of concentration camps and compounding the unending grief they caused, yet another act of sheer perfidy has come to light: it turns out that the camp at Auschwitz was in fact designed by Fritz Ertl, a former Bauhaus student in Dessau—not even "against his will as a prisoner, but as departmental head of building."[1007]

In the summer of 1928 Fritz Ertl enrolled at the Bauhaus in Dessau (matriculation number 259),[1008] that is to say, both Max Bill and Hanns Fischli might have met him in Dessau. Ertl arrived at the Bauhaus as a fully-qualified bricklayer but with only a middle-school certificate. Starting in April 1928, at the same time as Hanns Fischli, "he completed the foundation course, after which he was accepted into the building section by Hannes Meyer; following an extended leave of absence he rejoined the building section, under the new bauhaus director Mies van der Rohe after October 1930. In June 1931 he graduated with a diploma."[1009]

In 2007 a typewritten copy of a text written by Primo Levi in 1960 and now stored in the Yad Vashem Documents Archive in Israel was published in Europe in the Italian weekly *L'Espresso.* In this hitherto unknown document the great writer "presents a dry account of his *via dolorosa* from Italy to Auschwitz and back. He had already done that with supreme, shattering skill in his books *If This Is a Man* (1947) and *The Truce* (1963), but in these two previously unpub-

1007 Information kindly supplied by Dr. Ulrike Bestgen, Weimar, 27 September 2007

1008 Wingler 1962, p. 534

1009 Winkler 2003, pp. 28–29

1010 Franz Haas, "Nach Auschwitz und zurück, unbekanntes Dokument von Primo Levi," in *Neue Zürcher Zeitung,* 28 September 2007

1011 Max Bill, Zurich to Dr. Siegfried Salzmann, 18 March 1971, cited in *Paul Klee und seine Malerfreunde* 1971; this letter is not included in the Winterthur catalogue for the same exhibition

lished pages we learn, for the first time, the names of many of those who suffered alongside him. . . . In this document Primo Levi recapitulates those two terrible years starting in autumn 1943. He and his fellow partisans were captured close to the Swiss border (he also names the man who betrayed them) and taken to the transit camp at Fossoli before being transported to Auschwitz."[1010]

Primo Levi did not manage to reach Switzerland, like another Italian partisan, Angelo Mangiarotti, who was among the refugees that Max Bill helped at the time. When I telephoned Mangiarotti to ask about his connection to Max Bill, the first words he uttered were: "Bill gave me food."

Returning to Klee's Teachings on Theory

At the same time as working as a commercial artist and designing typographies, Max Bill consistently strove—from the early 1930s onward—to clarify his own ideas as to how he could radically advance his own art production.

Following constructive investigation and experimentation Bill, as he himself openly explained, would ultimately "return" to Klee's theoretical teachings, with the emphasis on theoretical, in the sense that Bill's style would henceforth no longer be beholden to Klee's work, it would not relate to the latter's "picture-motif-compositions" any more, as it had done during his time at the Bauhaus. "It was only through my own constructive investigations that I ultimately returned to Klee's theoretical teachings. Without previously having fully taken these in [Bill had, as he said, 'only intermittently' attended Klee's theoretical course at the Bauhaus] I retrospectively discovered that my findings were confirmed by his earlier experiments."[1011]

Besides designing the periodical *information,* he also created the masthead for the weekly *Die Nation* (another liberal-leftist, anti-Fascist periodical), which was first published in June 1932 on the initiative of Hans Oprecht and a non-partisan committee, with Peter Surava as its editor-in-chief.

Surava, who was admired and respected for his civil courage through out Switzerland in the 1930s in households that subscribed to *Die Nation,* was ostracized after the Second World War both politically and socially. It was not until Erich Schmid's film *Er nannte sich Surava* was released in 1995 that the country remembered the story of the avid Nazi opponent; for more on this, see *Abschied von Surava—eine Dokumentation,* ed. Erich Schmid (Zurich: Wolfbach Verlag, 1996).

With Jeanne Bucher's astute comment "we all love Klee" still ringing in his ears, Bill distanced his work from that of Klee and considered if and where there might be a different "point of contact" for him. And then he remembered learning how to create sandblasted glass objects from Josef Albers at the Bauhaus. As it happens, Albers once described how he negotiated that complicated technique. His "glass wall paintings" (see, for instance, *Tectonische Gruppe,* 1925, see p. 152) were "mostly made using a sandblaster (apart from the parts that are colored or kiln-fired with glass paints or porcelain paints). When you are sandblasting, the glass plate is first covered with specially prepared paper. I transfer the drawing by means of diazocopies (very fine, exact drawings!), then I cut out the sections that are to be white and sandblast down to the first sheet of glass through a colored (mostly black) overlay. If there are also matt areas in the design (on black these appear gray), I then cut out these areas and sandblast again, but only lightly. This technique requires some understanding of the materials: the nature of the overlays, the extent to which different paints can be fired, also tensions in the glass."[1012] Bill experimented with that technique around 1930—albeit not in strictly horizontal and vertical compositions, like Albers, but on glass with two circular excisions. And it was soon after that, around 1931, that Bill—by now a married man—deliberately embarked on a search for an entirely new artistic concept of his own.

A few days after his twenty-third birthday Max Bill learned with relief that his father—whose letters were so often overflowing with reproach—was moving away from Winterthur and, hence, further away from Zurich. The knowledge that there would now be a greater distance between father and son—at least geographically—came as a relief to Max.

Erwin Bill and his second wife, Lina Bill (née Wolf), moved to Ligerz am Bielersee, where he was appointed parish clerk in early January 1932 and thus embarked on a new phase of his life.

Freed from the troubling shadow cast by his father, Bill now started to make progress in his artistic work—as in the case of his *wellrelief* (1931–32, see p. 476), which can certainly be seen and appreciated as a precursor to Minimal Art. Within a few years Bill had also created sculptures such as *lange plastik* (1933), *konstruktion mit schwebendem kubus* (1935), and *unendliche schleife* (1935, see p. 559). As Bill himself said in 1942 in a draft curriculum vitae, in those early years he still did the main work on

1012 Josef Albers to Hans Hildebrandt, 2 October 1934, in *Hans Hildebrandt und sein Kreis* 1978

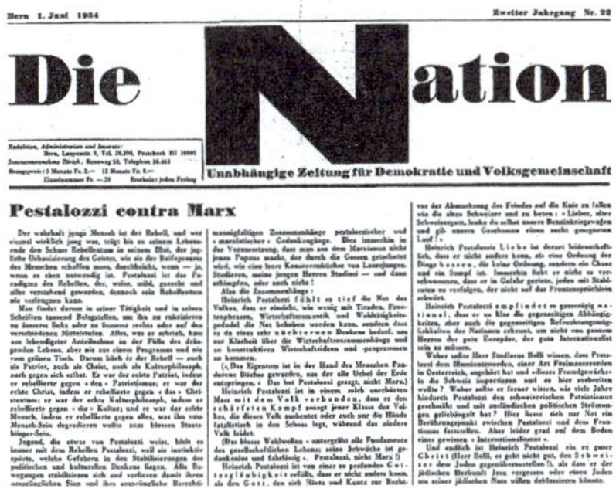

Bern 1. Juni 1934 — Zweiter Jahrgang Nr. 22

Die Nation

Unabhängige Zeitung für Demokratie und Volksgemeinschaft

Pestalozzi contra Marx

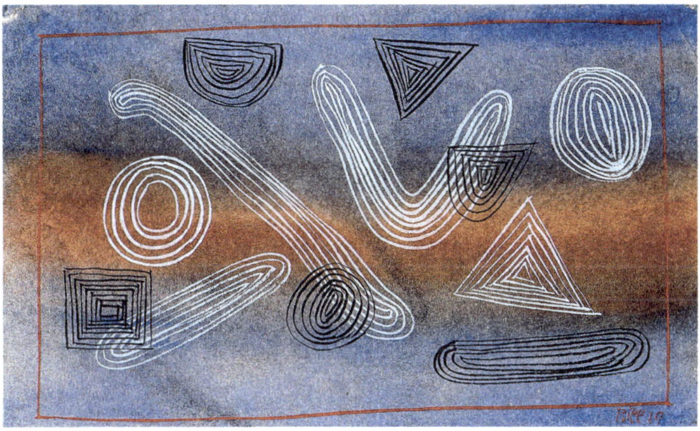

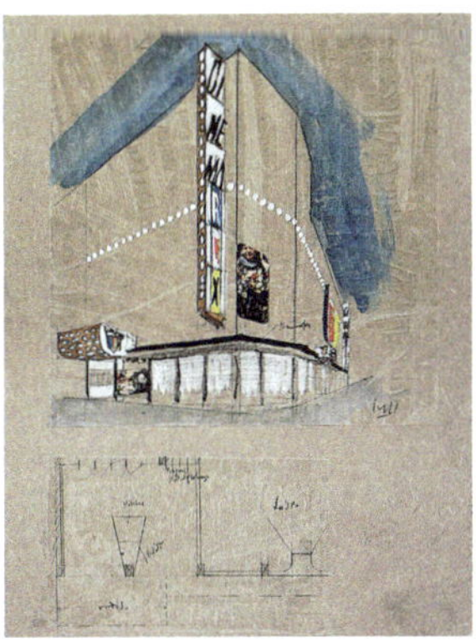

Max Bill, Masthead of the weekly *Die Nation,* 1933

Max Bill, *Teilung und Multiplikation,* 1929, gouache over watercolor on Japan paper, 16×25.7 cm

Max Bill, Design for signage for Cinema Rex, 1932, gouache and collage on tracing paper on card, 24×31 cm

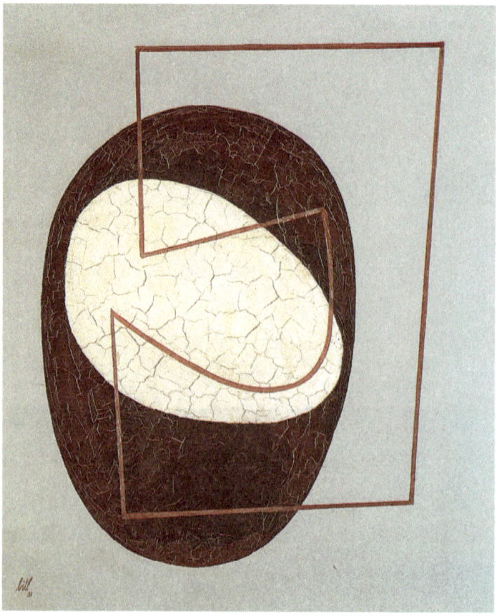

Max Bill, *komposition 2,* 1931,
oil on wood, 58×48cm

Max Bill, *glasbild,* 1930–31,
crystal glass, sandblasted on
one side, 60×100×0.5cm

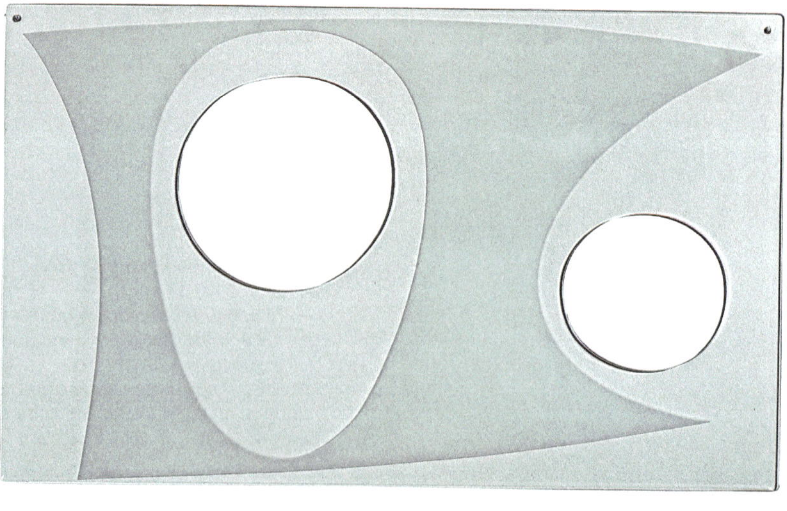

his wood or metal sculptures himself. At the same time he continued to earn an income for himself and Binia by working on commercial design commissions, such as the signage for Cinema Rex in 1932.

Concrete Art on Show in Zurich for the First Time

In 1932 a non-selective art exhibition was held in a newly completed office block, the Näfenhaus, in Bahnhofstrasse in Zurich. Max Bill, Hans Fischli, and Alfred Willimann reserved a wall together. Bill then discovered that the architect Alfred Roth was also working on paintings that could be described as Concrete, which he signed as "Aroth."

"Alfred Roth was in contact with Piet Mondrian back then; he was in Paris working with Le Corbusier and in 1927 took charge of the construction of Le Corbusier's buildings at the international Weissenhof Estate in Stuttgart. So Alfred Roth was already in contact with a lot of artists and he put together a collection in which the crowning glory was Piet Mondrian's *Composition with Red Blue and Yellow* (1930)."[1013]

Alfred Roth very generously donated that same Mondrian painting text to Kunsthaus Zürich, at a time when it was already worth millions. As it happens, when Roth was working for Le Corbusier, he also met Binia Spoerri in Paris, that is to say, before she and Bill met in Zurich in the late summer or autumn of 1930.

So Fischli, Bill, and Willimann invited Roth to exhibit with them at the Näfenhaus. Bill showed his *wellrelief* (see p. 476) for the first time. In fact this single exhibition wall provided the opportunity for a very small group of artists to be the first ever to show a selection of Concrete art in Zurich.

The exhibition wall with Concrete art by Aroth (Alfred Roth), Alfred Willimann, Max Bill and Hans Fischli is illustrated in *Dreissiger Jahre Schweiz,* Kunsthaus Aarau, 1981, p. 16.

In 2006 Christoph Bignens published a catalogue text on the "development of good taste" with particular reference to the work of Max Bill's friend Alfred Willimann. Soon after that exhibition at the Näfenhaus, Willimann and the photographer Hans Finsler were jointly appointed to run the photography class in the new extension of the Zurich Kunstgewerbeschule that was inaugurated in 1933.[1014]

1013 Bill 1991
1014 Bignens 2006

In the autumn of that year Bill designed the poster for *Tod und Leben*—an exhibition on "life and death" in the new extension of the Kunstgewerbemuseum (see p. 580).

Initially the title of the exhibition was to have been *Friedhof und Grabmal.*

In connection with this task, Bill acquired Ernst Fuhrmann's *Der Grabbau* (Munich: Georg Müller, printed in 1922, issued in 1923, with 103 black-and-white images from all across the world); it is inscribed inside in pencil by Bill with his name in lower case: "bill," that is to say, it was approved by him for inclusion in his growing library.

Besides the black that is associated in the Western world with death and mourning and the white that stands for life, there is a spray-painted background that ascends "heavenward" from a greenish yellow hue through blue tones into lilac.

Abstraction-Création

In a strange quirk of fate it was Jean Arp—the very artist whom Max Bill had dismissed in a letter to Hans Fischli in 1930 as an "abstract grandfather'—who advised Bill to become a member of Abstraction-Création in Paris, where he would come into contact with many international artists. That was eminently sound advice, which Bill and his friend Hans Fischli both followed. Illustrations of some of Max Bill's most recent works were soon included in the Abstraction-Création journal and on 22 December 1933—his twenty-fifth birthday—Bill personally delivered some of his works to the exhibition in the Abstraction-Création gallery on Avenue de Wagram. That was Bill's first participation in an art exhibition in Paris. When he arrived at the gallery, he found a small, elderly man cleaning the floor, who turned out to be the president of Abstraction-Création, Auguste Herbin.

Works by Max Bill are illustrated in nos. 2 (1933), 3 (1934), 4 (1935) and 5 (1936) of *abstraction-création art non-figuratif* (Paris: Éditions les tendances nouvelles, 1933–36).

The 1933 exhibition also included Georges Vantongerloo's sculpture *Construction des rapports des volumes qui émane de l'hyper-bole xy=k* (1929). Later on Vantongerloo gave this work to the architect Hein Salomonson in Amsterdam as a wedding present. It was destroyed during the Second World War.

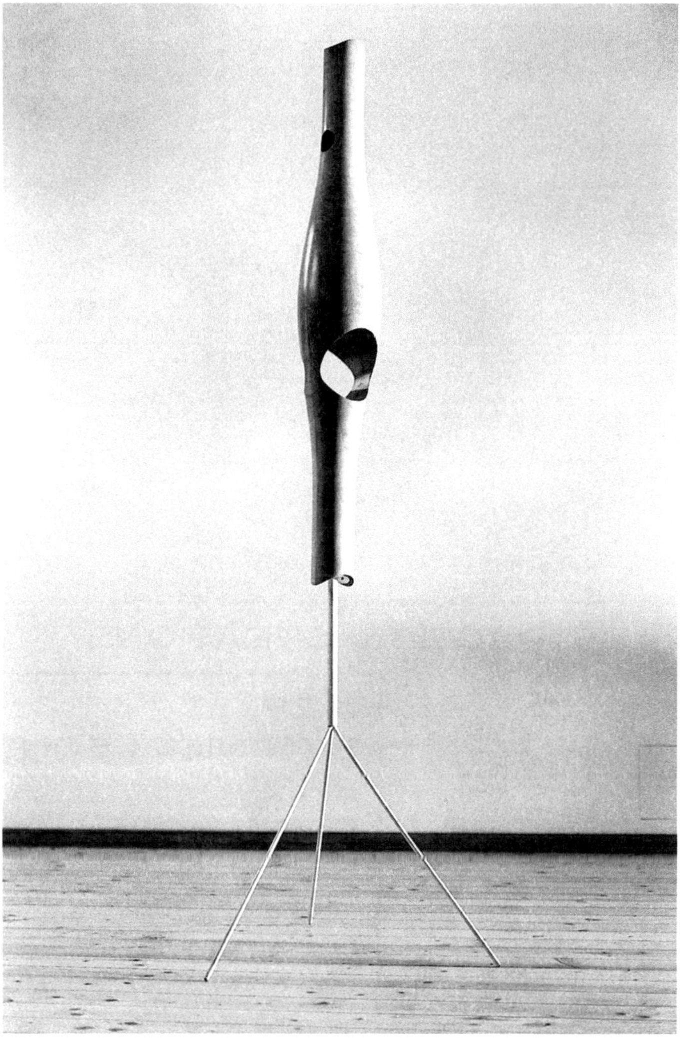

Max Bill, *lange plastik,* 1933,
iron and wood, height 2 m

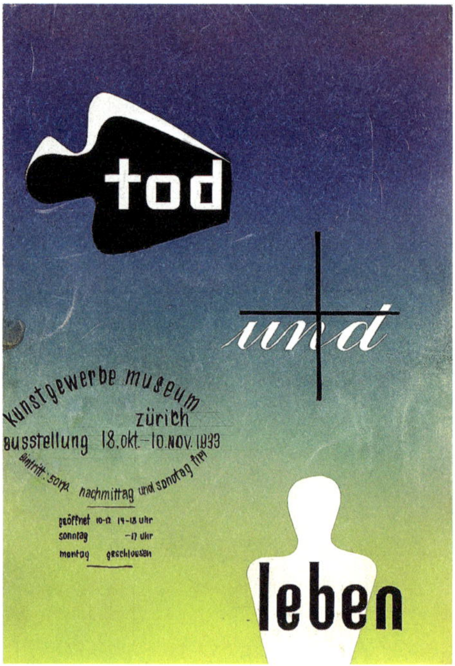

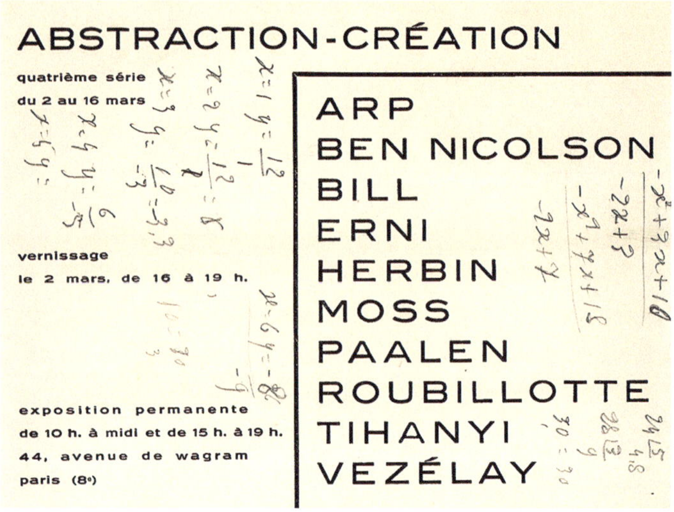

Max Bill, Poster design for the exhibition *Tod und Leben* at the Kunstgewerbemuseum in Zurich, 1933, collage, gouache, spray paint on card, 32×22.5cm

Invitation card for the exhibition *abstraction–création* (which included Max Bill) in Paris, 2–16 March 1934, with mathematical jottings by Georges Vantongerloo

In 1979—as Vantongerloo's executor, with the necessary authority—Max Bill had it constructed in a different material (painted brass) and with different dimensions (45×45×105cm). This version realized under Max Bill's supervision is now in the Max Bill estate left to Angela Thomas.

When Abstraction-Création was founded in 1931, one of the driving forces had been the Dutch artist Theo van Doesburg. On 24 January 1931 after two short-lived groups, Cercle et Carré and Art Concret, had ceased to exist, a number of artists met together at Van Doesburg's studio in Meudon on the edge of Paris. Those present included Van Doesburg himself, his neighbor Jean Arp, Auguste Herbin, and Jean Hélion (both Communist painters), and Alberto Giacometti (although Giacometti did not subsequently become a member of the new group). At a follow-up discussion, when Van Doesburg, Arp, Herbin, and Hélion were again present, they were joined by František Kupka, Leon Tutundjian, and Georges Valmier. And on 4 February 1931, again at Van Doesburg's studio, they drew up a constitution for the new association. That constitution was lodged with the authorities on 15 February 1931, which is why that is always cited as the date when Abstraction-Création was founded. However, during that early phase of Abstraction-Création, when its members were filled with new hope, news came that Van Doesburg had died in Davos on 7 March 1931. Hélion told the Belgian-Flemish artist Georges Vantongerloo of the sad news and encouraged him to join the group: "if we get painting away from 'nature' we will be able to set up a stable society with members ranging from Arp to Herbin and from Pevsner to you."[1015] Vantongerloo did become a member and took Van Doesburg's place on the board of Abstraction-Création.

Jan Brzekowski, a Polish poet living in Paris, was in close contact with artistic circles there in his capacity as secretary of the Association for Cultural Exchange between Poland and France.

Images sent by mail from Poland to France were published in Abstraction-Création's annual publications illustrating work by artists such as the former Tatlin student and innovative sculptor Katarzyna Kobro (a leading Constructivist in Poland), by her husband the painter Wladyslaw Strzeminski and by fellow sculptor Henryk Stazewski, who made several extended visits to Paris in 1929–34. Kobro, Strzeminski and Stazewski, along with the poet Jan Brzekowski, were all members of the Polish group Artistes révolutionnaires. Brzekowski persuaded

1015 Jean Hélion, Paris, to Georges Vantongerloo, Paris, 10 March 1931, Vantongerloo Archiv

some of the most talented, innovative artists of that time to donate works of their own to help to build up an international collection at the museum in the socialist city of Lodz. Schwitters, Léger, Vantongerloo, Van Doesburg and Sophie Taeuber-Arp were among the artists who were generous enough to participate in that enterprise, which still bears fruit today.

He already knew Sophie Taeuber-Arp and Jean Arp from Cercle et Carré, and now expressed great interest in the newly founded group, Abstraction-Création.

The international nature of the new group is well reflected in the list of artists who participated in the exhibition that opened at the Abstraction-Création gallery on 19 January 1934: Sophie Taeuber-Arp, the English sculptor Barbara Hepworth (who was already a friend of the Arps), Béothy, Closon, Fernandez, Hélion, Power, Prampolini, Seligmann, and Valmier. Sophie Taeuber-Arp designed the invitation cards and occasionally watched over the exhibits. On 26 January 1934 the members of Abstraction-Création elected a new board: Herbin was re-elected as president, Arp became the new vice-president, Vantongerloo took over as business manager, and the ordinary members were now Béothy, Fernandez, Freundlich, Gleizes, Gorin, Hélion, Kupka, and Sophie Taeuber-Arp—the only woman.

Bill suggested to his older colleagues in Paris that they should also accept his Swiss friends Alfred Willimann and Hans Fischli into Abstraction-Création[1016]; as a result his former fellow-student at the Bauhaus, Hans Fischli, did indeed participate in the group's activities.

On 2 March 1934 there was another opening at Abstraction-Création, and it is fair to assume that Bill would have made the journey from Zurich to Paris for that occasion because he was among the exhibitors. That exhibition also included works by Arp, Erni, Herbin, Moss, Nicolson, Paalen, Roubillotte, Tihanyi, and Vézelay.

1016 Bill 1991
1017 Gallati and Oechslin 1995–96, p. 5
1018 Bill 1990 [b], p. 35

Visiting Piet Mondrian

In December 1933 Binia and Max Bill met up with Jean Arp in Paris, and Binia took a number of photographs of him.

The portrait *Hans Arp, Clamart 1933* is illustrated in *Binia Bill—Fotografien* (Zurich: Scheidegger & Spiess, 2004), p. 99.

"Max Bill's wife Binia was the daughter of an entrepreneur whose specialty was the Far East.... As a photographer born into a wealthy family, her main interest was in cutting-edge fashion and the art scene."[1017]

Arp suggested they should go to see Mondrian and arranged a visit. At the appointed time the three went together to Mondrian's studio in Rue du Départ. At that time Max's French was still fairly rudimentary compared to Binia's. She had lived a very emancipated life as a music student in Paris before she met Max Bill, and was much more eloquent and at ease in conversation.

Bill remembered that occasion very clearly: "Mondrian was very correctly dressed, the room was extremely tidy, the seating order had already been decided because in that relatively small space order was the only survival strategy. What particularly took me by surprise was the main wall in the room. It was covered with large white panels in different sizes and rhythmically accented by colored squares in red, blue, and yellow. In front of the wall there was an easel with a painting on it, and two more paintings on the floor." In fact, Bill found that wall "disconcerting, if anything." The furniture also caught his eye: "Most of the furniture had been made by Mondrian himself from planks and slats. And the furniture was white, too—accented with the three 'primary colors.' Will Grohmann's new book on the Ida Bienert collection was lying on the table."

In 1926 Piet Mondrian had designed a small (unrealized) salon for Ida Bienert, who was mother-in-law to the dancer Gret Palucca. This salon for "Madame B." was only realized in 1970 for a gallery exhibition, with a reconstruction being presented at Fondation Beyeler in 2004.

"Mondrian showed us it with quiet pride.... We made several more, less formal, visits to his studio in Rue du Départ, until Mondrian moved to Boulevard Raspail in 1936 because the building he was living in was due for demolition. His studio then took on a new look."[1018] Max Bill particularly remembered that in Rue du Départ Mondrian had "barely any books" around him—in contrast to Bill later on, whose library would eventually contain almost all the available publications by and about Piet Mondrian.

It is interesting to consider whether Mondrian in fact created such progressive art "despite himself." Certainly, his ideology could not be described as progressive. He absorbed a lot of theosophical concepts, and Robert P. Welsh broadly defined Mondrian's ideology as "metaphysical-conservative."[1019] Could we in fact apply a term coined by Ernst Bloch—"non-synchronicity" [*Ungleichzeitigkeit*]—to Mondrian's ideology and work? Whatever the case, for Mondrian as an artist his interest in theosophy meant that he did not want to engage—in ideological terms—with his materials ("that which is most superficial" in the theosophical sense). Thus the application of color(s), which Vantongerloo went into in such depth, was much less important to Mondrian. Indeed, as Bill reported, when Mondrian progressed beyond his abstract-Cubist phase he became much more interested in structures than in color. Mondrian also reached a point where he wanted to free his paintings of the three-dimensionality that had been so important to the Cubists: "So I came to make only lines and brought the color *in* these."[1020] Mondrian's linear structures became purely instinctive, and he only added colors afterward to balance out the composition. Later on Mondrian used loose strips of paper to work out the linear structures in his compositions; in New York in the 1940s he replaced those strips of paper with monochrome strips of adhesive tape.

It seems that Bill's visits to Mondrian's studio in the 1930s prompted him to experiment with the idea of a square standing on one corner. But Bill approached that motif very differently to Mondrian, who was at least a generation older. In Bill's *zweiteilige konstruktion,* a study done in 1934 (see p. 541), an orange square is overlaid with the outline of a square standing on one corner with jagged incisions cut into its lower left side. Inside the orange square there are similar incisions and outside are triangles, all of which can be read as voids or negative forms. The seemingly simple *zweiteilige konstruktion* is in reality extremely complicated.

In 1920 Mondrian published *Le Néo-plasticisme—aux hommes futurs,* in which he wrote: "jusqu'à présent, le plus extérieur domine en tout. Le féminin et le matériel régissent la vie et la société et entravent l'expression spirituelle en fonction du masculin. Dans un manifeste des futuristes, la proclamation de la haine de la femme (le féminin) est entièrement juste. C'est la femme dans l'homme qui est la cause directe de la domination du tragique dans l'art."[1021]

1019 See Welsh 1966

1020 Piet Mondrian to James Johnson Sweeney, 24 May [1943], in *Piet Mondrian: The Earlier Years* (New York: Solomon R. Guggenheim Museum, 1957), p. [7]

1021 Mondrian 1920, pp. 3–4

1022 Mondrian 1925, pp. 9–10

This text by Mondrian, translated into German and now titled "Neue Gestaltung," was published as a Bauhaus book in 1925. In the English translation, titled *The New Art—The New Life,* this passage reads: "Up to the present, the most exterior has dominated in everything. The feminine and the material rule life and society and shackle spiritual expression as a function of the masculine. A Futurist manifesto proclaiming hatred of woman (the feminine) is entirely justified. It is the Woman in Man that is the direct cause of the dominance of the tragic in art."[1022]

Jean Arp, who had recommended that Bill be accepted into Abstraction-Création, but who then left the group on 1 June 1934 following upheavals largely of his own making, once expressed his admiration for Mondrian's art—as Bill himself said—in a very simple statement: "Every artist should buy a painting by Mondrian." Of course Bill was not yet in a position to buy one himself, but he was very impressed by Mondrian. Whenever Binia and Max were in Paris they went to see him and went dancing in nightclubs with him in the evenings, although, as Max told me, while Mondrian loved dancing with Binia on those occasions, it was always in his own very stiff, wooden way.

Uncharted Artistic Terrain

When Bill visited Paris in December 1933 he and the Belgian artist Georges Vantongerloo did not yet meet face to face. However, they were soon to correspond with each other, initially and in the following year in rather formal terms; in fact Vantongerloo's first two letters to Max Bill were sent on behalf of Abstraction-Création. By the mid-1930s the two men were starting to develop a very special, friendly relationship, which then endured uninterrupted until Vantongerloo died in the autumn of 1965. Georges Vantongerloo, the older of the two by a generation, became the closest of all Max Bill's friends.

Vantongerloo, whose native language was Flemish, spoke a somewhat entertaining version of French; Max Bill, who grew up as a German speaker and had to rely on the German translation of Le Corbusier's *Vers une architecture* when he was a student at the Kunstgewerbeschule in Zurich, adopted some of Vantongerloo's linguistic idiosyncrasies.

Vantongerloo's artistic aims were not exotic, nor was he trying to seek out the heart of darkness—as described by Josef Conrad in his book of that title, which Max Bill once read. Indeed, some might have kindly described the intellectual adventures that Vantongerloo pursued as naïve, but he was always searching for philosophical-aesthetic meaning. His thoughts revolved around topics such as space and brightness. In his later years, both in his thinking and in his art, Vantongerloo turned his attention to "unlimited space." And he ultimately worked his way through to astonishing artistic outcomes, to clarity and lightness. Nowadays Vantongerloo can be named in the same breath as other pioneers of modern art—leading figures such as Brancusi, Kupka, and Mondrian. The focus of Vantongerloo's life was also the focus of his art. He unerringly strove to achieve an innovative-aesthetic equilibrium. And although he spent most of his life in France, where he died at the age of seventy-nine in October 1965 following a fall in his studio, for decades it did not occur to any of the major French museums to present a retrospective of his remarkable oeuvre.

"... beyond what seemed to be ... the permissible limits of aesthetic existence"

Bill very quickly grew to admire Vantongerloo and, at a time when they had already been close friends for many years, he attempted to situate Vantongerloo's art in a wider context by comparing it with that of the Dutch artists Bart van der Leck, Piet Mondrian, and Theo van Doesburg. In 1917, when Van Doesburg founded the journal *De Stijl* in Leiden "Piet Mondrian was painting his 'plus-minus' compositions and, under the influence of Bart van der Leck, just starting to explore the idea of planar compositions with primary colors. Van Doesburg died in Davos in 1931 at the age of forty-eight. Piet Mondrian, the oldest, died in New York in 1944 at the age of seventy-two; van der Leck redirected his artist efforts.... The youngest, Georges Vantongerloo, was the most radical from the outset.... He set out his most important ideas in two publications, *L'Art et son avenir* (written in Menton in 1919–21, published in Antwerp in 1924) and *Problems of Contemporary Art: Paintings, Sculptures, Reflections* (New York, 1948). But those texts alone would not be enough to justify his artistic existence. He achieved that in his paintings and sculptures, in which he boldly struck out into uncharted artistic

1023 Max Bill, "Georges Vantongerloo," in *Neue Zürcher Zeitung*, 29 November 1956

1024 Bill 1973

terrain. He always pursued his experiments beyond what seemed to be, at that moment, the permissible limits of aesthetic existence, and it was only years later that others could properly understand them." And Bill concluded in his article, written in 1956, that the key to the potency of Vantongerloo's art lay in exactly those "aesthetic processes."[1023]

Marlow Moss's Studio— "... incomparably clean and harmonious"

When last-minute preparations were under way for the opening of the Abstraction-Création exhibition in Paris on 22 December 1933, Max Bill suddenly caught his first glimpse of Marlow Moss, whose given name was in fact Marjorie Jewell Moss.

Marlow Moss, born into a wealthy English family, moved to Paris in 1927. Her role models in art were Rembrandt, Van Gogh, and Mondrian, whom she only first met in 1929, when she had already been in Paris for two years. The two then met regularly up until his departure in 1938 and it was Mondrian who suggested that she became a member of the group Abstraction-Création. Marlow subsequently studied with Fernand Léger.

Bill remembered looking around at the works that had already arrived, when two ladies entered the room—each carrying a package. They unpacked and propped two paintings up. "One of the ladies was very small, very thin and slight, with a slender face and lively eyes, the other was strong and tall. They were dressed identically, with flat, wide-brimmed hats." Bill looked at the paintings they had brought and said, "I'm so glad these wonderful works by Mondrian have arrived at last." There was an icy silence, and the smaller of the two women—Marlow Moss—said, "Those paintings are by me."[1024] The tall woman was Nettie Nijhoff, a Dutch writer and Marlow Moss's partner.

As it happens Bill's faux pas was not so very wide of the mark; Moss had in fact painted those compositions when she was in close contact with Mondrian and there were certainly affinities between their approaches. However, a brief dispute did flare up between Moss and Bill at that exhibition. Moss maintained that she had invented the "double line," and there is no denying that "double lines" only started to appear in Mondrian's compositions somewhat later than in Moss's paintings. Bill pointed out that Mondrian had already done the same thing in the early twenties, although he did admit that it was in a different context and "with different intentions." But the dispute soon subsided and Bill was invited by the two ladies to visit them at their country mansion, Château d'Evreux, near Paris. On his first visit they were already waiting to welcome him at the gate to the property—with Marlow in elegant riding clothes.

In 1944 the Château d'Evreux and a large proportion of Marlow Moss's early works were destroyed in an air raid.

Inside the castle Bill saw Marlow Moss's studio—incomparably clean and harmonious—with works not only of her own but also by Piet Mondrian. "The playful table decorations and exquisite food" consummately fulfilled "their functions—just like the perfect paintings. Everything was bright, fresh, transparent."[1025] During their meal, Bill was initially confused to see nasturtium flowers on the salad, not yet aware that they were edible.

In the Bibliothek Max Bill there is a copy of the prestigious art journal *Cahiers d'art* from the first quarter of 1934; toward the end of that issue there is news of the latest exhibitions, some of which are also reviewed. Readers are informed that Galerie Jeanne Bucher in Paris, where Max Bill would very much like to have shown his work, was currently presenting works by Paule Vézelay (born Marjorie Watson-Williams in Bristol, England), who had been a member of Abstraction-Création for some time but who—as the critic points out—had not succumbed to the group's "dogmatism" and was "closer to Arp" than to the group's (unnamed) "promoters."

It is interesting to note that none of the women members of Abstraction-Création—not even the most prominent—ever had a solo exhibition at the group's gallery. Paule Vézelay had joined Abstraction-Création in 1934 and was certainly close to Jean Arp, as the critic had suggested. Indeed a photograph has survived showing Paule Vézelay in a bathing suit, in the south of France, next to the still fully clad Jean Arp.[1026]

1025 Bill 1973
1026 Alley 1987
1027 Alley 1987
1028 Unknown author, *Cahiers d'art* 9:1–4 (1934)
1029 For more on Vézelay's life and work, see the catalogue for the retrospective *Paule Vézelay,* which was presented at the Tate Gallery in London in 1983; Vézelay, who lived to witness that exhibition in her honor, died just nine months later, in March 1984
1030 *Cahiers d'art* 9:1–4 (1934)

In 1983, when I visited Marguerite Arp-Hagenbach, Arp's second wife, in Locarno-Solduno, and we looked at that photograph of Paule Vézelay and Arp, she remarked: "Arp liked women with plump thighs."

Two months after the Second World War broke out, Vézelay left France and returned to England. She spent most of the war in Bristol (1939–44), "where her work included some drawings of bomb damage."[1027]

"She avoided the pitfall that catches out most members of the Abstraction-Création group with whom she has been associated for some time, by not accepting their dogmatism that demands the irrevocable execution of the subject. Closer to Arp than to the promoters of this group, Vézelay always grasps the object."[1028]

Paule Vézelay was in fact born Marjorie Agnes Watson-Williams in Clifton, Bristol, in 1892. She lived with the Surrealist André Masson for four years, from 1939 to 1932. When she fell in love she was already thirty-six years old; he was three years her junior, married, with a child. Vézelay and Masson painted "side by side." Masson divorced his wife and in April 1932 wanted to marry Vézelay, who suddenly lost interest in him; following her separation from Masson, her own art also ceased to be at all "surreal": The most important influence on her from then onward was Jean Arp. She seems to have met him in or around 1933, and the two soon became close friends.[1029]

That issue of *Cahiers d'art* also reports on an exhibition devoted to the work of the late Van Doesburg: "Theo van Doesburg (Abstraction-Creation gallery)."

The black and red on this invitation card is an exception; all the other extant invitation cards for Abstraction-Création exhibitions are printed in monochrome black. This posthumous solo exhibition of the work of Van Doesburg ran from 16 to 30 March 1934.

"The works exhibited by friends of this artist, who died relatively young, take us back to the time of the first efforts to reject the motif in favor of non-figuration, which has now become the basis of a whole school. Van Doesburg, Mondrian, Vantongerloo and others have led this school."[1030] This is one of the rare examples of Vantongerloo being recognized as a "leader," as a pioneer on the same footing as Van Doesburg and Mondrian. That solo exhibition was immediately followed by another exhibition with not only eight living members of the group, including Freundlich, Gleizes, and Gorin, but also the late co-founder of the group, Van Doesburg (30 March–12 April 1934). Also in that same issue of *Cahiers d'art* Christian Zervos (editor-in-chief) published an article on Brancusi, whose work had been on display in New York until 13 January 1934.

Last, but not least, there was an article by Sigfried Giedion on the civil engineer and bridge-construction expert Robert Maillart ("Nouveaux ponts de Maillart").

This overview of events in Paris in *Cahiers d'art* also indicates that the Association des Écrivains et Artistes Révolutionnaires (A.E.A.R.) wanted to organize an exhibition in the Palais des Expositions in January and February 1935. The group's exhortation (also published in this overview) to artists to stand shoulder to shoulder with the "rising" class, "to integrate" themselves into this class—namely, the proletariat—is signed by figures such as Herbin, the president of Abstraction-Création, Laurens, Lurçat, Ozenfant and Signac ("c'est de l'intégrer à la classe qui "monte," elle seule peut restituer sa vraie fonction sociale.")

Many years later Max Bill published his book on Robert Maillart.

Zervos's article reflected the hope that many artists—mostly on the political left—would now invest in the "coming class," the proletariat. Zervos remarked that Brancusi, like others, wanted to bring moments of happiness to the wider public—but it was a one-sided love, which was not returned by "the people." That was the great tragedy: instead of being liberated from exploitation, ordinary people were now witnessing the ever-more horrifying expansion of Fascism. As Zervos put it in his exhibition review: "Brancusi's oeuvre is realized for the masses that he would have labored for had he not been prevented from doing so by the prevailing social circumstances and attitudes." That generation of artists who were no longer obliged to seek work from princes and the church now pinned their faith in the "citizen." "Brancusi has a strong desire to share his joy in creation ... and this is why his sculptures should in fact be seen as models of works to be executed on a large scale, for the pleasure of all the citizens who may like to install them in public spaces."[1031] Max Bill soon demonstrated the same ambitions—and as such he was a legitimate successor to Brancusi.

In the catalogue for the New York Brancusi exhibition (Brummer Gallery, 1933–34) there is a pithy, handwritten comment by the artist himself: "Don't look for obscure formulas or mysteries. I am giving you pure joy."[1032]

1031 Cited in Christian Zervos, "Réflexions sur Brancusi à propos de son exposition à New York," *Cahiers d'art* 9:1–4 (1934)

1032 Zervos, "Reflexions sur Brancusi"

1033 Georges Vantongerloo, Paris, to Jean Arp, Meudon, 6 June 1934, Vantongerloo-Archiv

Power Struggles in the "Comité"

By spring 1934 the Abstraction-Création committee was already entangled in power struggles. It was a perfectly simple problem: the committee had previously decided in a democratic vote that the reproductions of works by members in the group's own yearly journals should all be the same size. However, in April 1934, certain members wanted to ignore that decision, with those in favor arguing that the "better" works should receive preferential treatment in the form of larger illustrations. Vantongerloo spoke out against that undemocratic innovation.

In *Abstraction-Création* no. 3 (1934) the main focus—in large illustrations—was on works by members of the committee. Meanwhile, works by eight women artists (including Barbara Hepworth and Marlow Moss) and by Abstraction-Création members living abroad who could not leap to their own defense in Paris (such as Josef Albers in the United States and Max Bill in Switzerland) were only illustrated in small-format images. Those names alone demonstrate that the argument that "better" works should be seen in better illustrations was no more than a ploy—a shot across the bows in a conflict that would soon cause part of the group to break away.

The following artists each had one large image of their work reproduced: Arp, Béothy, Calder, Domela, Freundlich, Fernandez, Gleizes, Gorin, Hélion, Herbin, Kupka, Moholy-Nagy, Mondrian, Power, Seligmann, Schwitters, Taeuber-Arp (the only woman), Valmier, Kandinsky, Brancusi, González, Vordemberge-Gildewart and Vantongerloo (although the latter opposed the revised decision).

Robert Delaunay wrote to the committee in protest, objecting to the use of discriminatory image formats and again arguing in favor of a uniform format, thus coming down on Vantongerloo's side.

Robert Delaunay, a longstanding friend of the Arps, told Vantongerloo that the Arps were intending to step down. It is fair to assume that Jean Arp was the driving force in this move.

On 1 June 1934 Jean Arp, Sophie Taeuber-Arp, Fernandez, and Hélion all resigned from Abstraction-Création, directing their barbed complaints at Auguste Herbin, the president of the group. But Vantongerloo then objected to that move in a letter to Jean Arp, in which he cited Delaunay's objections: "It was specifically you [Arp] and Hélion who wanted to discriminate and decide which members are given large images and or not."[1033]

László Moholy-Nagy, Max's former master at the Bauhaus—one of the many artists now facing an extremely uncertain future—would soon leave Germany. However, before he emigrated he had one last chance to exhibit in Paris. As a member of Abstraction-Création he was able to present a solo exhibition of his work at the gallery on Avenue de Wagram, from 15 June 1934 until the end of the month—at exactly the time when the group was in turmoil. Moholy-Nagy traveled to Paris with his new partner, Sibyl, whose memories of that visit were dominated by the artists she encountered with Moholy-Nagy: "I don't remember how long we stayed. Any lesser impressions have been erased by the men we visited—Brancusi, Vantongerloo, Arp, Mondrian. They were Paris to me."[1034]

While the internal conflict at Abstraction-Création worsened, others were living things up in Paris. And at one of those parties, put on by Hans Schiess and Kurt Seligmann—two Swiss artists living in Paris—Meret Oppenheim met Sophie and Jean Arp.[1035] In fact Sophie Taeuber-Arp, Schiess, and Seligmann had good reason to celebrate because May 1934 saw the release of Anatole Jakovsky's new book *H. Erni, H. Schiess, K. Seligmann, S. H. Taeuber-Arp, G. Vulliamy*—ironically enough it was published by Éditions Abstraction-Création, that is to say, by the very group that Sophie and her husband had just split away from.

The book was designed by Sophie Taeuber-Arp; although this is not stated in the book, it is evident from a letter to Georges Vantongerloo from Sophie Taeuber-Arp herself.[1036]

Kurt Seligmann also had a studio in Basel where Meret Oppenheim remembered first meeting Max Ernst "in the late autumn of 1934." This was the encounter that ultimately led to the "passionate love on both sides"[1037] that we have already alluded to here in connection with Max Bill and Max Ernst's visit to La Barca in the Ticino.

Jean Arp urged Barbara Hepworth and her husband, Ben Nicholson, to leave Abstraction-Création. It is not clear if he also prompted Piet Mondrian to leave, but Vantongerloo certainly blamed him for Mondrian's departure, which he rightly felt was a serious blow to the group. César Domela and Hans Erni also left, as did František Kupka later on in September 1934.

Kupka addressed his letter of resignation to Vantongerloo, who was overseeing daily business in Herbin's absence: "My dear President, in my present state of health I must avoid becoming over-tired, and, unable

1034 Moholy-Nagy 1950, p. 113

1035 Oppenheim 2007, p. 195–96

1036 See Sophie Taeuber-Arp, Meudon, to Georges Vantongerloo, 23 January 1935, Vantongerloo–Archiv

1037 Oppenheim 2007, pp. 196

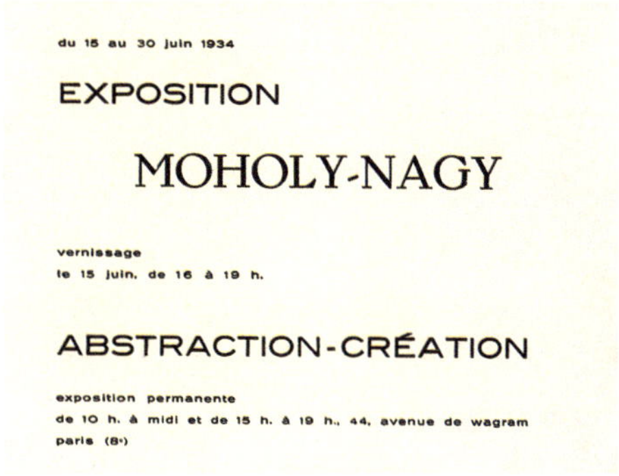

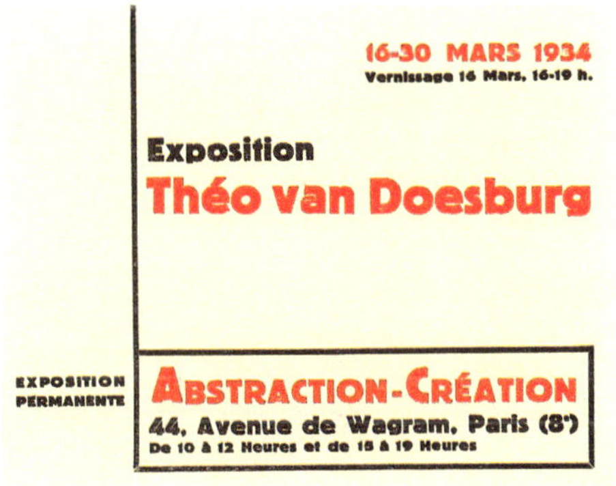

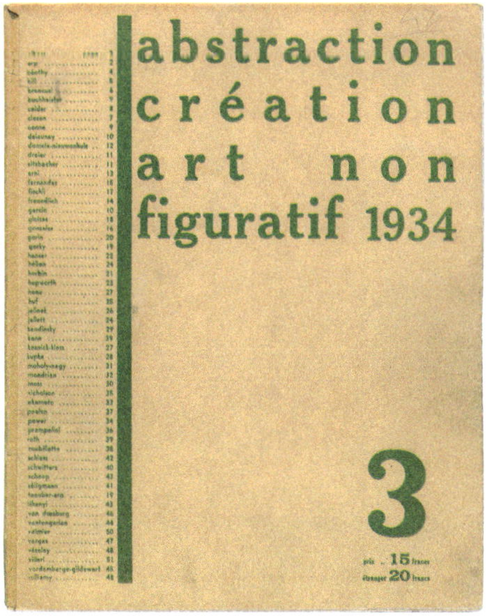

Invitation card for *Exposition Moholy-Nagy* at the Abstraction–Création gallery, June 1934
Invitation card for the post-humous exhibition *Théo van Doesburg* at the Abstraction–Création gallery, March 1934
Cover of *Abstraction–Création* 3 (1934)

Binia Bill, Max Bill with jazz musicians in his Steyr, on the paved drive outside the garage in Höngg, 1930s

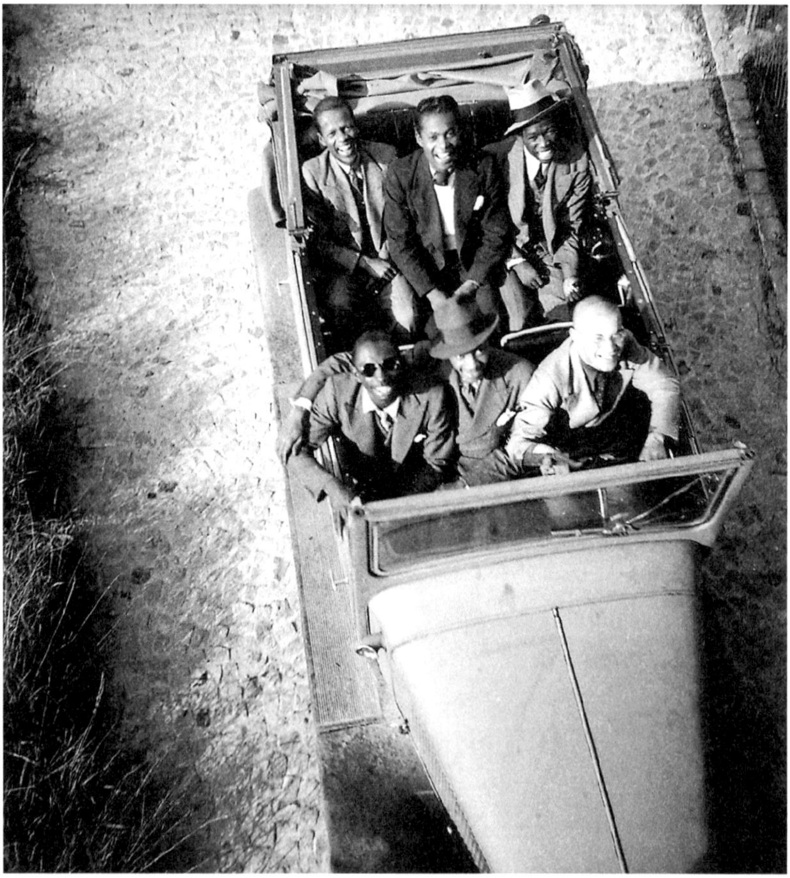

to see any chance of useful collaboration in Abstraction-Creation, I therefore ask you to kindly accept my resignation both as a committee member and as an ordinary member. Kupka."[1038]

Max Bill and Kupka did not meet at that time; they only met after the Second World War, in Paris in October or November 1945.

In a separate development Herbin, the president of Abstraction-Création, now found himself in serious financial straits and was no longer able to survive in the city, so he left Paris for the countryside.

Otto Freundlich, who wanted to fight on the side of the revolutionary proletariat, resigned in November 1934 and his partner, the painter Jeanne Kosnick-Kloss, left the group with him. Jeanne was also a trained pianist and had given recitals at the Bauhaus in the past. Freundlich explained his decision: "Dear Vantongerloo, in these crucial times the place of a revolutionary artist can only be alongside the revolutionary proletariat, and because I have taken this position, my artistic evolution is now solely linked to the progress of the revolution and I have no other interests. I wish your group good fortune. With cordial greetings, Otto Freundlich."[1039] Before long the Nazis would seize fourteen works by Otto Freundlich from German museums, some of which would subsequently go on show in *Entartete Kunst* in 1937.

Freundlich was interned in France in September 1939 but was released again in February 1940—partly because both Pablo Picasso and Sophie Taeuber-Arp pleaded his case. He managed to flee to Saint-Paul-de-Fenouillet in the eastern Pyrenees, only to be arrested there on 23 March 1943. Soon after that he was deported to Poland from Degostinet, a transit camp near Paris, and killed at the Lublin-Maidanek concentration camp in 1943.

Otto Freundlich's archive was rescued by Jeanne (Hannah) Kosnick-Kloss, who survived the Second World War. Since 1969 the Musée de Pontoise (France) has been home to the Association Les Amis de Jeanne et Otto Freundlich.

In 1988 an exhibition of paintings by Otto Freundlich, with loans from the Musée de Pontoise, was presented at the Musée départemental de Rochechouart, Limoges. This was accompanied by the first French-language monograph on his work: Alain Bonfand et al., *Otto Freundlich* (Paris: Éditions de la Différence).

1038 Kupka, 7 rue Le maitre, Puteaux, Seine, 14 September 1934, letter in *Abstraction-Création,* Vantongerloo-Archiv

1039 Otto Freundlich, 38 rue Denfert-Rochereau, Paris Ve, to Georges Vantongerloo, Paris, 22 November 1934, Vantongerloo-Archiv

Max Bill: Car Enthusiast and Jazz Fan

In August 1931, when Binia and Max Bill were still living in Zurich at Goldbrunnenstrasse 141, Bill bought a car—an Erskine. His next car was a Steyr, bought in early 1932. Bill was not the only fan of Steyr cars, Bertolt Brecht was another.

"It is a well known fact—and a barely excusable source of embarrassment in the Brecht community—that Brecht wrote a paean to a luxury convertible built by the Steyr automobile company and was given exactly that model by the company. His workings for the Steyr poem still exist in his notebook ('rear wheels pulsate separately')."[1040]

Brecht's texts with their Marxist dialectics appealed to Bill, who also liked singing texts of that sort.

Max Bill compiled some Brecht texts in a slim volume, with a typed cover design consisting of a horizontal line of the letter b intersecting with a vertical line of the letter b (estate of Max Bill left to Angela Thomas).

Brecht increasingly became an irritant to the Nazis and in July 1935 he was expatriated; with no option but to leave he then emigrated to the United States via Scandinavia and the Soviet Union.

In 1944–45 Max Bill took up a post teaching theory of form at the Kunstgewerbeschule in Zurich, the same institution that he had been expelled from as a student. It was Johannes Itten, now director of the Kunstgewerbeschule, who appointed him. Ernst Scheidegger, a student at the Kunstgewerbeschule at the time, remembered Bill's arrival: "... people had already been talking about Bill. We were standing outside the school building when he appeared in his Adler, an old-fashioned car, like a typewriter ... but then he just drove straight past us—it was very baffling. We were of course all thrilled that we could take his preliminary course."[1041]

Max Bill rarely talked to me about his son Jakob "Joggi" Bill, who was born in 1942 and enjoyed a "liberal but not anti-authoritarian upbringing." Just occasionally he would recall incidents involving his son—for

1040 Susanne Beyer, "Abschied vom Beton-Brecht," in *Der Spiegel,* 11 February 2008, p. 142

1041 Ernst Scheidegger, in Schmid 2008

1042 Max Bill to Georges Vantongerloo, Paris, 11 November 1946, Vantongerloo-Archiv

1043 Max Bill, Zurich, to Georges Vantongerloo, Paris, 23 November 1949, Vantongerloo-Archiv

instance, "when Jakob was still small, whenever he was bitten by a midge he would put one hand on his forehead and say, 'I've got a headache!'"

Jakob is left-handed and as an adult —in the right light conditions— he also paints. As painters, father and son took a different technical approach. And, as Max Bill once told me, "Jakob also varnishes his paintings very carefully, months after he has finished them—he waits as long as possible, until the paint is properly dry, unlike me," adding that Jakob always reproached him for that.

In November 1946 Binia and Max sent Jakob to Max's father Erwin Bill, in Ligerz on Lake Biel, for a short stay.

"my boy is at my father's, on holiday."[1042] By way of an exception here, Max Bill mentions his father in correspondence with his close friend Vantongerloo.

Afterward, when Jakob was back home again, Bill took his young son with him to look for bargains at a car saleroom.

In December 1949 Bill bought a Lancia Augusta; he needed a new car, as he told Vantongerloo, because just a week before the exhibition *Pevsner Vantongerloo Bill* closed at Kunsthaus Zürich on 13 November 1949 (a particularly important exhibition for Bill), he had written his present car off.

"a week before the end of the exhibition i destroyed my car, since which i have become a pedestrian. it's both convenient and very safe."[1043]

He did often drive rather fast. His next, even more impressive purchase of a car came in 1951. When Bill was awarded the very valuable grand prize for sculpture at the São Paolo Biennial, he was able to realize a dream he had had for a long time and acquired a Bentley Mark VI.

The date the Bentley was purchased is recorded by Jakob Bill in "Persönliche Notizen zur Geschichte des Hauses Bill in Höngg," in Arthur Rüegg and Jakob Bill, *Das Atelierhaus Max Bill 1932/33* (Zurich: Niggli, 1997), p. 96.

Years later Bill even bought a Rolls-Royce Silver Cloud—a "bargain," as he told me, a snip at "only 30,000 Swiss francs." It had the steering wheel on the right, it was silver-gray with fine lilac stripes, and Bill drove his "Jolls Joyce" as if it were a temporarily domesticated big cat that could at any moment pounce forward with all its might. The four garages attached to the house in Zumikon that Bill designed and built in 1967–68 were home to the Rolls-Royce, an Audi, and a red BMW that Binia drove.

Bill was always a keen jazz fan and one day—in his own, unconventional way—he brought five jazz musicians home with him in his splendid car. As they arrived at Höngg Binia photographed the delightedly laughing musicians with Max Bill at the wheel of his Steyr (see p. 594).

The jazz musicians are not named and the photograph is not dated. Since Binia and Max Bill left their rented apartment in Golbrunnenstrasse in Zurich on 1 April 1933 and moved into the new house in Höngg, built by Bill, that same month, the photograph cannot have been taken before April 1933.

In November 1934 Louis Armstrong and his band had a sell-out concert at the Tonhalle in Zurich. The audience cheered. And in December 1935 the world-famous jazz saxophonist Coleman Hawkins played in Zurich.

"With Warm Regards"

In January 1935 Bill sent Vantongerloo an image of a sculpture to be published in *Abstraction-Création* no. 4.

Vantongerloo replied by return of post "with warm regards" on 15 January. And just a few days later another letter arrived for Bill from Vantongerloo, in which the latter referred to the quarrels at Abstraction-Création and the resignations of certain committee members.

On 28 January 1935 Bill replied in German because he felt he could "only express himself imprecisely" in French. In this letter he was also mildly critical of the graphic design of *Abstraction-Création* (see pp. 593, 611).

Vantongerloo, who took his responsibilities at the artists' group Abstraction-Création very seriously, again replied by return post, on this occasion also expressing the hope that he and Bill might at last meet face to face.

Moholy-Nagy, in London by now, had heard of the trouble at Abstraction-Création and had been in touch with Mondrian about it: "Dear Vantongerloo ... I wrote to Mondrian telling him that I greatly regret the fact that many of our comrades are behaving so short-sightedly regarding their membership and are close to destroying all of A-C's achievements in these extremely hazardous times. Mondrian also expressed his regret but said that the cause was unfortunately dissent among the comrades

bill-zürich

bill zürich 10 limmattalstrasse 253 telefon 67.567 postcheck VIII 18.442

m. g.vantongerloo
"abstraction création"
paris XIV
7 impasse du rouet

ihre zeichen | ihre nachricht | meine zeichen | tag
28.1.35

betrifft
cahier no 4

lieber vantongerloo,

entschuldigen sie bitte, dass ich ihnen deutsch schreibe, leider kann ich mich französisch nur ungenau ausdrücken und möchte nicht, dass missverständnisse aufkommen könnten.

ich begraiffe ihre stellungsnahme gut, schade dass wir von diesem generalversammlungsbeschluss nichts wussten, sonst hätten wir natürlich nicht nach dem heft no.3 disponiert. wir hatten angenommen, dass jedem mitglied eine seite zur verfügung stehe und eine bestimmte klischeegrösse, da wir annahmen, dass ihnen die klischees,welche wir wünschten zu teuer zu stehen kämen, liessen wir diese hier auf unsere kosten herstellen und ihnen mit freipass zustellen, sodass ihnen die zollauslagen bei der rücksendung voll vergütet worden wären. ich wusste nicht dass das in paris solche mühe [illegible] macht und bitte sie deshalb vielmals um entschuldigung, es war in keiner weise unsere absicht.

ich bin der ansicht, dass kunstwerke im vornherein zu einer schlechten wirkung verurteilt sind durch die grafische reproduktion, deshalb glaube ich, dass an stelle der grösseren anzahl (2 stück) die grössere abbildung (1stück) treten sollte, wenn das betreffende mitglied das wünscht, eine ergänzung des generalversammlungsbeschlusses in dieser richtung sollte in erwägung gezogen werden.

ich sende ihnen beiliegend 2 fotos von derselben plastik, in der absicht beide zu zeigen, um ein imfassenderes bild davon zu geben. meine letzten bilder haben leider solche feinheiten, dass sie in der reproduktion vollkommen falsch erscheinen würden, was bei fischli im allgemeinen auch so zutrifft. die restierenden frs.5o.-lege ich ihnen gleichzeitig bei.

ich danke ihnen noch vielmals für ihre bemühungen und bitte sie die verschiedenen missgeschicke entschuldigen zu wollen.

ich bin mit den besten grüssen

ihr bill

beilagen: 2 klischeevorlagen / frs.5o in noten

Letter from Max Bill to Georges Vantongerloo, 28 January 1937, typewritten on "bill-zürich" letterhead

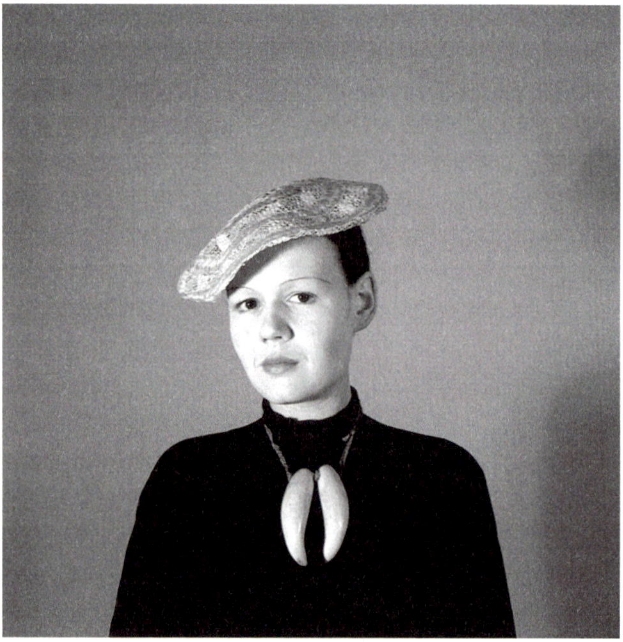

Binia Bill, Verena Loewensberg with hat
and walrus tusk pendant, 1934

Max Bill, Design for a wall painting
at the exhibition *Land- und Ferienhaus*
in Basel (interior of Hall V), 1935

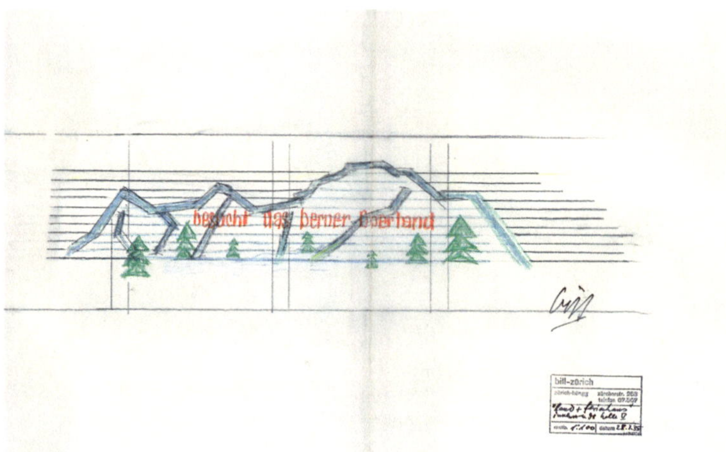

in Paris. What exactly is the situation? With very warm greetings, yours, L. Moholy-Nagy."[1044]

"In London I heard depressing accounts of the arguments at A.-C. and I am extremely sorry to see that the members want to destroy the very instrument that can give them security and the strength to face the world together."[1045]

The Brussels International Exposition—Expo 35

In early 1935 the architect Ernst F. Burckhardt once again called on Bill to collaborate on a project—this time it was the exhibition *Land- und Ferienhaus* in Basel. In response Bill created a 1:100 design for a wall painting with the words "besucht das berner oberland" (visit the Bernese uplands).

This two-part, colored design for the interior walls of Hall V, signed by Max Bill and dated 28 March 1935, has survived in the estate of Ernst F. Burckhardt in the gta Archiv at ETH Zürich. To the best of my knowledge it has not previously been published anywhere.

Bill was also commissioned to design the signage for the Swiss pavilion (with exhibition architecture by Hans Hofmann) at Expo 35 and to produce an image with Swiss mountains for the Schweizerische Verkehrszentrale (Swiss travel center) at the same exhibition.

In the spring of 1935 Binia and Max Bill traveled to Belgium with Verena "Vreni" Loewensberg and her husband Hans Coray. Verena Loewensberg (born in Zurich in 1912) was from a family of Jewish grain merchants who had immigrated from Germany. In the years immediately after the First World War Verena's father had a practice as a country doctor in Sissach (canton of Basel Landschaft).

"Verena had fond memories of accompanying her father on visits to isolated farms and of the rural atmosphere, although there were two sides to that: she loved the landscape and nature, but she hated the school with its harsh educational methods.... Her parents took an interest in cultural matters, even if their approach to art, literature, and music was relatively conservative."[1046]

1044 László Moholy-Nagy [handwritten in German], 7 Farm Walk, London NW11, to Georges Vantongerloo, Paris (28 August 1935), Vantongerloo-Archiv

1045 László Moholy-Nagy to Georges Vantongerloo, Paris, 12 February 1935, Vantongerloo-Archiv

1046 Bucher 1992, p. 10

Verena, whose mother abandoned her degree in medicine after giving birth to her, was the oldest of four siblings. Later on Bill was in contact with her brother Dieter, born in 1914, who became a physician.

Verena studied dance with Trudi Schoop for two years in Zurich and in 1932, at the age of twenty, she married the Romance philologist Hans Coray; her new father-in-law was the art dealer Han Coray, who was one of the first to take a keen interest in design as such. The newlyweds spent 1933 in Ascona before setting up home in Kirchgasse in Zurich in 1934.

The Corso building on Theaterstrasse near Bellevue was refurbished in 1934–35, and Verena Loewensberg and Hans Coray were among the first to rent an apartment there. Verena had a "large work table" in their small apartment, where she started to paint and—influenced by Hans Fischli—experimented with colored "drawings on plaster panels."[1047] Since the Loewensberg-Corays barely had any money Verena also worked in a photographer's laboratory. It was at the Corso that Verena first encountered the Bills: "I very soon met Max Bill and Binia Bill. Bill was in commercial art, Binia in photography. They were the first people with any real understanding of art that I got to know."[1048]

It is striking that in this statement, while Verena Loewensberg refers to Bill as a graphic artist, which is of course true—he had just designed the letter for the Corso sign—here is a major omission, namely no mention is made of the fact that he was an artist, who had, after all,already created such pioneering Concrete art works as *wellrelief* (1931–32) and *lange plastik* (1933), with the latter already having been exhibited in Paris at Abstraction-Création in December 1933. It may be that this in part reflects the squabbles about who first produced Concrete works. Following her time in Paris and visits to the studio Georges Vantongerloo, Verena Loewensberg starting producing Concrete art in or around 1936.

Verena Loewensberg, who was always extremely tastefully dressed and wore cashmere sweaters whenever possible, remained a lifelong friend of Max and Binia's. Yet, for all their friendship and mutual understanding, Verena always maintained a certain distance and Max Bill remembered her cultivating a "mysterious" aura, even on the occasions when she sat for Binia.

Following that trip to Belgium Verena Loewensberg briefly studied in Paris at the Académie Moderne, which had been founded by Edwige

1047 Bucher 1992, p. 11
1048 Verena Loewensberg cited in Bucher 1992, p. 13 note 14
1049 Auguste Herbin to Georges Vantongerloo, 1 September 1935, Vantongerloo-Archiv

Schlaepfer (from St. Gallen). Edwige Schlaepfer, who taught "engraving, etching, and aquatint" at the school, was a member of Abstraction-Création, as were two more teachers at the academy, namely, Auguste Herbin and Georges Vantongerloo.

It was Vantongerloo, head of "sculpture & mathématique" at the Académie, who helped to ensure that his colleague, Herbin, was appointed as a teacher of painting and frescos. This position allowed Herbin, a Communist in financial straits, to return to Paris from the provinces and to resume his duties as president of Abstraction-Création, where Vantongerloo (as vice president) had been standing in for him: "We will joyfully resume our good work and take up the good fight again in Paris."[1049]

Verena Loewensberg (who did not make any sculptures, as far as I know) studied with Herbin but was also very taken with Vantongerloo's aesthetic ideas. She greatly admired his work and later bought his painting *Lignes et intervalles* (1937).

In Zurich in 1937 Leo Leuppi founded Allianz, as an association for modern Swiss artists. The board consisted of Leuppi (president), Richard Paul Lohse (vice president), Walter Bodmer (a founder member from Basel), and Hans Erni (from Lucerne).

Bill told me that he had only signed the Allianz constitution once a passage that read "as regards politics and religion, the association is neutral" had been deleted, following his reminder to his colleagues that in the year 1937 there could no longer be any such thing as political neutrality.

From Max Bill's point of view—as he told me, looking back in 1975—Allianz was "primarily a joint venture to secure exhibitions and maintain an ideological stand against Fascism." Opponents of Allianz attacked and decried it as "Bolshevist."

Having spent some time drawing and painting shells and organic forms, in the late 1930s—not long after Max Bill first conceived his *fünfzehn variationen über ein thema* in 1935 and Hans Hinterreiter started work on his systematic paintings—Verena Loewensberg created the next examples of Concrete art in Switzerland. She now became a true pioneer of Concrete art. In 1937 she joined the Swiss artists' group Allianz, which Max Bill also joined, although he was not entirely at ease with the group's stylistic pluralism, that is to say, the convergence of influences from Surrealism, Cubism, and Concrete art.

Camille Graeser and Richard Paul Lohse, the other two Concrete artists working in Switzerland at that time and whose names are still familiar today, only really started to engage with the problems of systematic pictorial construction "in the early 1940s."[1050] Bill had clear memories of his first visit to Lohse in the Zett-Haus: "On the walls there were dark, Braque-like paintings," as he told me.[1051] Lohse also remembered those early days and told me that, among other things, he had "packed condoms" to earn money. His "shoe soles were made from cardboard" and in wet weather they squeaked so badly—he imitated the noise—that when he went to the exclusive Baur au Lac restaurant in Zurich he had to "enter by the back door."[1052] Of course he was not usually seen in exclusive restaurants but was more likely to be found in Restaurant Eintracht, which was frequented by leftists and others connected with Fritz Brupbacher, the physician who devoted his time to the poor and needy.

La Cambre in Brussels

On their trip to Brussels in spring 1935 the Bills visited Binia's older sister Klara and her husband Alex Bosshard. Binia got on well with Klara and when she was still studying cello in Paris, before she married Max Bill, she had often made the trip to Brussels, where she always stayed with Klara and Alex in their apartment (in a building designed by Bosshard) opposite La Cambre. After graduating from the Kunstgewerbeschule in Zurich, Klara Bosshard had continued her studies in Brussels at La Cambre, an *institut supérieur des arts décoratifs.* La Cambre, founded by Henry van de Velde, was both a school of architecture and a training center for various artistic occupations.[1053]

Max Bill had designed an address card for his sister-in-law: "klara bosshard bruxelles 38 avenue emile duray telf. 488514" (typography estate of Max Bill, collection of Angela Thomas). This address card, 10.5×4 cm, is mentioned in Max Bill, *Typografie Reklame Buchgestaltung* (Sulgen and Zurich: Niggli, 1999), p. 272, where it is dated 1933.

1050 Bill 1969 [a]
1051 Max Bill in conversation with Angela Thomas, 22 February 1976
1052 Richard Paul Lohse in conversation with Angela Thomas, 23 February 1976
1053 See Deleroy, Culot And Van Loo 1979
1054 Arthur Rüegg, "Concrete Construction? Three examples," in *Max Bill Arquitecto / Architect = 2G: International Architecture Review* 29/30 (2004) (Spanish and English), pp. 50–51
1055 Bill 1980 [a]

Max Bill would again be in contact with his brother-in-law, Alex Bosshard —an architect and young entrepreneur—in connection with Durisol, a "promising new" building material; when the Second World War broke out the production of Durisol was relocated from Belgium to Switzerland. The two men were in contact in 1942, for instance, in connection with Haus Villiger, which Bill was building in Bremgarten (Switzerland). "at the beginning of the 1930s [Alex Bosshard] had been involved in Belgium in the development of a building system that used the promising new material."[1054]

Bill was already familiar with the career of Henry van de Velde, who had set up the School of Arts and Crafts in Weimar, where he had remained until 1917. Since Van de Velde had been granted a German passport when he was appointed to his chair in Weimar, he was eventually expected to play a part in the war—but he could not countenance that as a pacifist and a socialist. In the end he managed he to escape to Switzerland with help from the psychiatrist Ludwig Binswanger.

Before he left Germany Van de Velde expressly stated his wish that Walter Gropius would continue to develop the work had done in Weimar. His wish was fulfilled, and Gropius took on the onerous role of first director of the newly founded Bauhaus in Weimar and subsequently in Dessau.

In 1926, eight years after the First World War had ended, Van de Velde received an invitation to return to his native Belgium "to take up a chair in the history of architecture at the University of Ghent and to become director of the new Institut supérieur des arts décoratifs in Brussels. This gave Van de Velde the opportunity to create a whole new curriculum. The new school in Brussels was to be housed in La Cambre, a former monastery. Among the young architects there we also find Victor Bourgeois, who was born in 1897. . . . Henry van de Velde was the director at La Cambre until 1935 and retired from his chair in Ghent a year later. In Ghent he designed both the library tower and the university's art history institute. Together with Eggerix and Verwilghen, younger colleagues from La Cambre, he designed the Belgian pavilion for Expo 37 in Paris and he also worked with Victor Bourgeois and Leon Stijnen (his successor at La Cambre) on the design of the Belgian pavilion for the New York World's Fair in 1939. In 1947, for health reasons, Van de Velde moved to Switzerland, where he participated in events at the Swiss Werkbund and also actively supported the founding of the Hochschule für Gestaltung in Ulm."[1055]

In the spring of 1935 László Moholy-Nagy was in Brussels, too, working on a commission for Expo 35; in fact, already uprooted by the political situation, Moholy-Nagy was on his way to London, where his loved ones were anxiously waiting for news from him. Another acquaintance of Max Bill's, Hermann Scherchen, was also in Brussels at that time. He was there to conduct Wladimir Vogel's *Wagadus Untergang durch die Eitelkeit* for solo voices, choir, and five saxophones (1930). It was in this oratorio that Vogel first gave a leading role to a "Sprechchor" (a "speaking" choir) —an idea that he had borrowed from worker's music-making.[1056]

A copy of *Wagadus Untergang durch die Eitelkeit* plus a recording of the oratorio on vinyl (Die Quadratbücher 18, ed. Hans Rudolf Hilty [St. Gallen: Tschudy, 1961]) is still in the Bibliothek Max Bill; this publication contains "ancient Berber minstrels' tales" recorded by Leo Frobenius, photographs, and the libretto of the oratorio; it was issued to mark the 65th birthday of Wladimir Vogel, who was born on 29 February 1896.

Aline Valangin, who was married to the lawyer Wladimir Rosenbaum, had trained as a pianist but a hand injury prevented her from pursuing it as a career on the instrument. Aline, "always ready to help anyone, took a particular interest in Vogel, the musician, and put all her energy into facilitating the performance of *Wagadu* that was planned for the World's Fair in Brussels."[1057]

Scherchen had originally planned to perform *Wagadus Untergang* with the choir of the Palais des beaux-arts, but difficulties arose. "Harry Goldschmidt, a journalist at the *National-Zeitung* in Basel at the time, put him in contact with a choir in Basel—the Sterk'scher private choir—which agreed to learn Vogel's oratorio." In the basement of the Müller-Widmanns' home in Basel, the French libretto was translated by a number of people "not in employment"—presumably émigrés without work permits. Having been "reworked (to fit the music) by Madame Aline in Zurich, together with J. P. Samson and the composer, it was then inserted into the vocal parts."[1058]

The writer Jean-Paul Samson played a part in this; he was Bill's former fellow performer at the short-lived, semi-political cabaret, the Krater in Zurich, and subsequently wrote articles for the anti-Fascist, wholly political periodical *information.*

After three months of rehearsals in Basel *Wagadus Untergang* received a "brilliant performance" at Expo 35 (to quote Vogel's biographer Hans Oesch). One wonders, did Bill and the others witness that moment? It seems highly likely, since Bill was already in close professional contact with Hermann Scherchen.

1056 See Pauli and Wünsche 1986
1057 Oesch 1967, p. 62
1058 Oesch 1967, p. 62

In 1937—as previously mentioned—Hermann Scherchen's music publishing house, Ars Viva, now citing Brussels as its place of publication, brought out a new score—*Joh. Seb. Bach, Musikalisches Opfer, Version Roger Vuataz, Partition*—with the standard cover design by Bill; Scherchen and Bill remained in contact and would soon meet again in Gstaad.

On that same trip to Expo 35 in Belgium the Bills and the Loewensberg-Corays, traveling together, bought a number of chow-chow dogs, who—left alone in a hotel room—prepared a surprise for their new owners by chewing up several cushions and sending feathers flying everywhere.

"Laissons ça, et travaillons!"

On his return from Brussels Bill wrote a registered express letter to Vantongerloo, mentioning in passing that he had been working at Expo 35. More importantly, he voiced some concerns he had about issue of *Abstraction-Création,* such as the fact that Fischli had not had a full page to himself as Vantongerloo had said he would, although he did concede that there might be some technical reason for this. He also asked why there were no illustrations of works by some of the group's leading members, namely Mondrian, Hélion, Calder, Arp, and Vordemberge, only reproductions of works by "inexact" artists and imitators (whom he does not name). Bill was clearly disturbed by these editorial decisions and was sure, as he writes, that Vantongerloo would be of the same opinion; indeed, as he adds, in a reactionary era such as their own it was all the more necessary for "*tous les abstraits*"—all the abstract artists—to stick together (as yet he makes no reference to any Concrete artists).

Vantongerloo replied on 11 May—as always, by return of post. He opens by saying that he had been very touched by Bill's candour. Making every effort to answer in good faith, as he says himself, he then goes on to explain that Fischli had had to share his page with another member of the group because of the acute financial difficulties currently facing the journal, partly because of the sums owed to the group by certain members, which he lists in detail. In response to Bill's reference to "imitators," he adds that in fact it was Piet Mondrian who had copied Miss Moss's "double lines," not vice versa.

Evidently Vantongerloo's list of monies owed by some of the "great" artists—Mondrian, Hélion, Calder, Arp, and Vordemberge—did not greatly interest Bill, nor was he interested in pursuing his complaint.

Instead, in his reply on 21 May 1935, he simply says, "*Laissons ça, et travaillons!*"—"Let's forget it, let's just work!"—and, still addressing Vantongerloo with the formal "vous," he adds how happy he would be to meet Vantongerloo on his next visit to Paris, whenever that might be. After that exchange of letters in May 1935 there was a lull in Bill and Vantongerloo's correspondence until 30 December 1935 when Vantongerloo again wrote to Bill.

The Swiss Werkbund Exhibition in Bern

At the Swiss Werkbund (SWB) exhibition at Kunsthalle Bern in 1935, both Max Bill and "Bill, Binia, SWB, Zürich 10, Limmattalsstrasse 253" were among the exhibitors.

Since Max Bill was registered as a citizen of Moosseedorf in the canton of Bern, the Bills were able to participate in the exhibition at Kunsthalle Bern. Egidius Streiff—whom Bill knew from their time together at the Krater cabaret—had taken over as director of the SWB [Schweizerischer Werkbund] in 1931 (*Werkbundausstellung Ortsgruppe Bern SWB,* exh. cat. Kunsthalle Bern, 24 August–22 September 1935, no illustrations).

Binia showed seven photographs including *Katze, Frau mit Schleier und Nelke, Puppen, Pingpongbälle,* and her portrait of the dancer *Marie-Eve.* Max Bill showed ten works: two posters, *Koffer-Duss* (lithograph, 1930) and *Negerkunst* (1931, see p. 475), and a number of brochures—notably for the Neubühl Estate in Zurich (1931) and for the Berghotel Scardanal (1935), newly built in the Grisons up above the village of Bonaduz in an avalanche-free zone. In autumn of that year, as Max told me, he and Binia traveled to Italy via France. In St. Tropez Binia photographed the French author Colette, but only from a distance. Colette had just opened a new boutique and Binia photographed her there with a group of other people outside the building.

1059 Emil Paryla questioned by police officers in Zurich, 11 May 1936, 8.10 a.m., Max Bill's fiche [state security files], (315:0)815, Bundesarchiv, Bern

1060 Lauterbach 1958

Who Was Alfred Thomas?

In 1935, most probably in October, the Bills, now in Höngg, took in a refugee from Germany—a politically active anti-Fascist. His name was Alfred Thomas, and in photographs that are still filed away today in the Federal Archive in Bern he creates a favorable impression with his honest, open gaze.

From autumn 1935 until spring 1936, Alfred Thomas found refuge in Max Bill's home in Zürich-Höngg. Thomas, born on 2 June 1906 in Kühschmalz, Prussia (now Kobiela, Poland), worked for the Rundschau-Nachrichtenagentur (RUNA), a Communist press agency in Zurich.

For some months Thomas lived with the Bills and moved around in Zurich unchallenged. However, following a written denunciation, which arrived at the Zurich police headquarters on 9 May 1936, he was suddenly arrested on a visit to friends in Zeltweg. Alfred Thomas, who occasionally used the alias "Max," was two-and-a-half years older than Bill. There are no records showing whether Thomas paid the Bills a nominal rent or not. In early 1936 (as we know from a letter to Vantongerloo) Bill was in some financial difficulty. He might therefore have asked for—or been offered—some rent.

Emil Paryla, an Austrian actor who used the stage name Emil Stöhr and who had lodgings in the home of a certain Frau von Fischer at Zeltweg 44 in Zurich, already knew Alfred Thomas from Breslau—from the time before his own engagement at the Schauspielhaus in Zurich in September 1933. "Our paths crossed at Farich's, an artist's café in Breslau. Thomas associated with actors there. He told me that he had done an apprenticeship as a locksmith. Later on he became an editor."[1059]

Max Bill's former teacher in the Bauhaus stage workshop, Oskar Schlemmer, also lived in Breslau from 1929 to 1932, having taken up a post at the Breslau art academy after leaving Dessau.

Schlemmer's neighbor in Breslau [now Wrocław], the architect Heinrich Lauterbach, recalled that time: "Schlemmer and I often saw each other at the academy, and almost daily at home. We were immediate neighbors in two of the terraced houses that I had built for the Breslau [Wrocław] *Werkbundsiedlung* in 1928–29. We often had a first early morning conversation over the garden fence. Our children went to the Waldorf school across the road.... Tut Schlemmer confided in me that it was the best, most fulfilling and most carefree time in her life with Oskar Schlemmer."[1060]

As it happens it was during this harmonious, satisfying period in the Schlemmers' family life that Oskar Schlemmer painted his now internationally renowned, much-reproduced painting *Bauhaustreppe* (1930). Other residents in Breslau at the time included the architect Hans Scharoun, who would later design the Philharmonie in West Berlin, and the painter Georg Muche, the former Bauhausler who drew up the plans for the Haus am Horn in Weimar—which Max Bill and I visited together in 1988.

When the academy closed in 1932, the Schlemmer family's carefree years came to an end, as they did for millions of others, including Alfred Thomas, who made his way to Zurich via Amsterdam and Paris. Having already lost his livelihood, Schlemmer was soon dealt another severe blow in January 1933, when news reached him of the death of his closest friend Otto Meyer-Amden. On the third anniversary of Meyer-Amden's death, he wrote in his diary: "I no longer have anyone to whom I can reveal my most secret artistic and personal thoughts in the certain knowledge of receiving the right response and answer."[1061] In 1935, in the same year that Alfred Thomas felt at least relatively secure for a while after being taken in by Binia and Max Bill in Zurich, Oskar Schlemmer—alone and still in his native Germany—was in despair: "It is a crime to kill an artist's love of creation and his artistic freedom."[1062] Oskar Schlemmer did not live to see the end of the Second World War; he died in poverty in 1943.

"Impoverished, churlishly greeted, loved by few: thus he entered life. Impoverished, ostracized, loved by few: thus he left life."[1063]

Max Bill was one of the few people who would not forget Oskar Schlemmer, who found himself obliged, mainly for financial reasons, to go into internal exile in Nazi Germany; see, for instance, Bill's article "Oskar Schlemmer 1888–1943" in the *Neue Zürcher Zeitung*, 6–7 September 1980.

After Alfred Thomas was arrested, the Zurich police opened an investigation into his circumstances. When they questioned Emil Paryla and his wife Selma on 11 May 1936, they began by asking when Paryla had first seen Alfred Thomas in Zurich.

Emil Paryla: "As far as I know he left Breslau shortly after the beginning of the Third Reich, I think he went to Holland, to Amsterdam. He wrote me a letter from there.... Thomas traveled from Amsterdam to Paris. I got a second letter from Paris and I then wrote to him that I would be here next year because I had signed up at the Schauspielhaus

1061 Schlemmer 1958, p. 346
1062 Schlemmer 1958, p. 340
1063 Lauterbach 1958

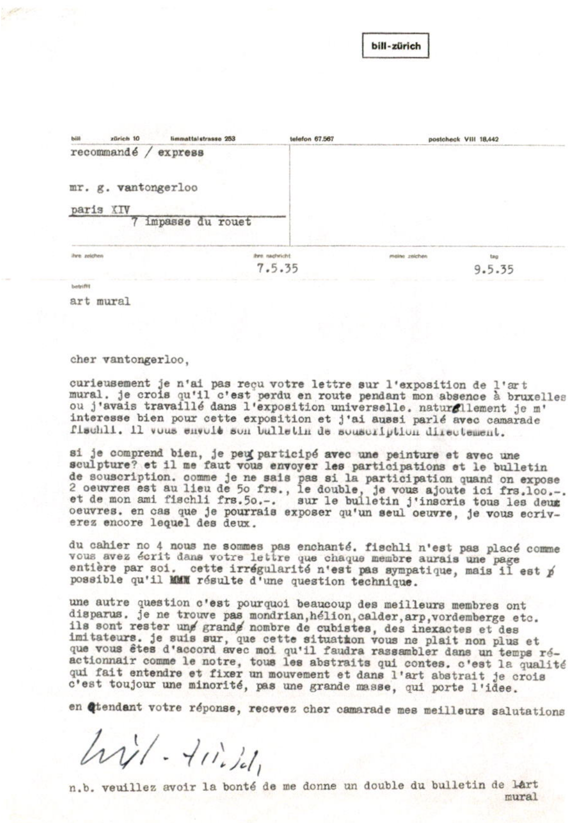

bill-zürich

bill zürich 10 limmattalstrasse 253 telefon 67.567 postcheck VIII 18,442

recommandé / express

mr. g. vantongerloo

paris XIV
7 impasse du rouet

ihre zeichen — ihre nachricht 7.5.35 — meine zeichen — tag 9.5.35

betrifft
art mural

cher vantongerloo,

curieusement je n'ai pas reçu votre lettre sur l'exposition de l'art mural. je crois qu'il c'est perdu en route pendant mon absence à bruxelles ou j'avais travaillé dans l'exposition universelle. naturellement je m' interesse bien pour cette exposition et j'ai aussi parlé avec camarade fischli. il vous envoie son bulletin de souscription directement.

si je comprend bien, je peux participé avec une peinture et avec une sculpture? et il me faut vous envoyer les participations et le bulletin de souscription. comme je ne sais pas si la participation quand on expose 2 oeuvres est au lieu de 5o frs., le double, je vous ajoute ici frs.1oo.-. et de mon ami fischli frs.5o.-. sur le bulletin j'inscris tous les deux oeuvres. en cas que je pourrais exposer qu'un seul oeuvre, je vous ecriverez encore lequel des deux.

du cahier no 4 nous ne sommes pas enchanté. fischli n'est pas placé comme vous avez écrit dans votre lettre que chaque membre aurais une page entière par soi. cette irrégularité n'est pas sympatique, mais il est possible qu'il résulte d'une question technique.

une autre question c'est pourquoi beaucoup des meilleurs membres ont disparus. je ne trouve pas mondrian,hélion,calder,arp,vordemberge etc. ils sont rester un grand nombre de cubistes, des inexactes et des imitateurs. je suis sur, que cette situation vous ne plait non plus et que vous êtes d'accord avec moi qu'il faudra rassambler dans un temps réactionnair comme le notre, tous les abstraits qui contes. c'est la qualité qui fait entendre et fixer un mouvement et dans l'art abstrait je crois c'est toujour une minorité, pas une grande masse, qui porte l'idee.

en atendant votre réponse, recevez cher camarade mes meilleurs salutations

bill-zürich

n.b. veuillez avoir la bonté de me donne un double du bulletin de l'art mural

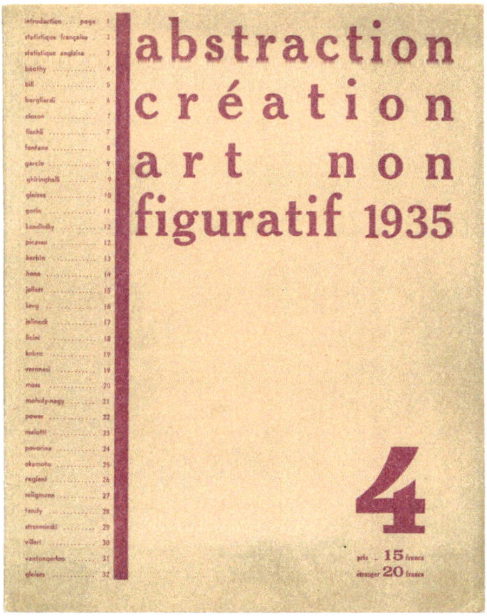

Letter from Max Bill to Georges Vantongerloo, 9 May 1935, typewritten on "bill-zürich" letterhead

Cover of *Abstraction–Création* 4 (1935)

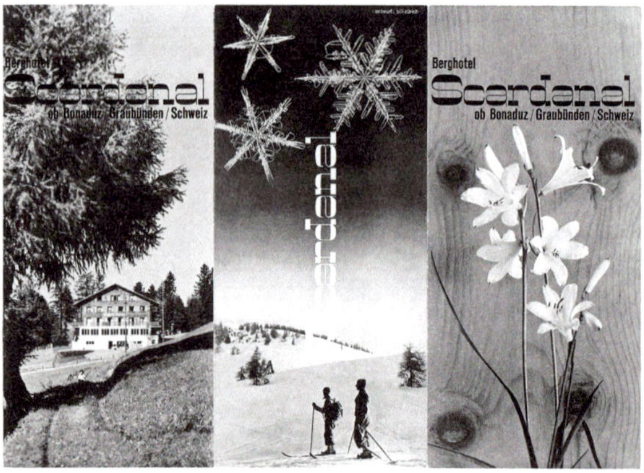

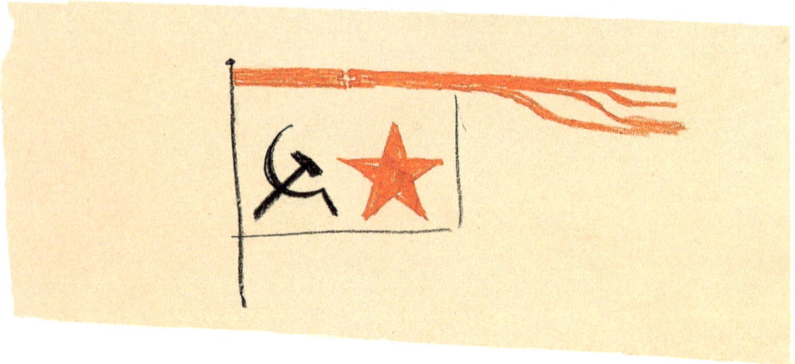

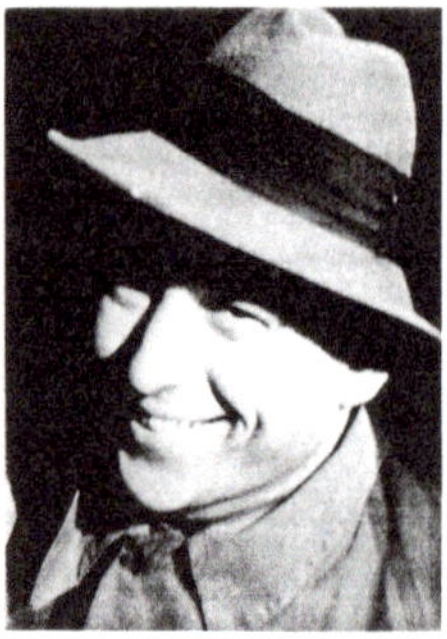

Max Bill, Brochure for "Berghotel Scardanal ob Bonaduz / Graubünden / Schweiz," 1935

Max Bill, Untitled (Sketch with red star, hammer, and sickle), Undated, colored pencil on tracing paper, 11.5 × 25.5 cm

Photograph of Alfred Thomas from a Zurich police dossier containing images of a number of émigrés in Zurich. The thing was, Thomas had lent me money in Breslau, about 1400 Marks. That must be noted somewhere in the immigration authority documents because I was asked about that at the time."

Police: "You shared Thomas's lodgings here?"

Emil Paryla: "Yes, in Anwandstrasse. Thomas had already been in Zurich for a month and collected me at the station. I didn't have a room and I didn't know Zurich. So I went with him and stayed in his room. I lived with him for a month."

Police: "Did Thomas state in 1934 that he had to leave Switzerland because he would no longer be granted a residence permit?"

Emil Paryla: "He told me that he would no longer be granted a residence permit . . ."

Police: "Do you know when Thomas left Switzerland?"

Emil Paryla: "In the summer of 1935. He sent a letter and photographs from Italy, of Alexander Moissi's grave. . . . I don't know how long he was in Italy, the theater was closed so I was in Austria. When I got back to Zurich he was here again."

Police: "Did Thomas often come to see you?"

Emil Paryla: "In the end I was even giving him a midday meal, for the last two, three months that is, about five times a week, he's very hard up."

Paryla was also asked about Alfred Thomas's work and political views.

Emil Paryla: "Thomas is on the left. He had to leave Germany, he's not a Jew." He had a "folder with a stack of foreign newspapers." "He read the papers and marked certain things. Sometimes he asked me if he could use my typewriter."

Police: "Where does Thomas live?"

Emil Paryla: "At Bill's in Limmattalstrasse, at two hundred and something."

Police: "Have you ever visited him there?"

Emil Paryla: "Yes, twice. He invited me. The Bill family were present. The conversation was about the theater. The first visit was this winter [1935–36]. I don't know how long Thomas had already been living there, I suppose about six months . . ."[1064]

Since Alfred Thomas had evidently shared his lodgings with Paryla, it is possible that Paryla—who was a member of the ensemble at Schauspielhaus Zürich—had taken him to Max Bill. In conversation Bill told me that Thomas had come to him "through people at the Schauspielhaus."

1064 Questioned by police officers in Zürich, 11 May 1936, 8.10 a.m., in Max Bill's "fiche" [state security files], (315:0)815, Bundesarchiv, Bern

In the Federal Archive in Bern, in the confidential Max Bill files, there is a photograph of the actor Paryla and Thomas.

Abstraction-Création no. 5

In August 1935 László Moholy-Nagy, Bill's erstwhile Bauhaus teacher in the metal workshop and now in exile in London, sent Vantongerloo his new address and inquired how things were at Abstraction-Création.

"Dear Vantongerloo, Dr. Giedion tells me I should immediately let you have my address here.... I am living in London now, see above for my permanent address.... I would be very happy to hear from you, how you are, and how A-C is faring? ... What is the situation now? With very warm wishes, yours, L. Moholy-Nagy"[1065] Vantongerloo replied in French: "... your constructive spirit always gives me great pleasure. Yes, it is unfortunate that some artists, even those considered to be very talented, have a very poor concept of community and believe that they can monopolize ideas about art."[1066] In his reply, on a postcard from London, Moholy-Nagy in effect suggested that if those artists could not be politically active, then they should at least participate in exhibitions. That was more urgent now than ever before.

"... I am very willing to participate again. I even think it is more vital than ever that we are active—at least in the matter of exhibitions. All the best! And best wishes to our comrades. Yours, L. Moholy-Nagy"[1067]

Moholy-Nagy remained loyal to the group. In December 1935 he wrote to say that he would be sending photographs of two of his recent works as his contribution to *Abstraction-Création* no. 5.

"My dear Vantongerloo, thank you very much for the invitation to contribute to no. 5 of *Abstraction-Création.* Naturally I am very happy to submit two items, only I haven't yet got round to photographing my latest works because of very demanding filming."[1068]

1065 László Moholy-Nagy, 7 Farm Walk, London NW11, to Georges Vantongerloo, Paris, 28 August 1935, Vantongerloo-Archiv

1066 Georges Vantongerloo, Paris, to László Moholy-Nagy, London, 2 September 1935, Vantongerloo-Archiv

1067 László Moholy-Nagy, London, to Georges Vantongerloo, Paris, 8 September 1935, Vantongerloo-Archiv

1068 László Moholy-Nagy, London, to Georges Vantongerloo, Paris, 19 December 1935, Vantongerloo-Archiv

And in late December 1935 Vantongerloo sent a friendly reminder to Bill—who was evidently tied up with more pressing matters at the time—that he still owed them a response to the official inquiry, sent on 16 November, concerning issue no. 5, and asked again if Bill wanted to have an illustration of his work included in it.

When issue no. 5 came out it did indeed have illustrations of two works by Moholy-Nagy on page 19, with the artist's name and the date, 1936, but no titles. However, this issue did not contain a text by Moholy-Nagy, as he had suggested in another letter, written in English in 1937, because the letter arrived too late—no. 5 was already out.

And as to the works by Max Bill—which are already illustrated on page 4 of issue no. 5, thanks to Bill's alphabetical "advantage" over Moholy-Nagy—the cube with excised triangular shapes (in the lower half of the page) is of particular interest. Casting a shadow as it lies on the ground, this work (dated "bill 1935") directly prefigures his *konstruktion mit schwebendem kubus* (1935–36), in which a cube is suspended in a white, neutral framework, so that it seemingly floats in the air. It is as if this illustration in issue no. 5 gives us a glimpse into Bill's experimentation, into a "work in progress." Maybe Bill had recently been re-reading Kandinsky's Bauhaus book *Punkt und Linie zu Fläche* (*Point and Line to Plane*), with its view of a room in the Constructivist exhibition in Moscow in 1921 (fig. 70). In the foreground there is a "triangular" framework supporting an object, and Bill's white metal framework is also in effect made up of triangles.

With regard to experimenting with positioning, with situating an object in space, Bill himself described how he handled the plaster version of his *unendliche schleife* (see p. 559), which was first suspended, then sawn into pieces and reassembled, and ultimately developed further lying on the ground. This was precisely the "learning by doing" that had been taught at the Bauhaus.

Financial Difficulties

In early 1936 Bill at last replied to Georges Vantongerloo's two most recent letters, explaining that, up until now, he had had neither the money to settle his debts nor any images of his works that he could send. However, he did now ask for the photograph he was enclosing to be published in the next issue and he assured Vantongerloo that he would pay what he owed as soon as possible. Vantongerloo reacted sympathetically and expressed his willingness to give Bill more time to pay. In early February 1936 Bill sent a second photograph to Vantongerloo and made a suggestion for the layout of the relevant page.

The reproductions of two of Bill's sculptures did then duly appear in issue no. 5, although Bill still had not made a payment. Now he was in debt to Abstraction-Création, just like Mondrian, Herbin, Arp, and others before him. Vantongerloo wrote to Bill—"I have to remind you that you still owe 150 francs. I know you are in difficulty at the moment"—and suggested that Bill might pay the outstanding amount in two installments. Bill did not immediately respond.

It was only toward the end of March that Bill wrote to Vantongerloo again, explaining that he was very busy with preparations for the Swiss pavilion at the Milan Triennial; he also pointed out that he had made it clear in one of his letters that his works should not be illustrated in *Abstraction-Création* no. 5 if he could not delay payment of the fee, which was why he now found Vantongerloo's insistence somewhat surprising. However, Bill concluded by telling Vantongerloo that since he currently had some funds in the bank, he was enclosing 150 Swiss francs. Vantongerloo replied by return that there had clearly been a misunderstanding, which he was very sorry about. Ever committed to Abstraction-Création, in this brief note he once again restates the cultural-political importance of the group's publications: "Our journal is, in short, a historic production that will be of use in the future."

Anonymous Denunciation

In those exceptional times Max and Binia Bill never hesitated to give protection to émigrés at their home in Höngg—they even took in refugees who were still actively trying to resist the forces against them, which they were not in fact legally permitted to do on Swiss soil. Max and Binia provided somewhere for them to say, either temporarily or for longer, as in the case of Alfred Thomas.

Those various émigrés are all named in the files kept by the Swiss intelligence service (known as the "political police"), in which they recorded both their own observations and third-party reports on Max Bill.

1069 See Stahlberger 1970, p. 95
1070 Stahlberger 1970, pp. 97–98
1071 Polizeiinspektorat Basel, Head of the Special Service to the office of the attorney general of Switzerland, Bern, 11 July 1951, Bundesarchiv, Bern

The records list émigrés such as a printmaker, by the name of Steiner, from South Tirol who later worked with the Concrete artist and printmaker Max Huber and who was apparently already in contact with Bill at that time. And there is also a note stating that an émigré from Austria, Rosa Trude Wiedner, stayed with Binia and Max Bill.

In spring 1936 Max Bill was taken up with preparations for the display in the Swiss pavilion at the Milan Triennial. However, just as he was about to leave Zurich for Milan, the Swiss police arrested Alfred Thomas, the German anti-Fascist who had taken refuge with the Bills. Bill once told me that this immigrant had "ill-advisedly let himself be seen in public," following which he was denounced.

At the time I did not ask who those "people at the Schauspielhaus" were, so in 2005 Erich Schmid and I traveled to Bern to seek out any information pertaining to those events in the Federal Archive. There are no records that might suggest how it was that Alfred Thomas came to be living in the Bills' home or who gave him their name. Could it have been Emil Oprecht? He published *information* (which Bill designed), was president of the board at the Schauspielhaus at the time and managing director of the new Schauspiel AG, but in light of the fact that Thomas was a committed Communist, it seems very unlikely that Oprecht made the connection since he had lost sympathy with Communism a long time ago. He had rejoined the Social Democratic Party of Switzerland in Zurich 3 in February 1926 and was now an advocate for democratic socialism.[1069] By way of an aside, the fact that Oprecht was a member of the Social Democratic Party of Switzerland casts a useful light on the much-repeated claim that Oprecht no longer wanted to go along with the Marxist arguments put forward in *information:* "This monthly was run by group of young, politically and artistically enlightened intellectuals, including Dr. Georg Schmidt, a Swiss citizen living in Basel. They were not dependent on any particular party or interest group or publisher and made it their business to fight all that was stagnant and backward looking and, broadly speaking, to breathe life into people's sense of history, progress, life, the struggle.... *information* took an extreme Marxist stand—often no longer shared by the publisher—against the bourgeoisie, against the existing capitalist economic order and against every national variant of Fascism."[1070]

The Swiss intelligence service kept a close watch on all kinds of political activities. In the records in the Federal Archive in Bern there is a file on Georg Schmidt, who later became director of the Kunstmuseum in Basel: "Schmidt-Hohl, Georg, Dr. Phil., born 17.3.1896, known for dallying with extreme left-wingers."[1071] Of course one of the "extreme left-wingers" moving in the same circles as Georg Schmidt will certainly have been Max Bill.

The denunciation that led to the arrest of Alfred Thomas and to the interrogation of Emil and Selma Paryla was written by someone who described himself as a "foreigner, but a straight talker" and was sent anonymously to the Zurich aliens office on 23 April 1936: "It is high time that attention be paid to the immigrant Alfred Thomas, also known in some places as Herr Max.... He [is a] covert resident, has not registered, has long been pulling the wool over the police's eyes ... have at last tracked him down again, although he uses disguises, spectacles, a moustache, always wearing different clothes, etc. He is almost a daily visitor in the home of the actor Stöhr, i.e. Paryla, Zeltweg 44, 3rd floor.... Thomas mainly sends his extremist literature to Spain. He takes things to the post office by bicycle between 6 and 7 in the morning. That rusty, very unsightly old bicycle can be seen leant against the wall for hours in the evenings.... This brazen con man deserves the same treatment as the 2 foreigners in the enclosed newspaper cutting. N.B.: Swift action is needed because the actors may already be leaving Zurich on 15 May and will not return until the autumn." This letter addressed to the "Esteemed Immigration Authority" still exists in the Federal Archive in Bern.

The person denouncing Alfred Thomas wished he would receive "the same treatment" as was described in a newspaper cutting (still in the Federal Archives but unidentified as such) that was included in his or her letter, describing the "Expulsion of Communist Agitators. AG. In accordance with Article 170 of the Federal Constitution, two foreigners, who evaded border checks and entered Switzerland without documentation, who specifically agitated on behalf of Communism by distributing party literature, and who in addition acquired Communist literature to smuggle to a neighboring country, have been expelled from Switzerland by the Federal Council."

Within a few days of the anonymous letter arriving at the aliens office, Alfred Thomas was arrested in Zurich at Zeltweg 44 and taken to police headquarters. On 9 May 1936 the Zurich police wrote a report, stating that "alleged Thomas, Alfred, ill. [illegitimate son] of Marie Thomas Communist alias 'Max' 2 June 1906 Kühschmalz, Upper Silesia, Prussia, subject of the German Reich, single, editor," refused to name his place of residence in Zurich. Unlike Emil and Selma Paryla, Thomas made no comment; maybe he already had experience of being questioned by police officers. Whatever the case, he did not name Binia and Max Bill. The official record reads:

"Arrested by the city immigration authorities." And Thomas was accused of the following misdemeanors: "Illegal entry and earnings, Communist propaganda; infringement of the Federal laws on foreigners' residence and settlement."

The Zurich city police, who could not persuade Alfred Thomas to reveal where he was living, summoned the Parylas to an early morning interview on 11 May 1936. At 8:10 a.m. the police commenced their interview with "Frau Paryla, née Schmidt, known as Frau Stöhr, Selma (Selly) Sybilla, formerly German, now of Vienna, born 4 March 1909 in Breslau ... married to Paryla since August 1935 ... actress, resident at Zeltweg 44." When she was asked, "Are you a Communist?," Selma Paryla replied that she was not a Communist, she was just against Hitler.

Police: "Do you know Mr. Thomas?"

Selma Paryla: "Yes, from Breslau. I met him there 5 or 6 years ago. He was introduced to me after a show."

Police: "Did you know what Thomas's occupation was at that time?"

Selma Paryla: "No ... I only heard later that Thomas was working for a newspaper. What that paper was called, or is called, I don't know."

Police: "When did Thomas first come to see you in Zurich?"

Selma Paryla: "He was here before us."

Police: "When did you and your husband arrive in Zurich?"

Selma Paryla: "My husband has been in Zurich for three years now. He is an actor at the Schauspielhaus ... I came to Zurich in April 1935 for a visit and stayed until the beginning of June 1935. Then I traveled to Vienna with Herr Paryla, who I already knew from Breslau. We were married there. My present husband had already shared a room with Thomas in 1934 ... on Anwandstrasse. Now I remember. They were already living together in the 1933–34 season ... but I don't know what made Thomas come to Zurich."

Police: "Did you meet Thomas on your first trip to Zurich?"

Selma Paryla: "Yes, when Paryla was already living at Zeltweg 44."

Police: "Was Thomas living there with your husband?"

Selma Paryla: "No. I don't know where he was living. But he was in Zurich for the whole time."

Police: "When did you and your husband return to Zurich from Austria?"

Selma Paryla: "... I didn't come back to Zurich until October 1935."

Police: "What was Thomas doing during the time when you were visiting Zurich and met him?"

Selma Paryla: "Thomas's fiancée, Tony [Antonie] Martin, was in hospital here, very ill. Thomas mainly took care of his fiancée."

Police: "How long has Thomas been visiting Zeltweg 44?"

Selma Paryla: "Since the spring of 1935."

Police: "And Thomas has been a daily visitor since October 1935?"

Selma Paryla: "I couldn't say if he was there every day. But he did often come after lunch. He only started coming every day, with very few exceptions, in early 1936."

Police: "Thomas would then always stay for the whole afternoon?"

Selma Paryla: "Yes. Although sometimes he might also run an errand. But I don't know what those errands were."

Police: "What did Thomas write when he was visiting you?"

Selma Paryla: "He sometimes used our typewriter. But I don't know what he wrote."

Police: "Which newspaper does Thomas write for?"

Selma Paryla: "The first I heard of that was on Saturday, from you."

Police: "So you didn't know until Saturday that Thomas writes and has always written for the *Rundschau?*"

Selma Paryla: "No."

Police: "But we have been informed that you always helped Thomas with his writing."

The police based this question on a line in the denouncer's letter: "... Mrs. Stöhr does his typing."

Selma Paryla: "That is not true."

Police: "Where does Thomas live?"

Selma Paryla: "Out in Höngg, with a family called Bill. When we visited him, which we did twice, we took the tram to the terminus. Then we had to walk another 5 to 7 minutes along the same road. The first time we visited him was some months ago, the second time was last week."

Police: "You knew that Thomas was living there but had not registered?"

Selma Paryla: "Yes."

Police: "But Theo [*sic*] Otto sometimes helped Thomas with his work?"

Selma Paryla: "Theo [*sic*] did sometimes visit us. But I don't know if Thomas and Theo are friends."[1072]

The police reports show that in their separate interviews both Selma Paryla and her husband stated that Alfred Thomas was living with the Bills in Höngg.

1072 Questioned by police officers in Zürich, 11 May 1936, 8.10 a.m., in Max Bill's "fiche" [state security files], (315:0)815, Bundesarchiv, Bern

1073 Police protocol sent to the office of the attorney general of Switzerland in Bern, 29 May 1936, Max Bill's "fiche" (315:0)815

1074 Teubner 1975, pp. 177–78

1075 Bruns 2007, p. 77

Emil Paryla: "I was there again last week. I was introduced to three people, two Swiss men and a women, just a moment, it was Thomas, a Swiss couple and another woman, a foreigner." On the strength of that statement the police then made inquiries as to the identity of the "foreign woman" staying with the Bills in early May 1936. In due course they established that it was a certain Rosa Trude Wiedner, born on 7 June 1900 in Freidorf, Austria, a seamstress, single. "... Wiedner has already been barred from entering the country."[1073]

Why were Emil and Selma Paryla so forthcoming when they were questioned by the police? The records show that, with regard to the actor's financial situation, Paryla's "wages" were "700 francs" and that the season at the Schauspielhaus lasted for "9 months." When questioned as to any ideology of their own, both Parylas denied being Communists. Presumably, they were fearful of reprisals—with good reason. At worst that could mean expulsion from Switzerland. And so it was that on 18 May the city police did indeed recommend to the Zurich sheriff's office [Polizeiinspektorat] "that the Parylas, husband and wife, and Theo [*sic*] Otto should be subjected to stringent immigration checks."

A book written some years later by Hans Teubner, a veteran of the Spanish Civil War, confirms that Paryla, Teo Otto (named by Selma Paryla under questioning), and other émigrés were all members of a very active Communist group at the Schauspielhaus in Zurich.[1074]

Hans Otto, not related to Teo Otto, who had been murdered in Berlin in November 1933—pushed out of a window because he refused to talk—was remembered by his colleagues each year in a memorial service at the Schauspielhaus. Hans Otto had lived in Berlin with the actor Wolfgang Heinz. They were prepared to flout the law if necessary and were active members of the Revolutionäre Gewerkschaftsopposition (Revolutionary union opposition), where Otto ran the film, stage, and music section.

"After his comrade was murdered Wolfgang Heinz moved to Zurich. In the season of 1934–35 he had parts in a number of Shakespeare plays at the Schauspielhaus, including *Hamlet* and *Othello;* in 1935 he also directed.... Heinz was a member of the inner circle of the Communist actors' cell led by Wolfgang Langhoff, which was in contact with resistance groups in Europe, including the Schulze-Boysen group in Germany."[1075]

Since Max Bill once told me that the émigré from Germany had come to him "through people at the Schauspielhaus," it might possibly have been Wolfgang Heinz or Teo Otto who asked Bill to take in the refugee who called himself Alfred Thomas (and who might have been using forged documents).

Up until 1938 and the Annexation of Austria, Wolfgang Heinz, Wolfgang Langhoff, Erwin Parker, their Schauspielhaus colleague Karl Paryla (the then already famous brother of Emil) and Teo Otto spent their summer vacations in Vienna: "Evidently it was during those summer months that they made contact with comrades elsewhere, including Prague."

In August 1936, a few months after the arrest and expulsion of Alfred Thomas, instigated by the Federal Council, it turned out that when the actors wanted to re-enter Switzerland, all of a sudden—in keeping with the threats already issued to them by the immigration authorities during questioning—they found themselves in difficulty. Fortunately the director of the Schauspielhaus, Ferdinand Rieser, was able to secure "another 'tolerated stay permit' for his actors."[1076]

In 1943, toward the end of the Second World War, Karl Paryla and Teo Otto were among those who paved the way for the creation of the Nationalkomitee Freies Deutschland (National committee for a free Germany).

"The aim of the KP Schweiz (the Communist Party in Switzerland) was now to disseminate the ideas of the National Committee for a Free Germany in work camps and among non-interned émigrés in the cities. . . . Because the most favorable conditions for this were at Schauspielhaus Zürich, on the suggestion of the party leadership in the Gordola camp the party grouping led by Wolfgang Langhoff at the Schauspielhaus took the initiative and founded the first Free Germany group. The founding members of that first group included both Communist and non-party-affiliated members of the ensemble, Teo Otto, Wolfgang Heinz, Karl Paryla, Mathilde Danegger, Erwin Parker, Jo Mihaly, and other anti-Fascists in Zurich . . . of course setting up any such groups in 'neutral' Switzerland was against the law . . ."[1077]

At Schauspielhaus Zürich Karl Paryla was seen in the premiere of Brecht's *Mutter Courage;* after the Second World War he returned to Vienna, where he died in 1996 at the age of 90.

1076 Bruns 2007, p. 77
1077 Teubner 1975, pp. 177–78
1078 Zurich City Police, Criminal Investigation Department, Zurich, 11 May 1936, Bundesarchiv Bern
1079 Report on the "Haftsache Alfred Thomas," Zurich City Police, 12 May 1936

An original set design for *Mutter Courage* by Teo Otto has survived in the collection of Peter Petrej in Zurich. In 1966 the set designer Teo Otto was awarded the Art Prize of the City of Zurich in recognition of his work.

A detailed police report of Thomas's arrest, dated 11 May 1936, is still held in the Federal Archive in Bern: "At 6:10 p.m. on 9 May 1936 Alfred Thomas was arrested ... in the apartment of the actor Emil Parila [*sic*], known as Stöhr, living at Zeltweg 44, Zurich. Besides Parila, the latter's wife and the stage designer Theo [*sic*] Otto, a German citizen, were also present in the apartment.... The arrest took place following the anonymous denunciation of said Thomas, who is alleged to be a Communist.... Thomas, also known as Max, is said to constantly alter his dress.... After his arrest, Thomas, at Police Station 7, refused to confirm his personal details.... In the usual Communist way he would not state his address, which we later established by other means.... According to his landlord, Max Bill, commercial artist, born 1908, Thomas has been living at his present address Limmattalstrasse 253 since early January 1936. However, according to personal notes made by Thomas he has been living there since October 1935.... Thomas is an editor at the *RUNA* in Zurich, a Communist enterprise that ... is constantly employing foreign nationals without authorization. Thomas has given no information as to his activities.... Thomas had 47.51 francs on his person. Of that sum 40 francs will be taken as a deposit for riding a bicycle without insurance and for taking on employment without a permit."[1078]

Yet more information emerges from another police report, dated 12 May 1936 and marked "Detainment of Alfred Thomas, Urgent," which is now held at the office of the attorney general in Bern: "... without ringing the doorbell detectives Stier, Bachmann 3, and I entered Frau von Fischer's apartment and I knocked on the door and immediately entered the room. Those present were Thomas, Paryla, his wife, and Otto. Thomas ... had no identity papers and also refused to give his name.... I examined the contents of stage designer Otto's pockets.... In the two rooms occupied by the Parylas we found a copy of the Basler Rundschau and 2 brochures from the VII World Congress of the Communist International [Comintern] with the speech by Dimitrow on the "Working Class against Fascism." Separate reports will follow on Otto, who appeared wearing an anti-Fascist, actually Communist neckerchief, and on the married couple, the Paryla-Schmidts. Otto's home was also searched."[1079]

Another report tells us more about what happened when Alfred Thomas's room at the Bills' house in Höngg was searched: "On the morning of 11 May when we arrived to search the house at Limmattalstr. 253, that is to say, the room occupied by Thomas, the main door of the house was locked. Despite our repeatedly ringing the bell, no one opened it. However, when we then opened it using the key found in Thomas's possession, a woman appeared by the name of Wiedner, Rosa Trude ... of Eichberg, Austria, born 7 June 1900 in Freidorf, Austria, seamstress, single. In response to our inquiry as to why she had not opened the door, she explained that Frau Bill had told her not to open the door to anyone. It subsequently became clear that Wiedner had been living, unregistered, at Bill's house for a long time and had also worked there. She has been charged with these offences. Wiedner has already been barred from entering the country."[1080]

It seems that, as well as letters, there were "around 170 issues" of *RUNA* in Thomas's room at the Bills.

"Appendix 10 is a very important document. It is dated 12 October 1935 and signed by Stefan, whose name you will know from the earlier RUNA files. Here you will find the alias 'Max' and the address of the German operative who currently sends the short reports on Germany. This is in fact Annemarie Jokl, Prague III, Zamecka 200. Max, in fact Thomas, must therefore be informing that operative ...

Appendix 14 is a letter from the Comité international pour la liberation de Thaelmann [a well known German Communist], which was sent to RUNA, Box 17626, Zurich, dated Paris, 2 March 1936."[1081]

The police also confiscated an astonishing array of foreign newspapers from his room: "In Thomas's portfolio there were one or more of the latest issues of the *New York Herald Tribune, Le Peuple,* Brussels, *Daily Herald, Daily Worker,* New York, *The Daily Worker,* London, *Westdeutscher Beobachter,* Cologne, *Deutsche Bergwerkszeitung, D'haagsche Post, Nieuwe Rotterdamsche, Courant Populaire,* Paris, *L'œuvre,* Paris, *Le Temps,* Paris, *Le Soir,* Brussels, *De Tribune, Het Volk,* Amsterdam, *Pester Lloyd,*

1080 Zurich City Police to the office of the attorney general of Switzerland in Bern, 23 May 1936, Bundesarchiv Bern

1081 Report on the "Haftsache Alfred Thomas," Zurich city police, 12 May 1936

1082 Zurich city police to the office of the attorney general of Switzerland in Bern, 23 May 1936, Bundesarchiv Bern

1083 The directorate of the police of the canton of Zürich to the office of the attorney general of Switzerland in Bern, 12 May 1936, Bundesarchiv Bern

Die Weltwoche, Zurich, *Neuer Vorwärts,* Prague, *Oesterreichische Woche, Das neue Tagebuch,* Amsterdam-Paris, *Youth News Service,* Wisconsin, *Die Tat* (brochure), Leipzig, 2 issues of *Die neue Weltbühne,* a brochure, *Kommunistische Internationale,* part 4 from 30.4.1936."[1082]

One wonders if, during the months that Thomas spent living in Höngg, from October 1935 until his arrest in May 1936, he allowed Bill to borrow those newspapers? If so, then both Thomas and Bill must have been extremely well informed at the time. And even if Bill did not have access to those papers, Thomas must have been a very informative, stimulating interlocutor for Max Bill and his wife Binia.

"Regarding the German Communist Alfred Thomas, currently held in custody by the Zurich District Attorney, you will receive from the Zurich city police documents relating to the expatriation of Thomas in accordance with Article 70 of the Federal Constitution. Should those materials, contrary to expectations, not suffice for expatriation by the Federal Council, please inform us so that we can without delay proceed with the expatriation of Thomas on the basis of the Federal Laws of 26 March 1931 on foreigners' residence and settlement."[1083]

"Bill, Max, re: Comm. Activities"

On 17 May, a few days after the police had searched the room occupied by Alfred Thomas and had applied to have him expelled, Max Bill himself was interviewed. A certain Detective Corporal Stier wrote up the minutes of that interview and added an extra note: "To the best of our knowledge the accused has often harbored foreigners without registering them. We regard the imposition of a hefty fine of no less than 20 francs for the infringement of the Federal Laws on foreigners' R. & S. [residence and settlement] ... as appropriate." As we know from one of Bill's letters to Vantongerloo, he was already very short of money in early 1936, so the police fine will certainly have come as a blow.

Max Bill later told me that on that visit to the city police in Zurich he had shown the detectives his contract for the Milan Triennial, issued by the Federal Department of Home Affairs in Bern, and had insisted that he had to immediately leave for Italy.

Following Bill's departure on 23 May 1936 the Zurich city police sent a note regarding his current location to the office of the attorney general of Switzerland in Bern: "Purely as a point of information ... currently, with the approval of the Federal Department of Home Affairs, Mr. Bill is in Milan where he is participating in the exhibition 'trienali [*sic*] di milano.'"[1084]

Bill had won that contract through a competition and had already sourced exhibits from all over Switzerland for the display in the Swiss pavilion in Milan. He had devised a widely diverse display of the latest arts and crafts in Switzerland alongside examples of modern Swiss painting, sculpture, and architecture.

On the day after Bill's interview, the Swiss Federal Council decided in favor of the application from the Federal Department of Justice and Police concerning the "expatriation of Thomas."

The Zurich city police also sent their comments on "Bill, Max, re: Comm. [Communist] activities" to the office of the attorney general of Switzerland in Bern:

12 May: "Det. Hüni sent a report to you stating that the Zurich city police had succeeded in arresting a RUNA agent, Thomas, Alfred Franz. . . . In the files it is said that this Thomas lived, unregistered, in the home of Bill, Max, of Moosseedorf, canton of Bern, born 22 December 1908 in Winterthur, son of Erwin and Marie, née Geiger, married to Binia, née Spoerri, no children, graphic artist, living at Limmattalstrasse no. 253, Zurich 10.

As we have discovered, Thomas already took refuge with said Bill in October 1935, and lived there illegally until his arrest. Bill has therefore been charged with a violation of immigration laws. . . . Bill claims he had no exact knowledge of the other's activities. However, he had assumed Thomas was writing a book. This "assumption" is a lazy excuse by Bill. The truth is that the latter knew said "Max" (Thomas Alfred) and thus also knew what he was doing in Zurich. It was for precisely this reason that he did not register him with the authorities. This Bill is far from unknown in Communist circles. This should be confirmed by the fact that at the time of the arrest of the Communist Heinz Neumann, alias Bieler, Karl, already known to you, we found in the latter's effects a visiting card bearing the name Bill . . ."[1085]

In keeping with the decision of the Federal Council, Thomas was then indeed expatriated, albeit to France—not to Nazi Germany (see p. 629).

1084 Max Bill's "fiche" [state security files], (315:0)815, in Bundesarchiv, Bern
1085 Max Bill's "fiche," (315:0)815
1086 Excerpts from the minutes of the Swiss Federal Council, 19 May 1936, Bundesarchiv, Bern

"Tuesday, 19 May 1936 ... the Federal Council of Switzerland ... in cognizance of a report from the office of the attorney general of Switzerland stating that Thomas, Alfred Franz ... at present in custody in Zürich, agitated in the Communist cause in Switzerland, and occupied a leading position in an international news agency with Communist leanings, where he, both organizationally and as a journalist, collected and wrote tendentious reports from foreign states, designed to create international difficulties for Switzerland.... In view of the fact that these activities endanger the external security of the country ... has come to the following decision: Thomas Alfred Franz is to be expelled from Switzerland.... The office of the attorney general will enact the expulsion."[1086]

With regard to the section that states Thomas's activities could cause "international difficulties" for Switzerland, it is worth noting that while the Federal Council hardly expected any such outcome, in all likelihood it responded in this way in order to prevent potential recriminations from Nazi Germany.

Erich Schmid (who was working on his film about Max Bill) and I endeavoured to discover more of what happened to Alfred Thomas after his expulsion and whether he survived the Second World War. We then commissioned two historians to conduct further research; they were able to establish that the Gestapo issued an international arrest warrant against Alfred Thomas, but were clearly never able to carry out any such arrest, otherwise his name would have been removed from the list of warrants.

Triennale di Milano: 1936

Bill's official remit for the Swiss pavilion at the Milan Triennial, which opened in May 1936, was outlined in Italian in the catalogue, *Guida Della Sesta Triennale,* as follows: "Max Bill, Zurigo," responsible for "*progetto e allestimento*" (project and installation) in the area of "*arte applicata e industriale, tessile*" (applied and industrial arts, textiles). The textiles he selected included, among other things, items by Elsi Giauque—a lifelong friend whom he and I visited together shortly before she died—and textiles by former Bauhaus master Gunta Sharon-Stölzl, which are listed in the catalogue under the company name: Sharon & Hürlimann, Stoffe. The Swiss pavilion also contained ceramics and glassware, Swiss jewelry—with a number of items by Bill's sister-in-law Klara Bosshard—clocks, fashion, items made from wood, and even a working marionette theater. The marionettes, which were seen in a comedy called *Kasane,* were by Carlo "Carl" Fischer, who had once taught Bill at the Kunstgewerbeschule in Zurich. The set was by Otto Morach.

In Milan Bill was surrounded by friends and at times almost *en famille*—the photography display opened with images by Binia Bill (first in the alphabetical sequence), followed by colleagues such as Hans Finsler, Gotthard Schuh, and Heiri Steiner. And there were also familiar names in the architecture section: Ernst F. Burckhardt, Hans Fischli, and Alfred Roth. The remainder of the space available for the visual arts had a relatively sparse display. Hans Erni from Lucerne, who had been a member of Abstraction-Création in the 1930s, and Alfred Williman are listed in the catalogue under "*pittura murale*" (wall paintings); as for the sculpture section in the Swiss pavilion, Bill restricted his selection to just three works of his own—which must surely have displeased his fellow sculptors in Switzerland.

The exact date of the opening is not given in the catalogue.

Max Bill, Binia, and the set-up team, spent around a week in Milan. A text by Max Bill on "the Swiss section at the Triennale di Milano in 1936" was published years later in *Dreissiger Jahre Schweiz: 1936—eine Konfrontation* (exh. cat., Aargauer Kunsthaus Aarau 1981, p. 95).

By the time of the 1936 Triennial the totalitarian Fascist regime had already been in power for well over a decade and had been caught up in the Second Italo-Ethiopian War since October 1935. That alone would have been reason enough to cancel any display in the Swiss pavilion in Milan. However, as it turned out, Bill took the Triennial as an opportunity—in Fascist Italy—to present a selection of anti-Fascist literature by the Italian émigré Ignazio Silone, who was now living in Switzerland. In a finely judged, subversive ploy, Bill succeeded in smuggling Silone's books into the Triennial; this was only possible because the books in the section devoted to "*arte del libro*" in the Swiss pavilion were listed not by author but by designer [493]—in Silone's case that was of course Max Bill, who had designed the jackets for both Silone's *Fontamara* (published by Oprecht & Helbling in April 1933) and *Der Fascismus: seine Entstehung und seine Entwicklung* (Zurich: Europa Verlag, 1933).

In the fight to establish the young Communist Party of Italy, Ignazio Silone, whose real name was Secondo Tranquilli, had led "dangerous missions at home and abroad in the 1920s"; "Fascist police and judiciaries were on the hunt for him as one of the most wanted scalps in all of Europe." There is documentary evidence of the pursuit of

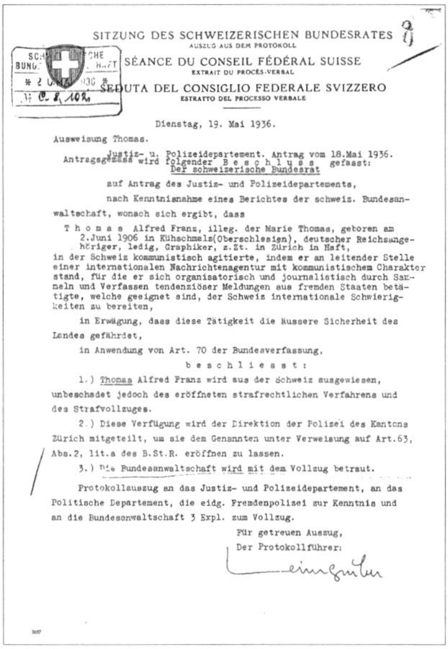

SITZUNG DES SCHWEIZERISCHEN BUNDESRATES
AUSZUG AUS DEM PROTOKOLL

SÉANCE DU CONSEIL FÉDÉRAL SUISSE
EXTRAIT DU PROCÈS-VERBAL

SEDUTA DEL CONSIGLIO FEDERALE SVIZZERO
ESTRATTO DEL PROCESSO VERBALE

Dienstag, 19. Mai 1936.

Ausweisung Thomas.

Justiz- u. Polizeidepartement. Antrag vom 18.Mai 1936.
Antragsgemäss wird folgender B e s c h l u s s gefasst:

Der schweizerische Bundesrat

auf Antrag des Justiz- und Polizeidepartements,

nach Kenntnisnahme eines Berichtes der schweiz. Bundesanwaltschaft, wonach sich ergibt, dass

T h o m a s Alfred Franz, illeg. der Marie Thomas, geboren am 2.Juni 1906 in Kühschmalz(Oberschlesien), deutscher Reichsangehöriger, ledig, Graphiker, z.Zt. in Zürich in Haft,

in der Schweiz kommunistisch agitierte, indem er an leitender Stelle einer internationalen Nachrichtenagentur mit kommunistischem Charakter stand, für die er sich organisatorisch und journalistisch durch Sammeln und Verfassen tendenziöser Meldungen aus fremden Staaten betätigte, welche geeignet sind, der Schweiz internationale Schwierigkeiten zu bereiten,

in Erwägung, dass diese Tätigkeit die äussere Sicherheit des Landes gefährdet,

in Anwendung von Art. 70 der Bundesverfassung,

b e s c h l i e s s t :

1.) Thomas Alfred Franz wird aus der Schweiz ausgewiesen, unbeschadet jedoch des eröffneten strafrechtlichen Verfahrens und des Strafvollzuges.

2.) Diese Verfügung wird der Direktion der Polizei des Kantons Zürich mitgeteilt, um sie dem Genannten unter Verweisung auf Art.63, Abs.2, lit.a des B.St.R. eröffnen zu lassen.

3.) Die Bundesanwaltschaft wird mit dem Vollzug betraut.

Protokollauszug an das Justiz- und Polizeidepartement, an das Politische Departement, die eidg. Fremdenpolizei zur Kenntnis und an die Bundesanwaltschaft 3 Expl. zum Vollzug.

Für getreuen Auszug,
Der Protokollführer:

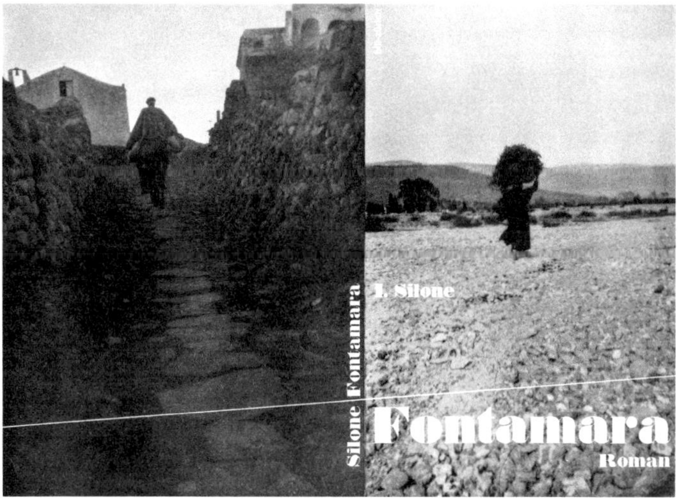

Expulsion order issued against the refugee Alfred Thomas, 19 May 1936

Max Bill, Dust jacket for Ignazio Silone's novel *Fontamara,* 1933

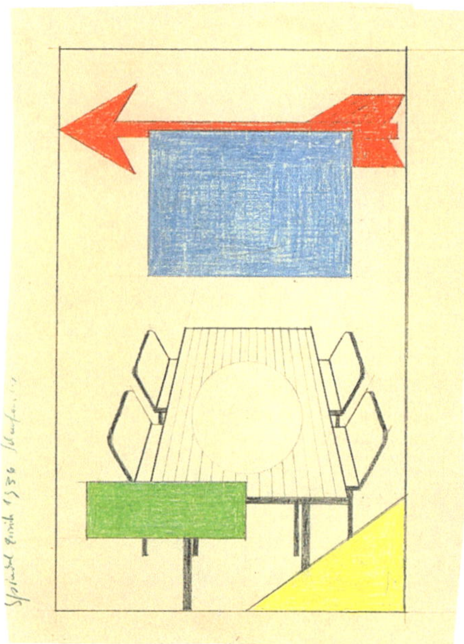

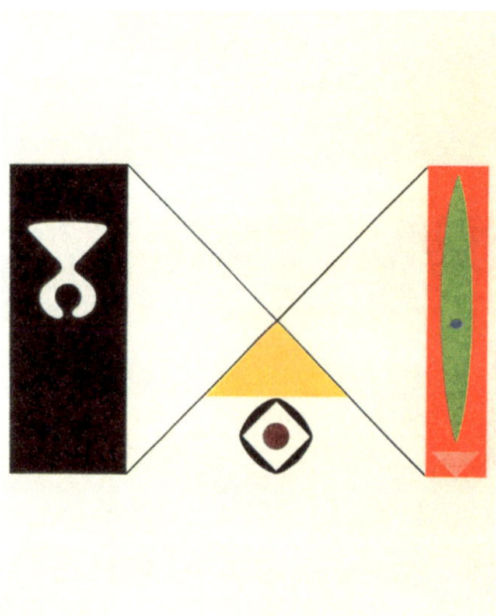

Max Bill, Design for a window display for the firm of Spindel in Zurich, 1936, colored pencil and graphite on paper, 39.7×29 cm

Max Bill, *3 variationen,* 1935, oil on plywood, 60×50 cm

Silone and records of "one concrete case where Swiss authorities provided help for the Mussolini regime."[1087]

Unfortunately the journalist, Paul L. Walser, did not go into any more detail regarding that "concrete case." In 1930, when Silone was in exile in Switzerland, he was excluded from the PCI [the Italian Communist Party], which left him with no party card. "First he was in trouble with his family and the neighbors because he as an active Communist and wanted by the Fascists. Later on, when he broke with the PCI, he had trouble with his new 'family,' his former comrades—there was never any real reconciliation. People remained suspicious of Silone, particularly since he had made his name as a writer abroad, far away from home."[1088]

His place of birth, Pescina dei Marsi, around a hundred kilometers east of Rome in the Province of L'Aquila in the Abruzzo region, was bombed by Hitler's Luftwaffe during the Second World War.

Hans Mühlestein, very moved by Silone's *Fontamara,* wrote a review in which he described it as "the most shocking and yet most poetic *document humain* that has come to my notice for many years. In it—by virtue of its unsurpassed objectifying creativity, of the kind only found in true masterpieces—the fate of a wretched Abruzzo village becomes a symbol for the misery of the disinherited and violated everywhere in humankind. This work has a spiritual, explosive power, which—beyond all politics, more elemental than all literature—instils in us the certain confidence that the spiritual force, which our culture once created, is still alive even in the most enslaved parts of Europe."[1089] Another reader in Switzerland who greatly admired Silone's writing was the cosmopolitan Jewish business man Bernhard Mayer, who met Silone several times in Ascona and in Zurich.

"In Ascona I met Ignazio Silone through Nettie Sutro, who translated his first books. I was already captivated at that first meeting and immediately ranked him alongside the very great minds, such as Kropotkin and Landauer. His first novel, *Fontamara,* came out soon after that first meeting; it created a huge stir. He gave me a copy with a full-page dedication, which I was very happy about.... Silone was a thoroughly political person. As a young man he had been a Communist youth leader in Italy; he had been in Moscow several times, but couldn't work

1087 Paul L. Walser, "Ignazio Silone und der Ort, wo er geboren und begraben wurde," in *Tages-Anzeiger,* 19 May 1979

1088 Walser, "Ignazio Silone," statement by residents in Silone's place of birth

1089 Hans Mühlestein, *information* 1:9 (April 1933)

with Moscow for very long, because they had no use for anyone with a mind of his own. There was a split. Silone then settled in Zurich, where I often saw him....

His second book was called *Fascismus.* Then came *Brot und Wein,* the next novel after *Fontamara,* and in 1943 *Der Same unter dem Schnee,* which also came out in the United States. Each of these books is a more mature continuation of its predecessors. All focus on the very poorest in society, with Silone's native village in the Abruzzo region as their point of departure. In the same way that Zola allowed us to discover unknown parts of France, Silone has shown us people whose lives we knew nothing of at all."[1090]

When Max Bill was designing the display for the Swiss pavilion for the Milan Triennial, he also as it were updated and took critical account of the aspirations of kindred spirits such as Charles Rennie Mackintosh, Henry van de Velde, and Walter Gropius.

For more information about the layout, technical organization and aesthetic structure, see Max Bill, "Section suisse d'exposition Triennale di Milano / Schweizer Ausstellung an der Triennale di Milano / The Swiss Exhibition at the Triennale di Milano," (May–October) 1936, in Alfred Roth, *Die Neue Architektur / The New Architecture / La Nouvelle Architecture 1930–1940* (Zurich and Munich: Verlag für Architektur Artemis, 1939), new edition by Girsberger (Zurich 1975), pp. 173–78. The entire production costs, including travel, hotel and wages amounted to 15,000 Swiss francs.

Crucially, when Bill analyzed problems he always considered potential solutions in light of their viability, not only from a technical point of view but also with regard to any economic and ecological implications. As a designer he always pursued a very clear path, seeking out the real basis of any commission and viewing his own actions as a problem-solving contribution to the way we shape the world around us. He had learned to take that approach in Josef Albers's preliminary course at the Bauhaus.

The Milan Triennial was widely reported, as far afield as Japan, and Bill could not help but feel that his work was better received abroad than at home in Switzerland. Every object in the display cases, every book, every photograph, every poster, every architectural design had been selected by Bill in the context of his own tireless effort to identify criteria that should be applied to design in daily life.

In later life, preparing exhibitions or as a pedagogue, Max Bill continued to develop the ideals he was already striving for in the Triennale.

1090 Mayer 1998, p. 104
1091 Thomas 1991 [a], p. 18
1092 Thomas 1991 [a], p. 18

The items on display in the Swiss pavilion were almost all the work of members of the Swiss Werkbund, which Bill had himself joined in 1930. However, when Bill's striking use of three-dimensional, spatial elements in the Swiss pavilion was awarded the Grand Prix at the Milan Triennial, the honor went not to Bill in person but—anonymously, so to speak—to the Swiss section.

This was the direct result of an intervention by the French member of the jury, Auguste Perret, who objected to the designer, Max Bill, being specifically named.

In the Italian section of the Triennial "Lucio Fontana [presented] his monumental sculpture *Victory* in the Sala della Vittoria." At the opening the Italian artist Luigi Veronesi (whom Bill knew from Abstration-Création) appeared "in full Fascist uniform," indeed many visitors came wearing Fascist "black shirts": "Interesting was the reaction of my Italian colleagues, who grasped the meaning of my gesture. All of them being Blackshirts . . ."[1091]

When it came to his own art production, Max Bill was now in a position to tackle problems of his own choosing, to decide on the materials and the processes he would explore. He himself described his own paintings and sculptures as "objects for spiritual use." In all his many different fields of operation, Bill always started by identifying the root of the problem.

In the late 1980s I talked at length with Max Bill about his connections with Italy, partly in preparation for a text that also touched on his work on the Swiss pavilion for the Milan Triennial.

"For years now Italy had been under a Fascist dictatorship and at that time it was at war with Abyssinia. This in itself was reason enough for me not to participate in the exhibition; on the other hand, it was also a reason for taking part, with the greatest possible coherence in the selection of the material to put on display." Bill thus made a conscious decision to smuggle certain anti-Fascist themes into the Swiss pavilion in Milan.

"Thus, as an exemplification of a very modern typographical style, I chose a few antifascist publications written by Ignazio Silone (pseudonym for Secondo Tranquilli in Italy on the most-wanted list; Silone was one of the first refugees to arrive in Switzerland. Since 1931 Bill had been collaborating with the writer. Silone was the editor of the anti-Fascist review *information,* published in Zurich; Bill was a contributor). And this, together with a rather unusual application of plastic spatial elements was enough to attract the attention of a great many visitors."[1092]

Ernesto Nathan Rogers

During that short visit to Italy Bill saw the Blackshirts with his own eyes, but in Milan he also met progressive Italian architects from the BBPR partnership. "Ernesto Nathan Rogers had excellent colleagues and the four of them made an excellent team at BBPR: Gian Luigi Banfi, Lodovico di Belgiojoso, Enrico Peressutti, and Rogers. Having all graduated at the same time in 1932, they had become an inseparable unit."[1093]

In 1944, some years after the Milan Triennial in 1936, Belgiojoso and Banfi were arrested in Milan.

The Fascist regime accused them of conspiracy. In the late autumn of 1943 Rogers managed to escape across the Italian border to Switzerland.

Just a few weeks after the Bills returned from Fascist Italy, there was a death in the family. Binia's father Ferdinand Jakob Spoerri—who had done business in Japan on behalf of the Winterthur company of Gebrüder Volkart—died on 20 July 1936 at the age of 71. Max Bill designed the announcement of his father-in-law's death using conventional uppercase and lowercase. Binia's family also expected him to design the inscription for the grave, which Bill only did, as he himself said, "extremely reluctantly." Ferdinand Jakob Spoerri was survived by his widow Ida Spoerri-Gross in Goldbach-Küsnacht on Lake Zurich and their three daughters (with husbands and children) Elsbeth Hodel-Spoerri in Riehen-Basel, Klara Bosshard-Spoerri in Brussels, and Binia Bill-Spoerri in Zurich. Ferdinand Jakob Spoerri was cremated and his ashes were interred at the cemetery behind Hohe Promenade in Zurich, the last resting place for members of many of Zurich's wealthier families. There is no longer any sign there of the gravestone designed by Max Bill.

1093 Max Bill in conversation with Angela Thomas for the text Thomas 1991 [a]

1094 Reported by Ernst Scheidegger in an interview with Angela Thomas in 2008

1095 Lohse 1981, pp. 100–101

1096 Lohse 1981, pp. 100–101

Zeitprobleme in der Schweizer Malerei und Plastik

By the mid-1930s various exhibitions at Kunsthaus Zürich had given the local population ample opportunity to acquaint themselves with high-quality, contemporary art. Looking back at the names of the artists whose work was shown there, one is struck by the unerring judgment of those exhibition makers. Art lovers in Zurich in those days were very spoiled and could hardly have been better informed.

In 1929 Kunsthaus Zürich presented the exhibition *Abstrakte und surrealistische Malerei und Plastik* where Max Bill—much to his frustration—was not among the forty international artists whose work was on display. That was followed in 1931 by special exhibitions with works by Wassily Kandinsky and Oskar Schlemmer and, in 1932, by major exhibitions of the work of Pablo Picasso, Juan Gris, and Fernand Léger.

As it happens it was Bill's friend Hanns Welti who had brought the first Picasso exhibition to Zurich in 1932.[1094]

In 1934 the group exhibition—*Neue Deutsche Malerei* (New German painting)—also included works by László Moholy-Nagy, who was of course Hungarian. And in October 1934 Kunsthaus Zürich presented works by Max Ernst, Jean Arp, Alberto Giacometti, Julio González, and Joan Miró.

Decades later Moholy-Nagy's art practice was presented to the public with great insight by Achim Borchardt-Hume, curator of the major overview exhibition that opened at Tate Modern in 2006 with a very judicious selection of works by two Bauhaus masters, Albers and Moholy-Nagy.

In early 1936 Sigfried Giedion and Leo Leuppi were involved in preparations for the exhibition *Zeitprobleme in der Schweizer Malerei und Plastik* at Kunsthaus Zürich (13 June–22 July 1936). They met in Leuppi's home, an old, half-timbered building that had originally been the railway station building at Zürich-Enge.

"Although the new station, built in 1924–26, had been finished for several years by then, the chalet-style wooden structure of the original station was still standing in the midst of an overgrown meadow, with bits of track lying about here and there. You had to climb a steep set of steps to visit Leuppi. It was like a wasteland in a William S. Hart movie from the twenties."[1095]

In these somewhat cramped conditions Leuppi and Giedion considered which paintings might be included in the exhibition.

According to Richard Paul Lohse, Giedion had criticized his compositions for being "painted with too little precision."[1096] Despite Giedion's critique, Lohse's work was represented in the exhibition—two paintings from that year, *Vogelbild I and Vogelbild II*—although they were not illustrated in the catalogue (see *Zeitprobleme in der Schweizer Malerei und Plastik,* exh. cat. Kunsthaus Zürich, 13 June–22 July 1936, p. 32, cat. nos. 114 and 115).

Richard Paul Lohse once gave his appraisal of Leuppi's ambitions and ideological thinking: "Leuppi was constantly preoccupied by the idea of an association of modern Swiss artists that would be capable of acting as an artistic counterweight to the GSMBA, that could take action and present exhibitions on its own account.... In Leuppi's view geometricizing art was *l'art abstrait,* as French art critics called it, by which they meant anything that was not traditionalist, i.e., not seeking to represent optical perceptions. For Leuppi abstraction was an expression of a modern, pantheistic life sense, of a universe that could accommodate both Lao-Tze and Beethoven's Ode to Joy. The wide horizons of Leuppi's world view explained not only his tolerant attitude to all forms of artistic expression but also his ability to collaborate with others, a year before Allianz was founded."[1097]

Zeitprobleme was in fact a selling exhibition with free entry on Sunday afternoons—making it accessible to all. In the catalogue the Kunsthaus director, Wilhelm Wartmann, expressed his gratitude to all those who had been involved in the exhibition preparations: "In Paris it was Jean Arp, with his longstanding, close connections to Zurich and Switzerland, in Zurich Max Bill and Leo Leuppi greatly assisted in the process. Besides the artists there was also Dr. S. Giedion, their friend and friend of the Kunsthaus, who, in addition to his extensive organizational work, weighed and measured the breadth and depth of the movement and the work of its Swiss representatives, and also wrote the introduction to the exhibition catalogue.... Messrs Le Corbusier and Max Bill also kindly agreed to formulate their personal convictions and artistic insights in their own introductions to the exhibition and the art of our time ..."[1098]

Although Bill never had special access to the circle around Sigfried Giedion and his wife Carola, because of some sense of animosity that seemed to be in the air, it was Bill who won the contract to design the catalogue and the poster.

Fourteen photographs, more than half of the total of twenty-one illustrations needed for the catalogue, were taken by Binia Bill. Max and Binia Bill worked together well as a team, and Binia Bill was given her due in the picture credits by Max, who designed the typography.

1097 Lohse 1981, pp. 100–1
1098 W. [Wartmann] 1936, p. 2
1099 Giedion 1936, p. 6

"Konkrete Gestaltung"— Concrete Forming

The exhibition catalogue, which has a relatively general text by Sigfried Giedion, also has a more personal text written by Le Corbusier. And it was in this catalogue that Max Bill published his first theoretical text (written in June 1936), with the title "Konkrete Gestaltung" (Concrete forming). In it he specifically makes reference to the brochure *AC* (Art concret) published in Paris in 1930 by Van Doesburg not long before he died. In his introductory text for *Zeitprobleme* Bill explains that since, in his view, Van Doesburg had been "somewhat unclear" about what exactly he understood by *art concret,* he would now attempt to clarify and define the phrase "concrete art" as a standard term.

Giedion's succinct statements in his introduction cast light on the human side of the artists' lives: "The painters and sculptors living in Zurich have very little close contact with each other." And Giedion expresses his surprise that "Arp, from Alsace" who had lived in Switzerland for a long time, had in fact spent "very lonely" years in Zurich. Nevertheless, Arp had certainly left "deep tracks" in Zurich.

Why does Giedion not mention here that Arp lived with Sophie Taeuber, first as her partner and later on as her husband?

In his text Giedion also discusses the work of various other artists, including Erni, Bill, Fischli, Glarner, Leuppi, Taeuber-Arp, Klee, and Le Corbusier. In Hans Erni's case, Giedion felt that "the forms seem to come entirely naturally to him."

Bill could only second Giedion's comment regarding Hans Erni; at the time Bill felt that Erni painted "more elegantly" than he did.

And as to Max Bill, Hans Fischli, and Fritz Glarner, he described them as "prudent in their dosage of effects, but then quickly and resolutely taking action, embracing and delving into sculpture, spatial design, and commercial art. ... Hans Fischli (Meilen, canton of Zürich): on one hand architect and builder of robust modern wooden houses, on the other hand, in his drawings, the poet among Swiss painters. He deftly peels back the outer layers of things. ... Fritz Glarner lived in Paris for a long time ... he paints from nature, which reveals itself to him as pictorial signs. ... Leo Leuppi "takes colored Cubism as his point of departure in the search for his own experimental field. ... Sophie Arp-Taeuber (Paris) has been a member of the movement since 1917. Her designs—progressively simplified—attain a fine balance of color and form."[1099]

It seems that soon after the opening Bill sent a copy of the catalogue for *Zeitprobleme in der Schweizer Malerei und Plastik* to Vantongerloo in

Paris. On 2 July 1936 Vantongerloo wrote from Paris thanking Bill for the beautiful catalogue, but also expressing some regret that the work of another Swiss member of Abstraction-Création, their "friend and comrade" the Surrealist Kurt Seligmann, had not also been represented in that exhibition.

In early June 1936, when Bill was still involved in preparations for *Zeitprobleme,* the French Comité de sûreté générale (Committee of general security) started to take an interest in the German Communist Alfred Thomas. On 11 June 1936 the Commissariat spécial d'Annemasse in Haute-Savoie contacted the Swiss attorney general with a request for clarification of "this affair."[1100] The Swiss authorities provided a detailed response in French. In addition to the information already cited here from the German records, a new detail emerges from a report marked "confident. C.8. 102, 23.6.36": "Thomas gave instructions for the compilation of reports on the movements of opponents to the German political regime." That would in fact suggest that Thomas was a key figure in the resistance movement.

In 1936, after his expulsion from Switzerland, it seems that Alfred Thomas traveled to Paris and "worked with Alpári."[1101] Gyula Alpári (also known as Julius Alpári), born in 1882, was a journalist and a founding member of the Hungarian Communist Party. Between 1921 and 1939 Alpári edited two Comintern publications, *Inprekorr* and *Rundschau.* As yet it has not been possible to establish how long Alfred Thomas spent in Paris or how long he worked with Alpári, although it is known that Alpári was arrested by the Gestapo in 1940 and killed at Sachsenhausen concentration camp on 17 July 1944.

One wonders, did Max Bill and Alfred Thomas develop a closer relationship during the time when Thomas was in Zurich? Did they meet again in Paris? In one letter to Vantongerloo, Bill certainly expressed his intention to be in Paris in the spring of 1937. On 24 February 1937 he wrote, "I look forward to seeing you and your wife in Paris in the spring."

1100 In the Bundesarchiv Bern

1101 Research by historian Katharina Morawietz, Universität Basel, email to Angela Thomas and Erich Schmid (23 June 2003)

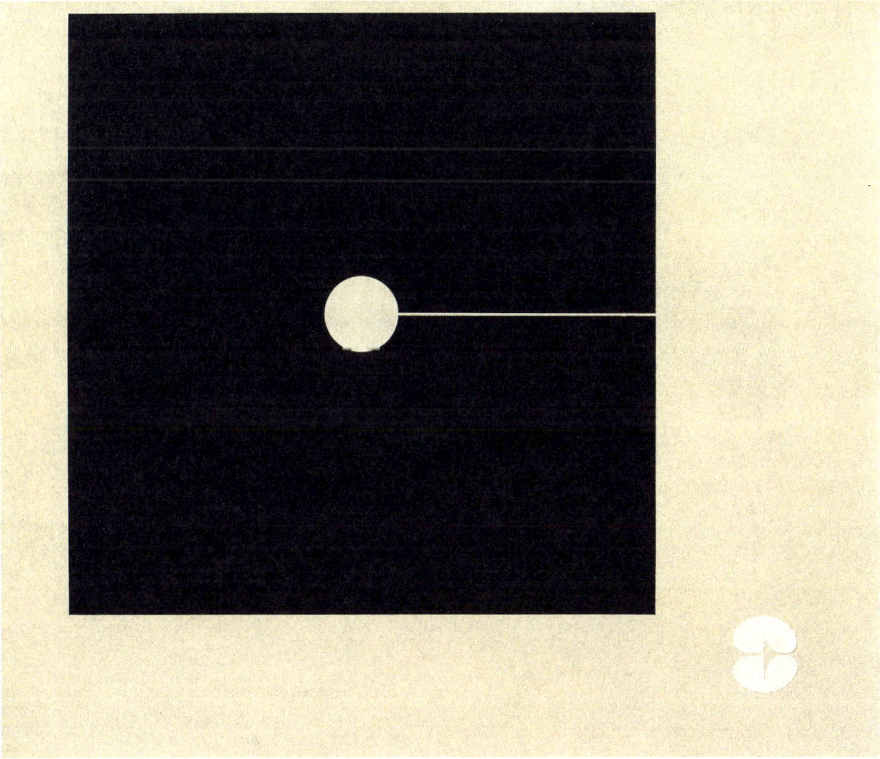

Max Bill, *konstruktion,* 1934,
oil on pressboard, 50×60 cm

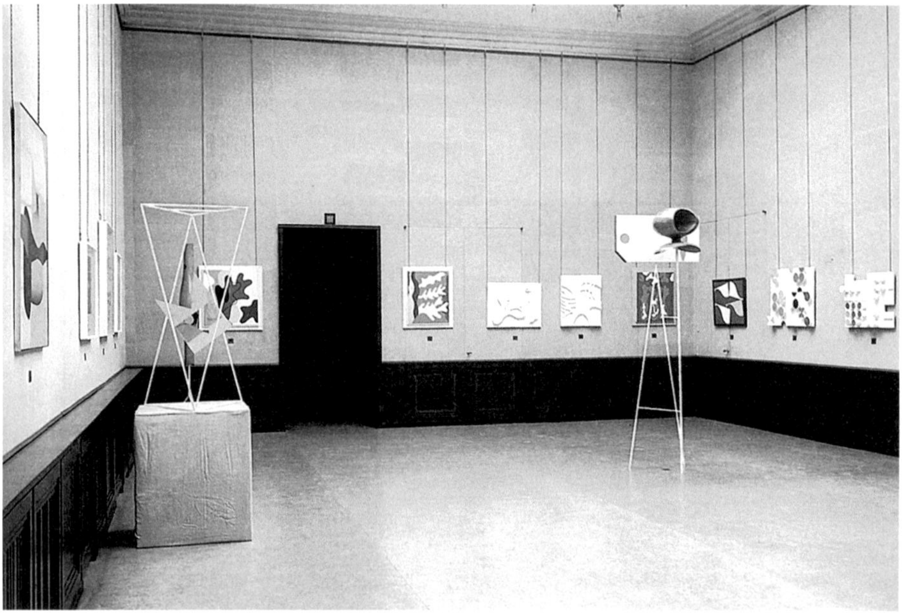

Binia Bill, View of the exhibition *Zeitprobleme in der Schweizer Malerei und Plastik* at Kunsthaus Zürich with works by Max Bill, Sophie Taeuber-Arp, and Clara Friedrich, 1936

Bill's "Design Logic" and Klee's Pictorial Thinking

Max Bill, in 1981: "The Bauhaus in Dessau ... played a part in the development of Constructivist art in Switzerland. Although it was not an art school, Wassily Kandinsky, László Moholy-Nagy, and Oskar Schlemmer all taught there. Despite their differences, all their pictorial compositions were underpinned by Constructivist principles.... Kandinsky and Klee formulated pictorial theories that perfectly complemented each other in their Constructivist logic. Klee's investigations in particular, with their wealth of ideas, were of inestimable value, above all with regard to the development of Constructivist art."[1102] At this juncture I would like to cite a statement by Bill (made in the letter to the art historian Dr. Siegfried Salzmann, which I have cited earlier here) and situate that statement in the wider context of Bill's ideological development: "It was only through my own Constructivist investigations that I ultimately returned to Klee's theoretical teachings. Without previously having fully taken these in, I discovered that my findings were in fact confirmed by his earlier experiments. Indeed, they were confirmed to such an the extent that I am still of the opinion that my 'design logic' is a direct continuation of what Klee meant by 'pictorial thinking'—albeit within the constraints of the structural, rhythmic, and means-of-expression issues relating to Constructivist art as I understand it."[1103]

Max Bill built his own artistic ideology on the foundations laid by Theo van Doesburg and Paul Klee. In the exhibition *Zeitprobleme in der Schweizer Malerei und Plastik* at Kunsthaus Zürich in 1936, Bill's experimental works from the early 1930s, his logical, perceptively artistic solutions were certainly the most radical exhibits. Bill was now creating work that was not immediately explicable to the viewer, although of course he could always explain it. He was gaining more influence.

The exhibition catalogue names the following as the owners of the works on display by Max Bill: "Max Wassmer, Bern, Anita Hug-Forrer, St. Gallen, E. F. Burckhardt, Küsnacht, Robert Blum, Zurich, F. Hodel, Basel." The first on that list, Max Wassmer, is the cement manufacturer with whom Bill had been in Strasbourg some years previously; the third is Bill's friend, the architect Ernst F. Burckhardt, with whom he had traveled to Paris. And it was in Paris that Anita Forrer, second on the list, purchased a work by Bill, most probably at the Abstraction-Création

1102 Bill 1981 [a], p. 24

1103 Max Bill, Zurich, to Dr. Siegfried Salzmann, 18 March 1971, cited in *Paul Klee und seine Malerfreunde*, 1971, p. 124

gallery. The list also includes the musician Robert Blum, Ernst F. Burckhardt's brother-in-law, and, last of all, Fritz Hodel, who was married to Elsbeth, one of Binia Bill's sisters.

In 1934 Bill had designed a "greenhouse with a one-room gardener's lodge," which was in fact constructed in Riehen (Basel) in 1936. However, it was demolished in the 1970s.

The residence for Fritz Hodel-Spoerri and his wife Elsbeth had been designed by Hans Schmidt. It was built in 1924–25 at Sonnenbühlstrasse 40 in Riehen and has survived more or less unaltered. From the outside it appears relatively conventional and, although it does not have a flat roof, this was Schmidt's "first advance toward industrialized building.... In collaboration with the Basel concrete manufacturers O. Christen he developed prefabricated, single-section, concrete-frame profiles for the windows and doors—he later advertised those frames in *ABC*."[1104]

Rassemblement universel pour la paix

In 1936 the first international congress of Rassemblement universel pour la paix (RUP, International Peace Campaign) was due to take place at the League of Nations headquarters in Geneva. However, the Swiss Federal Council refused to allow the congress to be held on Swiss soil because of Switzerland's status as a neutral country. The congress duly took place in Brussels instead. "It is the largest congress the world has ever seen: fifty thousand delegates from forty international organizations ... and seven hundred and fifty national organizations have come together to discuss how to avert the threat of war and to strengthen the League of Nations. Involuntarily, the Congress has taken on an alarming topicality following the latest news from Spain, where a bloody civil war has broken out. The Fascist General Franco has just been appointed head of government after a successful coup against the recently elected left-wing republic. On the Spanish battlefields, where opponents are locked in fierce combat, it is not just that Fascists and leftists are facing each other, this conflict looks like a dress rehearsal for the next, fast-approaching world war. While Franco is supported by Germany, Italy and Portugal, the Popular Front is backed by France and the Soviet Union, and thousands of volunteers in

1104 Suter 1993, pp. 143–44
1105 Bochsler 2004, pp. 383–84
1106 See Lang 1975 p. 309

international brigades are going to war to defend democracy. As a consequence the Spanish delegates to the Peace Congress receive the loudest applause. The appearance at the Congress of the renowned Spanish Communist Dolores Ibarruri, better known as La Pasionaria, instilled fear into all the bourgeois delegates as the crowd loudly chanted 'Planes for Spain! Cannons for Spain!' and started to sing the International. But the singers were quickly enjoined to cease, since the conference regulations expressly forbid the singing of this left-wing battle anthem."[1105]

The lawyer Wladimir Rosenbaum, who had a very successful practice in Zurich, actively assisted in the procurement of weapons for Spanish Republicans in their fight against Franco's Fascists. This ultimately led to his being charged with a criminal offence, indicted, and sentenced. Of the five presiding judges, three were in favor of convicting Rosenbaum. In mid-November 1938 Rosenbaum was sent to Pfäffikon district prison (canton of Zürich) to serve his sentence. Jean-Paul Samson had inadvertently played a pivotal part in the events leading up to Rosenbaum's imprisonment. He had approached Rosenbaum in a delicate, secret mission on behalf of the Republicans in Spain; this was of course the same J. P. Samson who (also in November 1938) provided a French translation of Bill's German text for his epoch-making folio of prints *fünfzehn variationen über ein thema* (1935–38).

The French writer Jean-Paul Samson regularly met up with R. J. Humm at the Rabenhaus on Limmatquai, along with the émigré writers Ignazio Silone and Bernard von Brentano. The physician Fritz Brupbacher, who cared for the poor in Zurich, also often joined them.[1106] Samson had translated seven books by Ignazio Silone.

By her own account, Rosenbaum's wife, Aline, knew very little of what was happening at the time, although in 1936 she did become aware that Jean-Paul Samson—who was living with them at the time—had started "whispering" with Ro: "Samson was left-wing, he often visited the Brupbachers and consorted with people with whom we ourselves had no contact.... The war in Spain was the main topic of conversation. Everyone was on the side of the Catalans and wanted to help them.... As I learned later, Zurich Communists, who Samson sympathised with, had approached him to ask if he could find a Swiss national who could act as a middleman between the Russians and the Spanish government and procure weapons for the Spaniards from Switzerland. He thought of Ro. The idea was to negotiate with a Swiss arms manufacturer. Naturally, Ro, in his euphoric willingness to help, was ready to step in and contacted the arms manufacturer Bührle, without any advantage to himself, since the aim was to serve the good cause ... and also to fight Hitler's despotism in neighboring Germany. At that time all arms deals with Spain were prohibited in Switzerland and punishable with a heavy fine. Switzerland was terribly afraid of upsetting the Germans."[1107]

"From late September 1936 to March 1937 the lawyer Wladimir Rosenbaum clandestinely acted on behalf of an anti-Fascist network in defense of the democratic Popular Front government in Spain. On the morning of 11 March 1937 he was arrested. The office of the attorney general had been alerted to his activities by information that came directly from the Schweizerische Kreditanstalt (Swiss Credit institution). The background to his denunciation had been an article that appeared in *L'insurgé,* a Fascist periodical in Paris, on 17 February 1937 ... which had come to the attention of the (Swiss) office of the attorney general. In the article there was a reference to 25 million [francs], which—following weapons deals with Comintern and the French Communist Party—had been paid into the Schweizerische Kreditanstalt in Zurich, weapons that were destined for Spain. The periodical could only have had access to this story through the police or a secret service."[1108]

On 15 November 1938, when Vladimir Rosenbaum had to report to Pfäffikon district prison, Aline drove him there by car. Her liaison with the writer R. J. Humm was over by now, but in the meantime she had become involved with the composer Wladimir Vogel. She stayed on in Zurich for a few days as a guest of Binia and Max Bill, at least geographically within reach of Rosenbaum as he started his sentence. She then left for Brussels, to rejoin Vogel, but not before "having promised to spend Christmas in Zurich. My friends Max Bill and his wife Binia invited me to stay with them. On Christmas Eve, Samson and I went to the prison in Pfäffikon to celebrate Christmas. A strange Christmas party."[1109] Rosenbaum was also visited in prison by Max Bill, who—as he told me—did not drop him (like many of Rosenbaum's friends) and even took him some pastries.

When Vogel was refused a work permit in Brussels (in a repeat of his experience in Switzerland), he and Aline traveled on to Paris, where they re-established contact with Sophie and Jean Arp, who were by now living in Meudon on the outskirts of the city. In March 1939, when Rosenbaum was released from prison, Aline collected him by car and took him

1107 Aline Valangin, in Kamber 1990, p. 189
1108 Kamber 1990, pp. 205–6
1109 Aline Valangin, in Kamber 1990, p. 236
1110 Aline Valangin, in Kamber 1990, p. 238
1111 Handwritten notes by Max Bill for his eulogy for Wladimir Rosenbaum
1112 Frosch 2004, p. 63

back to Paris with her. Having been convicted of a criminal offence Rosenbaum was now disbarred from legal practice in Switzerland. As it turned out, he chose not to live with Aline and Vogel in Paris; he was "really broken" when he arrived there. "He felt the urge to return to the Ticino, which was a blessing, because Hitler invaded France very soon afterward."[1110]

In 1984 Max Bill delivered the eulogy for Wladimir Rosenbaum in the courtyard at Casa Serodine, Ascona. And he cited his late friend: "Mr. Chairman, Gentlemen of the Jury, the Public Prosecutor has described me as Herr Rosenbaum from Zurich. Gentlemen, I am not Herr Rosenbaum from Zurich. Gentlemen, I am the Jew Rosenbaum from Lithuania. I am Rosenbaum—Swiss on paper only."[1111]

"... rejects from an oversaturated culture"

Bill's friend Hans Hinterreiter and his wife Mina Salm hiked through Spain in 1934 and were particularly impressed by the Moorish patterns at the Alhambra. Toward the end of 1935 they decided to move to the island of Ibiza because they felt that life there would be more comfortable than in Switzerland. However, shortly before the outbreak of the Spanish Civil War they received a visit there from Willy Hess—a mutual friend of Bill and Hinterreiter's from Winterthur—who persuaded them to come back to Switzerland. On his return Hinterreiter of course visited the exhibition *Zeitprobleme in der Schweizer Malerei und Plastik* at Kunsthaus Zürich, which ran until 22 July 1936. He was particularly taken with Sophie Taeuber-Arp's work and with the new Concrete works by Max Bill, whom he happened to run into in the exhibition.

Bill sometimes mistakenly cited 1938 as the year when he and Hinterreiter met again, for instance in his catalogue essay in *Hans Hinterreiter,* Galerie Meile, Lucerne 1990. However, the correct date has to be 1936, because Bill later remembered standing by his painting *Variationen* (1934) and talking with Hans Hinterreiter in the exhibition *Zeitprobleme in der Schweizer Malerei und Plastik.* Bill's *Variationen* is illustrated (no. 18) in the catalogue *Zeitprobleme in der Schweizer Malerei und Plastik,* Kunsthaus Zürich, 1936.

Despite a poor response in the press, the *Zeitprobleme* exhibition was a remarkable success. "*Zeitprobleme* attracted more visitors than any of the preceding or following exhibitions, with the sole exception of the very popular Courbet exhibition."[1112]

Nevertheless, even after an interval of two years, in a review of a Le Corbusier exhibition at Kunsthaus Zürich, one critic, Bernhard Diebold, clearly still felt the urge to vilify *Zeitprobleme.* Linking the two exhibitions, he declared that "the paintings we see here are of no value to anyone ... the paintings we see here ... are the detritus and rejects from an oversaturated culture.... It is not only in Germany that the term 'degenerate art' is heard in response to art of this kind."[1113]

Sometimes it seems that Diebold's tirade left its mark on the reception of Concrete art and still lingers on today in the dismissive attitude to Concrete art seen in certain sections of the bourgeoisie.

Bernhard Diebold, normally a theater critic, did not balk at using the Nazis' term of abuse in connection with Le Corbusier's paintings and the exhibition *Zeitprobleme*—which included Concrete works by Max Bill. This was just one of those instances when the Nazis' disastrous ideology spilled over into Switzerland. Perhaps emboldened by C. G. Jung's attack on Picasso in the *Neue Zürcher Zeitung* in the early 1930s, Diebold launched his own offensive against Le Corbusier and the Concrete artists, whom he accused—in pseudo-psychological terms—of "chronic art neurosis" and "dogged hatred of the bourgeoisie," of exhibiting works that were "degenerate."

Although Bill himself was not in personal danger at that time in early March 1938, his works were in a sense under threat and he was very disturbed by the atmosphere in his native country. In early 1936 he had already begun to consider emigrating to the United States and started to learn English with some determination. However, he was reluctant to rush into anything so uncertain. In 1938 he found himself in a dilemma: on one hand he achieved a "moral success" with his contribution to the exhibition *Neue Kunst in der Schweiz* in Basel, on the other hand, having been identified by the Swiss intelligence service as a "left-wing radical," he would immediately be interned if there were a Nazi invasion. He had to try to gauge the level of the threat he was facing. "I have to say, for all the ap-

1113 Bernhard Diebold, "Für wen ist das gemalt?," in *Neue Zürcher Zeitung,* 6 March 1938, cited in Frosch 2004, pp. 40–41. In her book about the artist Clara Friedrich, the art historian Eva Frosch notably cites and quotes excerpts from this article in the *Neue Zürcher Zeitung.* It was after reading her book that I ordered a copy of the incriminating article from the *NZZ* archives

1114 Max Bill to Josef Albers, 3 March 1938, Archiv Max Bill

1115 Letter inserted into the book *San Lazzaro et ses amis,* Bibliothek Max Bill

peal of going to the United States, I don't really have the courage to just go and try my luck. I wanted to represent Switzerland at the New York World's Fair, but now they're building a Swiss hamlet, I can't be doing with that." He also mentions a commission he is currently working on, "a sculpture for the Swiss National Exhibition in 1939, 12×12×12 meters. A huge thing and completely free rein. Wonderful."[1114] That "huge thing" became a modular sculpture, which Bill called *konstruktion aus 30 gleichen elementen* (1938–39).

Max Bill reproduced two views of this sculpture—which he created "in complete freedom"—at the beginning of a text he wrote in Zurich in March 1939; this text came out in French in the periodical published by his new friend Gualtieri di San Lazzaro: "La Maîtrise de l'espace," in *XXe siècle* 2:1 (1939). The same text also includes a reproduction of one work by Alexander Calder (*Mobile,* 1936), one by Georges Vantongerloo (*S×R/3,* œuvre cat. no. 93, 1936), one by Alexander Pevsner (*Construction,* 1937) and another sculpture by Bill himself (*konstruktion in messing,* 1939), which is now in the collection of Kunsthaus Zürich (see p. 666).

Bill's three images of his own works numerically "outdid" the images of works by his fellow artists: an undemocratic procedure that had echoes of the break-up of the international artists' group Abstraction-Création.

In 1959, when Bill considered reworking the article, San Lazzaro was in full support of the idea: "Dear Friend, I have just received your letter and am fully in agreement with the notes that you would like to add to that article, especially considering that it was written twenty years ago at the happy age of thirty! . . . with warm regards, San Lazzaro."[1115]

Hans Hinterreiter

In 1936–37 Hinterreiter was back in his home town of Winterthur, working on the first draft of a theoretical text, *Die Kunst der reinen Form.* However, in the late 1930s he became caught up in a chimera that would preoccupy him for years. Hinterreiter's idea was to use light projections to create a series of compositional grids with ever changing color combinations. His desire was to identify a temporal component in a sequence of alternating light projections that would transcend the usual rules and aesthetics. That temporal component, in the sense of a quick sequence, i.e., speed, remained important to Hinterreiter for many years. It was only in later life that he started to question this idea. Up until the late 1950s Hinterreiter continued to dream of a "color-play apparatus'—in fact something very close to the computers that we have today: "The ideal outcome would be an electron apparatus that could be used to build up images through combinations of elementary forms, fields of tension, and color norms as quickly as one can strike a chord on the piano."[1116]

Hinterreiter and his wife, in the best of spirits, celebrated the new year in 1939 back home in Central Switzerland, high up in Seelisberg. But their joy was short-lived. At the end of April 1939, soon after the birth of their daughter Liliane, Hinterreiter's wife Mina died in the cantonal hospital in Aarau, and a few months later, on 1 September 1939, the Second World War broke out. Hinterreiter vowed not to become a soldier and left for Ibiza. In early 1940 he was ordered to return to Switzerland "for medical re-examination." He deliberately did not tell the military authorities that he had also trained as an architect, "knowing full well that in an emergency I would be assigned to years of fortress-building; the examining doctor made fun of the fact that such a short-sighted person was a painter. . . . He could not measure the far-sighted spirit."[1117]

Years later Hinterreiter still felt that, theoretically, what he was doing could not be classified as painting "but rather as an entirely new, emergent *optical* art, which will also significantly involve an element of passing time. It will be between music and painting. It is a pure anachronism and a wretched waste of time that I still have to work with a brush and drawing utensils."[1118]

Only now, anyone viewing those compositions that Hinterreiter painted himself, is happily able to take real pleasure in what he once described as a "wretched waste of time."

1116 Hans Hinterreiter, diary, 16 July 1959, Hinterreiter archive
1117 Hinterreiter, diary, 16 July 1959
1118 Hinterreiter, diary, 16 July 1959
1119 Giedion-Welcker 1958, p. 41
1120 Max Bill, Zurich, to Georges Vantongerloo, Paris, 5 August 1945, Vantongerloo-Archiv

Constructions

In January 1937 the exhibition *Konstruktivisten* opened at Kunsthalle Basel, conceived and curated, installed and explained by Georg Schmidt. It proved to be an outstanding highlight in Swiss cultural life. Securing loans for the exhibition was very challenging because the barricades were already going up across Europe. And it proved all but impossible to obtain works by Soviet artists. Tatlin and Malevich had to be represented with reproductions since no original works of theirs were released for loan—in the Soviet Union under Stalin Constructivist art was ostracized and banned.

At the opening of *Konstruktivisten* Bill met up again with his closest friend, Georges Vantongerloo, who had come from Paris; he also met up with Sophie Taeuber-Arp, who was represented with twenty-four works, and with the Dutch artist César Domela. It was on that same occasion that Bill became acquainted with Naum Gabo's brother, the Russian sculptor Antoine Pevsner, who was living in Paris at the time. Carola Giedion-Welcker later reported that Pevsner had "specially prepared" the metals he used for his sculptures and she compared Brancusi and Pevsner's "dialogues with space": "The integral, organic core of Brancusi's work conducts an intense dialogue with the space around it. Here, through proportioning and the active inclusion of light, a spatial-cosmic life is almost magically attained and revealed.... Pevsner's sculptures, too, enter into a directly cosmic relationship by virtue of the way that the light falls on the specially prepared metal, generating different hues depending on the time of day and the seasons."[1119] Bill may have been particularly interested in Pevsner's handling of his materials and the effects they created.

In 1945 Bill wrote to Vantongerloo: "i have studied pevsner's work very carefully and talked a lot with him after i saw his constructions at the constuctivist exhibition in basel in '37, i was interested in them because i was also making similar constructions."[1120]

But there is no knowing if he was also moved by the "cosmic" component identified by Carola Giedion-Welcker. The art critic Anatole Jakovsky had also written an essay on Pevsner earlier on, discussing the works Pevsner was producing in bronze, celluloid, and "sky blue" glass.

"So Pevsner started by replacing the canvas with a celluloid surface, because he needed a greater translucency, a more vibrant substance to realize the dream of infinity he is obsessed with.... Pevsner has renounced sculptural solidity and immobility forever. His materials allow him to introduce the 4th dimension, time ... unlimited space in which opaque or transparent obstacles crystallize like islands.

That's why Pevsner, like his brother Gabo, likes both glass and celluloid. These materials facilitate the flow of cinematic rhythms."[1121]

This passage by Jakovsky is taken from a slim volume titled *Arp Calder Hélion Miró Pevsner Séligmann*. With a cover design by Arp, it was most probably published to accompany an exhibition in May 1933 with works by all five of these artists, presented by Pierre Loeb at Galerie Pierre in Paris.

Jakovsky particularly noted that Pevsner sought to avoid "solidity" and "immobility"—issues that Bill would of course have been very familiar with from his own sculptural work. No doubt Pevsner and Bill found plenty to discuss when they met in Basel.

Not long after that discussion took place Bill nimbly avoided the danger of a sculpture appearing too solid by working only with outlines and imaginary planes that are "permeable" to light and air, as in *konstruktion aus 30 gleichen elementen* (1938–39) which is made from stainless steel rods, and *konstruktion mit drei quadratgrössen* (*denkmal für pythagoras,* 1939–41/1978, see p. 351), which is made from gold-plated brass rods. A decade after that memorable meeting with Pevsner, its impact on Bill still lingered on in his *dreiteilige einheit* (1947–48). Unlike its predecessors *dreiteilige einheit* no longer consisted of rectangular outlines but instead took the form of gleaming, ingeniously intertwined chrome-steel curves, which won Bill the International Prize for Sculpture at the São Paulo Biennale in 1951. This sculpture—entirely made up of arcs, with not a single straight line—in fact harbors a secret, which Bill revealed in 1977: "The centers of the three circular bands mark the corners of a right-angled triangle."[1122] Later on, when Bill was working with granite he sometimes "dematerialised" it by having it polished, which makes it appear lighter—particularly when the work reflects its surroundings.

Sophie and Jean Arp spent some weeks in Basel in 1937 while *Konstruktivisten* was being exhibited at the Kunsthalle. Jean Arp—known as the *peintre-poète*—was not represented at Konstruktivisten because his art could not properly be described as Constructivist. However, this exhibition was very important to Sophie Taeuber-Arp who in fact had the largest group of works on display, and it made her name in Switzerland. She wrote to her sister full of joy: "Of course it is a very rare opportunity for me to exhibit so many works. The exhibition is wonderfully installed,

1121 Jakovsky [ca. 1933]
1122 Bill 1977 [a], p. 32
1123 Sophie Taeuber-Arp to Erika Schlegel, 8 February 1937, cited in Thomas 1983, p. 54
1124 Max Bill, "Sophie Taeuber-Arp," *Werk* 30:6 (June 1943), p. 171

the guided tours ... brilliant."[1123] Excited by curator Georg Schmidt's insightful guided tours, the Basel collector Marguerite Hagenbach purchased Sophie Taeuber-Arp's painting *Cercles mouvementés* (1934).

In my book *Sophie Taeuber-Arp* (Museo Comunale d'Arte Moderna Ascona, 1983) there is a photograph of Taeuber-Arp in the home of the collectors Annie and Oskar Müller-Widmann in Fringelistrasse in Basel (p. 54); Taeuber-Arp, who had worked on the interior design of the Müller-Widmanns' home is seen here with Domela, Vantongerloo and Pevsner, who also showed works in the *Konstruktivisten* exhibition at Kunsthalle Basel in 1937.

Although Max Bill had achieved some success in the 1936 Zurich exhibition *Zeitprobleme in der Schweizer Malerei und Plastik* and although he clearly took a Constructivist approach in certain works (e.g., *tektonische konstruktion,* 1937, and *konstruktion auf der formel* $a^2 + b^2 = c^2$, 1937), his reputation was apparently not yet sufficiently established for him to be invited to participate in *Konstruktivisten* in Basel. Bill naturally regretted this and it may have encouraged him in his desire to emigrate to the United States, which he actively considered from 1936 to 1938.

In the first illustrated text that came out after the tragic death of Sophie Taeuber–Arp in January 1943 at Bill's house in Höngg, Bill analyzed the motion inherent in *Cercles Mouvementés.*[1124]

In 1959, sixteen years after Sophie's death her collector in Basel, Marguerite Hagenbach, and Jean Arp married. Arp purchased Ronco dei Fiori, a property in Locarno-Solduno, which is now home to the Fondazione Marguerite Arp-Hagenbach.

"Forgive me, I have to write in German"

In February 1937 Max and Binia Bill went on a skiing holiday to the Engadine. They stayed at Hotel Waldhaus in St. Moritz-Dorf. Having seen Vantongerloo in January at the opening of the Constructivist exhibition in Basel, Bill now wrote to him on the hotel's notepaper, saying that he was looking forward to seeing Vantongerloo and his wife Puma again in Paris in the spring.

In the same month that the Bills went skiing in the Engadine, Wassily Kandinsky personally installed his retrospective at Kunsthalle Bern, where he met his former Bauhaus colleague Paul Klee for the last time. In an age that was not yet obsessed with attendance numbers, Kandinsky reported that his retrospective was "well attended, with 1250 visitors."[1125]

Vantongerloo reacted with interest to Bill's proposed book on the "relationship between Concrete and Constructivist art and architecture"—especially since the journal *Abstraction-Création* had in effect come to a halt.

Bill also returned to France in 1937, where he visited the *Exposition internationale des arts et techniques dans la vie moderne* (1937) in Paris and was in close contact with Wassily and Nina Kandinsky.

Architectural Projects

As we have already seen, around 1934–36 Max Bill designed a "greenhouse with a one-room gardener's lodge" for his brother-in-law Fritz Hodel in Riehen, near Basel.[1126] In the mid-to-late 1930s Bill also turned his attention to projects for several publicly advertised architectural competitions. However, perhaps because none of those designs was realized, he later rarely reproduced any of them in publications, with the result that they are barely known. A selection of those "*projets de concours*" was, however, published in the catalogue for his retrospective, *Max Bill,* in Geneva in 1972 (exhibition and catalogue conceived by Max Bill and Valentina Anker), which introduced his oeuvre to a much wider public in West Switzerland. The competition projects are all listed with their French titles: "Hall de congrès et de concert à Zurich" (1936), "Grand magasin Globus, Zurich" (1937), "Aménagement au bord du lac, Zurich" (1937), and "Restaurant Waid, Zurich" (1937). The high point of that series of projects is Bill's "Pavillon suisse pour l'exposition universelle de New York" (1938). These competition projects are illustrated in *Max Bill,* exh. cat. Musée Rath, Geneva, 6–30 April 1972, Geneva 1972.

1125 Cited in Frey 1995, p. 89

1126 On this see Arthur Rüegg, "Hodel Gardener House, Riehen 1934–1936," *Max Bill Arquitecto/Architect = 2G: International Architecture Review* 29/30 (2004) (Spanish and English), p. 70–73

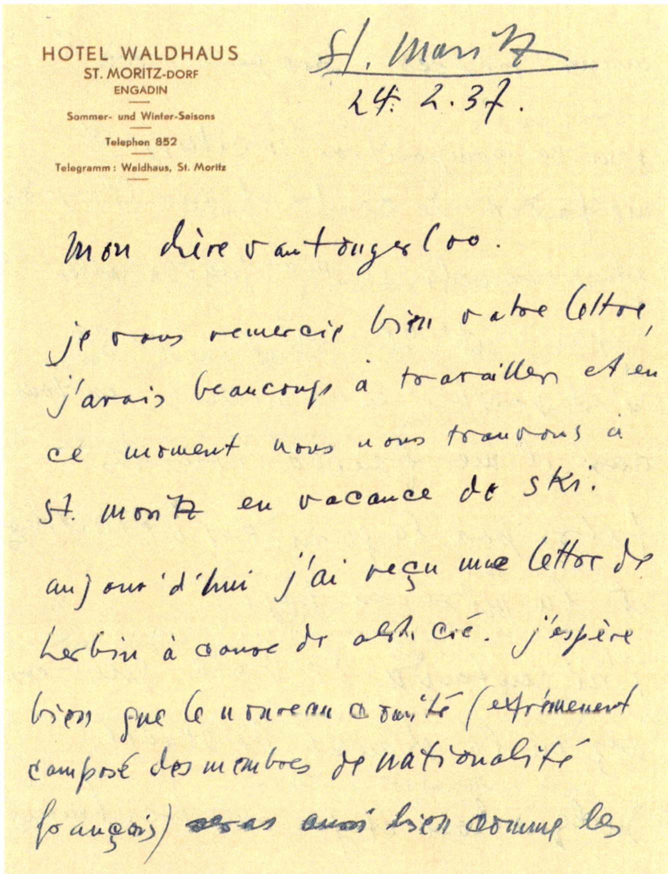

HOTEL WALDHAUS
ST. MORITZ-DORF
ENGADIN
Sommer- und Winter-Saisons
Telephon 852
Telegramm: Waldhaus, St. Moritz

St. Moritz
24. 2. 37.

mon cher vantongerloo.

je vous remercie bien votre lettre, j'avais beaucoup à travailler et en ce moment nous nous trouvons à St. moritz en vacance de ski.

aujourd'hui j'ai reçu une lettre de Herbin à cause de abstr. créa. j'espère bien que le nouveau comité (extrêmement composé des membres de nationalité français) ~~[illegible]~~ aussi bien comme les

Letter from Max Bill to Georges Vantongerloo, 24 February 1937, handwritten on Hotel Waldhaus paper

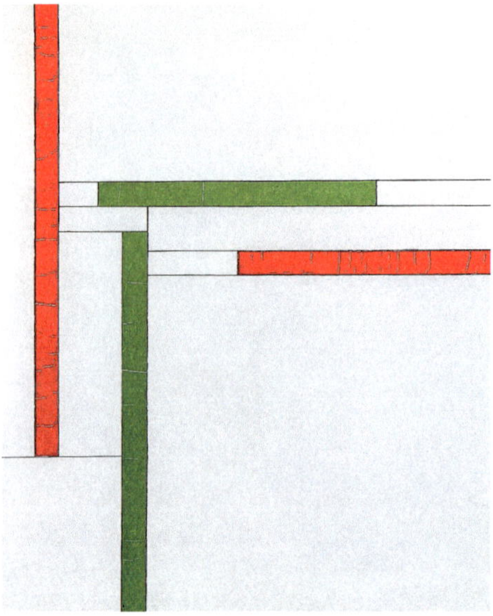

Georges Vantongerloo, *Fonction de lignes rouge-vert,* 1936, oil on triplex board, 79.4×66.1 cm

Max Bill, *konstruktion auf der formel* $a^2+b^2=c^2$, 1937, gouache and india ink on card, 30×50 cm

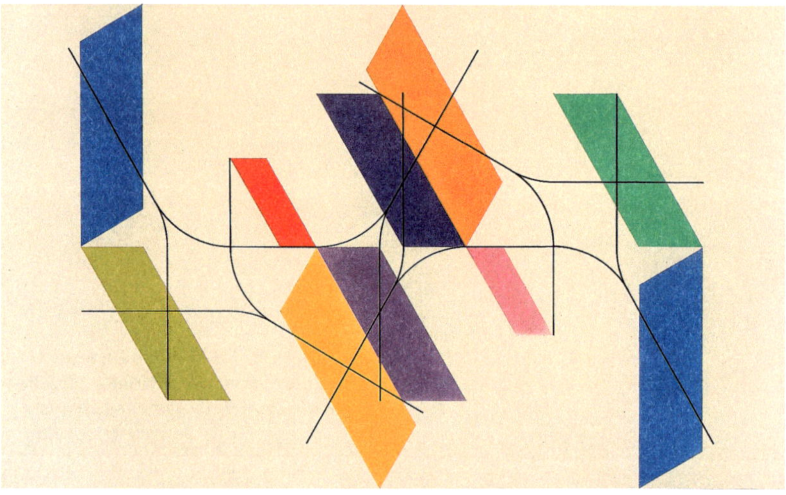

Neue Kunst in der Schweiz

In 1938, at the exhibition *Neue Kunst in der Schweiz* at Kunsthalle Basel (9 January–2 February 1938), Max Bill was finally able to show an entire group of works in a room of his own, which he and the left-wing art historian Georg Schmidt then discussed during public tours.

A black-and-white exhibition view showing Georg Schmidt and Max Bill talking together close to Bill's *konstruktion mit schwebendem kubus* (1935) was reproduced in Angela Thomas, "Max Bill und seine Konzeption von Konkreter Kunst" in *Tages-Anzeiger*, 9 January 1982, p. 41; despite a reminder from Max Bill, the *Tages-Anzeiger* subsequently failed to return the photograph to him.

After the exhibition had closed Binia and Max Bill again went on a skiing holiday, as they had done the year before.

In early March 1938 Bill wrote to Josef Albers and mentioned in passing that the artist Friedrich Vordemberge-Gildewart, who had left Germany, had by now been living with him in Höngg "for some time."

Soon after that Vordemberge-Gildewart and his wife Leda (whose Jewish heritage made life in Germany extremely dangerous for her) set off from Höngg for Holland, where they settled in Amsterdam; Vordemberge made contact there with the Expressionist Max Beckmann who had also fled Germany.

In the same letter he congratulates Albers on his upcoming fiftieth birthday.[1127] Bill also refers to the extreme needs of the people who were being forced to leave Nazi Germany to save their lives and who now had to find somewhere to live; many members of their own "Bauhaus family" had already suffered that fate: "half of the Bauhaus has left Europe since your last letter."[1128]

"Der Architekt jedoch entfloh / nach afri- od- ameriko" ("But the architect fled / to Afri- or Americo"): this is the last couplet of Christian Morgenstern's poem "Der Lattenzaun," which Max Bill occasionally recited to me by heart.

1127 Max Bill to Josef Albers, Black Mountain College, North Carolina, 3 March 1938, Archiv Max Bill

1128 Bill to Albers, 3 March 1938

Bill proudly told Josef Albers about the exhibition *Neue Kunst in der Schweiz:* "I had a room all to myself in it, and the moral success was not bad."[1129]

The artist Anna Baumann visited the exhibition and commented in her notebook: "The wonderful brass sphere by Max Bill. Fascinating."[1130]

However, that same month Peter Meyer published a fierce polemic against Concrete art in *Das Werk,* Switzerland's most important cultural periodical, declaring that this was a form of art that neither set nor acknowledged values, but that shattered values; it embodied "the intoxication of unleashed technology, the sadistic desire to suppress individual life."[1131]

As we have seen, in March 1938 the theater critic Bernhard Diebol, writing in the *Neue Zürcher Zeitung,* used the term "degenerate art" in a Swiss paper.[1132] Manuel Gasser immediately reacted to Diebold's "transgression" in *Die Weltwoche:* "Diebold's article has caused no small upset among Swiss art lovers ... who have instantly recognized the singularity of what is happening here for the first time in Switzerland ... with a journalist and an influential newspaper openly acknowledging a concept of art propagated by Hitler and Goebbels."[1133]

The Basel art collector Oskar Müller, for one, wrote a letter protesting against Peter Meyer's harsh, unjustifiable attack, his negative view of Corbusier's painting, and his sweeping denigration of Surrealist and abstract art—which, by implication, also included what Bill called "Concrete art." That letter, which had over fifty like-minded co-signatories and was published in the May issue of *Das Werk,* specifically stated that "by indiscriminately rejecting this art and defaming it as morally, even politically suspect, Peter Meyer has joined the ranks of those politicians who are out to destroy the standards we live by."[1134]

1129 Bill to Albers, 3 March 1938

1130 Diary of Anna Baumann-Kienast, January 1938, Angela Thomas archive

1131 Peter Meyer, "Moderne Kunst in der Schweiz," *Das Werk* 25:3 (March 1938), p. 76

1132 Bernhard Diebold, "Für wen ist das gemalt?"

1133 Manuel Gasser, "Grundsätzliches zu Bernhard Diebolds Aufsatz 'für wen ist das gemalt?,'" in *Weltwoche,* 11 March 1938, cited in Frosch 2004, p. 41

1134 Oskar Müller, "'Moderne Kunst in der Schweiz'—Ein Protest," in *Das Werk* 25:5 (May 1938), p. 160

1135 Peter Meyer, in *Das Werk* 25:8 (August 1938), p. 256

1136 Jaffé 1971, p. 83

Bill also took action against Meyer's attack and sent a circular letter asking for support from six fellow artists whom he held in high esteem (Gabo, Kandinsky, Mondrian, Pevsner, Vantongerloo, and Vordemberge-Gildewart).

The first response came from Vantongerloo who replied, as ever, by return, enclosing two sketches and a photograph.

In August 1938 *Das Werk* published Max Bill's response to Peter Meyer's accusations ("Über konkrete Kunst" [On Concrete art], no. 25:8, pp. 250–56). His text is followed by a note from Peter Meyer, in his capacity as editor of *Das Werk,* in which Meyer distances himself from Oskar Müller's "collective protest."

"Following the controversy on modern art in *Werk* 1938, part 3, page 74, and part 5, page 159, we happily hand over to an artist [Max Bill] who will set out the arguments relating to the subject of the differences of opinion, not to the latter as such. An attempt to cast light on the situation seems to us far more productive than massed protests."[1135]

At least Meyer acted fairly by giving Bill the right of reply.

Bill illustrated his text with one work each by the six artists he had written to, and one work of his own, his sculpture *unendliche schleife,* which he first conceived in 1935 (see fig. p. 433).

Vordemberge and Bill had been colleagues since their time as members of Abstraction-Création, although Vordemberge, born in Osnabrück in 1899, had joined in 1932 and Max Bill did not join the group until December 1933.

In the circular Bill sent in March 1938, Vordemberge-Gildewart's location is given as "Zürich," since—as Bill told Albers—Vordemberge was temporarily staying with the Bills in Zürich-Höngg.

Vordemberge's *Komposition Nr. 97* (1935) is illustrated first, given pride of place as Bill had done in his suggested layout, which was adopted by *Das Werk.* In 1937, when Friedrich Vordemberge-Gildewart and his wife Ilse Leda were living in Berlin, the Nazis had mocked Vordemberge's art in the Entartete Kunst exhibition in Berlin, so they left Germany for Switzerland, where they had stayed "with friends" in 1937–38,[1136] before moving on to Nicolaas Maes Straat 22 in Amsterdam. Another important work in Bill's layout was Mondrian's painting *Rhythmus von Linien und Farbe* (1937). Bill's circular with a request for images had reached Mondrian in Paris before he finally left for London. All the works illustrated in Bill's article, including Vantongerloo's painting *Fonction de lignes rouge-vert* (1936, see p. 654), were printed in black and white only. Vantongerloo's painting precedes Max Bill's *unendliche schleife,* which is seen in a photograph taken by his wife Binia, who is duly credited next to the image: "Foto Binia Bill SWB, Zürich."

Bill's *unendliche schleife* is followed by a double-page spread with images of sculptures by the Russian brothers Naum Gabo, *Raumkonstruktion* (undated), and Antoine Pevsner, *Konstruktion* (1937–38). Gabo's *Raumkonstruktion* is an extremely interesting, finely balanced construction with "solid" diagonal planes incorporated into a horizontal-vertical figure—which, to me, has a distinct visual affinity with Bill's *denkmal für pythagoras* (1939–41/1978, see p. 351). Bill in fact produced this monument in two versions, one solid and the other open, although in both cases the work is of course about planes, not volumes. The version with solid planes is now in the collection of Jakob Bill. In the "open" version (now in the collection of Angela Thomas), Bill in effect only realized the edges of the planes, giving the work an airy character. This version is balanced on just two of those edges, conveying an impression of extreme fragility and perfect balance, which is in fact underpinned by the mathematical equation $a^2 + b^2 = c^2$. The last image in Bill's article is Wassily Kandinsky's painting *Entassement réglé* (1938). Kandinsky's location is given as Neuilly sur Seine, near Paris, because he had by now finally left Nazi Germany.

One wonders why Bill did not approach any women artists or even name them in his article—figures such as Sophie Taeuber-Arp, who had been acclaimed for her works in the *Konstruktivisten* exhibition in Basel, and Verena Loewensberg from his own generation. The omission of Sophie Taeuber-Arp is perhaps all the more surprising since her work could in fact better be described as Concrete art, as Bill defined it, than as Constructivist.

Creative Concrete Art

Bill's aim in his article for *Das Werk* in August 1938 was to tease out certain art-historical concepts. Ironically, at the point in the article where Bill is discussing Naturalism, the typesetter made an odd error: instead of stating that "every form of naturalism is by definition *unschöpferisch*

1137 Bill 1938 [a], p. 253
1138 Bill 1938 [a], p. 250
1139 Bill 1938 [a], p. 250

[uncreative]," the sentence in question states that "every form of naturalism is by definition *unerschöpflich* [inexhaustible]." Bill corrected that error by hand in one of the reprints of the text. The sentence with the misprint occurs in the following context: "Naturalism in the broadest sense and the combined processes that reproduce nature, such as those seen in Cubism, Surrealism, Expressionism, etc., have nothing whatsoever to do with what we understand by Concrete art. Since every form of naturalism is by definition uncreative, is not creative in its own right, every creative artistic expression excludes any form of naturalism, i.e., the greater the distance to naturalism, the greater the possibility of pure expression."[1137]

For Bill, the naturalism seen in the work of artists such as his former teacher Eduard Bick—which he rejected as "uncreative'—was in fact the polar opposite to what he was striving for in Concrete art and to what had been achieved by his fellow artists in the recent works illustrated in his article for *Das Werk.* These works demonstrate what he was referring to as the "possibility of pure expression," the wealth of possibilities that are intrinsic to what he now called Concrete art and "which had previously generally been erroneously referred to as "abstract art."[1138]

One aspect of the article that Bill wrote on Concrete art in 1938, which particularly catches my attention and surprises me today, is that he admits to there being a "religious-philosophical" component in Concrete art. This is quite at odds with his correspondence with the free economist Fritz Schwarz, in which he rejected the notion of a religious component in the idea of a free economy. I was completely taken aback by the following passage, since I knew Bill as someone who never ever expressed or demonstrated any religious inclinations. And yet in this article, which can almost be read as a manifesto, he wrote: "We are convinced that society will arrive at a democratic view of art from a starting point that does not derive from an obsession with personal, hierarchical, or national self-representation, and that its contents will not, as in earlier great epochs, be sustained by beliefs such as the Egyptians' faith in their fantasy gods, the Greeks' faith in human-like gods and demigods, nor anything resembling the veneration of saints in the Middle Ages, but by a belief in real human beings and in the inherent power of nature itself. In that respect, Concrete art will have a religious-philosophical component."[1139]

Vantongerloo thanked Bill for the article in a letter from Paris, most probably written on 20 August 1938 (the letter is dated 20 July 1938, but since the issue of *Das Werk* that he refers to was not published until August, it seems Vantongerloo must have mistaken the month). He liked the layout of the article, but he criticized the inaccurate translation of an important passage in his own text and added a lengthy polemic against

Mondrian. There are no more letters between Vantongerloo and Bill from 1938 in the Vantongerloo-Archiv. But there is a business card left by Max Bill, evidently on a visit to Paris, with a note written in pencil: "je suis à l'hôtel raspail si vous revenez. salut bill 29.8.38" (If you come back, I am at Hotel Raspail).

The Death of Ernst Ludwig Kirchner

Bill first became acquainted with the work of Ernst Ludwig Kirchner as a teenager at Kunstmuseum Winterthur in 1924 when he joined guided tours led by Georg Schmidt. Later on Bill was especially impressed by Kirchner's *Drei Akte im Walde* (ca. 1933, see p. 661) because of Kirchner's strikingly unusual use of light as a compositional tool. Bill's interest in this painting is a telling example of the works he himself looked to when he was still establishing his own personal frame of reference.

This painting is now in the collection of the Wilhelm-Hack-Museum in Ludwigshafen am Rhein; when a retrospective of Max Bill's work was presented there on the ground floor of the museum in 1990, he specifically alerted me to the Kirchner painting on the upper floor.

Ernst Ludwig Kirchner died a "difficult death" on 15 June 1938, as his student Christian Anton Laely wrote in an article with the title "Why Ernst Ludwig Kirchner Shot Himself": "As yet the real motive for that deed has not come to light. One has read of inner attrition and attenuation, also of physical ailments. . . . This is not to say that all of that left no mark on Kirchner, but the defamation of his works and those of friends from his youth in the Third Reich outraged him! There are those in Germany today who accuse modern art of having been 'judaised.'"[1140]

An Article on Space

After some months of silence between Bill and Vantongerloo, their correspondence resumed in early 1939. Bill contacted his friend with a brief request for more illustrations for an article on "space" that he wanted to write.

1140 Christian Anton Laely, "Ernst Ludwig Kirchner †," *Das Werk* 25:8 (August 1938), p. 225

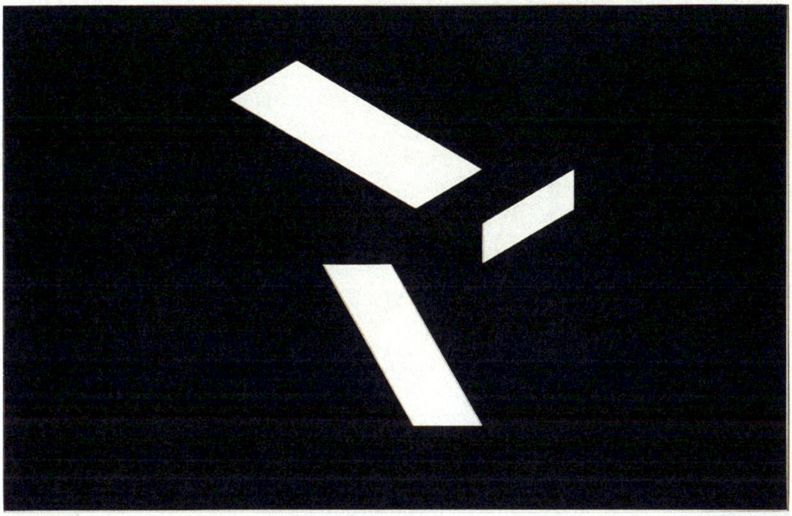

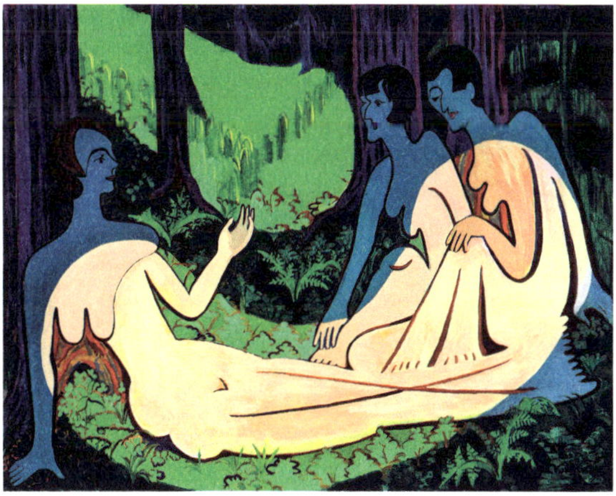

Max Bill, *konstruktion in schwarz,* 1939, cut card, 30×49 cm

Ernst Ludwig Kirchner, *Drei Akte im Walde,* 1934–35, oil on canvas, 149×195 cm

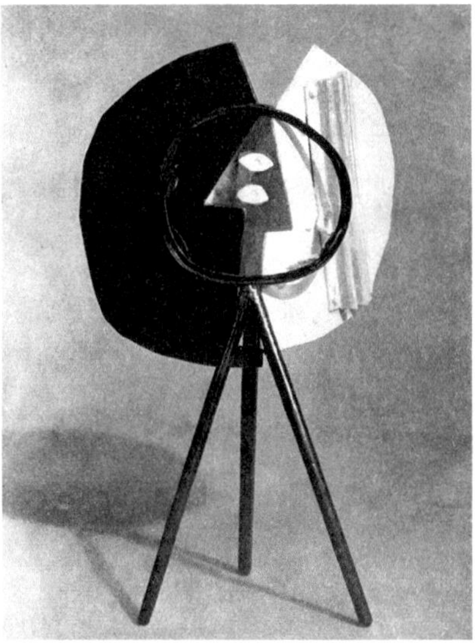

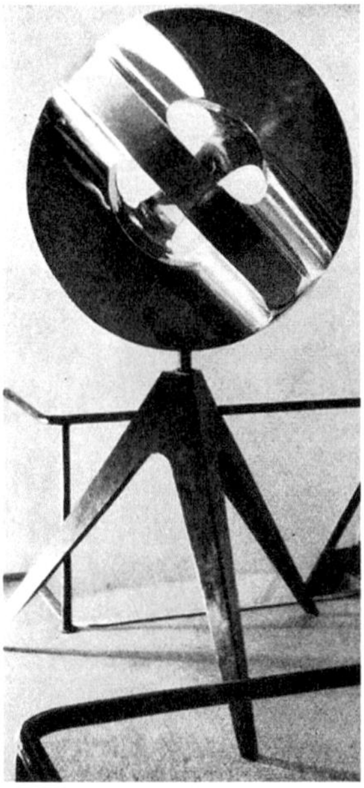

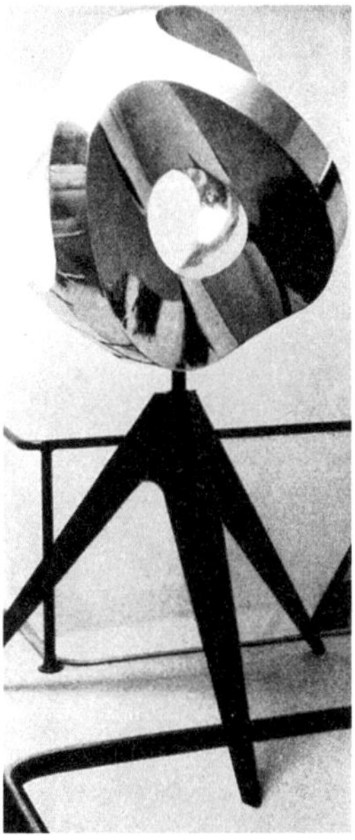

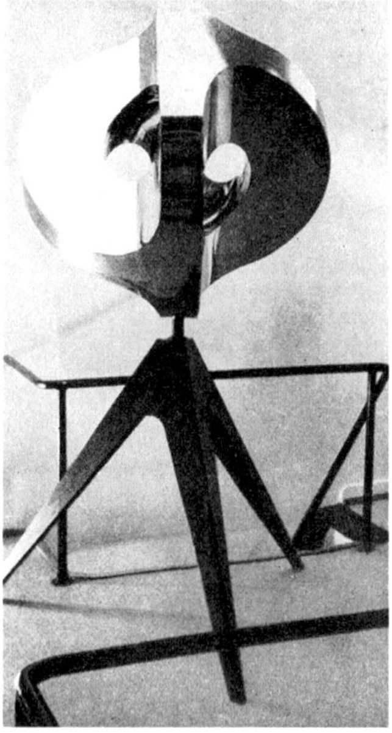

Pablo Picasso, *Tête,* 1928, brass and iron, painted, 18×11×7.5cm
Max Bill, *konstruktion in messing und eisen,* 1937, three views of the same sculpture, brass and iron

It was in the summer of 1939 that Max Bill and Georges Vantongerloo first spent a few days holiday together at Madame de Mandrot's castle.

Concrete Art: "... a truly democratic concept of art"

From 24 February to 10 March 1940 there was a "Salon Indépendant" at the Kongresshaus in Zurich. It was a selling exhibition with no admission fees for visitors and Bill participated in it with three sculptures and one painting. In the official exhibition catalogue the entry for Max Bill directly follows the entry for his former sculpture teacher Eduard Bick. In terms of its content and ideology Bill's work had long since outstripped the naturalism of his former teacher at the Kunstgewerbeschule.

Bill's brief statement in the exhibition catalogue (p. 11) reads: "Concrete art shapes form, color, and space independently of external natural phenomena. Balanced relationships between forms; harmonious and contrasting colors; spatial structures ordered according to artistic laws—all these combine to create what we call Concrete art. As a truly democratic concept of art its contents serve neither national, religious nor individual cravings for self-representation—only the aesthetic needs of humankind."

The participants in the exhibition had been asked to provide short statements. Bick placed the emphasis in his statement on "instinct": "the artist has to leave the crucial balance between art and nature to his instinct, reason and determination may help, but they cannot discover it alone" (p. 11). Eduard Bick's price for a bronze *Frauentorso* was 3,000 Swiss francs, exactly the same price as Max Bill had set for his *konstruktion in messing* (1939, see p. 666), if it sold. Master and student proposed the same prices.

Groups of Identical Elements

Max Bill's friend Hans Hinterreiter, who returned from Ibiza in 1940 having been summoned to appear in person for "medical re-examination," did not send any works to the Salon Indépendant because he was still grieving for his late wife. Opinions of his work were sometimes divided. The Zurich artist Richard Paul Lohse, already a well-known name by then, rejected Hinterreiter's work out of hand. However, Bill staunchly defended

Hinterreiter: "There can't be only horizontal-vertical works!"[1141] In fact the discussion about strictly "horizontal–vertical" compositions had already played out long ago in Paris at Abstraction-Création in the mid-1930s. But Lohse may well not have been aware of that debate, since he had not been a member of the group.

"Around this time numerous, hitherto dogmatic Constructivists in the group learned something from 'dissidents' such as Arp and Hélion, and Kandinsky, too, and made a radical, paradigmatic shift from the right angle ... to the curved or free floating line."[1142]

Unlike Lohse, Bill was heartened and stimulated by Hinterreiter's work, particularly by the idea of creating compositions from groups of identical elements. After all, in Paris in 1938 Max Bill had himself already published his fifteen variations on a theme that he had devised in 1935, which progresses from a triangle to an octagon and back again. That series had already featured arcs, drawn with the utmost geometric precision (but of course rejected by Lohse). And Bill had also assembled groups of identical elements, as in the sculptures *konstruktion aus 30 gleichen elementen* (1938–39, see p. 665), *konstruktion in messing* (1939, see p. 666), and *konstruktion aus drei quadratgrößen* (*denkmal für pythagoras,* 1939–41/1978, see p. 351).

A Subversive Sheen

Bill's sculptures gleam, but not only because he sometimes gilded the brass they are made from, as in his *denkmal für pythagoras.* There is never a sense of alienation in Bill's works; he always chose his own path. They have an aura of complete autonomy and a subversive sheen that never dims, not even in quite everyday situations. They remind us that every human being has the right to work without feeling alienated and should have chance to savour the ensuing contentment, although even today large swathes of society still do not enjoy that right.

A few years after he had made his *konstruktion aus 30 gleichen elementen* (1938–39, see p. 665) Bill provided a explanation: this sculpture "is a three-dimensional demonstration of a solution to the problem of progressively developing a shape into a rhythmic figure. The construction, based on the number six, starts at the left with six identical elements, the next group of six is crossed over by a vertical group of six, meanwhile the

1141 Max Bill in conversation with Angela Thomas

1142 Gassner 1994, p. 27

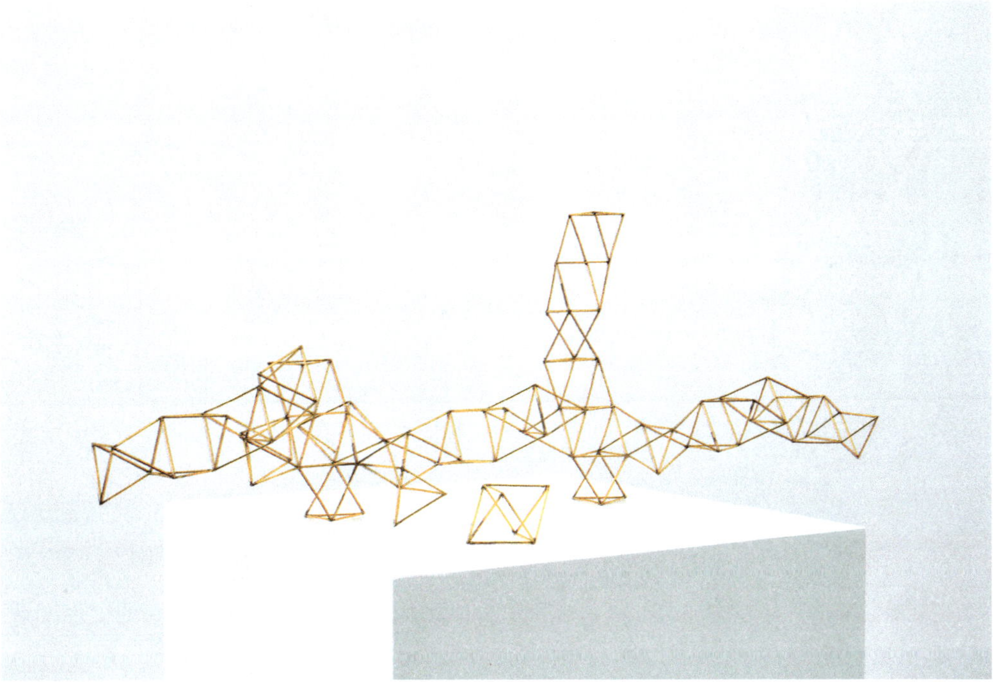

Max Bill, *konstruktion aus 30 gleichen elementen,* 1938–39, gold-plated sculpture, 30 × 90 × 16 cm

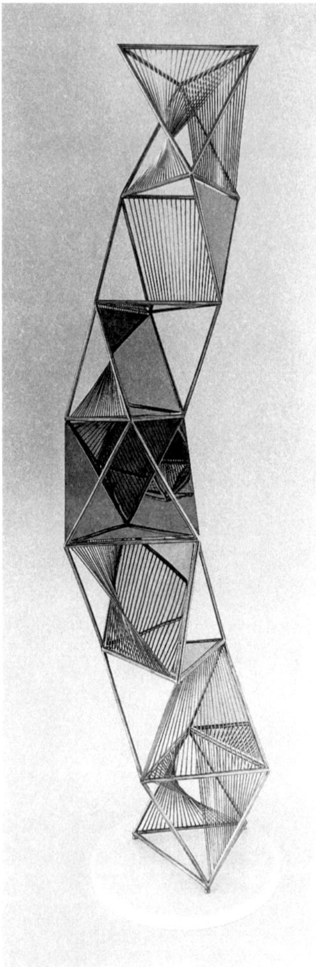

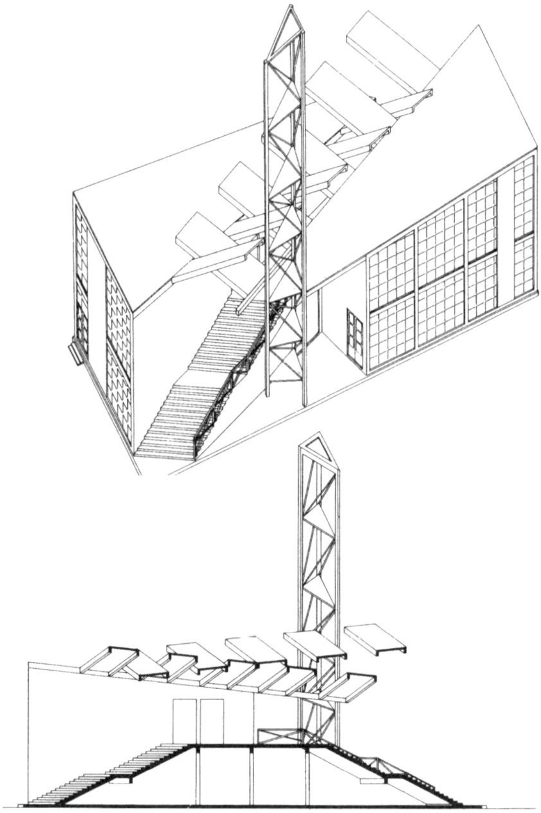

Max Bill, *konstruktion in messing,* 1939, brass, 142 × 36 × 36 cm

Konstantin Stepanovich Melnikov, Design for the Soviet Pavilion at the Exposition Internationale des Arts Décoratifs in Paris, 1925

first half of the last group of six is enclosed in six more elements and the second half of that group, like the beginning, fades quietly away. Below it there is one element as a single unit."[1143]

"In 1930 Hans Hinterreiter embarked on systematic investigations into colors and forms based on Ostwald's color theory. His method produced continuously connected color and form progressions."[1144]

It may be that, in addition to Hans Hinterreiter's "heartening" example, the Melnikov Pavilion (1925) with its progression of elements rising vertically upward—seen by Bill in Paris some years earlier—was also a source of inspiration, unbeknownst to Bill, for his *konstruktion in messing* (1939).

At one point Bill suggested to Hans Hinterreiter that instead of using his small-format studies for light projections, Hinterreiter could convert them into larger formats, into paintings that could be exhibited and viewed at leisure. And Hans Hinterreiter did then participate in the Allianz group exhibition at Kunsthaus Zürich in 1942, despite the differences in artistic ideology between himself and Lohse.

Looking Back: The American Dream

By now yet another acquaintance of Max Bill's—Xanti Schawinsky, whom he had first met at the Bauhaus in Dessau—had emigrated to the United States. Schawinsky had been appointed to a post at Black Mountain College in North Carolina, where Josef Albers was also teaching, and now took the opportunity to sing Max Bill's praises there, as Albers reported in a letter to Bill in January 1937: "Dear Bill, Xanti Schawinsky . . . has been telling me that you are an important exhibition maker."[1145]

By the time Josef Albers and his wife Anni, who was of Jewish descent, decided to leave Germany and managed to secure a passage to the United States (in 1933) "abstraction was over" in Germany, as Albers used to put it. A few years later, Albers wrote to Bill asking if he could put any exhibition opportunities in Europe his way. Schawinsky added a few handwritten lines to Albers's letter: "Dear Bills, a quick greeting, until I get round to writing a proper letter. We're floating in the most glorious holidays and muddling along together in American. Ahoi! Xanti."

1143 See Bill 1942

1144 Bill 1976 [b]

1145 Josef Albers, Black Mountain, North Carolina, to Max Bill, Zurich, 5 January 1937, Bibliothek Max Bill

That "muddling along together in American," as Xanti described it—that more relaxed lifestyle than in Europe—may also have made it somewhat easier for Anni and Josef Albers to negotiate life as a couple, in the sense that they were now in a situation where their very different backgrounds no longer mattered as much as before. Josef was from Bottrop in the Ruhr, Germany's main coal mining district, where his father was a house painter and joiner. Anni (Annelies), née Fleischmann, was a Berliner through and through. Her father owned a furniture factory and her mother was from the Ullstein publishing dynasty. Anni had grown up in Berlin-Charlottenburg, where she was looked after by an Irish nanny and attended to by a butler. "She was a dark beauty with her own proud charm, exquisitely brought up and socially adept; he—ten years her senior—was Catholic and blond, a rather sociable fellow with a didactic drift."[1146]

In 1936, in view of his lack of professional success as yet in Switzerland, Bill started to learn English with some determination. He was very motivated because he had a new dream: no longer yearning to go to the Soviet Union, he now had his sights set on the United States, and he wrote in that vein to Albers on 24 January 1937: "My successes here are such that I have diligently been taking English lessons for a month now and am planning, as soon as possible, to exchange this inhospitable realm in the midst of not precisely pleasing Europe for the United States and maybe soon to become involved in the World's Fair in New York [1938]." In response to Josef Albers's inquiry about potential exhibition opportunities, Bill outlined the current situation in Switzerland: "... no private galleries are interested in our work because there is little prospect of financial gain. The public galleries are always filled with group exhibitions." And it seems that the situation in Paris was no better. As Bill also reported in his letter, nothing had sold at Kandinsky's seventieth birthday exhibition at Galerie Jeanne Bucher.[1147]

In 1937, when Albers was already at Black Mountain College, Walter Gropius accepted an invitation to teach at Harvard University in Cambridge, Massachusetts. By now several Bauhauslers from Bill's time in Dessau—Albers, Moholy-Nagy, Gropius, and Schawinsky—

1146 Ludmila Vachtova, "Knall mit Wetterleuchten. Eine Künstlervita im Zweigespann als fortlaufende Erfolgsgeschichte: Josef und Anni Albers," in *Die Weltwoche,* 5 November 1998

1147 Max Bill, Zurich, to Josef Albers, Black Mountain College, Black Mountain, North Carolina, 24 January 1937, Archiv Max Bill

1148 Max Bill to Josef Albers, 3 March 1938, Archiv Max Bill

had emigrated to the United States and were working there. They had all responded very favorably to Bill's work on the Swiss pavilion at the Milan Triennial when news of it had reached the United States.

With a view to potentially emigrating to the United States, Bill now started work on designs for the Swiss pavilion at the New York World's Fair in collaboration with two Swiss architects, whose names he never mentioned to me but whom he did describe as already being well established in the United States. However, the competition entry that Bill and the Swiss architects submitted was not selected and that rather dissuaded him from leaving for the land of endless possibilities. In March 1939 he explained his thinking to Albers: "I have to say, for all the appeal of going to the United States, I don't really have the courage to just go and try my luck."[1148] At the same time, he had by now enjoyed welcome success in Basel at the exhibition *Neue Kunst in der Schweiz* in 1938 and had also already been commissioned to create a sculpture for the Swiss National Exhibition in 1939. The sense of frustration that had troubled Max Bill for a time subsided again, at least for a while.

Abstract Art in Amsterdam

Soon after Bill's participation in *Neue Kunst in der Schweiz* (9 January–2 February 1938), he also participated in the exhibition *Abstracte Kunst* in Amsterdam, which opened at the Stedelijk Museum on 2 April 1938. Bill showed two works: *konstruktion* (1937, see pp. 662 and 671) and *vier konstruktionen: variationen über ein thema* (1935–38).

These two works are seen together in a photograph reproduced in *Tentoonstelling Abstracte Kunst,* exh. cat., Stedelijk Museum Amsterdam, 2–24 April 1938, p. 15.

As it happens, one of the members of the jury was Mart Stam, whom Max Bill would very much have liked to accompany to the USSR some years earlier. Stam also helped to install the exhibition.

In Amsterdam Bill found himself in the company of other leading artists. Piet Mondrian was represented with four works and there were three works by Moholy-Nagy; there were also works by Antoine Pevsner, whose art had already particularly interested Max Bill at the *Konstruktivisten* exhibition. Five women also participated in *Abstracte Kunst,* including two English artists, Barbara Hepworth and Marlow Moss, and two French artists, Paule Vézelay and Jeanne Kosnick-Kloss, whose husband, Otto Freundlich, was represented there, too. However, of all the works shown by women artists only one—*Two Forms in Plane Wood* (1937) by Barbara Hepworth—was illustrated in the catalogue. Many of the exhibiting artists attended the opening, "including Arp, Brancusi, Vordemberge-Gildewart, Kandinsky, Pevsner, and Bill."[1149]

Although Wies van Moorsel names Brancusi among the artists who attended the opening in Amsterdam, I would question this, since Max Bill once told me, with some regret, that he had unfortunately never "personally" encountered Brancusi, whose work he greatly admired.

Gualtieri di San Lazzaro and *XXe siècle*

Max Bill spent longer than usual in Paris in 1938, in part to ensure that his first systematically developed series of prints, *fünfzehn variationen über ein thema,* was printed to the highest possible standard. Max Bill's works were not yet widely known in Paris at that time. Only art lovers with a taste for the avant-garde who attended the exhibitions at Abstraction-Création's own gallery, which featured works by Bill from December 1933 onward, would have been able to place him.

It was Gualtieri di San Lazzaro, from Sicily—the owner of Édition des chroniques du jour in Paris—who was willing to risk publishing Bill's folio, *fünfzehn variationen über ein thema* (1935–38). The folio also included an introduction by Max Bill, which was translated into English by A. J. Dakin and into French by Jean-Paul Samson—Bill's longstanding friend whom he had worked with both at the Krater cabaret in the late 1920s and at *information.* The series was printed in Paris by Fernand Mourlot, the preeminent printer who collaborated with both Pablo Picasso and Henri Matisse. Much to Bill's regret he never happened to run into Matisse—whom he so greatly admired—in Mourlot's studio. After Gualtieri di San Lazzaro's death on 7 September 1974, the writer André Pieyre de Mandiarques wrote a homage to him as the publisher "whose taste, in culture, always gravitated toward shock, renewal, and revolution."[1150]

San Lazzaro's biographer, Pierre Volboudt, presents his multi-faceted subject as a sceptical enthusiast, torn this way and that, who was driven by his own impulsive curiosity: "his cause was that of all the creations that decided the face of an era. He contributed more than anyone else to revealing them; he served them with a lucid fervor that an apparent

1149 Van Moorsel 2003, p. 234
1150 Pieyre de Mandiarques 1975

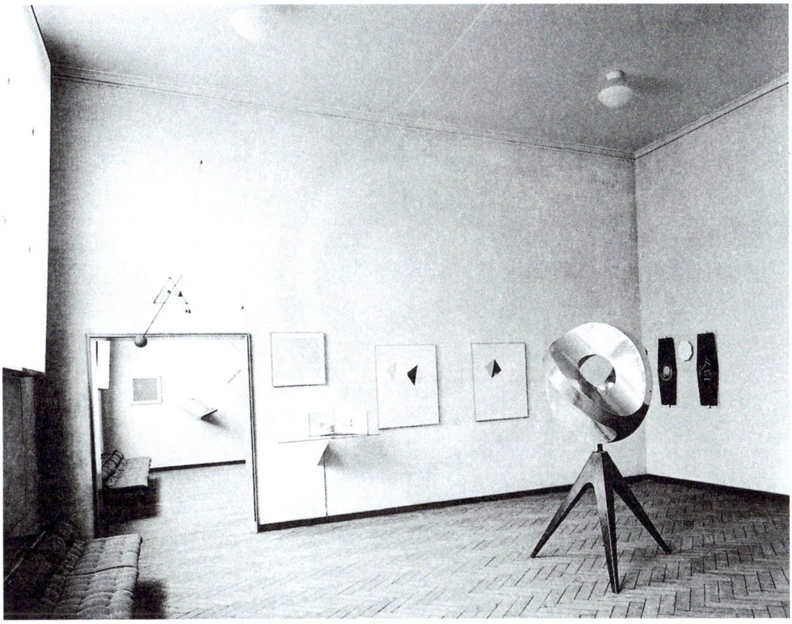

View of the exhibition *Abstracte Kunst* at the Stedelijk Museum, Amsterdam, 2–24 April 1938. Max Bill's *konstruktion in messing und eisen* (1937) has a prominent position

Cover of *XXe siècle* 4 (1938)

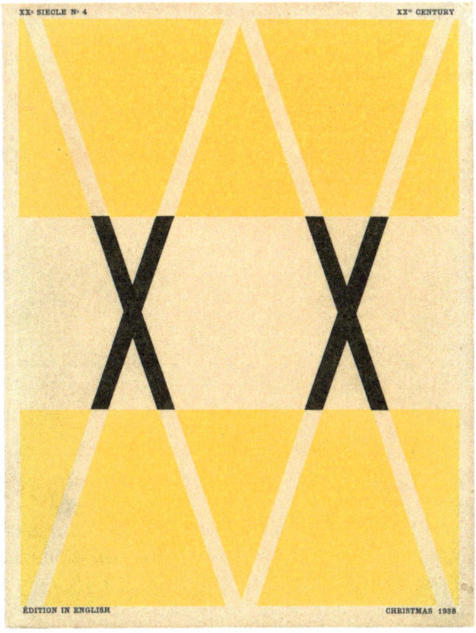

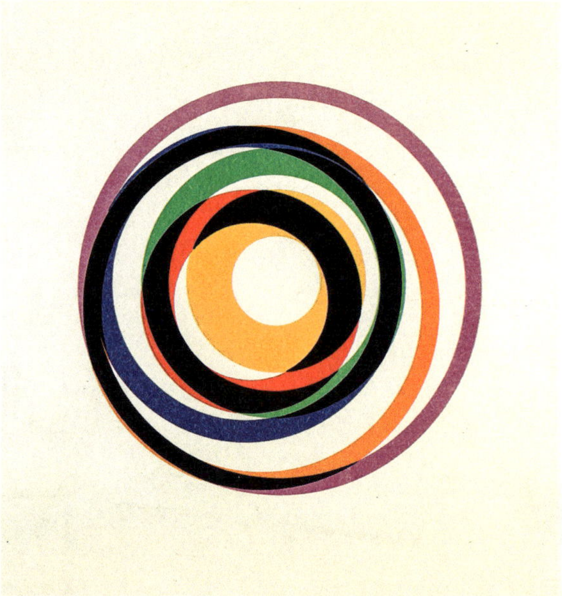

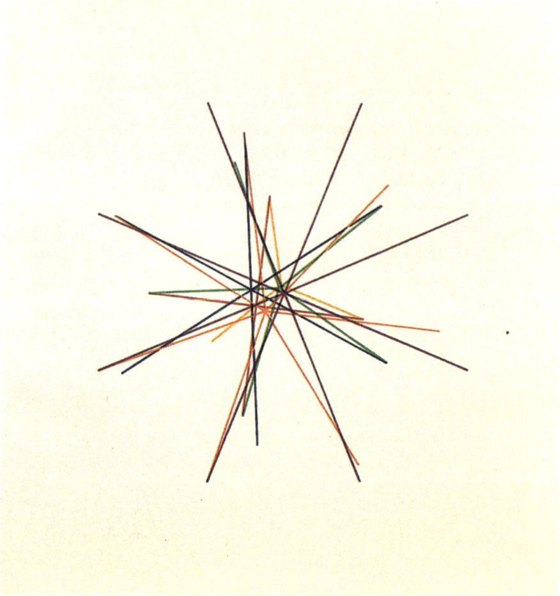

Max Bill, Two sheets from the series of prints *fünfzehn variationen über ein thema,* 1935–38, 30.5 × 32 cm

detachment barely concealed under a charming and distracted courtesy ... this manyfold San Lazzaro, always divided between himself and himself ... under the cover of an authoritarian timidity maintained as a kind of protective dandyism, this enthusiastic skeptic ..."[1151]

The publication *San Lazzaro et ses amis,* from which these lines are taken, was sold in a sturdy box which also contained original lithographs by Max Ernst and Max Bill, among others.

It is said that this little Sicilian often seemed cold, "impassively enigmatic," caught up in a puzzling, emotional stasis, cold-blooded. But this aloof demeanor was only a ploy to allow him to make judgments that were all the more precise and, in fact, impassioned: "San Lazzaro, cold and proper, would issue a ferocious judgment without batting an eyelid, with a fleeting smile followed by a comment conveying the most glacial of British humor." When he was listening he generally appeared distracted, deliberately concealing his ostensibly absent, unmoved gaze behind cigarette smoke. Yet this man who seemed undecided, sceptical to some, as if he were incapable of real spirit, in fact had the capacity to be a great, enduring loyal friend.[1152]

Some of San Lazzaro's contemporaries found him taciturn and distant, even mistrustful, but Bill got on well with him and they became good friends, with San Lazzaro feeling able to show Bill another more generous side of his character—revealing a touch of "*grande noblesse*"—and with Bill taking pleasure in San Lazzaro's flashes of subtle irony.

San Lazzaro's inner circle of friends in Paris included the Kandinskys and Nusch and Paul Éluard. He had first met Wassily and Nina Kandinsky in April 1930. In 1935 and 1936 San Lazzaro was in particularly close contact with the Kandinskys, who gladly took the opportunity to talk Russian with San Lazzaro's Lithuanian wife, Racha. The Kandinskys and the San Lazzaros often dined together in Paris.[1153] Bill may in fact have first been introduced to San Lazzaro by the Kandinskys or the Éluards, or by Jean Arp, who also knew him well.

Bill's past lover, Nusch Éluard, who by now had already modeled for several portraits by Picasso, also greatly impressed San Lazzaro. He marvelled at her as one of the only two "really beautiful" women—with their own mysterious sensuality—he had met during the course of his life. Indeed he felt that Nusch was not merely beautiful, she also had a "brilliant" aura. The other marvel was a wonderfully beautiful Russian woman who cared for Matisse in his old age with the kind of "devotion one associates with another age."

1151 Volboudt 1975
1152 Marchiori 1975
1153 See Jouffroy 1975

"Matisse lived separated from his wife, in an apartment on the boulevard Montparnasse, where a beautiful Russian lady took care of him with a devotion from another time ... she was one of the two really beautiful women and as if tempered by a secret voluptuousness, which he had known.

The other was Nusch Éluard, more spiritual, at least in the physical, of which Picasso had made a marvelous portrait."[1154]

On 13 March 1938, the day after Hitler's Annexation of Austria, the first issue of San Lazzaro's art periodical, *XXe siècle,* came out in Paris with a cover design by Max Bill. San Lazzaro, who was far from sectarian, would soon publish illustrations of a wide range of works in his periodical—from abstract to Concrete to Surrealist—anything that sought to oppose the menacing wave of ignorance and violence that was on the horizon.

Looking back, San Lazzaro summed up the atmosphere of that time: "in 1938, we already feared that we were on the brink of disaster ... shaking hands with artists—with the most diverse interests but all opposed to the sheer stupidity that we were not wrong to anticipate surging toward us—was a necessity, in terms of both humanity and history: resisting the imminent deluge."[1155]

XXe siècle did not, however, achieve the success that San Lazzaro had hoped for. Although he included illustrations of works by Surrealist artists, *XXe siècle* was not able to compete with *Minotaure,* the magazine published by Albert Skira and the Surrealists. *Minotaure* gave the Surrealists very considerable influence in Paris at the time, and their exhibitions subliminally kindled a persistent, stubborn aversion to the more daring modern trends—and hence to Concrete art in particular.

"the exhibition of the Surrealists had provoked a sneaky but tenacious aversion against the most daring tendencies of modern art."[1156]

As if oblivious to the wider political dangers, the same artists who had been united in their opposition to the nationalists now began to fight each other on stylistic grounds. San Lazzaro had to come up with something. In fact it was Jean Arp (equally at ease in both Surrealism and abstract art) who had given him the idea of publishing original prints in *XXe siècle.* San Lazzaro already put that idea into practice in the third issue of *XXe siècle* (July, August, September 1938), which contains an original colored woodcut by Kandinsky; readers also learned that issue no. 4 would contain "8 original prints by Henri Matisse, Henri Laurens, Miró,

1154 San Lazzaro 1966, pp. 187–88
1155 Gualtieri di San Lazzaro in *XXe siècle* 27 (Paris, December 1966)
1156 San Lazzaro 1966, pp. 187–88
1157 Courthion 1975, pp. 41–42

Arp, Magnelli, de Chirico, Zadkine, Hélion, and 2 lithographs by Marcel Duchamp and by Max Bill. . . . *XXe siècle* has been launched . . . and will become the best known of all art magazines."[1157] However, the invasion of France by the Fascists in 1940 stopped the presses at *XXe siècle* for many years, with result that Max Bill and his fellow artists no longer had the opportunity to reach a wider public through its pages. It was only after the liberation of Paris that *XXe siècle* could resume publication, with contributions from Arp, Louis Aragon, Max Ernst, Antoine Pevsner, and others.
The launch of the periodical *XXe siècle* (with original prints) on the international stage also marked the international launch of the work of Max Bill, which was now seen alongside works by leading artists such as Matisse, Arp and Duchamp.

XXe siècle was not only the name of the periodical that San Lazzaro assembled with such care and attention to detail, it was also the name of the gallery that he would later open in Rue des Canettes. Besides his activities as both publisher and gallerist, San Lazzaro was also a respected writer, the author of autobiographical books and, among other things, a monograph on Paul Klee, which was translated into German, English, Italian, and Portuguese (*Klee. La vie et l'œuvre,* ed. Fernand Hazan, Paris 1957).
Gualtieri di San Lazzaro's second wife was Maria Papa, an attractive and talented Polish sculptor.

Following the death of San Lazzaro, the Musée d'art Moderne de la Ville de Paris paid homage to this major figure in an exhibition: *San Lazzaro et ses amis, hommage au fondateur de XXe siècle* (19 November 1975 to 11 January 1976). The list of participants names many leading artists, including Jean Arp, Calder, Chagall, Robert and Sonia Delaunay, Max Ernst, Hartung, Kandinsky, Man Ray, Miró, Dorothea Tanning and Max Bill, who showed three works in this exhibition in honor of his friend.

The Breadth of Variation in Concrete Art

Bill had worked out the "theme" of his *fünfzehn variationen über ein thema* (1935–38) in 1935. Limiting himself to just six colors plus black, gray, and white, Bill rang the changes in his variations with the utmost precision. Moreover, when he published his *fünfzehn variationen* Bill in effect publicly demonstrated the breadth of variation that could be discovered in Concrete art—in a "*coup de génie*" that, as it happens, also debunked Peter Meyer's accusations. As Max Bill himself said: "The very fact that a single theme—a single basic idea—leads to such a wealth of possible variations within very strict parameters, to fifteen very different entities, in itself serves as proof that Concrete art contains within it endless possibilities."[1158] This first series of Bill's, with its truly exemplary aesthetic logic, paved the way for the subsequent development of Concrete art.

Many years later, in 1980, Bill told me that he sent a copy of his *fünfzehn variationen* to Piet Mondrian, who was no longer in Paris by then, having arrived in London on 21 September 1938. Mondrian sent a letter in response, explaining that the variations were "too naturalistic" in his view.

In his foreword to the *fünfzehn variationen* Bill had noted that "although geometry provided the material for this work ... the thinking that leads to forms of this kind is neither mathematical nor geometric. what is seen in the 'fünfzehn variationen über ein thema' is purely a game with forms and colors, with no external compulsion to be anything other than that, with the sole purpose of bringing joy."[1159]

Bill's use of rounded shapes evidently did not find favor with Mondrian. In 1938 Mondrian was sixty-six years old; Max Bill turned thirty in December 1938. Mondrian was evacuated from London in 1940 as the air raids increased and in September 1940 he settled in New York.

The devastating accounts by figures such as Barbara Hepworth, Ben Nicholson and Naum Gabo of the two years that Mondrian spent in London (September 1938 to September 1940) are well worth reading. See "Mondrian in London," *Studio International, Journal of Modern Art* (December 1966), pp. 285–99.

Years later, critics were still alluding to the importance of Bill's first systematic series in exhibition reviews. In 1976, for instance, in his review of the *Max Bill* retrospective in Hamburg, Gottfried Sello discussed the *fünfzehn variationen* at some length: "Four decades later the importance of this series of variations is readily apparent because we know what it has given rise to, we know of the countless artists who have pursued a similar path, which is still pursued now by young Constructivists in the seventies who work according strict mathematical principles.... What distinguishes Bill from his successors, what he demonstrates in his *fünfzehn variationen,* is that he is never dogmatic.... Bill, the artist, does what no mathematician or computer can do. He makes a choice from the

1158 Max Bill in conversation with Angela Thomas

1159 Bill 1938 [b]

1160 Gottfried Sello, "Das Dreieck wird rund," in *Die Zeit,* 12 March 1976

endless possible variables suggested by the theme 'from triangle to octagon': fifteen variations, not one more, not one less. And his selection criteria have nothing to do with mathematics; they are situated in the realm of sight and vision."[1160]

"... the deluge"

On 23 December 1938, the day after Max Bill's thirtieth birthday, Professor Hans Bernoulli—Bill's mentor from the free economy movement—received a letter signed by the president of the Swiss school board (the board of the ETH) informing him that his contract would not be renewed for the summer semester of 1939.

When Bill returned to Switzerland from the Bauhaus, the Free Economists held meetings, also attended by Bill, "every Monday, at 8 p.m., Bahnhofplatz 2, 2nd floor, in the premises of Tess-A.G." (from November 1929 onward); the discussions were led by "Prof. Bernoulli" (according to announcements in *Letzte Politik* 8:41, 1929, and in the following issue).

Hans Bernoulli, a native of Basel, is still remembered in Zurich today for the Bernoulli Houses that he built and now bear his name. However, few are aware that Bernoulli was obliged to resign from his teaching post at ETH Zürich because of his activities as a Free Economist and for his publicly aired critiques in December 1938.

The reasons given were nothing short of scandalous. Because Bernoulli had been publicly critical of certain developments he was now accused of launching "attacks against the most important Federal Offices." That in itself showed just how little public debate was allowed in Switzerland at that time; it was also symptomatic of the looming political "deluge" that was already making itself felt in Switzerland, as Bill's friend San Lazzaro had so aptly put it in Paris.

The letter that informed "Herrn Titularprofessor H. Bernoulli, Riehen-Basel, Bettingerweg 22" that he was no longer permitted to teach at the ETH, contains the following passage: "Dear Sir, with reference to your external activities promoting the doctrine of a Free Economy ... since 1933 these activities have led to multiple inquiries from others as to whether your attacks against the most important Federal Offices are compatible with your teaching responsibilities at a Federal institution. You are widely known as a teacher at the ETH.... However, with the Swiss Education Council already repeatedly having had to address your external activities and repeatedly having tried to draw a line between the outstanding expert in urban planning and the Free Economist, it believes it can no longer maintain this position.... The Swiss Education Council has thus ... resolved not to renew your teaching contract in the field of urban planning after the end of the winter semester."[1161]

Bernoulli's biographer, Werner Schmid, reported that "Bernoulli was greatly afflicted by that shock," not least because he was very devoted to his students. Bernoulli had told Schmid that "there had been no discussion with him for ten years." His dismissal also horrified Bernoulli's ETH students who vehemently protested against it, as did the Bund Schweizer Architekten (Association of Swiss architects).

On 18 January 1939 Hans Bernoulli approached the Federal Councillor Philipp Etter, the head of the Federal Department of Home Affairs, in an effort to have the "decision rescinded"; over two months later, on 24 March 1939, Etter informed Bernoulli that his request had been rejected. "Malevolent Etter," as Werner Schmid calls him, "insisted that this was a decision taken by the School Board and that the Federal Council had no capacity to intervene"; Schmid concludes that "the guardians of Swiss cultural life thus looked on as an outstanding expert in his own field, highly regarded at home and abroad—as the School Board itself agreed—was dismissed from his post because he had dared to hold and express a different political opinion."[1162]

The writer Werner Schmid, born in 1898 in Zollikon, canton of Zürich, also published biographies of the Free Economists Silvio Gesell and Fritz Schwarz, with whom Max Bill corresponded. For seven years Schmid ran the Büro gegen Amts- und Verbandswillkür (an independent ombudsman service), which was set up by Gottlieb Duttweiler, the founder of Migros, a co-operative retail company. Schmid, who was a member of the Zurich Gemeinderat (city parliament), the Zurich Cantonal Council, and the National Council, also became honorary president of the Liberal Socialist Party of Switzerland.

1161 The letter is reproduced in full in Werner Schmid 1974, pp. 43–44

1162 Schmid 1974, p. 4

1163 Peter Meyer, in his capacity as editor of *Das Werk, Schweizer Monatsschrift des BSA und SWB für Architektur, Kunst, Kunstgewerbe,* Zurich, to Alfred Roth, Architect BSA [Swiss Architects' Association], Doldertal 19, Zurich (14 December 1939), copy inserted into a publication about Alfred Roth, Bibliothek Max Bill

1164 Max Bill to Paul Klee, Bern, 16 December 1939, copy kindly made available by the Klee expert Stefan Frey, Bern, 2007

It is hardly surprising that Max Bill, appalled by the Swiss authorities' outrageous treatment of his free economy mentor, now became seriously concerned that his own professional life might be under threat due his personal interest in the idea of a free economy. That concern may well have strengthened his desire to leave Switzerland.

". . . the same dismaying impression of complete nothingness"

Max Bill's concerns were not unfounded given that Peter Meyer, for one, was still a hostile adversary. Having viewed Bill's *fünfzehn variationen,* Meyer reiterated his derogatory views on Bill's art in a letter to Alfred Roth: "I have looked at Max Bill's Variations and have read the text, only for both to leave me with the same dismaying impression of complete nothingness. . . . In both respects, the sensual and the intellectual, these Variations are arbitrary and unfounded." Furthermore, the theme chosen by Bill was "simply childish." And Meyer concludes: "I believe that one can of course toy with these things, but one should not abuse them . . . thus I cannot bring myself to recommend this work by Bill. . . . with best regards, yours, Peter Meyer."[1163]

Two days before that letter was sent to Bill's colleague, the architect Alfred Roth, indirectly accusing Bill of "abusing" art, of not producing serious art that needed to be taken seriously, Bill had himself sent a letter with birthday wishes to Paul Klee in Bern, who was not in good health: "I congratulate you most sincerely on your birthday today and wish you better health in the coming years than in the past year. . . . yours, Bill."[1164]

Spirals

Bill had a particular fondness for the "contrary-motion" or reverse spiral, which is seen in his *fünfzehn variationen* (1935–38) and which would reappear in his steel-wire *spirale* (1944–48). By contrast, Brancusi had a distinct aversion to reverse spirals, which he called "death spirals." As the art historian Carola Giedion-Welcker writes, Brancusi felt that the reverse spiral had something "fatal" about it: Brancusi drew "a spiral that did not open up like a growing leaf but that turned back in on itself! Egocentric development, he said, disoriented withdrawal from bright life into the darkness, which can lead to suicide. In his view ... it was a willful aberration of the grand destiny and rhythm of life. Klee also recognizes 'life spirals and death spirals' that either lead into open expanses 'filled with movement' or into a confined space, which is 'hostile to movement.'"[1165]

In 1993, when Max Bill and I returned to Zumikon from a trip to Paris, he told me that he had visited Paul Klee in Bern and had given him a folio of his *fünfzehn variationen über ein thema;* he also mentioned that Klee himself had painted some "spiral pictures" in 1938.[1166] In a letter to Siegfried Salzmann, Bill later noted that he had had "several opportunities" to visit Paul Klee in his home toward the end of his life, when he saw "new compositions and others that Klee was still working on ... our relationship was also influenced by the fact that he had grown up very close to my own home town and that we spoke a similar dialect, which he always preferred to High German. Klee once said he was astonished that although he did not remember seeing me in his theoretical classes, I was one of the few who had understood what he was trying to do with his theories."[1167]

The disease that Klee suffered from in his last years, which greatly troubled him, was probably an extremely rare, very acute form of scleroderma, an autoimmune disease.[1168] There are a number of potential explanations for its onset: "In the complex course of an autoimmune disease both external and internal influences have to be taken into account as possible causes. In Klee's case the disease could have been triggered by inhaling organic solvents used in his paints or by the traumas he underwent in Germany and his inevitable isolation as an artist on his return to Switzerland."[1169]

1165 Giedion-Welcker 1958, p. 199
1166 Handwritten note made by Angela Thomas on 31 March 1993
1167 Max Bill, Zurich, to Dr. Siegfried Salzmann (18 March 1971), cited in *Paul Klee und seine Malerfreunde,* 1971
1168 Suter 2006, p. 102
1169 Suter 2006, p. 107

Bill, Mondrian, and Duchamp Take Tea with the Pevsners

In the 1930s Max Bill took a keen interest in cultural and political developments in France. He met many artists living in Paris, both on his own account and as a member of Abstraction-Création. During one trip to Paris in 1938 Bill and Piet Mondrian were invited to tea at home with Antoine Pevsner, and it was on that occasion that Bill met Marcel Duchamp. The tea was served not only with caviar (not to Bill's taste) but also with *Rotoreliefs* brought by Duchamp, which he demonstrated on a portable gramophone placed on the floor. His six "rotating reliefs"—discs printed in color on both sides and played at slow speeds—did not meet with unanimous approval. The moving images generated by the *Rotoreliefs* —"Lamp," "Montgolfière," and "Poisson japonais" were the titles of some—somewhat resembled the naturalistic sequences seen in kinetoscopes earlier in the century. Three-dimensionality was conjured out of two-dimensional configurations by means of rotation—neo-Renaissance! As ever, when something perturbed Mondrian or seemed "too naturalistic" to him, he took refuge in silence.

Meanwhile Duchamp's *Rotoreliefs* came as a considerable shock to Max Bill. He immediately saw that those colored discs (when they were not in motion) had "a bewildering external affinity" with his own *fünfzehn variationen,* which were currently being printed. It may have been due to that initial shock that Bill was always drawn to Marcel Duchamp's work after that. Years later, in Zurich, Bill would be involved with exhibitions of works by all the other three artists who were at that tea party: Antoine Pevsner (1949), Piet Mondrian (1955), and Marcel Duchamp (1960).

In 1949, at Kunsthaus Zürich, Bill curated the exhibition *Antoine Pevsner, Georges Vantongerloo, Max Bill,* in which he presented three different concepts of Concrete art. Bill also designed the poster and the catalogue, which includes—besides texts by his two older colleagues, Pevsner and Vantongerloo—Bill's own essay on "Die mathematische Denkweise in der Kunst unserer Zeit" (in *Antoine Pevsner, Georges Vantongerloo, Max Bill,* exh. cat. Kunsthaus Zürich, 1949).

In 1955 Kunsthaus Zürich presented the exhibition *Piet Mondrian,* a comprehensive retrospective with 119 works on display. Bill installed the exhibition and designed both the poster and the catalogue (*Piet Mondrian,* exh. cat. Kunsthaus Zürich, 1955). He also wrote a lengthy introductory essay for the catalogue, in which he discussed topics such as "the hallmark of modern painting" and "the path that Piet Mondrian took."

And lastly in 1960, Max Bill, in collaboration with Arnold Fawcus and Serge Stauffer, curated and installed the exhibition *Dokumentation über Marcel Duchamp* at the Kunstgewerbemuseum in Zurich. Bill also designed the exhibition signage and the poster.

Bill and Le Corbusier

In 1938, during one of his longer trips to Paris, Bill worked in Le Corbusier's studio compiling and editing volume 3 of *Le Corbusier & P. Jeanneret: Œuvre complète 1934–1938* (Zurich: Girsberger, 1939, ed. Max Bill). Work on volume 3 had previously been held up for some time because Le Corbusier had been hospitalized in St. Tropez after a serious swimming accident.
In August 1938 Le Corbusier wrote from his sickbed to the publisher Girsberger in Zurich: "I have already started the text for the maquette Bill left me."[1170]
Bill grew impatient at the delay, but when he tried to cajole Le Corbusier into action, the latter expressed his irritation: "Vous pouvez vous vanter de m'empoisonner l'existence"—"you can brag about how you're poisoning my existence."[1171]

However, when the convalescent Le Corbusier returned to his practice in Paris, he and Bill were soon on good terms. Le Corbusier's studio was in long, narrow premises, barely three meters in width, at Rue de Sèvres 35. He was generally only there in the afternoons, leaving the day-to-day administration of the practice's architectural projects to his cousin, Pierre Jeanneret.

Bill went through the studio archive, seeking out unpublished materials relating to buildings by Le Corbusier. Bill and Le Corbusier then worked together on the project entries and on the picture captions for the newly retrieved photographs. They then met again in 1939 to read the final proofs in Switzerland at "the little house" (Villa Le Lac) in Corseaux on Lake Geneva that Le Corbusier had built for his parents in 1925.
This architectural masterpiece, with the simplest possible layout, is now a listed, historic monument owned by the Fondation Le Corbusier,

1170 Le Corbusier, Hôpital St. Tropez, to Hans Girsberger, Zurich, 25 August 1938, in Girsberger 1981

1171 Le Corbusier to Max Bill, cited in Girsberger 1981, p. 53

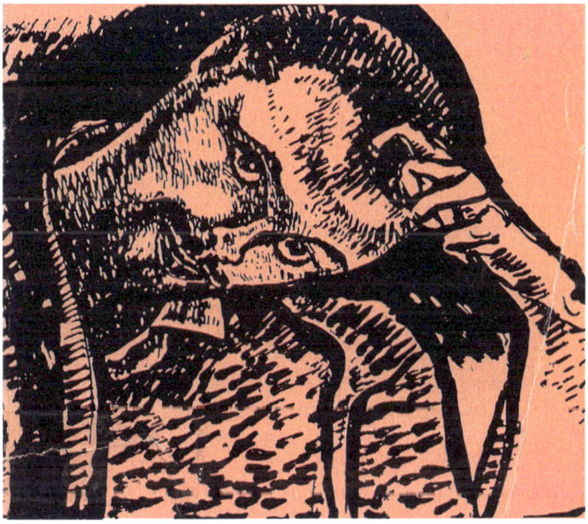

Paul Klee, *Junger Mann, ausruhend* (Self-portrait), 1911, cover image of the first edition of Paul Klee, *Journal*, published in French in 1959, Bibliothek Max Bill

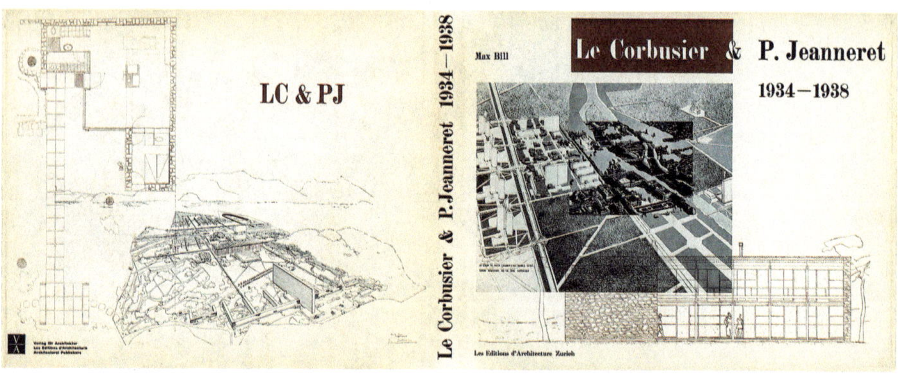

Max Bill, Book cover for *Le Corbusier & P. Jeanneret 1934–1938,* 1939

Paris; it is illustrated in *Le Corbusier und die Schweiz—zum 100. Geburtstag,* exh. cat., conception and texts by Prof. Dr. H. C. Alfred Roth, with contributions from Emil Miltchev (Bern: Bundesamt für Kulturpflege, 1987).

After the death of Le Corbusier's father in 1926, his mother Madame Jeanneret-Perret remained in the house. Le Corbusier's mother, whom he held in the highest esteem, was small, had an extremely lively mind, and gave piano lessons.

Le Corbusier and Bill worked in the garden of the house on Lake Geneva, shielded by a stone wall with a rectangular opening that revealed the vista across the lake. Sometimes they swam in the lake; Le Corbusier must have already recovered from the trauma of his swimming accident. It may even be that Bill remembered that "window" when he was planning his own house in Zumikon and created a rectangular transition between the concrete wall and the little wall by the terrace seating, guiding one's view—not across a lake, as Le Corbusier had done—but out to a cutting through the garden that leads down through the woods and on to Küsnacht gorge further down the hill.

The house in Zumikon is now home to the foundation I set up, namely, the Max Bill Georges Vantongerloo Stiftung.

Louis Soutter

On 15 July 1939, at the end of the day in Corseaux, Bill drove Le Corbusier to Vallorbe to catch the express train to Paris—and also to collect his friend Vantongerloo at the station, so that they could drive to La Sarraz together. But a strange meeting came about before they reached Vallorbe.

Le Corbusier asked Bill if he would mind stopping in a town near Vallorbe to meet someone. As they walked into a café, they were greeted by a man who looked astoundingly like Le Corbusier, almost like a caricature of him. He was wearing a slightly oversized bowler hat and was—as Bill told me in November 1981—"very delighted" to see them. His dark, baggy clothes seemed more like heirlooms from the past. He was wearing horn-rimmed spectacles, very like Le Corbusier's—maybe identical to them. Even his features resembled Le Corbusier's, they were "just more jumbled together." This was in fact Le Corbusier's cousin, Louis Soutter.

It was only years later that Bill learned that Le Corbusier and Louis Soutter were cousins, "the drawings that Le Corbusier took with him back then are now valuable collectors' pieces and Soutter a highly-regarded representative of Swiss art."[1172]

"The main difference between Louis Soutter and Le Corbusier was their neckwear; Le Corbusier generally wore a bow tie, but Louis Soutter was wearing a cravat—only, like a punk these days, there were safety pins hanging off his cravat, from top to bottom. We ate pastries and drank coffee." Then Soutter unrolled a bundle of drawings and allowed Bill and Le Corbusier to choose whatever they liked. Bill modestly selected just one drawing, one of the smallest sheets. "Time was running out and we said our goodbyes to Soutter."[1173] Le Corbusier left the café with the rest of the drawings under his arm and waved as he boarded the train. Bill later discovered that Le Corbusier greatly admired the work of his oddly dressed cousin; in fact Le Corbusier had already written about Soutter and had published some of his drawings.

By the time of that meeting Soutter was living a very lonely life in a residential home. Born in Morges (canton of Vaud) to a bourgeois Swiss family—his father was a pharmacist—Soutter had followed his rich American lover and future wife, Madge Fursman, back to her native land and had been appointed head of the art department at Colorado College in Colorado Springs in 1897. However, "in 1903 he gave up all hope of establishing himself socially and artistically in America and returned to Switzerland, physically and mentally weakened." He was unwell—he may have had typhoid fever—and confused. "He pursued a somewhat checkered career as a musician for the next two decades but also required financial support from his family because of his extravagant lifestyle."[1174] Soutter, who had studied architecture and music, initially made his living as a violinist in the Orchestre de la Suisse Romande; later on he had occasional engagements in sanatoriums and played for silent films. His family was ashamed of him and "appointed a guardian for their dandified family member so that he would no longer be a burden to

1172 Max Bill, "Le Corbusier," in *Sonntagszeitung*, 27 September 1987
1173 Bill, "Le Corbusier"
1174 Matthias Vogel, "Vom Geist des Schmerzes durchdrungen. Louis Soutter-Retrospektive im Kunstmuseum Basel," in *Neue Zürcher Zeitung*, 3 December 2002
1175 Vogel, "Vom Geist des Schmerzes durchdrungen"
1176 Card from Max Bill to Tine Vantongerloo, Vantongerloo-Archiv
1177 Thomas Ribi, "Mäzenin der Avantgarde—Hommage an Hélène de Mandrot im Kunsthaus," in *Tages-Anzeiger*, 13–14 February 1999

them. . . . In 1923 he was admitted against his will to a home for the elderly in Ballaigues in the district of Jura-Nord Vaudois,"[1175] where he remained for the rest of his life, despite trying to flee several times. It was only after he had reached that lowest ebb—only alleviated by occasional meetings with Le Corbusier—that he started to produce the precious works of art that Le Corbusier and Bill had been allowed to choose from in that café.

With Vantongerloo at La Sarraz

In the summer of 1939 Max Bill and Georges Vantongerloo spent a short time at Château de La Sarraz, just a few months before their correspondence would first be interrupted by the outbreak of the Second World War and then completely halted until after hostilities were over. On 15 July 1939, the day when Bill took Le Corbusier to the station at Vallorbe, he also met Vantongerloo off the express train from Paris at the same station. Vantongerloo was traveling alone—without Puma, his wife—so Max Bill sent her a friendly postcard from La Sarraz and also included greetings on it to Miss Moss, that is to say, the artist Marlow Moss, who was a member of Abstraction-Création like Bill and Vantongerloo.

"my dear puma [Tine Vantongerloo], it's a great shame that you weren't able to be here . . . with warmest wishes to you, yours, bill. and very best regards to miss moss and madame nijhoff."[1176]

Bill took Vantongerloo with him in his car to La Sarraz where they were expected as guests of Madame de Mandrot at her magnificent castle. Hélène de Mandrot had been a keen patron of the arts since her husband's death in 1920 and in 1928 she had played an important part in the founding of the Congrès international d'architecture moderne (CIAM). In 1922 she had created a *maison d'artistes* at La Sarraz as a meeting place for artists. Bill and Vantongerloo filled a double page in the visitors' book when they signed it. Vantongerloo drew a sketch of a work he had made three years earlier, and Bill drew two motifs, adding the words "pour la balance entre le blanc et le noir" (to balance black and white). He also (perhaps misleadingly) dated his stay at La Sarraz as 16–24 July 1939.

"The castle soon became an important meeting place for the leading lights of modernism. Moholy-Nagy, Max Ernst, Oskar Schlemmer, Sergei Eisenstein, Hans Arp, Le Corbusier, Max Bill—the list of visitors to La Sarraz between 1922 and 1947 is long and includes the most important figures in the European avant-garde."[1177]

The double page "Max Bill & Georges Vantongerloo" from the visitors' book at La Sarraz (1939) is illustrated in Georges Duplain "En feuilletant les 'albums' de la maison des artistes," Livres d'hôtes, La Sarraz (1939), in *Gazette de Lausanne,* 11 June 1960; it is also illustrated in Alice Rewald, "Max Bill à New York," in *Gazette de Lausanne,* 1–2 June 1963.

However, Bill was not to enjoy the rest and recuperation he had hoped for on that short break because it proved impossible to achieve any real "balance" between Vantongerloo and his aristocratic hostess. They did not get on at all well and Vantongerloo left earlier than planned. Bill stayed on at La Sarraz but insisted on telling Madame de Mandrot all about his closest friend Vantongerloo until, it seems, she burst into tears. Looking back, it seems that Bill and Vantongerloo only received their invitations to La Sarraz at a relatively late stage. In fact Madame de Mandrot generally took advice from Sigfried Giedion on the invitations she issued, and earlier guests at La Sarraz had included Moholy-Nagy (1935), Willi Baumeister (1932, 1937), Max Ernst (1935, 1936), Serge Brignoni, Fausto Melotti, Xanti Schawinsky, and Friedrich Vordemberge-Gildewart (no year dates were recorded for the last four).[1178]

When Friedrich Vordemberge-Gildewart and his wife Leda fled Germany, the Bills took them in at their house in Höngg (1937–38), despite Bill already having been fined by the police in 1936 for giving refuge to the "illegal immigrant" Alfred Thomas. After the war Max Bill invited Vordemberge-Gildewart to join the faculty at the Hochschule für Gestaltung in Ulm and appointed him head of the visual design department. Not long after that appointment Vordemberge-Gildewart had a solo exhibition in Ulm. Bill gave the address at the opening and Hans Curjel—whom Bill had worked with at the Corso theater and had had fun with at La Sarraz in July 1939—wrote an essay for the exhibition catalogue.

"In this presentation, with around fifty works spanning thirty years of creative activity, Vordemberge-Gildewart provides an overview of his artistic progress and the goals he has reached. This account of Vordemberge's work is of particular importance just now because he has recently been appointed to the teaching staff at the Hochschule für Gestaltung in Ulm by Max Bill. Thus an artist at the height of his powers has been called upon to pass on, as a pedagogue, artistic and intellectual principles that he has pursued with energy and logic,

1178 Baudin 1998, p. 319
1179 Curjel 1955
1180 Madame de Mandrot, La Sarraz, to Alfred Roth, Zurich, 27 July 1939, gta Archiv
1181 Roth 1988, pp. 61–63

uncompromisingly, and that—despite numerous setbacks—he has realized as a calm free spirit."[1179]

These various artists formed a strong network, which proved to be of particular benefit to them in the period after the end of the Second World War. Other guests at La Sarraz in July 1939, besides Bill and Vantongerloo, were Ernesto Nathan Rogers, Hans Curjel, and Alfred Roth, who did not stay as long as the others. After Vantongerloo had returned to Paris and Roth had also departed, Madame de Mandrot wrote to Roth in confidence about what the remaining guests were up to. She described them as "*épatants*" (splendid), and although they had very different mindsets, she felt that they perfectly complemented each other. She gave them her special seal of approval: "definitely re-invitable."

"Dear Roth, Bill, Curjel and Rogers are all fine examples of their kind, very nice and certainly worth inviting again. Their intellects are very diverse but they complement each other. Rogers is very attractive, the other two are stronger, a great support for him ..."[1180]

A few years later (1943–44) a house designed by the architect Alfred Roth would be built in Zurich for Madame de Mandrot.

Bill's friend Alfred Roth recalled that holiday in July 1939: "We spent those lovely summer days playing croquet, walking, talking. One day we read in the daily paper, *Le Matin,* that the world-famous film diva Marlene Dietrich would be spending a few days in Lausanne. We immediately decided to drive to Lausanne in the hope of catching a glimpse of the illustrious visitor somewhere there. Only by some dark means the lady of the castle had discovered our intentions and decided, for fun, to take the wind out of our sails. At this point the reader should be aware that Hélène de Mandrot was a quite extraordinary woman—extremely cultured, brilliant, averse to convention, critical and encouraging in one and invariably very elegantly dressed. She loved being admired by men and using her intellect and her charm to dominate any situation—she had little time for womanhood.... Hélène de Mandrot was the epitome of the grande dame.

To return to our proposed excursion to Lausanne for the sake of Marlene Dietrich. We were standing chatting in the courtyard when, all of a sudden, 'la grande dame' appeared—slowly, majestically descending the castle steps in the most elegant of outfits, dressed and made up to kill. Struck dumb by her sudden appearance out of nowhere, we immediately understood the deeper, true meaning of her arrival, namely, 'Here's your Marlene Dietrich for you, in person,' at which we were spontaneously overwhelmed with admiration for this 'diva' and spinelessly abandoned our excursion to Lausanne."[1181]

In Alfred Roth's *Amüsante Erlebnisse eines Architekten* (Zurich: gta/Ammann, 1988) there is a reproduction of a photograph (by Ernesto Rogers) of Max Bill, Alfred Roth and Georges Vantongerloo playing croquet in the grounds of La Sarraz in the summer of 1939 (p. 63).

Roth, for his part, wrote to Max Bill at La Sarraz, who in fact appears to have stayed there for sixteen days in all (without Binia): "[I]t's a pity the last days were so rainy and freezing cold. Have you had the fire on in the Knights' Hall, have you been roasting hogs on a spit? Your nearest and dearest in Zurich are very, very well, surprisingly so, yes indeed. Many greetings to our comrades-in-games."[1182]

"The aesthetic impact arises from a strictly observed system ..."

In addition to producing publications on Le Corbusier and publishing his own *fifteen variations,* in the late 1930s Bill was also closely involved in the publication of *Moderne Schweizer Architektur (1925–1945)* edited by "Professor Dr. Linus Birchler, Dr. Giedion, Ing. Werner Jegher, Arch. Peter Meyer, Dr. Georg Schmidt, Arch. Egidius Streiff." Bill was responsible for the typography, the layout, and the design of the illustrations; it was published under his name in 1949 by Verlag Karl Werner, Basel.

Peter Meyer wrote a review of volume 3 of Le Corbusier's catalogue raisonné ("edited by Max Bill, architect, Zurich") for *Das Werk.* He refers to Le Corbusier as an "avid doctrinaire" and is not wholly convinced by Bill's layout "... the principle of filling the page with text and pictures to the very edge is possibly taken too far." Peter Meyer also does entirely agree with all that Bill says in his introduction: "We beg to differ when Bill remarks in his introduction that the Swiss National Exhibition lacked 'any great dominant idea that might point the way forward' and has not left anything of lasting value."[1183]

At this point it is worth recalling that Bill greatly regretted not having the opportunity to realize an architectural commission for the *Schweizerische Landesausstellung 1939* in Zurich. Architects, even the great ones, have to be able to live with setbacks of that kind.

1182 Alfred Roth, Doldertal 19, Zurich, to Max Bill, visitor at La Sarraz Castle (26 July 1939), gta Archiv

1183 Meyer, "Le Corbusier & P. Jeanneret, *Œuvre Complète 1934–38,*" *Das Werk* 27:2 (February 1940), pp. XIII–XIV

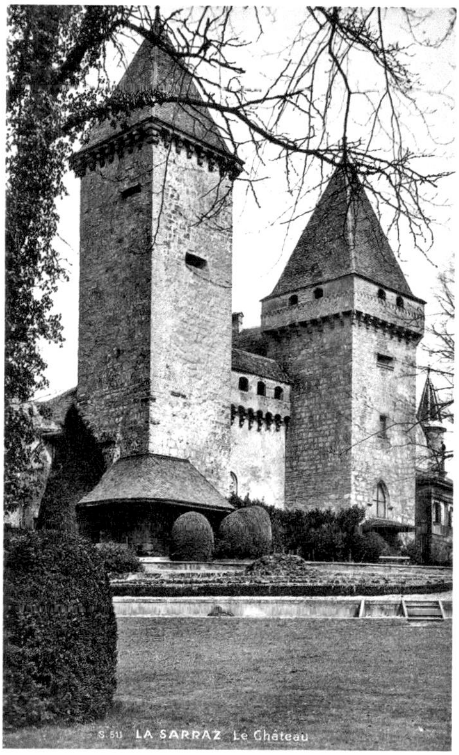

Le Château de La Sarraz, where CIAM was founded in 1928 and where Bill, Vantongerloo, Ernesto Rogers, and Alfred Roth were on holiday in July 1939

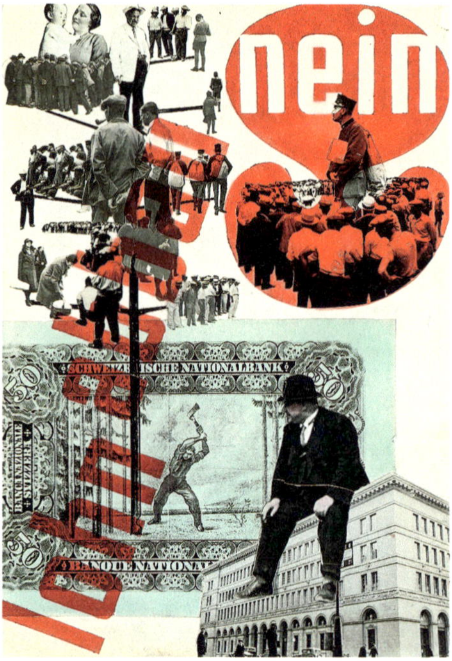

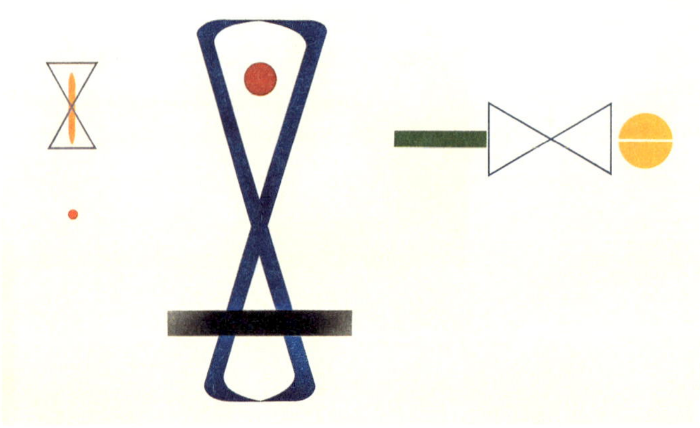

Max Bill, *Lohnabbau nein*
(No wage cuts), Poster design,
1939, photo montage and
gouache on card, 47 × 34.5 cm
Max Bill, *realization,* 1937,
tempera on card, 29 × 49 cm

And when it came to *Expo 64* in Lausanne, it was the Swiss architect Le Corbusier who was left on the sidelines, while Bill had a chance to make his mark as the architect of the section "Bilden und Gestalten" ("Educating and Creating").

Although Meyer questions aspects of Bill's design for volume 3 of Le Corbusier's catalogue raisonné, the section on "Exemplary Book Design" in the same issue of *Das Werk* contains a glowing review of another book designed by Max Bill: "*Die neue Architektur / La nouvelle Architecture / The New Architecture,* by Alfred Roth, Zurich, illustrated with 20 examples, with the participation of numerous co-contributors. Format 29×24. In a fixed grid consisting of 9 sections per page, the pictures are arranged according to their importance, in conjunction with drawings and texts, making the best use of the space. The aesthetic impact arises from a strictly observed system combined with a logical yet free arrangement of texts and images. The publisher is Dr. H. Girsberger, Zurich 1940; collaborator and designer of the layout is Max Bill SWB, Zurich."[1184]
This issue of *Werk* came with a small printed card that read "überreicht von der redaktion" ("a gift from the editorial team"), with a handwritten note added by Peter Meyer: "To Mr. Max Bill—in the hope of not introducing a new irritation but of ending the old irritation, yours, P.M."

The publisher Girsberger later looked back at the making of *Die neue Architektur:* "Friendship has always played an essential part in my life as a publisher. *Die neue Architektur*—a standard work produced by my publishing house when it was still in its infancy—could never have come about without my friendship with Alfred Roth and Max Bill. In a late-night conversation on the way home from Café Select, Roth and I decided to create a representative survey of modern architecture drawing on the best available examples. No effort was to be spared in the production of an out-of-the-ordinary book, a 'bible' of new architecture. Plans by the leading architects of the day, which came to us from all over the world, were redrawn in the most meticulous manner at Atelier Roth, and Max Bill, who at that time still liked to deal with typographical tasks, contributed to the look of this publication in a way that went far beyond mere design. The cover ... bespeaks his extraordinary talent as a designer."[1185]
The reception that greeted *Die neue Architektur,* with its outstanding design by Bill, could not have been more positive. The critic at *The Architectural Review,* a highly respected British journal, declared that it was "a Rolls-Royce among books." In 1970 Girsberger filled in the picture: "... but the Second World War, which broke out just

1184 Meyer, "Le Corbusier & P. Jeanneret," pp. XIII–XIV
1185 Girsberger 1970, p. 28

before the book was launched, put an end to that extremely promising initial success. Pre-orders from overseas had to be cancelled and it was only after the war had ended that the book became a resounding success and went into numerous editions. A similar fate befell volume III of Le Corbusier's catalogue raisonné, which was also published just before the war and designed by Bill."[1186]

In 1934 and 1938 Bill designed the Christmas exhibitions presented by the Werkbund and the Zürcher Kunstgewerbe (Zurich association of arts and crafts) at the Kunstgewerbemuseum in Zurich.

"From 26 November to 21 December 1938 the Zurich section of the SWB ran its customary Christmas exhibition. The exhibition design was by Max Bill SWB."[1187]

He had also designed several items of jewelry on his own initiative in recent years. There was of course no let up in his engagement with theoretical questions and he wrote a number of texts on a range of artistic issues. Bill was also commissioned to design a political poster for a campaign relating to the referendum on 28 May 1939 concerning wage cuts for Federal employees.

Bill's Critique of Swiss Authorities

On 1 September 1939 Germany invaded Poland, marking the beginning of the Second World War, and Bill and Le Corbusier would not meet again until after the war had ended. Over the years Le Corbusier had been "revered, decried, misjudged, mistrusted."

Le Corbusier, for instance, had proposed engaging in much-needed, large-scale planning projects, above all for dwellings, instead of wasting public monies on armaments: "Canons, munitions? merci! Somewhere to live, if you please!"[1188]

In Werner Oechslin's book *Le Corbusier und die Schweiz: Dokumente einer schwierigen Beziehung* (1987), there is open criticism of the Swiss authorities' treatment of "their own" creative artists.

1186 Girsberger 1970, pp. 29–30
1187 In *Das Werk* 25:12 (December 1938)
1188 Max Bill, "Le Corbusier," in *Sonntagszeitung,* 27 September 1987
1189 See Oechslin 1987
1190 Ernst Morgenthaler, cited in *Zürcher Maler,* 1947, pp. 18–19

As both a creative spirit and a prophet of doom he was equally "loved and opposed." And although he was "disregarded by many during his own lifetime," Le Corbusier was "one of the greatest Swiss of our century" in Bill's estimation. When the world bade farewell to Le Corbusier on 1 September 1965, in a ceremony in Paris attended by André Malraux, France's Minister of Culture, the *tricolore* was draped over his coffin.[1189]

Of the designs listed in volumes 2 (1929–34) and 3 (1934–38) of Le Corbusier's catalogue raisonné, more projects from the earlier volume were ultimately realized. In Bill's characteristically forthright introduction to volume 3, he returned to one of the aspects of a free economy that concerned him most and insisted that there had to be changes in the prevailing "system of ownership." He also made the point that "for certain personal reasons" the architect Le Corbusier had not been asked to do anything for the Swiss National Exhibition in 1939.

As it happens the painter Le Corbusier was treated rather differently in Zurich. Kunsthaus Zürich presented a solo exhibition of his work, *Le Corbusier, der Maler,* from 15 December 1937 to 9 January 1938.

It is worth noting here that in conversation with me in Restaurant Central in Zurich, on 30 November 1981, Bill suggested examining Le Corbusier's works in light of the influence of Louis Soutter on his human figures.

That exhibition was followed on 12 February 1938 by an exhibition of work by the painter Ernst Morgenthaler, Binia and Max Bill's neighbor in Höngg. Ernst Morgenthaler lived in Geneva from 1916 to 1928, which was where he met Sasha, his future wife, who was six years younger than him and a member of the Bernese aristocracy. Like Hugo Ball before him, Ernst Morgenthaler wrote a monograph on Hermann Hesse, who was also a friend of his. It was published in 1936 and considerably raised Morgenthaler's profile. In 1939 his wife, Sasha Morgenthaler, carried out a major commission for the Swiss National Exhibition and caused a nationwide sensation with the mannequins she created for the fashion pavilion. Subsequently, she became known at home and abroad for her immensely successful Sasha dolls.

Morgenthaler grew up in the countryside in the canton of Bern. His father insisted he had to train as a silk weaver, and it was only when he was 27 that he decided to abandon silk weaving and become a painter. He "took painting lessons with Cuno Amiet on Oschwand and also ... with Paul Klee in Munich."[1190]

The Morgenthalers' house in Höngg was designed by Hans Leuzinger. And as it turned out, the architect Hans Schmidt (who had returned from the Soviet Union in 1937) and his team member, Max Bill, would soon work together in a building at the Swiss National Exhibition that was also designed by Leuzinger. Schmidt and Bill were commissioned by two Swiss architectural associations (the Schweizerischer Ingenieur- und Architektenverein and the Bund Schweizer Architekten) to create an appealing, comprehensible display (using existing materials) on "urban and regional development" for the Plan & Bau section at the exhibition. Max Bill knew Schmidt very well. The two had already spent time together in Paris after Schmidt's return from the USSR and had similar outlooks on the problems of urban planning and regional development.

Urban Planning and Regional Development: A Touring Exhibition

"Under the arcades in a courtyard shaded by plane trees there is a small foyer dedicated to Swiss architects and the pioneers of Swiss engineering; visitors pass through it on their way into the main exhibition. On the walls of the elongated hall with its gallery-like upper floor, plans, drawings, and models afford an insight into the objectives of modern urban planning and, beyond that, of regional and national development. Three-dimensional maps of Switzerland introduce visitors to the most important topics in each of the four sub-groups."[1191]

Environmental protection issues were also raised in the display. In the section "Canton of Zürich. Sewage Treatment Plants" we read: "Our lakes, rivers and streams are becoming polluted due to the increasing volumes of wastewater that are being fed into them from densely populated areas, workshops, and factories. This pollution can be prevented by building sewage treatment plants connected to our sewage networks. There is an urgent need for the construction of sewage treatment plants, which are already required today for Lake Zurich, the Limmat, the Glatt, the Töss."[1192] Bill, who of course also had to consider wastewater management and hygiene in his own work as an architect, marked (among others) a relevant

1191 *Schweizerische Landesausstellung 1939,* Zurich, official guide with list of exhibits and map of the exhibition, p. 240
1192 Hans Schmidt in *Schweizerische Landesausstellung* 1939
1193 See Friedmann 1930
1194 Max Bill in conversation with Angela Thomas, 8 January 1994
1195 Bill 1949 [c], pp. 170–73

passage in a book he bought that year: "... the beautiful constraints of symmetry and harmony are also intrinsic to the applied sciences. Hippodamos, Pericles's architect, devised a rectilinear system for the streets of Piraeus, oriented toward the directions of the compass, in the certain knowledge that he thus best served both mathematics and hygiene."[1193] Bill acquired Hermann Friedmann's *Die Welt der Formen* (Munich: C.H. Beck, 1930) for his library and marked it with "bill 1939"; he added his own notes in the margins of the first three chapters.

In the end Max Bill was contracted to construct "a sewer system for the places along the Zürisee," because up until the "Landi" (Schweizerische Landesausstellung) in 1939, there was no such system in place—as he told me in conversation in Zurich on 30 November 1981.

The Swiss National Exhibition of 1939 was conceived as a touring exhibition, but the outbreak of the Second World War meant that the planned tour had to be put on hold for some years. It was not until 1943 that the exhibition opened again at the Gewerbemuseum in Basel, where it ran from 21 February to 21 March. Bill later remarked that his materials for that exhibition, with its four subgroups (town and country, transport, settlement, and recreation), had "disappeared without trace."

Robert Maillart's Cement Arch

It seems, as Bill told me in conversation, that it was also Hans Leuzinger who was instrumental in securing approval for the civil engineer Robert Maillart—one of Bill's heroes—to construct his Cement Hall at the Swiss National Exhibition in 1939.[1194] Although the Cement Hall—an open, arched shell—was not a functional structure as such, in its construction it was an outstanding example of Maillart's skills. If anything it was "an advertisement, a representative structure, that is to say, neither a pure work of art nor a utilitarian structure but a daring piece of propaganda. The site was developed by architects from the section 'Plan und Bau' and the Cement Hall was intended as a demonstration of the advantages of concrete as a building material ... and to publicise Portland cement.... The vault was made from sprayed concrete (gunite) just six centimeters thick."[1195]

On 8–11 July 1939, when the Swiss National Exhibition was still in full swing, there was a meeting of CIRPAC (the executive body of CIAM) in Zurich, to finalize preparations for the sixth Congress, which was planned for September 1939.

A list of meetings and congresses held between 1928 and 1939 has been published in *CIAM—Internationale Kongresse für Neues Bauen: Dokumente 1928–1939,* ed. Martin Steinmann, Institut für Geschichte und Theorie der Architektur, ETH Zürich (Basel and Stuttgart: Birkhäuser, 1979), p. 212.

Max Bill would also participate in the CIAM congresses in Italy and France: CIAM VII was held in Bergamo (23–30 July 1949), during which Bill went on the excursion to the Olivetti factory; during CIAM IX in Aix-en-Provence (19–21 July 1953) delegates, including Bill, went on an excursion to Marseille to visit Le Corbusier's newly completed *Unité d'habitation.* On the roof Le Corbusier walked up to Bill, pointed at a group of roof structures and said, "look at that! i've made the biggest sculpture in the modern era!"[1196]

"Design . . . at the service of the homeland"

The wider situation in Switzerland in the late 1930s was marred by deflation, unemployment, the devaluation of the Swiss franc, and political radicalization fanned by the impact of National Socialism. Uncertainty about political objectives was officially countered by "national self-reflection"—the so-called internal national defense strategy—at the Swiss National Exhibition in 1939. The artists exhibiting there avoided any kind of experimentation and largely relied on traditional forms of expression.

After Bill's success at the Milan Triennial in 1936 and his very notable involvement in a number of architectural projects during the 1930s, he hoped to win a major building contract for the Swiss National Exhibition. However, he fared no better than the already renowned Le Corbusier. He was met with a rebuff. The director of the Swiss National Exhibition

1196 Max Bill in conversation with Angela Thomas

1197 Hans Finsler, in *Zum Andenken an Egidius Streiff* [ca. 1952]

1198 Richard Paul Lohse, "Denkmalwettbewerb: 'Ehrung der Arbeit,'" in *Volksrecht,* 5 March 1943

1199 Max Bill in conversation with Angela Thomas, 1 July 1975

explained to Bill that what he had done at the Milan Triennial was less suitable for the National Exhibition and that, in any case, more or less all the contracts had already been awarded.

The National Exhibition of 1939 ultimately had a long-lasting, negative impact on creativity and design in Switzerland. "In the wake of the Swiss National Exhibition, the ideas of the Werkbund and notions of quality fell on hard times. Design was put at the service of the homeland. Egidius Streiff [who had taken over as secretary of the Swiss Werkbund in 1931 and who had previously been active at the Krater cabaret in Zurich] tried to allay the general confusion and to keep creative activities going, but the circle [of those who supported clear forms and good design] was becoming ever smaller. Alfred Altherr already resigned in 1938."[1197]

"On the occasion of the Swiss National Exhibition of 1939" the city council in Zurich launched a public sculpture competition (open to sculptors of "Swiss nationality") for a monument "in honor of work." The anonymous competition entries were to comprise "a model of the design in white untinted plaster on a scale of 1:5." Potential entrants were informed that they could collect a model of Helvetiaplatz on or after 8 September 1941.

Max Bill submitted his design for a monument with the code word "Werkplatz" (the last date for submissions was 15 January 1942). The city council had promised that all entries would be put on public display, and there was an exhibition of entries in due course—albeit it seems not until 1943—at the Kunstgewerbemuseum in Zurich. Richard Paul Lohse, Bill's fellow Concrete artist, reported in a press review that the jury had concluded that "none of the designs was ready to be executed."[1198]

Professor Bruno Reichlin kindly sent me a copy of the article Richard Paul Lohse wrote for *Volksrecht,* with a handwritten date: "5-3-1943." I will return to the contents of this article under the rubric "1943" in the second volume of this biography. For now, suffice it to say that Lohse staunchly defended Max Bill's competition entry.

Mobilisation

Bill was called up for several extended periods of military service between 1939 and 1944. "Everyone is equal in the Swiss military, and that's good for camaraderie," as Max Bill once said to me in 1975.[1199] However, he never developed any ambition whatsoever to pursue a military career. This clearly distanced from his mother, an officer's daughter, who had been a military enthusiast for years and, as the family often recalled, had once written a letter to General Guisan.

To escape the tedium of military service, at least for a short time, Bill drew on his own inner resources and wrote the article "Paul Klee—zu seinem 60. Geburtstag" (Paul Klee—for his 60th Birthday), which was published in the *Neue Zürcher Zeitung* on 17 December 1939, one day before Klee's birthday. Bill's article takes up a quarter of the page. The other three quarters are occupied by military topics, such as "Our Soldiers Write: Christmas Greetings from the Border," "Blackout Alarm," and "For Our Soldiers."

In September 1939, at the beginning of the Second World War, the Swiss army was mobilized, with soldiers deployed on Switzerland's border with Nazi Germany. In the following years, most European countries would suffer under unimaginable dictatorships, censorship, flight, destruction, deportation, internment, and murder.

However, these years are also marked by brave anti-Fascist resistance, political commitment, and solidarity with emigrants and others in danger. In Switzerland, which was spared the war's destruction, Bill tried to stay in contact with his friends and artists who were in occupied France, the Netherlands, Italy, and Hungary—and he supported them as much as possible.

The second volume of Max Bill's biography shares the often-tragic wartime experiences of these associates, along with the extended story of Bill's continued artistic career.

Acknowledgments

My deepest gratitude goes to Erich Schmid—my creative partner in life. With his feature length films, particularly with his documentary *Max Bill—The Master's Vision* (2008) he and I have visited over twenty countries for cinema screenings and have encountered many wonderful, remarkable people on our travels.

I would also like to express my heartfelt gratitude to my sister Barbara Bode in Berlin; she painstakingly transcribed the extensive correspondence between Max Bill and Georges Vantongerloo, which is preserved in Haus Bill in Zumikon. She also crucially helped me to track down materials during my protracted research into the cultural-historical background to Bill's life during this period. She encouraged me and was the first to read and comment on my manuscript.

In a brief moment ascending the stairs to the offices of Hauser & Wirth Publishers in Rämistrasse in Zurich, when I first encountered the translator, Dr. Fiona Elliott, and she asked one perfectly targeted question—whether I would like a literal or a gentler approach to the translation ("a gentler one!" said I), it was immediately clear to me that I could trust her to translate the moods and life events in my text into English. And that trust only increased when I found, to my surprise, that she also plays the French horn. Fiona then embarked on an extremely fruitful working relationship with the all-female team that produced this book: the publisher Dr. Michaela Unterdörfer, her colleagues Dr. Kristina Hinrichsen (associate editor) and Mélanie Letoré (editorial assistant), myself, Emily Fayet (Hauser & Wirth artist liaison), and our expert editor, Mary Christian, in New York.

Sonja Zagermann designed the book with great dedication. Nothing was too much trouble for her and she devoted herself to the realization of this task with the same precision and commitment as all the other ladies I have just named, whom I salute joyfully and with great gratitude.

Special thanks also go to

Dr. Bruno Maurer, Director of the gta Archiv/ETH Zürich
Dr. Daniel Weiss, gta Archiv/ETH Zürich
Dr. Stefan Frey, Klee-Nachlassverwaltung, Bern
Prof. Marek Wieczorek MA, PhD, University of Washington, Seattle
Dr. Robert Dünki, Stadtarchiv Zürich

Walburga Krupp, Stiftung Hans Arp und Sophie Taeuber-Arp, Rolandseck
Dr. Ulrike Bestgen, Weimar
Ruth Binde-Schwarz, Zurich
Thomas Kramer, Scheidegger & Spiess, Zürich
Riyoko Probala; Peter Petrej; Annarella Rotter-Schiavetti; Werner Merzbacher; Hendrik A. Berinson; Prof. Jacques Picard, Universität Basel; Deborah Holmes; Jürg Frischknecht; Peter Kamber; Dirk Scheper; Yael Aloni, Tel Aviv

Dr. Angela Thomas, July 2021

References

Archives and Sources

Archiv Christoph Geiger, Freienbach.

Archiv Max Bill, c/o max, binia + jakob bill stiftung, Adligenswil, Switzerland.

Archiv SIK, Schweizerisches Institut für Kunstwissenschaft, Zurich.

Archiv Stiftung Bauhaus Dessau.

Archiv Ortsmuseum Oetwil am See.

Archives de la Maison des Artistes. Château la Sarraz, Switzerland.

Bibliothek Max Bill, haus bill, Zumikon.

Bauhaus-Archiv, Museum für Gestaltung, Berlin.

Ernst Geiger's visitors' books, deposited at Museum Neuhaus, Biel.

gta Archiv, ETH Zürich.

Hans Hinterreiter-Stiftung, c/o Dr. Ferdinand Meyer, Meyer Lustenberger, Zollikon. Hans Hinterreiter, diary.

Hubelhüsi chronicle. Christine Gautschi Zuppinger, Bern.

Schawinsky-Archiv, c/o Ronald Schmid, San Nazzaro.

Wilhelm Ostwald Archiv, Deutsche Akademie der Wissenschaften, Berlin.

Fritz and Elly Schwarz archive, Schweizerisches Sozialarchiv, Zurich.

SCCPA. Schweizerisches Cabaret-, Chanson-, und Pantomimen-Archiv, Thun/Gwatt, H.U. von Allmen: Documents in the estate of Ernst F. Burckhardt relating to Der Krater.

Stiftung Hans Arp und Sophie Taeuber-Arp, Rolandseck.

Vantongerloo-Archiv. Angela Thomas, haus bill, Zumikon

Publications

Adriani, Götz. 1980. *Hannah Höch—Fotomontagen-Gemälde-Aquarelle.* Cologne: DuMont.

Alley, Ronald. 1987. *Paule Vézelay: Paintings and Constructions.* Exhibition catalogue. London: Annely Juda Fine Art.

Audoin, Philippe. [1970]. *Breton.* Paris: Gallimard.

Ausstellung. 1934. Exhibition catalogue, Kunsthaus Zürich, 11 October–4 November 1934. Zurich.

Avril, Nicole. 2001. *Moi, Dora Maar.* Paris: Plon.

Ball-Hennings, Emmy. 1938, 1987. *Blume und Flamme. Geschichte einer Jugend.* Foreword by Hermann Hesse. Reprint, Frankfurt am Main: Suhrkamp.

———. 1999. "Aus den Tagebüchern." In Berhnard Echte and Katherini Aemmer, *Emmy Ball-Hennings. 1885–1948; Texte, Bilder, Dokumente.* 208–11. Exhibition catalogue, Museum Strauhof, Robert Walser-Archiv, Stroemfeld. Frankfurt am Main: Roter Stern.

Bäschlin, Nathalie, Béatrice Ilg, and Patrizia Zeppetella. 2000. "Paul Klees Malutensilien." In *Paul Klee. Die Sammlung Bürgi,* edited by Stefan Frey and Josef Helfenstein, 183–97. Bern: Benteli.

Baudin, Antoine. 1998. "Hélène de Mandrot, ou quand la collection se confont avec l'action." In *Die Kunst zu Sammeln. Schweizer Kunstsammlungen seit 1848,* edited by Regina Bühlmann, 317–22. Zurich: Schweizerisches Institut für Kunstwissenschaft.

Berger, Renate, ed. 2000. *Liebe macht Kunst. Künstlerpaare im 20. Jahrhundert.* Cologne: Böhlau.

Bignens, Christoph. 1985. *Corso. Ein Zürcher Theaterbau 1900 und 1934.* Niederteufen: Niggli.

———. 2006. "Die Entwicklung des 'guten Geschmacks': Alfred Willimann als Grafiker, Künstler, Lehrer und Mitglied des schweizerischen Werkbunds." In *Hans Finsler und die Schweizer Fotokultur. Werk, Fotoklasse, moderne Gestaltung 1932–1960,* edited by Thilo Koenig and Martin Gasser, pp. 224–38. Exhibition catalogue, Museum für Gestaltung Zürich. Zurich: gta.

Bill, Jakob. 1997. "Persönliche Notizen zur Geschichte des Hauses Bill in Höngg." In *Das Atelierhaus Max Bill 1932/33. Ein Wohn- und Atelierhaus in Zürich-Höngg von Max Bill und Robert Winkler,* edited by Arthur Rüegg, pp. 87–102. Zurich: Niggli.

———. 2008. "Max Bill und das Corso in Zürich." In Max Bill. *Aspekte seines Werks,* edited by Kunstmuseum Winterthur and the Gewerbemuseum Winterthur, pp. 171–75. Zurich: Niggli.

Bill, Max. 1928. "interview mit bauhäuslern." *Bauhaus. Zeitschrift für Gestaltung.* 2/3: 24–25.

———. Ca. 1930. Curriculum vitae.

———. 1936. "konkrete gestaltung." In *Zeitprobleme in der Schweizer Malerei und Plastik,* 9. Exhibition catalogue. Zurich: Kunsthaus Zürich. Typography by Max Bill.

———. 1938 [a]. "über konkrete kunst." *Werk* 8 (August): 250–55.

———. 1938 [b]. *quinze variations sur un même thème.* Paris: Chroniques du Jour. Series printed by Mourlot for publisher Gualtieri di San Lazzaro. Another version appears in *Max Bill. Die grafischen Reihen.* Exhibition catalogue, Landratsamt Esslingen. Stuttgart: Gerd Hatje. 1995

———. 1938 [c]. "les paysans suisses et la forme absolue." *XXe siècle,* December.

———. 1942 [a]. *allianz vereinigung moderner schweizer künstler.* Exhibition catalogue. Zurich: Kunsthaus Zürich.

———. 1942 [b]. Curriculum vitae. 26 February.

———. 1943. "sophie taeuber-arp." *Werk* 30 (June): 167–71.

———. [1944] "wassily kandinsky." Reprint from vol. IX of the encyclopaedia *Die Grossen der Weltgeschichte,* Kindler.

———. 1949 [a]. "über die mathematische denkweise." In *Werk* 2 (March): 86–91.

———. 1949 [b]. "die mathematische denkweise in der kunst unserer zeit." In *Antoine Pevsner, Georges Vantongerloo, Max Bill.* Exhibition catalogue. Zurich: Kunsthaus Zürich.

———. 1949 [c]. *robert maillart,* Erlenbach-Zurich: Verlag für Architektur. In German, French, and English.

———. 1951. "kandinsky, l'éducateur." In *Wassily Kandinsky,* edited by Max Bill, pp. 95–98. Paris: Maeght.

———. 1953, "vom staatlichen bauhaus in weimar zur hochschule für gestaltung in ulm." In *Magnum 1.*

———. 1955. "der massstab der modernen malerei / der weg, den piet mondrian zurücklegte / das werk und seine auswirkung / was mondrian nicht tat / zur zürcher mondrian-ausstellung." In *Piet Mondrian,* edited by R. Wehrli, pp. 6–10. Exhibition catalogue. Zurich: Kunsthaus Zürich.

———. 1966. "meine erfahrungen mit der griechischen architektur." In *Griechenland,* pp. 3–6. Fribourg: Office du livre.

———. 1968. "le corbusier—texte und bezeichnungen; kritik, polemik und präsentation." In *Universitas, Zeitschrift für Wissenschaft, Kunst und Literatur* (August): 817–23.

———. 1969 [a]. In *Konstruktive Kunst. Elemente und Prinzipien,* unpaginated. Exhibition catalogue, Biennale Nürnberg, Kunsthalle Am Marientor. Nuremberg: Institut für Moderne Kunst.

———. 1969 [b]. "walter gropius—architekt und erzieher in unserer zeit." In *Universitas. Zeitschrift für Wissenschaft, Kunst und Literatur* 11 (November): 1145–48.

———. 1971. "rund um 'die augen.'" In *Hanns R. Welti,* unpaginated. Exhibition catalogue. Zurich: Galerie Scheidegger + Maurer.

———. 1973. Introduction. "begegnung mit marlow moss." In *Marlow Moss. Bilder, Konstruktionen, Zeichnungen,* unpaginated. Exhibition catalogue. Zurich: Gimpel & Hanover Galerie.

———. 1976. "begegnung mit otto morach." In *Otto Morach, 1887–1973. Ausstellung aus dem Nachlass Bilder, Aquarelle, Zeichnungen, Graphiken,* 15. Exhibition catalogue. Biberist, Switzerland: Verein der Freunde des Schlösschens Vorder-Bleichenberg.

———. 1977 [a]. "idee-konzept-werk: über ein thema." In *Idee-Konzept-Werk,* edited by Gerhard Altenbourg, pp. 28–39. Exhibition catalogue. Berlin: Akademie der Künste.

———. 1977 [b]."meine 30er jahre." In *Um 1930 in Zürich. Neues Denken—neues Wohnen—neues Bauen,* edited by Margit Staber, pp. 186–88. Exhibition catalogue. Zurich: Kunstgewerbemuseum Zürich.

———. 1979 [a]. "die kugel-pendelleuchte." *form + zweck, Fachzeitschrift für industrielle Formgestaltung* 3, p. 71.

———. 1979 [b]. "lehren am und aus dem bauhaus.," In *form + zweck, Fachzeitschrift für industrielle Formgestaltung,* 3, p. 66.

———. 1980 [a]. "einflüsse von pionieren der architektur in und aus belgien," paper delivered at the conference "Belgien und Europa," Académie royale des Sciences, des Lettres et des Beaux-Arts de Belgique, Brussels, 13 November.

———. 1980 [b]. "oskar schlemmer 1888–1943." In *Neue Zürcher Zeitung,* 6/7 September.

———. 1981. "bauhaus und 'abstraction-création' in bezug auf die entwicklung der konstruktiven kunst in der schweiz." In *Konstruktive Kunst 1915–45,* by Rudolf Koella, pp. 24–25. Exhibition catalogue. Winterthur: Kunstmuseum Winterthur.

———. 1983. "der gesamtkunstwerk-kreuzweg." *Züriwoche,* 24 March.

———. 1987. "le corbusier." *Sonntagszeitung,* 27 September, pp. 34–35.

———. 1990 [a]. In *Max Bill.* Exhibition catalogue. Tokyo: Contemporary Sculpture Center.

———. 1990 [b]. "räume von piet mondrian." In *Mondrian auf der Tube. Popularisierung und Trivialisierung der Ideale,* edited by Margit Weinberg Staber, 35. Exhibition catalogue. Zurich: Haus für Konstruktive und Konkrete Kunst, Stiftung für Konstruktive und Konkrete Kunst.

———. 1991. Invitation card text for *Alfred Roth, Prof. Dr. Hc., Architekt, Publizist und Maler. Sein malerisches Werk von 1922–1990,* Galerie Arteba, Zurich.

———. 1993. Text about Eduard Bick. Typescript. February.

Bill, Max, and Valentina Anker, eds. 1972. *Max Bill.* Exhibition catalogue. Geneva: Musée Rath.

Billeter, Fritz. 1997. "Ein Überlebender aus grosser Zeit—Serge Brignoni im Gespräch." In Fritz Billeter, *Serge Brignoni,* pp. 13–41. Zurich: ABC.

Blei, Franz. 1911. *Vermischte Schriften,* vol. 4: *Das Schwere Herz. Zwiesprachen und Gedichte,* pp. 149–76. Munich: Georg Müller.

Bloch, Carola. 1981. *Aus Meinem Leben.* Pfullingen: Neske.

Bloch, Ernst. 1962. *Erbschaft dieser Zeit.* 1935, Gesamtausgabe 4. Frankfurt am Main: Suhrkamp.

———. 1965 [a]. "Alpen ohne Photographie." In *Literarische Aufsätze,* pp. 488–89. Gesamtausgabe 9. Frankfurt am Main: Suhrkamp.

———. 1965 [b]. "Maloja-Chiavenna-Drift" (1934). In *Literarische Aufsätze,* pp. 498–503. Gesamtausgabe 9. Frankfurt am Main: Suhrkamp.

———. 2005. *Das Abenteuer der Treue. Briefe an Karola 1928–1949.* Edited by Anna Czajka. Frankfurt am Main: Suhrkamp.

Bochsler, Regula. 2004. Ich folgte meinem Stern. *Das kämpferische Leben der Margarethe Hardegger.* Zurich: Pendo

Borchardt-Hume, Achim. 2006 [a]. "Two Bauhaus Histories." In *Albers and Moholy-Nagy from the Bauhaus to the New World,* edited by Achim Borchardt-Hume, pp. 66–78. London: Tate Publishing.

Borchardt-Hume, Achim, ed. 2006 [b]. *Albers and Moholy-Nagy from the Bauhaus to the New World.* Exhibition catalogue. London: Tate Publishing.

Borngräber, Christian. 1977. "Ausländische Architekten in der UDSSR: Bruno Taut, die Brigaden Ernst May, Hannes Meyer und Hans Schmidt." In *Wem Gehört Die Welt—Kunst und Gesellschaft in der Weimarer Republik,* pp. 109–137. Exhibition catologue. Berlin: Neue Gesellschaft Für Bildende Kunst.

Brandt, Marianne. 2001. "Brief an die junge Generation." In *Marianne Brandt—Hab ich je an Kunst Gedacht,* edited by Hans Brockhage and Reinhold Lindner, pp. 45–49. Chemnitz: Chemnitzer Verlag.

Brendel, János. 1986. "Der deutsche Einfluss von Scheerbart und Wilhelm Ostwald auf die ungarische Konstruktivisten-theorie." In *Wechselwirkungen. Ungarische Avantgarde in der Weimarer Republik,* edited by Hubertus Gassner, pp. 173–78. Exhibition catalogue, Neue Galerie Kassel, Museum Bochum. Marburg: Jonas.

Bruderer-Oswald, Iris. 2004. "Die neue Optik. Kurt Schwitters, Carola Giedion-Welcker und Sigfried Giedion." In *Kurt Schwitters. Merz—ein Gesamtweltbild,* edited by Annja Müller-Alsbach and Heinz Stahlhut, pp. 22–31. Exhibition catalogue, Museum Tinguely, Basel. Wabern: Benteli.

———. 2007. *Das neue Sehen. Carola Giedion-Welcker und die Sprache der Moderne.* Bern: Benteli.

Brühl, Georg. 1983. *Herwarth Walden und 'Der Sturm.'* Cologne: DuMont.

Bruns, Brigitte. 2007. *Werft eure Hoffnung über neue Grenzen. Theater im Schweizer Exil und seine Rückkehr.* Leipzig: Henschel.

Bucher, Annemarie. 1992. "Verena Loewensberg—Versuch einer Rekonstruktion von Leben und Werk." In *Verena Loewensberg 1912–1986,* by Beat Wismer and Stephan Kunz, pp. 9–23. Exhibition catalogue. Aarau: Aargauer Kunsthaus.

Canetti, Elias. 1985. *Das Augenspiel. Lebensgeschichte 1931–1937.* Munich: Carl Hanser.

Carlepsch, Michael. 2007. *Picasso und der Nationalsozialismus.* Düsseldorf: Patmos.

Caws, Mary Ann. 2002. *Dora Maar. Die Künstlerin an Picassos Seite.* 2000, Frankfurt am Main: Fischer Taschenbuch.

Chatwin, Bruce. 1989."Konstantin Melnikow." In Chatwin, *Was mache ich hier,* pp. 91–100. Munich: Carl Hanser.

Courthion, Pierre. 1975. "San Lazzaro éditeur et animateur de l'art vivant." In *San Lazzaro et ses amis. Hommage au fondateur de la revue XXe siècle.* Paris: La Revue XXe Siècle.

Curiger, Bice. 2002. *Meret Oppenheim. Spuren durchstandener Freiheit.* 1982, Zurich: Scheidegger & Spiess.

Curjel, Hans. 1955. In *Vordemberge-Gildewart. Werke aus den Jahren 1923–1954,* unpaginated. Exhibition catalogue. Ulm: Museum Kunstverein Ulm.

Danuser, Claudio. [1995]. "Béla Bartók und die Schweiz." In *Béla Bartók 1945—50th Anniversary—1995,* Zurich: Migros-Genossenschafts-Bund.

Davidi, Sigal. 2001. "The Levant Fair 1934 and the Promotion of Modern Architecture in Eretz Israel." Unpublished paper, translated by Yael Aloni. Israel Institute of Technology, Haifa.

Delaunay, Robert. 1989. "La lumière" and "Über das Licht." Translated into German by Paul Klee. In *Der blaue Reiter. Dokumente einer geistigen Bewegung,* edited by Andreas Hüneke, pp. 401–4. Leipzig: Philipp Reclam.

Deleroy, Robert L., Maurice Culot, and Anne Van Loo. 1979. *La Cambre 1928–1978.* Brussels: Editions AAM Archives d'Architecture Moderne.

Dentler, Hans-Eberhard. 2006. "Johann Sebastian Bach. Der geometrische Komponist." *Du,* March.

Di San Lazzaro, Gualtieri. 1966. *Parigi era viva.* 1949, Milan: Mondadori.

Dietzsch, Folke F. 1990. "Die Studierenden am Bauhaus. Eine analytische Betrachtung zur strukturellen Zusammensetzung der Studierenden, zu ihrem Studium und Leben am Bauhaus sowie zu ihrem späteren Wirken," PhD dissertation, Hochschule für Architektur und Bauwesen Weimar.

Dosch, Luzi. 1980. "Neues Bauen in der Schweiz: Gewerbeschule und Kunstgewerbemuseum Zürich 1930–33 im Werk von Karl Egender." Licentiate thesis, Kunstgeschichtliches Seminar der Universität Zürich.

Drost, Julia. 2007. "Max Ernst in der Schweiz." In *Max Ernst—Im Garten Der Nymphe Ancolie,* edited by Werner Spies and Anja Müller-Alsbach, pp. 13–45. Exhibition catalogue, Museum Tinguely. Basel. Ostfildern-Ruit: Hatje Cantz.

Droste, Magdalena. 1984. "Beiträge zur Geschichte der Ittenschule in Berlin." In *Aus der Ittenschule Berlin 1926–1934,* by Magdalena Droste and Anneliese Itten, pp. 3–14. Exhibition catalogue, Galerie im Trudelhaus, Baden. Zurich: Itten.

Droste, Magdalena, ed. 1987. *Gunta Stölzl—Weberei am Bauhaus und aus eigener Werkstatt.* Exhibition catalogue, Bauhaus-Archiv Berlin; Kunstgewerbemuseum Zürich; Gerhard-Marcks-Stiftung Bremen; Kunstverein Hochrhein Bad Säckingen; Nederlands Textielmuseum Tilborg. Berlin: Kupfergraben.

Droste, Magdalena, and Jeannine Fiedler. 1988. *Experiment Bauhaus, das Bauhaus-Archiv Berlin (West) zu Gast im Bauhaus Dessau.* Bauhaus Dessau, GDR. Exhibition catalogue, Bauhaus-Archiv/Museum für Gestaltung. Berlin: Kupfergraben Verlagsgesellschaft.

Eckmann, Sabine. 1997. "Der Verlust von Heimat und kultureller Identität. George Grosz, Lyonel Feininger." In *Exil. Flucht und Emigration europäischer Künstler 1933–1945,* edited by Stephanie Barron with Sabine Eckmann, pp. 285–303. Munich: Prestel.

El Lissitzky. Maler, Architekt, Typograf, Fotograf. Erinnerungen, Briefe, Schriften. 1976. Dresden: VEB Verlag der Kunst.

Éluard, Paul. 1987. *Liebesbriefe an Gala (1924–1948).* Translated by Thomas Dobberkau. Edited by Pierre Dreyfus. Hamburg: Hoffmann und Campe.

Endicott Barnett, Vivian. 2005. "Hommage an Max Bill und Wassily Kandinsky." In *Max Bill. Maler, Bildhauer, Architekt, Designer,* edited by Thomas Buchsteiner and Otto Letze, pp. 22–23. Exhibition catalogue, Kunstmuseum Stuttgart. Ostfildern-Ruit: Hatje Cantz.

———. 2006. "From Both Sides of the Atlantic to the Pacific: Klee and America in the Twenties." In *Klee and America,* edited by Josef Helfenstein and Elizabeth Hutton Turner. The Menil Collection. Ostfildern-Ruit: Hatje Cantz.

Engemann, Friedrich. 1977. "Das Bauhaus in Dessau." In *Dessauer Kalender 1977,* pp. 4–14, Dessau: Rat der Stadt.

Ernst, Jimmy. 1985. *Nicht gerade ein Stilleben. Erinnerungen an meinen Vater Max Ernst.* Cologne: Kiepenheuer & Witsch. Original edition: *A Not-So-Still Life. A Child of Europe's Pre-World War II Art World and His Remarkable Homecoming to America.* 1984. Wainscott, NY: Pushcart.

Ernst, Max. 1934. "Was ist Surrealismus?." In *Ausstellung, 11 October–4 November 1934.* Zurich: Kunsthaus Zürich.

Feininger, T. Lux. 1994. "Die Bauhauskapelle." In *Das frühe Bauhaus und Johannes Itten,* edited by Rolf Bothe, pp. 374–78. Ostfildern: Gerd Hatje.

———. 2006. *Zwei Welten—Mein Künstlerleben zwischen Bauhaus und Amerika.* Translated from the English by Florian Bergmeier. Halle: Mitteldeutscher Verlag.

Fiedler, Jeannine, and Peter Feierabend, eds. 1999. *Bauhaus.* Cologne: Könemann.

Finsler, Hans. 1952. Eulogy, in "Zum Andenken an Egidius Streiff, " pp. 7–9. Obituary booklet. Zurich: gta Archiv.

Fischer, Guido. [1966]. "Ernst Geiger. 1 February 1876–16 December 1965." Obituary, in *Brugger Neujahrsblätter,* pp. 58–64. Brugg, Switzerland. Archiv Christoph Geiger.

Fischer, Lothar. 1969. *Max Ernst in Selbstzeugnissen und Bilddokumenten.* Reinbek bei Hamburg: Rowohlt.

Fischli, Hans. 1968. *Hans Fischli. Malerei Plastik Architektur.* Exhibition catalogue. Kunsthaus Zürich. With detailed autobiographical recollections, pp. 5–86.

Frehner, Matthias. 2004. "Der Engel des Lebens oder: zu Segantinis Motiv der Frau im Baum." In *Blicke ins Licht. Neue Betrachtungen zum Werk von Giovanni Segantini,* edited by Beat Stutzer, pp. 91–110. Exhibition catalogue, Segantini Museum St. Moritz. Zurich: Scheidegger & Spiess.

Frei, Annette. 1987. *Rote Patriarchen. Arbeiterbewegung und Frauenemanzipation in der Schweiz um 1900.* Zurich: Chronos.

Frey, Stefan. 1995. "Die Kandinsky-Retrospektive in der Kunsthalle Bern 1937." In *Kandinsky nelle collezioni svizzere / Kandinsky in den Schweizer Sammlungen / Kandinsky dans les collections suisses,* by Manuela Kahn-Rossi, 48ff. Exhibition catalogue, Museo cantonale d'arte Lugano. Milan: Skira.

———. 2000. "Rolf Bürgis Engagement für Paul und Lily Klee sowie die Gründung der Paul-Klee-Stiftung." In *Paul Klee. Die Sammlung Bürgi,* edited by Stefan Frey and Josef Helfenstein, pp. 199–217. Bern: Benteli.

———. 2003. "Paul Klee—Chronologische Biografie 1920–1931." In *Paul Klee. Lehrer am Bauhaus,* edited by Wulf Herzogenrath, Anne Buschhoff, and Andreas Vowinckel, pp. 220–52. Exhibition catalogue, Kunsthalle Bremen. Bremen: Hauschild.

Friedmann, Hermann. 1930. *Die Welt der Formen.* Munich: C.H. Beck'sche Verlagsbuchhandlung.

Frosch, Eva. 2004. *Clara Friedrich. Künstlerin und Sammlerin.* Zurich: Scheidegger & Spiess.

Gallati, Karin and Urs Oechslin. "Konstruktive Konzepte der Moderne. Einfamilienhaus Bremgarten 1942 Max Bill." Diploma thesis, Zurich 1995/96.

Gassner, Hubertus. 1994. "Realität der Sympathie. Parallelismus der Naturreiche." In *Élan vital oder das Auge des Eros. Kandinsky, Klee, Arp, Miró, Calder,* edited by Hubertus Gassner, pp. 25–38. Exhibition catalogue. Munich: Haus Der Kunst.

Gatje, Robert F. 2000. *Marcel Breuer: A Memoir.* New York: Monacelli.

Gautschi-Züricher, Margrit. 1988. *Gedenkschrift. Bertha Züricher 1869–1949, Ulrich Wilhelm Züricher 1877–1961, Gertrud Züricher 1871–1956.* Exhibition catalogue. Sigriswil, Switzerland: Zentenhaus Köniz.

Geiger, Ernst. N.d. "Robinsonade im Langensee." Handwritten text about his time looking after the island in Lake Langen. Freienbach, Christoph Geiger.

———. 1949. "Vor fünfzig Jahren. Auf Segantinis Pfaden." Manuscript. Archiv Christoph Geiger.

———. 1957. "Zur Geschichte des Stadthauses." In *Brugger Neujahrsblätter,* pp. 34–39.

———. 1969. "Rückblick, geschrieben im Winter 1921/22." In *Brugger Neujahrsblätter,* pp. 15–34. Clipping. Archiv Christoph Geiger.

Giacometti-Duperret, Odette. 1994. "Max Ernst im Bergell." In *Das Bergell. Heimat der Giacometti,* edited by Ernst Scheidegger, 176–77. Zurich: Ernst Scheidegger.

Giedion, Andres. 2007. "Biografische Notizen zu Carola Giedion-Welcker (1893–1979)." In *Das neue Sehen. Carola Giedion-Welcker und die Sprache der Moderne,* by Iris Bruderer-Oswald, pp. 385–401. Bern: Benteli.

Giedion-Welcker, Carola. 1958. *Constantin Brancusi.* Basel/Stuttgart: Benno Schwabe.

Giedion, Sigfried. 1936. "Zeitprobleme in der Schweizer Malerei und Plastik." In *Zeitprobleme in der Schweizer Malerei und Plastik,* pp. 3–8. Exhibition catalogue. Zurich, Kunsthaus Zürich. Typography by Max Bill.

Girsberger, Hans. 1970. *Stationen.* Zurich.

———. 1981. *Im Umgang mit Le Corbusier / Mes contacts avec Le Corbusier.* Zurich: Les éditions d'architecture Artemis.

Grohmann, Will. 1924. *Wassily Kandinsky,* Junge Kunst 42. Leipzig: Klinkhardt & Biermann.

———. 1954. *Paul Klee.* Geneva: Editions des Trois Collines; Stuttgart: W. Kohlhammer.

———. 1958. *Wassily Kandinsky. Leben und Werk.* Cologne: M. DuMont Schauberg.

———. 1968. "Über Max Bill." In *Max Bill,* pp. 18–21. Exhibition catalogue. Hanover: Kestner-Gesellschaft.

Grohmann, Will, ed. 1934. *Paul Klee. Handzeichnungen II 1921–1930.* Potsdam: Müller & Kiepenheuer.

Grote, Ludwig, ed. 1959. *Erinnerungen an Paul Klee.* Munich: Prestel.

Guggenheim, Kurt. 1999. *Sandkorn für Sandkorn.* 1959, Frauenfeld: Huber.

Hahn, Gustav A. 1977. "Über den Dessauer Komponisten Kurt Weill." In *Dessauer Kalender 1977,* pp. 62–65. Dessau: Rat der Stadt.

Hahn, Peter. 2008. "Bill und das Bauhaus." In *Max Bill. Aspekte seines Werks,* edited by Kunstmuseum Winterthur and Gewerbemuseum Winterthur, pp. 72–83. Zurich: Niggli.

Hahnloser, Hans R. 1973. "Erinnerungen und Briefauszüge." In *Künstlerfreunde um Hedy und Arthur Hahnloser-Bühler,* pp. 21–32. Kunstmuseum Winterthur.

Hahnloser-Ingold, Margrit. 2007. "Félix Vallotton in Winterthur und Zürich—Die Geschichte einer Freundschaft." In *Félix Vallotton in der Villa Flora. Aus der Sammlung Arthur und Hedy Hahnloser-Bühler und aus Schweizer Privat- und Museumsbesitz,* edited by Ursula Perucchi-Petri, pp. 105–25. Bern: Benteli.

Hans Hildebrandt und sein Kreis. 1978. Exhibition catalogue. Bremen: Kunsthandel Wolfgang Werner.

Hausenstein, Wilhelm. 1921. *Kairuan oder eine Geschichte vom Maler Klee und von der Kunst dieses Zeitalters.* Munich: Kurt Wolff.

Heinze-Greenberg, Ita, and Regina Stephan, eds. 2004. *Luise und Erich Mendelsohn—Eine Partnerschaft Für Die Kunst.* Ostfildern-Ruit: Hatje Cantz.

Helfenstein, Josef. 2000. "'Ort Der Verabredung'—Die Sammlung Bürgi." In *Paul Klee. Die Sammlung Bürgi,* edited by Stefan Frey and Josef Helfenstein, pp. 33–165. Bern: Benteli.

Herold, Marianne. 1991. *Roman Clemens.* Zurich: ABC.

Hertzberger, Eleonore. 1993. *Durch die Maschen des Netzes. Ein jüdisches Ehepaar im Widerstand gegen die Nazis.* Zurich: Pendo.

Herzogenrath, Wulf. 1980. "Josef Albers' Werk bis zur Zeit der Übernahme eines Teiles des Vorkurses." In Wulf Herzogenrath, *Josef Albers und der 'Vorkurs' am Bauhaus 1919–1933. Reprinted from Wallraf-Richartz-Jahrbuch, Westdeutsches Jahrbuch für Kunstgeschichte* 41 [1980], pp. 245–76. Cologne: Wienand.

Hinterreiter, Hans. Diary. Hinterreiter-Stiftung.

———. 1978. *Die Kunst der reinen Form.* Facsimile edition of the original manuscript of 1936–48. Ibiza/Amsterdam: Ediciones Ebusus.

Holmes, Deborah. 2005. *Ignazio Silone in Exile. Writing and Antifascism in Switzerland 1929–1944.* Aldershot: Ashgate.

Hörner, Unda. 1996. *Die realen Frauen der Surrealisten.* Mannheim: Bollmann.

Huelsenbeck, Richard. 1920. *En Avant Dada.* Hannover / Leipzig / Vienna / Zurich: Paul Steegemann.

Huggler, Max. 1969. *Paul Klee. Die Malerei als Blick in den Kosmos.* Frauenfeld / Stuttgart: Huber.

Huonker, Gustav. 1985. "Das Geistige Europa." In *Literaturszene Zürich. Menschen, Geschichten und Bilder 1914 bis 1945.* Zurich: Unionsverlag.

Isaacs, Reginald R. 1984. *Walter Gropius. Der Mensch und sein Werk,* vol. 2. Berlin: Mann.

Jaffé, Hans L. C. 1971. *Vordemberge-Gildewart. Mensch und Werk.* Cologne: M. DuMont Schauberg.

Jahn, V. 1917. Pastor: "Ulrich Geiger-Schwarz" Obituary, *Brugger Neujahrsblätter,* 59–60.

Jakovsky, Anatole. 1934. *H. Erni, H. Schiess, K. Seligmann, S.H. Taeuber-Arp, G. Vulliamy.* Paris: Éditions Abstraction–Création. With the dedication "Für B und M Bill in Freundschaft, S. H. Taeuber Arp."

———. "Pevsner." [ca. 1933]. In Jakovsky, *Arp Calder Hélion Miró Pevsner Séligmann.* Paris: Jacques Povolozky.

Jansen, Franz M. 1989."Von damals bis heute." In *Der blaue Reiter. Dokumente einer geistigen Bewegung,* 172–73. Leipzig: Philipp Reclam Jun.

Jeanne Bucher—une galerie d'avant-garde, 1925–1946. 1994. Exhibition catalogue, Les musées et l'Université de Strasbourg. Geneva: Skira.

Jouffroy, Alain. 1975. "San Lazzaro et Kandinsky par Nina Kandinsky," interview with Nina Kandinsky, in *San Lazzaro et ses amis. Hommage au fondateur de la revue XXe siècle.* Paris: La Revue XXe Siècle.

Kamber, Peter. 1990. *Geschichte zweier Leben—Wladimir Rosenbaum und Aline Valangin.* Zurich: Limmat.

Kandinsky, Nina. 1976. *Kandinsky und ich.* In collaboration with Werner Krüger. Munich: Kindler.

Kandinsky, Wassily. 1926. *Punkt und Linie zu Fläche, Beitrag zur Analyse der malerischen Elemente.* Bauhausbücher, vol. 9. Munich: Albert Langen.

Kassák Lajos 1887–1967. 1987. Exhibition catalogue. Berlin/GDR: Akademie der Künste.

Kerr, Alfred. 2004. *Der Dichter und die Meerschweinchen. Clemens Tecks letztes Experiment.* Edited by Günther Rühle. Frankfurt am Main: S. Fischer.

Kieren, Martin. 1990. *Hannes Meyer. Dokumente zur Frühzeit, Architektur- und Gestaltungsversuche 1919–1927.* Heiden: Niggli.

Klee, Felix. 1957. "Erinnerungen." In *Paul Klee. Tagebücher 1898–1918,* edited by Felix Klee, pp. 422–27. Cologne: M. DuMont Schauberg.

Klepsch, Michael Carlo. 2007. *Picasso und der Nationalsozialismus.* Düsseldorf: Patmos.

Koelbl, Herlinde. 1989. *Jüdische Portraits.* Frankfurt Am Main: S. Fischer.

Koella, Rudolf. 2008. "Bill vor Bill: zum Frühwerk des Künstlers." In *Max Bill. Aspekte seines Werks,* edited by Kunstmuseum Winterthur and Gewerbemuseum Winterthur, pp. 27–39. Sulgen/Zurich: Niggli.

König Sen., Friedrich. 1920. *Land und Leute des Moosseetales.* Münchenbuchsee: Verlag der Flurgenossenschaft des Münchenbuchseemooses.

Krüger, Werner. 1990. *Die Umwandlung von Energie in Kunst.* Video. Cologne: Artemedia Produktion.

Lang, Karl. 1975, 1983. *Kritiker, Ketzer, Kämpfer—Das Leben des Arbeiterarztes Fritz Brupbacher.* Zurich: Limmat.

Lang Jakob, Evelyne. 2003. "Die Architektin." In *Flora Steiger-Crawford 1899–1991,* pp. 110–39. Zurich: gta.

Lang, Lothar. 1965. *Das Bauhaus 1919–1933, Idee und Wirklichkeit.* Berlin/GDR: Zentralinstitut für Formgestaltung.

Lauterbach, Heinrich. 1958. "Ansprache von Heinrich Lauterbach [6 September 1958]." In "Oskar Schlemmer zum 4. September 1958." With handwritten dedication "Zur Erinnerung herzlichst zugeeignet von Tut" (Special publication for friends of the late Oskar Schlemmer).

Le Corbusier. 1926. *Kommende Baukunst.* Translated and edited by Hans Hildebrandt. Stuttgart: Deutsche Verlagsanstalt.

Le Corbusier und Pierre Jeanneret, ihr gesamtes Werk von 1910–1929. 1930. Edited and translated by O. Stonorov and W. Boesiger. Girsberger, Zürich.

Le Corbusier & P. Jeanneret, Œuvre complète, 1929–1934. 1934. Edited by W. Boesiger. Zurich: Girsberger. Cover design by Max Bill.

Le Corbusier & P. Jeanneret, Œuvre complète, 1934–1938. 1939. Edited by Max Bill. Zurich: Girsberger. Cover design by Max Bill.

Le Corbusier, Œuvre complète, vol. 1, 1910–1929. 1995. Edited by Willy Boesiger and Oscar Stonorov. Basel: Birkhauser.

Lerch, Fredi, and Erwin Marti. 2008. "Einführung—Der Kunstpublizist C. A. Loosli." In *Carl Albert Loosli, Hodlers Welt,* edited by Lerch and Marti, pp. 7–16. Zurich: Rotpunkt.

Liessner-Blomberg, Elena. 1990. "Romanisches Café." In *Russen in Berlin, Literatur, Malerei, Theater, Film, 1918–33,* edited by Fritz Mierau, pp. 336–38. Leipzig: Philipp Reclam Jun.

Lipchitz, Jacques. 1972. *My Life in Sculpture.* London: Thames & Hudson.

El Lissitzky. 1965. *Russland. Architektur für eine Weltrevolution 1929.* Vienna: Anton Schroll. 1930. Berlin: Ullstein.

Lissitzky-Küppers, Sophie. 1976. "Erinnerungen und Briefe." In *Maler, Architekt, Typograf, Fotograf. Erinnerungen, Briefe, Schriften,* 11–98. Dresden: VEB Verlag der Kunst.

Loew, Heinz. 1984 [a]. "Die bewegliche Plastik und die mechanische Bühne." In Joost Schmidt, *Lehre und Arbeit am Bauhaus 1919–32,* pp. 77–83. Düsseldorf: Edition Marzona.

———. 1984 [b]. "Joost Schmidt: Lehrer am Bauhaus." In Joost Schmidt, *Lehre und Arbeit am Bauhaus 1919–32,* pp. 7–9. Düsseldorf: Edition Marzona.

Lohse, Richard Paul. 1981. "1936, Prolog zur Allianz." In *1936—Eine Konfrontation,* pp. 100–101. Exhibition catalogue. Aarau: Aargauer Kunsthaus.

Maasberg, Ute and Regina Prinz. 2004. *Die Neuen kommen! Weibliche Avantgarde in der Architektur der zwanziger Jahre.* Hamburg: Junius.

Machlitt, Ulla and Hans Harksen. 1977. "Aus der Arbeit der Bauhaus-Werkstätten in Dessau." In *Dessauer Kalender 1977,* pp. 74–103. Dessau: Rat der Stadt.

Maciejewski, Franz. 2008. *Freud in Maloja. Die Engadiner Reise mit Minna Bernays.* Berlin: Osburg.

Magnaguagno, Guido. 1980. Introduction to *Linolschnitte zu Ignazio Silone,* by Clément Moreau/Carl Meffert, unpaginated. Berlin: LitPol.

Marchiori, Giuseppe. 1975. "San Lazzaro et les artistes italiens." Translated by Angela Delmont. In *San Lazzaro et ses amis. Hommage au fondateur de la revue XXe siècle,* pp. 109–15. Paris: La Revue XXe Siècle.

Mayer, Bernhard. 1998. *Interessante Zeitgenossen / Interesting Contemporaries / Lebenserinnerungen eines jüdischen Kaufmanns und Weltbürgers / Memoirs of a Jewish Merchant and Cosmopolitan 1866–1946,* edited by Erhard Roy Wiehn. Konstanz: Hartung-Gorre.

max bill. 1976. *du,* special issue, 424 (June):12–69.

Max Bill. Typografie, Reklame, Buchgestaltung. 1999. With contributions by Gerd Fleischmann, Hans Rudolf Bosshard, Christoph Bignens. Zurich: Niggli.

Mebold, Adrian. 2008. "Max Bill und Winterthur: Geschichten zwischen Heimat und Avant-garde." In *Max Bill. Aspekte seines Werks,* edited by Kunstmuseum Winterthur and Gewerbemuseum Winterthur, pp. 203–15. Sulgen/Zürich: Niggli.

Mehring, Walter. 1965. *Verrufene Malerei—Einst verkannt, geschmäht, verfolgt, heute weltberühmt und kaum mit Geld zu bezahlen.* Munich: Wilhelm Heyne.

Mendelsohn, Louise. 2004. "My Life in a Changing World." San Francisco, n.d. Unpublished manuscript translated from the English by Ita Heinze-Greenberg in *Luise und Erich Mendelsohn—Eine Partnerschaft für die Kunst,* edited by Ita Heinze-Greenberg und Regina Stephan. Ostfildern-Ruit: Hatje Cantz.

Meyer, Felix. 1995. "Sonate für zwei Klaviere und Schlagzeug." In *Béla Bartók 1945—50th Anniversary—1995,* edited by Migros-Genossenschafts-Bund. Zurich.

Meyer, Hannes. 1993. "Mein Hinauswurf aus dem Bauhaus. Offener Brief an Herrn Oberbürgermeister Hesse, Dessau." In *Bauhaus Dessau, Dimensionen 1925–1932,* edited by Andreas Bossmann. Exhibition catalogue. Dessau: Bauhaus Dessau.

Moholy-Nagy, László. 1929. *Von Material zu Architektur.* Bauhausbücher, vol. 14. Munich: Albert Langen.

Moholy, Lucia. 1972. *Marginalien zu Moholy-Nagy. Dokumentarische Ungereimtheiten. / Moholy-Nagy, Marginal Notes. Documentary Absurdities.* Krefeld: Scherpe.

Moholy-Nagy, Sibyl. 1950. *Experiment in Totality.* New York: Harper.

Mojzisová, Iva. 1986. "Moholy-Nagy in Brünn und Pressburg." In *Wechselwirkungen. Ungarische Avantgarde in der Weimarer Republik,* edited by Hubertus Gassner, pp. 282–83. Exhibition catalogue, Staatliche Museen, Neue Galerie Kassel, and Museum Bochum. Marburg: Jonas.

Mondrian, Piet. 1925. *Le néo-plasticisme—aux hommes futurs.* Paris: Editions de l'effort moderne, Léonce Rosenberg. 1920. German translation: Piet Mondrian, *Neue Gestaltung. Neoplastizismus,* Bauhausbücher, vol. 5.

Mühlestein, Hans. 1914. *Ferdinand Hodler. Ein Deutungsversuch.* Weimar: Gustav Kiepenheuer.

Mühlestein, Hans and Georg Schmidt. 1942. *Ferdinand Hodler 1853–1918. Sein Leben und sein Werk.* Erlenbach-Zurich: Eugen Rentsch.

Müller, Thomas. 2000. *Von Charlottenburg zum Central Park West. Henry Lowenfeld und die Psychoanalyse in Berlin, Prag und New York.* Frankfurt am Main: Édition Déjà-Vu.

Münster, Arno. 2004. *Ernst Bloch. Eine politische Biografie. L'utopie concrète d'Ernst Bloch.* Paris: Kimé. 2001; Berlin: Philo.

Muscheler, Ursula. 2016. *Das rote Bauhaus. Eine Geschichte von Hoffnung und Scheitern.* Berlin: Berenberg.

Nerdinger, Winfried. 1985. *Walter Gropius. Der Architekt Walter Gropius. Zeichnungen, Pläne und Fotos aus dem Busch-Reisinger-Museum der Harvard University Art Museums, Cambridge, Mass. und dem Bauhaus-Archiv, Berlin.* Exhibition catalogue. Berlin: Mann.

Neumann, Eckhard, ed. 1985. *Bauhaus und Bauhäusler. Bekenntnisse und Erinnerungen.* Stuttgart: Hallwag. 1971, reprinted Cologne: DuMont.

Nonne-Schmidt, Helene. 1984 [a]. "Joost Schmidt." In Joost Schmidt, *Lehre und Arbeit am Bauhaus 1919–32,* pp. 115–17. Düsseldorf: Edition Marzona.

———. 1984 [b]."Reklame-Unterricht 1930–32." In Joost Schmidt, *Lehre und Arbeit am Bauhaus 1919–32,* pp. 95–97. Düsseldorf: Edition Marzona.

———. 1984 [c]. "Typografie 1923 bis 1932." In Joost Schmidt, *Lehre und Arbeit am Bauhaus 1919–32,* pp. 19–22. Düsseldorf: Edition Marzona

Oechslin, Werner. 1987. *Le Corbusier und die Schweiz. Dokumente einer schwierigen Beziehung.* Zurich: gta/Ammann.

Oesch, Hans 1967. *Wladimir Vogel. Sein Weg zu einer neuen musikalischen Wirklichkeit.* Bern/Munich: Francke.

Oppenheim, Meret. 2007. In Werner Spies and Anja Müller-Alsbach, *Max Ernst—Im Garten Der Nymphe Ancolie,* edited by Werner Spies and Anja Müller-Alsbach. Exhibition catalogue, Museum Tinguely, Basel. Ostfildern-Ruit: Hatje Cantz.

Paul Klee und seine Malerfreunde. Die Sammlung Felix Klee. 1971. Exhibition catalogue, Kunstmuseum Winterthur. Duisburg: Wilhelm-Lehmbruck-Museum.

Pauli, Hansjörg, and Dagmar Wünsche. 1986. *Hermann Scherchen, Musiker, 1891–1966.* Exhibition catalogue, Akademie der Künste. Berlin. Berlin: Hentrich.

Pazitnov, L. 1963. *Das schöpferische Erbe des Bauhauses 1919–1933.* Berlin/GDR: Institut für angewandte Kunst.

Pech, Jürgen. 1991. "Max Ernst und 'Das goldene Zeitalter,'" in *Max Ernst. Fotografische Porträts und Dokumente.* Exhibition catalogue. Brühl: Raathaus Brühl.
Perrottet, Julia. [1989/90]. "Allar wird Bühnenbildner." In Suzanne Perrottet, *Ein bewegtes Leben,* pp. 233–35. Bern: Benteli.
Perrottet, Suzanne. [1989/90]. *Ein bewegtes Leben.* Bern: Benteli.
Pieyre de Mandiarques, André. 1975. "Héroïque San Lazzaro." In *San Lazzaro et ses amis. Hommage au fondateur de la revue XXe siècle.* Paris: La Revue XXe Siècle.
Poeschel, Erwin. 1922. *Augusto Giacometti.* Zurich: Rascher. With handwritten note by Max Bill: "bill—antiquarisch gekauft 1944" (bought secondhand in 1944).
Pohl, Karl Heinrich. 1994. "Eisner, Fechenbach und die Revolution in Bayern." In *Felix Fechenbach 1894–1933. Journalist Schriftsteller Pazifist,* pp. 42–59. Papers from symposium held in Detmold to mark the centenary of Fechenbach's birth. Detmold: Institut für Lippische Landeskunde und Kreis Lippe.
Posener, Julius. 1990. *Fast so alt wie das Jahrhundert.* Berlin: Siedler.
Prat, Marie-Aline. 1980. "Contribution aux archives de l'art abstrait en France. Le groupe et la revue 'Cercle et carré.'" PhD dissertation, Université de Paris, Sorbonne.
Prior, Ingeborg. 2002. *Die geraubten Bilder. Die abenteuerliche Geschichte der Sophie Lissitzky-Küppers und ihrer Kunstsammlung.* Cologne: Kiepenheuer & Witsch.
Radewaldt, Ingrid and Monika Stadler. 1997. "Sachsse Stölzl. Biographie." In *Gunta Stölzl. Meisterin am Bauhaus Dessau. Textilien, Textilentwürfe und freie Arbeiten 1915–1983,* edited by Stiftung Bauhaus Dessau, pp. 10–86. Ostfildern-Ruit: Gerd Hatje.
Radlach, Viola, ed. 2000. *Cuno Amiet—Giovanni Giacometti. Briefwechsel,* Exhibition catalogue, Schweizerisches Institut für Kunstwissenschaft. Zurich: Scheidegger & Spiess.
Rasch, Emil. 1971. "Mit dem Bauhaus Arbeiten." In *Bauhaus und Bauhäusler. Bekenntnisse und Erinnerungen,* edited by Eckhard Neumann, 183. Bern/Stuttgart: Hallwag.
Renner, Paul. 1932. *Kulturbolschewismus?* Erlenbach-Zurich / Munich / Leipzig: Eugen Rentsch.
Richter, Horst. 1958. *El Lissitzky. Sieg über die Sonne. Zur Kunst des Konstruktivismus.* Galerie Czwiklitzer, Cologne.
Roth, Alfred. 1988. *Amüsante Erlebnisse eines Architekten.* Zurich: gta/Ammann.
———. 1927, 1991. "Erinnerungen an den Bau der 'Weissenhofsiedlung.'" In *Zwei Wohnhäuser von Le Corbusier und Pierre Jeanneret. Fünf Punkte zu einer neuen Architektur von Le Corbusier und Pierre Jeanneret durch Alfred Roth.* Facsimile of 1927 edition. Stuttgart: Karl Krämer.
Roth, Michael. 1991. "Aus einem Gespräch mit Anton Stankowski." In *Anton Stankowski gewollt—geworden. Visualisierungen im freien und angewandten Bereich,* pp. 25–37. Exhibition catalogue, Ulmer Museum. Stuttgart: Hatje.
Sacher, Paul. "Begegnungen mit Béla Bartók," in *Béla Bartók 1945—50th Anniversary—1995.* Zurich: Migros-Genossenschafts-Bund.
Sachsse, Rolf. 1985. *Lucia Moholy.* Düsseldorf: Edition Marzona.
Schaarschmidt, Karl-Heinz. 2003."Grundlagen der Gestaltung—Plastik." Manuscript, lecture to design students at the Technische Universität Dresden. Rev. 2003.
Schaller, Marie-Louise. 1983. *Otto Morach (1887–1973).* Zurich: Schweizerisches Institut für Kunstwissenschaft/Munich: Prestel.
Schaub, Gerhard, and Ernst Teubner, eds. 2003. *Hugo Ball. Briefe 1904–1927.* Vol. 2. 1924–27. Göttingen: Wallstein.
Schawinsky, Alexander, 1927. "Xanti." Typescript on Bauhaus Dessau. Bauhaus-Archiv Berlin and Ronald Schmid, Schawinsky-Archiv, San Nazzaro.
Scheidegger, Ernst, director. 1998. *Max Bill—Maler, Plastiker, Architekt, Erzieher und Politiker.* Color film. 100 mins. Zurich: Scheidegger & Spiess.
Scheiffele, Walter. 2003. *Bauhaus Junkers Sozialdemokratie—Ein Kraftfeld der Moderne.* Berlin: form + zweck.
Scheper, Dirk. 1986. "Hermann Scherchens Zusammenarbeit mit Oskar Schlemmer." In Hansjörg Pauli and Dagmar Wünsche, *Hermann Scherchen, Musiker, 1891–1966.* Exhibition catalogue, Akademie der Künste, Berlin. Berlin: Edition Hentrich.
———. 1988. *Oskar Schlemmer—Das triadische Ballett und die Bauhausbühne,* vol. 20. Foreword by Max Bill. Berlin: Akademie der Künste.

Scheper, Renate. 2005. "Die Geschichte der Werkstatt für Wandmalerei am Bauhaus," in *Farbenfroh! Colourful! Die Werkstatt für Wandmalerei am Bauhaus / The Wall-painting Workshop at the Bauhaus,* pp. 8–40. Exhibition catalogue. Berlin: Bauhaus-Archiv.

Schilt, Jeroen, and Herman Selier. 1993. "Het leven van Lotte Stam-Beese." In *Lotte Stam-Beese 1903–1988, Dessau, Brno, Charkow, Moskou, Amsterdam, Rotterdam,* pp. 10–35. Rotterdam: Rotterdamse Kunststichting/Uitgeverij de Hef.

Schipper, Merle. 1974. "Jean Hélion: The Abstract Years. 1929–1939." PhD dissertation, University of California, Los Angeles.

Schlemmer, Oskar. 1958. *Briefe und Tagebücher,* edited by Tut Schlemmer. Munich: Albert Langen/Georg Müller.

———. 1990. *Idealist der Form. Briefe, Tagebücher, Schriften 1912–1943.* Leipzig: Reclam.

Schmid, Erich, director. 2008. *Bill—Das absolute Augenmass.* Color film. 93.5 mins. Zurich.

Schmid, Werner. 1974. *Hans Bernoulli. Städtebauer Politiker Weltbürger.* Schaffhausen: Peter Meili.

Schmidt, Doris. director. 1983. *Max Bill.* Color film. Zweites Deutsches Fernsehen.

Schmidt, Hans. 1976. "Erinnerungen an Lissitzky." In *Maler, Architekt, Typograf, Fotograf. Erinnerungen, Briefe, Schriften.* Dresden: VEB Verlag der Kunst.

Schnaidt, Claude. 1990. "Von der Diktatur der Maschine zur Diktatur des Proletariats." Manuscript from lecture at series "Moskau–Zürich" at ETH Zürich, 12 June.

Schoop, Albert. 1992. *Ernst Ludwig Kirchner im Thurgau. Die 10 Monate in Kreuzlingen 1917–1918.* Bern: Kornfeld.

Schreyer, Lothar. 1956. *Erinnerungen an Sturm und Bauhaus.* Munich: Langen-Müller.

Schumann, Thomas B., ed. 2002. "Wir verstummen nicht—Jo Mihaly (1902–1989). Portrait einer vergessenen Schriftstellerin, Tänzerin und Emigrantin. " In Jo Mihaly, *Auch wenn es Nacht ist: Roman.* Hürth bei Köln: Edition Memoria.

Schwarz, Dieter. 1998. "Die Sammlung Georg Reinhart, Winterthur." In *Die Kunst zu Sammeln, Schweizer Kunstsammlungen seit 1848,* pp. 345–54. Zurich: Schweizerisches Institut für Kunstwissenschaft.

Spies, Werner. 2008 [a]. "Die Desaster des Jahrhunderts." In Werner Spies, *Max Ernst. Une semaine de bonté,* pp. 10–71. Exhibition catalogue, Albertina, Vienna; Max Ernst Museum, Brühl; and Hamburger Kunsthalle. Cologne: Dumont.

Spies, Werner, ed. 2008 [b]. *Max Ernst. Une semaine de bonté.* Exhibition catalogue, Albertina, Vienna; Max Ernst Museum, Brühl; and Hamburger Kunsthalle. Cologne: Dumont.

Stahlberger, Peter. 1970. *Der Zürcher Verleger Emil Oprecht und die deutsche politische Emigration 1933–1945.* Zurich: Europa.

Stam, Mart. 1976. "Die Architektur-Konzeption El Lissitzkys." In *Maler, Architekt, Typograf, Fotograf. Erinnerungen, Briefe, Schriften,* pp. 394–95. Dresden: VEB Verlag der Kunst.

Steiner, Heiri. 1976. "Erinnerung an Ernst Keller 1924–27." In *Ernst Keller, Graphiker, 1891–1968. Gesamtwerk,* edited by Hansjörg Budliger et al. Exhibition catalogue. Zürich: Kunstgewerbemuseum.

Steinmann, Martin, ed. 1979. *CIAM—Internationale Kongresse Für Neues Bauen. Dokumente 1928–1939.* Institut für Geschichte und Theorie der Architektur. Conference papers. Basel: Birkhäuser.

Stiftung Bauhaus Dessau. 1997. *Gunta Stölzl. Meisterin am Bauhaus Dessau. Textilien, Textilentwürfe und freie Arbeiten 1915–1983.* Dessau: Stiftung Bauhaus.

Stutzer, Beat. 1979. "Ernst Ludwig Kirchner und Basel." In *Ernst Ludwig Kirchner. Die Sammlung im Kirchner-Haus Davos und die Werke Kirchners im Kunstmuseum Basel,* pp. 23–26. Exhibition catalogue. Basel: Kunstmuseum Basel.

———. 2004. "Biografie—Giovanni Segantini, 1858–1899." In *Blicke ins Licht—neue Betrachtungen zum Werk von Giovanni Segantini,* edited by Beat Stutzer, pp. 151–53. St. Moritz: Segantini Museum, and Zurich: Scheidegger & Spiess.

———. 2007. "Georg Schmidt, Ein Gang durch die Winterthurer Kirchnerausstellung 1924." In *Expressionismus aus den Bergen. Ernst Ludwig Kirchner, Philipp Bauknecht, Jan Wiegers und die Gruppe Rot-Blau,* edited by Beat Stutzer, Samuel Vitali, Han Stenbruggen, and Matthias Frehner, pp. 281–86. Exhibition catalogue, Kunstmuseum Bern, Groninger Museum, and Bündner Kunstmuseum Chur. Zurich: Scheidegger & Spiess.

Stutzer, Beat, Samuel Vitali, Han Stenbruggen, and Matthias Frehner, editors. 2007. *Expressionismus aus den Bergen. Ernst Ludwig Kirchner, Philipp Bauknecht, Jan Wiegers und die Gruppe Rot-Blau.* Exhibition catalogue; Kunstmuseum Bern; Groninger Museum; and Bündner Kunstmuseum, Chur, Switzerland. Zurich: Scheidegger & Spiess.

Suter, Hans. 2006. *Paul Klee und seine Krankheit.* Bern: Stämpfli.

Suter, Ursula, ed. 1993. *Hans Schmidt 1893–1972. Architekt in Basel, Moskau, Berlin-Ost,* Dokumente zur modernen schweizer Architektur. Zurich: gta.

Klee, Felix, ed. 1957. *Tagebücher von Paul Klee 1898–1918.* Cologne: M. DuMont Schauberg.

Teubner, Hans. 1975. *Exilland Schweiz—Dokumentarischer Bericht über den Kampf emigrierter deutscher Kommunisten 1933–1945.* Berlin: Dietz.

Thomas, Angela. 1983."Sophie Taeuber-Arp 1889–1943." In *Sophie Taeuber-Arp 1889–1943.* Exhibition catalogue. Ascona, Switzerland: Museo Comunale Ascona. Typographical design by Max Bill.

———. 1991 [a]. "Max Bill ed i suoi rapporti con l'Italia / Max Bill and Italy." In Max Bill, edited by Luciano Caramel and Angela Thomas, pp. 10–24. Exhibition catalogue, Milan: Lorenzelli Arte.

———. 1991 [b]. *Mit unverstelltem Blick—Bericht zu drei Künstlerinnen. Anna Baumann-Kienast, Alis Guggenheim, Sophie Taeuber-Arp.* Bern: Benteli.

Thümmler, Sabine. 1999. "Bauhaus-Tapete." In *Bauhaus,* unpaginated. Bramsche, Germany: Rasch.

Tolziner, Philipp. 1989. "Mit Hannes Meyer am Bauhaus und in der Sowjetunion." In *Hannes Meyer 1889–1954. Architekt Urbanist Lehrer,* edited by Werner Kleinerüschkamp, pp. 134–65. Exhibition catalogue; Bauhaus-Archiv, Berlin; Deutsches Architekturmuseum, Frankfurt am Main; and Museum für Gestaltung, Zurich. Berlin: Ernst.

Tupitsyn, Margarita. 1999. *El Lissitzky—Jenseits der Abstraktion. Fotografie, Design, Kooperation.* Exhibition catalogue, Hanover: Sprengel Museum.

Valdivieso, Mercedes. 2000. "Eine 'symbiotische Arbeitsgemeinschaft,' Lucia und László Moholy-Nagy." In *Liebe macht Kunst. Künstlerpaare im 20. Jahrhundert,* edited by Renate Berger, pp. 63–85. Cologne / Weimar / Vienna: Böhlau.

van Moorsel, Wies . 2003. *Durchschnitt reicht nicht! Nelly van Doesburg 1899–1975.* Sulgen/Zurich: Niggli.

Vaucher, C. F. 1996. *Aus meiner linken Schublade. Erzählungen eines Lebens.* Zurich: Rotpunkt.

Vogel, Wladimir. 1977. *Schriften und Aufzeichnungen über Musik. Innerhalb—ausserhalb.* Edited by Walter Labhart. Zurich: Atlantis Musikbuch.

Volboudt, Pierre. 1975. "Portrait de San Lazzaro." In *San Lazzaro et ses amis. Hommage au fondateur de la "revue XXe siècle."* Paris: La Revue XXe Siècle.

W. [Wilhelm Wartmann]. 1936. Introduction. In *Zeitprobleme in der Schweizer Malerei und Plastik.* Exhibition catalogue. Zurich: Kunsthaus Zürich. Typography by Max Bill.

Waldheim chronicle. Theodor Marty. Archiv Ortsmuseum Oetwil am See.

Weininger, Eva. 1994. "Lieber Lux." In *Das Frühe Bauhaus und Johannes Itten,* edited by Rolf Bothe. Ostfildern-Ruit: Gerd Hatje.

Weise, Anne-Kathrin. 2002. "Pariser Impressionen—Marianne Brandt und Frankreich." In *Das Bauhaus und Frankreich 1919–1940 / Le Bauhaus et la France 1919–1940,* edited by Isabelle Ewig, Thomas W. Gaehtgens, and Matthias Noell. Berlin: Akademie Verlag.

Weitemeier, Hannah. 1974. "László Moholy-Nagy—Leben und Werk." In *László Moholy-Nagy,* edited by Wulf Herzogenrath, pp. 8–114. Exhibition catalogue, Württembergischer Kunstverein Stuttgart, Kölnischer Kunstverein, and Kunstgewerbemuseum der Stadt Zürich. Stuttgart: Gerd Hatje.

Welsh, Robert P. *Piet Mondrian 1872–1944.* 1966. Exhibition catalogue, The Art Gallery of Toronto, Philadelphia Museum of Art, Gemeentemuseum, The Hague. Toronto: The Art Gallery of Toronto.

Widmer, Helny. 1974."Die Gründer der Sektion Aargau 1904–1954." In *Aargauer Almanach auf das Jahr 1975.* Lucerne: Buchdruckerei Keller.

Wingler, Hans M. 1962. *Das Bauhaus. 1919–1933. Weimar, Dessau, Berlin.* Bramsche: Rasch.

———. 1974. *Kleine Bauhaus-Fibel.* Berlin: Bauhaus-Archiv.

Winkler, Klaus-Jürgen. 1974. "Die Werkstätten für Wandmalerei und Bildhauerei." In Hans M. Wingler, *Kleine Bauhaus-Fibel,* 18–20. Berlin: Bauhaus-Archiv.

———. 2003. *Baulehre und Entwerfen am Bauhaus 1919–1933.* Weimar: Bauhaus-Universität Weimar, Universitätsverlag.

Wollsdorff, Christian. 1988. "Takehito Mizutani." In *Experiment Bauhaus, Das Bauhaus-Archiv Berlin (West) zu Gast im Bauhaus Dessau,* edited by Magdelena Droste and Jeannine Fiedler. Exhibition catalogue, Bauhaus Dessau. Berlin: Bauhaus-Archiv and Museum für Gestaltung.

Wood, James N. 1974. Introduction, in *Max Bill,* 19–36. Exhibition catalogue, Albright-Knox Art Gallery, Los Angeles County Museum of Art. 1975; San Francisco Museum of Art. 1975. Buffalo: Buffalo Fine Arts Academy and the Albright-Knox Art Gallery.

"Zum Andenken an Egidius Streiff." [1952]. Obituary booklet. gta Archiv, ETH Zürich.

Zürcher Maler. 1947. Exhibition catalogue. Zürich: Kunsthaus Zürich.

Index

Credits

For works by Max Bill: © 2022, ProLitteris, Zurich. Unless otherwise noted: Collection of Angela Thomas, Zumikon. Courtesy the max bill georges vantongerloo foundation and Hauser & Wirth

For works by Binia Bill, Herbert Bayer, Lucia Moholy, Alexander Rodchenko, Konstantin Stepanovich Melnikov, and Georges Vantongerloo: © 2022, ProLitteris, Zurich

For works by Josef Albers: © The Josef and Anni Albers Foundation/2022, ProLitteris, Zurich

For works by Pablo Picasso: © Succession Picasso/2022, ProLitteris, Zurich

For works by T. Lux Feininger: © Estate of T. Lux Feininger; for works by Jacques Lipchitz: All Rights Reserved—Estate of Jacques Lipchitz; for works by Otto Morach: © Estate of Otto Morach

Archiv Ortsmuseum Oetwil am See: p. 69; Bauhaus-Archiv Berlin: pp. 181 (bottom), 197–203, 231; Courtesy Belvedere, Vienna: p. 84; Galerie Berinson, Berlin: p. 161 (top left); © 2008, Bühnen Archiv Oskar Schlemmer, 28824 Oggebbio (VB), Italy: p. 248 (bottom); Hubelhüsi-Chronik, Bd. I, Burgerbibliothek Bern, FA Züricher, Inv. 324: pp. 12 (bottom), 43 (bottom); Christoph Geiger, Freienbach: pp. 11, 12 (top), 23 (bottom), 49, 50 (top), 64, 115 (bottom left), 139 (bottom), 395 (bottom); Sammlung Hans-Ulrich Geiger, Zurich: pp. 29 (bottom), 44, 170 (top); gta Archiv/ETH Zürich: pp. 514 (photo © Gotthard Schuh/Fotostiftung Schweiz), 567, 600 (bottom); Collection Huber, Offenbach, Germany: p. 352; Galerie Kornfeld, Bern: p. 91; Kunstmuseum Bern: pp. 54 (top), 63; Raymond Martin, Ligerz: p. 50 (bottom right) (photo A. Kölla, Brugg); max, binia + jakob bill stiftung, adligenswil: pp. 152 (top), 483 (bottom right), 533, 559, 594, 600 (top), 640, 666 (left); Private Collection. Courtesy Hauser & Wirth Collection Services: p. 102 (top); Courtesy Erich Schmid, haus bill: pp. 30 (bottom left) (photo: Zentrum Paul Klee, Bern), 454 (bottom); Schweizer Cabaret- und Chansonarchiv: pp. 445 (bottom), 454 (top); SIK-ISEA, Zürich: p. 30 (top); Stadtarchiv Brugg, F 001.866: p. 23 (top); Städtische Bildersammlung Brugg: p. 170 (bottom); Swiss Federal Archives, E3010A#1991/226#95*, ref. 207.1 P, Bill Max, 1949–1980: p. 612 (bottom), 629 (top); Angela Thomas, Zumikon: pp. 24, 29 (top) (photo: Angela Thomas), 30 (bottom right), 43 (top), 50 (bottom left), 53 (middle and bottom), 54 (bottom), 70, 83, 92, 101, 102 (bottom), 107 (photo: Peter Gaechter), 108, 115 (top and bottom right), 116, 127–32, 139 (top), 140, 151, 152 (bottom), 161 (top right and bottom right), 162, 169, 175–76, 181 (top), 182, 187–88, 204–17, 232–47, 251–52, 257–68, 283 (left), 284–91, 292 (photo: Angela Thomas), 301 (top), 301 (bottom)(photo: Angela Thomas), 302–33, 334 (photo: Angela Thomas), 341–51, 357–84, 395 (top and middle), 396–419, 420 (bottom), 429–30, 445 (top), 446–53, 467–75, 476 (top), 476 (bottom) (photo: Spreng, Basel), 483 (top and bottom left), 484 (top and bottom right), 484 (bottom left)(photo: Giorgio Hoch), 513, 519–28, 534–42, 560, 568–80, 593, 611 (bottom), 612 (top and middle), 629 (bottom), 630–39, 654, 661 (top), 662, 665 (photo: Jon Etter), 666 (right), 671–92, 734; Georges Vantongerloo Archive, haus bill: pp. 599, 611 (top), 653; Sammlung Elsa und Heinz Wehrli Hotz: p. 218; Wilhelm-Hack-Museum, Ludwigshafen: p. 661 (bottom); Stiftung Wilhelm Lehmbruck Museum—Zentrum Internationaler Skulptur, Duisburg, Germany: p. 420 (top); Winterthurer Bibliotheken, Sammlung Winterthur: p. 53 (top); Zentrum Paul Klee, Bern: p. 248 (top)

Cover

View from the Prellerhaus balcony at the Bauhaus in Dessau. Foreground, from left: Ursula Schneider, Anni Albers, Gunta Stölzl. Standing below: Max Bill, unidentified man. Seated below, from left: Bruno Streiff, Shlomoh Ben-David (Georg Gross), Gerda Marx, unidentified man, 1927

Bauhaus-Archiv Berlin

Jacket photograph

Angela Thomas in Haus Bill, Zumikon
Photo by Sim Canetty-Clarke

Every effort has been made to trace copyright ownership and to obtain reproduction permissions. Corrections brought to the publisher's attention will be incorporated in future reprints or editions of this book.

Translated from the German
by Fiona Elliott
Publisher: Michaela Unterdörfer
Managing editors: Kristina
Hinrichsen and Mélanie Letoré
Editorial support: Emily Fayet
Project assistants: Valeria Brucker,
Maria Elena Garzoni, Courtney
Meier-Neal, Nele Templin
Copyediting: Mary Christian

Book design and typography:
Sonja Zagermann
Pre-press: LUP AG
Production coordination: Christine Stricker
Printing and binding: DZA Druckerei
zu Altenburg GmbH

Cover Paper: Lessebo Design 1.3
Natural, 240 g
Dustjacket Paper: Lessebo Design
1.3 Natural, 200 g
Endpaper: Lessebo Design Natural, 90 g
Paper: Lessebo Design Natural, 90 g
Typeface: Univers

Printed and produced with friendly support from the max bill georges vantongerloo foundation.

The publishers wish to thank Scheidegger & Spiess for the generous permission to publish an English edition of the original book.

A heartfelt thank you also to Angela Thomas for her tireless support, enthusiasm, and generosity to access her archives. Countless images presented here for the first time to an international audience were kindly made available by the author and the max bill georges vantongerloo foundation.

Distribution:
Europe and the UK:
Buchhandlung Walther König
Ehrenstrasse 4
50672 Köln
Tel +49 221 20 59 6-53
Fax +49 221 20 59 6-60

All other territories:
ARTBOOK | D.A.P.
75 Broad Street, Suite 630
New York, NY 10004
Tel +1 212 627 1999
Fax +1 212 627 9484

ISBN: 978-3-906915-40-1
Library of Congress Control Number:
2020947105
Printed and bound in Germany

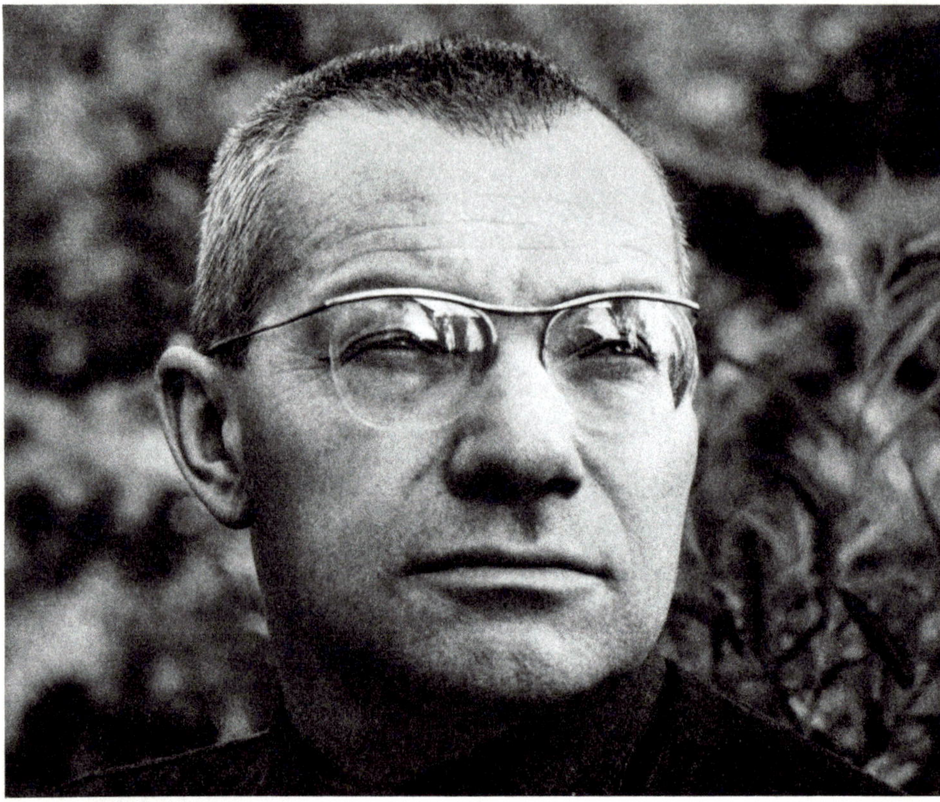

pour monsieur georges

und zum beginn des jahres 77
an angela

max bill